Shakespeare on
Television

Shakespeare on Television

AN ANTHOLOGY OF ESSAYS AND REVIEWS

Edited by J. C. Bulman and H. R. Coursen

UNIVERSITY PRESS OF NEW ENGLAND
HANOVER AND LONDON, 1988

TO KEN AND BERNICE

UNIVERSITY PRESS OF NEW ENGLAND

BRANDEIS UNIVERSITY DARTMOUTH COLLEGE
BROWN UNIVERSITY UNIVERSITY OF NEW HAMPSHIRE
CLARK UNIVERSITY UNIVERSITY OF RHODE ISLAND
UNIVERSITY OF CONNECTICUT TUFTS UNIVERSITY
UNIVERSITY OF VERMONT

Printed in the United States of America

Library of Congress Cataloging-in-Publication Data

Shakespeare on television.
  Includes bibliographical references and index.
  1. Shakespeare, William, 1564–1616—Film and video
adaptations. I. Bulman, James C., 1947–
II. Coursen, Herbert R.
PR3093.S54 1988   822.3'3   87–40511
ISBN 0–87451–435–5
ISBN 0–87451–442–8 (pbk.)

5   4   3   2   1

Contents

THE PRODUCTIONS

Preface

It is said that more people view a single television production of a Shakespeare play than all the people who have seen live productions of that play in four hundred years. If true, then the need to understand the nature of the experience of Shakespeare on television grows in proportion to the number of televised versions of plays that appear. As the essays in this anthology prove, however, little agreement exists on what the experience of televised Shakespeare is or how one should judge it—as theater? as film? as something inherently different from, and inferior to, those other media? Some critics suggest that Shakespeare's plays cannot work within the diminished space of a small screen. Whatever the merits of that viewpoint, television is the medium through which countless people experience and enjoy Shakespeare. This anthology attempts to illuminate that experience and to clarify the psychology of perception for the many who encounter Shakespeare primarily, even exclusively, on television.

Television has precipitated a revolution in how Shakespeare is taught in the classroom. Teachers have shifted their focus away from the text alone to the potentials of the plays in performance; and students, nurtured on television, have responded with enthusiasm. Videotaped productions have become an integral part of many courses. Inevitably, the BBC/Time-Life Shakespeare Series provided impetus for the revolution: these productions are now widely used at colleges and universities and at many secondary schools as well. Furthermore, their popularity has encouraged teachers to use videotapes of other, often older, productions: demand for them has never been greater. This revolution, in fact, has been so pervasive that a whole generation of students now understands Shakespeare primarily as a man of the screen.

It follows that this focus on television productions has created an abundance of critical and scholarly debate over the past dozen years. The debate has been waged in journals such as the *Shakespeare Quarterly*, in reviews written for major newspapers and magazines, and at conferences and seminars the world over. The problem is that these essays and reviews are widely scattered: no volume has collected the best material on television adaptations or provided a handy source for reviews, a bibliography, and a videography. This anthology provides these things. It is divided into three major sections. The first, "Wide Angles," contains general and theoretical essays which ad-

dress televised Shakespeare from a variety of perspectives—formalist, decon-
structionist, political, feminist. The second, "Closeups," contains essays
on individual productions or groups of productions, including accounts of
American and British versions made prior to the BBC Series. The third,
"Short Subjects," collects reviews from major newspapers and journals, focusing on conflicting assessments of all widely used productions: these reviews
demonstrate how perceptions of any one version may differ radically from one
another and be nonetheless valid. The three major sections are followed by a
bibliography and, finally, a videography of which cassettes are available and
where they may be rented or purchased.

We do not intend to provide a history of Shakespeare on television. Few, if
any, pre-1960 productions are available outside of specialized collections at
universities and libraries. We have, however, suggested the beginnings of televised Shakespeare and attempted in part to trace its evolution by reprinting a
few significant essays and by detailing early productions in the review section.
Reviews in the popular press are not often indexed and are therefore almost
as irretrievable as copies of the pre-1960 productions themselves. The anthology treats more extensively those productions that are currently available or
that may become available in the future; and while, inevitably, we concentrate on the popular BBC series, we do not suggest that BBC "house style"
represents the correct mounting for these plays. Indeed, that style varies drastically, as one is forced to notice in viewing the discrepant treatments of the
two sequences of history plays.

In addition to the BBC productions, the anthology gives ample coverage to
other televised versions, independently made, for which cassettes exist—the
Olivier *Lear*, the Eric Porter-Janet Suzman *Macbeth*—or for which cassettes
do not yet exist: for example, the Papp *Much Ado* and *King Lear* (with James
Earl Jones), the Hands *Antony and Cleopatra* (with Janet Suzman), the popular *Hamlet* with Richard Chamberlain, the Stratford, Ontario, mounting of
Taming of the Shrew, and the opulent Olivier *Merchant of Venice*, directed
by Jonathan Miller. Each of these productions provides useful contrasts with
other televised versions of the play. By paying particular attention to them,
we hope to encourage their availability in cassette form. An opportunity to
compare and contrast two or more television interpretations of a play can only
enhance one's sense of the manifold possibilities residing in the script itself.

While the anthology includes discussion of the differences between television and film, we have chosen not to deal with films available in cassette
form—the Polanski *Macbeth*, the Zeffirelli *Romeo and Juliet*, the Olivier
Henry V, *Hamlet*, and *Richard III*. These films may now, of course, be
viewed on a television set, but they remain films—more visual, less verbal,
less intimate than television productions, products of (to use Marshall Mc-
Luhan's term) a "hotter medium" than television. The same is true of Peter
Hall's *Midsummer Night's Dream*, which appeared on American television
in January 1970. These films are treated admirably by Jack Jorgens in *Shakespeare on Film* (Bloomington: Indiana University Press, 1970). Contemporary

reviews of some of these and other Shakespeare films are contained in Roger Manvell's *Shakespeare and the Film* (New York: Praeger, 1971). The only production customarily regarded as film which this anthology treats is the Wirth-Schell *Hamlet*: it originally appeared on Austrian television and is briefly considered in the context of other televised versions of that play. Regardless of its dissemination in a 16mm format, this Wirth-Schell *Hamlet* falls squarely into the genre of television. Much can be learned, of course, from comparing film and television versions of Shakespeare, even if films in cassette form suffer—as they inevitably do—from being reduced to the cramped dimensions of the television screen.

In sum, this anthology is designed to help scholars towards further research into a fertile new area of inquiry about Shakespeare, to help teachers incorporate televised Shakespeare into their classes, and to help students sharpen their perceptions of what they experience. We hope that as different productions of the plays become available in cassette—some from the vaults and archives where they now reside, others newly made—the richness and variety of Shakespeare's art will become all the more apparent, and the opportunities for understanding television as Shakespeare's ally will increase.

This volume, then, is but a beginning. It cannot pretend to be a definitive treatment of the subject. But insofar as it gathers material between two covers from diverse sources, we hope that it may prove a convenient reference. Our search for appropriate essays and reviews has been made easier by the encouragement and cooperation of friends. Among those friends we number Bernice Kliman and Ken Rothwell, whose *Shakespeare on Film Newsletter* has become an invaluable resource for anyone interested in how the media have treated Shakespeare; Herb Weil, from whose seminar at the International Shakespeare Congress of 1981 some of the best work on televised Shakespeare emerged; Graham Holderness, who allowed us to see early proofs of his Shakespeare filmography that appeared in *Shakespeare Survey*, 39 (1987) 13–37; John Lemly, whose researches in London saved us a trip; and Peter Saccio and Roger Manvell, whose suggestions helped to shape the present volume. We wish to thank Homer Swander, a pioneer in teaching Shakespeare through performance, and to thank as well Anne Britting Tobey, Al Fuchs, Dan Sullivan, Andy Ford, Roy Greason, Carmen Greenlee, Lloyd Michaels, Gini Linkovich, and Mary Ann Steinbeck; also John Ladley, Helen McCullough, Alan Bartlett, and the staffs of the Allegheny College and Bowdoin College libraries. We are grateful, too, to the Bowdoin College Research Fund and the Faculty Development Committee of Allegheny College for their support, and to the various editors, publishers, and reviewers who so generously have allowed us to reprint copyrighted material here. Individual permissions are acknowledged where appropriate.

15 September 1987   J. C. Bulman
                                                      Allegheny College
                                                      H. R. Coursen
                                                      Bowdoin College

Part One
WIDE ANGLES

The Bard and the Tube
H. R. Coursen

To say that Shakespeare is timeless is to utter an aphorism only half true. Shakespeare's seeming timelessness results from his ability to change with the times, to survive, even thrive, in different formats and in media undreamt of in his dramaturgy.

The media themselves have changed. Shakespeare has emerged from under a footlighted proscenium stage for which he did not write, has freed himself from massive and literal sets which he would not recognize as an adjunct to any of his scripts, and has found himself on rake-thrust stages which provide a kind of 3-D effect for the spectators, in suggestive spaces like Peter Brook's open-ended squash court, or in areas where lighting is the primary conveyor of atmosphere and image. Styles of acting have also changed and, today, vary with their context. Or *should* vary: to see histrionics that might work on the stage thrust at a television camera, *à la* Jon Finch as Bolingbroke or Emrys James as Enobarbus, is to recognize that some actors are either insensitive to their medium or inflexible in their technique.

Television has also changed, as David Marc has recently demonstrated.[1] The "burning issues" of a decade before become the laugh lines of the next, as "All in the Family" shows. And, regardless of programming or content, the techniques of television have evolved, as any reviewing of a 1950s show would demonstrate. It is more than a matter of color. It is also a question of the three-camera format for most taped shows and editing so skillful—as with all good editing—that we do not notice the myriad shifts and transitions that focus with automatic precision on two people talking, as seen from the waist up, on the speaker and on the other's reaction to what has been said. Other variations exist, of course, but we notice—if at all—that television does not even attempt to develop a "field of depth." The depth of the tube extends no further than the back of the set. If we contrast the "field of depth" of television with that of a wide-screen film, we notice that the film's illusion of depth is far greater. Suffice it that most television shows are shot in studios, sometimes in rooms no larger than the living room upon which they look. TV is an indoor medium for our indoors. Even scenes that purport to be outdoors are merely products of large sound stages. It is interesting, perhaps inevitable, that one of the few BBC scripts shot outdoors, *As You Like It*, was a drab production.

The director of a play by Shakespeare must, if he is translating the script to television, recognize that we have been conditioned, perhaps unconsciously, to "the way television does things." Again, regardless of content, the techniques of television have been perfected since those delightful early days when we could watch a live and trembling pair of hands preparing a sandwich with Kraft cheese. The most successful translations of literature to the tube have necessarily availed themselves of this perfection of technique. I think particularly of "Masterpiece Theatre," which employs the outdoors superbly, though sparingly, and specifically of the superb *Pride and Prejudice*.

A studio, with its limited size, and a stage would seem to be comparable performing areas. In the theatre, however, we watch what the director wants us to watch even though we have, theoretically, the entire stage in view. Entrances and exits, lighting, and carefully constructed lines of sight insist that we look at what the director wants us to see. If Shylock is slumped downstage right and all the other characters form a kind of arrow, headed by Portia, on a raked stage, and all are looking at Shylock, one only looks at Shylock. We have been conditioned, however, to have the television camera do the looking for us, and part of that conditioning comes from film. If we have ever seen what amounts to a filmed play—the Evans-Anderson *Macbeth* or the Olivier *Othello*, for example—we know that while each may be fascinating as a record of performance, as representatives of their medium they are pretty dull. In Olivier's Shepperton version of *Othello*, for example, I kept yearning for a glimpse of Venice, or of the harbor of Cyprus, with the rack dislimning and the Turkish wreckage bobbing in the surf. But what we got there— marvelous as the performances were—was not film but stage. In the studio-bound BBC *Hamlet* a graveyard scene shot at The Church of the Holy Trinity at Stratford would have been magnificent, but it was not to be. When a television director employs a static camera, as Jonathan Miller tended to do in his *Taming of the Shrew* and *Othello*, the results are deadly; our attention is called to a director who has not mastered the rudiments of his medium. No act of dedication or devotion permits us to focus on the issues of life and love or life and death.

If we grant that television is a limited, if "perfected," medium that can recreate literary texts like *Pride and Prejudice*, *The Golden Bowl*, and *Our Mutual Friend* effectively, we might believe that Shakespeare, who provides a script ready-made, would be easy for the tube. Not so. A script "in being," particularly of a well-known play, represents a rigidity, a centuries-old codification that one tampers with at one's peril. It is there. All that language. Shakespeare's plays were produced out of doors, with the possible exception of the "command performances" some scholars posit for *A Midsummer Night's Dream* and *Macbeth*, before Shakespeare's company acquired the indoor Blackfriars Theatre late in his career. Shakespeare's stage was a "bare island," unencumbered by sets, depending upon available lighting and moderate temperatures, and prey to sudden squalls, as depicted by Olivier's Globe Theatre in his great film of *Henry V*. The language of the plays compensated for all that Shakespeare's stage could not accomplish—it gives us Verona's dawns, Scotland's darkness, Egypt's heat, the murky morning of the Battle of Bosworth Field ("Not shine today!" Richard complains of the sun, which will not show him his lucky talisman—the hump on his back), the bloody sun that illuminates the showdown at Shrewsbury, and storms that sink Turks, madden an ex-monarch, and evaporate with the wave of a magician's wand.

The language is not intended to compensate for our lack of imagination. It forces our imaginations to transcend our disbelief. We are, literally, watching actors in makeup and costumes on a stage that we know is not the "real world." We are meant to accept the weather the words describe. McLuhan's theories would seem to make drama a "cool medium," that is one "high in participation or completion by the audience."[2] "And speech," he claims, "is a cool medium of low definition [i.e. not well filled with sensory data] because so little is given and so much has to be filled in by the listener."[3] Shakespeare's speech is usually poetry, of course, in which our senses are appealed to via imagery, and to which our senses must respond. Unless we interact with the language—and that is to do much more than merely to "understand" what it means—the dramatic experience is lost to us.

Film, a "hot medium," does not need much language. As Gloria Swanson says in *Sunset Boulevard*, "Dialogue? We had faces!" Film depends upon sound for only some ten to fifteen percent of its effect. The medium is visual and the image is the message. If one looks at some of the films that appeared fairly soon after Al Jolson said, "Wait a minute! Wait a minute! You ain't heard nothing yet," one notices an over-reliance on "talk." The directors, given either a new toy to play with or a new dimension to explore, often went too far. Many of those films rely on bombastic perorations during which the camera stands static and self-conscious or roves down a row of expressionless faces being asked to "win one for the Gipper!" Film evolved from the silent screen. No amount of talking will erase that heritage. The sound track exists to augment and emphasize the image, not to replace it. When it tried, it failed. Augmentation itself could become ludicrous, as when a thousand twangling violins began to swell towards that kiss that Gary Cooper or Jimmy Stewart or Cary Grant or Van Johnson or John Wayne or Clark Gable was about to plant on Myrna Loy or Ann Sheridan or Ida Lupino or Ingrid Bergman or Vivian Leigh or Katherine Hepburn.

Suffice it that to translate Shakespeare to film, a radical transition must be made. Olivier's *Henry V*, for example, gave us the very Battle of Agincourt that Shakespeare's Chorus claims cannot be depicted:

> Can this cockpit hold
> The vasty fields of France? Or may we cram
> Within this wooden O the very casques
> That did affright the air at Agincourt? . . .
> Think, when we talk of horses, that you see them
> Printing their proud hoofs in the receiving earth.
> For 'tis your thoughts that now must deck our kings. . . .

The battle scenes in Olivier's film are superb. They demonstrate what film can do. True to the "Epic Tradition" that has found its way into the American Western, Olivier's Henry and the Constable of France square off in a final *mano a mano*. Shakespeare's King seems relatively inactive during the battle. We see him set it all in motion, send his men off with a rousing locker room oration, order the killing of prisoners, grieve at the murder of the boys guarding the rear echelon, confer with Montjoy, and ascribe the victory to God. We get a sequence of scenes that suggest that a great battle is swirling around Henry. Olivier gives us the battle.

More recent film versions of Shakespeare have virtually eschewed the word. *Throne of Blood*, Kurosawa's magnificent translation of *Macbeth* into medieval Japan, relies on the Oriental Noh tradition of acting, which uses posture and mime to convey attitude and meaning. Kozintzev's monumental *King Lear* is also virtually wordless, emerging as it does from the Russian silent film tradition of Sergei Eisenstein. Franco Zeffirelli's brilliant *Romeo and Juliet* cut the text drastically, but thereby captured the teenage nubility of Olivia Hussey, who was in no way capable of handling long stretches of blank verse. The film gave us the flaming opulence of the Capulet ball, the sweaty dust of swordplay in Verona's square, as recorded by a hand-held camera, and a high-renaissance patina across face and landscape. Zeffirelli's film turned literary art into visual art and used art *per se* to create and to enhance his effects. Kozintsev's film is quasi-documentary, a black and white flickering as if we are following a Nazi camera into Poland in 1939. Fire licks at the edges of the celluloid, people die by the sides of the road, and the camera does not pause for them. For Zeffirelli death is elegant, if ironic: the uninvited guest who ends the masquerade, as in the Jerome painting which the film employs for a brilliant instant, as Tybalt and a Capulet retainer hurry from the stones on which Mercutio's life drains out.

Television is not film. Television's tradition is not the imagery of the silent screen but the sound of radio. Radio employed what were called "sound effects" to convince us that doors were squeaking open into some Inner Sanctum, that The Shadow was chuckling out of his invisibility, that coshes were cracking on skulls so that Mr. North could wake up after the commercial and groan, "Where am I?" and that police with sirens wailing were racing down urban canyons to bust gangs. After a great crash and a lot of laughter, a final tin cup would drop from Fibber McGee's closet. It happened every time and it was always funny.

Television's origins remain obvious today. It is possible to listen to television—"60 Minutes" being an example. Here I disagree with McLuhan, who says that "TV will not work as background."[4] It is film that won't work as background. It is not just the darkened auditorium and our decision to pay to be sitting there. Nor is it the relative absence of sound. The image demands our attention. It is huge and it is all we can see. We have to close our eyes to escape it. Any sound is designed to call our attention to the image—the increasing tempo of the music, the cry of "Look there!" or "Sail ho!" The tube accommodates sound easily, partly because of its heritage—the original television sets were tiny screens dwarfed by the framework of the radio around them—and partly because the word is needed to amplify the mere nineteen inches or so of the screen. Although some television shows like "All in the Family" claim to be presented before live audiences, the "laugh track" is another of television's inheritances from radio, as well as a reminder of television's early "live" days when what were basically radio variety shows were televised from large auditoriums in New York City.

As I have noted, the substance of Shakespeare's plays is their language. Television can incorporate more language than film. Films made *for* television, for example, follow a different set of conventions than films made for the cinema. When the Bard meets the Tube, then, the transition should be much easier than it is when Shakespeare is translated to film.

The climate for Shakespeare and television would seem to be excellent. But even if we grant excellent productions featuring strong acting, intelligent directing, and a smooth application of the techniques to which television has conditioned us, Shakespeare encounters difficulties when he confronts the tube. It is not just that television trivializes by squeezing its "message" onto a small screen and between commercial breaks. Newton Minow's image of a "vast wasteland" remains aridly accurate. Shakespeare's scripts are not deserts—which for him meant any wild and uninhabited space—but, like any living thing, they tend to dry up in the desert. And while the problems that must occur when greatness has television thrust upon it are unlikely to be resolved, other problems do exist.

The fact of a script "in being" demands an adjustment *to* the dialogue. The director cannot say to his writers, "Rewrite this scene." It is there already and must seem to emerge naturally from context, not as in a soap opera where dialogue is a mumbled afterthought accompanied by a shrug. In Shakespeare, dialogue *creates* context. It becomes difficult, if not impossible, for a director to create a kind of "natural" or "casual" or "modern" environment out of which Shakespeare's highly poetic and relatively archaic speeches come. We do not have that problem with the stage. We assume its artificiality and willingly suspend our disbelief in our act of dramatic faith. The mechanical quality of television and its un-surreal and documentary quality—it is superbly suited for black and white narratives about Dachau—makes our suspension of disbelief almost impossible. During the best moments of the BBC Shakespeare Series, my response was that I could hardly believe that I was watching television. That response involved a mild and momentary transcendence of the "reality" the medium imposes upon us and of the lack of expectations that anything other than the passage of time can occur within that reality, unless we are watching a sporting event, the news, or a documentary about the SS.

Stephen Hearst points to the problems of the spoken word on TV. His observations would seem to apply particularly to that troublesome entity known as a "script-in-being:"

> a written text on the right-hand side of any script page which makes com-
> plete sense by itself is a bad text. What are the pictures there for? . . . The
> words, except in exceptional circumstances, need to follow the pictures. . . .
> Pictures have their own grammar, their own logic . . . and cannot easily be
> kept waiting. . . . To such a picture you could speak no more than about 25
> words. . . . Language seems to play a secondary role in television.[5]

What Hearst says becomes truer as television moves further and further
away from its radio origins. Television is becoming literally more and more a
filmic medium. If "Television is a medium whose form dominates its content," as Hearst maintains, Shakespeare is a dramatist whose language tends
to dominate and, indeed, incorporate considerations like setting and lighting.
As TV becomes more filmic, the problems for Shakespeare on TV must, it
would seem, increase.

On stage, Shakespeare presses us past obvious artifice, even as he incorporates it as a basic metaphor in many of his plays, and towards something far
more deeply interfused, something that becomes "reality" for our psyches and
our imaginations. Television as medium—for all of McLuhan's insistence
that "It engages you. You have to be *with* it"[6]—lacks a theatrical sense of
levels and depths. Furthermore, as William Worthen suggests:

> Perhaps because TV performances are transmitted by the camera, across
> a visibly domestic space, TV acting rarely tests its fictive boundaries. *King
> Lear* constitutes a certain kind of role for the spectator by requiring a range
> of response from him, a response both to the drama and to the acting of it.
> The TV camera requires different responses—more "receiving" and less
> "doing"—and so constitutes a rather different role for us, one that seems
> partly incompatible with the challenges of the play.
> By protecting us from the particular kind of challenge that *Lear*—and
> perhaps any stage play—creates in performance, the camera constitutes an
> inadequate role for the TV viewer. The challenge to feeling remains, but
> the difficult challenge to presence, the challenge that the theatrical spectator
> shares with and experiences through the actor, is simply not a part of the
> play.[7]

Furthermore, television, like radio before it, has conditioned our span of
attention. We are accustomed to commercial time-outs in our football games,
and ever-increasing "messages" towards the end of late-night movies, until
they become a kind of Doppler effect. Shakespeare is "too long" for television
and must go to the barber's with Polonius's beard. Even for today's stage the
longer scripts—*King Lear*, which is two texts conflated into one, and *Hamlet*—must be edited down to some three hours' running time. Even if public
television has seen fit to assume some of the annoying punctuality of the
networks, it is more flexible than they can be. Nonetheless, public television
cannot afford, it seems, to give us more than two minutes' intermission in
three hours of Shakespeare, a niggardliness that can become a problem even
for those of us who have no intention of switching over to see what is on the
commercial channels. We the audience, however sincere our intentions,
have been conditioned away from the length and the depth that Shakespeare
tends to represent.

We do not expect that anything of quality can be free. Yet television is "free." It sits there awaiting the twist of two fingers, or perhaps the flick of a button from the bored humanoid in his lounger. Given the necessity of having a tube and given an unseen electric meter whirring away out there in the smog or snow, we notice the difference when we make the effort to get to the cinema or the theatre and plunk down from ten to a hundred dollars for two seats. Our commitment to the tube involves no more than the random temptation presented by another channel. It is an extension of what Meredith once called "Modern Love." Our tube, of course, is surrounded by the amenities and temptations of a "living" or a "play" room—a fridge full of beer, a phone that may ring, and random crisscrossers who have only contempt for our choice of channel. Even ads on TV are created out of that conflict. "As long as you aren't doing anything. . . ." I heard that when I was reading for exams in graduate school, and the words might force a layabout from the assassination of Caesar, the rejection of Falstaff, the final words of Cleopatra, the coming-alive of the statue of Hermione.

PBS, apparently, cannot afford or risk more than a one-minute intermission twice during its Shakespeare telecasts. The intermission in the theatre permits the spectator to grab a cup of coffee, to visit with his fellow spectators and, while relaxing, to absorb and crystallize the dramatic experience as it has occurred thus far. He or she is then ready to reengage the play. At any rate, PBS coerces an attention that is exhausting for the best-intentioned of us and totally defeating to those of small commitment. Even the best of the BBC productions have met this response: they have simply strained our attention-span to its limits. It is not merely that TV has conditioned us to bite-sized chunks of tube-fare between commercial breaks, but that this is Shakespeare. He demands our complete attention.

While our surroundings and attention-span condition our ability to attend to Shakespeare on the tube, so do our expectations of the medium *per se*. Television is a luller—often, literally, a baby-sitter. Before television, children played. Now they watch children and puppets playing for them, as the watchers get dirty and perspire only vicariously. We *can* become involved in the "cool medium" during its documentary phases. As McLuhan suggests, "The [John] Kennedy funeral . . . manifested the power of TV to involve an entire population in a ritual process. By comparison, press, movie and even radio are mere packaging devices for consumers."[8] And so is television most of the time. McLuhan goes on to suggest a central paradox inherent in TV, one that relates to the problem of putting Shakespeare on the tube: "the Kennedy event provides an opportunity for noting a paradoxical feature of the 'cool' medium. It involves us in moving depth, but it does not excite, agitate or arouse."[9] Theatre—as practiced by the great Greek and Elizabethan dramatists—does excite, agitate, and arouse. Most television is more a form of relaxation than even of entertainment. Perhaps the best that Shakespeare can do on TV is to entertain, though at a level beyond whatever we expect of the medium. TV is the opiate of those who are otherwise insulated from the "drug-culture." Shakespeare did appeal to the mass audiences of the cosmo-

politan London of the late 1500s and early 1600s, and still does so occasionally to the sophisticated audience of New York City—those who can afford
$35 a ticket for a fine Royal Shakespeare Company performance of *Much
Ado About Nothing*. Today's masses, obviously, have been conditioned away
from a lively appreciation of Shakespeare's art.

Television, unfortunately, has conditioned us to expect the most simplistic
of allegories. This in spite of the development of the medium for which Marc
argues persuasively. In the case of television, the technique is usually superb,
the product usually lousy. In the case of Shakespeare, paradoxically, the product is superb, while the technique has seldom matched it. But beyond technique lies the probably inescapable fact that, for all the reasons why Shakespeare should work on TV, a deeper set of reasons dictates that the tube is an
impossible medium for Shakespeare. The basic problem, of course, is that
Shakespeare wrote for living theatre. While the space within which actors
work for a TV show may resemble a stage in size and shape, we as audience
are not within the space within which the action occurs, as we are in live
theatre. We tend to receive a production from the tube mechanically, largely
because it has been mechanically reproduced for delivery *via* a machine.
While some of the BBC productions have transcended their medium, they
have done so only during brilliant "spots of time." Seldom, if ever, has one
of the productions achieved a fully satisfactory aesthetic fulfillment. Indeed,
several previous television productions of Shakespeare have been superior to
almost all the BBC productions.

But the BBC productions are what we have, and they have already become
normative. The point of my critique is to suggest what we have in them, what
we cannot have in them, and how a diminished thing like TV might still
stretch its built-in limits as it attempts to incorporate material considerably
better—and far more difficult—than it usually essays.

1. David Marc, "Understanding Television," *The Atlantic* (August 1984), 33–44.
2. Marshall McLuhan, *Understanding Media* (New York: McGraw-Hill, 1964), p. 22.
3. McLuhan, p. 23.
4. McLuhan, p. 312.
5. Stephen Hearst, "It Ain't Necessarily So," *The New Review*, 5, 1 (Summer 1978), 3–13.
6. McLuhan, p. 312.
7. William Worthen, "King Lear and TV," *Shakespeare on Film Newsletter*, 5, 2 (May 1983), 11.
8. McLuhan, p. 337.
9. McLuhan, p. 338.

From "Shakespeare in Film, Radio, and Television"
John Russell Taylor

Before we start to consider the chequered career of Shakespeare in these new media, there is one thing worth pointing out. Though like all theatre Shakespeare's drama is a visual art, and even has its occasional purely visual *coups de théâtre* (the descent of the 'statue' of Hermione from her pedestal near the end of *The Winter's Tale*, for instance), the prime accent is on sound rather than sight; scenes are set by what we hear, not what we see, and many of the most familiar passages of Shakespeare are long speeches, like Hamlet's soliloquies, Jaques's Seven Ages of Man speech, Ulysses's discourse on Order, Enobarbus's 'The barge she sat in . . . ,' which present virtually nothing for the physical eye to see at all. These are not all Shakespeare, or anything like it, but on the other hand they are essential to Shakespeare; you can't just take them away on the grounds that if Shakespeare had been writing for the modern theatre, with all its resources, or for the cinema, he would not have written like that. Or at least you can, but in doing so you run into the obvious difficulty that your audiences may refuse to recognize the result as 'Shakespeare' any more, and if this happens you have thrown away all the built-in advantages, to replace them probably only with resentment and suspicion.

Now it stands to reason that the more the medium you are dealing with inclines to expression in primarily visual terms, the more you are going to be dogged by this difficulty. Especially if it is a new medium, not yet quite established in respectable opinion as an art in its own right. If you put on an opera called *Othello* or a ballet called *Hamlet* nobody is going to complain very loudly that 'It isn't Shakespeare'; of course it isn't—it's opera or ballet first, and the fact that the theme comes from Shakespeare is more or less coincidental. At worst audiences may complain, as with Andrée Howard's ballet *Twelfth Night* a few years back, that the plot is too involved to be conveyed satisfactorily in terms of ballet, or something of the sort. But offer a film or a radio production called *Othello* or *Hamlet* which omits or rewrites a lot of Shakespeare's text and you will probably be in for trouble; on the credits of the first talking Shakespeare film, *The Taming of the Shrew*, with Mary Pickford and Douglas Fairbanks, the fateful note 'additional dialogue by Sam Taylor' caused such a flurry that it has not yet been forgotten.

This means that the new media best calculated to swallow Shakespeare whole without indigestion are the purely aural ones, radio and the gramophone record. Film, though not—as the older pundits, brought up in the silent cinema, would have us believe—almost exclusively a visual art, is still visual to an extent which makes wholesale transfer of Shakespeare from stage to screen a dangerous undertaking. Television, still the newest and least

Reprinted, with permission, from *Shakespeare: A Celebration, 1564–1964*, ed. T. J. B. Spencer (Baltimore: Penguin Books, 1965), pp. 99–103, copyright © Penguin Books, 1965.

formed of the four, hovers awkwardly in between, enjoying some of the advantages of radio and suffering from some of the film's disadvantages where Shakespeare is concerned. It is not surprising, therefore, that radio and the gramophone seem up to now to have acclimatized Shakespeare most successfully. There are at least two complete recordings of Shakespeare's works on long-playing records under way in this country, both offering uncut texts and a minimum of discreet background music and effects. This unobtrusive 'adaptation,' almost always with some cutting to fit in with programme schedules, has generally been found the most effective way of putting Shakespeare on radio, and in the course of its existence BBC radio has presented on one or other of its three domestic channels productions along these lines of all Shakespeare's plays but two, *Titus Andronicus* and (rather surprisingly) *The Comedy of Errors*—though this latter, with all its juggling with two pairs of identical twins, might reasonably claim to be the most visual of all Shakespeare's plays. The most popular of Shakespeare's plays on radio to date has been *The Tempest*, with no fewer than fourteen full-scale productions; after that came *Twelfth Night* with eleven, *Hamlet* with nine, and *Othello, The Merchant of Venice*, and *Romeo and Juliet* with seven each.

Television, though in its pre-war beginnings almost as educationally orientated as sound radio, has tended until recently to fight shy of Shakespeare in Britain, and even more so in America, apart from one or two wild prestige productions in early days, when everything was done live and all sorts of things could go terribly wrong (Maurice Evans has some scarifying stories of his renowned television *Hamlet* in New York). The first full-scale Shakespeare production on television seems to have been the BBC's modern-dress *Julius Caesar* in July 1938; a few months later they relayed a stage production of *Twelfth Night* complete from the Phoenix Theatre and then shortly before the wartime shutdown they did a full-dress studio production of *The Tempest*. After the war things began again slowly, and television Shakespeare, despite isolated attempts on both BBC and Independent channels, cannot be said really to have caught on until the BBC's ambitious series of Shakespeare histories in 1960 under the general title *An Age of Kings*. This took up an idea previously tried on radio: that of treating the main body of Shakespeare's history-plays from *Richard II* to *Richard III* as a coherent sequence with a continuity of theme running right through. The texts were somewhat cut (particularly in the *Henry VI* plays) and rearranged into fifteen episodes running in regular series from April to November, with the same actors playing the same parts throughout and the same producer and director (Michael Hayes and Peter Dews respectively) in charge of the whole series. A similar arrangement was essayed in 1963 with the classical history plays, grouped under the title *The Spread of the Eagle*.

An Age of Kings probably offers the fairest ground to date for judging television's potential in adapting Shakespeare; certainly it is the most extensive. Television, it is often said, is an intimate medium for watching in intimate, familial surroundings. This is to a large extent true (as it is, incidentally, of radio). Television is also a visual medium, and this means that if it does not have necessarily to convey its meaning largely or entirely in visual terms, it does at least have to keep the eyes occupied, because if the eyes wander the mind wanders too. Both of these qualities are in themselves mixed blessings where Shakespeare is concerned, and moreover each complicates the problems which arise from the other. The first means that quiet, intimate scenes are in general better suited to television than expansive rhetorical scenes, Richard II's more introspective moments rather than Henry V's clarion calls to arms. Effects can of course be graded, as they can on radio, by varying the distance of the speaker from microphone and camera, but here the visual nature of the medium steps in to complicate matters. If you hold an actor in close-up while he soliloquizes you are likely—unless the actor commands a quite exceptional degree of personal magnetism—to find your audience's attention drifting because one face in close-up for some length of time is not all that interesting to watch. Equally, if you move your actor far enough away for the big, demonstrative moments he is likely on the normal home screen to be so small and insignificant-looking that again he cannot magnetize attention. And if you do everything in medium shot it will just look dull anyway. (This last was the pitfall *An Age of Kings* most often fell into.)

But put like that, this argument seems to suggest that all drama should be impossible on television. This obviously is not true, but what it really resolves itself into is more than anything a matter of timing. Television must be able to mix up close, medium, and long shots, to move cameras around a lot or have a lot happening in front of them. Most stage-plays offer possibilities of all of these things, but as it were in slow motion; they dwell in moods that television should ideally just touch on, they take time to make transitions which television can do in a flash. There is hardly a stage play written of which the author, once properly schooled in television techniques, could not equally well convey the essence for television in an hour.

Does this then mean that Shakespeare and other classics should not be done on television at all? Strictly speaking, yes, that is precisely what it does mean—that no plays should be performed on television but those written for television; swift, fluid, *nuancé*. But clearly no one is going to speak as strictly as that. Even if the effect of Shakespeare on the television screen is, even at its very best, considerably less than in a passable stage performance, television production still has a number of advantages other than strictly aesthetic; for instance, the number of people who can see a single performance (it is estimated that more people saw the Royal Shakespeare Company's television *As You Like It* in March 1963 during one showing than had previously seen the play during its whole earlier history on the stage), and the durability of a taped production as a record. Shakespeare on television still has a lot to offer, provided we know clearly in advance just what we may hope to get out of it.

From "Boxing the Bard: Shakespeare and Television"
Graham Holderness

Parallels between the television medium and the Elizabethan drama have been expressed consistently by those involved in producing Shakespeare for the BBC. In 1947 George More O'Ferrall wrote of his production of *Hamlet*: 'Why should we claim that television is especially suited to Shakespeare? Because in its method of presentation it comes nearer to the Elizabethan theatre, for which the plays were written, than the modern theatre can do'.[1] The parallel characteristics cited are diversified acting areas, swift sequence of scenes and the possibility of intimacy between actor and audience. John Wilders, Literary Consultant to the BBC/Time-Life Shakespeare series, pursued this analogy to claim that television reproduction of Shakespeare could emulate or at least approach the freedom and flexibility of Renaissance popular drama. Television can restore to the plays an 'unbroken continuity' by rapid cutting, the equivalent of rapid scene-changes in a theatre without scenery; can place the actor in a close proximity to the audience and enable him or her to speak at the more 'conversational' pitch and pace probably possible in the 'acoustically lively' Globe Theatre; can equal, by the alternation of long-shot and close-up, the rapid alternation of disparate conventions in the diversified medium of the popular Elizabethan drama.[2]

Raymond Williams has shown[3] that in all developed broadcasting systems the characteristic organization is one of 'sequence' or 'flow'. In all communications systems before broadcasting, the essential items were discrete, independent units: in broadcasting the real *programme* is offered as a sequence of these and other similar events, which are then available in a single dimension and a single operation.

Broadcasting in its early stages inherited this problematic, and—since in general the *form* of the technology developed prior to any corresponding content—operated in a parasitic way upon it: the philosophy of broadcasting was 'transmission', the *relaying* of events (musical concert, play, public address, sporting event) to a general audience. *Programming* was a matter of arranging these discrete televised events into a series of timed units, with the appropriate mix, balance and proportion.

In Williams' view the important change was the movement, inherent in the nature of the medium itself, towards a concept of sequence not as *programming* but as a continuous *flow*. This is recognised instinctively in the way we talk of 'watching television' rather than watching a particular unit, and in the familiar reluctance to 'switch off' after a unit is completed. What the viewer experiences is thus not the published programme of discrete units, but a planned flow which is in both form and content the real 'broadcasting'.

Reprinted, with permission, from *The Shakespeare Myth*, ed. Graham Holderness (Manchester University Press, 1988).

From its inception, BBC television began to dramatise productions of Shakespeare, the first occurring in February 1937. There was already a strong tradition of broadcasting Renaissance drama in general on BBC *radio*—a tradition the history of which remains to be written[4]—but BBC television, with some exceptions, has never followed this, choosing always to paddle in the safer shallows of Shakespeare.

The challenge of adapting Shakespeare for television was certainly taken up at an early stage; but a close attention to the particular forms employed can be instructive. The first complete production (of *Twelfth Night*) was broadcast in January 1939: but prior to this there had been some twenty broadcasts in the form of a series called 'Scenes from Shakespeare'. The programmes would be about twenty-five minutes in duration, comparable with other types of programme. Programming information foregrounded the *actors* rather than the play or the dramatist, in keeping with a similar emphasis for light entertainment programmes, music, comedy and so forth. Caution should be exercised in drawing inferences from this form: since before the war television broadcasting was in a very early experimental stage and the technologies relatively undeveloped. Notwithstanding, it can be suggested that initially television incorporated and assimilated Shakespeare into, and employed methods of production and transmission appropriate to, its own medium. Despite the strong and evident influence of the theatrical profession (at its strongest in the 1950s), television did not seek to come to terms with Shakespeare on grounds defined by the theatre or literary criticism. Whole plays were broken into 'scenes from', short units compatible with normal programming requirements. Duration of programme units was not in itself a technical inhibition: in March 1937 a relatively full fifty-minute version of *Macbeth* (longer than many a supposedly complete silent production) was broadcast in two halves. The format was the result of programming decisions: Shakespeare was programmed as 'entertainment' rather than as 'education' or 'information'. The emphasis on the distinctive qualities of actors, derived directly from the contemporary theatre, paralleled the star cult of 'variety' common both in the contemporary cinema and in television itself.

Initially, then, television approached Shakespeare in a manner very different from the broadcasting techniques we have become accustomed to. The material was treated as entertainment, incorporated into a pattern of mixed programming without any unusual emphasis or special foregrounding, and regarded as not essentially different from any other item placed within a particular programmed sequence. Nor is there any manifestation, in these early stages, of the ideological appropriation of Shakespeare which later became commonplace. On St. George's Day in 1936 there was no broadcast of *Henry V*: instead there was a documentary about another national culture hero, King Arthur. The *Radio Times* of 1937 carried an enormous amount of media 'hype' around the coronation of George VI: even by the standards of contemporary media servility towards royalty, the number of programming references and exploitations of popular monarchist interest was extraordinary. There were programmes on heraldry, royal families, and even archery appropriated as 'toxophily—the sport of kings'. There were advertisements using the occasion for commercial opportunism: the Marchioness of Cambridge, identified in terms of her royal consanguinity, apparently suffered some dryness of the skin from playing lacrosse, and was wont to emolliate her complexion with 'Ponds Cold Cream'. A smiling Beefeater assured some children that he had been using Gibb's 'dentifrice' consistently 'since the last coronation'. There was a broadcast performance of Edward German's *Merrie England*. But there was no Shakespeare. Even BBC radio offered only a paltry twenty minutes of *Henry* V, compared with the whole of Act 3 of Wagner's *Walküre*; and to supply a more patriotic air, 'the song of a nightingale, broadcast from a wood in Surrey'.[5]

After the war BBC television moved into Shakespeare production in a much more confident way, and by the early 1950s the modern format of BBC Shakespeare, monumentally established in the BBC/Time-Life Series, was more or less fully formed. Where the early broadcast performances integrated the productions into the programmed sequence of variety and entertainment, adapting the material to the rhythms of the medium, from the early 1950s the Corporation began to make Shakespeare broadcasts into special occasions by programming on particular seasonal dates—*Twelfth Night* at Christmas, *Henry* V on St. George's Day; by using a particularly significant 'slot' such as Sunday evening; and by inserting write-ups and feature articles into the *Radio Times* to prepare the viewer for an isolated, special experience. In the late 1940s plays were broadcast in complete versions from studios and by outside broadcast.[6] The first production of *Hamlet* in December 1947 sprawled magisterially across four evenings. The *Radio Times* carried a feature article by the producer, which claimed in his support the theatrical and academic authority of Dover Wilson and Granville-Barker.[7] The production was highlighted in the 'recommended viewing' column, 'Talk of the Week'. *Hamlet* was followed in 1949–50 by the other three 'great tragedies', each accompanied by supportive feature articles in the *Radio Times*.[8]

By the early 1950s everything possible was being done to *isolate* a Shakespeare performance from the flow or sequence of the medium. A special kind of privileged attention was being focussed on the play by accompanying 'programme notes' and quasi-academic discussions. The practice of flanking a performance with educative ancillary material was beginning to appear: on the evening of 'Shakespeare's Birthday', 1952, to herald a production of *The Taming of the Shrew*, a panel discussion on televising Shakespeare featured producers, actors and critics.[9] In the *Radio Times* a visual technique of boxing information on the play, to separate it from the contamination of the surrounding contextual *bricolage*, began to be employed.

A useful example of the latter is to be found in the *Radio Times* for May 15, 1953. The programme note on the play, a production of *Henry* V, is boxed off from the surrounding page in a design resembling a theatrical programme (and beyond that, the 'society' invitation card from which the latter derives). A short article by Michael Macowan, the BBC producer, is incorporated into the programming information, describing the acting company and its methods. The company in question was called the 'Elizabethan Theatre Company':[10]

> With very little money, and using the barest minimum of setting and the most elementary Elizabethan costumes, a dozen to a score of young men and women, mostly from Oxford and Cambridge, set out last summer to play Shakespeare wherever they could find an audience and a place to play in. Sometimes it was an inn-yard, sometimes a college garden or the hall of an ancient house (the kind of conditions which Shakespeare's own company met on their tours), sometimes a town hall or an ordinary theatre. Despite many imperfections, the soundness of the principles on which they were working and their own vitality and talent created a great impression—particularly during the Edinburgh Festival.

This touring company, based on the principle of reviving the Elizabethan *ensemble*—playing in extra-theatrical locations, without pictorial scenery, doubling parts—is nothing less than a forerunner of the early RSC, a characteristic product of what Alan Sinfield has called 'culturalism'.[11] A product of the relative cultural fertility of post-war Britain, this intervention attempted to offer an alternative to mainstream theatrical tradition, aligning Shakespeare more closely with notions of accessible popular entertainment. The production was directed by John Barton, and subsidised by (among others) the Arts Council.

Without making extravagant claims for the radical potentiality of this embryo which is now a monumental national institution, it can be suggested that the kind of dramatic intervention made here was culturally a potential point of radical energy in Shakespeare reproduction, and its presentation on television a challenge to the dominant theatrical and naturalistic conventions. Thirty years later Jane Howell's productions of the first tetralogy for the BBC/Time-Life Series, based on similar principles, stood out with remarkable boldness and clarity as a radical cultural intervention.[12]

Yet this remarkable production of *Henry V* appeared as the BBC's official contribution to the festivities for the coronation of Elizabeth II. The *Radio Times*' 'Television Diary' juxtaposed 'The Elizabethan Theatre Company' against a BBC film on 'The Second Elizabeth'. A potential growth-point of post-war British culture, which was attempting by a reappropriation of Elizabethan theatrical practices to harness some of the popular energies of the Renaissance theatre, was in turn appropriated by the BBC and manipulated into a curtain-raiser for the New Elizabethan Age. By the operation of institutional forces, an opportunity to bring the populist and democratic medium of television into an alliance with the popular aspects of Shakespearean theatre was rendered little more than an ideological affirmation of historical continuity, institutional hegemony and state power.

1. George More O'Ferrall, "The Televising of Drama," *Radio Times* 19 March 1947, 4.
2. John Wilders, "Adjusting the Set," *Times Literary Supplement*, 10 July 1981, 13.

3. Raymond Williams, *Television: Technology and Cultural Form* (London: Fontana, 1974), pp. 88–90.

4. The only historical study I know of is an unpublished M.A. thesis by Margaret Horsefield, "Shakespeare on Radio," Shakespeare Institute, University of Birmingham. Janet Clare has compiled a list of radio productions in *Theatre of the Air: A Checklist of Radio Productions of Renaissance Drama, 1922–1986; Renaissance Drama Newsletter, Supplement Six*, University of Warwick, 1986. It is evident from this list that BBC radio has broadcast some 100 productions of non-Shakespearean Renaissance plays, compared to over 200 productions of Shakespeare; BBC television has broadcast just over 100 Shakespeare productions, and only sixteen non-Shakespearean plays. Stuart Evans discusses the technical problems of dramatising Shakespeare for radio in *Shakespeare Survey*, 39 (1986).

5. Philip Brockbank informs me that he recalls listening to this broadcast. The nightingale, unpatriotically insensible to the occasion, failed to show up.

6. After the war studio production became the norm, but there were several outside broadcasts from the Open Air Theatre, Regent's Park. *As You Like It* was adapted for studio, and *A Midsummer Night's Dream* broadcast from Regent's Park, in July of 1946. See Ian Atkins, "Open Air Theatre to Studio," *Radio Times*, 12 July 1946. See also Holderness and McCullough, "Filmography," p. 16 and p. 28.

7. *Hamlet*, produced by George More O'Ferrall, broadcast between 5 and 15 December 1947.

8. See J. C. Trewin, "Every Inch a King," *Radio Times*, 20 April 1948, and "A Tragedy of Darkness," *Radio Times*, 18 February 1949, 25; and Lionel Hale, "*Othello*—A Play Bursting with Energy," *Radio Times*, 21 April 1950, 43.

9. Panel discussion on "Shakespeare and Television," broadcast on 22 April 1952.

10. *Radio Times*, 15 May 1953; see p. 15 for feature article, "New Elizabethan Actors."

11. Alan Sinfield, "Royal Shakespeare," in Jonathan Dollimore and Alan Sinfield, eds., *Political Shakespeare* (Manchester: Manchester University Press, 1985), pp. 164ff.

12. For discussions of Jane Howell's BBC productions, see Graham Holderness, "Radical Potentiality and Institutional Closure," in Dollimore and Sinfield, *Political Shakespeare*, pp. 197–99; and (with Christopher McCullough), "Boxing the Bard: The Cultural Politics of Television," *Red Letters*, 18 (1986), 23–33. See also Stanley Wells, "The History of the Whole Contention," *Times Literary Supplement*, 4 February 1983, p. 105.

Decentering the Bard

The BBC-TV Shakespeare and Some Implications for Criticism and Teaching
Gary F. Waller

The late Louis Althusser once remarked that our age might well be remembered for its drastic revaluation of the most ordinary of human activities—reading, writing, and sight.[1] No student of contemporary culture needs to be reminded that we live in an age of rapid changes in the ways we perceive and interpret plays, poems, novels, art, film, television—indeed, any experience that involves the complex, deceptive (and self-deceptive) act we call interpretation. We live, it is often argued, at the end of an era in our civilization, in a time when old paradigms no longer seem adequate to our moral, philosophical or day-to-day experiences, and when new ways of projecting our desire for meaning upon reality are struggling to be born. Relativism, dislocation and discontinuity characterize our age; and believers in the traditional humanities, like art or literature, seem to be overwhelmed by despair or paralysis.

Shakespeare's plays have traditionally been accorded a primary, even untouchable, place in our culture. Yet they have been read and produced and interpreted—"concretized" as the fashionable jargon has it—within continually changing horizons of expectation, even while each successive age has asserted that its dominant mode of concretization is natural, true-to-life, or whatever the current cliché may be—if not God-given, at least Bard-authenticated. Reading Johnson on Lear or Mrs. Jameson on Shakespeare's heroines we became uncomfortably aware that our own interpretations may come to be as quirkish; certainly we may appreciate that, as Alan Dessen puts it, Shakespeare's plays have "for centuries . . . functioned as a Rorschach test wherein individuals and even entire cultures consciously or unconsciously have discovered themselves." [2]

One of our preconceptions is that such relativism is inevitable. To read is always, as Derrida has taught us, to rewrite; or as Harold Bloom would put it, to read is necessarily to misread. So when Raymond Williams argues in his 1975 inaugural lecture as Professor of Drama at Cambridge that "drama is no longer . . . coextensive with theatre," that "most dramatic performances are now in film and television studios" [3] and further that no society has ever been so self-conscious about "acting," that drama "in quite new ways" is built into the rhythms of our everyday life, [4] especially through the omnipresence of television, then we realise that by asking "What is *our* Shakespeare?," we are necessarily asking further questions: To what extent do film and, more latterly, television versions of his plays express and determine *our* culture's rewriting or misreading of Shakespeare? What changes can we see coming over the ways we respond to, teach, write criticism about his plays? Is it true that today, after sixty years of serious movie-going, we inevitably imagine Shakespeare filmically, i.e. instead of speaking of "adapting" Shakespeare to film, we find ourselves within a discourse that conceives more naturally of a filmic Shakespeare? At the very least, we must surely consider Jack Jorgens' point that since "millions of people each year . . . experience Shakespeare on the screen . . . it will become increasingly impossible for teachers and critics to ignore these productions." [5]

Shakespeare's teachers and critics now have another disruptive challenge. Since 1978, we have seen, at the rate of six a year, the BBC's noble effort to produce what Cedric Messina announced as "basic 'classic' interpretations" designed "to make the plays in permanent form accessible to audiences throughout the world." Noble, I'll suggest, but naive: Messina's very terms, "classic," "basic," "permanent," set up theoretical and, indeed, ideological barriers to the realization of his other announced aim, to make the plays "as vividly alive as it is possible for the production teams to make them."[6]

Mind you, I (like, I'm sure, most others) am still partly in what Barthes calls the hysterical stage of interpretation[7]—when we forget that a text is a fiction and we lose ourselves in its sheer impact (like, perhaps, the proverbial old lady who got out of her theatre seat during a performance of Othello and started to attack Iago with her umbrella). It is, indeed, marvelous to be able to turn on one's television and see, and hear, and luxuriate in, Shakespeare's plays—and equally so to be able to use and refer to them in the classroom. But teachers and critics, after all, are peculiarly burdened by having to articulate more than being overwhelmed or appalled by a performance. So we all go through Barthes' other three stages: the "fetishistic," where (in traditional pedagogy) we concentrate on discrete elements, words, details of staging or verbal phrases, worrying them, attacking them with a dictionary, a thesaurus, blocking charts; the "obsessional," where we look for systematic patterns (moral, philosophical, historical) to which we can relate the work; or the "paranoiac," where we sense the work has designs upon us, and we contemplate what insights and pressures the performance has brought to our lives.[8] In short, if we want to find ways of moving beyond mere chit-chat about the BBC Shakespeare, we have to find some powerful theoretical models within which we can locate our experience of these productions. Such terms as "hysterical," "fetishistic," "obsessional" or "paranoiac" may not be those by which we would all want to describe the productions, but they do provocatively underline our crucial challenge—to search for a contemporary language by which Shakespeare can enter our history, rather than be a part of our gossip.

Ironically, it is only in the past ten or so years that academic criticism has allowed Shakespeare's plays, once again, to function as theatre. For forty or more years, the dominant strand of Shakespearean criticism read the plays, in effect, as poems or historical documents or novels rather than as scripts. Work by such critics as J. L. Styan, Alan C. Dessen, Michael Goldman and E. A. J. Honigmann has gradually directed our attention to the performative, open-ended nature of the Shakespearean text.[9] In Shakespeare and the Energies of Drama (1972), for instance, Goldman declared that the critic should "seek a meaning for each play in the human significance of our response as audience, in the life it awakens us to, the awareness it builds upon." Above all else, he argued, in theatre "there is a unique focus on the body. The play may rise in Shakespeare's imagination and come home to our own, but it takes place between two sets of bodies, ours and the actors'." Similarly, Honigmann attempts to "study the dramatist's technical skills in guiding audience response," suggesting that the plays are built on "fluctuations of feeling" within the audience, and that Shakespeare often deliberately leaves his spectators in uncertainties.[10]

Such theatre-centered criticism has made a significant breakthrough, and today most Shakespeareans would recognize as unsatisfactory any criticism (or teaching) that dehistoricizes the Shakespearean script into a static monument. We recognize perhaps that even in his own age, each time Shakespeare himself saw one of his own plays performed, he would have seen it in a new guise, modified by factors over which he had no control.[11]

However, one of the ironies of our present situation—again underlining the dislocating nature of contemporary culture—is that, as usual, academics are in the rearguard of cultural adaption. Having been dragged screaming into the theatre, we must face the possibility that, as Ronald Bryden is reported to have apprehensively (and tellingly) stated, Shakespeare will be further "liberated from us"[12]—that Shakespeare's plays are not only theatre, but they are also (indeed have been for sixty years) film and now, television. So here we are, all subject to what Derrida calls "the symptoms of fear before the dangers of the festival,"[13] asking all over again what *are* the demands and pressures, the advantages and limitations, put upon the dramatic text by the new medium? What are the necessities and possibilities of television Shakespeare as opposed to Shakespeare in the theatre—or even Shakespeare on film? I think such questions are especially important to ask when we consider the culturally peripheral nature of traditional theatre and the fact that television, for better or worse, has taken on what Fiske and Hartley call a "bardic function"—i.e., providing a common centre, articulating the myths of our society, its very power a pressing reason for our taking it seriously.[14]

In what follows, I want to develop two major arguments. The first is that we are bound, when considering the television Shakespeare, to see productions within the semiotics of television itself. There has been some criticism along these lines and, in a sense, all I will do will be to suggest that the detailed studies of the dynamics of television made by such scholars as Stuart Hall, Umberto Eco, Roland Barthes, and others need to be applied to Shakespearean criticism. More substantial, I think, is my second argument, in which I will apply some seminal ideas of Benjamin to the Shakespearean text as a cultural phenomenon—and then go on to draw some parallels with developments in contemporary literary criticism. In each case, the television Shakespeare is considered as "text," and thus some of the current critical ferment on the nature of textuality and dissemination generated by Derrida, Foucault and others will be relevant.

First, then, to pay some attention to the distinctive codes of television. We are obviously going to fundamentally misunderstand the BBC Shakespeare plays if we view them as televised theatre; but also, I suggest, if we see them as televised film. I stress this latter distinction because Cedric Messina's original intention was, quite explicitly, to transfer the conventions of film into television—and I suspect this intention helps account for the unsatisfactory nature of many of the early productions. Regardless of intention, the dynamics of television, its peculiar strategies as a medium of communication, and the ways it intersects with the deep semantic structures of our culture make it distinctively different from film. Having said that, I must of course stress the differences from theatrical production. At times in the BBC productions we can see the director uneasily trying to approximate theatrical conditions—by rapid closing or distancing to give the sense of shifting sightlines or perspective, or by using occasional panning or tilt-shots to break the conventional television technique of over-the-shoulder shots. But the essential nature of television makes it fundamentally different from the theatre. Both film and television, for instance, have greater visual and temporal flexibility. With both, we have to discuss montage, cutting, camera movement and angle, visual as much as verbal symbolism, cinematic motif, shot length, and— above all else—the directive viewpoint of the camera: the way in which the lens controls our access to the action. Film and television also share a greater flexibility than theatre in the use of spectacle. One thinks of the spectacular use of the beach at the opening of Polanski's *Macbeth*, the use of the castle battlements and the sea in Kozintsev's *Hamlet*, or the luxuriant grace of the forest in the television *As You Like It*. On the other hand, there are some obvious dangers: one of the reasons the BBC *Tempest* is such an unsatisfactory production is the way the visual codes, through repetition and duplication, unintentionally parody the Shakespeare script. Not only is the TV image granular, volatile and imprecise, but for drama it provides, crucially, a virtually two-dimensional acting space. Necessarily, static and intimate scenes dominate; more than two or three people are hard to handle; and when there are scenes with movement, Z-axis staging and concertina zooms are crucial stratagems. Television has difficulty in providing a panorama in depth, and it is relatively unable to record rapid motion by sweeping.

However, television does have one enormous strength—its intimacy. The primary reality of television drama—and here it is somewhat unlike film—is not spectacle, but the intimacy with which it records human emotions. Some theatre-oriented critics have protested that "television's use of the close-up enforces an intimacy with the individual characters which Shakespeare does not always choose to give us,"[15] drawing attention to talking heads, torsos rather than whole bodies, or not being able to watch off-camera characters (the silent Angelo in Act 5 of *Measure for Measure*, for instance). But behind the protest is not only a nostalgia for an impossible monumentality of Shakespeare's script, but also a reluctance to use the strength of the medium. Just as the Elizabethan theatre's predominant focus on the space between the pillars would have dominated an Elizabethan production and the proscenium stage a nineteenth-century one, so the voyeuristic intimacy of television is its determinative characteristic. Its most powerful image, at once metonymy and metaphor, is the human face. The television actor expresses himself not, as on the stage, in body movements, but in facial change. Whereas in Act 3 of *Julius Caesar* Keith Michell's rendition of Antony's speech lacked atmosphere, as a group of ten actors attempted to stand in for (what in film) could have been hundreds, in *Henry IV* Anthony Quayle compellingly shocked us as he glanced away from the action and directly into our living rooms as we watched, just as the conspirators in *Julius Caesar* stared uneasily at us, eyeball to eyeball. As Robert E. Knoll pointed out, not totally approvingly, the focus of the play became the psyches of the conspirators [16]—or, as I would prefer to put it, *our* sense of the shiftiness and the risk of conspiracy. But at such moments we may realize that a performance of Shakespeare is best concretized, for us, not in a theatre, an alien building with an aura of a church or a museum, but in our own rooms. Television creates an intimacy between two rooms, ours and that of the screen. We peer through the screen as if into another person's private life—and that is why the best moments of the BBC productions have been when they are, literally, in rooms, and we peer, moving unseen like voyeurs, between Angelo and Isabella, conscious of the unperceived closeness of their faces to ours. Williams argues, in fact, that ever since Ibsen, drama has dealt predominantly with "enclosed rooms on enclosed stages" and that there is a "direct cultural continuity" with the rooms in which we now watch "the framed images of television." [17]

If, as is often said, the soliloquy was the key technical strategy for Renaissance stage drama, especially for tragedy, then such intimacy is our equivalent. As film developed earlier this century, the soliloquy underwent a shift inward by the frequent use of voice-over techniques (as in Olivier's *Hamlet*) and by being broken by cutting and varied angle-shots. In television a further displacement occurs as—even though we lose the physical isolation of a character alone on a stage—we become the privileged participant in a voyeuristic revelation.

I have been arguing so far that the strategies of television—its system of signs, the fact that it is primarily a visual, iconic, sign system with strong but supplementary aural-verbal support—should make fundamental differences to the way we teach and write about Shakespeare. Now I want to turn to a more speculative area, where I concentrate on ways in which cultural content is transmitted, especially in the way that television serves to bring to the surface, often in disguised or repressed forms, the deep semantic structures of our society. [18]

Where television's greatest distinction as a medium (and not only for Shakespeare) lies is simply in the scope of its audience and the consequent desacralization of Shakespeare as sacred text. Here I turn to Walter Benjamin's famous essay, "The Work of Art in the Age of Mechanical Reproduction." [19] Benjamin argued that just as printing, lithography and, in this century, the reproduction of sound and colour have dramatically changed the way we perceive art, so the authority, what he terms the "aura," of the work of art is put in jeopardy when the authenticity of the art-work is put into question. [20] He suggests that film in particular, by substituting a "plurality of copies for a unique existence" and thus meeting "the beholder or listener in his own particular situation," has emancipated the work of art from a quasi-religious status. [21] John Berger has extended this argument into a consideration of art reproduction, showing the way photographic reproductions multiply and fragment the meaning and status of an original. [22]

Now, consider the argument in relation to the play—and, by extension, to theatre, film, and television. There still remain, in Shakespeare criticism, the vestiges of a view of the sacred text and, indeed, the sacred author, "an author-creator who, absent and from afar, is armed with [a sacred text and] keeps watch over, assembles, regulates the time or the meaning of representation."[23] But what theatre-centered criticism and now the further dissemination of film and television show us is that the play (perhaps more than any other art-work) is always already decentered. There is no original: no original performance, no original "text." A play is a script, decomposing as it is composed and recomposed as it is performed. It never makes meaning until it is loosed into the world as performance: in short, until it enters the textuality of history. What directors have often said, usually to the horror of the academic establishment, is given further support by the dissemination of television productions. When, for instance, Kozintzev remarks that he always regards half the text of any play as diffused remarks "to acquaint actors as thoroughly as possible with the heart of the action to be played,"[24] or Jonathan Miller argues that since Shakespeare left no "collateral instructions" it is impossible to know if we were "in the presence of a version wherein the text was speaking for itself,"[25] then we become aware, perhaps disturbingly so, that it is the role of each audience, each reader or spectator, to become the guardian of the play—to carry out, as creatively as possible, the inevitable rewriting that constitutes attention, response, study, and criticism.

I want to draw out some implications for Shakespearean criticism from my appropriation of Benjamin's argument. What I have termed the inherently decentered nature of the play—the fact that we can never objectively privilege any concretization of it—clearly calls into radical question any lingering concept of a fixed, classic reading of a play. Meaning in drama, even more evidently than with other art-forms, does not inhere in the work: the work may initiate performances of meaning in a continual unraveling and interplay between itself and successive spectators.[26] The text provides us with the signs: as Roland Barthes puts it, "reading," or in our case viewing, does not simply follow a text. The text becomes the point of departure.[27]

In accord with the truism that good criticism always takes account of its own historicity, we can see the history of Shakespearean criticism illustrating the changing ways the plays have been read and produced—the shifting fashions (and rewritings) of *Lear*, the obsessive concentration on Hamlet's inwardness or delay since Coleridge, the unprecedented popularity of *Troilus and Cressida* in this century, the changing evaluation of the comedies, even the dividing out of new categories of plays like the romances or the problem plays, not to mention variations, emphases and readings of individual plays. The test of success of a production (or a reading) is clearly not to be related back to an original text (which is waiting to be produced or read) but to the coherence and vitality of the play's impact. To these well-recognized instances, we can now add the BBC's emphasis on what I have called the voyeuristic intimacy of the plays, just as in the 1960s we added the dark, brooding cruelty of Brook's *Lear* and *A Midsummer Night's Dream*.

If we stand back from the line of argument I am pursuing, we can see as well how the production and reproduction on videotape of Shakespeare's plays reinforce some of the most important developments in contemporary literary theory. We can no longer pretend that the text is a fixed, historical entity: it is historical only in the sense that most of its history occurs after, not before, it is written, and part of that history takes place in our studies, our classrooms and (especially) our living rooms. We can no longer presume to authoritatively fix the "meaning" of a play—Barthes's "obsessive" phase, you recall—since we can observe the text opening up in us meanings which, in our own history and our own language, we are struggling to articulate. Inevitably, we realize, we build into our readings our own preconceptions, obsessions, anxieties or desires of which we may be unaware, and which (like those of the author) are class or culturally as well as linguistically determined. No discourse is innocent—neither Shakespeare's nor ours. Since meaning is never a static entity, the task of interpretation, as Nietzsche and Derrida put it, is necessary and joyfully endless;[28] the perennial task of interpretation is the struggle to articulate as persuasively and powerfully as possible the ever-renewed and renewable life the performed text opens up in us. Meaning is a process of dissemination—it is split, spread, always potent.

Now to move to some implications for Shakespeare criticism. If my argument is, even in part, granted, some of the long-treasured tenets of two dominant schools of criticism, at least in the Anglo-American world, are thereby called into question. The first is the school of organic formalism, best represented by the New Critics or F. R. Leavis, for whom a play succeeds insofar as it has organic or symbolic unity and coherence. But if there are, finally, as Derrida puts it, no texts but only an infinite textuality, always on the move, a differential network without fixed origin; if a text articulates sociocultural pressures of which neither it nor its author is aware and is open to perpetual *difference*—changing fashions of production, cutting, reading, all different concretizations in different minds, theatres, eras—then organic unity disappears. Yet perhaps no single idea has had such a stubborn hold over the critical fashions of our century as that of textual unity or wholeness. As an increasing weight of criticism has shown in recent years, however, texts are always riddled by abysses, unsettled by repression; their apparently solid ground is no rock but thin air.[30] Indeed (and Shakespeare's plays are often uncanny evidence of this) the most interesting literary works are those that, by organicist criteria, appear imperfect, unfinished, disruptive rather than soothing and resolved.

The implications for teaching, as well as for understanding, the dynamics of watching Shakespeare are tremendous. To stress the performative dimension of the play is to avow that criticism and teaching are participatory, not passive, experiences. Our classrooms become communities of interpreters. And, unlike theatre performances, film and television productions are reproducible—we can stop the television, we can rewind our films, we can compare productions in ways that theatrical productions cannot be compared. We will be able to rewatch Olivier's *Hamlet* or Miller's *Antony and Cleopatra* for years—and because we will be able to do so in our living rooms as well as our classrooms, we may find that readings of these productions will no longer be restrained by the usual canons of academic criticism. On this point we connect with another of Benjamin's arguments in "The Work of Art in the Age of Mechanical Reproduction," in which he pointed out that with film (and, we can add, television) the art-work has undergone a radical democratization, in that the existence of audiences unfamiliar with the traditional reification of art as a sacred object encourages a different, less controllable mode of spectator participation and response than occurs even in the theatre. Perhaps we romanticize the Elizabethan age when we say that every artisan, apprentice, and gallant had his own opinion of Hamlet or Hieronimo, but that is certainly a possibility with the television Shakespeare. The bard is loosed into our world.

Secondly, where does this leave the other, perhaps the dominant, mode of Anglo-American Shakespeare criticism of our time? Historical criticism has insisted that, finally, Shakespeare's plays are explicable only within what used to be termed the "Elizabethan world-picture." Studies of Shakespeare's plays considered in terms of their "background" (a static concept which in effect detaches the plays from their history) continue to appear, although as Mark Rose recently remarked, they make us uncomfortably aware that while our sense of reality has drastically altered, much of our critical vocabulary remains static.[31] When, twenty years ago, Jan Kott's *Shakespeare Our Contemporary* appeared, it was given a hostile reception by historicist critics for what was seen as its projection upon Shakespeare of ideas and perspectives foreign to his age and to his "intentions." Since that time such notions as "the Elizabethan point of view," "Shakespeare's contemporary outlook," or "seeing things as Shakespeare saw them" have become increasingly questioned, even ridiculed. Every age—and especially those like Shakespeare's with an especially dominant cultural power like the Monarchy and Court—tries to exclude either by direct censorship or by consent any experiences or social forces which challenge its hegemony. One of the crucial functions of art is that it unmasks and demystifies the apparent "truths" of a society, opening up the contradictions and silences within its seeming coherence and showing the ideological distortions that are going on.[32] If, as Williams puts it, art is one of the central means by which a society expresses its sense of being a society,[33] then it does so in ways that operate at a level far below the explicit or commonplace thought of an age—at what Foucault calls the archaeological level rather than that reified by historical scholarship in the past fifty years.[34] Our role as critics and readers is to show how our own distinctive place in history allows us to speak of what the text cannot speak—as feminist critics have done in recent years, and as a new mode of structural historicism promises to do.

What I am outlining as a revisionist approach to literary history may seem a long way from the BBC Shakespeare; but my digression is necessary, I think, to bring out one distinctive feature of the productions. I spoke initially of the "hysterical" stage of appreciation, and I want now to try to move beyond that.

However welcome they may be to our screens, however brilliant some of the performances, all are exercises in cultural nostalgia. In costume, setting and indeed in intention, the productions—with the partial exception of Miller's *Antony*—have been antiquarian. To ask what are the distinctive features of our concretization of the plays is to pay attention not merely to a closed and formal universe of signs, but to the way these signs interact with and reinforce or challenge the dominant ideology of our own culture.

Television's critics have frequently accused it of not merely being superficial and trivialising, but of reinforcing some of the more authoritarian and retrogressive forces within our society. Like a hieratic or "theological"[35] work of art, television demands a passive public of consumers, for whom it acts as both creator and reflection of insecurities for which it provides temporary and therefore never-ending palliatives. A similar point can be made about capitalism's power to absorb, neutralize and employ any potentially challenging medium—the newspaper and periodical in the nineteenth century, or rock music in our own time, are classic examples. What in the late nineteenth century seemed to promise a democratization of choice, decision and experience have become more firmly controlled by the cultural hegemonies of our time—in publishing, by mass-circulation page-turners, consumer magazines and a culturally controlled press. These are particular examples of how the discourse approved and promulgated by our society conceives of its audience as a mass to be administered and manipulated, and not as a direct participant (except under carefully pre-coded conditions). All these criticisms are well-known and have been advanced by such critics as Enzenberger, Hall, Williams and others.[36]

And yet just as the ideological strains of a work emerge despite its author or the text itself, so when we consider it in relation to the dominant structures governing its reception, even the most nostalgically conceived and ideologically neutralized work of art may contain the most revolutionary potential. Here we connect with another part of Benjamin's argument. The very reproducibility of the plays, their invasion of our homes, our living rooms, our mental and emotional presuppositions, mean that potentially at least, we are letting loose within our culture, in ways not matched since Shakespeare's own age, one of our history's most powerful counter-cultural forces. Alvin Kernan has written of the way, in the forty years after Shakespeare's death, his plays did indeed become revolutionary. Along with those of his fellow dramatists, they released into the common consciousness of their time—often in the form of the enacted fantasies and repressed urges of underprivileged and thwarted classes—forces that would eventually emerge in the revolutionary struggle in mid-century. What, asks Kernan, is the act above all others feared by the Elizabethan and Jacobean Court? Regicide. What is the most common act, performed or sought with resounding emotional impact, on the Jacobean stage? The killing of the king. Kernan is not tracing a direct connection: what his example does point to is the way art may function as the articulator of hidden desires and pressures, the way such desires and pressures become, despite official pronouncements of the dominant ideology of an age, habituated.[37]

In Shakespeare's age, the drama—at least that part that could escape the direct control of the court—acted as the vehicle of counter-dominant cultural forces that would have a profound and permanent effect on our history. It did so by transforming a residual and in many ways archaic cultural form, the theatre, showing how it could be used in a dazzling combination of populism and avant-garde daring, to embody and direct the age's most radical drives.

How does this apply to Shakespeare on television? Unlike the Elizabethan theatre, television may appear to be a radically new medium, and yet it has quickly been appropriated by our society's dominant cultural forces to become an essentially conservative, even reactionary, medium. The crass verisimilitude at which most television drama aims is a case in point: it is a nostalgic return to the bourgeois realism that revolutionized and then overwhelmed the eighteenth- and nineteenth-century novel. "Realism" is a distinctive and ideologically specific mode of observation which tries to exclude or render marginal alternative ways of seeing. In our century it has been adapted by pulp fiction, Hollywood movies and the bulk of television drama as an expression of cultural nostalgia. That the BBC productions have, by and large, chosen to stay within its limits is revealing—especially given the genuinely revolutionary possibilities of television to which Benjamin's arguments point.

Yet inherent in television are features that do, in fact, challenge the dominance of bourgeois realism and embody, perhaps in the way Kernan argues the Jacobean drama did, forms of experience that break with those approved by the dominant socio-economic forces of corporate capitalist society. Ironically it is in commercials, in live sports television, and in some "fringe" programming that the most sophisticated, disruptive and dislocative techniques, akin to many of those found in postmodern fiction or art, can be found: discontinuity, irrealism, dislocating effects of sound, colour, perceptual changes, split-screens, slow-motion and instant replays from a variety of angles—all ways of exposing the ideological repression of bourgeois realism, just as the fiction of Becket and Pynchon, Vonnegut and Sukenick, or the painting of Oldenburg or Warhol, have done in print and paint.

What bourgeois realism has tried to do and what the bulk of television does is to limit the responses of its audience to the known, the approved, to the consensus outlook of the dominant classes of society. But just as a text ravels itself together at one end while always unraveling at the other, so television, in spite of itself, contains the seeds of transformation, the possibility of opening its audience to experiences and forms that go beyond its declared or desired intentions. Here Benjamin's emphasis on the potential democratization of film (and television) is unusually important—and it is here that the BBC Shakespeare has, perhaps, a central role to play in the cultural crisis of our time. Could it be that Shakespeare on television may open us to the unsettling challenges Kernan argues it provided his own time? Could it inspire a generation of television watchers to demand more substantial, provocative drama on television? Could it unsettle the viewers, even a little, into challenging the residual values the medium reinforces? Could it use more radical techniques to bring about the equivalent of what Peter Brook terms "living theatre?"[38] Could teachers and critics and directors demand that the surprising and disruptive technical possibilities of the medium be used not to reinforce our society's fearfulness and paralysis, but to suggest ways we can make our history?

To answer "yes" to any of these questions may be unrealistically optimistic (to answer "no," especially for educators, may be cynical despair). But to have answered "yes" to similar questions about the theatre in Shakespeare's time might have appeared to be even greater folly. What we have learned in the past fifty years, as the bourgeois-capitalist hegemony has been challenged, renewed itself, become dislocated and paralysed, is that a dominant culture always produces the possibility of counter-cultures from within itself, and that it is the essential nature of texts (including television) to be open-ended, to be what Barthes terms "writerly"—always requiring completion, application, (mis)reading and rewriting by each new audience.[39]

Here is our potential, tiny as it may be, and our justification for celebrating, hysterically if we like, the very fact of the BBC productions. But it will require more than welcome: it will require criticism, analysis, deconstruction, demystification and certainly more than the genteel appreciative or deprecative remarks that have passed for criticism so far. Only by taking it seriously, by making it undergo the difficult and infinite unraveling of reading and teaching and criticism, can we hope to let the Shakespeare text, once again, enter our lives and our history.

1. Louis Althusser and Etienne Balibar, *Reading Capital,* trans. Ben Brewster (London, 1970), pp. 15–16.

2. Alan C. Dessen, *Elizabethan Drama and the Viewer's Eye* (Chapel Hill, N.C., 1977), p. 6.

3. Raymond Williams, *Drama in a Dramatised Society* (Cambridge, Eng., 1975), p. 3.

4. Ibid., p. 5.

5. Jack J. Jorgens, *Shakespeare on Film* (Bloomington, Ind., 1977), p. 3.

6. "Wilders Interview at MLA," *Shakespeare on Film Newsletter,* 4:1 (1979), 3; Cedric Messina, "Preface" to the *BBC-TV Shakespeare* volumes (London, 1979-), quoted by Maurice Charney, "Shakespearean Anglophilia: The BBC-TV Series and American Audiences," *SQ,* 31 (1980), 292.

7. Roland Barthes, *The Pleasure of the Text,* trans. Richard Miller (New York, 1975), p. 63.

8. Ibid.

9. See my "Speaking What We Feel: Shakespearean Criticism in the Late Seventies," *Dal. R.,* 58 (1978), 550–563.

10. Michael Goldman, *Shakespeare and the Energies of Drama* (Princeton, N.J., 1972), pp. 4, 6, 10; E. A. J. Honigmann, *Shakespeare: Seven Tragedies* (New York, 1976), pp. 1, 2, 4.

11. John Russell Brown, *Free Shakespeare* (London, 1974), p. 48.

12. "Messina at the SAA Meeting," *Shakespeare on Film Newsletter,* 4:2 (April 1980), 1.

13. Jacques Derrida, *Writing and Difference,* trans. Alan Bass (Chicago, 1978), p. 244.

14. John Fiske and John Hartley, *Reading Television* (London, 1978), p. 86.

15. Jacqueline Pearson, "Shadows on the Shadow-box: The BBC Shakespeare," *CQ,* 21:1 (Spring 1979), 69.

16. Robert E. Knoll, "The Shakespeare Plays: The First Season," *Shakespeare on Film Newsletter,* 3:2 (April, 1979), 3, 5.

17. Williams, *Drama in a Dramatised Society,* p. 9.

18. Stuart Hall, *Encoding and Decoding in the Television Discourse* (University of Birmingham Centre for Contemporary Studies Stencilled Occasional Paper: Media Series SP no. 7, 1973), p. 11.

19. Walter Benjamin, "The Work of Art in the Age of Mechanical Reproduction," in *Illuminations*, ed. Hannah Arendt, trans. Harry Zohn (New York, 1968), p. 223.

20. Ibid., pp. 221–23.

21. Ibid., p. 223.

22. John Berger, *A Way of Seeing* (New York, 1973); cf. Benjamin, "The Work of Art," p. 231.

23. Derrida, *Writing and Difference*, p. 235.

24. Grigori Kozintsev, *Shakespeare: Time and Conscience*, trans. Joyce Vining (New York, 1972), p. 215.

25. Ralph Berry, *On Directing Shakespeare* (New York, 1977), p. 9.

26. Cf. Wolfgang Iser, *The Act of Reading* (Baltimore, 1978), p. 27.

27. See Roland A. Champagne, "Between Orpheus and Eurydice: Roland Barthes and the Historicity of Reading," *Clio*, 8:2 (1979), 231.

28. See e.g. Derrida, *Writing and Difference*, p. 12.

29. See e.g. Jacques Derrida, "Signature Event Context," *Glyph*, 1 (1977), 185.

30. Susan R. Suleiman, "Varieties of Audience-Oriented Criticism," in Susan R. Suleiman and Inge Crosman, eds., *The Reader in the Text* (Princeton, N.J., 1980), p. 40. Cf. J. Hillis Miller, "Deconstructing the Deconstructors," *Diacritics*, 5:2 (1975), 31.

31. Mark Rose, "Changing Criticism," YR, 66 (1977), 463.

32. Terry Eagleton, "Text, Ideology, Realism," in Edward W. Said, ed., *Literature and Society: Selected Papers from the English Institute* (Baltimore, 1980), p. 160.

33. Raymond Williams, *The Long Revolution* (London, 1961), p. 30.

34. See e.g. Michel Foucault, *The Order of Things* (New York, 1973), p. xi.

35. Derrida, *Writing and Difference*, p. 235.

36. Peter Uwe Hohendahl, "The Use Value of Contemporary Literary Criticism," NGC, 7 (1976), 6.

37. Alvin Kernan, "The Plays and the Playwrights," in *Revels History of Drama in English*, Vol. 3, ed. J. Leeds Barroll et. al. (London, 1975), p. 251.

38. Peter Brook, *The Empty Space* (Harmondsworth, Eng., 1978), ch. 1.

39. Roland Barthes, *S/Z*, trans. Richard Miller (New York, 1974), pp. 4–5.

Wooden O's in Plastic Boxes
Shakespeare and Television
Sheldon P. Zitner

Royal jealousy; accused queen dies; schoolboy prince felled by psychoso-
matic illness. Princess abandoned in diapers as chief of mission is eaten in
animal encounter. But younger generation heals all wounds as king repents
and maternal statue walks off pedestal.

What is unthinkable in this parody is not so much the plot of *The Winter's
Tale* as the style of *TV Guide*. The television ambience—even its flack—is
saturated in the television style: vividness through disconnection; 'relevance'
no matter how irrelevant; diction that leapfrogs fact and logic to land with a
thump on cliché and pizzazz. The style is enveloping, as our instant recognition shows. In contrast, there is no pervasive 'theatrical' style. We rarely
experience a staged play by Shakespeare in the context of other plays. Only
reviewers attend the theatre night after night, so for most of us the foil and
context of stage performance is the daily round. But the foil and context of
Shakespeare on television is other television. *All's Well* and *Macbeth* are
time-slots between Whatever and the Eleven O'clock News, items in the
weekly line-up—of which the general viewer watches enough hours a day to
constitute something like a university teaching load. I am, however, less concerned about the possible contamination of *Titus Andronicus* by *Kojak* or
about the operation of Gresham's Law of Show Biz than about some consequent differences between the situations of the theatre and television
audiences.

For the stage play, even for the movie, not only an actor, but an audience,
prepares; for television one merely turns a knob. The stage-play ritual begins
with planning: for tickets, for transportation (to another city, sometimes another country), for dinner, for clothing. It is a venture, a budget item, an
occasion. It is also a ceremony, generating expectations, attitudes, behaviour.
Film-going is more casual but still has something of preparation and of distinction from the daily round. Not so with television, however nasal the ancient instruments or pitted the Folio type that, as truncated time-warp,
announce the plays. These maimed rites of television viewing and the accompanying transformation in the circumstances of its audience are the first matter I should like to discuss. The second is the difference between the stage and
television definitions of the locus of dramatic action. Both topics are large,
and I can hardly make even a beginning with each. Yet it seems to me that

Reprinted, with permission, from *University of Toronto Quarterly*, 51 (Fall 1981), 1–12.

their historical development exhibits some common features; in both cases there is a clear progression from theatre to film to television.

Let me put this in the form of two paradigms. From stage to film to television, the audience changes from active collective to passive collective to passive individual; and the locus of dramatic action from primary definition by the physical stage to primary definition by the moving vantage of the camera and finally to primary definition by the television screen. In addition, the oval of vision is—largely because of screen size—least mobile in television and, like its audience, given fewest options. Both the novel situation of the television audience and the way in which television circumscribes the locus of action lead, I think, to some common effects. But for the moment I want to return to a further consideration of the audience, specifically to some consequences of the de-ritualization of television viewing. For those who never or rarely see a staged play by Shakespeare, or indeed by anyone, this de-ritualization may very well put an end to real or imagined social barriers. That Shakespeare is caviar to the general is not what makes him caviar, and no one can reasonably regret the size of the new audience for Shakespeare. But this should be no bar to taking a sober look at how they are getting their Shakespeare. The issue is not the fact, but the conditions of access.

Literary genres can be defined—and so Aristotle defined them—by their manner of presentation: through a single lyric voice, through the many voices of the play, or through the novel's combination of narrator and characters. But, especially since the primacy of print, the literary 'kinds' have also been characterized by their particular conditions of accessibility. Verse and fiction have come to bear the imprint of their audiences of solitary readers: verse with its need of devices to prompt and sustain intensity through repeated readings of complexities; long fiction with its need of devices to prompt and sustain anticipation and intermittent reading. But theatre audiences neither re-read nor do they declare their own intermission. Nor are they solitary. These are not only conditions of the audience, but conditions of the dramatist's text and of the collaborative company text that is performance. Shakespeare adapts the poet's devices of incremental repetition and the novelist's devices of synecdoche. But more important are those strategies necessitated by the fact of a collective audience.

The actualities of Elizabethan audience behaviour lay somewhere between the verve sentimentalized and envied in academic descriptions of 'those nut-cracking [and head-cracking] Elizabethans' and the presbyterian solemnity of audiences at Stratford, Ontario. But, however expressed, the response of a live audience makes itself elaborately known and is taken account of by actors and dramatists. The alternating current from audience to troupe flows nowhere but in the theatre. A different current flows, but weakly, between spectators at a film, although the responsiveness that is an excitement in the theatre is largely a nuisance in the movie house. But the theatre's tuning of performance to response is not a factor in television viewing. Nor is the there any of the flywheel effect of live audience reaction which modifies the responses of individual theatre-goers, exaggerating some, damping others. Television transforms all drama to closet drama, to plays for ones, if not for one.

The possible effect of television's lack of a collective audience on actors is more obvious than the possible effect on plays. Some dangers and opportunities that the dramatist seizes or avoids, as well as the strategies he develops for each, are no longer relevant. The writer of serious drama, for example, is at the mercy of the most ticklish boob in the house. Stray laughter is the occupational hazard of tragedy, and the only insurance available against contagious titter lies in placing it where it can be accommodated. The 'lightning rods' for laughter that Shakespeare placed so cannily in the middle acts of *Lear* to attract needed release lose some of their function outside the theatre. One wonders if Shakespeare's characteristic sawtooth pattern of intensification and release is not inevitably less effective on the television screen since it no longer answers to a pressing need, and the desirable variety in the character of audience attention is, in any case, achieved by the necessary varying of camera angles.

One thinks uneasily also of some important moments in Shakespeare in which the audience is spoken to over the heads of other characters. When the dying Henry IV deplores Hal's ingratitude, invoking it as both excuse and punishment of his own transgressions, his 'See, sons, what things you are' is hardly directed only to the princes in attendance. 'The foolish over-careful fathers,' of and to whom he speaks, are also many and—since 'canker'd heaps of strange-achieved gold' were their object—not even necessarily aristocratic. The actor must not only help to convey the plot-occasion but touch on the life-errors and rationalizations in the audience that are its origin and echo. Such moments, relatively rare even in Shakespeare, in which the actor becomes the hearer's story—immediately rather than through generalization from the fable—depend in part on the mutual cues possible only in live theatre. And the multiple analogues in Shakespearean plot that prompt what Yeats called 'The Emotion of Multitude,' the feeling of being surrounded rather than only appealed to by the motifs enacted onstage, seem to demand that we experience them in a parallel communion, as members slightly varying a unison. The pattern of illusion and interruption of illusion—of appeal from *locus* to *platea*—that Shakespeare and his contemporaries adapted from medieval practice[1] depended on a sensibility different from the one that produced later stage illusionism. But it depended also on the presence of a responsive live audience to which to make the appeal. Lacking such an audience, television is less flexible, less able to create and then abandon dramatic illusion in the Shakespearean manner. Consequently those scenes that gain their effect through direct address, as does the pirouetting of Richard III, or through an appeal to contexts outside the immediate stage scene present particular difficulties for television.

All this leads to a larger consideration I can only mention here. Some

critics—John Holloway, for example[2]—view the form and power of Shakespeare's plays, especially of his tragedies, as related to the supposed origins of
drama in ritual. To the extent that one shares this view the deritualization of
the television audience—not merely through casualness, but through the absence of collective response—sets a limit on the depth of feeling one can
expect from televised versions of Shakespeare's plays, or of anyone else's for
that matter. I don't happen to share this view. It is far less reasonable, in any
case, to go on insisting that television is a bland and limited medium than it
is to acknowledge the problems and attempt to find intensifying devices in the
new form. And it is wholly *unreasonable* to deplore as theoretically impossible television productions that have been successful indeed.

My second concern, the effects of television's way of defining the locus of
dramatic action, can be discussed with more precision. If the situation of its
audience makes scenes that break through dramatic illusion difficult for television, there are similar results from television's way of defining the locus of
dramatic action. Part of the effect of Shakespeare on the stage comes from the
fact of the stage itself and from our consciousness of it—not of the particular
construction of the Globe, but of any stage. With Shakespeare in the theatre
we are always *in* the theatre. 'We know,' as Dr. Johnson put it, 'that we are
neither in *Rome* nor *Pontus*.' But, more than this, the physical fact of the
stage, whatever its form, is necessary to the meaning and effect of all those
references to 'the wooden O,' those allusions to scenes natural and unnatural,
to parts, actors, acts and acting. The metaphor of the theatre, the most telling
of Shakespeare's organizing and reflective metaphors, becomes remote and
less effective without the theatre's real presence and without the visual rever-
beration between illusionary and physical acting space. That most successful
of the film versions of Shakespeare—Olivier's *Henry V*—was unable to summon up an equivalent in its own medium and so had to begin by recreating
the Elizabethan theatre; like incunabula it leans on the older medium for
what it did not re-invent, defining the state of a problem that film adaptation
has yet to solve.

A related difficulty that is only partly visual should, none the less, be mentioned here. It arises when Shakespeare uses theatrical archaism for purposes
of theme or texture. There are some telling scenes and one entire play which
depend on the dramatist's self-conscious allusion to the earlier theatre, not as
a metaphor but as embodying a particular style with characteristic ideological implications. Falstaff's send-up of Lyly in 1 *Henry IV* presents no
particular problem since it is primarily verbal burlesque, and Falstaff's mock-
euphuism—even when an audience does not recognize it as such—is appropriate as underdog amusement at the expense of the court. But when we come
to the Players' scenes in *Hamlet* and to the archaizing construction of *The
Winter's Tale* we are dealing with conscious allusion that is both burlesque
and tender, and both local and thematic in its implications. In *Hamlet* the
Players' arthritic Senecanism of speech sets the play apart from the play-
within-a-play, makes the artifice of Hamlet's situation 'real' with respect to

the greater artificiality of the Players' theatre. But it also gives us an equivalent of the black-and-white world of Hamlet's own naively polarized moral categories, categories wholly inadequate to the world of complex moral grayness in which he has to function. Hamlet, in short, thinks like an old play—and the anomaly should be obvious. The creaky machinery of *The Winter's Tale* has the effect of severely qualifying the cozy and reassuring implication of the play's fable. 'Well can they judge of nappy ale / And tell at large a winter's tale.' So the poet Thomas Campion extolled the rustic Jacks and Joans who told these artless tales of perils, marvels, and happy endings, tales we weary city-folk love but can't believe in. Shakespeare's verbal and structural archaism (his models were such tales and plays like *Mucedorus*) acknowledges that his play offers us naive wish-fulfillment. And this in turn reinforces a reminder of what actuality is: the unreasonableness of Leontes' jealousy and Florizel's love; Polixenes' self-contradictory opposition to Perdita; the undeserved death of Mamilius, the sadness of Hermione's lost years. The BBC version gave us some, but not enough, of this toughness. Adequate translation of this aspect of the play would require some equivalent television modes of allusion, and they are probably not available. I shall not lament long over this problem, however. The toughness and qualifications are largely lost even in the theatre, since the tradition of theatrical romance against which the play worked has been long forgotten.

The main problems for television adaptation of Shakespeare, however, are the more obvious ones of transferring plays written for a highly stylized stage to a medium whose typical visual imagery is more realistic in detail and effect, and whose visual and emotional frames are much more restricted. The mobility of the camera and the possibilities of realistic spectacle create a dilemma for both film and television. To ignore the chance to make Birnam Wood's coming to Dunsinane seem less an empty trick or to forgo the visual 'values' of a real Dover Cliff in *Lear* is to deny the particular genius of the camera. An impression of trickery, however, may be just what we want to validate Macbeth's (and Shakespeare's) ultimate view of the witches in *Macbeth*; and if in *Lear* the theme of language as lie is to reach its climax in Edgar's poetic subterfuge,[3] perhaps the real Dover Cliff is the last thing we ought to see. In any case, to allow the camera to 'do the thing it most does show' is to abandon the visual stylizations that Shakespeare's plays depend on. The actual woodland locations in the BBC *As You Like It* undercut the spirit of that comedy, since what Shakespeare's play demands is pastoral, and what the camera provides is Arden's coarser grandam, Nature. On the other hand, when television gives us a highly stylized theatrical set, as in the BBC *Winter's Tale*, we are also disappointed. The camera's Ariel liveliness and magic promise something more than a squat and serviceable geometric form appropriate only to a fixed set to which the eye, confined to a physical stage, knows it must often return in diverse dramatic contexts.

Solving the problems of translating Shakespeare's virtual space (I appropriate Susanne Langer's term here) to the more 'real' space accessible to the camera is more difficult for television than for film, largely because of television's small screen. But this limitation does have some advantages. Television puts a tighter frame around language, which tends to dissipate into the larger and deeper screen-space and auditorium of film, thus accelerating the detextualizing tendencies of modern performance in all media. Since its spoken words loom larger in the total sensory input, television can go further than film towards restoring the Elizabethan theatre's primacy of words.

Yet the most urgent questions raised about the BBC television versions of Shakespeare—apart from those about acting and interpretation that can be raised about any production—have to do with the effects of television's restricted locus of dramatic action, about its depth and angle, as well as its size. The stage is at home in a virtual middle distance; film is at home in a real or virtual everywhere; but television is most at home in rather cramped and shallow real space. The long shots that help make Kozintsev's *Lear* so memorable a film must shrink to mite-size on the television screen and dwindle also in effect. Large ceremonious scenes, of which there are so many and of such variety in Shakespeare, are at best difficult for the most tactful television camera. Visible shapes (as Aristotle remarked in the *Politics*) can embody something of human character and passion, and their bulk as well as their contours can be made significant. Briefly, or in documentaries, size can be accepted neutrally as perspectival; but in sustained imaginative works ant-size tends to convey ant-emphasis. Hence television's weakness in the formal ceremonial scene. But screen size does not undermine the strength that early theorists like Pudovkin attributed to the camera, its ability to interrupt dialogue in order to render psychological states through close-up, and historical development through montage.

Film is a space-time continuum. What would be an intolerable interruption on stage is acceptable when film converts time to space, drawing it out to accommodate a change in the eye's vantage. The new space of close-up can halt the progression of dialogue with the privileged explanation of a need to burrow through to hidden motive. There is a gain in psychological immediacy. But when close-ups are dictated only by the medium's need for camera variation, and imposed on an Elizabethan play, something is lost but—worse—something added. The close-up tends to overpsychologize soliloquy, for example. The detailed and prolonged image it requires solicits from the actor a facial pose and variations more elaborate than the relevant speech-time on stage. There is a consequent change in the observed ratio of inwardness to exposition, or to rhetorical art for its own sake, or to the connection of the words with plot and theme. All of these, in a fully calculated balance, make up the soliloquy—and indeed all the dialogue—in Shakespeare. As the camera moves, the text doesn't change, but its meaning, its emphasis, and its effect do.

In scenes of aside or overlooking, which are so amusing in *Twelfth Night* and *Troilus*, so revealing elsewhere, close-up can prejudice the balance between covertness and fun by emphasizing the former, with perhaps a darker result than the dramatist intended. Further, the close-ups of Angelo in the BBC *Measure for Measure* made—so my students complained—Angelo's sudden changes of mood, which they fully understood and accepted as written, seem arbitrary rather than intelligible. This is an instance in which the relative forces of the close-up and the conventionally acted representations are different and in which the tact of the theatre's middle distance helps cover the difficulties of the text. I suppose that such observations return us to an earlier point: that filmed drama's strength lies in the 'real,' the palpably expressed, while the stylizations of Elizabethan theatre are more forgiving of idea and abstraction.

As the visual focus narrows from group to individual, body to face, face to eye, the implications of the visual field shift from the social to the psychological, and this inevitably prompts directors and actors to offer a psychologized construction of the text. But (to deal brutally with a complex matter) Shakespeare is not a psychological—or any other sort of—determinist. His plots and dialogue are not typically the outcome and distillation of personality. In any case, inadvertent psychological 'modernizations' through the bias of the camera have even less warrant than the psychological modernizations of interpretative criticism.

One of the questionable efforts of the BBC *Richard II*—and indeed of all its versions of the second tetralogy—was the effort to 'clarify' the text.[4] In *Richard II* the camera cuts to Bolingbroke in exile, informing us that before he returns to England he knows about the death of his father and about Richard's proposal to confiscate his property. Not so in Shakespeare: we learn that Bolingbroke has mustered an invasion force in the very scene that shows us Richard resolving to seize Bolingbroke's lands. Shakespeare here prepares our scepticism about Northumberland's later assertion that Bolingbroke comes 'but for his own.' The BBC version makes scepticism certainty, thus reducing the force of the alternative motives that lead others to join the rebellion, and obscuring the tacitness of the 'tacit vice' of opportunism that is the essential Bolingbroke. But it is not only Bolingbroke who is 'clarified.' The camera also shows us Richard bracing himself to 'act' his role in I.i. It becomes a character the dramatist never thought of, an explanatory narrator (more the presiding voice of a novel than of a play) whose explanations are more in the style of a C. P. Snow than of a Shakespeare. In clarifying character the BBC histories simplify it—and with two important consequences: they alter the relation between audience and play, and they alter the play's conception of history.

Where Shakespeare prompts attention to anomaly in character and events and offers opportunities for judgment, the screen asks only acceptance of what the camera 'proves,' forestalling query by providing the conclusive evidence of close-ups and corridor whispers (as in *Henry VIII*). No doubt the camera is acting in the service of what is thought to be 'political realism.' But the result is unlike the imperfectly grasped equivocal information on which we customarily attribute political motives, and all too like the banal clarity of the melodrama of political intrigue. Shakespeare's strenuous efforts to keep present motives and past events obscure[5] in *Richard II* are jettisoned at the outset, and with them Shakespeare's characteristically cool attitude towards power. Shakespeare insists on the limitation of what we can know. We see only so much of Hal and Westminster, of Caesar and Rome. No matter how vividly he represents occasion, he never forecloses interpretation: the event or the character never dwindles to a thesis. This allows an equivalent of the ambiguity arising from distance which is an inevitable part of our own understanding of politics. All too often the BBC versions impart certainties and turn Shakespeare's histories into History according to Shakespeare—quite another enterprise. In clarifying what Shakespeare omitted by way of causes and explanations the televised histories sometimes give us a hardboiled naivety destructive of the play. Not to be told—and Shakespeare does not tell us—why Hal is absent from Gaultree Forest when his brother tricks the rebels into surrender is to be offered the chance to learn more about the circumstances of power than further knowledge of the absence could tell. Shakespeare's apparently wayward 'here's one thing and now—perhaps unconnected—here's another' is actually far more tough-minded in its acceptance of the contradictory and the unintelligible. The BBC depiction of corridors and faces may seem initially a voluntarist view of history that places the outcome of events in the hands of individuals with specific motives. Yet what the BBC 2 *Henry IV* tries at times to give us is a more tightly determined causal chain of events than in the play. And some of its most memorable images—as in the coronation scene—are the Chief Justice muffled in his robes and Hal as a poster king, depersonalized by haircut and crown. Shakespeare's plays, in contrast, offer neither overdetermined events nor the stylizations of the camera. We must infer the meaning of Gaultree Forest for ourselves, puzzle out cause or no cause in the interstices of plot, focus on whole persons, and allow for Fortune, the goddess-enemy not only of historical figures but of explanations of history.

Shakespeare's plays were written for Shakespeare's theatre. And what his theatre provided most often was humanity seen not in the all-defining close-up of psychology or at the far and narrowed distance of sociology or through the historical retrospect of montage but in the open middle distance of social relation. Shakespeare's is a relational not an essentializing or ideologizing stage: not a stage pre-empted by convictions that must focus on one causal chain, psychological or sociological, but a stage closer to the tenor of encountered experience in which causes and motives of all sorts jostle. It offers whole human figures disposed in patterns that exhibit what is primarily a social (often familial) meaning in space that can—when the meaning dictates—be both Rome and Egypt, and on occasion convert up and left to heavenward and sinister. The solitariness of his characters onstage is generally painful and undesired; their immersion in crowds violent, fearful, or silly. For this sort of stage his plays were meant. What the camera can instantly suggest—enclosing sociology with a long shot, defining private states with a close-up—Shakespeare must do by other, more elaborate, means, and usually does not do at all. In sum, the simplicity and flexibility of the Elizabethan stage do not provide encompassing environments. But film and, more emphatically, television—despite the two-dimensional screen—give a priority to time, place, and objects, and so create environments in which human actors are expressions of a context rather than its creators.[6] To re-define the locus of dramatic action, its characters, its size, its depth, the angle from which it is viewed, is thus to tamper with the conceptual foundations of the Elizabethan text. It is also to create a new medium, one that will certainly demand different kinds of words, at times even no words at all. But if one wants to preserve the old words, one has to discover in the medium some equivalents of the old. This, rather than the conventional problems of interpretation, is the challenge of televising Shakespeare's plays.

I make no plea for archaeological productions of the plays. But since alternative televised versions are unlikely in the near future, directors have a special obligation to think twice. The BBC plays have so far been exemplary in this respect. At their best they have combined caution with ingenuity. When *The Merchant of Venice* ventured into that play's rather tricky sexual subtext, it did so not only with great tact but with an ingenious respect for the medium. The closing moments that gave us a lonely Antonio in silhouette, his back to us as the credits unrolled between us, said all that had to be said about what the departing new couples had defeated or surrendered, and about how a play completed dwindles from metaphor back to print.

For the most part the BBC productions have respected the text. By this I mean only that similar interpretations have appeared, say, in the *Shakespeare Quarterly*, without subsequent loss of subscriptions or editors. But Cleopatra as slut—the word is the producer's—does strain one's patience, though rather less than the idea strains the text. Yet the exceptions to playing within rather than with the text have been fewer than the record of stage productions over the last two decades might have led one to expect. In the theatre, however, the wildest violation leaves no scar; it will be superseded shortly by an interpretation better or worse—no matter which. But on the television screen the ingeniously faithful version can be as pernicious as the worst because the flicker promises to become an eternal fire. Not only will the BBC series be shown and reshown, but university media centres acquire the videotapes as soon as they become available. One can already anticipate growing difficulties in the struggle to persuade students to read the text—a struggle that will unfortunately coincide with the current fashion for what is called 'teaching through performance.' But another difficulty promises to become even more insidious. Too many of my contemporaries have had the experience of growing up with the late Beethoven quartets à la Budapest, and having to hear the Amadeus or Guarnieri versions ten times over before concluding that there was a world elsewhere. One of my recurring nightmares is having to deal year after year with the teabag *Tempest*. However, I do not propose to conclude with such grim possibilities.

I should like rather to pursue the question of the locus of action further and comment briefly of some scenes in the BBC *All's Well* and *The Winter's Tale*. *All's Well* was a splendid instance of discovering equivalents in a new medium. The work was played as a sequence of duets and trios in the shallow depth in interiors, their space often defined to the rear by shadow, to the fore by tables. Surfaces and space were varied and made interesting by the play of firelight or by movements in and out of significant close-up. They were given a further richness of detail and social reference by frequent visual allusions to Vermeer. But the relations among that play's leading figures particularly lend themselves to the comfortable, slightly formal intimacy that is wholly within the compass of the television camera. Luck, however, comes only to ability.

The Winter's Tale presented much greater difficulties, most of which were nicely solved. But the statue scene has always been a problem. I have seen Hermione's de-lapidation, as Dr. Johnson might have called it, done badly, and I have seen it done well. When I saw it from the second balcony it did not work. The acting was good enough, but the queen's supposedly miraculous step from the pedestal seemed, visually, too perfunctory to rival loaves and fishes. This disappointment was, I think, largely a matter of perspective. Only the real gods can look *down* on miracles; for the second balcony the age of miracles is past.

At a New York performance in Central Park along with the other groundlings I had to look *up* at the stage. The statue scene then was indeed a miracle, a double miracle since a stiff breeze ruffled the wispy, shroudlike gown worn by Salome Jens as Hermione, making her appear disturbingly in and of the flesh. The statue scene and others that evoke the ceremonious or the holy should, I think, prompt the director to give his audience the advantage that Shakespeare's groundlings had over the toffs in the galleries; should prompt him to employ the metaphysics of position that was part of Elizabethan stage vocabulary. When Tintoretto or Veronese places the eye of the observer below a noble banquet or a deposition, he employs the vantage of respect and adoration. When we look at Edward Hopper's 'Night Shadows' as from the third-story window of a solitary watcher, the urban scene dwindles to an answering alienation. Shakespeare—who showed in the cliff scene in *Lear* that he understood the aesthetic import as well as the fact of perspective—had only to accept his theatre as a given when he wrote the statue scene. The pedestal from which Hermione descends and Paulina's language gave him what he needed. But the camera's mobility demands more. The BBC *Winter's Tale*, admirable though it was, gave us Hermione now from slightly above, now almost level. The angles were chosen presumably in order to include the noble spectators. Perhaps they were thought necessary as surrogates for our wonder, but their positions were cramped and awkward so that they would fit into the frame. Farce may romp in a closet, but miracles can't be crowded. The scene didn't quite come off. Ideally one does want the spectators' variations upon awe and wonder. Shakespeare's stage could offer that, and for many of his audience the positional correlative as well. The television director must go through a series of trials to discover screen equivalents. It is not an easy task.

Some of what I have described as the characteristic difficulties of the television medium—the fragmented audience, the small screen—can be dealt with quite easily. The videotape of *As You Like It* is, I assure you, remarkably better when seen on a four-foot screen in the company of a class of thirty than when watched at home with a cat. Indeed, when one leaves the restraints of living rooms and neighbours all things seem to improve. As a friend of mine remarked: 'Until I heard the videotape with the sound turned up, I didn't realize that Autolycus was behind the bush actually pissing.' Japan is prodigious in the production of wonders and I understand that the wall-size home TV is a possibility. We may not survive the soap ad as apocalypse, but we may have the small satisfaction of seeing some of the problems we have discussed disappear.

1. See Robert Weimann, *Shakespeare and the Popular Tradition in the Theatre* (Baltimore, 1978), pp 73–84.
2. John Holloway, *The Story of the Night* (London, 1961).
3. See *Some Facets of King Lear*, ed R. L. Colie and F. T. Flahiff (Toronto, 1974), pp 20–21.
4. This discussion of the history plays is indebted at several points to observations made by Virginia Carr, Paul Cubeta, Irene Dash, and Peter Saccio during a panel discussion at the 1981 NEMLA meeting in Quebec City.
5. Wilbur Sanders, *The Dramatist and the Received Idea* (Cambridge, Eng., 1968), pp. 158ff.
6. See G. K. Hunter, 'Flatcaps and Bluecoats,' *Essays and Studies*, 33 n.s., (1980), 21ff.

From "Television Shakespeare"
Stanley Wells

. . . One distinctive feature of the BBC series, "The Shakespeare Plays," is its completeness. It is a grand, perhaps grandiose scheme: to present all the plays at the rate of about six a year, over a period of six years. What, I wonder, are the supposed merits of this plan? It is said to have an educational purpose. John Andrews, interviewing Cedric Messina, said "I gather that one of the things you hope for is that you will . . . create a library of Shakespearean video productions that will last for quite some time."[1] Messina did not deny this; and in the edition of *Romeo and Juliet*, the first play to be shown, it is

Reprinted, with permission, from *Shakespeare Quarterly*, 33 (Fall 1982), 261–77.

said that "The guiding principle . . . is to make the plays, in permanent form, accessible to audiences throughout the world." It would, I suppose, have been possible to accomplish such an aim by drawing on existing films and tapes where satisfactory ones were available, and by filling in the gaps where they are not. But apparently some consistency of approach was thought desirable, and one can see that this would have its merits. It may also be relevant that financial backing was to be sought. "The Complete BBC Shakespeare" is a far stronger selling-point than productions of various, lesser-known plays to fill the gaps in a collection.

Although one may understand why the concept of completeness had its appeal, it must have been obvious that it also has certain disadvantages. It creates relentless pressures. It entails the risk of routineness. The cameras must keep turning, whether or not the ideal director or actors for a particular play are available. This is bound to create the sense of an obstacle-race in which the competitors grow more and more exhausted as they approach the thirty-seventh hurdle. At a press showing of one of the plays, a BBC official said "After this, and the *Henry VI's*, we've only got twelve more plays to go." As the editor of a complete edition, I know just how she felt. Some productions are bound to be less successful than others. Indeed, the series failed to get off the ground with a resounding non-start when the first play to be taped, *Much Ado About Nothing*, turned out to be completely unacceptable; it has never been publicly shown. There have been demands that others be remade. Charles Shattuck, at the end of the first season, wrote in his Presidential Message to the Shakespeare Association of America that one of the six plays (he refrained from saying which) "has provoked such indignation (here I choose a mild term) that the management ought to consider withdrawing it, filming it again with another cast and director, and sending it to us again in another season. The play on which it is based is too well known, too much in demand, for it to be represented permanently by so wretched a production." He called upon members of the Association to "monitor the quality of each film in the bank" because, he said, the project "can affect the teaching of Shakespeare for at least the next quarter of a century."

You will have observed that somehow the concept of completeness is felt to entail a degree of permanence: the productions "will last for quite some time;" the plays will be made accessible "in permanent form;" they will go into a "bank" from which they can be repeatedly extracted for at least a "quarter of a century." The notion here is laudable enough. There are, and there probably always will be, far more people reading and studying Shakespeare's plays than there are performances for them to see. Even in England, where one might expect performances to be most readily available, there was no major stage production of *All's Well That Ends Well* between 1967 and 1981. The 1981 production, by Trevor Nunn, in which Peggy Ashcroft plays the Countess, is an excellent one; it will, unless the normal pattern is completely broken, have a few dozen performances in Stratford-upon-Avon, Newcastle-upon-Tyne, and London, and be seen by perhaps 100,000 people, before receding into theatrical history. In the meantime the television production, also excellent, will be available for showing all over the world, can be taken out of the "bank" and slipped into a viewing machine at any time of the day or night, can be supplied with subtitles or alternative—or even duplicate—soundtracks, and will enable interested persons to see the play for at least twenty-five years. The play will repeatedly jump vibrantly to life at the touch of a switch.

Is there not, perhaps, more than a little wishful thinking in such a scenario? What happened to the BBC tapes of *The Wars of the Roses*, and *The Spread of the Eagle*? to Jonathan Miller's *The Merchant of Venice*, and to his *King Lear*? Why is Miller at present directing a new production of *King Lear*—with the same actor in the title-role as last time—if he might have saved hundreds of thousands of pounds by taking his previous production out of the vaults and restoring it to circulation? Has there ever, in the whole history of television (such as it is), been a production of Shakespeare which has borne repetition more than a few years after it was made? A few—a very few—of the many cinema films of Shakespeare have acquired classic status and can still be seen with pleasure, though increasingly they are becoming period pieces, of interest as documents in the history of filmmaking, or as records of performances by great actors of the past. Would we recommend that a school-child or undergraduate see Reinhardt's *A Midsummer Night's Dream*, or Olivier's *Hamlet*, as a way of getting to know the play? Would we not even be wary of sending him to see Olivier's more recent, and fuller, *Othello*? Even if television could achieve productions of this stature, what reason have we to think that they would have a longer life? Jonathan Miller himself, in an interview with Anne Pasternak Slater, [2] offered a powerful illustration of the way in which productions come to seem out of date. He said "There's a wonderful book by Anne Hollander about costume, in which she has a series of photographs of productions of films and plays about Queen Elizabeth I, going from 1920 to 1960. Each of those periods presumably thought that they were producing an authentic version of the costumes, but what comes off each of the photographs is the period in which they were done, rather than the period to which they refer." There is no way in which this aging process can be arrested. Acting styles change; new technological devices are introduced. For all we know, three-dimensional television may be standard in twenty years' time. Performers develop in new ways, so we look at them differently; they grow old and die, their reputations fade; styles of incidental music change; new interpretations of the plays, both academic and theatrical, may come between us and the transfixed images of yesteryear; our attitude may be affected by so small a matter as a style of haircut or a fashion for beards. And, of course, competitors may arise; already more than one American critic has called for a transatlantic challenge. Maurice Charney, reviewing the second season of the series, wrote: "An American version of the 37 plays might not be able to compete with the BBC version for authority and authenticity, but I think it could compete on the grounds of vitality, originality, and vivid imagination.

And it would certainly have a better crack at being the spontaneous, informal, culturally relevant, and 'vividly alive' entertainment that Cedric Messina so earnestly hopes for. Let American television producers sit up and take notice."[3]

Needless to say, excessive claims or hopes for the lifespan of the BBC series do not invalidate it in the shorter term, and it is evident that the planners had in mind some of the dangers that I have mentioned. This is reflected in the attitude towards the text, though tensions are apparent in various statements that have been made about policy. Educational aims appear to argue for fullness. John Wilders, Literary Adviser to the series since it started, writes that

> There were good reasons why we should produce every play complete and uncut. . . . On the other hand, . . . one reason why we were embarking on this venture was to encourage people to enjoy Shakespeare, to win for his plays viewers who might approach them with reluctance, even hostility. What, for example, would the Australian in the outback or the Mexican in his *hacienda* make of the opening dialogue of . . . *Romeo and Juliet*:
>
> > SAMSON Gregory, on my word, we'll not carry coals.
> > GREGORY No, for then we should be colliers.
> > SAMSON I mean, an' we be in choler, we'll draw.
> > GREGORY Ay, while you live, draw your neck out of collar.
>
> At that point, the very people in whom we hoped to arouse an enthusiasm for Shakespeare which they would pass on to their grandchildren would probably switch off, determined to give the remaining 36 plays a miss.[4]

Here, the argument for cutting is to remove obscurity. But length has also been a consideration. Alan Shallcross, designated script editor for *Romeo and Juliet*, is reported in the edition of that play as saying "Experience shows that the maximum length for a television play to hold the viewer's attention is about two and a half hours." And during the two years in which Messina was producing the series most plays were cut so as to fit within this limit. There was even a plan, happily abandoned, to perform plays referred to, in what may be accounted a new Shakespearean sub-genre, as "'the biggies' (*Hamlet*, *Lear*, etc.) in extenso, probably across two nights." The BBC editions helpfully indicate all the intentional cuts and textual changes. They also include articles based on interviews with directors, actors, designers, and others which, for all their maddening retention of hesitations, qualifications, confusions, and self-contradictions, nevertheless sometimes vividly illuminate the production process. The director of *Romeo and Juliet* is quoted on the cuts: "One is torn. Cedric's brief was to make it as definitive as you can. To do a definitive version you have to do the whole text really. One didn't want to cut too much, but as a showman you don't want to bore the pants off your audience, so some sort of compromise has to be made. But whoever does Shakespeare, it will always be true—certain things you cannot make sense of and they should be cut."

Under Jonathan Miller's management, even long plays such as *Troilus and Cressida* and *Othello* have been given with few cuts. But policy has not been constant, and has sometimes imposed visible strain on David Snodin, who writes a page or so about the text in the editions. *The Taming of the Shrew*—not a specially long play—was shorn of the entire Induction, inducing painful contortions in Mr. Snodin: "Under Jonathan Miller's rule . . . we have at all times tried to remain aware of the fact that every play will be seen by millions of people who have never seen, or indeed read, a Shakespeare play before; and that these people should therefore be given the chance to see a version of the play that sticks as faithfully as possible to the text. At the same time, however, such a ruling should never be enforced to the extent of possibly hampering a viewer's understanding, enjoyment and general involvement . . ." and so on, betraying evident embarrassment that for once, and for reasons which may have been perfectly well considered, Dr. Miller and his colleagues had decided to reduce a play by an entire dimension.

To a Shakespearean, this decision may seem deplorable. Yet it is at least arguable that translation of Shakespeare to a different medium requires, and justifies, free treatment of the text. Olivier's film of *Henry V*, regarded by many as the best of the film adaptations, omits about one half of the lines; so does his *Hamlet*. Grigori Kozintsev, in his fascinating book about the genesis of his film *King Lear*, writes: "one should keep as much of the text as possible. However it was not at all easy. . . . It seemed that there had not been one occasion when the filming of a scene from a Shakespeare play based on the text had been more effective than exactly the same scene in the theatre. The best parts of Orson Welles's films seemed to me those which had no mention in the play: Iago in the iron cage hoisted up in the air (the prologue to *Othello*); the coffin of enormous proportions which is dragged along the ramparts (Falstaff's funeral)."[5] And Jack Jorgens, in *Shakespeare on Film*, tells us that in Peter Brook's film of *King Lear*, "The poetry has been cut to the bone (so anxious was Brook to avoid a dead museum piece that he once considered using a text 'translated,' as if a foreign classic, by Ted Hughes)."[6] And that seems to me not at all a bad idea. When I saw Zeffirelli's film of *Romeo and Juliet*, so pretty to look at, so uncomprehending in its treatment of the lines, I wished the whole script had been in modern English prose, making a film of the story of Romeo and Juliet, not of Shakespeare's play of the same name. If adaptation has to occur, I think it should be thorough. Then it has a chance of creating an independent, if related, work of art—like Verdi's opera *Falstaff*, or Berlioz's dramatic symphony *Roméo et Juliette*, or, in its own way, Colley Cibber's *Richard III*, for a couple of centuries probably the most popular play on the English stage. Ted Hughes might, indeed, have made a *King Lear* which would have spoken in filmic terms to our generation in a similar way. I do not say that it is impossible to make successful films, for either the cinema or the television, using all or most of Shakespeare's words. I do say—as Kozintsev said—that it is "not at all easy."

But, of course, television adaptations of Shakespeare which omitted, rearranged, or rewrote large sections of the text would not serve the purposes of educators committed to instructing students in Shakespeare's dramatic crafts-manship, nor would they be likely to appeal to sponsoring bodies. So there is a tension between the demands of the medium and the demands of the pos-tulated public. I am sure that this tension may exist within many of our minds, too. Do we want good television drama or pure Shakespeare? Are we really being true to Shakespeare if we are faithful to the letter of his texts but fail to convey their spirit?

The problem of authenticity rears its head, moreover, in relation to setting and costumes. The plays were written to be performed on more or less bare stages with, we believe, little attempt at naturalism. In the theatre, naturalism came increasingly to be sought until about a hundred years ago, since when non-representational stylization has been experimented with in varying de-grees. We cannot speak now of a uniform modern convention of staging Shakespeare: styles in recent years on the English stage have included the neo-Elizabethanism of Peter Gill's National Theatre *Much Ado About Noth-ing*, the stylized modernism of Peter Brook's *A Midsummer Night's Dream*, the Victorian theatricalism of Ron Daniels' *A Midsummer Night's Dream*, the symbolic austerity of John Barton's *Hamlet*, and the Edwardian natural-ism of Trevor Nunn's *All's Well That Ends Well*. "Updating" of setting and costumes has been intelligently and illuminatingly used; in Buzz Goodbody's modern-dress *Hamlet* and in John Barton's *Much Ado About Nothing* it seemed especially valuable as a means of revivifying social conventions that would not have been apparent to a modern audience. The process has be-come so common that a reviewer recently declared that a production of *A Midsummer Night's Dream* at Stoke was "straight Shakespeare" while going on to say that it was performed in late-nineteenth-century dress. I don't find it easy to think of many successful Shakespeare productions of recent years which have used Elizabethan settings and costumes. In the history plays, admittedly, a certain continuity of convention may be observed; though set-tings for these plays may be more or less stylized, costumes are usually of the period in which the action takes place. Otherwise, directors have often been most successful when freed from the constraints of authenticity.

Directors of the BBC television series, however, have been hampered in this respect by two factors. One is that the conventions of television drama, and thus the expectations of a television audience, favor naturalism. There is no ready-made equivalent in television terms to the bare platform stage of Shakespeare's time. John Wilders describes how this problem presented itself to the planners:

> The television equivalent of Shakespeare's stage would be an empty studio
> and that, I originally thought, was what we should use. I am now certain,
> however, that we were right not to adopt this style for all the plays, though
> Rodney Bennett used it for the battlement scenes in *Hamlet* and Jane How-
> ell came close to it in her production of *The Winter's Tale*. How austerely
> academic our productions would have looked! Moreover, an empty studio

would have made a very different impression on the viewer from that created by an empty stage on Shakespeare's own audience. To the television viewer, accustomed as he is to such representations of reality as football matches, news films and thrillers filmed on location in California, the opening scene of *Macbeth* would not have been "an open place" but Studio I of the Television Centre, White City.[7]

The other factor inhibiting the directors' imaginations appears to be an initial decision that updating of setting as well as textual tampering was to be avoided. Jonathan Miller is quoted as saying that his main problem in taking over the series was "the original contract with the American co-producers—it had to be so-called traditional, in the costume of the period (whatever that meant). There was no chance of shifting period—above all, no modern dress." For Miller himself, this seems not to have been a serious obstacle. "The brief was No monkey-tricks—and I think monkey-tricks is at least 50 per cent of what interesting direction is about. . . . But it so happens that the requirement that I stick to something which is recognisably period happens to coincide with an interest of mine, which has been growing in the last year or two, in trying to return to the 16th century because it is interesting in its own right."

These, then, are some of the considerations which affected the choice among the options open in relation to setting and costumes. To some extent they are negative factors—no modern dress, no experimental settings—but they have led to more positive decisions, some more fruitful than others. Two productions have been taped on location, one—*Henry VIII*—successfully. It seems significant that a history play responds best to this treatment. The other, *As You Like It*, seems by general agreement to have been less successful; John Wilders calls the decision "a mistake:" "by placing *As You Like It* in a real forest we forced the realism of the location to conflict with the artificial conventions of the play. It became that much harder to believe in." My own memory of the production is that the actors fought a losing battle against long grass that entangled their calves, and midges that had constantly to be swatted away from their faces. Location settings have not been used since Jonathan Miller took over.

More fruitful has been the decision "to make the productions look like paintings." Stating the case for this, Dr. Wilders writes,

> The television screen resembles the stage in that it depicts characters who move and speak, but its two-dimensional surface, rectangular shape and surrounding frame also make it look like a picture. This is the feature of the small screen which has been exploited by Jonathan Miller, whose version of *Antony and Cleopatra* was designed to recall the paintings of Veronese, and by Elijah Moshinsky, whose *All's Well* contained visual quotations from Rembrandt and Vermeer. It is, I am sure, the most satisfactory answer the directors have yet found. It calls attention to the artifice of the plays and does justice to those tableaux which are as much a part of Shakespeare's dramatic language as is his dialogue. But can the appropriate style of painting be found to match every play? And how many viewers were aware of the pictorial allusion?[8]

I don't think conscious awareness of the allusion in the viewer is necessary to the success of this technique; surely it is enough if the viewer recognizes the beauty of the pictures while perhaps having some notion that they are not entirely original. I agree that the pictorial technique has been successful in giving visual pleasure, but this alone will not rescue a production that is deficient in other respects. It is not enough to do justice simply to the "tableaux." That very word suggests a freezing of the action which is a denial of drama. A successful visual style would be one that is effective when the play is moving fast as well as when it is moving slowly, and above all one that allows for rapid and easy transitions. There are beautifully composed pictures in the BBC's A Midsummer Night's Dream, but the play seems to me nevertheless to be one of the weaker productions.

Although Jonathan Miller has declared that the limitation to "period" costume is not one that cramps his own style, he has also said that it represented an insuperable obstacle to the engagement of directors whom he would have wished to work for him. This is one of the inevitable problems of a house style. The drawing up of guidelines has the advantage of working towards uniformity and consistency of approach, helping to create a recognizable style for the series. It may have the advantage of stimulating directors by creating an initial challenge; but it may also inhibit individuality and discourage the participation of artists who find the guidelines unsympathetic. Reviewing one of the productions, I wrote that "the medium has reduced the message." A distinguished friend and colleague argued that the limitations were not in the medium but in the use made of it: that a better director could have found ways of making the play work on the screen by using the medium more creatively. He suggested that Ingmar Bergman would be the right man for the job—perhaps thinking of Bergman's delightful translation into television terms of Mozart's The Magic Flute. Why, he asked—he thinks big—had the BBC not employed Bergman?

The answer, I later found, had already been given by Miller, stating that "the original contract with the American co-producers" specified conditions under which "some of the best directors I might have got refused to work." He had tried Bergman, who "wasn't available." He had tried Peter Brook, because it was important, in "a series of Shakespeare plays which are meant to stand as a document—to have at least one version of a great director's work on tape. But he wouldn't do it, unless we worked with his actors, in his theatre, in Paris, filming under his own direction," which was impossible both because of the expense and also—an odd reason, perhaps—because "many of his own troupe wouldn't have spoken well enough for transmission in America." (I can't make out whether that is an insult to Americans, supposing that they can understand only if spoken to at dictation speed, or a compliment to them for refusing to accept anything but the best. In no way can I construe it as a compliment to Brook's actors.) Miller had wanted Brook for Antony and Cleopatra; he also tried Trevor Nunn, who "turned it down," William Gaskill, who "turned it down," and Ronald Eyre, who "turned it down." All these except Bergman are best known for their work in the theatre, and all are experienced directors of Shakespeare.

In the event the directors employed have, except for Miller himself, tended to be ones who have worked mainly for television, and who have little or, in more than one case, no previous experience in directing Shakespeare in any medium. Such circumstances seem likely to result in competent rather than brilliant productions. It is interesting that the director of the production for which I have heard the most general praise—*All's Well That Ends Well*—is a young man whose talent had displayed itself in productions of operas at Covent Garden but who had little experience with Shakespeare and who had never previously directed a television play. In this case, individual talent appears to have overcome the drawback of inexperience. It is interesting too that the same director's production of A *Midsummer Night's Dream* had a poor critical reception in England. Each play represents a distinct challenge.

Difficulty of enticing the most desirable-seeming directors is not the only practical problem that has faced Dr. Miller and his colleagues. They have not always been able to employ the actors they wanted. Asked what he was "going to do with *Othello*," Miller replied "I don't know for certain, because it depends very much on who I can get. It's eight months ahead, and very few actors will commit themselves. I'm interested in Ian Holm, among others, and someone like Frank Finlay as well." In the event neither actor was involved. Finance, too, is bound to be a problem, however generous the sponsorship. Miller has spoken of "inadequate rehearsal facilities," saying that "you only have about a month to rehearse, and six days to tape. Most people who really take Shakespeare seriously feel that at least six weeks are necessary to rehearse, with 12 days of taping." There are, then, serious practical problems of various kinds, some of them inextricably bound up with the circumstances that make the series possible at all, and I think we should bear these in mind in passing judgment upon it.

[The second part of this essay deals largely with productions directed by Jonathan Miller. See Wells's assessment of Miller's achievement in Part II of this volume and his reviews of *Shrew, Troilus, Timon,* and *Winter's Tale* in Part III.]

1. *Shakespeare Quarterly,* 30 (Spring 1979), 137.
2. All statements by Jonathan Miller cited in this text are from *Quarto,* 10 (September 1980), 9–12.
3. *SQ,* 31 (Summer 1980), 292.
4. "Adjusting the Set," *Times Higher Education Supplement,* 10 July 1981, p. 13. The script as printed shows that the first two lines were spoken, the second two omitted.
5. *King Lear: The Space of Tragedy* (London: Heinemann, 1977), p. 53.
6. (Bloomington: Indiana Univ. Press, 1977), p. 244.
7. "Adjusting the Set," p. 13.
8. Ibid.

The BBC Shakespeare and "House Style"
James C. Bulman

The BBC Shakespeare has established itself firmly in the American curriculum. Over one hundred colleges and universities have purchased the entire series, and countless others have bought or rented tapes of individual plays.[1] It is fair to surmise, then, that tens of thousands of students watch at least one of The Shakespeare Plays annually; some watch many more than one. Teachers have been quick to applaud the series as a tool by which to teach the plays through performance, not merely as texts: Shakespeare—so goes the cliché— wrote for the stage, not the page; and if a television studio is not the same as a legitimate stage, it is the next best thing. Yet there are dangers inherent in showing the BBC Shakespeare to students. For the uninitiated—those who have not learned to *read* Shakespeare intelligently—the tape may *become* the play, as fixed as any Hollywood production, not merely an interpretation of the play. Worse, the lazy student may allow viewing the tape to serve as a *substitute* for reading the text and be never the wiser. Furthermore, if the production is only mediocre (as, at best, some have been), students may never wish to encounter the play again.

It is crucial, therefore, that students continue to be taught to read Shakespeare responsibly, even to imagine a "performance" as they read, before they are asked to see a tape and respond to it critically. Just as importantly, before they can use the BBC Shakespeare as an effective tool for critical analysis, teachers must understand how the series evolved—how producers shaped the productions under their command, and how the different biases of those producers betray a fundamental conflict in their conceptions of what the series was to be and what audience it was to reach. In the following pages, I shall draw some distinctions between the Messina years (1978–79) and the Miller years (1980–81), when a majority of the "popular" plays—those read most often in college—were produced. Shaun Sutton, who took over the series when Miller returned to the practice of medicine, has exerted less control over his directors than his predecessors did, and in fact has used directors who worked under them; productions done under his aegis, therefore, bear no particular stamp, or when they do they continue to reflect the biases of Messina and Miller. If teachers understand the tensions inherent in the making of the BBC Shakespeare, they may use the series more circumspectly as an instrument for interpretation.

Cedric Messina originated the series, a fact of which he is justly proud. He spoke at the outset of doing *definitive* productions that for years to come would bring Shakespeare to the masses as Shakespeare was meant to be. He wanted "to make the plays, in permanent form, accessible to audiences throughout the world."[2] To Messina, accessibility seemed to mean two things:

Reprinted, with permission, from *Shakespeare Quarterly*, 35 (Special issue, 1984), 571–81.

the availability of the tapes themselves, and the ease with which they could be comprehended. Messina aimed to educate the audiences of the world by making them *enjoy* Shakespeare: "the plays are offered as entertainment," he insisted, "to be made as vividly alive as it is possible for the production teams to make them. They are not intended to be museum-like examples of past productions."[3] Perhaps not. But neither were they radically to depart from traditional interpretations. There was to be little pruning of texts, no modern dress. Messina even instructed his directors to "let the plays speak for themselves,"[4] as if they were capable of such speaking without directorial interpretation.

Jonathan Miller, who took over from Messina, laughed at the notion that any production could be definitive. As a man of the theatre with considerable background in staging Shakespeare, he realized that any re-creation is by nature an interpretation; and his impulse in the theatre had always been to seek out new angles on old texts. But bound by an obligation to be "orthodox"[5]—to leave texts pretty much intact (as he had *not* done, for example, in his 1970 *Merchant of Venice* with Laurence Olivier) and to stage conservatively—Miller decided to make the best of the situation by redefining orthodoxy as an academic challenge. He set out to present the plays as Elizabethans would have understood them, to view them through the Elizabethan imagination, to re-create for each play an authentic Zeitgeist in matters moral, political, religious, and aesthetic. In their responses to Shakespeare, therefore, these two producers could not have been more distinct; and any accurate appraisal of the series must acknowledge the distinctions between them.

Messina gave his directors a number of guidelines—principles, if you will—on which to base their productions. First, he wanted to fulfill the expectations that a television audience would bring to any program, even Shakespeare. These expectations would be different from those an audience would bring to a stage production. In the words of Sheldon Zitner, "filmed drama's strength lies in the 'real,' the palpably expressed, while the stylizations of Elizabethan theatre are more forgiving of idea and abstraction."[6] To play to film's strength, Messina advised his directors to keep the audience unaware of theatrical conventions, omit as much artifice as possible, and dedicate themselves to the principle that Shakespeare, to be done right, must be done *naturalistically*. This accounts for why *As You Like It* was filmed on location—and why, as a result, pastoral artifice yielded to barnyard realism. Furthermore, as the essence of good television is action, Messina insisted, directors ought to provide it: fast-paced entertainment and a keen cinematic eye will catch a first-time viewer as "idea and abstraction" never will. Desmond Davis, who directed *Measure for Measure*, attests to how Hollywood references served Messina's popular approach to Shakespeare:[7]

> I wanted to do a rather colloquial production . . . for example, the long sequence in the jail: I made it like an AIP horror movie jail, flambeaux and red lighting and dwarf jailers. You wouldn't have been surprised if Peter Lorre had walked through the background. And I tried to make Mistress

Overdone's brothel a bit like the *Destry Rides Again* saloon. I had the men smoking cigars and young ladies parading along the balconies. I wanted to make it like a western, with gambling games—so it's recognisable to a modern audience.

Understandably, Messina selected directors with proven television track records. It made no difference to him whether they had ever directed Shakespeare before; in fact, he may have preferred that they come to Shakespeare fresh. Directors who have done Shakespeare on the stage may be inclined to do dangerously unorthodox things with him, whereas a director like John Gorrie, whom Messina chose to direct *The Tempest*, could be counted on to preserve the most sacred critical commonplaces about each play—no doubt those he remembered from school—and never to rock the boat with invention. With a naiveté that must have delighted Messina, Gorrie admitted to having no particular approach to *The Tempest*: "but I must say that it didn't worry me greatly, because I believe if you cast good actors and allow it to happen in rehearsal, the combination of the actors and the play will show you the way to go." [8] Perhaps for this reason, Messina's directors were partial to actors who had played their roles before. Michael Hordern had played Prospero many times, most recently at Stratford-upon-Avon in 1978, where Gorrie apparently had seen him; Derek Jacobi returned from a two-year tour in Tony Richardson's *Hamlet* to walk into rehearsals for the BBC *Hamlet* directed by Rodney Bennett, who, typically, had never directed Shakespeare in his life. Messina, then, was determined to satisfy popular taste. He depended on the use of "realistic" film techniques to make Shakespeare palatable for a mass audience; his directors resorted to traditional interpretations of the plays; and by preserving the status quo, they apparently satisfied Messina's criteria for definitive production.

Miller was less conservative. He—and the few directors he chose to work with him, all but one experienced in the theatre—came to the series armed with ample knowledge of stage history and an assumption, antithetical to Messina's, that television ought to preserve theatrical artifice and find its own analogues for stage conventions. As Shakespeare wrote plays and not movie scripts, Miller thought it important to eschew the kind of cinematic realism for which Messina strove. Jane Howell, who directed *The Winter's Tale* and had staged the play twice before, defended Miller's philosophy. Television is *not* a realistic medium, she argued; all that need be real is the actor's performance. One must honor the original rules of stage performance, she said, "both the social history and the physical shape of the theater, because . . . you break those rules at your peril." [9] She continued to play by "the original rules" in subsequent productions: her staging of the first history tetralogy in one colorful, stage-like set playfully attests to her interest in re-creating the original conditions of performance. Of her production of *The Winter's Tale*, she admits that she first tried a realistic conception, then grew exasperated with it and changed her mind: "I'm more interested in an essence than in 'reality'—I get very *bored* with 'reality.'" [10]

The essence of Shakespeare, for Miller and his crew, lay not in cinematic realism, but in a less material truth to Elizabethan attitudes—a sort of "period verisimilitude" rooted in history, sociology, and psychology, Miller's passion. Miller subscribed to the notion that any work of art mirrors the society in which it is created: thus Shakespeare, in his plays, both consciously and unconsciously reflects the social and political attitudes and conflicts of his day. Believing that productions of the plays ought likewise to reflect those attitudes and conflicts, that directors ought to view the plays as windows on Elizabethan society, Miller parted company with Messina as radically as the new historicism departed from the principles of New Criticism. And the analogy is fitting, for Miller's productions beg to be understood in terms of social history as resolutely as Messina's productions demand to be understood apart from it.

Like the new historicists or their British counterparts the cultural materialists, Miller turned to recent work by social historians to establish contexts in which to probe character and motive in Shakespeare's plays. He wished to discover what the Elizabethans (and, presumably, Shakespeare) would have thought lay behind Antony's decision to return again to his Egyptian dish or behind Kate's shame that women are so simple. By research, Miller claimed to validate all his directorial decisions. As often as not, however, "research" provided an excuse for him to indulge his own biases.

Take puritanism, for example. Miller saw the rise of puritanism reflected everywhere in Shakespeare, in Octavius as much as in Malvolio. Miller thus strove to redeem The Taming of the Shrew from the commedia dell'arte tradition by declaring it a treatise on obedience in sixteenth-century marriage, particularly among the puritan squirarchy. To prepare for his production, he steeped himself in literature on "the rise of the Elizabethan puritan movement and the bringing back of the Calvinist notions of a fallen world, one which required magistrates and disciplinarians to keep order."[11] In the sixteenth century, Miller argued, "the authority of the father and husband is a sine qua non of the family being smoothly run," and it was precisely this point that he thought Shakespeare was driving home in Shrew. "You can't slip and slide around the notion of obedience just because it offends our beliefs about the independence of women; they did not think that way then. . . . If everything is done in the light of what we think it's a sort of historical egocentricity . . . what T. S. Eliot calls 'historical provincialism.'"[12] Good sentences and well pronounced. In them, Miller defends his "straight" reading of Kate's final speech, his emphasis on characters in the "act of self-examination," his addition of a psalm sanctifying marriage at the end, his cutting of Sly's Induction—such revisions as would have appalled Messina—all in the service of a "moral seriousness" which, he argues with remarkable sleight of mind, is more faithful to Shakespeare's true intent than Shakespeare himself was.

According to Miller, the physical production, too, should register fidelity to the Elizabethan conception of history. Cinematic realism, filming on location, adulterates Shakespeare, he claimed; but reference to Renaissance and

Baroque painting might provide an imaginative analogue for stage pictures. As John Wilders, the series' literary consultant, commented, "the television screen resembles the stage in that it depicts characters who move and speak, but its two-dimensional surface, rectangular shape and surrounding frame also make it look like a picture."[13] Thus Miller decided that set and costume designs must look as though they had been done by Rembrandt, Titian, Vermeer; and iconographic allusion became crucial both to the interpretation of the text and to the preservation of theatrical artifice.

Let me illustrate how Miller's aesthetic differed from Messina's. Each man produced one Roman play. Messina chose Herbert Wise to direct *Julius Caesar* because Wise had had popular success directing *I, Claudius*; and one good Roman, after all, deserves another. Both men concurred that *Caesar* is one of Shakespeare's most direct, least subtle plays—"one of the simpler pictures of empire"—and thus a good education tool for those who get their history lessons from television instead of books.[14] For this reason, they agreed that they had to be scrupulously accurate about historical presentation. Romans had to be noble Romans; their conflicts, unambiguous and straightforward. Wise strove for a clarity of exposition that would make the play easy to understand; and to enhance that clarity, he instructed his designers "to leave it crisp and simple."[15] His Rome was to be the Rome of every schoolboy's imagination, the abstract or essence of "classical" architecture. To Messina's delight, Wise wound up recycling sets he had used for *I, Claudius*, perhaps hoping that familiarity would breed respect. When asked if he had considered doing the play in Tudor style, Wise replied, "I don't think that's right for the audience we will be getting. It's a not jaded theatre audience seeing the play for the umpteenth time . . . for an audience, many of whom won't have seen the play before, I believe it would only be confusing."[16]

Miller, in contrast, sounded as though he did have a jaded audience in mind. Undertaking *Antony and Cleopatra* as his first project, he was intent on avoiding the marmoreal quality of *Julius Caesar*. But he complained that he was "obliged to be orthodox" and "had to find something which would nevertheless not be a simple, literal-minded reproduction of a classical antiquity which is incompatible with the quality of the text."[17] These sound suspiciously like words to the Wise. What Miller found to satisfy the series' "requirement" was late sixteenth-century Italian Baroque painting, "notional landscape—painterly in its richness, but not literal-minded in its realism." He focused in particular on Veronese's *The Family of Darius at the Feet of Alexander*, because "it is created by a sixteenth-century iimagination into which are fed the images of the classical past but altered and dissolved and finally crystallized in the imagination."[18] In other words, Miller imaginatively participated *with* Veronese in recreating a "period;" and if the resultant vision of Rome and Egypt is not typical of past productions of the play, if Miller's conception of those places is not *our* conception, it nevertheless attempts to approximate the *Elizabethan* conception, and in so doing it challenges our intellects as Messina's conception of Rome never does.

Wilders thought that such "visual quotation" was "the most satisfactory answer" that directors had found to the problem of translating Shakespeare to the screen. "It calls attention to the artifice of the plays," he said, "and does justice to those tableaux which are as much a part of Shakespeare's dramatic language as his dialogue."[19] During the Miller years, then, the art gallery replaced Hollywood as a source of visual inspiration. Miller created a "house style" more distinct than Messina's. "House style" is Stanley Wells's term, and it captures Miller's theatrical bias very well.[20]

Miller aimed his rationalizations at seasoned theatregoers. Just as he assumed that an audience would know that *Shrew* is, by tradition, regarded as a farce, so he assumed that an audience would be familiar with the heroic legend of Antony and Cleopatra; and he proceeded to challenge that familiarity by demonstrating that Shakespeare's text is *not* a reverent history lesson. The Antony and Cleopatra he served up were a most mortal pair; no Mars and Venus for him.[21] His casting was as unpredictable as Messina's was predictable. He chose Colin Blakely to play Antony not for grandeur, but for his "ruffian" quality—that "of a rugby forward in one of those Midlands sporting clubs who's just beginning to fail." Likewise he chose Jane Lapotaire as Cleopatra because, he claimed, using "research" to spite the play, Cleopatra's sexuality and prowess were myth, not grounded in history. And who else would have thought of casting John Cleese, of *Monty Python* fame, as Petruchio for his "moral gravity"?

One thing is certain: under the same rubric, Miller and Messina gauged their productions for widely discrepant audiences; and their different intentions indicate that Miller fundamentally departed from Messina's philosophy for undertaking the series. Messina, in his perhaps over-easy assumption that a television audience would require its Shakespeare straight and simple, focused on what he took to be central to each play. There were no surprises. His *Julius Caesar* attempted to account "classically" for the fall of Republican Rome; his *As You Like It* had to show—what else?—love in the woods. Messina preserved our time-honored notions about the plays, apparently without realizing that safety can be dramatically dull, and simple clarity un-Shakespearean. Miller may have leaned too far in the other direction. His productions were full of surprises. In assuming that his audience was familiar with—even tired of—traditional interpretations of the plays, he went out of his way to illuminate what was not so obvious, what was ambiguous, what was ironic, what was subtextual. He showed us the puritanism of *Shrew*, the tawdriness of "legendary" middle-aged lovers; he showed us a *Shrew* without slapstick and an Egypt without pyramids. He risked making central what, in Messina's view, was peripheral. His *Shrew* had little farce; his *Antony* little grandeur. These productions seemed to be aimed at an educated and privileged audience just as surely as Messina's were aimed at an ignorant multitude. Miller challenged our preconceptions; Messina had pandered to them.

This is not to suggest that every director simply adopted the "house style" of his producer. Some of the most acclaimed productions in the series were made by directors who deviated from the dictates of their producers and approached the texts by way of some middle path. Certainly one could not accuse David Giles of slavishly following Messina's prescription for "realism" in action or "clear and simple" characterization in *Richard II* or *Henry V.* Giles saw these plays as "unabashedly theatrical" and knew that anything less than a stylized production would discredit them.[22] His productions were boldest when they found analogues for theatrical artifice. The Chorus in *Henry V*, who stepped out from a crowd in a stylized set, spoke directly to us as the camera tightened in on him, then turned to reveal a new set into which he faded as just another bystander. The tableaux in *Richard II* recalled medieval ecclesiastical art—Richard in profile as a saint, flanked by petitioners. These techniques more closely resembled Miller's visualization of Shakespeare than Messina's.

Even directors who accommodated the "house style" often asserted their independence to good effect. Desmond Davis, whom we have already heard discussing how Hollywood influenced his production of *Measure for Measure,* explained with far more theatrical acuity that the core of the play, for him, lay in the psychological mirroring of Angelo and Isabella, in their struggle to deny that "eroticism is just the other side of purity," the flip side of one coin.[23] As a visual metaphor for this idea, Davis used the same set, slightly redecorated, for the brothel, the convent, and the jail—all distorted images of one another, all mirrors of social repression. His metaphoric approach to *Measure* was similar to Elijah Moshinsky's approach to *All's Well That Ends Well.* Moshinsky found *his* central metaphor in the First Lord's line, "The web of our life is of a mingled yarn, good and ill together." This line suggested to him that the play, too, was of a mingled yarn—"a chiaroscuro—light and shade, age and youth, good and bad."[24] Thus he cast actors very young and very old to artificially heighten the conflict in generations; he pitted those of a mannered school against those of "an ultra-naturalistic school;" he explicitly invoked works by Rembrandt, Hals, Bosse, and Vermeer to create contrasts in light and texture, interiors in which one was always conscious of action going on in a room beyond, as if to suggest the workings of unconscious, unexpressed depths of feeling. These productions achieved a subtlety unknown to most in the series, and they did so because their directors approached the texts—problems of tone, color, and motivation—with more open-mindedness than preconception. Davis may have used Hollywood to guide his eye, but his ultimate concern was with psychological and moral conflict and a visual metaphor by which to express it, *not* with "action" or "realism." Moshinsky may have adopted Miller's iconography, but he used it to illuminate problems that were central to *All's Well*, not peripheral to it. Davis and Moshinsky achieved their integrity by moderating, though not ignoring, the biases of their producers.

The worst productions, however, illustrate how these biases, if followed to excess, can damage Shakespeare. I shall discuss two of them briefly to demonstrate that when they went wrong, they went wrong because Messina and

Miller too insistently imposed their versions of "orthodoxy" on the texts. *Romeo and Juliet* is a case in point. Its director, Alvin Rakoff, was an embarrassing choice. Apparently a friend of Messina, he bragged that he "knew Cedric would offer" him a play to do, but feared it might be one he "didn't understand." He was relieved when offered *Romeo*: "At least I could read it and understand it without too much help."[25] And why did Cedric choose Rakoff for this particular play? Because "Alvin's very good at romantic stuff," and he is also "an action director, and *Romeo* has enough action to satisfy him."[26] They agreed that the play was "so encrusted in tradition" that they had no choice but to honor it: they did so by setting it "in high Renaissance Tuscany." Jonathan Miller would probably have winced to think that Verona had gone south on holiday. But Messina and Rakoff also agreed that "the play should be done as naturalistically as possible." Why? Rakoff reasoned that "You're asking the audience today to do a hell of a thing: the most real medium in the world is television; they're watching the news at nine o'clock and they're seeing real blood and real violence and suddenly we're saying, 'Come to our pretend violence.'" Any stylization would "alienate a hell of a lot of the potential viewers."[27]

Rakoff wasted no time in getting down to cases. Mercutio, he said, was not to be seen as afraid of Tybalt. "Tybalt is the Jack Palance character in a cowboy movie, he can outdraw anybody, but Mercutio thinks he's as good. Their fight could be both classic, tiring and funny." Rakoff's idea of "classic" bowed to the divinity of the American western. By contrast, Romeo and Tybalt were to have "a bloody great brawl. It has to be sordid, as sordid as possible—a street brawl. Romeo can't fight Tybalt. . . . It's just that Romeo is incensed, passionate. . . . Romeo kicks Tybalt in the balls, puts his sword in, and continues plunging with the knife—it's not even a clean rapier wound, it's a dagger, plunged in again and again."[28] Here's where Rakoff's heart was. Here lay his sinews and his bones! But lest we think the realism ceases with the fight scenes, let's consider the casting of Juliet. An actress of only fourteen, the poor girl got roundly panned by critics. She couldn't act. Rakoff sympathized with her. "She does have limitations—which you're bound to have at that age—but at least she is fourteen. She looks like a young child killing herself."[29] Messina defended the choice more sentimentally. She reminded him of his own daughter, seven-and-a-half; and when she killed herself, he wept at the pathos. Together, Messina and Rakoff got hung up on details that did not fit their scheme of realism. How old, for example, was Lady Capulet? Why was the Nurse so much older? And what about her husband? How short *were* life spans way back then? Rakoff concluded with a shrug: "Whatever Mr. Shakespeare wanted to say at the moment, he said. This is why you see all the professors going through hoops trying to make it make sense. But there's no way you can."[30]

Miller's production of *Othello* failed for just the opposite reasons. It was refined out of existence. Seeing *Othello* as a drama of emotion and psychological conflict, Miller decided it should be played scaled down, without the heroics or the great moral crises of tragedy. The whole production was shot in interiors, replicas of the Palace of Urbino, a maze of rooms suggesting claustrophobia, imprisonment: no exteriors were appropriate for the small "domestic play" that *Othello* was for Miller.

Anthony Hopkins discussed the many sessions during which he and Miller worked out the complexities of Othello's character. It soon became apparent that Miller was firmly in the camp of Leavis, who thought that the essential traitor was within the gates, that Iago was but a catalyst for Othello's neurosis:

> Miller's idea at first was that this was Othello's flaw, that he has always been a jealous man; we had a psychological run-down—that it was to do with his mother being taken from him and all that. We tried to establish that Othello was a punctilious man, that he had risen to supreme rank by punctilious attention to detail, to himself, repressing tremendous volcanic powers within himself over the years, burying and burying and ramming them down. . . . Othello has always been aware that deep down inside him is chaos and horror, horror and hell, and Iago spots it, knows how to unleash the hell.[31]

Miller confessed that his diminutive model for Othello was King Hussein of Jordan. "A remote giant" of an Othello would not work: "our horror would be merely stimulated by the spectacle of a person of grandeur falling." Miller was obviously not satisfied with Renaissance tragedy. "What is interesting," he says, "is that it's not the fall of the great but the disintegration of the ordinary, of the representative character. It's the very ordinariness of Othello that makes the story intolerable."[32] The story, I would ask, or the production? One hears Miller return time and again to his anti-heroic song, as loud here as in *Antony*—to his determination to whittle away at tragic greatness, to make all his characters lie down on an analyst's couch from which they never rise the same.

To convey the "ordinariness" of Othello, Miller opted to do two things that make a mockery of Shakespeare's play. The first was to tone down Othello's passion, the *rhetoric* of tragedy, and have Hopkins speak soliloquies in *sotto voce*, reduce them to a domestic, intimate style. The second was to deny the importance of Othello's blackness. Messina had earlier tried to cast James Earl Jones as Othello but was forbidden to do so by British Equity. Jones, of course, had made a distinguished stage Othello, so it would have been a typical choice for Messina, tried and true—nothing left for the director to do but to let Jones be Othello still. Miller claimed, however, that blackness would be a distraction. "It didn't seem to be a leading issue in the play really. It would still work perfectly well if the lines referring to blackness were eliminated and the play simply allowed to proceed."[33] How did he justify his claim? He adopted a scholarly air: "To the Elizabethans, Moor just meant dark stranger." Pseudo-historical research once again came to the aid of Miller's bias. "The dark strangeness really doesn't help one to portray his character"—or, if it does, it does so for the wrong reasons. It encourages us to equate blackness with susceptibility: "you tend to equate the supposed simplicity of the black with the exorbitant jealousy of the character. If one were to accept what anyone of mature understanding would—that jealousy has nothing whatever to do with any peculiarities of character that you can readily identify in advance—the blackness becomes a distraction."[34]

One must admire Miller for his psychological sensitivity and his insight into prejudice. Unfortunately, his understanding of character is not the same as Shakespeare's; and by imposing his own analytical bias on *Othello*, he robbed the play of an essential racism with which Shakespeare did confront his audiences and pared down a great tragedy until it was no more than closet melodrama.

It is crucial to understand the fundamental differences in "house styles" when one uses the BBC Shakespeare as a teaching tool. Each style, each bias, gives a particular shape and color to a production; and by demonstrating to students how that happens, one makes them aware that there are alternative ways to interpret and to stage a play.

For pedagogical purposes, even the worst productions can be useful. They tend to magnify the problems of a rigid approach. They demonstrate that too mechanical an application of "house style" can close off rather than open up a play, can leave too many potentials of the text unaddressed. Students who have read the text responsively will pick up on those unaddressed potentials and ask questions: Is pastoral love the same as love in a "real" wood? Did Shakespeare mean *Romeo* to be as raw as a spaghetti western? Is Cleopatra's allure really more cerebral than physical? Isn't Othello's color important? Such questions lead students to a fuller appreciation of the play and of the power of performance to manipulate their responses to it.

The better productions, on the other hand, insofar as they employ a "house style" imaginatively to address the cruxes of a play, may allow students to discover potentials in the text that they had never dreamed of in their reading. In an essay written before any of The Shakespeare Plays were broadcast, Jay Halio warned that the "availability of films and performances threatens to supplant the old reliance upon a close reading of the text." The word "threatens," he explains, communicates his "concern that without proper care the study of Shakespeare could degenerate into entertainment without insight, a joyful but vacuous apprehension of the plays leading to, at best, a sophisticated appreciation of staging techniques or, at worst, a debased taste for gimmickry."[35] Given the popularity of the BBC Shakespeare in the classroom, Halio's warning is even more apt today.

The first place a student should see Shakespeare played is in the theatre of the mind. Then, and only then, will viewing a production—studying how its particular approach illuminates certain aspects of the play, fails to account for others—help students to a richer understanding of Shakespeare.

1. Information was provided by Time-Life, Inc., which has co-produced the series with the BBC. Though in the United States the series bears the title of "The Shakespeare Plays," I prefer to identify it by its British origins.

2. Quoted in a preface to the BBC editions of the plays he produced. These editions, under the title *The BBC-TV Shakespeare*, reprint, with interviews and production material, the texts edited by Peter Alexander in 1951.

3. Ibid.

4. Messina's brief to his directors is sharply contradicted by one of Miller's directors, Elijah Moshinsky, who, in discussing his production of *All's Well*, says, "People think the plays should 'speak for themselves'! Plays *don't* speak for themselves—you interpret them by casting, by editing, by designing. They *need* interpretation."

5. The word is Miller's own, quoted in the introduction to the BBC edition of *Antony and Cleopatra* (London, 1981), p. 18.

6. "Wooden O's in Plastic Boxes: Shakespeare and Television," *University of Toronto Quarterly*, 51 (Fall 1981), 7.

7. Quoted in the introduction to the BBC edition of *Measure for Measure* (London, 1979), p. 19.

8. Quoted in the introduction to the BBC edition of *The Tempest* (London, 1980), p. 24. Shaun Sutton sounds as though he shares the bias of Messina and his directors. In an interview with the Associated Press, Sutton claimed to have three priorities in filming the plays: "The first one is to make them entertaining. . . . Second is to cast them up, to put the money on the actors. And third is to avoid obscure gimmicks."

9. Quoted in the introduction to the BBC edition of *The Winter's Tale* (London, 1981), p. 18.

10. Howell, p. 19.

11. Quoted in the introduction to the BBC edition of *The Taming of the Shrew* (London, 1980), pp. 18–19. The books that Miller found particularly inspiring were Lawrence Stone's *The Family, Sex and Marriage in England 1500–1800* (New York: Harper & Row, 1977)—a book from which John Wilders, the series' Literary Consultant, quotes—and Michael Walzer's *The Revolution of the Saints* (Cambridge, Mass.: Harvard Univ. Press, 1965).

12. Miller, *Shrew*, p. 18.

13. In "Adjusting the Set," *Times Higher Education Supplement*, 10 July 1981, p. 13.

14. Quoted in the introduction to the BBC edition of *Julius Caesar* (London, 1979), p. 19.

15. Ibid., p. 24.

16. Ibid., p. 20.

17. Quoted in the introduction to the BBC edition of *Antony*, p. 18.

18. Ibid.

19. "Adjusting the Set," p. 13.

20. See "Television Shakespeare," *Shakespeare Quarterly*, 33 (1982), 269.

21. It is, of course, fashionable to treat the heroism in *Antony* with skepticism, and Miller revealed his wish to do so when he tried to get Peter Brook to direct it for the series. Brook had just directed a spare, unheroic *Antony* for the RSC. When he refused Miller's invitation—perhaps because he objected to Miller's "house style"?—Miller took the assignment himself.

22. Quoted in the introduction to the BBC edition of *Henry V* (London, 1979), p. 19.

23. Introduction to *Measure*, pp. 24–25. Davis describes in some detail how, to establish that Angelo and Isabella are mirror images of one another, he shot their two interviews with "two opposed cameras. . . . It was a visual idea: he was rather large, shot from waist level, and she was a minute figure, shot using the whole depth of the room. Then slowly they come together."

24. Quoted in the introduction to the BBC edition of *All's Well That Ends Well* (London, 1980), p. 17.

25. Quoted in the introduction to the BBC edition of *Romeo and Juliet* (London, 1978), p. 19.

26. Ibid.

27. Ibid., p. 20.

28. Ibid., p. 25.

29. Ibid., p. 23.

30. Ibid., p. 30.

31. Quoted in the introduction to the BBC edition of *Othello* (London, 1981), pp. 22–23.

32. Ibid., p. 23.

33. Ibid., p. 18.

34. Ibid.

35. "'This Wide and Universal Stage': Shakespeare's Plays as Plays," in *Teaching Shakespeare*, ed. Walter Edens, et al. (Princeton: Princeton Univ. Press, 1977), pp. 273–74.

The British *Shakespeare Series*
A Prolegomenon
Susan Willis

As the myriad Shakespeare festivals across the North American continent attest, Shakespeare's plays are probably performed more frequently in America
than in Britain. That fact does not, however, make Stratford-upon-Avon a
suburb of St. Louis or Shakespeare a Yankee Doodle Dandy. Shakespeare
comes from another time and, for Americans, also from another place, even
when the words are spoken with an American accent. America has so successfully adopted Shakespeare as its own that British perspectives on his work
can sometimes come as a surprise. The BBC Shakespeare series is a case in
point. Although the BBC intended to make productions of the 37 plays available world-wide, their Shakespeare series is nonetheless British in ways more
pervasive and far-reaching than accent, ways that point up the differences
between British and American television; and those differences account for
much of what the series became in the United Kingdom and in the United
States.

Consider one of the basics of the situation—scheduling. Any American
picking up a television schedule in Britain is struck by the unusual times
programs start—8:53, 9:14, 11:02—different on every channel, different
every day. The U.S. is so accustomed to the unvarying order of half-hour and
hour time slots that British programming appears chaotic. But it is also much
freer than American programming, for every show need not be trimmed to fit
the slot; the slot can be chiseled to fit the show. In the BBC's initial planning
of the Shakespeare series, the two-and-a-half hour maximum was suggested
by the American underwriters, worried about audience attentiveness. Of
course, the BBC had similar concerns about the raw material Shakespeare
offered them as television drama and would naturally have edited without
American prompting, though not just to fit an arbitrary time slot. Only the
"great tragedies" were originally exempted from the two-and-a-half hour
mold, and the first two years of the series consistently upheld the guide-
line—and chopped some scripts in the process. One of Jonathan Miller's first
actions as producer, however, was to argue for using full texts; when he pre-
vailed, it posed no problem in Britain but endless problems for American
programming, now faced with tapes running 108 minutes or 3 hours and 43
minutes rather than the usual tidy, prefabricated time units. The Americans'
first response to such gaps was to fill them with a performance of period music
or with those specially-taped interviews that so annoyed scholars in the U.S.
(they were never shown in England); and when that funding ran out, the
American programmers had no choice but to edit the tapes. As WNET's Jac
Venza explained, "When they would go three minutes over the half hour, we
felt that if they [the BBC] couldn't cut three minutes out of three-plus-hours,

we could." Two or three minutes here or there will probably not cause a great flutter, but anyone who has seen the *Henry VI-Richard III* productions only on American television has not seen Howell's productions at all, so heavily edited were they, losing not minutes but well over an hour of tape in the American transmission. Furthermore, the editor at WNET felt virtuous doing it. If so seemingly elementary a difference as scheduling yields such problems, it is not surprising there are contrasts in aesthetics and context.

Criticism of technical elements in the BBC series has abounded. Early on, television-savvy American academics lamented what they wrongly perceived as the constant use of two-camera taping in the BBC productions, but the greater item for comment among television professionals was Jonathan Miller's reliance on single-camera scenes. Not only did WNET series coordinator Roger Downey say they were impossible to edit, but Jac Venza explained, "The idea of never having a cut in the midst of a long literary speech sounds right, I mean, when Jonathan [Miller] describes it. The fact is, it belies that there is an audience looking at very sophisticated cinematic editing and cutting, so that if anything, this will look more strange. . . . He [Miller] took the position that whole scenes should just be performed for the literary style, and there should be no interruption of intercutting, . . . but I'm not sure it served the dramatic impact of the pieces as well as it might." In addition to these concerns, there were comments about the prevalence of triangular blocking, i.e. two speakers in the foreground of a shot with another figure in the rear, as a standard device in the series.

More than on camera work, however, technical criticism of the series centered on its pacing. To some extent pacing is a subjective matter; what is fine or subtle for one viewer may be slow and laborious to another. But, in general, American television—epitomized by "Three's Company" and "Miami Vice"—is very fast-paced, full of quick cuts that are partly dictated by the need to overcome commercial interruptions. Briskness makes good television and anything less prompts impatience, or so the aesthetic maxim runs. Even "Sesame Street," the mainstay of children's educational television in America, is programmed in 30-second modules. Accustomed to that rhythm and reinforced by the visual assault of rock videos, some viewers find anything less than scarcely contained chaos a slow pace. BBC programming, on the contrary, because it is based on a non-commercial system, is not driven by commercial breaks. Devotees of "Masterpiece Theatre" appreciate the uninterrupted development and juxtaposition of scenes, the careful building of effect over time. Admittedly, the British see far more of American television than Americans see of British. Consequently, Britons notice the difference between American television pace and some of theirs; Americans, for lack of comparison, do not. Some people at the BBC agree with those at WNET who felt that a few of the Shakespeare productions were very slow; but the American response in general results from overlaying an American standard on the BBC without acknowledging differences.

The technical element that provoked most concern, though, was the sound; WNET and PBS repeatedly complained to the BBC that the audio was bad, that the actors could not be heard. Critics, too, registered concern throughout the series, one saying *Measure* was "a production marred only by this series' continuing annoying variation in sound levels" (Drew), another charging of *Timon* that Miller "could have at least made sure every actor was adequately miked; some of the speeches evaporate into air downstage" (Brown).

To anyone observing BBC taping and editing practices, such criticism is at least ironic. Of the seemingly eight thousand technical aspects a BBC production staff has concern for, sound is far from overlooked. During taping the sound supervisor virtually wears a path between the sound gallery and the director's chair. In the Shakespeare series, at the sound supervisor's behest, horses' hooves have been swathed in booties, silver lids have been padded, once actors even removed their shoes and sock-footed their way across shot to avoid inappropriate sound. In fact, so earnest is the sound crew to capture every syllable of Shakespeare that the most prevalent visual flaw in the series is boom shadows. And in editing, sound levels are carefully monitored so that each line is clear and audible. For their part, the British comment on the bland uniformity of American sound: "it all sounds alike," all levels evenly high. The difference is not technical; it is aesthetic. The British have another standard: they unapologetically value perspective sound, which means if a character speaks far from the camera, he should *sound* far from the camera, even if that means faint. *Timon* is a case in point, for in that production any number of characters either speak from afar or exit speaking at the opposite side of the studio; they not only sound far away but occasionally a word is even garbled or lost. *Othello*, too, has a striking example of this approach to sound. As Iago asks Cassio about Bianca they sit in a window seat in the main hall; Othello is hidden behind the open door to the next room. The scene is almost entirely shot from behind Othello, so we see what he sees and, more importantly, hear what he hears—snatches of the deceptive dialogue, Iago's muttered questions, Cassio's muffled replies. A cut to one brief 2-shot shows us Iago chuckling and jollying Cassio along, then it's back to the distant view. Though not every word is audible here, we share the subjective effect of the 'revelation.' To the British this is not bad acting or bad audio—it is perspective sound, realistic sound effect that establishes the depth of the picture.

Nonetheless, not every director in the series favored perspective sound. Elijah Moshinsky, for one, insisted that he wanted American sound, no variance, and fought to avoid perspective sound in *Love's Labour's Lost*. The dilemma about audio also from time to time prompted videotape editors across the Atlantic to bump up the BBC sound level. In other words, in transmitting them, WNET to some extent Americanized the productions, editing for speedier pace and more uniform sound. Clearly these productions were not seen as works of art, valuable as created; for the implication of this

American response is either that the BBC does not know what it's doing or does it badly, though neither is in fact the case. They know what they're doing and mean it. The two countries are divided by their views of a common medium.

The rigor of these aesthetic differences points up how closely linked television is to popular culture. We all know the accepted patterns and methods; if those are diverged from, we tend to see the divergence as a problem or flaw rather than a creative difference. Some of the American response to the Shakespeare series may have been affected, for instance, by the contemporary vogue for television mini-series, lavishly filmed affairs involving big name stars and extensive location work. By comparison, the Shakespeare series may have seemed cramped or confined in the studio and certainly not lavish. The battles came in for special criticism in this regard; with the exception of Achilles' pushing Hector's battered head into the slime during *Troilus and Cressida*, several television professionals found the studio battles unworkable and, as the only feasible approach, sanctioned instead the work of Olivier and Kurosawa, i.e. film work, not television.

In another sense, too, the aesthetic differences deserve reckoning, and that reckoning concerns the issue of medium itself. Were Americans given novels rather than television productions, they would immediately recognize their British context and call any quick criticism based entirely on American cultural values a misreading. Yet a comparable response to the Shakespeare series is not called a misviewing. What we get from the Shakespeare series, however, is partly determined by what we see and partly by how we see and what we look for.

Consequently, there is the British cultural context of the series to consider. Theory of the television medium asserts that "the television message is made meaningful only at the moment when the semiotic codes interlock with the cultural awareness *supplied by the viewer,* whose own context will play a part in shaping the cultural awareness" (Fiske & Hartley 123–24). The BBC Shakespeare series provides an excellent laboratory for testing and proving the ways this statement is true, starting with casting.

Americans have almost no way of fully appreciating the contributions of casting to the series except where John Gielgud, Claire Bloom, Roger Daltrey, and now probably John Cleese and Derek Jacobi are concerned. They have quick recognition in the U.S. But all the fine British television actors who took part in the series go unnoticed across the Atlantic because they have not been weekly visitors on American sets as they have been back home. Americans lose the *frisson* of recognition, the extra edge of watching an actor move from weekly series to classical drama. What would the effect of such a series be for Americans if they saw Alan Alda in jerkin and codpiece spouting iambic pentameter?

Consider an example. Though the name of Leonard Rossiter is not a household word in the U.S., it is in Britain, where he was (before his untimely death between the taping and transmission of *King John*) revered for his comic characterizations. As one interviewer proclaimed: "On the television screen, all Leonard Rossiter has to do is give one of his famous shifty looks and he has me—and the rest of the country—rolling around clutching our sides. . . . Even now, years afterwards, Reggie Perrin and the dreadful Rigsby are as vivid in the memory as they were on the screen." Playing the executive Perrin in the long-running series "The Rise and Fall of Reginald Perrin" and the seedy, lecherous landlord Rigsby in "Rising Damp," Rossiter gained a wide British following; his facial expressions in these roles became so well known that one critic of *King John* observed: "The unaccustomed beard which he adopted in the central role could not conceal the occasional wild and oddly lunatic leer which was the essential rampant Rigsby" (Slim). Yet no American would see Rigsby in Rossiter's King John. No American could feel what so many British reviewers, admittedly in a eulogistic mode, lamented as the unexplored classical abilities of this fine actor. A similar case in the same cast is John Thaw, who played Hubert, previously seen in Britain (without beard) chasing criminals as star of "The Sweeney" series. Americans have no way of appreciating the effect such casting has on the British audience; even a list of the actor's credits evokes no connotations or memories for an American audience.

But this is good casting, better than most Americans can know, and it happens repeatedly in the Shakespeare series, encouraged by Miller's inventive tapping of John Cleese as Petruchio and carrying through to the end. When Elijah Moshinsky called to offer TV comedienne Maureen Lipman the part of the Princess in *Love's Labour's Lost*, she paused and then responded, "But . . . I'm Maureen Lipman!" implying "I don't do classical drama." Nevertheless she showed she can do classical drama, bringing a lively refinement to her performance and stunning the studio with her delivery of the emotional change at Marcade's entrance and news: on every take her eyes filled with tears as the banter and laughter left her lips. After the last take, as several cast members gathered to congratulate her, one actress could be heard paying her honest tribute: "How did you do that?" If Goldie Hawn or Gilda Radner had played the part, we might have a response analogous to the British seeing Maureen Lipman. The associations a performer has for the audience are not an inconsequential part of the BBC Shakespeare productions in Britain, though they are lost in America.

In other areas of production, too, the British cultural context figures significantly. From the cockney Luce in *Comedy of Errors* to *Winter's Tale's* west country Perdita, the class and regional accents used throughout the series—that vocal shorthand that tells the British ear so much—to foreign listeners can seem an aural impediment, the words harder to discern. Accent does not say to an American audience, certainly not to a classroom on first viewing, what it quickly says to a British audience more discriminatingly born to the manner of class distinctions. Because accent often functions as an interpretive signal in British drama, a character's entire background and world view can be suggested in a few syllables if the audience knows the "code." Of course, there were two different kinds of accent at work in the series—natural and assumed. National origin was subject to comment by British critics with Anthony Hopkins' Welsh lilt and Ian Charleson's Scots burr, and Edward Petherbridge was accused of sounding American as Gower in *Pericles*. Americans usually protested any non-Oxbridge sounds: "[Miller] tends to cast his British television productions from ranks so Cockney they sound like leftovers from the first stage run of *My Fair Lady*" (*Boston Globe*, 37), or "some BBC presentations can be a tiresome sort of challenge to us poor 'hempen home-spun' Americans, sometimes unable to cut through the thicket of British accents" (McNally B5).

This issue of accent complements a related aspect of the series' presentation and its audience's perception—that the BBC Shakespeare series was part of the fabric of contemporary British dramatic production and demonstrated its fashions and fads. Moshinsky's punk Puck, that Brixton tough of a sprite, was in 1981 part of a spate of punks on British stage and television, even Shakespearean punks that ranged from the beige *Dream* fairies at the National Theatre to the young and provocative punk witches of the RSC's 1982 Brechtian *Macbeth*. Even Tamora, Queen of the BBC Goths, as carefully period-costumed as she was, also conveyed a wildly up-to-date ferocity with her nose-ring, large bone-and-bead jewelry, and shocking cascade of red hair. Such characterization reads on several levels to a British viewer, and while Americans pick up some of the connotations, these are not as rich or full as they are to those viewers confronted by punks every day in the street or on the Underground. Punk is a political and social statement in British society, whereas it is derivative, more nearly a rock video fashion, in America. The context thus provides more nuances for the British viewers.

Even within the medium of television, there is a richer context for viewers of televised Shakespeare in Britain than in America: as the BBC Shakespeare series began in 1978 the RSC was just televising two of its productions on ITV, perhaps as a competitive challenge—the Ian McKellan-Judi Dench *Macbeth* and Trevor Nunn's musical *Comedy of Errors*, both using very different production values and styles than the BBC, as reviewers remarked. On the other hand, were it not for the occasional televised Joe Papp/Shakespeare in the Park production on PBS, Americans would see even less than the very little American Shakespeare now on television. William Ball's lively *Shrew* from the American Conservatory Theatre (also shown on PBS) and a few Hallmark Hall of Fame broadcasts can be singled out because of their rarity as non-cable televised Shakespeare.

It even makes a difference which channel the BBC Shakespeare series was shown on, BBC 2 in Britain and PBS in the United States. Though BBC 2 does have a somewhat higher-brow reputation than Britain's Channel 4, it is nonetheless one of the "regular" channels, having a place more like ABC's or CBS's in the U.S. Households that have never even clicked by PBS in

America would have turned in to BBC 2 in England. But PBS was founded on the premise of specialized programming, in contrast to the nature of programs on the three major American commercial networks, and consequently "self-selects" its audience more than BBC 2 does. Even though the series had comparatively small ratings shares in each country, the BBC Shakespeare production office chose to be sanguine in its interpretation of the figures, where the American programmers, seeing the audience often fall below even that of most other public television shows, so much going for so little, began to endure rather than enjoy the series as it moved toward its close.

In one other area, too, the British and Americans have demonstrated their distinctive attitudes and orientations toward the series—in marketing it for education. From the beginning, in both countries, the BBC project was billed as exceptional in its pedagogical potential: students and others who had only read the plays in school or only heard of Shakespeare as a cultural icon could now see the plays in performance and experience their vitality. In the U.S., the series' three underwriters—Exxon, Metropolitan Life, and Morgan Guaranty Trust—also sponsored a carefully coordinated program of printed materials, designed by Tel-Ed, Inc. and offered free to every secondary school in the country. These materials included summaries of the plays, questions for discussion, prepared stencils, and posters; some packets on the major plays also had a record with comments from leading actors and the director as well as speeches from the performance. In addition, Metropolitan Life provided free viewer guides for the general public, with some efforts at wide dissemination early in the series. Otherwise, this general audience was left to its own devices.

In Britain, however, the educational outreach used broadcast media just as the plays did. With arms in radio and television and an established and active educational division, the BBC—committed by mandate to inform, to educate, and to entertain—mobilized its own resources. Every BBC Shakespeare production was preceded (within a day) by both a radio program about production history or character interpretation done by a famous performer (the likes of Sir Michael Redgrave, Janet Suzman, Judi Dench, Anthony Quayle, Dame Peggy Ashcroft) and a half-hour television program of background and commentary on the play—independent of the production—given by a wide variety of well-known figures such as Germaine Greer on *Romeo and Juliet*, Lord Chalfont (Minister of State in the Foreign Office 1964–70 and widely published on foreign policy) on *Henry V*, Stephen Spender on *Winter's Tale*. These low-budget, one-camera affairs took some justified abuse from critics for their technical aspects (though they were filmed in some remarkable locales, the camera work was elementary); but in terms of the information disseminated, they were in most cases impressively efficient and thorough—and readily available to anyone who might be considering tuning in one of the plays, whether a student or John Q. Ratepayer. In fact, for some productions the audience was larger for the "Shakespeare in Perspective" program than for the play itself, and the free book list was much in demand by schools and universities. Moreover, when the BBC sold the series in Britain, they offered it with the accompanying "Shakespeare in Perspective" program, a package that has proven very popular. These alternate approaches to outreach speak volumes about the variant assumptions each culture has regarding use of media, education, audience, and Shakespeare. Only near the end of the series in America did the short-lived, experimental "Shakespeare Hour" emerge on television, re-formatting selected plays into weekly one-hour units with filmed mini-essays on relevant themes and issues when time allowed. Its educational potential was never fully reached, however, for PBS stations let it be known that they were satiated with Shakespeare, and so the program was not renewed after its initial season.

Americans—whether they consider the BBC Shakespeare on technical, aesthetic, interpretive, or educational grounds—must acknowledge their special and sometimes limited perspective on what the series is. From underwriters to academics, American have somehow assumed the Shakespeare series was made especially for them. It wasn't. As Cedric Messina, founding producer of the series, was fond of saying, only the BBC could have conceived the project and only the BBC could have carried it through. Moreover, when finished, the series bore the mark of its origin; it was made for a British audience and then successfully marketed world-wide. In planning, production, and aesthetic, the BBC Shakespeare series is very British indeed, a fact that both limits and enhances its effect on its international audience.

Boston Globe, Apr. 19, 1982. (Review of *Dream*.)
Brown, Ben. "A Good Pedigree Can't Save Poor Play," *Detroit News*, Dec. 14, 1981. (Review of *Timon*.)
Drew, Mike. *Milwaukee Journal*, Apr. 11, 1979. (Review of *Measure*.)
Downey, Roger. Telephone interview, Nov. 11, 1984; and personal interview, June 13, 1985.
Fiske, John, and John Hartley. *Reading Television*. London: Methuen, 1978.
McNally, Owen. *Hartford Courant*, Apr. 24, 1982, B5. (Review of *Dream*.)
Moshinsky, Elijah. Personal interview, July 8, 1986.
Slim, John. *Birmingham* (Eng.) *Post*, Nov. 26, 1984. (Review of *King John*.)
Venza, Jac. Personal interview, June 12, 1985.

From "Radical Potentiality and Institutional Closure: Shakespeare in Film and Television"
Graham Holderness

Television constitutes the only really 'national' theatre our society is likely to have. The medium of television would appear to offer unique opportunities for a democratic recovery of Shakespeare: a reappropriation of jealously-guarded fortresses of high culture for the popular audience which initially embraced and fostered the Elizabethan drama. Television is (unlike the Elizabethan theatre) a national institution in a genuinely universal sense; its place that fundamental space of social life, the home; its mode of communication direct, populist and general; its content largely constituted by the 'entertainment' and information widely regarded as the staple necessities of our contemporary culture. Some writers have drawn a close parallel between television and the Elizabethan theatre: a cultural comparison which appears to underlie the BBC Shakespeare series. Terry Hawkes actually proposes the television medium as a successor or reconstitution of the Elizabethan theatre's cultural potentialities,[1] and John Wilders, literary adviser to the BBC Shakespeare series, follows this analogy to propose that TV reproduction of Shakespeare's drama can emulate or at least approach the freedom and flexibility of Shakespeare's contemporary stage.[2]

Whether in practice television adaptations of Shakespeare genuinely fulfill these ambitions—and, indeed, whether the Elizabethan theatre can be properly regarded in retrospect as the central focus of national culture—remains open to question. A different kind of populism emerges from within the BBC itself: where academics envisage television as a means of reconstituting the Elizabethan theatre, producers think more in terms of translating theatre into the familiar discourse of television itself. For Cedric Messina, the original producer (replaced after the first two years by Jonathan Miller), the 'primary purpose of the series' was 'to provide good entertainment . . . because that's what Shakespeare wrote them for.'[3] 'The guiding principle . . . is to make the plays, in permanent form, accessible to audiences throughout the world.'[4] Within this alliance of academics and broadcasters there naturally arose a certain tension, between, on the one hand, scholarly and educational concerns, and on the other the values of popular entertainment, with the TV medium usually imposing its own solution, as John Wilders indicates: 'The television equivalent of Shakespeare's stage would be an empty studio. . . . I am now certain however that we were right not to adopt this style. . . . To the television viewer, accustomed as he is to such representations of reality as football matches, news films, and thrillers filmed on location in California, the opening scene of *Macbeth* would not have been "an open place" but Studio I of the Television Centre, White City' ("Adjusting the Set," p. 13).

Reprinted, with permission, from *Political Shakespeare*, ed. Jonathan Dollimore and Alan Sinfield (Manchester University Press, 1985).

None the less, within that alliance of the camera and the pen, these discrete ideologies, the scholarly/democratic and the media/populist, seem to have coalesced into unity; and the tendency of the resultant approach to Shakespeare must necessarily move towards a devolution of cultural authority.

The argument for 'accessibility' is greatly strengthened by the (now familiar but actually very recent) developments in the manufacture and marketing of video technology. Broadcasting itself makes the complex and expensive products of an intensely centralised culture immediately available to the whole of a society; but the availability remains at the mercy of centralised planning bodies and not at all subject to popular participation or democratic control. Video technology increases that availability enormously, and (however severely constrained by restrictive copyright legislation and the absence of a licensing system) confers much more power on the consumer. The planners of the BBC Shakespeare had this in mind from the outset: Cedric Messina accepted the suggestion that one hope of the planners was for the creation of 'a library of Shakespeare video productions that will last for quite some time.' This aspiration involved commercial as well as cultural considerations: '. . . the plays are actually starting to pay for themselves. The plays are selling already around the world . . . ' ("Cedric Messina Discusses The Shakespeare Plays," p. 135).

It has already been argued in relation to film that in one sense, and particularly for those operating within the educational apparatus of 'Literature,' the translation of Shakespeare into a non-literary form must necessarily be potentially radical: subverting the cultural hegemony of literature itself, disturbing the equilibrium of received cultural traditions. Similarly, if one symptomatic strategy of bourgeois culture is to preserve certain figures of cultural authority for specialised participation by a social and intellectual elite, then the extension of participation in Shakespeare to a much wider constituency via that audience's most familiar medium must necessarily exert some pressure on the bases of cultural power. But these propositions bring us up against the truly fundamental question: is the extension of high culture to be seen as a democratic appropriation of cultural wealth by the people, or simply as an extension of centralised cultural power by the transmission of authority, in the form of an art which cannot choose but be reactionary and pacificatory in its ideological effects? After all Matthew Arnold, and the Newbolt Report, and Scrutiny, all spoke of the desirability of taking Shakespeare to the masses, often in a rhetoric of intense radical populism, but they were certainly not fostering or proposing a radical cultural politics.

Although productions of Shakespeare on TV are nothing new, the project of the series, in its ambitious scope and scale and massive investment of cultural capital, clearly represents the most significant intervention to date into the reproduction of Shakespeare on the screen. And other, more material investment was required to get the series off the ground: the BBC entered into partnership with the American company Time-Life TV, which in turn raised financial backing for the series from three big private corporations in the USA—Exxon Corporation, Metropolitan Life Insurance Company and Morgan Guaranty Trust of New York. This alliance between the BBC and American private enterprise indicates how the series was generated from the very highest levels of economic and cultural power. Clearly it is inadequate to write the series off as a predictable symptom of its institutional and capitalistic origin, but it is important to trace and measure the constraints and determinants built into the series itself as a consequence of its economic and institutional basis.

The scale of investment and the nature of commercial underwriting (as distinct from commercial *sponsorship*) imposed one very obvious requirement on this enterprise: it should be economically viable—that is, give an economic as well as a cultural return on capital investment. This condition necessarily entailed the preservation of the plays in a consumer-durable form (video-cassette) rather than restriction to one-time transmission, and an international marketing operation. Conscious of this dependence on the market rather than on patronage and subsidy, the planners insisted that productions should aim for 'high quality' and 'durability.' What 'high quality' originally implied in such a context is predictable: 'great' directors, 'classical' actors, 'straightforward' productions:' . . . these productions will offer a wonderful opportunity to study the plays performed by some of the greatest classical actors of our time' (Messina, *Richard II*, p. 8). This insistence on building into the productions that isolating quality of 'excellence' is familiar from the Arnoldian practices of literary criticism, though it is perhaps unusual to find critical excellence and market value, the common pursuit of true judgment and industrial quality control, quite so firmly identified. The concept of 'high quality' in fact entailed a conservative respect for 'traditional' values in Shakespearean production. Jonathan Miller has described the 'problems' he inherited in taking over the series, among them ' . . . the original contract with the American co-producers—it had to be so-called traditional. . . .'[5] Cedric Messina had accepted this constraint even more readily, in the belief that only 'traditional' productions would 'stand the test of time': 'We've not done anything too sensational in the shooting of it—there's no arty-crafty shooting at all. All of them are, for want of a better word, straightforward productions' ("Cedric Messina Discusses *The Shakespeare Plays*," p. 137).

Despite expressed reservations, Jonathan Miller accepted the executive producership of the series after the second season. Whatever his capacities as a stage director, Miller believes in the absolute determinacy of the television medium, which imposes its own constraints on dramatic production. Television is incurably naturalistic and translates everything into naturalism.[6] Miller is therefore averse to any attempt to theatricalise television: TV productions should display no manneristic theatrical styles, no expressionistic acting and no mixing of conventions. It is impossible to reproduce Elizabethan theatre conditions in a television presentation: 'What is characteristic about the Elizabethan stage condition is that the audience is part of that condition. . . . In television you automatically eliminate the audience. It isn't present at the production. It's absolutely hopeless to try and reconstitute the wooden "O" inside the electric square' ('An Interview with Jonathan Miller," p. 9). Olivier's film version of *Henry V* was therefore mistaken in trying 'to set up within one medium the conventions of another.' Miller's consistent adherence to naturalism is admitted as an explicit commitment to illusionist representation: the audience should be 'unaware of the fact that they're in the presence of an art-form.'

In fact there is greater diversity of production styles in the series than these theoretical pronouncements would suggest. But there can be little doubt that overall a conservative 'drag' is applied by a combination of factors: the constraints of commercial underwriting; the consequent concern of the BBC to build high-quality prestige into the series; the conservative cultural views of the original producer and the willing submission of his successor to the dominant naturalistic style of television drama. The conservatism of the whole series can best be measured against one remarkable exception, Jane Howell's production of the first historical tetralogy.

The most appropriate contrast of detail to be made is that between the productions of the second historical tetralogy (which belong to the first and second 'seasons' of 1978–79), directed by David Giles under the producership of Cedric Messina; and the 1982 productions of *Henry VI* and *Richard III*. Messina foregrounded the English history cycle, allowing these plays to dominate the first two seasons (*Richard II* and *Henry VIII* in 1978; the *Henry IV*s and *Henry V* in 1979). These programming decisions suggest a nationalistic desire to celebrate the course of English history; but the 'British' quality emerges also from Messina's thoroughly conventional view of the plays: 'These histories are a sort of curse of the House of Atreus in English'. This view was supported by an ancillary broadcast featuring right-wing pundit Paul Johnson: 'According to the orthodox Tudor view of history the deposition of the rightful and anointed king, Richard II, was a crime against God, which thereafter had to be expiated by the nation in a series of bloody struggles. . . .'[7] Messina wanted to organise the plays into a coherent historical totality; and it was originally the producer's hope that the plays would share a uniformity of style, knitting them even more closely together into an integrated unity. Asked by an interviewer what he would be doing to 'assure continuity,' Messina spoke of maintaining character castings, and indicated that he thought it would be 'right and proper' to keep the same director ("Cedric Messina Discusses *The Shakespeare Plays*," p. 137).

This didn't, in the event, happen, and the consequences are instructive. The second tetralogy is a characteristic example of conventional 'high-quality' Shakespearean production: performed, in Messina's words, 'by a splendid company, including many of the leading names in our classical drama' (Messina, *Richard II*, p. 9). The central actors tend to be classical old stagers or modern stars: John Gielgud, Wendy Hiller, Anthony Quayle, Derek Jacobi and Jon Finch. The overall style of production is overwhelmingly naturalistic; the director David Giles was chosen as an experienced *television* director regarded as 'adept at dealing with English history and the English character' (e.g. *The Forsyte Saga*) (*ibid.*, p. 19). The combat-scene in *Richard II* (I.iii), a formalised heraldic ritual which hardly invites naturalistic presentation, was done in this mode: 'You can't do it realistically in a television studio and yet we didn't want it to get too stylized: that's why we used real horses. If we had gone too stylized with the list scene we would have had to stylise the play all the way through, and stylization on television is very difficult' (David Giles, *ibid.*, p. 20).

The second tetralogy emerges from this production as a constituent element in an inclusive and integrated dramatic totality, illustrating the violation of natural social 'order' by the deposition of a legitimate king. The plays are produced in 'classic drama' style with predominantly naturalistic devices of acting, *mise-en-scène*, and filming. Actors are identified wholly with their roles, growing old in them; settings are more naturalistic than conventionalised; camera movements and angles are always 'straightforward,' with no 'artycrafty' shooting.

In the case of Jane Howell's productions of the first historical tetralogy, the director's whole conception of the Shakespearean history play diverges strikingly from that propounded by Cedric Messina and evidently accepted by David Giles. Where Messina saw the history plays conventionally as orthodox Tudor historiography, and the director employed dramatic techniques which allow that ideology a free and unhampered passage to the spectator, Jane Howell takes a more complex view of the first tetralogy as, simultaneously, a serious attempt at historical interpretation and a drama with a peculiarly modern relevance and contemporary application. The plays, to this director, are not a dramatisation of the Elizabethan World Picture but a sustained interrogation of residual and emergent ideologies in a changing society.[8] Commenting on Talbot's dilemma in 1 *Henry VI*, IV.v–vi, Howell defines the drama as a disclosure of the contradictoriness of chivalric values: 'When Talbot finally comes face to face with his own son who will not leave the battle although he knows he is going to get killed, then Talbot has to come face to face with his own values; because if the values of chivalry mean you have to sacrifice your son . . . ' (1 *Henry VI*, p. 31). At the same time Howell wanted to explore the plays' potentiality for contemporary signification: 'We felt it shouldn't be too medieval . . . we talked about Northern Ireland and Beirut and South America, about warlords and factions.'[9] This awareness of the multiplicity of potential meanings in the play required a decisive and scrupulous avoidance of television or theatrical naturalism: methods of production should operate to open the plays out, rather than close them into the immediately recognisable familiarity of conventional Shakespearean production.

Howell's basic conception of the plays entailed a refusal to attempt naturalisation: Jonathan Miller's insistence that the TV medium *enforces* naturalism, and that the conventions of theatre would not work within it, seems to have been systematically ignored: 'At the outset she had made the clear decision to avoid any attempt to scale down the action to make it more "televisual." The energy, she felt, was essentially theatrical and she therefore made a number of theatrical decisions—the company would double parts as they do in the theatre; the action would all take place on a single set, which would change in mood from play to play . . .' ("Dialogues of Disintegration,"

p. 20). One important consideration here was a historical one: Howell felt that the plays would work better in the kind of theatrical situation they were originally produced in, on a relatively bare stage with minimal, emblematic props and scenery, by a company of actors operating as an *ensemble*. The set, modelled on an adventure playground in Fulham, was designed to suggest the locations of popular drama—'we thought of fairgrounds and circuses and mystery plays' as well as familiar modern environments, a children's playground or a burnt-out building site. It was constructed to appear deliberately non-naturalistic: thus allowing the play to express both historical and contemporary meanings. Oliver Bayldon, the set-designer, explained his decision to use a modern parquet floor as a deliberate violation of illusionist representation: 'It stops the set from literally representing . . . it reminds us we are in a modern television studio.'[10] Stanley Wells commended this aspect of the production: 'Jane Howell has dared to encourage us to remember that the action is taking place in a studio.'[11]

It will be apparent to what extent Jane Howell's practice contradicts or negates the definitive pronouncements of Cedric Messina and Jonathan Miller on how Shakespeare should be televised. This director found it possible to reject television naturalism in favour of the theatricalising of television, to mix the conventions of one medium with those of another, and to recreate some of the radical potentialities of the Elizabethan theatre. Even Jonathan Miller's persuasive point about TV's elimination of the audience was solved here by constituting members of the cast, for certain scenes, as a vociferous and participating audience (e.g. the Jack Cade scenes in 2 *Henry VI*), as well as by extensive use of the direct address to camera, the equivalent of actor-audience dialogue.

All these devices are defamiliarising, estranging, 'alienating'; they induce the kind of alert and vigilant curiosity sought by Brecht's 'epic' theatre. The actors double parts, thus preventing any illusionary identification of actor and character. Nor are the actors the familiar Shakespearean stars of the BBC *Richard II*, their personalities so subdued to what they work in that they appear to be characters from Shakespeare. Furthermore, under the director's influence there is a general rejection of Stanislavskian method: her advice to her actors insistently recalls Brecht (see BBC 2 *Henry VI*, p. 24). This 'epic' style provides much greater flexibility and freedom to the actor, who is no longer imprisoned within the naturalist concept of a coherent psychological identity, but able to play out those psychological incoherencies which can disclose sociological truths (see BBC 1 *Henry VI*, p. 30).

The radical potentialities of television Shakespeare, evident enough from these examples, are in practice systematically blocked, suppressed or marginalised by the conservatism of the dominant cultural institutions. Overall the BBC Shakespeare series operates to confirm the cultural authority which in turn confers the status of high culture upon the BBC itself, and on those powerful capitalist corporations which financed it—a circular process which effectively closes out the people for whom the series is supposedly produced.

Once the production becomes completed and packaged in video-cassette form it becomes universally available, but also permanently fixed, unchangeable: the radical and subversive potentiality of performance is translated back into something closer to the authoritarian dominance of the literary text. The BBC Shakespeare series is in fact the most perfect consummation to date of a process which commenced in Shakespeare's own time with the Tudor government's systematic destruction of the national religious drama, the professionalising of theatre by the licensing of a few acting companies and the building of the first purpose-built playhouses, the privileging of metropolitan over national culture, and the incorporation of the drama into the cultural structure of an emergent bourgeois nation-state. A 'national' culture is, in bourgeois terms, the production by a centralised cultural apparatus, operating from the capital, of high-quality aesthetic objects which are then transmitted to the 'nation,' which in turn acts as passive recipient of a pre-packaged cultural commodity. The active, democratic participation and intervention of the Elizabethan audience actually generated a process which reduced that audience to an inert constituency loyally consuming liberal doses of what one is tempted to call, following Peter Brook, 'deadly television.'[12]

Film and television reproductions of Shakespeare are in essence no different from other forms of reproduction, in theatre or education: they have specific commercial and cultural functions within the economic and ideological apparatus of a bourgeois-democratic society. Spaces are created within that cultural apparatus for radical intervention, and such opportunities have to a limited extent been seized. The most promising space for cultural intervention remains, despite systematic attacks on the system, that of education, where film and television productions can be introduced into literature courses, posing fundamental cultural questions, liberating radical possibilities of meaning, and contributing to the much needed politicisation of the 'Shakespeare' institution.

1. Terence Hawkes, *Shakespeare's Talking Animals* (London: Edward Arnold, 1973), p. 231.

2. John Wilders, "Adjusting the Set," *Times Higher Educational Supplement* (10 July 1981), p. 13.

3. "Cedric Messina Discusses *The Shakespeare Plays*," *Shakespeare Quarterly*, 30 (1979), 137.

4. Cedric Messina, "Preface" to *The BBC TV Shakespeare: Richard II* (London: BBC, 1978), p. 8.

5. Ann Pasternak Slater, "An Interview with Jonathan Miller," *Quarto*, 10 (1980), 9.

6. Tim Hallinan, "Jonathan Miller on *The Shakespeare Plays*," *Shakespeare Quarterly*, 32 (1981), 134.

7. Paul Johnson, "*Richard II*," in Roger Sales, ed., *Shakespeare in Perspective* (London: BBC/ Ariel Books, 1982), p. 33.

8. Henry Fenwick, "The Production," *The BBC TV Shakespeare: Henry VI, Part One* (London: BBC, 1983), pp. 22–23.

9. Henry Fenwick, "Dialogues of Disintegration," *Radio Times* (1 January 1983).

10. *The BBC TV Shakespeare: Henry VI, Part Two* (London: BBC, 1983), p. 20.

11. Stanley Wells, "The History of the Whole Contention," *Times Higher Educational Supplement* (4 February 1983), p. 105.

12. See Graham Holderness, *Shakespeare's History* (Dublin: Gill and Macmillan, 1984), Introduction 3: "Drama and Society."

The Moon in the Morning and the Sun at Night
Perversity and the BBC Shakespeare
Scott McMillin

Perversity is what Petruchio does to Kate when he makes her declare that the sun is the moon before she can continue the journey to her father's house (*Taming of the Shrew*, IV, v). My purpose is to choose two instances of apparent perversity in the BBC series of Shakespeare plays, one apiece from the Cedric Messina and Jonathan Miller regimes, and attempt to explain why the Miller example is the more promising from a political point of view. I also want to account for the failure of that political promise. Genuine perversity, Miller's kind, always shows a flash of the subversive in contradicting what everyone takes for granted (established power depends on what everyone takes for granted). Why that flash so often fails to ignite anything—why, indeed, it usually becomes part of an established lighting design after all—has to concern anyone interested in radical politics.[1]

My first example comes from 1 *Henry IV* and it concerns the lighting of the scenes just before the battle of Shrewsbury. The viewer will remember that the rebel leaders in IV, iii, meeting at night in front of Hotspur's tent, stand in lovely moonlight. By contrast, when the royal forces make their appearance one scene later and receive emissaries from the rebels (V, i), they are all ruddy in the rising sun: "How bloodily the sun begins to peer / Above yon bulky hill," the King says, although it looks as though he is being roasted by a Birmingham coke oven. The perversity comes at the beginning of the next scene, when the rebel leaders return to their camp. They are shown outside their tent again, and the moon is shining once more! The angry sunlight has disappeared, and it is night again. Either someone forgot the time of day, or the Petruchio principle is at work here; and if there is one thing the BBC can be counted on to know, it is the time of day. Petruchio seems to be in charge:

PET. Good Lord, how bright and goodly shines the moon!

KATH. The moon! the sun—it is not moonlight now.

PET. I say it is the moon that shines so bright.

KATH. I know it is the sun that shines so bright.

PET. Now by my mother's son, and that's myself,
It shall be moon, or star, or what I list . . .

The other example of perversity comes from Miller's *Antony and Cleopatra*. Toward the end, in the monument, as the Queen is dying, Charmian ends her lovely speech about "a lass unparallel'd" by saying "Your crown's awry, / I'll mend it"—and then she doesn't. She doesn't straighten the crown.

She doesn't do anything. She just stands there. I suppose that Cleopatra dies with her crown atilt, although the scene of Caesar's arrival is shot from behind her and one cannot tell what she looks like.

There is a distinction to be made between these two cases of perversity. The first can be made to fit the text, and the second cannot. That moonlight outside Hotspur's tent, bathing the rebels in a lovely glow even as the royal forces are being fired by a bloody sun, has designs upon us. We recognize Hotspur as a headstrong romantic and we recall a famous line of his about plucking honor from the pale-faced moon. Now on the eve (?) of battle, Hotspur's romanticism has turned to suicidal foolhardiness, and yet that lush moonlight still shines outside the tent. Moreover, this production has given us an even more brilliant moonlight scene early in the action. The robbery at Gadshill trembles with painterly moonlight, the visual representation of Falstaff's "Let us be Diana's foresters, gentlemen of the shade, minions of the moon." The visual repetition of this lighting at the rebels' tent tells us, as the moon language of the text does too, that Eastcheap roguery belongs to the same world as foolhardy rebellion. And what is that sometime moonlighter Prince Hal doing when we learn this? He is standing in the bloody sunlight, ready to join his father in bringing disaster upon the lunatic rebellion.

The perverse moonlight, in other words, can be explained as part of a coherent interpretation of the text, and that is exactly what is troublesome about it. The technology of these shows has a staggering power to produce ready-made, complete, coherent interpretations of Shakespeare, and when such authority is consolidated in a state agency like the BBC, one should ask, upon whom is the power to be used? I refer not just to the technology of lighting effects in the studio but also to the technology of filming these shows for the twin purposes of preserving them for ages to come and exporting them for commercial gain. Monuments and profits—these motives have been known to occur together before, especially in countries once stirred by imperial possibilities, and the answer to the question of who will receive the enlightenment of these productions takes on global proportions. "The task," said the *Times* review of 1 *Henry IV* (17 December 1979) is "to present Shakespeare not to audiences of a few hundred faithful but to millions both across the globe and down the years to come." In other words, the natives. Across the oceans and down the ages, the natives are waiting for Shakespeare, and natives had better not be given their Shakespeare without reinforced guidelines of correct interpretation. Let the text of sun and moon be therefore radiant with the finest lighting in our studios, so that subversives like Hotspur and Falstaff will be kept in the dark, Hal will emerge bloody and victorious in the light, and the danger of misunderstanding in the colonies will be kept under control.

In the long run, then, this is not perversity after all. It is a form of cultural control in which a coherent literary interpretation takes hold through the technology of mechanical reproduction. (Besides, it is cheaper to shoot those two moonlit tent scenes at once.) This is not the genuine touch of Petruchio at all, but rather a simple economical example of cultural imperialism.

For a true reflection of Petruchio, one turns to *Antony and Cleopatra* and its director, Jonathan Miller. Here the intention is to contradict the text—not to reinforce it through cultural interpretation, but to thwart it, deny its meaning at crucial moments, reverse its most obvious points just when cultural piety likes to take hold. This motive must be seen through the smokescreen claim to historical accuracy the director has laid down for each of his productions. How the Renaissance mind worked is no mystery to Jonathan Miller, who has been to all the galleries in search of the Baroque image for this play, the Dutch interior for that one. This Renaissance pictorial overlay has nothing to do with the "accurate" representation of a Shakespeare play, but it does provide an attractive camouflage while perversity moves into position and takes aim at the standardized interpretations of the text. When Miller's Charmian does not straighten the Queen's crown, this is just the final touch in a production which has consistently opposed the language of grandeur and exoticism, leaving a knobby-kneed Antony and a scrawny Cleopatra looking for a Veronese painting in which to compose themselves. The men are boozy and bedraggled; the women rub their thighs a bit—so much for the claim to Roman nobility and Egyptian sensuousness. Petruchio has visited this text and reversed its most obvious meanings.

Miller's other productions are charged with the same impudence, although *The Taming of the Shrew* and *Timon of Athens* bid fair to be exceptions, and I shall turn to them shortly. Miller usually goes after the big moment, the cultural fixture. Othello speaks "put out the light, and then put out the light," but he does not put out the first light, the candle. There it burns on the bedside table, while Othello then manages to direct "thou flaming minister" to Desdemona. This Othello is a dark-tanned white man (now turning pink as my tape ages), so that all such references as "black as mine own face," "thick lips," and "sooty bosom" make no sense at all. Miller talked at one point of eliminating the references to blackness in order to harmonize with casting a white actor for the part, [2] but such pious chatter should not obscure what he actually did. He actually let the language of blackness stand and contradicted it with Anthony Hopkins.

In *Troilus and Cressida* the leading example of textual subversion occurs in the debate between Hector and Troilus over the value of Helen of Troy. This is the major philosophical debate in the Trojan camp, Hector's argument for objective value being posed against the subjective idealism of Troilus and Paris. When Hector gives in to the younger idealists, disaster lies ahead for Troy. Miller turns this argument into an exercise in tactless twaddle by the simple device of putting Helen herself, and the other women of Troy, into the scene. The men are discussing Helen to her face, and the issue changes from their reasoning to their rudeness. There she sits, this pearl whose price hath launch'd above a thousand ships, listening and panting furiously ("these men!"). Her silent rage contrasts with the next scene, which begins with the wonderful volubility of a drag-queen Thersites, played by a superior transvestite actor named The Incredible Orlando.

Such jolts to orthodoxy are now distributed world wide. School children for ages to come will wonder why Othello is not black nor Cleopatra beautiful. They will have been taught, correctly, that Othello's "there where I have garner'd up my heart" is a stunning speech, but they will not be able to hear much of it through the choked up sobbing of the actor. If they *do* hear it, they will hear nonsense, for Othello changes the fountain which is to be kept "as a cistern for foul toads" to one kept *in* a cistern for foul toads. So many lines are gagged in this production that a transcript would read like a Bad Quarto.

Anyone who mistrusts the cultural imperialism of the BBC project must take some pleasure at the damage Miller has inflicted from the inside. By turning Petruchian perversity against the text, he initiates questions about authority instead of disposing them to lie low in a thicket of correct interpretation. And in the case of *Antony and Cleopatra*, he has picked the perfect play. It is about *real* imperialists, for one thing, and for another, watching it on American television reminds us that Caesar is still gaining ground. To hear that "This production is made possible in part by grants" from the oil company, the bank, and the insurance firm reminds us that the empire reaches very close to home—although all one needs is the Time-Life symbol that appears at the beginning, with that happy little G-major chord behind it. The imperialism of this project is not confined to England. It extends to a western capitalist culture in which the English and the American are hard to separate. It is a good thing Miller blended Rome into Egypt—he reminds us that when it comes to empire, the apparent differences between the leading agents are meant to disguise underlying similarities.

But aside from *Antony and Cleopatra*, where the imperialism in the play is treated to the same reduction as the imperialism in the BBC project, not much can be said for the political range of Miller's solid and genuine perversity. His cheeky irreverence reminds one of the central modern tradition in British anti-authoritarian comedy, a tradition which goes back to the music halls and "The Goon Show," and which is now best known through *Beyond the Fringe* and "Monty Python." None of these shows has made an impact on contemporary radical politics, one reason being that all of them base their hilarity to some extent on a misogyny which contemporary radical politics has learned to disown.

Consider Miller's *Troilus and Cressida* once more. The juxtaposition of Helen and Thersites that I mentioned earlier shows the director's hand most clearly: the beautiful woman is positioned where she must remain silent among men; the woman manqué, Thersites in drag, takes the foreground of the next scene and no one can shut him up. He stands between the viewer and the other characters. This is the kind of "woman" who can tell what is going on. He is one of the two commentators on the action, the other being Ulysses. Credit Miller with finding the common ground in this pair. Ulysses gives the prologue as a voice-over. He knows what is coming and can guide

us to it even in his absence. His speech on degree and his immediately following strategy for tricking Achilles into action are played as equally reasonable.
The contradiction between them receives no attention. This wise man knows
what is up. He also doesn't like women. His only troubled moment is when
Cressida arrives in the Greek camp and, flirting with everyone else, refuses to
kiss him. He gets even—sadly, wisely—when he takes Troilus to spy on her
unfaithfulness with Diomed. Thersites is the other spy to that scene, and one
sees how accurately Miller perceives the similarity between foul-mouthed
scurrility and voice-over wisdom: they both know a whore for a whore, and
don't mind peeping in.

Miller is drawing out the anti-feminism of these two commentators, but
his own treatment of the female characters reduces them to objects fit for the
misogynist's eye. Helen is all bosom, whether it is panting furiously as she
listens to the debate over whether to send her back, or is offering herself to
Paris's hand and the camera's eye during Pandarus's love song. Cressida is
made to deliver "tear my bright hair, and scratch my praised cheeks" stretched
on the bed she shared with Troilus, her head outside the frame and only the
torso visible. The terms of this dissection are reversed—all face, no body—
when she identifies her fault, and the fault of all women:

> Ah, poor our sex! this fault in us I find,
> The error of our eye directs our mind.

The plays to which Miller was most faithful are *The Taming of the Shrew*
and *Timon of Athens*. There is no need to dwell on misogynism in *Timon*,
where the only identified women are whores. Miller has only to play the text
as written, adding an extra touch by casting a former film-beauty, Diana
Dors, as one of the whores. *The Taming of the Shrew* is a more complex case.
Miller defined his production as "Puritan" in pre-production commentary,
and sealed the point with a Puritan hymn in praise of order and obedience,
sung by the assembled husbands and wives at the end.[3] Miller's only significant change lay in omitting the Sly prologue: to suggest that the play is intended to fool a drunken tinker would, I presume, not fit the moral plan. In
all other respects, Miller's version is a straightforward piece of shrew-bashing.
Casting John Cleese as Petruchio was at first greeted as a sign of zaniness, but
the anti-feminist inheritance from "Monty Python" was here being turned to
explicit purpose. Miller knew that his actor would only have to temper the
method, not change it. Kate's concluding speech about the simplicity of
women is the most centered and valorized moment for an actress in all of
Miller's productions. Compare his shot of Desdemona when she is killed—an
arm sticking up from below, a hand fumbling for her husband's beard.
Women are frequently dismembered in Miller's camera-angles, but not the
submissive Kate. She commands the scene. For the Puritan, an ordered marriage leads to an ordered family, and these lead to an ordered state—the orthodoxy is seamless so long as the woman submits.

This is a skimpy version of the Puritan doctrine of marriage, which held that women should be valued as freely-choosing partners within the terms of subordination they accepted in marriage. There is nothing about starving them into submission, as Petruchio does to Kate. Petruchio is no more representative of Puritan husbands than the Elizabethan stage was of Vermeer interiors. It has been noted that such historical allusions help attract a special audience to Miller's productions—not the broad popular audience for which Messina designed his correct interpretations, but an intellectually hip crowd fond of cultural range and beholden to established institutions.[4]

The question to ask of this audience is not whether they participate in radical politics (they don't), but whether they notice issues of feminism and misogyny. Do they notice anything offensive about Miller's summing up Cleopatra as "a treacherous slut?"[5] Do they wonder about the implications of his turning Othello into an ordinary man[6]—as though all men are prepared to strangle their Desdemonas in the interests of justice? The director who thinks this way and knows he has an audience for the results is bound to violate the Shakespearean text in perverse ways, but the perversity fails to stake out an opposition to the BBC's cultural imperialism. Miller's opposition is personal and stubborn, determined to cross authority in the interests of male-centered individualism, mindful of the opportunity for gaining effects at the expense of women, and for those reasons incapable of arousing radical political interests.

All this is a far cry from early Puritanism, in which the anti-feminism was beginning to give way to respect for the individual rights of women, and in which a radical politics was taking hold. No radical politics takes hold in Miller's productions, which have the true touch of Petruchio in more ways than one. When Petruchio calls the sun the moon, he is abusing the woman he married for money. Sometimes male perversity extends no further than making a woman knuckle under.

1. See, for example, Graham Holderness, "Radical Potentiality and Institutional Closure: Shakespeare in Film and Television," *Political Shakespeare*, ed. Jonathan Dollimore and Alan Sinfield (Manchester University Press, 1985), pp. 182–201.
2. In the Introduction to the BBC edition of *Othello* (London, 1981), p. 23. See James C. Bulman, "The BBC Shakespeare and 'House Style,'" *Shakespeare Quarterly*, 35 (1984), 580.
3. See "Jonathan Miller on *The Shakespeare Plays*," *Shakespeare Quarterly*, 32 (1981), 134–145.
4. Bulman, "The BBC Shakespeare and 'House Style,'" pp. 575–577.
5. "Jonathan Miller on *The Shakespeare Plays*," p. 143.
6. Bulman, "The BBC Shakespeare and 'House Style,'" p. 580.

Part Two
CLOSEUPS

Tragedies

Shakespeare On TV
An Optimistic Survey
Marvin Rosenberg

Four times (at the time of this writing), Shakespeare has had major engagements with television in 1953–1954. Twice, he came off more or less with honor. The best that can be said of the other two times is that the playwright was the victim of technical knockouts.

But this record is better than it sounds. Shakespeare showed, even in defeat, that he is still the champion in any dramatic medium—if properly handled. His work can be made to fit the television screen admirably; and, for modern audiences, it can even gain impact through the intimacy of the new form. It is worth remembering here that in the relatively small theaters for which Shakespeare wrote—even in the outdoor Globe—the audience was pretty close to the action—perhaps even much closer than we used to think, if Leslie Hotson's recent arena-staging theories[1] have any validity. Many scenes, played far forward on the platform—or perhaps centrally at Whitehall—were virtual close-ups. This was especially true when the rapidly succeeding scenes were played in different stage areas, which became for the moment specialized locales cut off from the rest of the acting space. The audience then focused on localized action, something the television camera can do now for viewers. In the close relationship TV establishes, a brilliant clarity can often be given to the music of the verse as well as to its meaning; and the latter can be illuminated by subtle, intimate stage business, legitimately suggested by the lines, that sharpens both the stage action and the characterization. Beyond this, scene can follow scene with the speed Shakespeare was working for.

Reprinted, with permission, from *The Quarterly of Film, Radio, and Television*, 9:2 (Winter 1954), 166–74. © 1954 by the Regents of the University of California.

This is what television *can* do. In the last year, it came a long way toward learning how to do it. In the first major undertaking of *Hamlet*, in the spring of 1953, many of the problems of producing Shakespeare in the medium became apparent, and some were solved on the spot. This *Hamlet* was an ambitious production, for television: a two-hour show with a big-name cast—Maurice Evans as Hamlet, Sarah Churchill as Ophelia, Joseph Schildkraut as Claudius—and at a cost of many thousands of dollars. If the production was less than consummate—as it was—it was not for lack of effort and investment. It was clearly good enough to have been worth doing, and it taught television a lot.

First of all, there was the question of time. Two hours straight on network television is a fabulous slice of paid-for eternity, at the going video rate; and to ask a sponsor to give us more may be sheer ingratitude. But until more time is available, we are not going to get all of any Shakespearean play in one showing. Some of the lines will have to go. Well, some of the lines had to go in Shakespeare's time. The playwright himself mentioned a playing span that matches television's—"the two hours' traffic of our stage"—and, though we need not take this or other similar contemporary statements literally, it seems very likely that the plays then took some two or three hours. Shakespeare's actors may have spoken a little faster than ours; but it seems most unlikely that they should have spoken *Hamlet* trippingly enough on the tongue to get through the whole play, business and all, in the time allowed. More likely, if the actors had tried, they would have tripped completely over their tongues, and their words would have sounded like gibberish to a representative London audience. Both logic and contemporary evidence suggest that the plays were trimmed for the Elizabethans as customarily—if not as severely—as for our own.

This was not—and is not—necessarily unfortunate. In his best plays, Shakespeare has soft spots that are better excised; and it is often doing him a favor to eliminate them. I have nothing against the purists who like to produce Shakespeare entire, untouched; but too often the result is the preservation of stage relics rather than the production of living theater that the playwright would probably have preferred. On the other hand, the plays will take only so much cutting before they are mortally wounded; they bled badly in two of the television presentations I will discuss.

Hamlet came off fairly well in the 108 minutes of actual playing time,[2] though it lost in mood, in character, and even something in plot from the cutting. The fine, sinister mystery of the opening encounter on the battlements was chopped away, and with it the suspense that usually carries through the first court scene and our introduction to the melancholy Hamlet. This early omission seemed the less happy because it was replaced, with no saving of time, by a pantomimed court pageant. Fortinbras and the diplomatic complications springing from his impetuousness were missing—as they frequently are—and were missed, too, to the extent that they removed a foil for Hamlet's contemplative character; thus, the moment was lost when he was to say "How all occasions do inform against me . . . " and harden his resolve to act instead of think. The deleted comedy of silly Osric could be spared; rather less, that of the gravediggers. Many a favorite line here and there had to go in intermittent editing, as well as some of the loveliest poetry—notably the lines on Ophelia's suicide.

The *Hamlet* production also pointed out one of the specific pitfalls of dealing with Shakespearean spectacle on the tiny television screen. If there is a law about staging for the medium it seems to be this: on television, background clutter is poison to complex drama, and especially to the plays of Shakespeare with his temptation to elegance. The genius of the medium is its selectivity of focal points for the combined perception of eye and ear; the line of action must be clear; the form of speech, unblurred by visual distraction. In a large theater, the complementary stage movement of a minor character may easily function as an aid to audience focus; but in the television studio this may be as dangerous as a flaring signpost pointing away from the action. Similarly, the appearance behind the actors of scattered backgrounds as conflicting shapes of black and grey—especially when they are in poor perspective (and this is sometimes unavoidable at the present technical level)—confuses the eye and interrupts the eye-ear perception. In the televised *Hamlet* production, there was a praiseworthy attempt, usually successful, to avoid the clutter of action; but there was a less careful attention to elimination of scenic hodgepodge. Each of the palace interiors suggested a kind of old-fashioned drawing room, with tables, chairs, and other paraphernalia; and, in depth shots, these interiors strove hard with the actors for visual attention. Another distraction was the over-all costuming. Snappy, dark, modern uniforms of the military, against the vaguely Victorian-Ruritanian flavor of the ensemble, worked in opposition to the viewers' time orientation.

A device favored by the play's producers (Hallmark Theater) was that of looking at the actors through tricky points of view—from beyond a window, through a fire, etc.—and, although this was an interesting technical novelty, it had the disadvantage of reminding the viewer of what an interesting technical novelty this technical novelty was. Another trick used extensively in *Hamlet* was to end scenes on a long close-up of the face of a character expressing some emotion. This grew to be very painful, particularly when the actor was Schildkraut, a "high style" man whose frozen agony as he waited for the camera to leave him was surely as embarrassing to him as it was to the audience. (This trick, as we shall see, was used by the Hallmark company much more infrequently in a second, better Shakespeare show.)

The virtuosity of the television camera is a great temptation to the producer. It can go almost anywhere, at any time; and it can look at people from many angles, including those from which we would never dream of looking at them. But unlike the film camera—which it apes in this capacity—the television camera that follows a live performance can never know if a tricky shot looks merely tricky until the action has been played out. Hence, television demands the most rigorous planning, creative previsualization, and clear-cut rehearsal on the part of director and producer; and the whole craft will have to learn from the mistakes of the pioneers. Probably never again will *Hamlet* end on television with a full-screen close-up of the dead hero, if there is even a remote chance that circumstances might cause his eyes—as they did Maurice Evans'—to blink widely and unmistakably under the pitiless stage lights.

Apart from its pioneer excesses, *Hamlet* was a heartening show to watch. It gave a large audience some excellent entertainment and a good taste—if not a full bite—of one of Shakespeare's best plays. It added to the common knowledge of Shakespearean production.

The next televised Shakespearean play, *Othello*, indicated that some lessons had been learned from *Hamlet*—but not enough. This was called a one-hour production, but bits were inevitably lost here and there for commercials and introduction. To consider cramming *Othello* into so brief a period was imprudent—and *impudent*—enough; but what the cutters did to the play was sheer murder. Even the story line was lost; a narrator tied together the butchered limbs of the tragedy with threads that were borrowed from some hack writer's leftovers. Iago was hardly recognizable, Desdemona barely appeared, and only the merest surfaces of Shakespeare's motivations were communicated. About the editing of this play, the less said the better; and the whole production could have been passed over with a single, despairing sigh except for some first-rate presentation of what was saved. The action came out cleanly against simple backgrounds of wall and arch forms that let the words and the actors' movements carry the weight of the tragedy. Furniture and other properties were at a functional minimum, so the stage area was left free without looking bare. When depth perspective was needed, a view through an arch provided enough sense of distance and kept the eyes inside the frame of action. The crowd scenes were well handled; groups moving through the viewing area emphasized the central action but did not distract from it. There were many scenes between two characters in the play, and these were enriched by a sensitive use of business to bring out the humanity of the lines. In two hours or more—and with an Othello more passionate than the star in the TV production—a first-rate job might have been done.

Everything that could have been learned from the two productions already described was completely disregarded in the Orson Welles *King Lear*. This performance went into history as a stern lesson in what not to do with Shakespeare on TV. If director Peter Brook—a highly recommended man from England—had deliberately set out to clutter up the small television screen, he could hardly have succeeded more effectively. From beginning to end, the action was difficult to keep in focus; in an effort to achieve constant depth, the director succeeded mainly in achieving visual confusion. Too many people were too often doing too many things, and the shifting backgrounds kept claiming the eye. There was even confusion as to who was saying what and, beyond this, confusion as to what was said. This was particularly true of the Fool, a restless acrobat who tried ineffectively to talk as he bounced.

The production was strangled in its own complexity. Thus, the hovel in the storm had to be an Alfred Hitchcock-type windmill; we saw it first in an obviously phony long shot in an obviously phony storm. And the interior was again Hitchcockian, with slant shots of the windmill competing for attention with the lines. If there is one place in *Lear* where the audience comprehension demands concentration on the human action, it is in the weird, wild night scenes after Lear is turned out into the storm. Yet in the TV production, the scene was broken up by the camera into ill-assorted pieces, and the whole was never brought together. The only really direct communication in this scene was a brutal inset showing Gloucester being blinded: an ugly close-up, Grand-Guignol style, as a brutal thumb dug into Gloucester's eyeballs and rooted them out.

What made the blinding scene the less acceptable was the cutting which had so abbreviated Gloucester's background that any parallel between his suffering and Lear's was hard to find; his experience carried no suggestion of retribution, but was only a kind of exercise in sadism. The linked pathos he shared with Lear was diminished. By curiously crude staging, Lear himself was deprived of the supreme pity he was designed to evoke. Thus, at the end, Welles came on wailing, dragging behind his murdered daughter Cordelia by the edge of her skirt. This might have had its impact in a large theater, as part of a massive stage picture; on television, it was ludicrous. And this kind of thing happened too often. The camera would frequently either close-up on Lear's face when, to understand his stature and his declined status, the audience needed to see him in context; or it would lose him in a moving multiplicity of detail when the audience needed to focus on him.

Lear is a hard play to do, but—despite Lamb—it can be done. Perhaps the TV production showed how by showing how not to do it. Another time, there will be less cutting, the story and characters will have a better chance, the subplot will be better integrated with the main one, and the camera will keep the whole in focus against a clean, clear background. I personally would not mind seeing Welles in it again, under better auspices. There is a good deal of the ham in him, but anybody who is fond of the Elizabethans probably needs a partiality to ham in moderate amounts; certainly, Lear has to be larger than life-size if any Shakespearean character does. Welles showed in the first scenes that he had the giant voice the old King needed and the sense of size; and with better direction, in sounder stage pictures, he might have carried the play off.

It is a pleasure to approach the end of this report on a happy note. Maurice Evans returned to television less than a year after his *Hamlet* with a production of *Richard II*—a play that had brought him fame in the legitimate theater. It was good Shakespeare, and good television. Much had been learned since the earlier production, and the learning showed.

The play was easier to cut in order to fit into almost two hours' time, and it preserved Shakespeare's basic story and characters. Missing was a part that I have always liked: the fine scene where the Duchess of York stands up for her traitor-son Aumerle. The absence of this scene was particularly noticeable because it could so easily have replaced some badly wasted minutes at the beginning of the show where the producers, in an effort to "tie in" the play with something of "popular interest," ran very poor newsreel shots of Elizabeth II's coronation. Except for this poor exchange, I did not mind the deletions here and there; and I felt fortunate to see a competent job done.

Richard II had a good deal of elegance, but this was mainly kept in hand. Except for some visual confusion in the early court conflict between Mowbray and Bolingbroke, where the director seemed impelled to a certain busyness, the action and background were well controlled. In this second Shakespearean production by Hallmark, there were still some tricks that were too obviously tricks—seeing characters through a fire or through the leafy branch of a tree—but these were mercifully few. Gone were the scene endings fixed on agonized faces; interscene action was much smoother. All that really bothered me in the scenery was a massive castle front, so seemingly genuine that I could not help but wonder about its presence in a television theater. (It turned out to be a leftover prop in an old Brooklyn film studio where the play was produced.) I would have been willing to settle for something much less bulky on the small screen and for less pretentious shots than the distorted perspectives that were made necessary when a horseman sat in the court and parleyed with Richard on the battlements. Still, nothing looked phony about the battlements, and perhaps the general effect contributed to the audience enjoyment. The acting suited the tone of the production: it was competent and controlled. Evans himself did not display the range of anguish that made his stage performance as Richard so memorable; but this was certainly partly from design, from his awareness of how close the audience would be. He knew what he was doing; and, to the end, he carried a show of hope and dignity mixed with despair which suggested that he might somehow outlive his deposition.

This reminds me wistfully of a comment on the production by a California newspaper reviewer. He noted that TV audiences seemed especially to enjoy *Richard II* because the story was unfamiliar to them, and they did not know how it was going to come out. What a luxury—not to know how a Shakespeare play will come out! For those of us too familiar with the canon, it is hard to appreciate the suspense and excitement that a "first time" could have; but the thought is heartening that television, as it comes of age, may bring a first time for all of the plays to thousands of spectators who might never otherwise come to know them.[3]

The plays, since they must be cut, will have to be cut judiciously in order to preserve character, story, and meaning. They must be acted against simple, nondistracting backgrounds that will provide a minimum platform for the lines and the action to emerge in clear outline. The actors must have a knowledge of and respect for the music, significance, and drama of Shakespeare's language; and they must have a capacity to communicate its essences in the style the intimate new medium demands. Television can do this, and I believe it will.

1. "Shakespeare's Arena," *The Sewanee Review*, 61:3 (Summer 1953), 347–61.
2. We are likely to have commercials always with us, unless we achieve something better through subscriber television. Meanwhile, the paid announcements—at least those shown in the intermissions of the plays discussed here—were not intolerable. They were in reasonably good taste (though the plug for Mother's Day cards seemed to follow hard upon Hamlet's closet scolding of Gertrude) and were little enough to sit through for the privilege of seeing Shakespeare for nothing. (I would guess that the Elizabethans would have been happy to get into the Globe free if it meant only that they had to hear the wares of London tradesmen commended during intermission.)
3. In a generous gesture, the film of Evans' TV *Richard II* has been made available to education groups in the United States.

The Setting in Early Television
Maurice Evans' Shakespeare Productions
Bernice W. Kliman

In the heyday of live television, Joyce C. Hall, daring President of the Hallmark Card Company, sponsor of the Hallmark Hall of Fame, agreed to an innovative experiment: live Shakespeare in a two-hour production, not only the first "complete" Shakespeare on American television, but also the first dramatic production of that length in the medium.[1] To accommodate the experiment, NBC delayed other scheduled broadcasts. It was 1953, and one of the principal Shakespearean actors was Maurice Evans, who, only a few years before, had produced and acted in the successful G.I. *Hamlet*, performed in the Pacific theater for American soldiers during World War II, with George Schaefer, a young sergeant, as director. The soldiers had responded to a Hamlet living in a state of siege, where every man wore a uniform, where the sense of imminent disaster was palpable. This *Hamlet*, produced on Broadway shortly after the war, in 1946, was the basis for the Hallmark production.[2]

Reviewers, hopeful about what the experiment boded, were ecstatic.[3] As late as 1975, Cecil Smith, columnist for the *Los Angeles Times*, said that the two-hour *Hamlet* "made Hallmark a television standard for the rest of the industry" (22 October 1975, 4:20). This production was followed by many

Reprinted, with alterations, from *Shakespeare and the Arts*, ed. Cecile W. Cary and Henry S. Limouze (Washington, D.C.: University Press of America, 1982).

others starring Evans. These early live broadcasts, fortunately saved by the kinescope process,[4] offer valuable insights into television during its "golden age," give those too young to have seen him a sense of Maurice Evans as an actor, and form the basis for the whole interesting topic of Shakespeare on television in that they offer an opportunity for an experiment in criticism. The four television productions I am concerned with—*Hamlet, Richard II, Macbeth, The Taming of the Shrew*—were all directed by Schaefer, starred Maurice Evans, and were produced live during a three-year period in the fifties.[5] With so many significant constants, perhaps one can decide what makes Shakespeare on television successful. These four indicate, by demonstrating the range of television possibilities, that Shakespeare on television works best when producers do not try to imitate the illusion we expect of movie space, but opt for a semi-illusionist setting like that of the proscenium-arch stage, or for the even more suggestive and imaginative bare television setting.[6]

First, *Hamlet* (26 April 1953): The opening shot of King Hamlet's tombstone (1830–1890) tells us it is the nineteenth century. In a dissolve, we move to I.ii, the first court scene, to see a fussy interior. Nothing could be further from Olivier's moody set in his 1948 filmed *Hamlet* than this Victorian clutter.[7] Having once settled on a definite time, however, the producers are committed to a specific kind of space. In drawing rooms and sitting rooms, we see urns, crystal, candlesticks, statues, couches, portraits, china, inkstands, cushions, chests, pilasters, clocks, bric-a-brac of all kinds, all over. These environmental trivia are not only distracting but also contrast ironically with the elemental passions of the play—either that or they swamp any passions entirely.[8] The setting opposes the atmosphere that the uniforms were to help create; the setting for the Evans/Schaefer stage production was much simpler. The producers seem to be aiming for the measure of illusion that movie sets afford. But the set, not large enough to represent convincingly a castle interior, inevitably clashes with the solid weight of so many objects. The spatial relations of one part of the set to another are studio-like, that is, unrealistically close to each other, while in any one shot, realism dominates the frame. . . . This mix of artifice and reality is not quite right, though it is difficult to pinpoint the specific errors of judgment and taste. . . .

Several creative settings suggest what the whole production might have achieved. The nunnery and prayer scenes take place in the set's most believable section, which has few distracting objects. A wrought-iron doorway allows for some attractive shots, especially of Hamlet peering through it at the praying Claudius. Also workable is "The Mousetrap" setting, which, like the nunnery setting, provides opportunities for scenes in mid- to long-shot with at least two planes of action. Perhaps the use of such long shots derives from illustrations of *Hamlet*, where long shots can vary with close-ups, as W. G. Simmonds' illustrations do; perhaps from film models, such as Olivier's *Hamlet*. The "To be" soliloquy precedes the play-within-a-play. Its setting, as we soon see, is the players' backdrop showing the orchard scenery for their play. It begins with an overhead close-up of Hamlet's reflection in a birdbath, then widens out to include the painted scenery behind him. This artificial setting is more congenial to the verse than the "realistic" settings of other segments.

Even when some of the cluttered areas of the set are used, creative camera work sometimes minimizes the oppressive effect. When Horatio, for example, confronts Hamlet for the first time (I.ii.159), the camera shoots from outside a window. Though something of a movie cliché, the shot has its usefulness here. Since the resolution of the television picture is not sharp enough to present scenes with much depth of field, Horatio, behind Hamlet, is almost a blur. In effect, Hamlet, isolated, concentrates our attention. The director also controls response with tight shots. Camera work throughout is varied, with high-angle, low-angle, close- and long-shots. In the closet scene, mirror shots are effective, first for views of Hamlet and Gertrude at her dressing table—a traditional view now in moving images—and then for a representation of the ghost's appearance to Hamlet only. While effective shots do compensate for the set for a time, inevitably it intrudes again.

This is not to say that had the *mise-en-scène* been different, Evans' would have been a great *Hamlet*. . . . We sense no informing intelligence desperate to communicate with a receptive yet agonistic audience (to use George Steiner's formulation). There seems to be no overall interpretation.[9] We do not grasp motivations, relationships and their connectedness to the whole. It is "Let's run through *Hamlet*, Gang," with interpretations only within scenes. Is Claudius friendly or not? Gertrude does not let Claudius finish his pompous lecture on mourning (I.ii.87–106), yet Claudius motions her to persuade Hamlet to stay at Elsinore (in the pause between lines 117 and 118). The courtiers do not react to the news that Hamlet is heir. Is it therefore an empty promise in this version? Or were the supernumeraries not rehearsed? Later, Ophelia and Laertes exchange a knowing look—"Oh, no, not again"—when Polonius advises Laertes (I.iii.58–81). This is a mistake, because Ophelia and Laertes must respect as well as love their father, however he may appear to others, or their subsequent behavior is inexplicable. For the sake of an easy laugh here, the producers rip the web of connections. Similarly, in the same scene, Ophelia shakes her head, objecting to Polonius' aspersions against Hamlet, but then she says "I shall obey" without being pressed. The two responses are at odds. Hamlet, in his scene with Ophelia, shows his love for her, making unintelligible Claudius' cruel declaration, "Love! His affections do not *that* way tend" (pointing at her). From behind the wrought iron doors, Claudius and Polonius presumably see that Hamlet becomes bitter only after Ophelia reveals the spying by looking towards them. Since in this production she realizes fully, with deep chagrin, that she has given herself away, her last speech of the scene, "Heavenly powers, restore him!" (III.i.138), is incongruous; she knows very well how to account for Hamlet's agitation.

Such inconsistencies continue throughout the production. The producers unfortunately place Ophelia's mad scene at her bed, with a doctor and nurse in attendance, making it difficult to understand how she gets away to drown herself, especially after Claudius urges the nurse to "give her good watch." There is no willow scene to tell how it happened. On the other hand, the rag doll Ophelia cradles in her arms is effective; it was a prop used also in the stage production. And since Laertes does not jump into the grave (there is none—the scene takes place inside at the altar where Claudius was praying and near the spot where Ophelia and Hamlet had their last "private" talk), Hamlet's passionate outburst seems unmotivated, because Laertes' outcry has not borne such an emphasis.

Evans' mannered and declamatory style, furthermore—with quaver in voice and quiver on lips—may have been, even in 1953, an exaggerated and outmoded "Shakespearean" acting technique. But other problems of acting and casting are graver. Sarah Churchill is too forthright and steady a soul to go mad. In closeup, Evans, at fifty-two, seems old for the part, older than Claudius, played by Joseph Schildkraut, fifty-eight. Gertrude, perforce, has to be older than Hamlet, limiting her credibility as a sensuous woman, her low-cut gowns notwithstanding, and Ruth Chatterton, fifty-nine, who plays her, forgets some lines. Her smile is grotesque, a false-looking grimace that flashes on and off. Our last view of her is indeed strange. As she literally sings out the word "poisoned," those around her, in rear frame and under the cover of others blocking the view, spirit her off the set before she falls. Hamlet says no "adieu" to her. The director here returned to an earlier stage tradition, when Gertrudes presumably did not like falling onto the stage or pretending to be dead for dozens of lines.

. . . Although failures of conception, downright poor acting by some of the supporting cast, and old-fashioned acting by Evans hinder this production, the sets finally spoil it because by imposing, with those artifacts, an artificial kind of realism on the play, they highlight all the other defects, which in essence are failures of verisimilitude.

Richard II and *Macbeth* (from Hallmark's third and fourth seasons, respectively) are superior to *Hamlet* because the settings, which the producers did not update, serve both concepts and acting styles. *Richard* (24 January 1954), an intelligent and well-conceived production, uses a variety of sets. The interiors are illusionistic while the exteriors are quite obviously studio shot. Film clips of Queen Elizabeth II's coronation (June 1953) introduce the television production. Such spectacles demonstrate that television can capture the pomp and ceremony of grand scenes, even if heads in some shots must be seen as pinpoints. The large-scale prologue lends plausibility to the public scene that follows in the play, which opens in a large, medieval interior.[10] Gothic windows and soaring clusters of slender, engaged columns banded by shaft rings recall features of Westminster Abbey (where Queen Elizabeth II's coronation had taken place). The only unauthentic touch in this room is a multi-cusped doorway arch that looks like something out of *Dr. Caligari*. The smaller room where Gaunt confronts Richard is a well-realized, intimate medieval setting, with casement windows, fireplace, and a few well-chosen artifacts. In a room filled with natural-looking light, low camera angles provide good views of the room's beamed ceiling. In other interiors, a brazier lights the tent where York and Bolingbroke contend (II.iii), and the prison at Pomfret, a cavernous setting, has bone-chilling stone walls, weak candlelight and barred windows. Throughout these interiors, the illusion of reality holds.

The outdoor scenes, with their flat studio floors for ground, artificial leaves and paper maché stones, include the approach to Gaunt's room; the orchard where most of Isabel's scenes take place (including, rather strangely, II.iii, for when York says, "Come, cousin, I'll dispose of you," it is rather a shock to find her still there in III.iv); the dock where Bolingbroke embarks and disembarks; the coast of Wales and the exterior of Flint Castle. The set designer, Richard Sylbert, who also designed *Hamlet* and *Macbeth*, merely nods toward illusion for these, fully half the scenes of the play.

. . . Just as the set is part illusionistic and part not, so too is the acting. Evans' natural geniality and urbanity serve him well in the early scenes of this production. Quavering utterances are often completely absent, and when there seem to fit Richard's self-pity better than they did Hamlet's introspection. He pauses within verse lines more infrequently than he did in *Hamlet*, especially in the first part when his whole demeanor breathes confidence and competence. Yet when the camera catches Richard's entry not in mid-act but in a frozen tableau, we are not seeing an imitation of reality.[11]

But if setting and acting are sometimes contradictory in the effects they evoke, the interpretation is unified and coherent. Evans spans the character's full emotional breadth. We see a king boyishly well pleased with his ability to manipulate those around him, a spoiled playboy who has never had anyone say "nay" to him. His arrogant entrance with two wolfhounds characterizes him well. Although this production eliminates I.ii and thus Gaunt's implication of Richard in Gloucester's death, Richard implicates himself by the look he exchanges with his friends when Bolingbroke accuses Mowbray. Immediately plunged into the ambiguity of the play, we are forced to feel ambivalent about the antagonists, the present and future kings. Richard later becomes a pitiable spectacle as he recognizes his own vulnerability, but when he confronts Bolingbroke at the deposition he achieves a grandeur and a stature that had eluded him at first. Richard, a deeply flawed king who nevertheless does not deserve his fate, reaches tragic dimensions through self-recognition.

. . . While they make the production something different from Shakespeare's play, cuts and transpositions not only keep set changes to a minimum but also emphasize the struggles between Richard and Bolingbroke. With no women besides Isabel and her ladies, the Duchess of Gloucester and the Duchess of York are gone and so therefore is the Aumerle plot. With no tournament, Richard decisively banishes Mowbray and Bolingbroke immediately—and apparently meant to do so even before they came forward, for he had the bills of banishment prepared in advance. The gardener's scene (III.iv), which follows the deposition, merges with Richard's and Isabel's farewell (V.i). Instead of being a preparation, then, for the deposition, the gardener's speech about weeds is an *ex post facto* rationalization. For the most part, the changes are intelligent, and though we may miss the balance of characterization or the sweep of history afforded by the missing scenes (including the one that mentions the truant Hal), given the producers' need to reduce the play to one-and-three-quarters hours (fifteen minutes for commercials), the cuts are unobjectionable.

Pleasing transitions, with metaphoric content, connect disparate scenes and settings, supplying the connective thread missed in *Hamlet*. A close-up of cups raised by Bushy, Bagot and Green in I.iv dissolves to a close-up of Gaunt's cup of medicine in II.i, aptly pointing the contrast. Near the end of II.i, as the King, Queen and others, after Gaunt's death, leave the medieval room, the camera frames them as they walk outside past the casement window. After they have gone by, the camera tracks up to the window to show the rebels, Northumberland, Ross and Willoughby, looking out at the departing royal party. Then, with a cut to the inside, the scene is completed. Later, the fire in the prison scene (V.v) dissolves to the fire in the grating of Gaunt's room for the Exton-Bolingbroke scene and then back to the prison again. The break in this scene, much like the dissolves in the 1978 BBC production, suggests that Richard's musings cover a span of time. The fire, used here to underline, also harks back to its use analogically in II.i when, just as he opens the grating, Gaunt says "His rash fierce blaze of riot cannot last, / For violent fires soon burn out themselves" (lines 33–34). Because the Exton-Bolingbroke conversation takes place in the same room, by the same fire, Gaunt, as it were, not only describes Richard but prophesies about Henry.

The connection is emphasized by one profound change from Shakespeare's text. In a scene derived from Marlowe's *Edward II* V.iv, King Henry talks personally to Exton, instead of Exton talking to his servant as in V.iv in Shakespeare.[12] Speaking Lightborn's part, Exton reveals himself as totally evil, an assassin who is proud of the several ways he has disposed of victims for clients. Henry, taking Mortimer's role, gives him a bag of money and tells him never to return unless he eliminates Richard. This is far from the hesitant, questioning Exton of Shakespeare's play or the repentant Exton from Holinshed. Correspondingly, Hallmark's Exton kills Richard treacherously: after Richard rushes out, Exton stabs him in the back. He expresses no regret. Plotting directly with Exton blackens Henry's character considerably, especially since no mercy scene with Aumerle mitigates his crime. This Henry is less the enigmatic politician, more the ambitious hypocrite, especially when he repudiates Exton in V.vi. Though we cannot altogether blame him for the usurpation, for we recognize that Richard, through misrule, has forfeited his right to the crown, pity for Richard grows as a result of the textual change. Ironically, too, the scene takes place in the same setting where Richard, by his callous indifference to Gaunt, has most alienated our sympathy.

For *Macbeth* (28 November 1954), the producers chose a set that seems much smaller than the one used for *Richard II*.[13] We see for most of the play a primitive castle interior with bare flagstone floors, stone walls, arched windows and doorways, stone balconies, with pools of light created by torches. Jack Gould, in his *New York Times* review of this performance, deplored its realistic sets because he felt they distracted the viewer.[14] But for a viewer of *Macbeth* today—more obviously than for *Hamlet* or for *Richard II*—these interiors do not create the illusion of reality. The producers here seem to be aiming for the level of realism possible on film but instead fortuitously achieve the level possible on the proscenium-arch stage. We are to imagine the imposing entrance hall of a castle in a cramped studio space. The drawbridge is a squat little thing. Stairways sweep upwards about ten feet. High-angle shots used to attempt a sense of spaciousness and to place the audience in position of judge cannot overcome the set's limitations. Welles's insistent wide-angle lens in his filmed *Macbeth* (1948) succeeded in creating the illusion of deep space in a small set because the film medium responds better to such tricks. Exteriors in Evans' *Macbeth*, as in *Richard II*, are frankly studio shot.

Whether by intention or not, the stagy contrivance of the set is an asset in the Hallmark performance because Judith Anderson's Lady Macbeth and Maurice Evans' tremolo Macbeth, both larger than life, need the artifice of a stage background to be acceptable. Setting, objects and acting do not clash.

. . . As in *Hamlet*, however, no strong overall concept unifies the work. Banquo should not be suspicious of Macbeth from the start, for that does not match Evans' portrayal of him as a good man who disintegrates. More importantly, this production suffers, in spite of its effective touches, because Evans' depiction of Macbeth falls short of the variety of his Richard portrayal. He lacks the driving force of evil; a weariness at his center saps the play's energy. Evans amplifies the effect of his persona by transposing the announcement of Malcolm as heir from I.iv.35–42 to just before scene vii. In the text, the earlier announcement stirs Macbeth's murderous ambition, but then Duncan's geniality reactivates Macbeth's conscience. In Evans' version his conscience awakens on the heels of the announcement. Like the *Hamlet*, this production is sometimes too obvious, as when Macbeth points to crown and scepter as he says the words,

> Upon my head they placed a fruitless crown
> And put a barren scepter in my gripe.

> (III.i.61–62)

When Hallmark decided to repeat *Macbeth* in 1960—still directed by Schaefer, with Evans and Anderson as principals—off they went to Scotland to film the drama in color on location.[15] Live television was dead by 1960. This is a film rather than a television drama.

Virtually anything can be filmed, but not everything filmed is a film. Television, like film, can accommodate many formats, many kinds of content: lectures, lessons, advertisements, serials, drama "magazines"—the range is almost limitless. Television, however, is most itself, at least today, when a video camera is pointed at someone in the street who has witnessed a robbery, who has an opinion, whose house has just burned down. It is the real and now, Queen Elizabeth II's coronation or Charles' and Diana's wedding. Shakespeare, obviously, is not real and now in the same way. But when a television production repudiates the real, cuts its easy connection to the mundane by avoiding illusionist settings, it liberates us from the conventionality of the everyday that undermines what Shakespeare is—an assault on the audience's intellect, emotion and sensibility, a subversion of our usual white-noise existence. What can startle in the real after we have seen presidents and popes shot? Onstage, too, for present sensibilities, Shakespeare seems to respond best to the barest stage, allowing for quick exits and entrances and the creation of space in the audience's mind by Shakespeare's words.

The Taming of the Shrew, broadcast 18 March 1956, with Evans, Schaefer as director, and a charming Lilli Palmer as Katherine, cuts those connections to the real. The set, created by Rouben Ter-Aruntunian, is a large, almost empty space with clowns carrying on props as needed in this commedia dell'arte production.[16] Though twenty-five years old, it stands up very well. One might say that Shrew, after all, is a comedy and thus has a better chance at success than the tragedies; but this is unlikely, because Maurice Evans is better known for his tragic than for his comic characterizations, and because Shrew is so full of vexing questions of male-female relationships that it could be difficult to present a widely-acclaimed version. Shakespeare, of course, deflects criticism by treating it as a play within a play, framed by the "real" play of one Christopher Sly. Although the Hallmark production omits Christopher Sly (along with Gremio, the widow and other subsidiary characters), the non-illusionistic setting constantly informs us that these hi-jinks are not really serious and that those who dislike the play's politics are making earnest out of game. In spite of the artifice of the setting, however, the audience can accept the characters and their dilemmas as real enough to empathize with because the emotional states of the actors are realistic.

As a distancing effect, a pair of adagio dancers dressed like Kate and Petruchio re-create as part of the wedding entertainment the wooing, wedding and taming of Kate, whip and all—except this Kate makes the last move, breaking a paper hoop over her husband's head. (The male looks like Douglas Fairbanks, perhaps an allusion to the 1929 Taming of the Shrew with Fairbanks and Mary Pickford; also like Fairbanks, Evans wears a ring in one ear.)

The medium is used throughout to good effect, with unexpected camera angles, wipes from right and left (an anti-illusionary transitional device), and traveling camera. Baptista's house is a raised scaffold between two enclosed boxes that represent the interior. The scaffold quickly becomes a boxing ring for Petruchio's and Kate's first encounter, with bells, handlers, and ringside audience to complete the conceit. When Petruchio and Baptista walk in the arbor, the arches that represent it suddenly appear in the frame, held by white-clad clowns, as the two walk towards the camera, which tracks back with them. Petruchio's horse is a man in a horse costume, the church a two-dimensional facade. Petruchio's home, walled with hanging furs, expresses his uncouthness.

All is light, bright and joyful—and not a little of the effect is owing to the creative bareness of the set that allows space for infectiously exuberant acting. Suddenly Evans, who in 1953 looked too old to be a credible Hamlet, in 1956 at fifty-five is as youthful a Petruchio as one would want, illustrating that perception is based on style rather than form.

The interpretation is clear and unexceptionable but unified and satisfying. Petruchio's boasting, with its bombastic excess, is stretched to the edge of the ridiculous through the camera angle (very low), the music (parodic) and the reactions of his auditors (delighted). He is having fun. In this same spirit he woos Kate, and since he loves her and is immediately drawn to her energy, neither his words nor actions offend. Kate, too, responds to him. She rises in our estimation through comparison to her sister, whose characterization comments on those men who prefer coy passivity to forthrightness. Much worse than Shakespeare's character, this Bianca is depicted as mercenary, choosing her lover solely on the basis of riches, and as shrewish, for she has the widow's part at the banquet. At the end, then, she and Kate each occupy the original position of the other, but with more truth. Petruchio tames Kate, first by physical force (he literally pins her down, withholds food and rest) and second by showing two mirrors to her: the mirror of what she truly is, by describing her as sweet and loving, and the mirror of how she is acting, by behaving as shrewishly as possible himself. Kate can change because she *is* curst for policy. What else can she do with a simpering blonde sister? She is not innately an angry person, for our first view of her shows her smiling at a bird.[17] She is tamed when she joins the fun.[18] Setting gives physical dimension to the concept and helps to determine the acting. The process is dialectical: the shaping energy of the text flows outward to the setting, that of the setting inward to the text.

Probably no one way of televising Shakespeare will work at all times for all plays. Since television does not yet have the depth of field of film, to attempt a cinematic kind of realism seems to be a mistake. Live television performances, moreover, with no opportunity for reshooting defective moments, for moving from one to another space readily, are inherently more likely to be nonrealistic than film treatments, more likely, in fact, to be akin to stage performances than to film. In emulating theater, television has two choices, something equivalent to the proscenium arch, with its own version of realism, or the bare set, with actors alone providing the illusion of reality. A survey of television productions preserved on kinescope, tape, and film could tell us which methods or combinations of methods have been most successful. The example of the four live Evans productions, however, seems clear: the bare set is best. Next is the overtly theatrical semi-illusionist set. Either of these complements the artifice of the plays. Either gives Shakespeare the last word.

1. *TV Guide: The First 25 Years*, comp. and ed. Jay S. Harris, in assoc. with the editors of *TV Guide* magazine (New York: Simon & Schuster, 1978), pp. 203–5. Two-hour productions were not, however, to become a television norm for some years. Hallmark sponsored only a few such productions in the '50s.

2. See *Maurice Evans' GI Production of Hamlet by William Shakespeare: Acting Edition, with a Preface by Maurice Evans* (Garden City, N.Y.: Doubleday, 1947). Stage directions reveal this as similar in concept to the television production. Photographs and sketches, however, show that the stage setting was non-illusionistic.

3. See, for example, Jack Gould, "Television in Review," *New York Times*, 27 April 1953, p. 29, and Philip Hamburger, "The Dane," *The New Yorker*, 9 May 1953, pp. 67–68.

4. Kinescopes may be seen at the University Film Study Center, M.I.T.; ATAS/UCLA Television Archives, Los Angeles; Museum of Broadcasting, New York City. I am grateful for a S.U.N.Y. Faculty Research Grant (1981) that afforded me the opportunity to view these productions.

5. According to a letter he sent me, for *Hamlet* Schaefer "cast and directed the actors" but did not work with the camera, the responsibility of Executive Producer and Director Albert McCleery. See also Ernest Roderick Diehl, "George Schaefer and the Hallmark Hall of Fame: A Study of the Producer-Director of a Live Television Drama Series," Diss. Ohio State Univ., 1964, pp. 34–68.

6. I use the work "illusionist" much as John Styan does throughout *The Shakespeare Revolution: Criticism and Performance in the Twentieth Century* (Cambridge: Cambridge Univ. Press, 1977)—to describe a theater that attempts to create the sense that the audience is looking, as it were, through a window on reality. Styan finds spatial realism to be a distortion of Shakespeare's intention (p. 30).

7. Although we expect realism in film, Olivier upsets that convention to provide a poetic setting. See Sheryl W. Gross, "Poetic Realism in Olivier's *Hamlet*," *Hamlet Studies*, forthcoming.

8. Marvin Rosenberg, "Shakespeare on TV: An Optimistic Survey," *Film Quarterly*, 9 (1954), 166–74, deplores the setting because "background clutter is poison to complex drama." On the other hand, Alice Venesky Griffin, "Shakespeare Through the Camera's Eye—*Julius Caesar* in Motion Pictures; *Hamlet* and *Othello* on Television," *Shakespeare Quarterly*, 4 (1953), 331–36, says that the 60' x 70' set is "visually helpful and generally uncluttered." Hallmark's setting was lavish compared to those of some other television series, such as Studio One's *Julius Caesar* (6 March 1949) and *Coriolanus* (11 June 1951).

9. Bernard Grebanier, *The Heart of Hamlet: The Play Shakespeare Wrote, with the Text of the Play* (New York: Crowell, 1960), p. 307, says this also of Evans' stage *Hamlet*.

10. It was actually shot in "NBC's huge new Brooklyn studio," according to *Time*, 1 February 1954, p. 59.

11. Commercials in the '50s began just so—in frozen tableaux—and then, as if at a signal, the woman starts mopping her floors, or whatever. Current conventions, however, call for capturing an action in progress.

12. Thanks to Peter Saccio for identifying the interpolated scene as Marlowe's. Evans' Broadway version did not make this substitution, according to the two prompt books at the Lincoln Center Performing Arts Library.

13. Perhaps they were affected by Jack Gould's criticism of the impersonality of huge sets and long shots in his review of *R2*: *New York Times*, 25 January 1954, p. 25. If so, they got small thanks, for Gould criticized the *Macbeth* for too many close-ups, giving the play a disjointed, episodic feeling: *New York Times*, 29 November 1954, p. 32.

14. Gould misses the artifice of the proscenium arch, but to me this production comes as close as a television production can to the ambience of the proscenium-arch stage. This is a semi-illusionist setting, effected by the studio look. The fact that Gould finds this set too realistic tellingly demonstrates that willingness to accept a given performance as realistic varies with time and technology.

This *Macbeth* won five Emmy awards, including one for best direction.

15. The earlier version had been broadcast both in black and white and in color, but apparently color technology was not at a high level then. At least Jack Gould criticized the garish color. *Cue*, 11 December 1954, says only a few thousand color sets existed at the time. I have seen only the black and white versions of all four productions.

16. Jack Gould's review, *New York Times*, 19 March 1956, p. 63, called it "infectiously inventive." On 23 April the *Times*, p. 23, announced that Evans got an American Shakespeare

Theatre and Academy Award for the production. Olivier was one of the other recipients, for his production of R3.

17. Gould objects that Palmer is not spitfire enough at the beginning, but he misses the point. Her Kate is only playing the role of termagant because until Petruchio arrives she has no other choice.

18. For illuminating discussion of the text, which shows that *rather* than being tamed Kate joins the fun, see Irene Dash, *Wooing, Wedding, and Power: Women in Shakespeare's Plays* (New York: Columbia Univ. Press, 1981), pp. 57–61.

Three Televised Hamlets
H. R. Coursen

In 1960, Franz Peter Wirth directed *Hamlet* with Maximilian Schell for Austrian Television. Ten years later, Peter Wood directed Richard Chamberlain in *Hamlet* for NBC's Hallmark Hall of Fame. And ten years after that, the BBC released its *Hamlet* directed by Rodney Bennett and starring Derek Jacobi. In discussing these productions, one is tempted to make vast historical generalizations. 1960. 1970. 1980. What they show us, though, is not something about history, but something about conceptions of Hamlet and *Hamlet*.

The 1960 version employs a stark and barren set of columns and platforms as a context for Schell's occasionally vivid performance. The 1970 production is more ornate, as it must be to compensate for Chamberlain's wooden prince. The 1980 rendition brings us probably the most complete *Hamlet* we are likely to encounter and, of course, features Jacobi's energetic Hamlet.

I saw the Wirth-Schell *Hamlet* in August, 1986, in the 16mm version. But it had the *feeling* of its origin—a TV production. It seemed cramped and dark even on the larger screen. That so much of the script was delivered *sotto voce* and that so many of the shots were closeups made the larger screen inappropriate to the "scale" of this production. The production seemed rushed, or perhaps too evenly paced. Crucial moments like "Gonzago" moved past without pause for emphasis. Still, Wirth's treatment of that scene avoided the overelaborated silliness of Olivier's version.

The production incorporated some good moments. Perhaps that is typical of televised Shakespeare—spots of time, but seldom the sense of a fully realized production that theatre can achieve. Wirth anticipated Kozintsev by having Hamlet wander through the exiting court as the First Soliloquy rattled dryly through his brain via voice-over. The scrims through which Claudius and Polonius viewed Hamlet and Ophelia in the nunnery scene and through which Hamlet watched the court coming to the play suggested that, as "Gonzago" begins, Hamlet controls the forces of appearance vs. reality that have been confusing him so far. At the end of the Nunnery Scene, Polonius spoke of the "extremity for love" he had suffered in his youth, a transposition that nicely set up Claudius's rebuff of the Polonius thesis on Hamlet's madness. Hamlet moved from Ophelia's side to poke his head between the two throne chairs and comment on a "Gonzago" that seemed aimed primarily at Gertrude. He then shifted to Claudius's side of the royal dais and forced the King to break "Gonzago" up. Here, as in the script, it was Hamlet who interrupted the play for the final time. Claudius merely acceded officially to the disturbance the Prince was making. The plans for the final plot against Hamlet were conducted effectively by Claudius and Laertes in the graveyard after Ophelia's funeral.

Other moments were not so good. Perhaps because this was a television production, much of the action was private, intimate—the discussion between Gertrude, Hamlet, and Claudius in I.ii, for example. Wirth's treatment robbed Claudius of the politic emphasis which Patrick Stewart captured so well in the BBC version. The production lacked any trace of humor, perhaps because Polonius was cast as a Munster bureaucrat and with the exception of Schell's applauding himself after he realized that his shouted "villain" had been enough to wake even Claudius. Like Olivier, Wirth shifted the dull "To be or not to be" to a place after the nunnery scene. We heard it while watching Schell's eyes through an open space in a staircase, but this effect did even less for those leaden clichés than did Olivier's raging sea and dropping bodkin. The biting and ironic "How all occasions do inform against me" was cut, as was Fortinbras. While Hamlet's greeting of Rosencrantz and Guildenstern contrasted neatly in its cool formality with his earlier embrace of Horatio, the former two were allowed to drift away in search of Tom Stoppard. As in the Olivier film, Wirth led us to believe that Hamlet overhears the plot of Polonius and Claudius to "loose" Ophelia in the lobby. I think that such an approach makes mincemeat of the Nunnery Scene, which is a "discovery scene," no matter how different productions vary on what it is that is discovered therein. The Ghost's instructions to Hamlet about the latter's mind and Gertrude's ultimate destination were left in—effectively, particularly in view of Hamlet's later "Follow my mother" to Claudius, also left in—but Hamlet's lines about "guilty creatures sitting at a play" being "struck so to the soul that presently / They have proclaim'd their malefactions" were cut. The deletion robbed us of one intriguing potentiality of the play scene. I was disappointed that Hamlet could not run Claudius through at the last, but had to close his eyes and nick the King on the shoulder with the envenomed point. The lines suggest, as do most Hamlets, that the feeling level crashes through the rational persona one last time before the Prince slumps to silence.

Schell was particularly strong with the skull of Yorick, really reawakening his love for someone he had long forgotten. Schell provided some interesting readings: "No, good mother, here's mettle *more* attractive," and "Cain's jaw-bone, that did the *first* murder." The former provided an Oedipal gracenote to a production fortunately not very Freudian, while the latter reminded us of Claudius and suggested that a lot of murders had been done since Cain's and that a lot more were to come.

Lillian Wilds, who praises this *Hamlet qua* film, talks of Schell's "human-istic" and "tender" Hamlet and notes Hamlet's "gentleness and sadness" as he addresses the cooling corpse of Polonius. Schell does not talk about "lug[ging] the guts into the neighbor room," nor does he inform Horatio about the executions of Rosencrantz and Guildenstern, "not shriving time allow'd." The editing permitted Schell to be an engaging and attractive—a "lovable"—Hamlet.[1]

The 1970 production, with Richard Chamberlain, was a no-nonsense, black-and-white version, notable chiefly for its placement in the Napoleonic Era. Thus Hamlet became a Beau Brummell, contrasting in black tie and jacket against the more ornate costumes of the rest of the court.

Perhaps the best aspect of this production was the beginning. The first scene was brisk and nicely edited—words and muskets worthless against a diaphanous wisp of a Ghost. Hamlet watched in extreme closeup as Clau-dius's coronation pageant entered under the opening credits. The new King was accompanied by a boys' choir singing "Alleluia" and carrying massive candles. Claudius's first speech was read from a parchment. He then turned to Hamlet on "my cousin" and smiled at Gertrude on "my son." He was attempting to personalize a sudden new set of relationships by not deploying the royal "our." Yet he insulted Hamlet when he said, "'Tis [pause] unmanly grief." Hamlet's "I shall in all my best obey *you*, madam" was bitter. Claudius covered Hamlet's rejection of this unwanted family with "a loving and a fair reply." Hamlet's first soliloquy was cued by a festival flower which he held as he said, "But two months dead!" He then let the petal fall. The recessional chorus behind him ended. The soliloquy featured Chamberlain's cheek-bones, accented by the curve of his sideburns. Finally, as he recognized Hor-atio, he smiled. The opening sequence captured the mystery of the parapets, Hamlet's attitude towards his problems, Claudius's emphasis on "orderly tran-sition," and Gertrude's genuine concern for her son.

Except for random moments, the focus of the production lapsed markedly after the effective sweep of the first two scenes. The effort to tell *the* story, as opposed to *a* story, left us to observe an edited outline of the plot, television's approach to Classic Comics.

Richard Johnson's Claudius tended to be an unctuous stereotype. Michael Redgrave's Polonius remained merely self-satisfied, and had a disconcerting way of looking like a Gilbert Stuart portrait of George Washington. He was doing well enough, as he showed by tugging at his robe as he lectured about clothes to Laertes. Margaret Leighton's Gertrude remained merely worried about Hamlet, even crawling to him at the end to warn about "the drink." In fairness to her, however, much of her ambiguous role was excised, including much of the closet scene. Thus she could not avail herself of the context within which Eileen Hurley (opposite Olivier and Burton) or Claire Bloom (opposite Jacobi) could work. Chamberlain's Hamlet was handsome and well-spoken. Chamberlain underplayed the role, appropriately for TV, but the result was a bland performance. He seldom asked that we identify with him. The performances, however, may have been a function of a medium that punishes over-acting most cruelly.

That Claudius might confess publicly during "Gonzago" was not a possibility in this version of the play. "Gonzago" became merely a medium for Hamlet's revenge. Chamberlain shouted in a courtyard about "the conscience of the King" as loudly as had Olivier sprinting through a sleeping palace. As in the Olivier film, the play-within here was merely pantomime, so that the uneasy verbal comments of Claudius and Gertrude did not emerge. But Johnson did not squirm, as if on an inconvenient hill of ants, as did the diminished Claudius of Basil Sydney in the Olivier film. Johnson, insulted, bashed his alter-ego, Lucianus, from the stage and exited in a rage. That was an effective moment within an unrealized scene.

Other good moments included Laertes's exit for France in an elegant barouche and Ciaran Madden's long pause after her father's command that she reject Hamlet. Her "I shall obey, my lord" contrasted in its heartbreak with Hamlet's bitter "obedience" to Gertrude and with Gertrude's later acquiescence with Claudius's trap for Hamlet in the nunnery scene. She saw nothing wrong in the scheme and did, indeed, hope that her younger and shorter look-alike, Ophelia, would prove to have been the cause of Hamlet's antic behavior. If Hamlet *had* been attracted by this Ophelia, the pull had been his brief recognition that she looked like his mother.

Gielgud's filmy Ghost, framed beneath a solid archway, created a neat ambiguity by saying, "Leave *her* to heaven." Claudius, we inferred, was to be sent elsewhere. If so, however, how could Hamlet escape the "taint" of revenge?

Another vivid moment found Hamlet carrying the sword he had not driven into Claudius into Gertrude's chamber. The sword leaped out with an alacrity towards Polonius, the weapon seemingly a function of Hamlet's immediately prior wish to use it. The splendid rhythm of this sequence demonstrated the script's continuity, and found Hamlet deeply disappointed at his murder—not that it was Polonius, but that it was *not* Claudius. Hamlet had carried his motive in his repressed right arm from the previous scene.

Claudius and Laertes plotted Hamlet's death in the very chapel where Claudius had failed at prayer. The setting captured the King's descent from his awareness of the need to repent because of how things are "above" to the extroverted, this-worldly goals that had prevented his prayer and that deny him all that he would retain in his over-subtle plotting.

One of the few arresting visual moments in the production was the closeup of the as-yet-unidentified skull of Yorick, as the single Gravedigger sang, "For such a guest is meet." The only other creative use of the camera occurred when it rose above Fortinbras at the end. He stood in the midst of four strewn corpses—the basis for his ascent to kingship.

The production sank to a few silly sequences. When the "poor wretch," Hamlet, entered reading, we discovered that he had blindfolded himself. He identified Polonius as "fishmonger," it seemed, by the smell. Derek Jacobi's skull mask at the beginning of the play scene was a brilliant adaptation of Jacobi's stage production. Hamlet was filling the role of a Yorick we had yet to meet. But what on earth was the point of Chamberlain's blindfold?

In the nunnery scene, Chamberlain glimpsed a pair of eyes peering out from behind the royal bookcase. Hamlet began to shout and shoved Ophelia towards a huge globe, which began to spin. "This distracted globe," one assumed. Hamlet then flipped a book at Ophelia's feet and exited. Any feeling of a prior relationship between the two—an element that can make the scene a moving, if perverse, love scene—was lost here. The scene, like much of the production, functioned only superficially, at best.[2]

In the BBC production, Jacobi's strength lay in his recognition that Hamlet is characterized as "inconsistent." The would-be-perpetual graduate student is shattered by external events. His behavior becomes, to put it mildly, erratic. He "swings," as Jacobi says, "into suddenly intensely traumatic states."[3]

Jacobi's finest moments occurred during the climactic play-within-the-play scene. Here, theatricality was nicely accommodated to the tube. Jacobi borrowed from his Old Vic stage performance and donned a skull-mask as emblem of his "idleness." "How fares [pause] our cousin Hamlet?" Claudius asked with sour amusement. The skull-mask anticipated the graveyard scene and reminded us that, among other roles, Hamlet plays that of jester, the function vacated by Yorick over two decades before. The court of Claudius is characterized accurately by Michael Long in *The Unnatural Scene* as "manipulative, expeditious and politic, a matter of espionage and the political use of man by man against man," a place that holds "psychic energy [in] contempt."[4] Some of Hamlet's energy must flow towards the role of "fool," alter ego, "foil," and Jungian "shadow." Claudius can afford no jester, yet it is precisely the purpose of the play-within-the-play to activate the alter ego in Claudius, signalled by his earlier tortured aside: "How smart a lash that speech doth give my conscience!"

Jacobi extended his Yorick *into* the "Gonzago" sequence, upstaging the actors, who were discomfited by Hamlet's invasion of their space. Having introduced the play *via* his jester, Hamlet allowed his manic energy to go too far. Had he allowed his fool to rest and watch the play? Well, it is a question this production raised. As it was, Jacobi's Hamlet destroyed the great potential of "Gonzago" and allowed Claudius to evade the trap without giving anyone a glimpse of his guilt—except Hamlet, who saw what he wished to see.

The skull-mask that Jacobi plucked from the Players' prop-chest linked "Gonzago" with ancient drama. While "Gonzago" is more modern than is the Player's speech, which reports, *à la* Greek drama, rather than imitates action, "Gonzago" is an "old" play. It is cast in sententious couplets, held firmly within its melodramatic generic premises, and solidly embraced by the so-called "unities." It stands as anti-type to the sprawl of the play surrounding it. The outer play represents the "reality" in which Prince Hamlet lives. But the inner play, for all its antique formalism, might have had the power to translate the outer play into something other than a tragedy. Hamlet, the university student who knows what is "caviare to the general," would disapprove of the play *he* is in. Here, as elsewhere, Shakespeare's characterization of Hamlet is profoundly ironic. Jacobi is the only actor I have seen equal to the irony I describe. Hamlet, the critic of theatre and dramaturgy, rejects his own standards, as the character is delineated by Shakespeare. The intellectual, of course, tends to repress the feeling level. Jacobi showed feeling exploding through the rational surface, as Hamlet merged with Lucianus, "nephew to the *king!*," and destroyed his potential masterpiece, a play that might have forced a guilty creature to proclaim his malefactions. Jacobi's Hamlet became a character Hamlet would scorn (as he does, at times) within a play of which Hamlet would also disapprove. Jacobi's Hamlet became, among other good things, the tragedy of the "detached" literary critic ambushed by his own psyche.

If Hamlet is a victim of the simplistic dichotomy of binary opposition—what should such fellows as I do, crawling between earth and heaven—a simplification that occurs within a consciousness that Hamlet accepts as reality (about my brain!)—then Jacobi, at least, made Hamlet his own victim, and therefore tragic.

Bernice Kliman is right, I think, to suggest that "the more bare the set . . . the more immediate our apprehension of the enacted emotion."[5] One thinks of the unit set—a kind of playground—that Jane Howell employed so brilliantly to undercut the pretentious politicians of 2 *Henry* VI. The BBC *Hamlet* suffered in the graveyard scene, however, from its wide, blank, and uncemeterial ramp. Otherwise, the minimal background allowed Jacobi's Hamlet to emerge. It was, as John J. O'Connor says, not "melancholy or hesitant," but "passionate and impetuous."[6] Jacobi, says John Lardner, tended "to drown Hamlet's wit and charm in petulance and self-loathing."[7] Kenneth Rothwell described Jacobi's Hamlet as "hyped-up [with] a tinge of feline hostility not always pleasant to contemplate."[8] "It *hath* made me mad," Jacobi said to Ophelia, as if suddenly realizing that woman's makeup, when artificially produced, is one dimension in his own sudden and involuntary tantrums. When charged with that pressure known as emotion, Hamlet's thinking function lashes out inevitably and in spite of itself in flashes of impetuous action, and, when he cannot act, in radically negative judgments that include himself within their excoriation. Jacobi captured this ebb and flow between fruitless introspection and frantic activity better than any Hamlet I have seen since Richard Burton in 1964.

Glib categorizations hide more than they reveal. Thinking makes it so. Schell's Hamlet is for those who love the Prince and who must believe in Horatio's angel chorus. Chamberlain's is for those out there in television-land who have no particular opinion about this or any other Dane and who do not wish to be troubled with one. Jacobi's is for those who question the purity of the Prince, as Hamlet seems so often to do himself.[9]

1. Lillian Wilds, "On Film: Maximilian Schell's Most Royal Hamlet," *Literature/Film Quarterly*, 4:2 (Spring 1976), 134–140. For a fuller version of my review, see "A German Hamlet," *Shakespeare on Film Newsletter*, 11:1 (December 1986), 4.

2. The Chamberlain *Hamlet* is treated briefly, along with the Olivier and Burton versions, in Jay L. Halio, "Three Filmed Hamlets," *Literature/Film Quarterly*, 1:4 (Fall 1973), 316–320.

3. Derek Jacobi, WNET *Dial* (November 1980), 28.

4. Michael Long, *The Unnatural Scene* (London: Methuen, 1976), pp. 127 and 144.

5. Bernice Kliman, "The BBC *Hamlet*: A Television Production," *Hamlet Studies*, 4:1–2 (1982), 105.

6. John J. O'Connor, "TV: Derek Jacobi in BBC's *Hamlet*," *New York Times*, 10 November 1980.

7. John Lardner, "The Changing of the Bard: BBC's No-Nonsense *Hamlet*," *Washington Post*, 10 November 1980.

8. Kenneth Rothwell, "The Shakespeare Plays: *Hamlet* and the Five Plays of Season Three," *Shakespeare Quarterly*, 32:3 (1981), 395–401.

9. For fuller comments on the Jacobi *Hamlet*, see my "The Shakespeare Plays: *Hamlet*," *Shakespeare on Film Newsletter*, 6:2 (1982), 5 and 8, and "Shakespeare and Television: The BBC-TV *Hamlet*," *Shakespeare and the Arts*, ed. Cecile W. Cary and Henry S. Limouze (Washington, D.C.: University Press of America, 1982), pp. 127–133.

Stage and Screen: The Trevor Nunn Macbeth
Michael Mullin

Macbeth is notoriously difficult to stage. Despite its popularity with readers as one of the great tragedies, its consistent failure in the theatre has made it a shibboleth—the "Scots play" among theatre people, who think it is bad luck to speak the play's name or any of its lines. Nor has film or television succeeded where the theatre so often failed. A fundamental reason is common to any of Shakespeare's plays—the differences in theatrical conventions between his times and ours, in particular the special demands of Shakespeare's poetic verse drama and non-scenic production style. Television exacerbates the distinctions between Shakespeare's theatre and ours by its closeups and its realism. More than many of Shakespeare's plays, *Macbeth* is set firmly in time and place; it insists on a medieval, barbaric Scotland that realism can betray into a stuffy museum piece. Or, if the supernatural depends too much on special effects, the Witches and Banquo's Ghost can provoke titters from audiences. To reduce a great tragedy to a horror show *manqué* presents a temptation to which several filmmakers have yielded, most notably Orson

Reprinted, with permission, from *Shakespeare Quarterly*, 38 (Autumn 1987), 350–59.

Welles, Roman Polanski, and, standing to one side, Akira Kurosawa in
Throne of Blood.[1] To treat it as a history play presents another temptation the
theatre has largely avoided in this century, but one which has appealed to
filmmakers, most especially George Schaefer, and to television producers—
here I think of the recent effort by the BBC starring Nicol Williamson. Attempts to "package" the play within already established television genres—
horror or history film—rob it of its tragic scope, however fine the acting and
however powerful individual scenes may be.

In modern times, the theatre has most often treated *Macbeth* as a surreal
psychodrama, with the ghost located ambiguously between Macbeth's consciousness and the otherworld of the Witches. To achieve these effects, set
designers have created non-realistic heaths, often with suggestions of modern
European warfare, and interiors with warped, angled perspectives that suggest
a world onstage mirroring Macbeth's distorted perceptions.[2] Unavoidably,
such an approach shrinks the play's scope by diminishing its societal concerns. Yet, as a modern equivalent for the horror of witchcraft and Satanism
in Shakespeare's day and as an antidote to the nineteenth-century penchant
for "illustrating" the play with massive historical sets (whose changing
crowded out as much as a third of the text), the twentieth century's internal-
ization of evil into Macbeth's psyche seems apt.

Readers and literary critics, for whom non-specific performances in the
mind's eye can hold in suspension several impossible theatrical choices, enjoy
a liberty unknown in the theatre and television, where every moment is the
sum of choices—the director's, the actors', the designers'—that perforce must
exclude other unchosen possibilities. To the specificity of theatre, television
of course adds its own, insofar as the television director selects not only what
the audience sees (as does the director in the theatre), but also from what
angle and at what distance. What one loses in making the script's possibilities
specific in the theatre and on television, one may gain in intensity.

In this process of intensification television enjoys a special advantage. Its
selection of images controls not only how the audience sees the play, but also,
through jump cuts and panning, at what pace the action unfolds. Where
theatre may be constrained by the physical realities of staging—the moving
of sets or actors through space—television is free to compress or extend stage
time. All these advantages Trevor Nunn and the Thames Television director
Philip Casson exploited in their extraordinarily successful production of *Macbeth*, which has been broadcast in numerous countries around the world.

The production concept was simplicity itself: the play was treated as a ritual
reenactment. "It was quite obvious to the audience that it was a performance,
a celebration or enactment of something, and it was happening in a defined
space. It certainly wasn't happening on a blasted heath or in Inverness. There
was only one location, and that location was being transformed into different
places by people who were enacting the story," said Trevor Nunn.[3] In The
Other Place, the RSC's small studio theatre where *Macbeth* opened on 4
August 1976, the audience of about 200 surrounded the bare stage on three

sides, sitting only three-deep on ground level seats and two-deep on the balcony. Rough timbers and a makeshift ambience removed any sense of reverence or pretension. In this small space, unlocalized by any scenery, the action took place within a chalk circle twenty feet across. Just outside it, around the perimeter, the actors sat on stools and beer crates, coming and going as required, and watching the action attentively. What Trevor Nunn had sought, his audience responded to: an enactment of a ritual, a performance that partook of exorcism and Satanism.[4] The audience joined the actors as silent participants in this quasi-religious ceremony.

Within the ritualistic framework, the acting itself was intensely realistic. The small space demanded naturalistic acting without the large gestures and voice projection of the main stage. Macbeth (Ian McKellen) appeared as a lithe, angular warrior, his hair slicked back with brilliantine, sensual, enthralled by his wife before the murder, horrified at his bloody hands after it, and put beside himself with gibbering fear and rage by Banquo's ghost. Lady Macbeth (Judi Dench) seemed to have sensuality and passion held just in check, their power spurring Macbeth and then consuming her. Not only in the title roles, but in every part the acting excelled. The saintly, fragile Duncan (Griffith Jones) seemed every inch a Christian king. Each Witch took on individuality: the elder, turbanned First Witch (Marie Kean) seemed to preside, the Second Witch (Susan Dury) abetted her, and the Third Witch (Judith Harte), a crazed, demented young woman, seemed to possess second sight, her trancelike statements guiding the others. An older, craggy Banquo (John Woodvine) deserved Macbeth's suspicion: he was a powerful adversary who knew of Macbeth's crimes. Macduff (Bob Peck) came across as a strong, virile soldier, quick in moral judgment. With Malcolm (Roger Rees) he made the long scene in England, often thought to be boring and therefore cut extensively, a play-within-a-play—full of shifting, high-powered emotion as the two men first sparred with each other, then joined forces, and, at the shock of Macduff's grief, moved numbly away towards the battle at the play's end. The Porter (Ian McDiarmid) played his part for laughs with a music-hall Scots accent and the arch panache of a stand-up comic. Even the murderers (David Howie and Bob Peck) provoked sympathy at their fear of Macbeth. Omnipresent, Seyton (Greg Hicks) affected his master's slicked-back hair style. Ross (Ian McDiarmid) became an equivocating toady with an upperclass accent. In every part the actors responded fully and realistically to the play's psychological and emotional complexities. Doubling some of the smaller parts added to the sense of enactment and ritual. In the theatre, the presence of the actors sitting or standing outside the circle as witnesses made the experience strange and macabre. "I felt," said Maurice Daniels of the RSC, "like a voyeur watching with horror and fascination as Lady Macbeth and Macbeth became aroused, really unable to keep their hands off each other, as they planned Duncan's murder."[5]

The production avoided either historicity or modernism by choosing costumes and props that defeated any strict chronological period. Duncan's royal vestments seemed appropriately medieval, as were the swords and daggers. Other touches were less dateable: Macbeth's long leather trenchcoat, Malcolm's cable-knit white sweater, Lady Macbeth's black jersey dress and black headscarf. The costumes were black and white, with only a touch of silver or gold in the jewelry and ornament. The minimal setting made the props powerful visual symbols—Duncan's royal robes on a stand, the voodoo dolls the Witches hold before the eyes of the drugged Macbeth in the cauldron scene and which he will later cradle as if their magic protected him. Off to one side hung a thundersheet, as if to remind the audience that they were watching play-acting, not a representation of real life. The lighting too avoided photographic realism, pinspotting some, plunging others in shadows, crosslighting to sharpen the angles of a face. A surreal, nightmarish atmosphere pervaded the performance, enhanced by touches of black magic: the Witches prepared their broth between two candles, as if celebrating a black mass. When Macbeth began to "grow aweary of the sun" he stared upwards into a worklight glaring down and shoved it violently aside, sending it swinging in high arcs and casting harsh light on the faces of everyone in the theatre.

After opening in 1976, the production was tested and refined, moving from one theatre to another. Only after months in repertory did it come to Thames Television's Studio Two (in two sessions, 7–12 March and 27–29 May 1978). The shooting script shows that it was filmed in the order of the play, with breaks for a change of camera from time to time (repeating a moment so that different shots could be cross cut). But what is most remarkable is that, instead of re-conceiving the production for television, the television director Philip Casson seems to have set himself the task of finding ways in which television could re-create the experience of the theatre. Herein lies its success and its special interest.

From the outset, the conventions of television realism are denied. The video begins with an overhead shot of what at first looks like an abstract star pattern of white on black until we realize that it is the actors, standing around the circle, casting shadows outwards from a bright light overhead. The absence of background, the unusual, patchy lighting, and the sometimes uncomfortable closeups carry over from the theatre the sense of surrealism and the eerie feeling that there are people nearby, out of the frame but coming unexpectedly into the action—as indeed there were when the actors were sitting outside the circle. Seyton in particular appears when not expected. For example, in the scene in which Lennox and Another Lord assess the sorry state of Scotland (III.vi), an eavesdropping Seyton forces them to be elliptical and equivocal. Instead of sitting with the audience outside the stage space, the camera moves in close so that the viewer sees the action as if part of it onstage. In themselves no special innovations, such shots and camerawork nevertheless keep the viewer aware that he is within the play, even to the point of being addressed directly in the soliloquies. A special case, one might say, for Shakespeare, but still wonderfully effective. At the opening of Act Three, for instance, after Macbeth solemnly dons the royal cape and crown with the court watching, Banquo's face comes into the frame, and he speaks his doubts about Macbeth directly to us, as if we were one of the courtiers. Just as the theatre production contravened realism, so too did the television rendering, and in so doing confirmed the play's unreal, supernatural mystery.

In both the theatre and the television productions there comes a sense of powerful emotional and spiritual realities evoked within (or by) a stylized ritual. Besides the bare stage setting, the indefinite backgrounds, and the symbolic props, within the play itself the director introduced ceremonies as stage business: At his first appearance, Duncan is praying and murmuring "mea culpa" as organ music plays. His prayers alternate with the two other Witches performing some unholy terror—is it a birth strangling?—on the shrieking young Third Witch. Before proclaiming Malcolm apparent heir, Duncan is solemnly crowned and dressed in his royal cape. So too is Macbeth crowned and caped at the beginning of Act Three. These, with a swell of organ music now and then, kept alive an aura of ritual and liturgy.

In a curious way this ritualization points up a fundamental dissonance between theatre and television. Because television conventionally assumes a literal or photographic depiction of reality, its treatment of drama often makes television versions of stage plays merely recordings of drama, not drama in their own right. Because this Macbeth depended on the audience accepting its non-illusionistic framework, the conventions of theatre and television coincided as they seldom otherwise do. Put simply: it worked both on stage and on television.

How? To see, we need to look at three scenes in detail, using the promptbook, the shooting script, and the video to explore what happened and how the transition was made from theatre to television: (i) the letter scene, in which Lady Macbeth learns of the prophecies, invokes the spirits, and finally greets her husband; (ii) the banquet scene, always a challenge to actors and directors for its multiple focal points and for Banquo's ghost; and (iii) the cauldron scene, a famous trap into which many productions have fallen when spook effects convulse skeptical audiences.

In the letter scene, the script calls for four main actions: Lady Macbeth reading the letter (I.v.1–28), her reaction to the messenger and his news of Duncan's coming (29–36), her invocation of the spirits that tend on mortal thought (37–53), and her greeting of Macbeth (54–71). The promptbook's diagram shows Lady Macbeth in the center of the circle, with other actors arranged on their seats in a semicircle upstage and outside the circle. The directions in the promptbook give only the barest clues to what happens. At the beginning of the invocation ("Come you spirits . . . ") it says merely "Lady kneels C[enter stage]." Further along, at "Make thick my blood" it says "Lady rises, turns U.S. [upstage] then D.S. [downstage] kneels again D.S." Here and throughout, the television shooting script follows the staging used in the theatre, as a moment-by-moment comparison of the promptbook and shooting script confirms. The cues are somewhat more explicit. At the beginning of the scene for "shot 52," the shooting script specifies "ON 2 [camera two] LOW ANGLE LADY MACBETH" and continues "HOLDING" until "shot 53," when she "breaks out of fr[ame]" saying "top-full of direst cruelty," as if in response to the spirits. Camera one takes over—"She turns into it," "LOW ANGLE Lady Macbeth," "HOLDING, ON 1"—to the end of the scene. As the last part of the scene builds to its climax—Lady Macbeth and Macbeth nuzzling and kissing as they whet each other's appetite for the killing—the camera zooms in to a tight two-shot, their faces fill the screen, and we are made to feel uncomfortably close to that obscene and disturbing love making. Apparently, Judi Dench imagined that Lady Macbeth had a physical reaction to the spirits—hence her startled scream as she jumps up; they have indeed filled her full of direst cruelty, and she feels it as a sharp pang. The camera responds to that interpretation, and moves in to observe it closely, feeding an interest that borders on voyeurism. The art of television reveals the art of the theatre.

The letter scene, one might argue, is made for television's ability to move in close; the audience may even respond more fully at television's close range than they do at the theatre's greater distance. The banquet scene (III.iv), however, demands the full stage. It is a crowded scene, with the full cast of Scots nobility present. In a realistic production these numbers might be swelled by extras as servants, lords attendant, and ladies in waiting. Yet only eight actors performed the scene in the theatre and on television. Upstage are the Macbeths' "thrones" and in a semicircle downstage, the courtiers' "table"—in fact nothing more than the stools before which they stand at attention. Enhancing the ceremonial, attended by Seyton, Macbeth goes to each guest with a huge silver goblet, presents it for a ritual sip, hands it to Seyton, and moves on to the next guest. His asides to Seyton he slips into the intervals between guests. At the end, he toasts Lady Macbeth ("Sweet remembrancer") and drains the cup, while the assembled court claps in time. Then the ghost "appears" but only in Macbeth's tormented vision. In a masterful *coup de théâtre*, looking on nothing but a stool, Ian McKellen turned into a snarling, defiant lunatic, beside himself with rage and fear, frothing at the mouth and lashing out with his hands and arms as Judi Dench tried to restrain him. "His [McKellen's] most spectacularly successful scene is the haunted feast," Benedict Nightingale reported (*New Statesman*, 17 September 1976), "an ambitious combination of laughing bravado, foaming rage and a grotesque mimicry of the genial host—a pseudo-playful slap of someone's cheek, a woozy wave at the departing guests." By placing Seyton next to Macbeth, at the start Nunn brought together two of the scene's disparate foci. By keeping Macbeth relatively close to Lady Macbeth (who "keeps her state") and facing him out to the audience, the director kept attention on Macbeth's reaction, not on the ghost (or its absence), thus avoiding one of the dangers posed by this scene's multiple foci and abrupt shifts in emotional perspective.

To capture this scene, the camera became extremely active. The shooting script suddenly grows dense with notes to the cameramen, telling them to "crab," "zoom," "pan," "crane;" the active camera peers at Macbeth as he goes round the circle with the cup. Then, when he drinks to Banquo and sees him, he points directly at us—it is as if the camera were that ghost, an unwanted presence at the feast, whom only Macbeth can see. Of course such a link between Banquo and the camera eye ought not be taken too far (if so, how can we see when Banquo's ghost is not present?). But it is interesting to think that Nunn put the audience, and especially the television audience, in the perspective of an unseen observer to whom Macbeth suddenly responds. That response allows us to see the scorpions that have filled his mind and that impel him to seek by any means to defy fate. The horror of his deeds—the murderers pounding their clanking knives into Banquo again and again, the stocking-masked man who slides a knife into Macduff's son as he jiggles the boy playfully on his knee—these horrors the television forces us to witness and to understand as the outcome of the teeth-gnashing dementia we see let loose in the banquet scene.

In the letter scene and in the banquet scene Nunn stressed the perversion of the ceremonies of greeting (the Macbeths kissing) and feasting (the disrupted banquet). In the cauldron scene, where Shakespeare explicitly calls for witchcraft, the director re-imagined the occasion as a perversion of religious ritual. In keeping with the earlier ceremonies of Christianity and kingship—Duncan's praying and robing, for instance—the cauldron scene becomes a kind of black mass. Two candles on a low table form the altarpiece; a battered metal goblet is the chalice in which they brew the hell broth; and a polyphonic interweaving chant—"Double, double, toil and trouble," sung as a round—gives an eerie sense of liturgy to their preparations. In his leather trenchcoat, Macbeth enters. During his conjuration (ending "answer me to what I ask you," IV.i. 50–61) the Witches listen attentively, their delight growing as he names the evils in nature that may attend their answers. They disrobe him, pulling the coat down over his shoulders so his arms are pinned. With grey slime they daub a cross on his naked back, chest, and forehead; he takes the chalice, drinks it off, and falls, writhing, back against the altar into the arms of the First Witch, who cradles his head against her breast. Candles either side of his face, he speaks to the voodoo dolls they hold up as if the dolls could answer back. When he asks about Banquo's issue, they blindfold him with his neck scarf and then bring the candles up to his covered face ("Show his eyes, and grieve his heart"), as if their light could create the images of Banquo's progeny. Moaning, he writhes and struggles as if harrowed with pain. They desert him. He removes his blindfold and squints at Lennox and Seyton, unmindful of his indiscretions. Without special effects or gimmickry, the director thereby has suggested that the apparitions, perhaps aided by something psychotropic, arise from the coincidence of Macbeth's fears and the Witches' riddling replies. They express the modern horror of psychopathic dementia, not demonic evil.

Again, the television production takes advantage of a seeming limitation. The tight closeup and three-shots or four-shots make it difficult to concentrate both on the reactions of the individuals and on their placement as part of the group. Thus the director uses what the television cannot see to create surprise, shifting the camera angle, swirling it around when Macbeth drinks and suddenly finds his coat pulled off him by the Witch. In the theatre, that surprise may be tempered because we see that the "1st Witch rises, x's [crosses] behind seated Macbeth"—as the shooting script says. With the camera, her approach can be concealed until she strips off Macbeth's coat.

One might happily examine the production's many other excellences, successfully discovered and refined in the theatre, transformed and preserved through television. In scene after scene, Nunn creates mini-dramas with their own intrinsic interest—the Porter, Malcolm and Macduff, and Lady Macduff's murder are three that come to mind as unexpectedly engrossing. What lessons can be learned from this *Macbeth* about the relationship of Shakespeare in the theatre to Shakespeare on television? At the risk of being prescriptive or oversimplifying, I venture five general principles that contributed to the success of Nunn's *Macbeth*:

1. The theatre production had been tested and refined in repertory: the actors and directors discovered what worked, and they made every scene work.

2. The small stage space in three-quarters round created a close-up production style that carried over to television.

3. The ceremonial or ritual style suited television because the audience was not asked to believe in the physical reality of the action but in the reality of the emotions (seen in closeup) that performance released. It did not become a "filmed play."

4. The rhythm of the camerawork followed the emotional rhythms of the script. For the most part the camera looked at the action as if it were a spectator onstage, one of the actors who was not speaking and who sometimes stood or sat just outside the circle or sometimes moved into it. In a fundamental sense, the production was "made for television."

5. The television medium was kept subordinate to the drama—no special effects or tricky camerawork remind us that we are watching television.

Obviously, there can be no formula for predicting success in either the theatre or television. Yet if these observations have application beyond this particular *Macbeth*, they should alert television producers; Shakespeare plays produced in small studio theatres offer unusual opportunities. As the broadcast record of this *Macbeth* shows, the audiences for Shakespeare are vast, and the cost of production relatively low when months of preparations have already been made in actual theatre performance. Thus to create television Shakespeare is to serve not only theatre history, but also art, and such artists we all wish Shakespeare.

1. For further discussion of these and the film by George Schaefer, see my "Macbeth on Film," *Literature/Film Quarterly*, 1 (1974), 332–42.

2. For further discussion of twentieth-century *Macbeths*, see my "Auguries and Understood Relations: Theodore Komisarjevsky's *Macbeth*," *Theatre Journal*, 26 (1974), 20–30; "Rhythm, Pace, and Movement: *Macbeth* at Stratford-upon-Avon, 1955," *Shakespeare Studies*, 9 (1976),

269–82; "Strange Images of Death: Sir Herbert Beerbohm Tree's *Macbeth*, His Majesty's 1911," *Theatre Survey*, 17 (1976) 125–42; and "*Macbeth* in Modern Dress: Royal Court Theatre, 1928," *Theatre Journal*, 30 (1978), 176–85.

3. In an interview published in *The English Programme* 1980–81, an ITV publication, p. 12.

4. "The atmosphere was that of a satanic initiation rite," wrote Frank Marcus, *Sunday Telegraph*, 8 September 1977.

5. In conversation with the author.

Olivier's Lear and the Limits of Video
R. Alan Kimbrough

In the classroom as well as in the critical columns of both scholarly periodicals and the popular press, responsible commentary on a production of a script demands attention to the medium of that production. And to measure a production's success means to recognize the potential and the limitations of its medium. Commentary on Shakespeare productions has—for some time and with much astuteness—insisted on the inherent differences between stage and film. The borders between film and television are somewhat more blurred, and the process of defining them often relies heavily on the inferential or inductive conclusions that comparisons between film and television productions of a single text invite. The widely disseminated BBC Shakespeare productions have provided ample material for such comparisons; the 1982–83 Granada Television production of Laurence Olivier's *King Lear* invites similar comparisons even more enticingly for several reasons. First, it follows two very important and highly praised film versions of *Lear*: Grigori Kozintsev's in 1970 and Peter Brook's in 1971. Second, its costs for film and video library acquisition are quite modest. And third, unlike many of the BBC productions, it has elicited considerable acclaim. The recent release of Akira Kurosawa's *Ran* only increases the invitation to compare film and video treatments of *Lear*.

Yet a rather simple test is surely in order. When a Shakespeare production—whether on stage, film, or television—has managed to breathe fresh life into a familiar script, making us aware of possibilities we had forgotten or never realized, making us notice details that had escaped our attention, making us rethink our interpretations of Shakespeare's text, we can usually point to several significant images that have jarred us out of complacency by their thematic or characterizing resonance. With Kozintsev, Brook, and Kurosawa, identifying such images is easy. The same cannot, I think, be said of Olivier's

Lear. Why? Is the difference a result of the medium? I am very reluctant to answer in the affirmative. Indeed, I think we should resist any rapid conclusions about the differences between film and television as media for dramatic productions, especially of Shakespeare, that would result from contrasting Olivier's *Lear* with Kozintsev's, Brook's, or Kurosawa's.

Some critics' attention to Olivier's *Lear* would foster such comparisons. "Make no mistake about it, this is a 'King Lear' designed carefully for television, not for the theater," wrote John J. O'Connor (C20). Catherine Hughes labelled it "an ideal television adaptation" (112); Bill MacVicar found it "an uncommonly well thought-out and produced play for television" (69). And the reviewer for the *Library Journal* confidently predicted, "This award-winning production will no doubt become the standard against which all future Lears will be measured" (Hagloch 85).

As one might expect, most of the critical focus was on Olivier's performance and interpretation. The context—especially Olivier's age and his history of debilitating illness, not to mention his vast contributions to both theater and film throughout his long career—made the dominant raves predictable. But neither Olivier's acting nor that of his supporting cast is the issue here. Nothing suggests that the choice of medium determined the casting decisions (although a staged *Lear* would surely have been impossible for Olivier by 1982), nor has the choice of medium clearly determined the delivery of particular lines. Olivier himself, commenting on the difficulties he now finds in doing stage work, has said, "I don't see much difference between television and film, except that you do the television work in about a tenth of the time" (Cowie, *NYT* 25).

But one might be pardoned for thinking that the choice of medium is responsible for certain other features of the production. John Simon asked the question directly: "But is TV the right medium for this transcendent tragedy?" (68)[1] Simon's answer begs the question we are addressing, for he faults both film and television as media for *Lear*, insisting that the "living presences of great actors are needed, with just enough framing landscape and architecture, to convey the tremendous, brutal or noble, humanity of these personages, of this play. . . ." Benedict Nightingale goes much farther with two very apposite observations for the issue here, observations specific to this *Lear* but inviting extension to the medium generally:

> For instance, by focusing tight on faces and figures and treating even the lush English countryside as casually as any painted backdrop, [Michael Elliott's production] did much to solve the perennial problem of putting a non-naturalistic play on to a medium with an inbuilt bias towards naturalism. . . . We should have guessed that [Olivier] would score at precisely those points where his talent is supposedly weakest but TV strongest: those demanding contact and inwardness, telepathy and soul. (26)

These two issues deserve separate exploration.

The first—the medium's "inbuilt bias towards naturalism"—may be as true of film as it is of television. For some highly stylized theatrical devices, the distance of a stage is far more sympathetic and convincing than the sharply focussed, detailed clarity of either film or television. But setting aside the question of just how non-naturalistic *Lear* (or any other of Shakespeare's plays) is, we might still question Nightingale's implied prescription for success. He suggests that "a medium with an inbuilt bias towards naturalism" does well to obliterate or deemphasize the setting. The *Lear* films and much of what has succeeded on television strongly suggest otherwise. Kozintsev's rocky terrains and primitive castle interiors and Brook's frozen tundra show that naturalistic photography can work with enormous effect *if* the settings are right for the production. Much of what works well in Franco Zeffirelli's Shakespeare films also derives its impact from Zeffirelli's careful choice or construction of settings whose images will add substantially (in both senses of that word) to his productions. The BBC Shakespeare plays and Olivier's *Lear* alike suggest that the problems for television are not dissimilar. The choice or construction of setting becomes the issue. And the obviously fake—the built-in danger of nearly all non-contemporary settings, especially with limited budget studio sets—becomes only distraction when it is subjected to the clarity of the camera. Paradoxically, the dangers of stylization are less, for audiences can adjust to stylized conventions (witness Kurosawa's success). When the fake pretends to be real, the danger is far greater. The studio "henge" and the bizarre costuming of Olivier's *Lear* demonstrate the danger all too painfully.[2]

Nightingale's second point—that television is strongest when "contact and inwardness" are demanded—reinforces the standard observations about television's sympathy for very close-range photography. The cause-effect that Marion Perret implies is typical: "Designed as a tv film rather than as a movie, [Olivier's *Lear*] was photographed mainly in closeup" (1). Tucker Orbison's question—"Is the persistent employment of the close-up a necessary concomitant of the television screen?" (61)—thus rightly challenges one of the most widely held assumptions about television as a medium. It is true that the smallness of the television screen makes close-ups less intimidating and reduces their potential for the grotesque that can come from the hugely enlarged images of close-ups on a large film screen. But such close focus on faces carries the equal demand that the faces reveal character tellingly. And the close-ups of both Kozintsev and Brook—e.g., the numerous eyes, human and animal, in Kozintsev, the full frame face of Paul Scofield's Lear in Brook—say more than the close-ups in Olivier's *Lear*. The casting decisions become crucial, and filmmakers like Kozintsev and Brook have carefully sought out the faces that their cameras can capture in significant images. The faces are film faces. Despite the extensive film and television experience of many actors in the cast (particularly John Hurt, Leo McKern, and Diana Rigg, in addition to Olivier himself), Olivier's *Lear* gives us the faces of stage actors trained in using broad gesture and vocal inflection for expression, with far less reliance on the nuances of facial expression that theater audiences are too far away to see.

Yet generalization about televised Shakespeare is at best suspect, just as generalization about Shakespeare on film can be very wrong-headed. Nearly a decade ago, Jack Jorgens pointed out the weaknesses in what had then already become semi-established ways of categorizing Shakespeare on film. Citing Roger Manvell, Donald Skoller, and Peter Woolen, Jorgens noticed that critics "often sort out Shakespeare films by measuring their relative distance from the language and conventions of the theatre." And he labelled the principal categories of these "modes" as the "theatrical," the "realist," and the "filmic" (7). Citing Stanley Wells and Thomas Clayton, he noticed a parallel categorization for "three means of treatment which describe a film's relative distance from the original text—presentation, interpretation, and adaptation" (12). Such categories can be applied to Shakespeare on television with equal ease. And the Olivier *Lear* blends—in Jorgens' terms—theatrical and realist modes in a presentation of Shakespeare's play.

In an interview with Ronn Smith, Roy Stonehouse (the production designer of the Olivier *Lear*) partially confirmed this labelling of the production's mode as intentionally and self-consciously "realistic:"

> Television traditionally approaches the Bard in one of two ways: either in a very stylized manner . . . or in a very realistic way. The latter, however, is usually shot on location and ends up looking rather ordinary. It's very hard to suggest period on location. . . . Had we filmed *King Lear* on location, the finished product would have been judged as a film. It would also have been compared to other films of Shakespeare's plays. As it is, this production will be judged on whether it succeeds as Shakespeare-in-a-studio. (Smith 12)

Stonehouse repeatedly stresses this *Lear*'s studio aspect, detailing the four composite sets used in the three-and-a-half-week shooting schedule and explaining the difficulties of making anything look old on television:

> Television lighting enhances colors, and the high quality camera makes everything look beautiful. . . . We therefore took particular pains to stress and age the *Lear* sets. This, too, gives a certain authenticity to the realism we were after. I say "realism," but what I should say is "stylized realism." It isn't real in the sense that it can be documented. It's more like an impression of what we *think* was real. (Smith 12)

As I have indicated above, the "authenticity" Stonehouse was aiming for proved highly elusive indeed. The clarity of close-range television photography can only subvert such sets, self-consciously "aiming for impression rather than accuracy" (Perret 7). Robert Brustein's assessment was more blunt: "Reputedly the most expensive production ever made for British TV, this *King Lear* looks tacky" (26). But the chief point underlying Stonehouse's comments underscores the need to avoid any broad generalizations about television as a medium for Shakespeare based exclusively on this or similar productions. Televised "Shakespeare-in-a-studio" does not equal all of "Shakespeare on TV."

Peter Cowie points to yet another aspect of Olivier's *Lear* that seems significant. Observing that this production "looks very much a collaborative effort," he expands:

> Michael Elliott, the stage director known recently for his brilliant work at Manchester's Royal Exchange, discussed with Olivier and the designer, Roy Stonehouse, an abridged and visually persuasive version of the play that could grip the attention of TV viewers. (*Sight and Sound* 78.)[3]

I find Cowie's characterization of the production very telling, for if I read it correctly, it accounts far better than the limitations of the studio for the major disappointments of the production. And I trace those disappointments to what I see as a severely modest—if not indeed patronizing—notion of what could persuade and "grip the attention of TV viewers." The result is simply a literalism that does not warrant inflation as "realism" or "naturalism." And the literalism is patently obvious both visually and verbally.

Visually, the production's camera work fosters stagnation and suggests a directorial vacuum. The shooting is predominantly close range and straight angle, with predictable zooming in for the soliloquies (Edmund's "Thou, nature" directly into the camera). Reaction shots are rare; when the cameras do cut away from the speaker we are hearing, they usually focus on the person being referred to in the speech. The few overhead shots (e.g., the initial establishing of the much-criticized pseudo-Stonehenge setting) are clichés. Imaginative use of cutting is nearly nonexistent. And all too often the entire background is obliterated in the standard shadows of soap opera, depriving speakers (or their speeches) of significant social and dramatic context.

Productions of *Lear* must always wrestle with the tensions between the public-political and the private-domestic tragedies bound together in Lear's fall. It *may* be true that the small screen is inherently more hospitable to a focus on the private, with the vast social panorama of, say, Kozintsev's *Lear* requiring the large screen, even the enlarged large screen of cinemascope. But Peter Brook has shown that film can capture the inner turmoil and psychological disintegration of Lear with striking visual force. In the Olivier *Lear*, the entire burden of such revelation is put on Olivier's shoulders, or, more precisely, on his voice and—to a lesser extent—on his face. In other words, the television viewer's experience is markedly like that of the theater viewer's, except not live and at closer range. The cameras for this production merely record instead of helping to interpret. And one looks in vain for anything beyond the most literally obvious (the 900 gallons of rain, for instance, or the notorious addition of stage business requiring the mad Lear to disembowel a rabbit and eat its viscera raw) that would suggest any affinity with Kozintsev's *sine qua non* for filming Shakespeare:

> The problem is not one of finding means to speak the verse in front of the camera, in realistic circumstances ranging from long-shot to close-up. *The*

aural has to be made visual. The poetic texture itself has to be transformed into a visual poetry, into the dynamic organization of film imagery. (Cited by Jorgens, 10 n29; emphasis added.)

In a word, the Olivier *Lear* is simply dated.[4] Part of the evolution of television can be charted by paying attention to the shift from aural to visual, reflected in the ratio between what is thoroughly intelligible to a non-seeing listener and what requires attention to the visual images on the screen. (This evolution reinforces the earlier suggestion that the differences between film and television are becoming fewer and fewer.) For all their differences, both Kozintsev and Brook use frequent and lengthy shots with no dialogue at all. The signifying becomes exclusively visual. The same cannot be said of the Olivier *Lear*.

Despite some abridging, the Olivier script remains almost slavishly faithful to Shakespeare's text. Only three scenes (III.i, IV.iii, and IV.iv) have been cut entirely. On a few occasions (III.iii.36–60; III.vii.1–27; IV.vi.70–80; V.i.38–69; and V.iii.152–75) the sequence of lines and speeches has been modified. Most of the other cuts—some of the Fool's songs, Edgar's asides in IV.i, otherwise without observable pattern—seem to have been motivated principally by a desire to keep the video at about two and a half hours rather than by any coherent or consistent interpretation of character. Olivier himself is on record as saying, "I don't think the medium will hold the interest any longer [than a little over two hours]" (Cowie, *NYT* 25).[5] Teachers looking for a production that students can follow easily in their texts will be pleased, particularly since the visual usually does little more than illustrate or duplicate the verbal and students miss very little by keeping their eyes on their texts. Mindless fidelity and simplistic clarity determine all. The words are relentless, and the acting depends far more on actors' voices than on their faces or bodies. Since the screen usually shows little other than a close shot of the speaker's face, visual attention often becomes superfluous. On only three occasions do the words stop for any significant length of time: at IV.vi.80, for the crudely sensational rabbit-gutting incident and the visual substitute for the description Cordelia gives of the mad Lear in the excised IV.iv (with "Come o'er the bourn, Bessy, to me" reassigned from III.vi to Lear here; cf. Cordelia's "singing aloud" at IV.iv.2); early in V.ii for a tedious overlay curiously allowing us to see both the blind Gloucester and fragments of the battles he can only hear; and in V.iii for the obligatory but dull fight between Edgar and Edmund.

By way of contrast (although still with a largely uncut script in a studio production) I would point to the imaginative use of the medium in the opening of V.v in the BBC *Richard II*. For that soliloquy, director David Giles used his medium to obtain advantages not available in the theater, showing Richard's protracted imprisonment and torture by splitting the speech into segments and indicating the passage of time between segments. The device gives us glimpses of Richard's progressive enlightenment and ennoblement, i.e., his growth in tragic stature. And the very adroit use of the crucifix on the cell wall and the shadows of the prison bars work to pick up and affirm the many religious images elsewhere in the script that encourage serious attention to Richard as martyr and Richard as God's anointed king. In that segment we come far closer to seeing some of television's capacity as a medium for Shakespeare than we ever do in Olivier's *Lear*.

When I try to remember televised productions of other Renaissance plays that have succeeded powerfully, I immediately think of the 1970 BBC telecast of Marlowe's *Edward II* (shown in the U.S. in the fall of 1975 as part of the PBS "Classic Theater" series, originating from Boston's WGBH), a gripping production in a style very different from that of Olivier's *Lear* or the BBC Shakespeare series. Featuring Ian McKellen and the Prospect Theater Company and originally designed for the 1969 Edinburgh Festival, the production was filmed in London's Piccadilly Theater and made no attempt to disguise its "theatrical" mode. Yet director Toby Robertson was able to make Marlowe's tragedy visually compelling and convincing. Such a production reminds us that televised Shakespeare can admit a greater variety than we have seen recently, particularly if we seek to delineate the effects that a medium may have on productions. And it may be fruitful, too, to extend this investigation to telecasts of non-Renaissance plays that have worked well on the small screen.

The history of Shakespeare in the theater would suggest we have seen only the beginnings of television's potential as a medium for creative and illuminating productions of Shakespeare. The limits of video are scarcely to be defined by Olivier's *Lear*, and as we try to answer questions about the different necessities imposed by the media of television and film, the data available today may make inductive answers still exceedingly premature.

1. One answer to Simon's question appears in Benny Green's 13 April 1983 review of Olivier's *Lear* for *Punch*: "*King Lear* is one of those big plays which will not be squeezed into a small box. Reduced, as it must be by television, to spacial bankruptcy, it cannot meet its emotional commitments . . . " ("Television" 66, quoted by Orbison 68, n12).

2. But see Stephen Urkowitz's persuasive praise for the leather butcher's apron Cornwall puts on to gouge out Gloucester's eyes (3). I would consider that a notable exception to the rule; Urkowitz, by contrast, maintains, "The dress always seems to fit the action."

Tucker Orbison's explication of the Stonehenge setting (particularly its druidical significance, reinforced by the oak tree and its leaves later in the production) is surely among the more elaborate attempts to justify this production's sets.

3. See, too, Lloyd Rose's note—on the authority of David Plowright (Granada Television's managing director and Olivier's brother-in-law)—that Olivier and Elliott "worked out the production's concept together and collaborated in editing the text" (92).

4. Stanley Wells' review suggests that the production, at least its sets "in the pictorial tradition of the nineteenth century," is dated even in terms of the theater: "Irving and Wolfit would have been at home in this setting" (353).

5. See Richard Corliss: "Olivier has pruned the text significantly but fairly" (77). Joseph Sobran, on the other hand, sees a more pointed result—an "ingratiating" Lear—from the omission of "some of Lear's more savage lines" (56). Close examination of the cuts would not suggest such an intention, unlike the deliberate excising of Hal's savagery in Olivier's *Henry V* film.

Brustein, Robert. "Olivier's Lear," *The New Republic*, 6 June 1983, 26–27.

Corliss, Richard. "Lord Larry's Crowning Triumph," *Time*, 16 May 1983, 77.

Cowie, Peter. "Olivier, at 75, Returns to 'Lear.'" *New York Times*, 1 May 1983, sec. 2, pp. 1, 25.

————. "The Olivier Lear," *Sight and Sound*, 52 (Spring 1983), 78.

Hagloch, Susan B. "Audiovisual Reviews: *King Lear*," *Library Journal*, 1 October 1985, 85.

Hughes, Catherine. "British Television: As They Like It," *America*, 10 September 1983, 112.

Jorgens, Jack J. *Shakespeare on Film*. Bloomington: Indiana University Press, 1977.

MacVicar, Bill. "Raging at the Dying of the Light," *Maclean's*, 21 November 1983, 69.

Nightingale, Benedict. "Closed Circuits," *New Statesman*, 8 April 1983, 26.

O'Connor, John J. "TV: Olivier, at 76, Stars in a British 'King Lear.'" *New York Times*, 26 January 1984, C20.

Orbison, Tucker. "The Stone and the Oak: Olivier's TV Film of *King Lear*," *The CEA Critic*, 47:1&2 (Fall-Winter 1984), 61–77.

Perret, Marion. "The Making of *King Lear*," *Shakespeare on Film Newsletter*, 8:2 (April 1984), 1, 7.

Rose, Lloyd. "A Winter's Tale," *Atlantic Monthly*, February 1984, 90–92.

Simon, John. "Is TV Big Enough for Olivier's *Lear*?," *Vogue*, January 1984, 68.

Smith, Ronn. "Focus: Theatre on Video," *Theatre Crafts*, April 1983, 12.

Sobran, Joseph. "Lear's Show," *National Review*, 9 March 1984, 55–56.

Urkowitz, Steven. "Lord Olivier's *King Lear*," *Shakespeare on Film Newsletter*, 8:1 (December 1983), 1, 3.

Wells, Stanley. "The Sweetness of Age," *Times Literary Supplement*, 8 April 1983, 353.

Two Lears for Television
An Exploration of Televisual Strategies
Hardy M. Cook

The fifth season of *The Shakespeare Plays* opened in America on October 18, 1982, with the last play that Jonathan Miller directed for the series. The result is a provocative version of *King Lear* that marked the third time that Miller had cast Michael Hordern in the role of the foolish old king.[1] Fifteen months later, on January 26, 1984, Americans finally got to see the much heralded Laurence Olivier's *King Lear*. This version, taped earlier in England for Grenada Television, was directed by Michael Elliott and produced by David Plowright. These two productions of the play differ radically, each with instructive strengths and weaknesses. Having these two recent productions of the same play to compare and contrast provides us with a valuable opportunity to assess the possibilities for "translating" *King Lear* to television.

The acting styles in these two *Lears* differ in many significant ways. Michael Elliott conceived of his *Lear* as existing in a mythic world with characters who appear somewhat larger than life. Naturally following from this is his emphasis on individual performances. There is little doubt that the casting of Olivier in the title role was the principal reason for the production, but Olivier had a splendid cast to back him up, and the members of that cast

Reprinted, with permission, from *Literature/Film Quarterly*, 14:4 (1986) 179–86.

turned in some memorable, indeed unforgettable, performances. The *mise en scène* and editing of this production call attention to these individual performances with a preponderance of closely framed one-shots and rapid cutting—the effects of which are to accentuate the faces of the actors and the slightest nuances of expression that flicker across them. I shall consider in a moment what this strategy denies us on television.

In Jonathan Miller's production, the emphasis is exactly the opposite. Miller's actors perform in ensemble, consistent with his view that in *Lear* the family is a metaphor for the state. Michael Hordern graciously defers to the other members of the cast, who all give subdued performances consistent with Miller's beliefs about how Shakespeare should be acted for television. Miller uses a relatively static camera, which records fairly long takes of the actors generally in medium two-shots, three-shots, and four-shots, as opposed to Elliott's shorter takes and dominating one-shots.

Both of these productions of *King Lear* last approximately three hours. However, because each makes different aesthetic assumptions about the play, each reveals much about the possibilities available for producing Shakespeare for television. Miller's version is faster-paced than Elliott's. This pace is established in several ways—through transitions between scenes, the illusion of cross-cutting, the deletion of one scene, and the shortening of others. The pace of Elliott's *Lear* is slower because Elliott chose to take a more "cinematic" and less "televisual" approach in his production. Elliott, like Miller, gives the impression of cross-cutting between II.iv and III.ii–vi, but Elliott cuts more of the text. Three complete scenes are excised—III.i, IV.iii, and IV.iv (as opposed to Miller's one—IV.iii), and some speeches and scenes are noticeably shortened. As a result, Elliott has additional screen time that enables him to create new scenes which emphasize visual elements over verbal ones.

These new scenes call attention to the lavishness of his production. I.ii opens with Edmund's soliloquy on the now-deserted Stonehenge set. After it, Gloucester enters, and the two discuss the letter supposedly from Edgar. Rather than continuing the scene as the text does, Elliott creates a new scene at the stables of Gloucester's castle. Edgar rides in on a horse, followed by Edmund, also riding. After they dismount, the textual scene continues. A similar expansion happens at the end of I.v. After Lear and his retinue leave Albany's castle, a brief new scene, without dialogue, is added in which Lear and the Fool on the lead horse are followed by Lear's train. This expansion sets up another one that opens II.iv when, still on horseback, Lear and his men ride through the heath. The first few lines are delivered, and then a new scene begins after they enter the gates of Gloucester's compound. The most noticeable expansion occurs in IV.vi. After Gloucester vows to "bear affliction," he and Edgar walk off in a dissolve to Lear washing his rags in a stream. Lear snares a rabbit, opens it with a knife, eats its entrails, and drinks from the stream. There is a cut to Lear making and wearing chains of wildflowers before he says, "No, they cannot touch me for coining. I am the king himself." Lear recites a few more lines and sings a song that is not in the text. Only then does he run into Gloucester and Edgar, the dialogue of the scene continuing with Edgar's "Sweet marjoram." These changes reveal Elliott's more "cinematic" approach to the play, as he creates visual equivalents to the spoken word. We know from the text that Lear has gone mad—in Elliott's version we *see* much of the madness that we would normally *hear* more about; consequently, Elliott has no need for IV.iv, in which Cordelia discusses her father's condition with the Doctor.

Elliott, then, employs a more "cinematic" and less "televisual" approach than Miller does. His choices emphasize editing and visual equivalents as opposed to techniques that allow Shakespeare's language to carry a greater weight than is usual in cinematic versions of the plays. Since this distinction mimics a controversy that dominated film theory and film production up to the theoretical revolution of the mid-1960s, it will be useful to examine some of the theories of André Bazin, who in the 1950s distinguished between directors "who put their faith in the image and those who put their faith in reality."[2] Bazin sets the techniques of *montage* against those of *depth of field*. He first differentiates between two orders of montage: (1) images joined according to some abstract principle (a technique associated primarily with the silent cinema) and (2) images joined according to psychological montage whereby an event is broken down into those fragments which resemble the changes of attention we might naturally experience were we physically present at the event (a technique associated with the coming of sound). In opposition to these, Bazin sets depth of field techniques which permit an action to develop over a long time on several spatial planes, constructing dramatic interrelationships *within* the frame rather than *between* frames.[3] Although contemporary theoreticians convincingly call into question the use of the term "realism" by Bazin and others,[4] much of what Bazin has to say about depth of field techniques relates to the distinction that I am making between "cinematic" versus "televisual" approaches to Shakespeare on television.

Bazin explains that with depth of field techniques, dramatic effects which had formerly relied on montage can be created out of the movements of actors within a fixed framework where whole scenes are covered in one take with the camera remaining motionless.[5] With this approach, montage is partially replaced by frequent panning shots and entrances, based on "a respect for the continuity of dramatic space and, of course, of its duration."[6] From Bazin's theories, we may conveniently label those televisual strategies that are similar to Elliott's *montage technique* and those that are similar to Miller's *depth of field* technique. These two techniques rarely appear in unadulterated form, yet they describe the two major approaches that have been employed to translate Shakespeare's plays to television.

. . . Elliott's use of montage technique establishes interrelationships primarily by cuts between frames. Miller's use of depth of field technique establishes interrelationships within the frame. There are many accompanying differences between these two techniques. Elliott's takes are short; Miller's are long. Elliott frequently uses reaction shots; Miller uses them selectively. Elliott uses a highly fluid camera; Miller's camera is largely static—he moves his actors within the frame, and therefore blocking is extremely important. Elliott uses tightly framed one-shots; Miller uses looser, generally medium, ensemble shots.

I contend that Miller's televisual approach is ultimately more effective for realizing Shakespeare on television than Elliott's, which depends more upon cutting and visual equivalents. . . . Realizing Shakespeare for television alters the dynamics of television as a cinematic subgenre because the density of Shakespeare's language must of necessity be sacrificed in more "cinematic," montage approaches. In a highly visual medium like film, images can often be in competition with Shakespeare's language. Roger Manvell notes that "there can be little doubt that the full-scale spoken poetry of Shakespeare's stage and the continuous visual imagery of the cinema can be oil and water."[7] Charles Marowitz, an assistant to Peter Brook during the filming of Brook's 1970 *King Lear*, makes a similar observation:

> When we came to consider how the words should actually be treated on the screen, we realised that the power of Shakespeare's writing—particularly its evocative power—is so enormous that although one can find images which may seem appropriate, images become unnecessary or even unwanted—they can actually get between the audience and the power of the words.[8]

Because of the differences in image quality and the relation of the audience to the screen, in television the spoken word carries more weight than it does in the cinema. This is an especially important difference when dealing with a Shakespeare play in which language is paramount. As Sheldon P. Zitner points out, "Since its spoken words loom larger in the total sensory input, television can go further than film towards restoring the Elizabethan Theatre's primacy of words."[9] Therefore, my contention is not that Miller's televisual approach is more "realistic" than Elliott's, but that it better establishes a relationship between the spectator and the object on the television screen, replicating an experience with Shakespeare's plays that is similar to the theatrical one. To illustrate this contention, I now propose to examine Elliott's and Miller's televisual choices in I.i.

Elliott opens his *King Lear* with ominous background music. The first shot, which establishes the scene, is a high-angle long-shot of the enormous Stonehenge-like set as the sun rises behind it in the mists of the morning. Characters are seen moving to the inside of the circle of stones as the camera cranes down. It continues moving to set up a two-shot of Gloucester and Kent on the outside perimeter of the stone circle. As Kent begins speaking, the camera continues to move in to frame a much tighter two-shot. At Kent's "Is not this your son, my lord," Elliott cuts abruptly to a three-shot that now includes Edmund, viewed from the back. As Gloucester says, "His breeding, sir, hath been at my charge," there is another abrupt cut to a closely framed reaction shot of Edmund in which we see a slight raising of his left eyelid in response to his father's statement. This shot is held during Kent's "I cannot conceive you," at which time Elliott cuts back to the two-shot of Kent and Gloucester. After Gloucester's " . . . ere she had a husband for her bed," we are given another very quick reaction shot of Edmund before returning to the three-shot. At Gloucester's "But I have a son, by order of law . . . ," Elliott returns to the two-shot of Kent and Gloucester. When Gloucester says " . . . who yet is no dearer," Elliott has Gloucester move toward Edmund with the camera following in a pan that sets up a two-shot of Gloucester and Edmund. Gloucester moves back to reform the two-shot with Kent and says, "Though this knave came somewhat saucily to the world before he was sent for." At "there was good sport at his making," the camera tightens the two-shot; then Elliott cuts back to the three-shot and continues with it until Edmund's "My services to your lordship," which is delivered in a close one-shot. Next, there is a cut back to the three-shot for Kent's response, a cut to a one-shot of Edmund's reply, and then a return to the three-shot. After Gloucester's "He hath been out nine years," Elliott cuts to a reaction of Edmund at "and away he shall again" and then cuts back to the three-shot for "The King is coming." At this point, Kent and Gloucester turn to enter the circle of stones as Gloucester signals to Edmund not to follow.

What I have just described takes less than a minute and a half of screen time. In that time, Elliott cuts thirteen times, with some of the takes (especially Edmund's reactions) lasting only a second or two. In many respects, this opening is a perfect example of the montage strategy. Rather than show-ing the reactions of the characters within the frame, Elliott presents them to us in reaction shots through cuts between the frames. The cuts isolate indi-vidual performances in these reaction shots, such as the one featuring Ed-mund's raised eyelid; further, they replicate psychological changes in atten-tion. However, they are completely under the control of the director. They give spectators little choice about where to direct their attention. This to me is a major shortcoming of using the montage technique for presenting Shake-speare on television.

Miller's version of these same opening lines also takes about a minute and a half, but there is not a single cut during that time. Miller opens his scene with a long-shot of the darkly lit, relatively artificial interior of Lear's palace. Kent and Gloucester enter the set from the extreme right in deep field and walk to the front and center of the frame. Even before Kent begins to speak, Edmund, who had been sitting with several other courtiers on a bench to the right in deep field, rises and walks into the mid-field between the two Earls, creating the first of innumerable triangular blocking patterns in this scene. Edmund's body language suggests that he is trying to overhear what the two Earls are saying. Kent and Gloucester speak in hushed voices as if they do not wish to be overheard by the others present in the room. Kent looks over his shoulder, and Edmund's attitude implies that he is attempting to act casual, hiding his real purpose. The exchange between Kent and Gloucester contin-ues, and Kent once again looks over his shoulder and asks, "Is not this your son, my lord?" Edmund's and Kent's eyes meet. As Gloucester responds, Edmund moves behind his father to the right, establishing another triangular pattern. Sometimes this movement is only the slight turn of the body or the head. Gloucester, for example, in the middle of this threesome, directs his remarks to Kent and then turns to look at Edmund's reactions. When Gloucester announces, "The King is coming," the three move out of the way to let Lear enter from the right front. Rather than cutting, Miller has his actors move *within the frame*: we see all three all the time.

Miller, therefore, directs this same portion of scene one quite differently from the way Elliott does. Miller establishes relationships within the frame rather than between frames. We still have the reactions of Kent, Gloucester, and Edmund to what is being discussed, but we may choose how we wish to direct our attention during these interactions. With this strategy, the emphasis is less upon individual performances and more upon the interrelationships among the characters. This is just what the montage strategy denies us.

I want to make a few other points about the differences between these two versions of I.i before drawing some conclusions. After Gloucester and Kent enter the stone circle, Elliott continues the scene at a leisurely pace with music and the ceremonial entrances of Goneril and Albany, Regan and Cornwall, and Lear and Cordelia. After these entrances, Elliott moves in for a close one-shot of Lear, to an overhead shot of the interior of the circle, to another quick one-shot of Lear, to another overhead shot, and then to a shot of Lear on his throne. These cuts at times create the impression of a slide show; they are obtrusive and are not, in my view, as seamless as they should be. Throughout this production, Elliott cuts between frames to establish relationships. When Lear explains his intention of dividing his kingdom and retiring from active rule of it, Elliott cuts between one-shots of Lear and two-shots of Regan and Cornwall, two-shots of Goneril and Albany and one-shots of Cordelia. This montage strategy denies us the simultaneous impact of Shakespeare's language upon all the major characters in the frame (their collective reactions to what is happening) and the choice of where to direct our attention during those interactions.

The depth of field technique allows viewers to exercise more control over what they see. In this approach, blocking within the ensemble shots is extremely important, as it is in the theatre. Miller's blocking in this scene is a visual essay on the shifting relationships among the characters, and it is appropriate to consider some of these triangles and their effects.

The first triangular pattern, after Lear enters the frame, occurs when Lear, in the center of the foreground, examines the map, while in deep-field to the left are Regan and Cornwall and to the right are Goneril and Albany. After Lear's "while we / Unburden'd crawl toward death," Miller makes his first cut to a close one-shot of Lear. The camera then dollies back, setting up another triangle: the elder sisters and their spouses remain in deep-field in the same positions as the last triangle; at the apex of this new triangle in the center foreground is Cordelia; Lear sits on his throne slightly in front of Goneril and

Regan and almost in the middle of the three points. Goneril declares her love for her father to the right of a triangle formed by Cornwall, Albany, and Lear. Cordelia's reaction to her eldest sister's remarks is addressed to the Fool in another triangle: the Fool to the left in the foreground, Cordelia to the right, with Lear at the apex in deep-field. Regan declares her love in a triangle composed of herself, Cornwall, and Lear, and Cordelia's reaction is presented in the same pattern as before. When Lear asks Cordelia "what can you say," Goneril and Regan are together at the apex of a triangle with Lear and Cordelia on either side in the foreground. As Cordelia explains her reply of "Nothing," Kent moves into the apex, replacing Goneril and Regan. As Lear's anger increases, he steps to the right and blocks out Kent. As Kent bids goodbye, he does so in another triangular pattern: Lear is at the apex in deep-field; Cordelia and the Fool are together at the left foreground, while Kent is at the right. When Burgundy and France enter, they too form a triangle with Lear at the apex. The camera then dollies and pans to set up a triangle with the Fool and Cordelia at the apex and Burgundy and Lear at the other points in the foreground. When Cordelia pleads, "I yet beseech your Majesty," she does so in a triangle composed of herself, Lear, and France. During France's "My Lord of Burgundy," France, Cordelia, and Burgundy are blocked in yet another triangular pattern, while a triangle during France's "Fairest Cordelia" is composed of France, Lear, and Cordelia. When Cordelia bids her sisters farewell, they form another triangle, and the scene concludes with a triangle formed by Goneril, Regan, and Edmund. Most of these triangles are created within the frame primarily by the movement of the actors, with some movement of the camera, usually slow and gentle.

Miller's blocking thus replicates the shifting relationships among the characters. It also enables viewers to shift their attention among those characters. Miller's blocking places his characters in the dramatic space that we observe, and in that respect it controls emphasis as a director in the theatre does. However, with this technique, we have more freedom to direct our attention where we wish than we do with montage technique, and this strategy restores to Shakespeare's language the primacy that it loses with montage technique. There is no denying the power of the performances in Elliott's *Lear*. The difficulty is that the viewer is not permitted to observe a large portion of those performances because the camera often excludes from our sight many of the actors who are present. With Miller's strategy, we see most of the actors present in a scene most of the time. In this ensemble performance, we see more of the simultaneous effects that language has on the characters. With depth of field technique, the language is not as much in competition with the visuals, and thus a greater emphasis is given to the spoken word.

. . . Miller's version creates a televisual analogue to the theatrical experience—one in which Shakespeare's language is not sacrificed to the images. Montage can create competition between the visual and the verbal elements in a production. Those who direct Shakespeare's plays for cinema generally accept that this competition exists and substitute visual equivalents, paring down the verbal texts—often by as much as one half, as in the Reinhardt and Dieterle *A Midsummer Night's Dream* and the Olivier *Henry V* and *Hamlet*. Further, theatrical versions of Shakespeare's plays in cinema, such as Stuart Burge's *Othello* with Laurence Olivier, do not work well for the very reason that the visuals are uninteresting. This does not mean that one cannot have a satisfying experience with a filmed version of a Shakespeare play. Quite the contrary, many Shakespeare films are true to the spirit of the plays from which they were derived; but the importance of Shakespeare's language alters the dynamics of television as a cinematic subgenre. Therefore, a more "cinematic" approach to Shakespeare on television is not as effective a use of the medium as the depth of field technique.

Miller's televisual strategies enable viewers to watch Shakespeare on television in a manner that is similar to the theatrical experience. As H. R. Coursen notes, "The best TV productions gradually erase our concentration on technique and draw us into that attentiveness similar to what happens to us in the theater." [10] This, I contend, is what Jonathan Miller's production of *King Lear* does and what Michael Elliott's does not do. Miller's style accomplishes this through a greater, uninterrupted continuity of dramatic space and time, a more active relationship between the spectator and the object, more choice about where and how to direct one's attention while viewing a production, and a greater weight given to the spoken word.

1. Production credit was given to Shaun Sutton, who took over the reins of series producer from Miller.

2. André Bazin, *What Is Cinema?*, vol. 1, trans. Hugh Gray (Berkeley: Univ. of California Press, 1967), p. 24.

3. Cf. Dudley Andrew, *The Major Film Theories* (New York: Oxford Univ. Press, 1976), pp. 156–57.

4. Dudley Andrew, *Concepts in Film Theory* (New York: Oxford Univ. Press, 1984), p. 48.

5. Bazin, p. 33.

6. Bazin, p. 34.

7. Roger Manvell, *Shakespeare and the Film* (New York: Praeger, 1971), p. 15; cf. p. 107.

8. Quoted in Manvell, p. 138.

9. Sheldon P. Zitner, "Wooden O's in Plastic Boxes: Shakespeare and Television," *University of Toronto Quarterly*, 51 (Fall 1981), 6.

10. H. R. Coursen, "Shakespeare and Television: The BBC-TV *Hamlet*," in *Shakespeare and the Arts*, ed. Cecile W. Cary and Henry S. Limouze (Washington, D.C.: Univ. Press of America, 1982), p. 127.

Lear's Mock Trial

James P. Lusardi

For the tragic protagonist and for the audience alike, 3.6 of *King Lear* promises a moment of respite. After the ordeal of the storm-swept heath, the maddened Lear and his little band of shocked and shaken allies are provided by Gloucester with shelter "where both food and fire is ready" (3.4.151):

> Here is better than the open air; take it thankfully. I will piece out the comfort with what addition I can. I will not be long from you. (3.6.1–3.)[1]

Such comfort, however, gives Lear no relief from the "tempest in my mind" (3.4.12), and the developing scene projects the audience into the realm of the phantasmagoric. Apparently seizing on the ordinary furnishings of the place, the suffering king's hallucinating imagination transforms it into a court of law for the purpose of arraigning and judging those "she-foxes," his daughters Goneril and Regan. The scene becomes a grotesque expression of Lear's new concern with justice as he appoints his fellow sufferers as judges, the "naked wretch" Poor Tom, the frantic Fool, and the agonized Kent.

Harley Granville-Barker thought the episode "admirable on the stage," and others have echoed his verdict.[2] Yet surely the scene poses a complex challenge to anyone interested in performance. Precisely because it is "technically daring" it puts special demands on director and actors and presents a series of puzzles to students of stage images. Indeed, the omission of the mock trial itself (17–55) from the Folio may indicate that the heart of the scene was not always performed by Shakespeare's own company.[3] I propose to explore some of the theatrical possibilities of the scene, particularly the mock trial, in the context of the play and then, since the scene is rarely omitted from modern productions, to discuss two recent and readily accessible treatments of it—in the BBC production, with Michael Hordern, directed by Jonathan Miller, and the Granada TV production, with Laurence Olivier, directed by Michael Elliott.

The scene embodies at least three theatrical components that prove to be powerfully suggestive elsewhere in the play: the ritual, the trial, and the use of dramatic artifice. By "ritual" I mean ceremonial occasions, usually reflecting archetypal models, by which society seeks to order itself. Such occasions are exemplified in the play by the formal love-test in 1.1, the reconciliation of Lear and Cordelia in 4.7, and the chivalric trial by combat in 5.3. Even when the performance of the rituals is ill-advised or flawed, as in the case of the love-test that Lear couples with the division of the kingdom, these occasions still exhibit the characteristics of being "public," "deliberate," and "predictable, in outline if not in detail."[4] Though indubitably an attempt to invoke a time-honored social ritual, Lear's mock trial shares none of these qualities. It is carried out not in any public arena, whether castle or camp, but in a place of concealment, a farmhouse or outbuilding on Gloucester's estate, among a group of outcasts. It is not deliberate but unpremeditated, the sudden product of crazed inspiration on Lear's part. And it is completely unpredictable, in both outline and detail, with respect to its course and outcome. There is in fact no outcome, since the trial is abruptly broken off by the imagined escape of the imagined defendants. In short, the invoked ritual has been converted to parody.

A "trial" is of course a certain kind of ritual, and by using the term I mean to identify situations involving more or less formal arraignments, judgments, and sentences of alleged offenders against the values and hence the well-being of the community. The play offers plenty of instances: Lear's disinheritance of Cordelia and banishment of Kent in 1.1; Gloucester's rush to a verdict on Edgar in 1.2 and 2.1; Cornwall's stocking of Kent in 2.2; Goneril's and Regan's judgment on Lear in 2.4. All these occur prior to Lear's mock trial. It is immediately followed by the scene in which the "form of justice" (3.7.26) is the blinding of Gloucester at the hands of Cornwall and Regan. Ironically, Lear's court is now made up of those on whom judgment and punishment have been visited by the powerful, of those at the farthest remove from authority. The only other character in the scene is Gloucester; not actually present for the trial, he exercises the authority he retains on borrowed time, as 3.5 has made clear, and he will suffer terrible punishment for the good offices he performs for Lear and his fellows. But the supremely ironic presence is Lear himself, now the victim of his own original failure as a dispenser of justice; he presides at a trial where he is also a plaintiff and really a defendant. Formally, this trial is again a travesty of legal procedure. But, as Granville-Barker remarks of the stage picture conjured up, "Was better justice done, the picture ironically asks, when Lear presided in majesty and sanity and power?"[5] Curiously, Lear's mock trial is the only one among the many that achieves anything like a just condemnation of the truly guilty. As there is wisdom in folly and reason in madness, so there is justice in legal anarchy.

If rituals and legal proceedings are analogous to theatre, the third component of the scene partakes more directly of the thing itself. By the "use of dramatic artifice" I mean role-playing and the creation of dramatic fictions within the play. No doubt Edmund is the most consciously skillful actor and improviser of such fictions that we encounter, beginning with the elaborate deceptions he perpetrates on both father and brother in 1.2. While Edmund chooses to practice the theatrical art as a means of securing status and power, others have it thrust upon them and pursue it more tentatively. Kent becomes Caius in 1.4 because it is the only way he can continue to serve Lear. Edgar becomes Poor Tom in 2.3 out of fear, desperation, and the aching sense that "Edgar I nothing am." Circumstance forces him to sustain and elaborate his role-playing in ways he cannot anticipate, and at length, as he grows more accustomed to performance and more convinced of its transforming effects on himself and others, he invents well-meaning fictions, such as the solemn charade with Gloucester on Dover Cliff in 4.6. As the theatrical art is associated with Edgar's existential progress through the play, so it is with Lear's. But with Lear the practice is less conscious and more willful. In effect, as king, as father, and as mere man, he repeatedly stages scenes in which he casts himself in the dominant role as either the primary agent of justice or the primary victim of injustice. Yet, as Robert Egan observes, Lear's expanding vision of experience discredits his various attempts at dramatic artifice.[6] By the time he reaches the farmhouse in 3.6, he has been thoroughly unhinged by his ordeal, and in this setting he mounts what is ostensibly the most artificial of his dramatic fictions.

With the words "It shall be done; I will arraign them straight" (20), Lear seeks to transform the rude shelter into a courtroom. Immediately he begins to assign roles and block his characters. The gibbering Tom o' Bedlam is directed to take his seat as a "most learned justice" (21) or, as he is later styled in acknowledgment of his blanket-wrapped loins, "Thou robed man of justice" (36). The hysterical Fool, a "sapient sir" (22), benches by his side, "his yoke-fellow of equity" (37). Even the long-suffering Kent, in sorrowing sanity, must take his part: "You are o' th' commission, / Sit you too" (38–39). To be sure, a trial requires defendants to answer charges as well as evidence to incriminate them, and Lear calls for both: "Bring in their evidence" (35); "Arraign her first; 'tis Goneril . . ." (46). Here an ultimate tax is put on the theatrical imagination, that of performers and audience, since both evidence and defendants must be improvised. Though Lear's own madness is the most cogent evidence of the injury done him, he is hardly in a position to offer it as such. Instead, he claims that Goneril "kicked the poor King her father" (47–48), a demonstrable abuse, and in doing so he may well point to physical "bruises," correlatives of the internal hurt he has endured. The Fool, if not Lear himself, invents the correlative for the defendants:

> FOOL: Come hither, mistress. Is your name Goneril?
>
> LEAR: She cannot deny it.
>
> FOOL: Cry you mercy, I took you for a joint-stool
>
> (49–51).

Seizing on the device, Lear now indicts Regan, "another, whose warp'd looks proclaim / What store her heart is made on" (52–53). Then, with the strain on illusion at its greatest, Lear suddenly announces the disappearance of one, and thus both, of the defendants: "Stop her there! . . . False justicer, why hast thou let her scape?" (53–56). At this point, the trial collapses, Poor Tom muttering to the perplexed old man, "Bless thy five wits" (56), an allusion to the deranged mental powers that generated the illusory spectacle.

At once solemn and absurd, Lear's mock trial remains the truest dramatic fiction he has created.[7] Egan notes that the involvement of others, the community of participants, gives it special force:

> For the fiction . . . is not, like his previous visions, a private attempt to wield his experience into an orderly aesthetic pattern; it depends for its fulfillment not merely on Lear's own imagination and utterance but on those of a gathered, ritually participating community as well. . . . For a moment, a true moral need is thus expressed and fulfilled through dramatic artifice.[8]

The nature of this "moral need" is clarified in Victor Turner's *From Ritual to Theatre*. An anthropologist who employs the suggestive analogues provided by drama in analyzing social conflict, he offers a summary formulation of the way groups react in a state of crisis:

> As the conflict swells to crisis and the excited fluidity of heightened emotion, where people feel at once more enclosed in a common mood and loosened from their social moorings, ritualized forms of authority—litigation, feud, sacrifice, prayer—are invoked to contain it and render it orderly.[9]

Lear and his fellows, in this bizarre episode, are making such a response to their own crisis. But the small, disenfranchised, and alienated community that participates in the mock trial cannot possibly "contain" the chaos in the larger world of the play; it is rather a "ritual of affliction" that they perform. Still, it is the means by which they give sacramental expression to human values betrayed or abrogated in that larger world: "Ceremony is all the more precious because it is so terribly perverted to unjust ends, and conversely the picture in Shakespeare of disrupted ceremony gains significance because of the ideal of ordered behavior that it implies."[10] Here the whole process entails a curious inversion. The interruption of a ritual act or its conversion into parody ordinarily robs it of its sacramentality.[11] But in the "liminal" state through which Lear and his fellows are progressing, the ordinary sanctions are suspended. In this transitional phase of the rites of passage, images of disorder may become images of order. The same is true of the mock trial regarded as a dramatic artifice. The trial collapses when the defendants escape, but, as Egan points out, the trial as play includes within its fictional frame the disruption that ends it:

> Much of the efficacy of the play-trial and the stability of the image of moral order it sets forth derives from its participants' awareness that they are enacting not a real trial but a ritual imitation of a trial, and from the artwork's formal recognition of the chaotic realities over which it has no material power.[12]

While it is arguable that Lear, at any rate, can distinguish the imitation from the thing imitated, the fact remains that he dramatizes and thus encompasses formally the "corruption" (54) he can neither deny nor evade.

The language of the scene, like the stage imagery, is rich in complex associations. Virtually all of the leading motifs in the play are represented. There are references to gods and demons, sanity and madness, majesty and misery, parents and children, human beings and animals, as well as to sight, sex, sleep, clothes, food, fire, and "nature." Especially persistent and powerful in the scene are Edgar's evocations of the fiends that haunt and torment Poor Tom:

> Frateretto calls me, and tells me Nero is an angler in the lake of darkness. Pray, innocent, and beware the foul fiend. (6–8.)

At the outset he conjures up a picture of hell and its punishments, where Nero as the type of the tyrant fishes, perhaps for his lost soul. Lear, an "innocent" and yet "A king, a king!" (11), seems to respond by extending the imagery of hell: "To have a thousand with red burning spits / Come hizzing in upon 'em—" (15–16). Such associations help to establish the nightmarish quality of the scene and provoke in Lear the vision of judgment of which his trial is the corollary. Fraught as it is with apocalyptic imagery—"Arms, arms, sword, fire! Corruption in the place!" (54)—the scene anticipates Lear's expanded vision of "this great stage of fools," with its extremities of suffering and injustice, in 4.6. Similarly, shortly before he surrenders to exhaustion, Lear will put one of the ultimate questions of the play: "Is there any cause in nature that make these hard hearts?" (76–77). The scene is thus proleptic also of the final panel, the "promis'd end" or "image of that horror" (5.3.267–68).

In mounting the scene, director and designer must sort out the verbal images and decide which among them are merely imagined or hallucinated and which might have some relation to actual stage images. In a realistic or highly representational staging, for example, there might actually be a fire in a fireplace over which meat broiled on spits—Gloucester promised "food and fire"—all of which Lear converts to the iconography of hell. More stylized renderings would depend less on properties and more on the actors and the language, perhaps even eliminating properties altogether. In such renderings, ambiguities would abound, as they were probably meant to. The only physical properties that Shakespeare's script, and thus Shakespeare's staging, seems to call for are cushions (34), one or two joint-stools (51–52), and maybe a bench (38). Even if all properties were eliminated, there would still be plenty of interpretive choices to be made. For example, when Lear declares the court in session and turns to the "she-foxes," Edgar exclaims, "Look, where he stands and glares. Want'st thou eyes at trial, madam?" (23–24). Is the "he" who stands and glares the judge who faces the accused? Is this in the nature of a stage direction for the actor playing Lear? Or is the bedeviled Poor Tom, whose last speech and next fix on the "foul fiend" (17, 29), conjuring up an infernal spirit? That is, should Poor Tom be played as fully entering into Lear's make-believe trial or as merely pursuing "his own train of delirious or fantastick thought," as Dr. Johnson supposed?[13] Or what does his question mean about Goneril or Bessy or whatever "madam" wanting "eyes" at the trial? Eyes of spectators to look at her? Eyes like those of Lear or the fiend that glare at her? Or eyes of her own to see with? According to the way Edgar, by gesture or delivery, nuances the line, he may project for the audience a woman who is primping or one who is frightened or one who is blind and struggling to see. One might, as those who mount a play must, go through the scene line by line putting such questions to the script. In fact the choices to be made, like Poor Tom's devils, are legion. And I have said nothing about costuming and decor, blocking and movement, lighting and sound, all of which involve critical decisions about stage images. I think the best way of suggesting some of the theatrical possibilities of this visionary scene is to examine the treatments of it in the BBC and the Granada TV productions.

As the scene opens in the BBC version, Gloucester and Kent speak downstage in near darkness, the flame of an open lamp flickering between them. It is hard to tell much about the setting at first because of the prevailing darkness, and the details continue to be obscure throughout the scene because the guttering lamp remains the only effective source of light. The shelter is in any case a rude one, with a large opening upstage left, through which now and again lightning flashes in the distance as thunder rumbles. The reminder of the storm and the chiaroscuro technique employed in lighting the scene create an appropriately eerie effect.

We gradually make out the other characters, with an important exception. Behind Gloucester and Kent, the aged Fool sits at a wooden table where the lamp rests, and the nearly naked Edgar stands in the background by the entrance. But Lear is not in evidence. Not until Gloucester and Kent fade upstage and Edgar comes down to the table do we detect his presence. When the Fool begins his question, "Prithee, nuncle" (9), a bundle to his right moves and makes a sound, and suddenly Lear raises a shrouding blanket from his head to answer, "A king, a king!" (11). For this "discovery" the camera guides our attention to Lear's wild and wrinkled face, and then it moves back to fix the frame in a medium shot of the table and its occupants illuminated by the lamp. Turned toward the Fool, Lear seems to take his inspiration for the trial from the old man's self-consciously sage advice about misplaced trust. Announcing the trial, he calls on Edgar, who stands behind, to sit at the table on his right hand. Kent remains standing just upstage of Lear and the Fool. This is the basic blocking for the trial sequence.

On "Now, you she-foxes" (22), Lear himself rises and bends forward over the table gazing downstage left. Looking up, Edgar sees Lear "stand and glare" and then turns his eyes in the same direction; his jibe at "madam" draws an approving laugh from Lear. Lear's eyes remain on "her," his mouth moving slightly, as the Fool intones his lines about Bessy and Edgar rubs his belly and rebuffs the "black angel." His engagement with the visionary woman is so intense that he virtually ignores Kent's appeal that he rest. Kent in turn ignores Lear's attempt to seat him with the others, turning away briefly and then looking back sadly. "Let us deal justly" (39), says Edgar, suddenly dignified. Arraigning Goneril, Lear raises his hand to recite his oath and make his charge. Though the line is a mere formula as Hordern delivers it, its very inconsequence sorts ironically with his earlier oaths and maledictions. When the Fool addresses the accused by name, Lear speaks to him confidentially, and when the Fool equates her with a "joint-stool," Lear laughs.

In a stage production, a director would have to make certain decisions about the joint-stool. Is there really to be one (or two)? Does Lear point it out? Or does the Fool first make the equation? But since this is television, the camera determines what the audience sees or doesn't see, expanding or confining the space within the frame. Here the frame stays fixed on the group around the table, with the attention of all directed beyond the frame. It is up to us, responding to the mix of signals given, to imagine what may or may not be there. The effect is uncanny. By refusing to illustrate the text, the director forces the audience to do so, letting us create our own surreal combinations of fact and fantasy, our own stage images.

Lear's demented playfulness abruptly dissipates. Even as he gestures toward "another" with "warp'd looks," he cries out, "Stop her there!" (53). In his anxiety and frustration at the escape, he turns to Kent and the Fool, reproaching the Fool, and then stands helpless, yelping in his distress. This marks a new beat in the scene, characterized by a gathering together of the others in their care and concern for Lear. The Fool, now silent, reaches out to touch and stroke Lear's arm. Kent combines "pity" with an anguished rebuke for Lear's failure to retain "patience." And Edgar, who in this production is not only bare and begrimed but crowned with thorns, momentarily drops the mask of Poor Tom: "My tears begin to take his part so much," he says, with eyes shut and hands folded, "They mar my counterfeiting" (59–60). As Poor Tom again, he chases the dogs that bark at Lear—"Tray, Blanch, and Sweetheart." A tide of pathos threatens to engulf the scene when Lear sinks to his seat again. But Lear's next action counteracts it. From a dish he picks up a mangled meatbone and probes it: "Then let them anatomize Regan" (75). He pulls off a strip of flesh and eats: "see what breeds about her heart" (75–76). He flourishes a morsel: "Is there any cause in nature that make these hard hearts?" (76–77). He puts the question off-handedly, chewing. This blend of the pathetic and the grotesque is more compelling than either would be alone, and it expresses the spirit of the whole scene.

Having asked an ultimate question, Lear is ready to accept the ministrations of Kent, who comes to the table and leads him upstage to his long-delayed rest. As the old king settles on the cushions, he pulls imaginary curtains around him and collapses under his blanket in exhaustion. The faces of first Edgar and then the Fool in the foreground also reflect pain and weariness. The Fool, with almost all of his clown-like make-up wiped away, pronounces his final line like an epitaph and then literally puts down his head and sleeps at the table. But there is to be no rest. The remainder of the scene is given over to Gloucester's urgent warnings and the rapid decamping of the others with the comatose Lear. Only Edgar remains at the table in the flickering lamplight, taking what comfort he can from the "fellowship" of suffering.

When all is said, the BBC treatment of the scene is rather conservative. It is spare, though effective, in its use of stage images and close to the received text. By comparison, the Granada TV version is baroque in its imagery and prolific in its cuts. The pattern of difference seems clear. While Miller in the BBC version exploits the medium of television, he still treats *King Lear* as a play. Elliott, in the Granada version, means to turn the play into a film.

The Granada version reduces the scene by one half, omitting about sixty lines. Some of the same lines were also cut in the BBC production, such as Edgar's pastoral effusion (41–45) and his exorcism of the dogs (65–74), probably no great loss. The largest single piece of text omitted is Edgar's soliloquy at the end of the scene (102–15). This is also missing from the Folio, but it is not a matter of Elliott's following the Folio rather than the Quarto text, since he also includes lines from the Quarto and omits others from the Folio. Some of the cuts are surprising, such as Lear's initial naming of the judges

(21–22), his outcry against "Corruption in the place" (54), Edgar's aside on his tears (59–60), and, most of all, Lear's anatomizing of Regan and his question about "hard hearts" (75–77). There are also some changes in the readings of lines, of which more later. The point is that these modifications involve a re-making of the scene.

What is lost in language and the meanings it may convey Elliott seeks to supply in cinematic images. As the scene begins with a rush of background music, the camera is zooming through a driving rain over a thatched rooftop. It zeroes in on a hole in the roof to offer an aerial view of the white-haired Lear sitting on a bale of hay, the Fool also sitting and clinging to his right arm, and the convulsive Edgar thrashing at his feet. This tableau is presented four times from various angles. Now inside the barn-like structure, the camera at ground-level offers a rear-view that includes in the background Kent standing and Gloucester planting a torch in an upright. Other torches are already in place, and the scene is brightly lit throughout. The camera cuts to a close-up of Kent and Gloucester for their brief exchange and, with Gloucester's exit, back to the rear-view of the Lear group with Kent approaching it. As the angle is reversed, we see Lear, still in his kingly robes, staring down at the gravel-voiced Edgar muttering his hellish imprecations and then turning to the Fool, young but wan, to answer "A king, a king!" The next ten lines are collapsed into three, all Lear's: the excited "To have a thousand with red burning spits / Come hizzing in upon 'em" (15–16) inspires "It shall be done; I will arraign them straight" (20). The gesturing king attempts to rise on the last line but, weak as he is, can do so only with the help of the Fool and Kent. Once on his feet, he turns on "Now, you she-foxes?" (22), his next line, and the camera shifts away to show Lear and the others in the background and a single joint-stool looming large in the foreground. Now standing to Lear's right, Edgar points downstage with the line, "Look, where *she* stands and glares" (23). The ambiguities in the text are eliminated by changing the gender of the pronoun in the first half of the line and by simply eliminating the second half. One may say that the camera angle does make the joint-stool seem formidable.

Swelling music signals a change in mood as the trial begins. Gone is the lassitude Lear showed in the early tableau. The ritual invigorates him. Busily, he arranges Edgar, the Fool, and Kent to his left, who stand rather than "bench," the camera following him closely and then returning downstage to frame the joint-stool. As Edgar rasps out his call for justice, Lear points at "Goneril," cranes his neck toward the "honorable assembly," and waves his arms for the charge. Also gesturing, the Fool takes a step downstage to address the defendant, his high-pitched voice counterpointing Lear's sonorous assurance. Unable to contain himself, Lear bustles downstage on the line "Here's another" and scrambles to the right of the joint-stool after a cackling hen, which he seizes in triumph. "Ha," he cries, holding it up, "'tis Regan!" This reading replaces "Stop her there!" (53). The director thus eliminates another ambiguity and introduces an action and an image. We are shown Lear's chortling triumph and then, as the hen flutters from his grasp, his whimpering defeat. Moreover, as played here, it is a defeat at his own hands. Turning to pursue the escaping bird, he reproaches not one of the others but himself as the "False justicer."

The collapse of the trial leads directly to the collapse of Lear. While Kent and Edgar rush to his side, Lear weeps openly and sinks onto the bale of hay. His disappointment is inconsolable. He also shows self-pity. Hallucinating the "little dogs," he lovingly remembers "Sweet-heart" and makes kissing sounds, only to whine in protest that "they bark at me" (62). As he lies back to rest, he gasps out his last lines faintly. Here pathos is the dominant note. The cutting of lines 64–80 excludes any qualifying dissonance. And the handling of the rest of the scene reinforces the pathos. Lear's "We'll go to supper i' th' morning" is immediately followed by a close-up of the stricken Fool for his "And I'll go to bed at noon" (83–85). The bustle of Gloucester's urgent return still permits the camera to linger over the sleeping Lear and his tender removal by Kent and Edgar to the litter. There is also a close-up of the departing and despairing Edgar. But the end of the scene is given to the Fool in a style that recalls its beginning. We first see him from the rear sitting alone on the bale of hay as the others leave. After the cut to Edgar, the angle is reversed for the camera's zooming return to the abandoned and shivering figure. That last shot is of the Fool's face, mouth twitching and eyes shut against the pain of approaching death.

That Lear's mock trial should fare so well in such different productions takes us back to the power of the scene as a theatrical event. While the text may be variously realized in performance, since production is always interpretation, Shakespeare has provided the distinctive components on which to raise a structure of compelling stage images.

1. All citations are to *The Complete Works of Shakespeare*, ed. David Bevington, 3d ed. (Glenview, Ill.: Scott, Foresman, 1980).

2. Harley Granville-Barker, *Prefaces to Shakespeare*, ed. M. St. Clare Byrne (Princeton: Princeton University Press, 1970), vol. 2, 33n, 71. See also J. L. Styan, *Shakespeare's Stagecraft* (Cambridge: Cambridge University Press, 1971), p. 216, and Robert Egan, *Drama Within Drama* (New York: Columbia University Press, 1975), p. 43.

3. See Roger Warren, "The Folio Omission of the Mock Trial: Motives and Consequences," in *The Division of the Kingdoms: Shakespeare's Two Versions of 'King Lear'*, ed. Gary Taylor and Michael Warren (Oxford: Clarendon Press, 1983), pp. 45–57. Warren argues, on the evidence of the Folio text, that Shakespeare himself must have cut the mock-trial segment as a result of difficulties with it in rehearsal or performance (p. 45). Far from regarding the episode as "admirable on the stage," Warren views it as marred by "eccentric individual detail" that is bound to distract and confuse an audience (pp. 46–47, 50). Yet, as he also notices, the only modern production to omit the mock trial is Glen Byam Shaw's Stratford-upon-Avon production of 1959 (p. 53). Modern producers seem to think that the episode, despite its challenges, does work, and in the present essay I mean to suggest why and how it may work.

4. William Frost, "Shakespeare's Rituals and the Opening of *King Lear*," in *Shakespeare: The Tragedies*, ed. Clifford Leech (Chicago: University of Chicago Press, 1965), p. 192.

5. Granville-Barker, p. 34.

6. Egan, pp. 36–38.

7. Cf. James R. Siemon, *Shakespearean Iconoclasm* (Berkeley: University of California Press, 1985), p. 267. Siemon regards the scene as merely another example of the functioning of Lear's

oversimplifying "emblematic vision:" "he believes strongly enough in schematization to attempt the arraignment of Regan in the person of a joint-stool."

8. Egan, pp. 42–43.

9. Victor Turner, *From Ritual to Theatre* (New York: Performing Arts Journal Publications, 1982), p. 106. For "rituals of affliction," see pp. 109–10.

10. David Bevington, *Action Is Eloquence: Shakespeare's Language of Gesture* (Cambridge, Mass.: Harvard University Press, 1984), p. 172. On the "liminal" state, see pp. 3–5, 38, et passim.

11. Lynda E. Boose, "The Father and the Bride in Shakespeare," *PMLA*, 97 (1982), 330.

12. Egan, p. 45.

13. *King Lear: A New Variorum Edition of Shakespeare*, ed. H. H. Furness (New York: Dover, 1963), p. 207n.

Shakespeare in Miniature
The BBC Antony and Cleopatra
Richard David

Antony and Cleopatra raises many major questions, for Shakespeare provides fewer and less clear indications than in his earlier plays as to how the spectator should react; or, rather, these indications are here contradictory. Where, between the estimates of Caesar and of Cleopatra, are we to 'place' Antony? Where, between those of Charmian and Philo, Cleopatra? Then, too, this play, like all the others in the canon, is bound to provoke the usual arguments as to whether particular actors are well cast for particular roles, or whether the verse, here especially dense and subtly modulated, is effectively projected. In this paper I shall concentrate on those problems peculiar to the translation of the stage play into television.

Chorus, in *Henry V*, apologises for the attempt to contract 'the vasty fields of France' within the 'cockpit' of the Globe. How much more daring to confine Shakespeare's most wide-ranging and high-embattled play to the dimensions of 'the box.' Scale is, indeed, a major problem for this medium. It possesses, in one sense, a facility for expansion and contraction quite impossible in the constant focus of the theatre. On the other hand, both extremes, at least, are accompanied with serious disadvantages. If one attempts a broad effect on the screen and shows a crowd or even a number of figures in excess of four or five, these figures will be so reduced in size as to lose all reality and personal impact. The alternative, to switch to and fro between one and another of the elements in a crowded scene, destroys a characteristic Shakespearean effect, which derives from the *simultaneous* contemplation of opposing forces and their interreactions. At the other extreme the single figure, framed by the apparatus, especially in close-up, tends to become too insistent. Shakespearean soliloquies, which one might expect would come over well in the intimacy of the screen, are among the trickiest things to manage on TV. It is the interchanges between two, or at most three, actors that in this medium are most effective.

A second characteristic of the medium is its ability to focus upon, and so underline, particular points in the action. In this way the TV director acquires a power, infinitely greater than that of his counterpart in the theatre, to impose on the spectator his own particular interpretations, to nudge him into seeing this or that incident in one particular light. This magician's power can render invaluable assistance to the viewer but, misused, may turn his stomach.

I begin with matters of scale. Emrys Jones, in a stimulating introduction to *Antony and Cleopatra* in the New Penguin Shakespeare, has drawn attention to the construction of the play, built brick by brick of a multiplicity of short, often very short, mostly intimate or domestic scenes. From this Jones concludes that the play was probably written for the Blackfriars, that it is, in effect, closet drama, and that its central interest is purely psychological and not political. This concept, whether consciously or unconsciously adopted, enabled the director, Dr. Jonathan Miller, at least to present the drama with concentration and consistency. There were no wide panoramas, no outward-looking shots at all. The action all took place within enclosed spaces, mostly in small interiors ingeniously diversified by means of a minimum of decor, perhaps a single drape, red or purple, in the background combining, in Venetian richness, with a clear yellow or viridian costume in the foreground. In this almost claustrophobic confinement the emotional actions and reactions of the characters could be studied under the microscope.

I cannot myself, however, go all the way with this approach. Antony, Caesar, Cleopatra, are not just private individuals. Again and again the point is made that, however personal their behaviour, upon it depends the fate of millions; that the death of Antony 'Is not a single doom; in the name lay / A moiety of the world.' There are, in my view, at least five scenes that must be presented, if this universal dimension is not to be lost, on something greater than a domestic scale. They are the opening of the play, the first confrontation of Antony and Caesar, the banquet on Pompey's galley, Thidias' embassy, and the final tableau.

For the opening scene Dr. Miller employed a favourite technique—it became almost a mannerism—that was effective enough. Canidius and Ventidius (substituting for Philo and Demetrius) appeared in close-up. With 'Look where they come!' they drew apart to allow the more distant entry of the court to be sighted between them. As Antony and Cleopatra advanced towards the foreground, their Roman critics faded out of the picture; but the initial emphasis placed on them ensured that their critical presence was not entirely forgotten. Similarly, in the Thidias scene, the avenging Antony appeared in the background as Cleopatra and Thidias, whose foreground play had hitherto masked him, sprang guiltily apart. This scene, however, surely demands much more spaciousness. True, Antony is no longer surrounded by kingly attendants who, 'like boys unto a muss,' start forth to do his will. But the spectator needs to be reminded at this point that that court did indeed exist: the empty chamber, the half-hearted orderlies, need to be visually appreciated.

On the banquet scene I have little comment. The director, taking his cue from the ship's low-roofed cabin in which the entertainment takes place, succeeded in concentrating the scene, as if reflected in a convex mirror, without at all diminishing its robustiousness. But it was a pity, and not only because of the duplication, to make a banquet also of the first formal meeting between Antony and Caesar. The object was partly, no doubt, to bring the parties into a common focus round the table (including Enobarbus, who, the text makes clear, is *not* a full member of the delegation), and partly to provide the latter with opportunities to 'casualise' his 'The barge she sat in' speech by gobbling fruit or quaffing wine between paragraphs. Nevertheless, and however surprisingly, this speech was a perfect marriage of realism and poetry. I have had in the past to criticise this brilliant actor, Emrys James, for some gross comic exaggerations; it is all the more a pleasure to praise his Enobarbus almost without reservations.

The final tableau was the least satisfying of these 'grand' scenes, and its failure illustrates a major dilemma of TV. One needs here to see both the dead queen and Caesar as witness to and commentator upon her fate. In the theatre there is no problem, for a stage has breadth and the two elements can be opposed, one on either side of it. On TV this opposition in breadth is impossible without a fatal reduction in the size of the figures, and contrast can only be made in depth (the stage, of course, has this dimension as well). In this performance only the back of Cleopatra's head was seen, but this won't do: her dead image, 'looking as though she would catch another Antony,' is as much a summary of the play as Caesar's comment. We need both.

Lesser, but strikingly successful, examples of Dr. Miller's contrast-in-depth technique were, first, Antony's sentimental farewell to his attendants, performed in the background, with Cleopatra and Enobarbus, as puzzled commentators, occupying the foreground. A second was Caesar's reception of Antony's death. After a first outburst close to, he strides distractedly to the back of the picture but remains visible while his courtiers, in the foreground, whisper about the conflict of emotions that racks him. I might also mention, in a simpler vein, the ravaged face of Octavia in close-up while Caesar and his followers withdraw up-stage to plan revenge for her desertion. A pity, I think, that this picture did not conclude part 1 of the production, which instead went on to show the preparations for battle but stopped before the battle itself.

It is to be noted that Pompey's first colloquy with his associates, Menecrates and Menas, is couched in (for this play) uncharacteristically stiff and pompous verse. This was well mirrored by positioning the trio very formally, in a straight line facing the camera, and without much movement during the scene. Unfortunately this foreground-trio arrangement was repeated in the following scene between Caesar, Antony, and Lepidus and later became, like the contrast-in-depth, almost a mannerism. Lest, however, I may seem to be suggesting that the production as a whole was too static with too little variation in focus, I must express my particular admiration for the director's skill in modulating, continuously, smoothly, and appropriately, from group to close-up and back again. From dozens of good examples I cite Antony's complaint to Octavia, set as a bedroom scene (and, like so many other scenes, extremely attractive visually); and the scene in which Antony tells Enobarbus of Fulvia's death, which in control and timing could hardly have been bettered.

A television production is bound to be reduced not only spatially, to within the limits of the 'box', but temporally, to within a strict time-schedule. Cutting is inevitable. In a medium, and in a conception of the work, where what is emphasised is the intimate and the personal, it was no surprise that the major cuts were in just those elements that stress the play's wider geographical and political environment. Ventidius in Parthia of course disappeared: the scene is a regular casualty even in stage productions (but why retain the cue for it in II.iii?). Caesar's roll-call of Antony's kingly allies was shed, along with other more casual mentions of classical names. This was understandable, but closed one window onto the wider world. There were no soldier witnesses to Enobarbus' death; and it was hard to forgive the omission of the marvellous scene where other common soldiers hear 'music under the stage' and recognise the moment when Antony's luck finally leaves him, a scene that extends the connections of the play even beyond the natural world. To another painful cut, the total extinction of Treasurer Seleucus, I shall return.

Just as *Antony and Cleopatra* demands, if I read it rightly, that certain weight-bearing scenes should be presented with some grandeur, so there are certain speeches that crystallise the import of key moments in the action and whose prophetic quality must not be weakened under the pressure of too much realism. The most striking of what I may call these 'motto speeches' is Cleopatra's 'O withered is the garland of the war,' and this, for me, was irreparably ruined by being interspersed with gasps and even howls of hysterical anguish. A somewhat similar case is Antony's 'Sometimes we see a cloud that's dragonish.' This began well but went off, again because the hysteria that might well in actuality colour such an admission of total failure became too obtrusive for the speech to perform its function of pictorialising Antony's final dissolution.

As I proposed at the outset, I have (except when touching on the verse-speaking) concentrated upon the problems that the play poses for the *television* director in particular, but I cannot altogether omit reference to more general matters of casting and direction. With Colin Blakely's Antony I was really very well satisfied. He succeeded admirably in suggesting both the basic opportunism of the man and the geniality and generosity that make him, however clearly his faults may be seen, so beloved by his followers. He lacked only physical stature: references to Hercules as his ancestor and prototype were discreetly edited out, and when Cleopatra cries to him 'I would I had thy inches,' she was seated and Antony conveniently on his knees. This inevitably had some effect in diminishing the larger-than-life quality that I think (the director may not agree) this hero, above all heroes, requires.

I was not so happy with Jane Lapotaire's Cleopatra. She was lively, varied, pointed; but the wrangling, hopping, teasing queen must, above all things, remain regal, and in this she did not for a moment convince me. She also lacked something of the mystery, the never-ending unpredictability of the character. Some of the blame for this must fall on Dr. Miller for his direction of the last movement of the play. The trouble, indeed, began earlier, with the scene with Thidias. There could be no doubt that Cleopatra *did* 'mingle eyes' with Caesar's lackey, and to some purpose; but from the moment of Antony's entry her entire and unswerving loyalty to him could not be questioned. The two sequences just did not square. In the final movement nothing was allowed to cast doubt on the fixity and purity of her intention to follow Antony in death: witness the cutting of the scene with Seleucus which, although its place in the plot may well be to disguise from Caesar that Cleopatra is 'absolute for death,' yet has different overtones for the audience in that it shows us the lady of infinite variety maneuvering to the last. A pious widow, even an Isolde, is, to my mind, a poor substitute for Shakespeare's serpent of the Nile.

I have already praised Emrys James' Enobarbus, although a similarity in the trim of his beard to Antony's puzzled some viewers I know. Tribute must also be paid to Ian Charleson's Aberdonian, but by no means inhuman, Caesar, a more subtle portrait than what we are usually given. A black Iras nicely differentiated the two waiting-women and added a welcome touch of the exotic.

Three curiosities. It was surely a mistake to introduce part 2 with a written prologue that attempted to explain what happened at Actium. Even if this had not been written in a script that was hard to read, even if we had been given time to read it, the shift in the medium from drama to literature would still have struck a wrong note. Secondly, could not something more have been made of the monument? It was absurd for Cleopatra, in fear of capture if she left her monument, to refuse Antony a last kiss when he was already within easy kissing distance. And is it because it is hoped to show the production in India and China that all embraces were banned and kisses confined to the hand?

Finally one has to ask who would have benefited from this showing of the play on TV. I cannot believe that one who had neither read the play nor seen it on the stage could have made much of it here; but that is perhaps too much to expect. The student, with some instruction in the piece but no opportunity of seeing it in the theatre, might have received some help in understanding how it operates and would perhaps have gained in appreciation of some of the poetical set-pieces. To the professors, *any* production of the play should provide food for thought about Shakespeare's extraordinary *tour de force*. I must nevertheless confess that to me it seems that the necessary miniaturisation for TV must be more damaging to *Antony and Cleopatra* than to any other play in the canon.

Production Design in the BBC's Titus Andronicus
Mary Z. Maher

The final play produced for the BBC Shakespeare was the seldom performed revenge tragedy *Titus Andronicus*. As a guest of executive producer Shaun Sutton, I was allowed to audit and record during the process of translating a difficult and bloody play into a production that might appeal to a general audience. A number of the BBC's production staff shared insights and information with me, including director Jane Howell, lighting director Sam Barclay, costumer Colin Lavers, properties buyer Magda Olender, and visual effects designer Colin Mapson. This behind-the-scenes account of the production process provides a perspective on what the video viewer actually sees.[1]

Jane Howell is a veteran director for the series. Her credits include the three parts of *Henry VI*, *Richard III*, and *The Winter's Tale*. In a *New York Times* interview, Howell said,

> I was given a choice of six Shakespeare plays and *Titus* seemed impossible—so I decided to do it. I couldn't make sense out of it to start with, but there's a scene where someone kills a fly and Titus asks, "How if that fly had a father and mother?" Until then I wasn't sure if the play was by Shakespeare, but that beautiful simple image told me it was. Also in that scene Titus' grandson, Young Lucius, makes his first appearance, and it was the boy that made me decide to do it.[2]

The visual emphasis on the grandson of Titus and the eldest son of Titus' eldest son Lucius is perhaps Howell's biggest departure from Shakespeare's text. In Shakespeare's play, Young Lucius' presence is not called for by the playwright until 3.2. Yet Howell chose to tell the story as if the boy were a master observer of the action. Young Lucius is played by Paul Davies-Prowles, an actor who looks like an English schoolboy.

Howell's directorial concept was that the story could actually be the dream of Young Lucius. She carries out this idea by overlaying the actual Shakespearean text with a "video text," not only interjecting Young Lucius more prominently into the scenes in which Shakespeare has written him, but also featuring him as a powerful visual image in scenes where he does not appear in the original text. Consequently, Young Lucius shows up in the video production far sooner than 3.2. Howell's conception comes partly from her own son's experiences with nightmares at the age of nine, and partly from Titus' line at 2.1.251: "When will this fearful slumber have an end?"

In the BBC production, Young Lucius is introduced as the leader of the Roman procession to the Andronici tomb for burial of the sons killed in the recent capture of the Goths. By the end of 1.1 Titus has become enraged at yet another of his sons, Mutius, and has cut his throat in anger. The director breaks this scene at 1.1.385 by having Young Lucius retrieve Mutius' cloak and the knife that killed him after the fray is over. Thus innocence has its first look at the pattern of family revenge.

Young Lucius is interpolated into the action at other crucial points. He appears in the famous fly scene, reading a book quietly at first and then appearing in reaction shots during the conversation between Marcus and Titus. When Titus kills the fly, he takes Young Lucius' dagger, not Marcus', as the text implies. The boy is also closely integrated into the episode where Lavinia names her attackers by scratching their names in a sandy plot. His presence in all of these places astonishes us because we wonder what happens to children who view such grisly events. In 5.2., Young Lucius is added to the camera shots and actually takes part in the scuffle to apprehend Chiron and Demetrius. As their throats are cut shortly after, Howell ends the death ritual with a closeup shot of the boy's face silently reacting to yet another gory act.

It is in the final Thyestean banquet that Young Lucius actually becomes an accessory to murder. In the opening shots, it is his role to pour the libations over his father's hands for the "feast." He is also included as one of the three servers at the banquet, along with Titus and Lavinia, and it is Young Lucius who slips the dagger to Lavinia, the murder weapon intended for Tamora. As irony would have it, the dagger is first used by Titus on Lavinia.

The last of the multiple killings that follow is Lucius' stabbing of Saturninus. Howell has Young Lucius leap upon his father's neck, crying "No, no!" This gesture implies that despite the temptation to revenge and retribution, the boy retains an ultimate sense of morality. To watch his own father commit murder is too much for him emotionally—he cannot stay uninvolved as a passive observer.

The final accession scene has been separated from the banquet scene as if it happened later and was intended to be a formal burial ceremony as well. In it, Howell places Young Lucius beside the corpse of Titus, weeping. Although Marcus requests that Young Lucius kiss the corpse, he declines and instead goes to a place beside the entrance of the tomb, where the camera picks him up, gently holding the small black coffin containing Aaron's baby son. In the final shots of the production, the camera features Young Lucius' face. At first he looks at the baby, then his face is briefly obscured by Marcus closing the lid, and then we see his face upturned with an expression of sadness and confusion.

Howell's concept is directly reinforced by the costume designer. She asked costumer Colin Lavers to create a pair of steel spectacles to rim the boy's eyes. These glasses attract the viewer's attention because they are not Elizabethan nor Roman, but eighteenth-century. The glasses have a peculiar horn-rimmed effect and drape over the boy's ears rather than behind them. They are indeed an arresting stage property, and the camera catches them in a number of close-up and reaction shots. Also, Young Lucius never changes his costume throughout the play. He is constantly clad in a uniform of a neutral tan color.

Thus, Howell shifts the point of view of the narrative structure of the play by enlarging the role of Young Lucius and using the camera's ability to select visual images of the boy and interject them in strategic places. The viewer receives the impression that this story is told from the angle of vision of Young Lucius: the play is in part about a boy's reaction to murder and mutilation. We see him losing his innocence and being drawn into the adventure of revenge; yet, at the end, we perceive that he retains the capacity for compassion and sympathy. It is a privileged commentary created by the director within the television medium.

Costumer Colin Lavers felt that the shock of all the gore and blood in the play needed to be tempered with special costume touches. Thus the Roman soldiers are clad, for early parts of the play, in tunics of tan (to represent sand) trimmed in red (blood). Toward the end of the play, when Lucius returns with an army of Goths, the soldiers' costumes are mostly red, trimmed with tan. By this time, the soldiers are "far steep'd in blood" and their costumes reflect this decline into barbarism. However, Howell decided not to move to the other extreme and to "stylize" the play with scarves and symbols of bloodshed, as has been done in productions in the past:

> I've done it reasonably realistically. . . . I think it would look strange to see red ribbons on the [television] screen and so, when throats are cut, there are rivers of blood. I suspect it will seem shocking, but the play is very like what is going on today. It is set at the end of the Roman Empire when the Goths were sacking Rome, but you can't shrug it off as some past barbaric age. People are still having their hands cut off. Women are still being raped. People are still being slaughtered.[3]

Costumes were designed to reflect the differences between the Romans as civilized and well-governed countrymen and the Goths as lawless barbarians. For example, colors are sharp and defined on a Roman costume, diffuse and textured on a Goth. The costume period, said Lavers, is "reminiscently Roman rather than authentically Roman." The generals wear sparely styled tunics to suggest a tailored dress uniform. Foot soldiers have pre-shaped leather vests over their uniforms.

The aristocratic Romans (Saturninus, Bassianus, Lavinia) are attired in flowing costumes of polyester; this fabric is often chosen because it drapes softly and holds its shape well. The Emperor's corpse is attired in a royal purple color; the aspirants wear cornflower blue and lavender. The men wear soft suede boots made for the production and color-coordinated with their costumes. During the succession scene in Act 1, scene 1, both Saturninus and Bassianus wear white drapes over their costumes as symbols of candidacy (expecting to be elected by the Senate); they are referred to in the text as "candidatus" and the costume was copied from those actually worn during the historical period. At the Emperor's funeral, the senators wear black mourning drapes over their senate robes. After the funeral, the senators wear grey-colored togas with grey-colored masks which are molded from an acetate roofing material. At first, only the servants wore masks, but Howell liked the effect and felt that putting masks on the senators contributed to the idea of anonymity—of the "faceless crowd" they become when making decisions for Rome. When the foot soldiers and servants wear masks, interestingly enough, the masks have no mouths. All this tells the audience that the world of the Andronici is not characterized by political freedom and democratic ideals.

All the rituals of Rome—election, funerals, sacrifices—were well re-searched by the production design people to include burning of incense, washing of hands, burning entrails (sometimes animal, sometimes human), and the addition of ritual blood ringing the soldiers' eyes during ceremonies involving death.

The Goths are attired in skins, hides and furs—coarse-grained fabrics with nap and texture. Demetrius' and Chiron's costumes were inspired by Kiss, the rock-music group. The brothers look like huntsmen in rough, leathery ma-terial trimmed with bits of fur. Both wear chains around their necks as well as small skulls or dead animals dangling from their belts. Their hairstyles are suggestively punk and spiked; Tamora especially looks like a punk queen in a shock of unruly red and orange hair with small ghouls braided into it. She also wears a gold ring through one side of her nostril, and her necklace is made of chunky, irregular beads. Her make-up is overdone, looking very much like paint, and she appears in a gown cinched with a corselet made of what looks like fish scales—a creature who has no doubt oozed from the slime. All of these details contribute to the savage, animalistic effects desired. After Tamora becomes Empress, her costumes start to resemble Saturninus': she wears more softly-draped dresses. Just before she marries Saturninus, her costume emphasizes her breasts, her sexuality. After she has given birth, her costume allows her breasts to fall loosely, as if she were a nursing mother.

Although he accompanies the Goths, Aaron is attired more stylishly than the brothers (Chiron and Demetrius) he manipulates. He wears a buff-colored suede jacket with full, puffy sleeves and fur around the neckline. Diamond-shaped steel studs are splayed over one shoulder and down one sleeve. His bare chest is adorned with a shiny necklace that looks as if it is constructed of large brass washers welded into a primitive design. He wears form-fitting tights of dark rough wool and buff-colored, studded suede boots. In Act 4, scene 2, where Tamora's black baby is delivered to him, he dons a long, silvery caftan that reminds us of his Moorish ancestry. Both his costumes and Tamora's tell us that these two are very physical, sensual people. As Howell says, "The Goths have no shame about their actions."[4]

In the scene where Tamora and her sons Chiron and Demetrius appear as Revenge, Rapine and Murder, the costumes connote a kind of morality-play feeling. Tamora is attired in a dark-purplish silk robe that was dyed to create the effect of dried blood. Prior to production, the designers contemplated having the characters wear masks; however, these proved to be unwieldy and slightly unnatural to speak through in performance, so the faces of the characters were made up to look like masks instead. Tamora's make-up is white with grey shadows that shape her face into a skull. Chiron's and Demetrius' make-up is a slanted slash of black (each character's slash going a different direction) across the eyes. This make-up design gives the impression of forest animals, perhaps raccoons or wild birds of prey. When Titus kisses Tamora at 5.2.148 (a piece of stage business not in Shakespeare's text), we get what Howell calls "a kind of pornographic excitement." Indeed, Tamora is acted in such a way that discussions of murder arouse her; even Aaron suggestively sheathes and unsheathes his sword in dialogue spoken about his paramour.

Because of budget restrictions, "doubles" of costumes could not be constructed. Out of about five "takes" of Lavinia spitting her tongue out during Marcus' long speech of woe at 2.4.11–57, the final take was used because her costume was sufficiently soiled by that time to look realistic. Also, as Howell pointed out, the actors were by then so thoroughly sickened and slightly hysterical from the gore of that particular scene as to give genuinely extraordinary performances. A similar thing happened during the throat-cutting of Chiron and Demetrius. Once the blood containers were tapped, the mess was so great that it would have necessitated totally reapplying the make-up and also costume changes. Since there was only one set of costumes for the final banquet scene as well, five hours of camera rehearsal went into it: there were four killings in this scene, and at one point Titus crawled up on the banquet table to stab Tamora. Viewers might notice, too, that the meat pie is oversized, very large, so that one cannot miss the point of Tamora's sons being baked into it.

Set designer Tony Burroughs created another of the "unit sets" that Jane Howell favors and first used in the Henry VI plays. For Titus, he designed a kind of amphitheatre arrangement of stair units that could be wheeled into place and moved around to suit the scene. The set included a large structure that represented the 500-year-old Andronici family tomb (used for both the opening and closing burial scenes), several archways on the lower level (in which centurions stood or corpses were hung), bleacher-like arrangements that held tiers of people, either senators in session or Goths in a camp conference. Changes in lighting, rearrangement of set pieces, and draping the set pieces were ways by which the basic unit was transformed into an amphitheatre, a forest, a banquet hall, a crypt, or a pit into which Titus' sons fall.

This forum-like arrangement worked very well for formal processions and for the scenes in the Senate; but of course, it had to undergo a metamorphosis to look like the forest to which the characters periodically retreat. It is perhaps ironic that the "green world" of Titus is not a place for purification and reorganization of values, but a place where atrocities and secret crimes are plotted and committed, well out of the sight of day. To create the woodsy effects, banks and levels of the set were draped with large fishnets sewn with khaki-colored rags that suggest greenness and leafy texture. Trees were added to this environment, but few were leafy—most were stickery-looking and bare, to increase the appearance of threat. At one point, seven mattresses were dragged in to provide the bottom of the pit that Quintus and Martius fall into.

Lighting changes, of course, made each transformation complete. The forest scenes were not shot in bright sunlight because the events of those scenes were violent and depressing. They were mostly shot in "overcast" light, making the day seem ominous and gloomy. These effects were accomplished by surrounding the brightest of the television ceiling lamps with huge lamp-shades. Also used was a technique where hard bright lights were bounced off a cyclorama encircling the set in order to create softer, more diffuse lighting effects. When the boys fall into the pit in 2.3, green light emphasized the unnaturalness of the incident and the eerie plot that Aaron concocted to have the two boys accused. Campfire effects were created by using flashing lamps to give the impression of firelight on the backdrops; smoke machines were brought in to increase the feeling of gloom and indistinctness, and smoke from the torches added to this atmospheric anxiety.

Certain special effects deserve description because of the care and handling of detail. All of the decapitated heads and severed hands were researched at the Royal College of Surgeons for authenticity. The properties builders looked at cadavers and pieces of bodies from autopsies. When Chiron's and Demitrius' throats were cut, special care was taken to build a kind of abattoir. A small covered pavilion was put up and carcasses of meat were hung about. Some of these were constructed by the properties people, but one genuine lamb carcass was ordered from a butcher, and this one would get most of the frontal shots from the camera. In an unusual moment, a stagehand spread Vaseline on the hanging meat to make it gleam under the lights. Under their vests, Chiron's and Demitrius' chests were strung with plastic blood tubes hooked to large pumps of fake blood. Then the boys were trussed up (just like the meat) in harnesses and hung upside down for the actual killing. Rehearsals had to be carefully timed, of course, because the actors could not hang upside down for long. Once the boys' throats were cut, rivulets of blood ran down their faces in true horror-story fashion. Chiron especially was heard to squeal like a pig as the knife neared his throat. This was an important night on the set because the scene could be shot only once. To avoid resetting for this difficult sequence the next day, the production ran overtime.

These design elements are not just interesting in and of themselves, but are part and parcel of the interpretation of the play. Since *Titus* is not a well-known play, one of the director's chief tasks is simply to get the plot across;

with eighteen deaths in the script, it is important that the audience know whose side each person is on. *Titus* also is full of action and highly over-wrought classical references, so the performers have a singularly heavy task in conveying simple narrative information. Nevertheless, Jane Howell made this her own production by the addition of Young Lucius' point of view. Through his eyes, we ask the consummate question about the Andronici and their vicious enemies, the Goths: Who really are the barbarians? We find a glim-mer of hope in the young grandson, that somehow the interlocking patterns of revenge can be broken with one heir who retains his moral sensibility and mourns the death of innocent children.

Finally, what we learn about television is how "the BBC standard" evolved. Meticulous attention to detail and thorough research backing up the minutiae of scenery and properties are what contribute to excellence in BBC drama. Even though a viewer might not catch that tiny flowerlet embroidered on the bedsheets or that specially made hairpiece on a supporting actor, the produc-tion staff ensures that the details are correct—on camera or not. The motto of the BBC is "the highest production standard in the world;" that standard was maintained throughout the very last production in the Shakespeare series.

1. Parts of this essay previously appeared in *Shakespeare Bulletin* and *Shakespeare on Film Newsletter* and are reprinted with permission here.

2. "Shaping a Gory Classic for TV," *New York Times*, 14 April 1985.

3. Ibid.

4. Ibid.

Comedies

Anachronism and Papp's Much Ado
H. R. Coursen

Frank Kermode, in his discussion of recent Shakespearean films in *The New York Review*, tells of the way Peter Brook took *King Lear* apart, even asked Ted Hughes to render a modern version, and finally became convinced of the power and validity of the Shakespearean treatment. The process worked. For all of its flaws and for all of the adverse critical reaction it has received, Brook's *Lear* is a moving reintegration of the inherited text. The Papp-Antoon *Much Ado About Nothing* recently aired on CBS demolishes Shakespeare's play very effectively, but it leaves in its place a cultural disaster.

For some incomprehensible reason, this *Much Ado* is set in 1910 America. The production is defeated at the outset by its conception. Aristocratic love and Italianate intrigue collide in mid-air with small-town America, bands, balloons, and Blue Ribbon Beer. Language, "By my troth," clashes with spats and gramophones, turkey trots, and Keystone Cops. The cops might almost be forgiven were they capable of some of the superb visual jokes that Mack Sennett achieved, but these police are embarrassing parodies of a silent screen whose conventions Director Antoon has not studied. A trombone and banjo accompaniment of "Hey, nonny nonny" competes for first place as the production's worst moment against a host of strong contenders. The others would demand a tedious listing, but surely Beatrice's vibrant soliloquy ("What fire is in mine ears?") becomes a trifle dampened when delivered into the splatter and spray of a Victorian sprinkler system. Such gimmicks quench what fire is in the play. The Elizabethan cuckold's horns simply don't suit a set for *Ah Wilderness!*—and *vice versa*.

Conceptual problems are augmented by Mr. Antoon's inability to pursue the play's dramatic curve. *Much Ado* is intricately but carefully crafted, creating its structure primarily by contrast, insight against obliviousness, one character against another, these lovers against those, this scene against the one before and the one after. As in so many of Shakespeare's plays, *genre* plays against *genre*, the melodrama of Claudio-Hero, the comedy of Beatrice-

Reprinted, with revisions, from the *Maine Times*, 23 February 1973.

Benedick, the farce of Dogberry-Verges. Mr. Antoon delivers what Sedulus in *The New Republic* accurately calls "a big, loud, indiscriminate bundle of farce, tragedy, melodrama, and fairy tale." With equal accuracy, Day Thorpe of the *Washington Evening Star* asserts that "Papp's travesty of Shakespeare has no wit, no pace, no point." Mr. Antoon so overpowers the inherited text with his 1910 clutter that, while the production may work in some way for someone not acquainted with the text, it must baffle someone who knows the play. Here, even a little knowledge is a dangerous thing. Dogberry tends, for example, not merely to confuse words but to reverse meanings ("benefactor" for "male-factor"). While he *might* say "monocles" for "manacles" as Antoon has him say, the confusion is hardly Dogberry's linguistic best. Knowledge of optics would suggest that "monocle" cannot be within the Shakespearean canon. The first O.E.D. entry of the word is dated 1858.

The question of "monocle" might seem a quibble, but it raises the question implicit in Papp's production, that of anachronism. Brook sets his *Lear* in some pre-history shortly after the invention of the wheel, thus surrendering the opportunity to project the play's renaissance opulence. But *Lear* does seem to emerge from some dim folkloric landscape, when Stonehenge stood unscarred on Salisbury Plain. Brook makes a choice, giving something up and, one hopes, gaining something else. We may criticize that choice, but we must recognize it as a valid option. *Much Ado About Nothing* does not offer 1910 America as option, any more than *Troilus and Cressida* offers Civil War America or *Julius Caesar* the Italy of Mussolini. Yet the problem with Orson Welles's production was not merely its displacement in time, but that the displacement defined the very complications which Shakespeare leaves unresolved in his play. Brutus may be a kind of Woodrow Wilson, but Shakespeare's Julius Caesar is hardly a Mussolini. When the director, even someone as brilliant as Welles, replaces the Shakespearean imagination with his own, rather than attempting to recapture some of its dimensions, as Brook does in his *Lear*, the result is almost always disappointing. Occasionally, sheer visual brilliance can atone for obtuse editing and amateur acting, as in Zeffirelli's *Romeo and Juliet*. While Zeffirelli allows Rembrandt and Vermeer to vie with Raphael and Botticelli, his Verona is realized in a way which magnificently complements his admittedly controversial conception of the play.

Yet, one may ask, how can Antoon be indicted for cultural miscegenation or anachronism? Is not Dogberry as out of place in Sicily as Elizabethan spirits in Athens, or striking clocks in pre-imperial Rome? Or *Much Ado* in 1910? Shakespeare's anachronisms have with the passing of time blended into the fabric of his plays. It is the province of scholars to tell us that striking clocks were a medieval invention and Elizabethan fairies were survivals of pagan gods treated very differently by historical Athenians like Aeschylus and Sophocles. And the question of Shakespeare's anachronisms misses a vital point. As Anthony Burgess says in his tongue-in-cheek book on Shakespeare, "Our heads swim at the ease with which the Elizabethans fuse, or confuse, disparate times and cultures." There, Burgess is being serious. Historical accuracy was hardly Shakespeare's concern. He went behind and beyond history, ignoring chronology and cultural distinctions when he could make a better play, when he could penetrate more deeply into the motives of his characters, as in his making contemporaries of Prince Hal and Hotspur. If true of Shakespeare, however, why cannot it be true for Antoon? Partly because our own age is so "historically aware," has been conditioned against "inaccuracy." Let a television aerial be seen behind Eliot Ness, let a phone ring in the Ponderosa, and the network vice president is inundated with outrage. We are, it seems, attuned so to detail that we cannot achieve that flexibility which Mr. Antoon imputes to us, that sense of timelessness in time which characterized the Elizabethan view of history. And certainly we cannot bridge a gap between cultures when those cultures are as confusingly fused as they are in this *Much Ado*.

When we claim we suddenly "understand Shakespeare" because some director, disciple of Jan Kott or not, has delivered an updating to us, we are kidding ourselves. At best we understand something about our post-human era that Shakespeare also perceived. We may understand in new ways the Oedipus, Orestes, Electra, or Antigone myths when recreated by a Cocteau, Sartre, Giraudoux, or Anouilh, but we must understand the Greek plays on *their* terms. We may glimpse the myth of ambition more completely when we see Kurosawa's superb *Throne of Blood*, but the film is a complement to *Macbeth*, not a substitute for it. A "modern" Shakespeare will move us closer to the mystery of *the* Shakespeare primarily by chasing us back to the text, to rediscover the complexity and suggestiveness which modernizing tends to insult and flatten. Antoon's *Much Ado* reproduces with incredible fidelity the form and pressure of 1910 America but, in doing so, it obliterates whatever Shakespeare may still be saying to us with *his* play.

Sedulus suggests that Antoon produces a schizophrenic combination "with the Shakespearean play rendered hysterical by its competitor." Certainly this is one impression the production produces. My own non-psychoanalytic theory is that someone said something like, "Nothing can come of *Much Ado About Nothing*—hell, it's an old play by someone who died a long time ago—so let's ignore it as much as possible and do *our* play." This, too, is an impression the production produces.

Conceivably, this *Much Ado* might have been less disturbing on a full screen, which could have accommodated the amount of junk which crowded the foreground, background, and middle-distance. True, the bust of Shakespeare on Don Pedro's mantel-piece is wryly amusing, but the introduction of a plastic bard is finally an archetype for this production. Sedulus tells us that he saw the production on a movie screen at the Folger Library. It was too much for him, and when crammed into an area of some 350 square inches, it was much too much for me. Watching a television production on a large screen usually creates palpable distortion—closeups are too large and suggestive background cries for explicit detail. Still, the size of the larger image might have helped this production accommodate its "grandmother's attic." A larger picture, however, would probably have made the acting even more painful than it was. Mr. Antoon and Mr. Papp have much to learn from Howard Zieff, director of TV's Alka Seltzer ads, where background is suggestive but authentic, not overly specific, not dominant. Not only do Mr. Papp and Mr. Antoon not know their play, they do not know their medium. The medium is not totally the message, but its dimensions dictate an intelligent response, which, in this case, we do not have.

Papp's production can be contrasted on many counts—conception, voice and acting, and visual quality—with Peter Hall's A *Midsummer Night's Dream*, also produced for CBS. Perhaps it is unfair to pit big-time New York impresarios against the Royal Shakespeare Company. The former are after something other than "the Shakespearean moment." The latter capture it superbly, and, as I have witnessed, the latter approach can work, even with young people, even with an Archie Bunker who can be wheelbarreled to the show. Papp panders to the young and to the "sophisticated" and to the Bunkers by translating difficulty into their idiom, by refusing to permit Shakespeare to teach them *his*. The Royal Shakespeare Company *Dream* moves us towards the Shakespearean idiom, "educates" us to it, convinces us of its validity, wraps us into the world of the play, then releases us to the pondering of our own identities, to those moments after the play is over that tell us that we have experienced drama, not "entertainment." Papp reflects a society. The Royal Shakespeare Company recognizes a culture and entertains us superbly as it excites our own recognitions. But, as I suggested, the comparison is unfair. Talent is in short supply in New York, money is plentiful, and Papp can only work with what he has.

The pretentiousness of the CBS operation can be measured by the "teacher's guide" which the network saw fit to mail out prior to the debacle. Like most "teacher's guides," it reduces difficult questions to the level of easy answers, historical problems to the level of contemporaneity, intelligence to the level of insult. I hope *no* teacher cooed the following questions: "What does the room a person lives in, or the clothes he wears, tell about his character? (What do your own physical surroundings or choice of clothing reveal about *you*?)" Well, if you are a beribboned military hero named Don John, fresh from Pershing's Mexican Campaign, you are obviously spacy about peace. Such discontent may be manifest in Richard III and Faulconbridge or latent in Iago, but we are asked what the ribbons and gold leaves reveal about Antoon's Don John. We must ask in return, why does he suddenly so vividly betray his recent past? Or do some military men become villains in peacetime, like the Vietnam Veterans Against the War—as opposed to the platitudinous and patriotic bomber pilots so recently repatriated from North Vietnam? I do not find the question implicit in *Much Ado*. It *is* relevant when Shakespeare's plays ask it—Richard III's sudden fashionableness, Petruchio's sudden unfashionableness, Richard II's pursuit of Italian styles, Hamlet's nighted color, the new or improved garments noted by Lear and Gonzalo, the new clothes that don't fit Macbeth. The question of "fashion" reaches deeply into *Much Ado*, particularly through Claudio, but the "guide" does not touch these dimensions. One assumes that Papp will never undertake *Love's Labour's Lost*.

Strangely, after quoting both Jack Kroll and Leonard Digges on the primacy of Beatrice and Benedick, the "guide" suddenly makes Claudio and Hero "the central figures." The latter viewpoint can be defended, of course, but its *a priori* assertion renders the "guide" a wee bit schizoid. Whether the statement reflects Antoon's opinion is moot. He is quoted as saying that he wishes "to strip away what everybody says the play is all about and just tell the story." Such a statement is more than a neat evasion, it represents an abrogation of responsibility. A director need not accept received critical opinion, but he should be cognizant of it. Suffice it that Mr. Antoon wishes to tell some story about 1910 America. Obviously, he put his study into that area, and that area alone. Suffice it further that the director as storyteller is at best a romantic metaphor and at worst a vivid confusion between drama and prose fiction.

"Were the 'tough minded women' of 16th Century Sicily different from the women of 1910 America?" asks the "guide." How does anyone begin to answer that one? Which of several possible biases are we supposed to detect behind the question? The answer, I guess, one that should satisfy the most barnacled male chauvinist and the most encrusted female liberationist, is, Hell no, they were women, weren't they? The "guide" asks students to discuss "post-Vietnam America." Answer: when will that be? The "guide" asks, "How does Shakespeare portray the transition of Beatrice and Benedick from love's mockers to love's victims?" Answer: he doesn't. "How would Dogberry tell the story?" An exercise in point-of-view which would delight Henry James, Scott Fitzgerald, and Percy Lubbock. Answer: not as confusingly as Antoon tells it. "Do you think people would have acted that way in 1910?" Answer: irrelevant, immaterial, and requiring an opinion of the witness which only at least two former lifetimes could provide—one which had simultaneously absorbed the conventions of aristocratic Sicily and Elizabethan England, and one which had been expended in small-town 1910 America. And a third, of course, which could objectively view the former lives. "Would Beatrice have fainted away?" Answer: no, she would not have been caught at the same altar with Claudio. I belabor the "guide" not merely as target practice, but because, in its own benighted way, it so accurately reflects the production. Pity its compiler. She, Gloria Kirshner, was ambushed between falsehood and schizophrenia.

Conception, direction, acting and voice, accommodation to the medium—these are criteria one must consider in assessing any production of Shakespeare. Mr. Papp and Mr. Antoon fail vividly in each area. They neatly destroy the Shakespearean play, but all the king's whores and all the king's money do not put it together again.

Shakespeare and Anti-Semitism
Two Television Versions of The Merchant of Venice
Marion D. Perret

Almost every new production of The Merchant of Venice, a play that scholars assert is not primarily about religion, [1] is greeted by a protest that Shakespeare is anti-Semitic, which is then countered by an assertion either that as a man of his time he could hardly be otherwise or that his humanity transcended the prejudice of his age. [2] Seeking to make this play less offensive to current sensibilities, productions now tend to present Shylock more as victim than as villain and to treat the Christians as harshly as they have treated the Jew. An outstanding example of the effort to emphasize the playwright's sympathy for Shylock by focusing on the moneylender is the British National Theatre's 1970 production, starring Laurence Olivier, which with only slight changes [3] was telecast in the United States in 1974 as an ABC Theatre presentation. The 1981 BBC production for television, also attempting a version more palatable to modern taste, avoids this tightening of focus on Shylock, played by Warren Mitchell, but asks us to ponder who is the victim, who the victimizer. Jonathan Miller, who was involved with both productions, [4] insists that this "is a play about anti-Semitism . . . totally symmetrical in its prejudices." [5] The National Theatre presentation emphasizes Shylock; the BBC, symmetry of prejudice. Comparing the versions for television illuminates ways of attempting to present the play as not anti-Semitic; surprisingly, it also reveals that the first approach may, by trying too hard, suggest the opposite of what it intends.

We need not detail all of a production to grasp its particular quality: before one has watched twenty minutes of each, one can detect the National Theatre's emphasis on money, the BBC's on love. The massive Victorian furniture and pervasive bric-a-brac convey the stifling materialism of the National Theatre's version; in contrast, the golden light rippling through Venice and the silvery light bathing Belmont give a sense of spaciousness to the BBC version. What Miller says of the play itself neatly captures the difference in atmosphere of the two productions: "It's the world of legislation versus the world of mercy." [6] This essay will concentrate on III.i and IV.i, because these scenes—which contain the famous pleas for compassion, Shylock's "Hath not a Jew eyes?" and Portia's "The quality of mercy is not strained"—focus for us how each production as a whole deals with the problem of anti-Semitism.

The National Theatre version is, as one reviewer delicately understates it, "not exactly the play that Shakespkeare wrote." [7] Another reviewer is considerably more blunt about the purpose of this reshaping: "The main, astounding achievement . . . is to make horrifyingly credible . . . the gruesome old bargain at the heart of the play. [This production] virtually rewrites the origi-

Reprinted, with permission, from Mosaic, special issue on "Film/Literature," 16:1–2 (Winter/Spring 1983), 145–63.

nal to do so. Out goes much of the comedy, out Belmont's fairy-tale romance. Instead, there's the assumption that the central, unavoidable experience of the play is that explosion of frank, murdering tribal hatred at the core of it; that the task of any revival is not to skirt around this, but to create afresh a believable world from which it can spring."[8] How much of the adaptation was due to Miller, how much to Olivier, whose Shakespearean films show extensive tampering with text, is unclear. In any case, the manipulation eliminates as much as possible motives for revenge unflattering to Shylock.

The National Theatre production rearranges scenes into large blocks[9] to make the love plots twined by Shakespeare easier to follow and to emphasize the elopement of Jessica, though not her love for Lorenzo, because the pain it causes Shylock becomes his primary motivation for demanding the pound of Christian flesh. Shylock still underlines the irony of Antonio's seeking to borrow from one he has condemned and mistreated as a usurer (I.iii.103ff.), [10] but because the Jew's soliloquy (I.iii.38ff.) has been cut we get no indication that Shylock is masking the vindictiveness Shakespeare has him express as Antonio comes toward him:

> I hate him for he is a Christian,
> But more for that in low simplicity
> He lends out money gratis and brings down
> The rate of usance here with us in Venice.
> If I can catch him once upon the hip.
> I will feed fat the ancient grudge I bear him.

> (I.iii.39–44)

Also cut is Shylock's explanation to Tubal: "I will have the heart of him, if he forfeit; for, were he out of Venice I can make what merchandise I will" (III.i.119–21). It is easier to sympathize with a Shylock who seeks Antonio's death because his daughter has betrayed him than with a Shylock who seeks Antonio's death because the merchant has undercut his price. Focusing on the more attractive motive invites us to feel that depth of love for Jessica has become twisted into bottomless hate for Antonio by a kind of psychological *lex talionis*: his beloved daughter, his heart, has been taken from him by a Christian, so his revenge will be to remove the heart of a Christian. But we are asked to make the equation by this presentation, not by Shakespeare, who discourages us from doing so by showing that to Shylock a daughter is a possession less valued than ducats and by giving us before we even know of Jessica the uglier motive that the National Theatre has excised.

What makes it possible to cut these explanations of Shylock's behavior is that this whole production emphasizes the transcendent importance of money. Unabashedly intellectual, Miller has explained that he considers this production an "experiment" designed to show, as Hannah Arendt has shown, that "modern anti-Semitism . . . [is related to] 19th-century capitalism and politics rather than [to] biblical theories about the death of Christ;" he has thus set the play in the nineteenth century to put Shylock "within the context of the Rothschilds Banking House."[11] When we first meet Shylock at his desk, busily signing papers while Bassanio asks for money, the Jew seems the image of a successful financier, thoroughly at home in his bank. How central money is to his life becomes apparent as he prepares to leave; we realize, with a slight shock, that the "bank" is his home. This is a Shylock who, needed but not socially accepted by the genteel Gentiles, puts a top hat over his skullcap in a fruitless effort to seem one with the frock-coated gentlemen who speak frostily to him.

Setting this production in the financial world of the late nineteenth century lowers its emotional temperature. Black-coated men converse stiffly, seldom touching; real feeling, especially affection, is on the whole repressed, though irritation frequently ruffles the polite surface. By making us constantly aware of money, the setting effectively "unmasks the romantic element as so much flimsy sentimental decoration. The whole apparatus of treacly late-Victorian sensibility is wheeled into position to reduce the love-affairs to so much beribboned marzipan, pastiche Mendelssohn. Portia's boudoir bursting with tastelessly ornate furnishings and status-affirming dresses, all bespeak a greedy philistine society whose real life goes on in counting houses and legal chambers." [12] The omnipresence of riches reminds us particularly of the Jew, for though the Christian is likewise concerned with money, we see Shylock devoted solely to increasing and protecting his goods. . . .

An emphasis on commerce and distance between word and emotion marks the opening of III.i. Solanio tries to extract new information about the fortune of their friend from Salerio, who is absorbed in reading his newspaper. As he triumphantly produces the most recent bulletin of disaster, Solanio appears more pleased with having the latest information than concerned about Antonio's fate. That these men do not seem to love or hate deeply makes us more aware of the intensity of Shylock's emotion.

The Jew, who appears, obviously agonized, at the door of his house, endures their gibes until on "There I have another bad match" doubled resentment drives him to whirl on them. Fuming with rage, frustrated by impotence, back turned to the Christians' scorn, he pauses in seething silence atop the bridge over which they have come. This moment of suspended movement and speech, electric as the instant just before a storm breaks, is crucial, because as we share Shylock's experience, we make with him the connection between lost daughter and lent ducats. We see what he sees—a house across the canal whose blanked-out second story windows and central door give it an uncanny resemblance to a dead face. And we hear what he hears—a funeral knell. While the bell continues tolling, the moneylender turns slowly: "Let him look to his bond." Shylock comes forward as he meditatively asserts his humanity ("Hath not a Jew eyes?"), then spits out his anger at being treated like a monster—like the winged serpent in the sculpture we see over his shoulder. This framing reminds us that the indignation hurled at the Christians is the wrath of a dragon severely wounded yet still dangerous. "Revenge"—as though driving his point home with a dagger, Shylock emphasizes the word by striking his hand over and over; then he strides past the Christians, touches the mezuzah on his doorpost, and enters the house. In retro-spect, the play's coolness up to this outburst seems carefully calculated not only to make a statement about a society in which money counts more than feeling but also to contrast with the emotional intensity of Shylock's great scene.

Cutting and rearranging of text effectively underscore the lack of affection in Venice, where Lorenzo and Jessica do not appear together (II.vi has been cut), so that we will think of her as deserting Shylock rather than joining her lover. The only physical expressions of affection have been the kiss with which Bassanio greets Antonio and the pat on the hand Shylock gives his daughter on "Do as I bid you" (II.v.54), whose emotional weight is increased by the Victorian context. In the rest of III.i, Shylock's passionate intensity is set against the formal restraint of Tubal, whose stiffly correct appearance and lack of a yarmulke remind us of the society to which Shylock is alien.

In this scene, which does not build to its own emotional climax but is continually more passionate than all the scenes preceding it, Olivier again and again gives us striking visual images that epitomize the Jew's emotion. At "Hast found my daughter?" Shylock's right hand holds Jessica's portrait against his heart; his left hand first strokes the picture, then sifts through ducats. On "Would my daughter were dead at my foot" he hurls her picture to the floor, smashing it. Shylock acts out extreme love turning to extreme hate, which he transfers to Antonio, over whom he has some power. On hearing of the Chris-tian's loss, Shylock pounds Tubal's chest in delight, explodes into laughter and a grotesque jig—a dance of death for Antonio. Tubal smiles at this child-like indulgence, but soon his eyes grow sad, for he knows what he must also tell. Lest we lose sympathy for the vengeful moneylender, we are given sen-timental vignettes of Shylock more sinned against than sinning: hearing of the ring traded for a monkey, Shylock stoops over his wife's picture, kissing it, sobbing; opening a desk drawer, he takes out a prayer shawl, kisses it and puts it on, covers his eyes, then lifts them to heaven. The words that accompany this emotional icon, "I will have the heart of him," are given an attractive context by the memorable visual images reminding us that Shylock is driven to hate by loss of a loved one. We are invited to respond to the prayer-shawled figure rocking back and forth in speechless grief without reflecting upon the words just uttered. We are encouraged to forget that he invites Tubal to the synagogue to plan the legal butchering of a human being; instead we are to recall Shylock the loving father, the devoted husband, the devout man. The scene is designed to wring sympathy for the revengeful Jew from even the hardest Christian heart.

So is IV.i, though it goes about this differently, building to a wrenching emotional climax after most of the scene has been played down so much that one reviewer could remark, "In the long history of The Merchant of Venice the trial scene can never have generated so little excitement; it is as flat as a puncture."[13] Antonio is allowed no closer to dying than removing his jacket in preparation, because the more we sympathize with him, the less we sympathize with Shylock. In this production Shylock carries a briefcase rather than a knife; Bassanio addresses "Why dost thou whet thy knife so earnestly?" not to Shylock, whose hands are serenely folded, but to one of the Jews who accompany him. We are reminded how little distinguishable from the Christians the Jew is, when Portia, apparently oblivious of the moneylender's skullcap, directs "Is your name Shylock?" to the merchant. In explaining to the Duke why he chooses to "follow thus / A losing suit," Shylock sounds like a professor patiently trying various ways of explaining an idea to a slightly dull class. Until he rises to leave, the issues of the trial are presented more abstractly than emotionally.

Because of the underplaying until Shylock's last moments, the action in this judicial chamber, which resembles a boardroom rather than a court, seems controlled less by the players, who deliver many of the important speeches sitting down, than by the long table occupying most of the room, a physical barrier representing a spiritual one. The actors appear more or less trapped between the table and the wall, with nowhere to move except to the other side of the table. With movement limited, what little there is acquires significance: the blocking becomes an ironic commentary on the action. When Bassanio begs the Duke "to do a great right, do a little wrong," what we see is the Duke in the center, at the head of the table, Bassanio to the left angrily proffering money, Portia to the right forbidding such settlement. Beyond them, on either side, are Shylock and Antonio, paired so that the one who has wanted money and now will not take it is aligned with the one who offers money, and the one who needs mercy is aligned with the one who has advocated mercy but now insists on the law. Portia sits on Antonio's side of the table when she gives, with some asperity, a lecture on mercy to Shylock, who sits opposite; she sits where Shylock had been sitting when she gives the Jew, now in Antonio's place and position, the law he had invoked. This shaping of what we see engages our intellect more than our emotions, so that intense sympathy is reserved for Shylock's collapse.

Powerfully presented, Shylock's capitulation disturbs us and those we watch react to it. With Portia's "Tarry, Jew! . . . if it be proved against an alien . . . ," the racial issue at last becomes openly and legitimately relevant to the trial. Barely tolerated by Venetian society because of his usefulness, the Jew will become useless, intolerable, if his wealth is confiscated. Shylock, stricken, bends over, grasping a pillar for support, only to hear that he must also give up his faith. In this production, the provision that the Jew be converted clearly stems from human vindictiveness rather than from Christian concern for a lost soul: Antonio, eyes gleaming, all but sneers the words. As Shylock crumples to the floor, his fellow Jews rush to his side; so, shortly, does Portia. They lift him; she, almost tenderly, lifts his head, checking to see that he is still alive. Then, relentlessly, she pursues her demand: "What dost thou say?" The life has gone out of this man; the head Portia raises has eyes that are blank, uncomprehending for a moment before they stare wildly as Shylock snaps rigidly upright, grasped by the men and his passion, like a madman physically restrained. We hear his high-pitched "I am content;" we see the image of a frozen scream, which when Shylock leaves the room will thaw into a keening that ceases to sound human long before it fades away. The camera shows us, in turn, the faces of Portia, Bassanio, Antonio and the Duke. Their horror is real, sustained for a minute before business resumes as usual.

Life goes on, but haunted by the Jew's torment, for as Bassanio's reaction to Shylock changes, Bassanio's relationship to Antonio changes: freed from the danger of losing his own heart, Antonio seems to have lost Bassanio's. As Shylock draws ever closer to obtaining his pound of flesh, Bassanio moves from touching Antonio's arm to comfort him; to putting his hands on the seated merchant's shoulders, stooping over him and sobbing; to embracing his friend in anguished farewell; to retreating to the door, turning away from what he cannot bear to see. (That Shylock and Portia are underplayed makes him seem almost overly demonstrative.) Bassanio's deepening experience of the suffering that Shylock causes seems to make him empathize with the suffering that Shylock experiences. While Portia coldly details the punishment for an alien who seeks the life of a citizen, Bassanio's troubled face appears over her shoulder. Until the Jew's piercing lament drives Antonio to bury his head in his arms, only Bassanio seems to grasp the cost to the moneylender of becoming a Christian. Raising a hand in futile protest, Bassanio looks around at each of the others, then drops his hand, disheartened. He gropes for a chair and sinks into it, his back to the rest. When the Duke reminds Antonio that he should "gratify" the advocate, Antonio thrusts the bills—Portia's, with which her husband had tried to save his friend's life—at Bassanio, who clearly does not want to touch this blood money. Disgusted, Bassanio offers the three thousand ducats, which he emphasizes are "due unto the Jew," over his shoulder to Portia, who refuses, demanding his ring, which he withholds until Antonio acerbicly presses him to let his love "be valued." After the others leave, Bassanio finally rises from Shylock's seat and turns to face the older man, who sits across the table; Bassanio looks off in the direction of Shylock's wail, spreads his hands in helpless resignation, and sighs heavily before walking to the door, coldly calling over his shoulder "Come, Antonio," as though summoning a dog. The men go together to Belmont, but Shylock's alienation goes with them.

Challenging our settled sympathies for the second time within this scene, this treatment of Bassanio is disquieting. For most of IV.i, he expresses what we feel: pity for Antonio, anger at Shylock, irritation at Gratiano, who repeatedly voices a loathing for the Jew so exaggerated that we side with Shylock against him—Bassanio, after several times touching his friend's arm to quiet him, finally in exasperation cuffs his shoulder to shut him up. Yet Bassanio walks out of the chamber seemingly as contemptuous of Antonio as Gratiano had been of Shylock. Our last vision of the trial scene is of Antonio following Bassanio, who has just exited, much as Bassanio followed Antonio at the end of I.i.

In this production, Act IV, scene i contains many visual echoes. Bassanio's bending in grief over Antonio and Shylock's doubling over in torment recall for us Shylock's tearful stooping to kiss his dead wife's picture. Portia's disdainful slapping down of Bassanio's gloves ("You teach me how a beggar should be answered") reminds us of Bassanio's refusing to tip the waiter who offered him his gloves in the café where I.i is set. Where the visual images in III.i direct our sympathy toward Shylock by summarizing his pain, those of IV.i underline an irony that is a caution against prejudice: Antonio's malicious insistence on the Jew's conversion has apparently cut the merchant—as well as the moneylender—off from the society he treasures.

. . . The emphasis of the National Theatre version on commerce and anti-Semitism leads to a slightly cynical de-emphasizing of romance: except for the last, the scenes at Belmont are played for laughs.[14] In the BBC production warmth of feeling is characteristic of both Belmont and Venice, and people everywhere are valued not for financial soundness but for fullness of humanity. The standard of humane wholeness, which makes the play seem more of a piece, makes us more aware of the dramatic architecture pulling together different kinds of bonds and setting Jew and Christian against each other to reveal the prejudice that must be overcome by love.

. . . Laughter, pleasant or unpleasant, rings throughout this whole production. It voices the high spirits and hostility of the young men, the joy of the lovers, and the intelligence of the Jew, who uses humor to ingratiate himself with the Christians. That we laugh "with Shylock and at Shylock"[15] makes the Jew less alien and threatening to us, but Shylock's chuckle does not bring him closer to the Christians he manipulates by its means or bring the Christians who mock him understanding of what they ape. Mitchell's Shylock, unlike Olivier's, does not try to imitate the Christians' accent or appearance, but he does imitate the behavior of those he hates, who in turn imitate his. As Miller remarks in introducing the BBC production, "The Christians are shown to be just as merciless and heartless as the unjust Shylock." This symmetry of prejudice in action keeps us from blaming only the Jew: that the inclination to torture is inhumanity common to all men is shown both in III.i, where Christians cruelly make sport of a Jew whom they accuse of cruelty, and in IV.i, where a Jew torments a Christian by insisting upon the letter of the law, then is tormented by another Christian in the same way.

III.i is a triptych whose primary theme is suffering, whose secondary theme is torture. The central panel shows Salerio and Solanio tormenting Shylock; one side panel shows us Christians concerned about a Christian's losses, the other, Jews concerned about a Jew's losses. Because we only *hear* about Antonio's woes, whereas we *see* Shylock's, as the scene progresses our sympathy is distracted from the Christian about to suffer at the Jew's hands to the Jew now suffering at the Christian's hands. In this production, the scene builds sympathy as well as redirects it: the most moving moment is not Shylock's plea for compassion but his final speechless anguish over the loss of Leah's ring. Despite this dramatic crescendo, we are not allowed to lose our intellectual awareness in emotion. The exchange between Tubal and Shylock is shaped to make us note that while the Christians are united by the intensity of their love and pity for Antonio, the Jews are divided by the intensity of Shylock's love of money and pity for himself. In II.vii Salerio and Solanio's mocking imitation of Shylock's "passion so confused" between his daughter and his ducats lessens our respect for the Christians; in II.i, Shylock's demonstration of this passion lessens our respect for the Jew. Characterized by constant undercutting of approval based on religious identity, the BBC production forces us to recognize how Shakespeare leads us to question sympathy that is based on theology rather than on humanity.

Appalled as we are by Shylock's inhumane insistence on his bond, we are equally repelled by Salerio and Solanio's inhumane treatment of Shylock. In this production the framing of their physical abuse and mockery of the Jew up to his climactic "And if you wrong us, shall we not revenge?" gives their silent response to Shylock's plea as much dramatic importance as Shylock's speech. This widening of the usual tight focus on Shylock seems designed not to distract us from the Jew's appeal, but to make us intensely aware of the need for it; the iconoclastic technique ensures that we, unlike Salerio and Solanio, cannot disregard the suffering immediately before us. We pity the Jew for his inability to respond to physical abuse with anything except words until those words shock us into realizing that, by the law of measure for measure, the Christians' torture of the Jew becomes ultimately the Christians' torture of the Christian, as Shylock demands that Antonio make good his word. The widening of focus shows the ripple effect of prejudice.

In this production Shylock unintentionally invites the mockery of the Christians by seeming to take part in their verbal game: Shylock's anger at Salerio and Solanio for assisting his daughter's "flight" leads them to refer laughingly to Jessica as a bird; to Solanio's "It is the complexion of them all to leave the dam," Shylock retorts bitterly, "She is damned for it." The Christians reduce action which hurts the Jew into wordplay. When the Jew seems to continue the wordplay, they applaud him and thereafter hear his words only as a stimulus for punning action. On Shylock's "My own flesh and blood to rebel!" Solario lunges for the Jew's genitals, as though Shylock had spoken of sexual desire, and Salerio locks his arm around the Jew's neck, half in playful embrace, half in stranglehold. This physical bond seems to remind Salerio of another, for he asks Shylock about Antonio's fortune. In response, Shylock catalogs Antonio's mistreatment of him, protesting "What's his reason? I am a Jew." At this, Salerio and Solanio first feign exaggerated surprise, then explode into laughter, aping Shylock to each other. On "Hath not a Jew hands?" Salerio imitates Shylock's characteristic gesture; on "organs," Salerio makes the horns of the cuckold. When Shylock says "If you prick us, do we not bleed?" Solanio pretends he has been stabbed; when Shylock says "If you tickle us, do we not laugh?" the two Christians tickle the Jew. To them Shylock's impassioned plea is merely a cue for artificial passion. Because of, rather than in spite of, their increasing insensitivity, we are far from indifferent to Shylock's frustration. The scene becomes almost unbearable.

The unnaturalness and wrongness of the situation is driven home to us not only by the discrepancy between the Jew's words and the Christians' actions, but by the discrepancy between the Jew's words and his own actions: though Salerio and Solanio have been tickling Shylock, none of the three should be doubled over with laughter at his "If you poison us, do we not die?" Shylock's "And if you wrong us, shall we not revenge?" no longer imploring, no longer attempting to reason, but desperate, strong and determined, comes as a shock to stop all laughter. Salerio and Solanio now listen carefully as Shylock instructs them: "The villainy you teach me, I will execute." Though it diverts our attention from Shylock's "Hath not a Jew eyes?" the Christians' mockery emphasizes for us that in tormenting others, both Christians and Jews imitate what they hate.

The last part of Act III, scene i presents variations on the themes of torture and suffering. No sooner do Salerio and Solanio leave than Shylock is tormented by his well-meaning friend Tubal, whose news catches him uncertainly between joy at Antonio's loss of income and grief at Jessica's wasting of her father's money. Until the end of this scene Shylock's suffering gets small sympathy from us, partly because his friend gives him little, partly because he gives himself much, partly because his unattractive vengefulness directs our concern from the moneylender to the merchant. In this production Tubal is clearly critical of the way Shylock's grief has so distorted his perspective that he believes "The curse never fell upon our nation till now" and "No ill luck [stirs] but what lights o' my shoulders." Tubal twice tries to hush these exclamations, and when Shylock declares "I would my daughter were dead at my foot," Tubal, horrified at his friend's disregard of natural bonds, finally stops his mouth by putting his hand over it. Even this only temporarily halts the flooding self-pity, so Tubal, shrewdly sizing up the situation, adopts the tactic of shifting Shylock's attention from his own losses to those of Antonio. This works well: the Jew who spoke so movingly to Salerio and Solanio of humanity, the common bond between all men whatever their faith, turns to thanking God for the merchant's misfortune. Henceforth, whenever Shylock begins to bemoan his loss of money, Tubal reminds him of Antonio's loss. But Tubal is not entirely successful in manipulating Shylock, because half of the time he is as indifferent to the effect of what he says as Salerio and Solanio are to the effect of what they do. Again and again Tubal consciously lifts Shylock's spirits by speaking of Antonio's downfall, then unconsciously, almost compulsively, by coming back to Jessica's wasting of her father's gold destroys the mood he has created. "Thou stick'st a dagger in me," Shylock tells the friend who harps on daughter and ducats as much as on Antonio. The friend's response, telling Shylock that his daughter traded his wife's ring for a monkey, effectively twists a knife in the wound. We see and hear a new depth of pain behind "Thou torturest me, Tubal."

In this part of the scene, blocking emphasizes Shylock's isolation in self-pity. All of Tubal's lines are directed to Shylock; if Tubal speaks from behind or beside his friend, he touches him to draw his attention and ensure contact. Shylock, however, seldom looks at Tubal except when trying to get from him news of Jessica or Antonio; he rehearses his losses with his back turned on his friend. Even lines suggesting direct address, such as the repeated "Go, Tubal," are delivered with Shylock looking away from his friend. This gives emphasis to the few lines he whirls to deliver directly, lines which bespeak his alienation from any community of caring: "The curse never fell upon our nation till now," "I would my daughter were dead at my foot," "Thou stick'st a dagger in me." When at the end of the scene the camera moves in to a closeup on Shylock's agonized face—the closeup most critics wanted on "Hath not a Jew eyes?"—we feel the full weight of his alienation. We cannot remain unmoved by his anguished rending of his cloak. Neither can we tell precisely the cause of his mourning: is it the loss of his wife, his daughter or his ducats?

Our pity for the suffering we see is somewhat checked by this ambiguity and by what we have just heard: "I will have the heart of [Antonio], if he forfeit; for, were he out of Venice, I can make what merchandise I will." We are allowed neither to feel for Shylock without thinking nor to indulge in unfeeling prejudice against him.

As with Shylock's plea in Act III, scene i, Portia's plea in the first scene of the following act is framed to emphasize imitation. While Portia speaks of the "quality of mercy," the Duke appears over her shoulder. His presence lessens any suspense about the outcome of her address because it reminds us not only that what we see must be public justice rather than personal settlement, but also that the Duke's "How shalt thou hope for mercy, rend'ring none?" has already presented the argument Portia uses, which has failed to soften Shylock. Though most of the action in the courtroom scene is verbal, the way this production uses its medium makes what we see almost more striking than what we hear—and what strikes us is that the love of these Christians often causes pain to others.

Blocking emphasizes first Shylock's isolation from the Christian community, then his apparent accord with the "Daniel come to judgment," then his entrapment by that Daniel and that community. Shylock has to break through a barrier of Antonio's friends to come where he can claim his forfeit. Unquestionably in a hostile courtroom, he is unquestionably hostile; he enters bearing his bond, scales and a knife. However, as Portia goes over the details of the bond, Shylock literally and symbolically comes around to her side, believing—despite her suggestion that he provide a surgeon at his own cost—that she or the law embodied in her is with him. When Antonio's friends gather at his side to strengthen him for death, Shylock stands alone against them only momentarily, for Portia soon comes to stand behind him, her hand with his on the knife, insisting, as he insisted, that he take what his bond allows. As Shylock learns the cost of cutting he is visibly trapped, surrounded by Christians, until Salerio and Gratiano throw him to the floor to beg the mercy he would not grant. The "converted" Jew, sick at heart, staggers to his feet unaided; Shylock leaves as alien as he came through the still hostile crowd he must now consider brothers in Christ.

Symbolic stage business directs our sympathy. On the one hand, Antonio, arms spread and chest bared to the Jew's "justice," is an image of crucifixion suggested verbally as well as visually, since it follows hard upon Shylock's reference to Barabbas. The pose seems designed to prevent our becoming too sympathetic to Shylock, for at the moment we watch Shylock realize that he is caught in his own trap, we see that Antonio has not yet recognized this: he remains in the attitude of crucifixion, still awaiting his death. On the other hand, because it suggests circumcision, Gratiano's otherwise inexplicable stroking of Shylock's nose with his knife as the Jew is about to be sealed in his new religion emphasizes the painfulness of this "conversion." Gratiano's cruel gesture, recalling Salerio's and Solanio's mockery in Act III, scene i, does not present the Christians as striving to imitate Christ.

Because closeups are rare in Act IV, scene i, we notice that two of these focus on a kiss: repetition calls attention to the similarity between the Jew caught by his insistence on his bond and the Christian caught by his insistence on a "remembrance" for Antonio's deliverer. In this courtroom the quality of mercy is somewhat strained, and as the stricken Shylock, warned that the Duke may "recant" his pardon, agrees to the conditions Antonio stipulates, his skullcap is thrown from him. The anguish and horror on Shylock's face as Salerio drops his cross over the Jew's head proclaim that Shylock regards its chain as the noose Gratiano wished upon him. Nonetheless, Salerio forces the cross against the Jew's lips. This constrained kiss evokes sympathy for the man forced to abandon a faith that means much to him. So does Bassanio's kissing of Portia's ring as he reluctantly relinquishes it under pressure from Antonio. Though the supposed Balthasar has argued persuasively against Bassanio's keeping it, Antonio argues even more persuasively. He has shown that he values Bassanio's love more than his own life; can Bassanio value Antonio's love less than a ring? Antonio's plea that the advocate's "deserving and my love withal / Be valued" effectively forces Bassanio to choose between love of Antonio and loyalty to Portia. Antonio demands Bassanio's heart as surely as Shylock demanded Antonio's. When the trial scene ends with the camera closing in on the unused scales and knife, we weigh for ourselves how much justice has been done and how much mercy shown, and by whom.

The trial scene brings out something unattractive in each of the major characters. Though she advocates mercy, Portia shows none: not content with sparing Antonio's life she goes after the Jew's—something Antonio himself does not do—with the letter of the law. Shylock, who had nodded his willingness to act the caricature of cruelty Antonio and Gratiano believe a Jew to be rather then give the "gentle" (Gentile) answer the Duke wants, chooses to preserve his life rather than his religion. Bassanio earnestly but too easily assures Antonio that he would give his heart for him, then hesitates to give his ring to the one who saved his bosom friend's heart.

Sufferer and torturer change roles so often that we wonder whether the cycle can ever be broken, whether Christian and Jew will ever respect each other's humanity instead of imitate each other's inhumanity. The BBC production is shaped so that at the end of the scenes containing the famous pleas, we feel not that Jews are bad and Christians good, but that the humanity of anyone who tortures another is flawed. This production is prejudiced against cruelty, not against Jews.

. . . *The Merchant of Venice* will probably never be produced without someone's complaining about anti-Semitism. Despite the fact that in the BBC production three key people—the producer, the director and the actor of Shylock—are Jewish, as Miller points out in the interview broadcast with the play, it still drew protests in the United States, though not in Britain.[16] It is true that this is a play about anti-Semitism and that the Jew is not its hero. It is also true that a twentieth-century audience, haunted by memories of Buchenwald and Dachau, is likely, as Wertheim notes, "to respond to the persecution of the Jew with a pathos that is now almost conditioned reflex."[17] Shylock's Jewishness can no more be removed from the play than his occupation can be, but his Jewishness can be presented in a way that draws the sympathy of a modern audience: by emphasizing the suffering that, in Shylock's words, "is the badge of all our tribe." This is essentially what the National Theatre production does, appealing strongly to the audience's emotions. Effective as it is, when followed too enthusiastically, this approach encourages deliberate distortion of the text. Shakespeare clearly did not intend to portray Shylock favorably: to focus a primarily flattering light on the Jew, one must cut lines, even whole scenes, and visual effects have to be played against the words. If we assume that Shakespeare can be made non-anti-Semitic only by being made non-Shakespearean, simple logic suggests that Shakespeare is indeed, for whatever reasons, anti-Semitic. Behind the National Theatre's adaptation seems to lie the assumption that being unflattering to this particular Jew is tantamount to being prejudiced against all Jews.

Can Shylock be portrayed negatively without the production's being accused of anti-Semitism? Not really, suggests Miller, himself a Jew: "There's no satisfying Jewish groups . . . [who] want every single virtue the Jews hold up embodied in one man."[18] This desire, however understandable, is neither realistic nor helpful in dealing with Shakespeare's play, which was never intended to correct the injustices of twentiety-century history. As Miller notes in articulating the theory behind the BBC version, the task of the producer today is to "address the real problem of anti-Semitism, not whitewash the victim."[19] A production that like the BBC's casts unflattering light on anyone, Jewish or Christian, who torments another shows prejudice against cruelty, not religious bias.

To emphasize that both Jews and Christians are a mixture of good and bad is true to Shakespeare's text. Where the National Theatre production compels us to listen to "Hath not a Jew eyes?" the BBC production invites us to consider a larger question, "Have not human beings hearts?" This unspoken question resonates throughout the play, giving it unity and making possible a production that is indeed not anti-Semitic.

1. For example, Bernard Grebanier, *The Truth About Shylock* (New York, 1962), 175–80, and Warren D. Smith, "Shakespeare's Shylock," *Shakespeare Quarterly*, 15 (1964), 198–99, see Shylock's being a Jew as only incidental to his being a usurer.

2. To see this, one has only to look at the *New York Times* review section and its Drama Mailbag for about a month after the opening of any production. The problem is analyzed in relation to the National Theatre version by Fred M. Hechinger, "Why Shylock Should Not Be Censored," *New York Times*, 24 March 1974, sec. 2, pp. 23, 47, and by John J. O'Connor, "If Shylock Were Not Jewish," *New York Times*, 19 March 1974, sec. 2, p. 21; in relation to the BBC version by Michiko Kakutani, "Debate over Shylock Simmers Once Again," *New York Times*, 22 February 1981, sec. 2, p. 1, 30. same queries

3. Here and there large theatrical effects have been adapted to take advantage of the new medium: for example, instead of seeing Shylock from the rear as he dons his prayer shawl, we see a closeup of his face. Other actors play Gratiano and Jessica. The only significant difference seems to be that the comic scenes with Gobbo, often mentioned in the reviews of the London version, have been eliminated, further darkening the atmosphere of the play.

4. Miller directed neither video presentation, but produced and directed the original British National Theatre version and, as executive producer of the BBC version, articulates in interviews his conception of the play and its production. He may have influenced Jack Gold's direction of the BBC presentation: the interviewer for the London paper *The Stage and Television Today* reports Miller as saying of himself that "he [is] not one who could just sit on the sidelines and direct operations" ("No Modern Dress in Miller's Shakespeare," 28 June 1979, p. 20).

5. Interview accompanying the play, first broadcast in the United States on 23 February 1981.

6. Tim Hallinan, "Interview: Jonathan Miller on *The Shakespeare Plays*," *Shakespeare Quarterly*, 32 (1981), 141.

7. Irving Wardle, "Merchants All," London *Times*, 29 April 1970, p. 9.

8. Ronald Bryden, London *Observer*, 3 May 1970, p. 33.

9. For example, a sequence moving from II.i to II.vii to II.ix to III.i, which relates to the pursuit of Portia, and a sequence in two movements, from I.iii to II.i.166 and from II.iii through II.iv, which relates to the flight of Jessica. II.vi, II.viii, and III.v have been cut.

10. All quotations from the play are from *The Complete Works of Shakespeare*, ed. David Bevington, 3rd ed. (Glenview, Illinois, 1980).

11. Peter Ansorge, "Director in Interview," *Plays and Players*, 16 (March 1970), 53.

12. Wardle, p. 9.

13. Harold Hobson, London *Sunday Times*, 3 May 1970, p. 33.

14. Ansorge, review in *Plays and Players*, 16 (June 1970), 41.

15. Michael Manheim, "The Shakespeare Plays on TV: *The Merchant of Venice*," *Shakespeare on Film Newsletter*, 5 (1981), 11.

16. John J. O'Connor, in his review for the *New York Times*, 23 February 1981, p. 18, observes that Americans are more inclined to protest than others; he points out that "this BBC production created scarcely a ripple of objection in Britain, even in Jewish publications."

17. Albert Wertheim, "The Treatment of Shylock and Thematic Integrity in *The Merchant of Venice*," *Shakespeare Studies*, 6 (1970), 75.

18. Kakutani, p. 30.

19. Kakutani, p. 30.

Trivial Pursuit
The Casket Plot in the Miller/Olivier Merchant
June Schlueter

In III.ii of *The Merchant of Venice*, after Bassanio has chosen the lead casket, Portia offers him her ring, sealing the union for which Bassanio has sought her endorsement. Reluctant to "claim her with a loving kiss" until their union is "confirmed, signed, ratified" by Portia, Bassanio delays responding to the gentle scroll—or to the stage direction of many an editor; and in many productions he kisses Portia only after she gives him her ring. The moment of endorsement is a special one in the play, celebrating as it does not only the simultaneous fulfillment and promise of love but Portia's integrity and Bassanio's worth. Portia could have taught Bassanio "how to choose right" but, unwilling to be forsworn, trusted his love to find her out. Bassanio, having passed through the danger designed by Portia's father, has proven the value of both the lead casket and himself: the world may still be "deceived by ornament," but Bassanio is not.

Despite the importance of the casket plot in furthering the play's commentary on the mercantile morality of Venice and as a touchstone for distinguishing between fool's gold and true gold, modern directors have taken pleasure in exploiting its comic possibilities. Every recent production of *Merchant* I have seen has emphasized the pretentious heroics of the scimitar-wielding Morocco and the extratextual swishiness of Arragon. To their credit, directors have limited their fun to Portia's unsuccessful suitors (II.i, II.vii, II.ix) and played the final casket scene (III.ii) as a serious pursuit: Bassanio does not know which casket contains fair Portia's counterfeit, and Portia will not compromise her father, herself, or her love for Bassanio by telling. Jonathan Miller, however, who is not known for his restraint, extends the comic handling of the casket plot into III.ii, escalating directorial pleasure into diabolic delight. In his televised *Merchant* of 1973, which grew out of the 1970 National Theatre production starring Sir Laurence Olivier as a Victorian Shylock, Miller's persistently comic treatment of the casket plot seriously compromises Portia's integrity and Bassanio's worth, reducing the quest for Portia to a trivial pursuit.

This is not to say that the worth of Bassanio has not already been diminished by the comic treatment of Morocco and Arragon. As Jonas Barish points out in his recent SAA *Bulletin* comments (8:1, January 1985), reducing these suitors of rank and dignity to caricatures turns Bassanio's success into a hollow achievement: opponents must be worthy if the hero's triumph is to be sweet. Morocco and Arragon are not "contemptible" but "limited," and they deserve credit for having the courage to choose, which previous suitors had not. Still, the limitations of the two are so apparent in their orations that a director who ignores the comic possibilities in their portrayal might well have to fight against the text. Morocco is swollen with self, mightily impressed with his military conquests and confident that, were he able to determine the outcome through bravery, he would earn the lady. But in refusing to permit his "golden mind" to stoop to "shows of dross," he discovers that "all that glisters is not gold." Arragon, too, though he voices the lesson of inner worth that Bassanio must learn, refuses to rank himself with the "barbarous multitudes" and gets what he deserves—though the portrait of a blinking idiot hardly coincides with his own estimation of self.

There is inherent ironic humor in a situation that provides the contrary of what a character expects and a smug, self-congratulatory humor in an audience's sense of its superiority. So also is there humor in the strange appearance of these two exotic suitors: "a tawny Moor all in white" and a swarthy Spanish prince, both visually as well as temperamentally distant from the fair maiden of provincial Belmont. In portraying the two, though, directors might take counsel from Nerissa, who reminds her mistress (in I.ii) that "they are as sick that surfeit with too much as they that starve with nothing. It is no mean happiness, therefore, to be seated in the mean. . . ."

Miller approaches Portia's unsuccessful suitors in a spirit so "sick" with "surfeit" as to be subversive. With Morocco he is perhaps no more extravagant than other modern directors, but certainly he is not less so. In our first look at Morocco in this production, the camera shows us a Moor pressing snuff to his nostrils, without yielding the proud posture of a military man. Epaulets upon his shoulders, a banner of honor around his chest, the scimitar at his side, Morocco speaks with confidence of his exploits, kissing Portia's hand hungrily as he advances toward the caskets. His right arm bent formally at his waist, he offers an occasional gesture with white-gloved hand as he reads the inscriptions. Somewhat embarrassed at his own caution, the warrior laughs at his need to survey the caskets again, as Miller allows his erratic speech rhythms to dominate the scene and to turn him into both an innocent and a fool. Rejecting the lead casket, he moves in for a camera closeup as his voice shifts into high gear for his silver casket rumination; he slows the declamatory pace only on the repeatedly mispronounced "deserb." Coyly asking, "What if I strayed no further but chose here?," the Moor slides his arm around the startled Portia's waist, the lady recoiling from his forwardness. Morocco returns to the triple-armed pedestal on which the caskets revolve, rereads the inscription on the gold one, and summarily decides that "what many men desire" is the lady. His proud bearing, boyish confidentiality, and boldly simplistic vision of self all create a theatrical pomposity that lends a special humor to his naked disappointment when he opens the gold casket. The lively rhythms of his flamboyant speeches give way, simply, to "Oh Hell."

If Miller exercises some restraint in the portrayal of Morocco, he is unrestrained in presenting Arragon as a comic grotesque. Traditionally played as a haughty and effete aristocrat, the Spanish prince, armed with spectacles rather than scimitar, appears in this production as a nearly blind, bent, doting old man who can barely find his way to the caskets. Coming immediately after the Morocco scene, which is a conflation of II.i and II.vii, the second suitor scene begins with playful piano music that speeds up to accompany the prince in processional on Portia's arm. The expectant Nerissa catches sight of the suitor at the same time the audience does and turns toward the camera to express her amusement at this implausible match. Clad in tails and white tie, white hair wildly erect as though responding to an electrical charge, Arragon walks blindly past the caskets, submitting to the two women's pushes in finding his way. As the impatient Portia fans herself and sighs, the lethargic prince leans his nearsighted eyes toward the inscriptions and tediously mutters them. Speaking contemptuously of the "barbarous multitudes," he pulls out a knotted handkerchief, looks at it in bewilderment, then returns it to his pocket. Portia offers him a cup of tea, and, as he continues his expostulation, he extracts sugar cubes from the sugar bowl she holds, one by one, depositing seven in his cup before returning the eighth to the bowl. When Arragon does choose, still not having drunk his tea, he peers into the silver casket, where he finds Miller's version of a "blinking idiot," a mirror. Allowing Portia to direct him to the door, the self-pitying old man totters off, promising to keep his oath never to marry.

But Miller's decrepit prince hardly seems a candidate for marriage at all. If there is any merit in Arragon's judgment or in his claim to be a suitor, Miller's rendering of him as the impotent *senex amans* repudiates it. In agreeing to the conditions of the test, he has hazarded nothing, for the prospect of continuing his royal line through a legitimate—or any—heir is as laughable as it is unlikely. The spirit of the test was to limit suing to those worthy of Portia, a strategy that has worked with the suitors from foreign lands who have earlier taken their leave. But the reduction of Arragon to dotage makes a mockery of this purpose. If under her father's conditions such a man as this may woo Portia, then the prize may be bestowed unearned. The test is merely a lottery.

By the time Miller's Bassanio makes his bid, we have already seen the fault of a plan designed not merely to control Portia from the grave but to protect a "richly left" daughter from the undeserving. We have applauded Nerissa's fast action in turning the casket pedestal when Arragon nearly inserts the key not in the silver casket he has chosen but in the lead. The motif of hazarding all, begun in the bond plot with Antonio's sealing with Shylock for a pound of flesh for Bassanio's sake, must prevail in the earlier casket scenes if Bassanio's risk is to be respected. But the context in which Bassanio makes his choice has been established as one in which those who hazard are no worthier than those who decide Portia not worth the risk, a context in which her father's plan is hardly foolproof. If Portia does not teach Bassanio "how to choose right," she may indeed "miss" him.

Still, the scene between Bassanio and Portia begins seriously enough in the Miller production. Having just returned from riding, the two are dressed in riding habits and top hats, visually suggesting a compatibility that Portia and her other suitors did not have. The two remain outdoors for their early lines, in which Portia pleads with Bassanio to tarry, to "pause a day or two" and stay election so she may enjoy him longer, and Bassanio confesses that until he chooses he lives upon the rack. Iterating her commitment to her father's will, Portia insists she will not be forsworn and then precedes her young suitor into the house, where he will survey the caskets and choose.

Joined by Bassanio, Portia asks that music be played, spending some eleven lines discoursing on music, first as swan song for her unrewarded lover, then as celebration should he succeed, and finally—lines spoken as she approaches Bassanio—as "dulcet sounds . . . / That creep into the dreaming bridegroom's ear / And summon him to marriage" (III.ii). The song, of course, is "Tell me where is fancy bred," which, with its suggestive emphases on the short "e" and full rhyming of "bred" with "lead," may well cast suspicion on Portia's integrity. Is the song a hint to Bassanio, her way of assuring that her lover not miss? By this time, Portia knows which casket contains her portrait. (Indeed, in this production she clearly knows all along, sighing in relief when Morocco summarily dismisses the lead.) Does she hope that Bassanio will understand the hint in the rhyme and connect the "ding dong bell" with base lead?

Miller staged the musical prelude to Bassanio's choice so unsubtly that Bassanio would not have been in a more privileged position to choose had all three caskets been displayed with their lids ajar. The production not only admits Portia is cheating, but challenges its audience to resist laughing at the shamelessness with which she directs her show. As Bassanio soberly surveys the caskets, a cello and other strings play off-camera. Then two identically dressed women enter, their hair swept up to frame Oriental smiles. More appropriate to a Gilbert and Sullivan operetta than to a Shakespeare play, the sopranos project their vibrato voices into the face of the astonished Bassanio as they begin the strains of "fancy bred," positioned on either side of the lead casket. The two periodically bow their heads in prolonged glances at the treasured casket, so obviously pointing it out that only a blind man or a fool could miss the hint. The amused Bassanio casts a backward glance at Nerissa, who smiles in silent understanding, then patiently folds his arms, waiting for the women's exit and the moment of his choice.

If we have not laughed enough at these garrulous beauties, we laugh in incredulity when the dense Gratiano, standing alongside Bassanio throughout, points decisively to the gold casket, inviting Bassanio's wise response: "The world is still deceived with ornament." But Bassanio's confidence here has little to do with moral maturity, based on the recognition that outward show may not be the appropriate measure of worth, and much to do with the piece of intelligence he has acquired. Sighing and smiling, Bassanio selects the lead casket, feigning incredulity as he exclaims, "What find I here? / Fair Portia's counterfeit!"

For the rest of the scene, fancy's knell rings false, and all that Bassanio says seems contrived. The successful suitor's poetic praise of fair Portia's eyes and lips and hair and eyes again sounds less like an expression of joy and more like a ritualistic paean to the fairytale princess he earlier described to his benefactor. But at this point, Portia should be more than a conventional princess, for the transforming power of love has moderated Bassanio's vision of her, revealing her as a partner of integrity and value. Bassanio's deference to this choked-up, watery-eyed, disingenuous ingenue, who turns to claim the husband she knew she would secure, does further injury to Bassanio, suggesting a vulnerability and a weakness one can hardly admire. And Portia's accounting of her own worth, in which she employs the language of mercantile Venice, registers not as a transformation of Bassanio's rhetoric in the service of greater worth but as testimony to the endurance of Venetian values over Belmont's.

Miller, to his credit, rejected Olivier's ingenious suggestion that Bassanio play all three suitors: disguised as Morocco, he would try the gold; as Arragon, he would elect the silver; and, finally, as Bassanio, he would choose with certainty the lead, having eliminated the alternatives. Such an interpretation would lend a special significance to Bassanio's "The world is still deceived with ornament," if indeed Portia were. Olivier did not say whether Portia would have been privy to the scheme that would carry out her father's wish and still assure Bassanio's success. But whether she is in on Bassanio's deception or not, this playing would mean that Bassanio was never more than a fortune seeker in pursuit of the "richly-left" lady. If Portia did not see through his disguise, even while the audience did, she would appear the ignorant fool; if she did, she would be accomplice to a deception that severely compromised the spirit of her father's will, leaving her forsworn.

Such dismissive treatment of the relationship between Portia and Bassanio and of their characters, whether in Olivier's conception or Miller's, is rendered more perverse by the production's juxtaposition of scenes. Here the casket plot, beginning with Morocco's appearance in II.i, continues through II.vii, II.ix, and III.ii, interrupted only by III.i. In that scene, Shylock pleads for a Jew's humanity and pledges revenge. Still laughing from exposure to Miller's comic suitors, an audience is thrust into a scene of extraordinary emotional intensity, in which Olivier weeps over the loss of his daughter and dances in glee at the loss of Antonio's ships. Still haunted by the final image of Shylock wrapped in a prayer shawl, we are returned to Belmont for the amusing, but surely trifling, climax of the casket plot. With Shylock as sympathetic and as powerful a human figure as he is played here, how can Bassanio and Portia compete? Indeed, if this play is to remain on the right side of comedy, any director treating Shylock with such respect, such compassion, such admiration is almost obliged to trivialize others.

But in trivializing the casket plot, Miller destroys the rich connections that plot has with the rest of Shakespeare's play. We feel little of the connection among the play's several bonds and none between the comically deflated pretensions of the casket scenes and the deep essence of commitment and sacrifice in the bond plot. The scene in which Bassanio and Portia are united creates a material connection among the three plots: casket, ring, and bond. Bassanio's choice of the lead casket ends the casket plot; Portia's giving of the ring begins the ring plot; and Antonio's unhappy letter intensifies the bond plot, revealing the complication that prompts both Bassanio and Portia to rush off to Venice. Bassanio has hazarded all for Portia, Antonio has hazarded all for his friend, and Portia as Balthazar will put Bassanio in the impossible position of choosing fidelity to his friend or to his wife, in either case risking the love of the other. More importantly, the centrality of the contract should be apparent here, coming as it does as the happy consequence of Portia's keeping her moral bond, even as Shylock insists on keeping his legal but immoral agreement and the stage is set for Bassanio's breaking yet keeping faith with his wife.

If Bassanio's wooing of Portia becomes a trivial pursuit, as it does in the Miller production, Shylock is free to dominate the action: the play flattens to a one-dimensional treatment of the letter and spirit of the law, and the casket plot becomes a sideshow. Theatrically delightful as Miller's Morocco, Arragon, and the Gilbert and Sullivan duo might be, collectively they impoverish the play, preventing the casket plot from illuminating the value of its participants and adding to the personal, thematic, and structural riches that are the play's full sum.

As You Like It *and the Perils of Pastoral*
J. C. Bulman

"As You Like It was the catalyst that precipitated the plan to televise the whole canon of Shakespeare's plays for the BBC."[1] In retrospect, given the reception of that production, this statement may read like a bad joke. The BBC Shakespeare was the brainchild of Cedric Messina, and the story of its birth is worth recounting. Messina was directing Barrie's *The Little Minister* at Glamis Castle and grew enchanted with both the castle and its surroundings. "I went for the burn walk, and it seemed to be the most wonderful sort of forest," he recalls. "It occurred to me that if one were to do a location production of *As You Like It*, then this was the place to do it" (p. 20). Do it he did, in June of 1978; and that production inaugurated the series. But the *if* clause proved to be the problem. For most who saw the production, the location that appealed to Messina as "wonderful" seemed far too earthbound, too specific for the elusive joys of the Forest of Arden.

In principle, pastoral poses problems for producers of Shakespeare. In both ethos and form, pastoral is highly artificial: it signifies retreat to an ideal; it is a state of mind. At its most romantic (as in Lodge's *Rosalynde*), the green world is a world of play and game, not a place where shepherds tend sheep and maidens milk goats; at its most political (as in Spenser's "Shepheardes Calender"), it depicts an allegorical world of good government. Contemporary theater has sought various ways to present pastoral artifice. Perhaps taking its cue from Peter Brook's minimalist *Midsummer Night's Dream*, the RSC's staging of *As You Like It* in 1980 used mere poles for trees, and sheepskins stretched between them suggested shelter; The Acting Company's postmodernist staging of 1985 used parti-colored umbrellas to suggest the play world of Arden, and they were rolled about to suggest another part of the forest. In such productions, the conventions of pastoral romance are something to which we can willingly surrender—the love at first sight, the miraculous conversions, the theophany of Act 5.

Television, however, makes its own demands on a Shakespeare text. Chief among them is the demand for realism. Audiences unused to modern theatrical productions and nurtured instead on films shot "on location" are skeptical of stage conventions—indeed, sometimes downright derisive. Thus the directors of Shakespeare's comedies for the BBC, including Basil Coleman, who directed *As You Like It* for Messina, have had difficulties knowing how to stage obviously unrealistic situations (women playing men, male and female mistaken for identical twins, middle-aged courtiers living happily in the woods) for a medium in which the camera reveals each blemish, exposes each fake, and destroys romantic fictions that might be easily tolerated in the theater.

Other BBC directors came to terms with this problem in ways different from Coleman. Jane Howell, for example, chose to stage the pastoral scenes of *Winter's Tale* in a bare, white studio to evoke a feeling of endless space, broken only by a blasted tree and a rock—a set evocative of *Waiting for Godot*. By making the set so minimal and artificial, she directed our attention to the poetry, where the true pastoral vision resides, and thereby encouraged us to participate in creating an imaginary world. With perhaps more success, Elijah Moshinsky conceived of the Renaissance canvas as an apt analogue for the television screen and thus invited us to expect artifices similar to those used by Rembrandt, Vermeer, and others. At its most allusive, his *Dream* recreates Rembrandt's *Danae in Her Bower* for Titania; and his set for the Athenian woods—dominated by a pool of water through which characters pass to effect their metamorphoses, and by a moon ever smiling on their inconstancy—richly employs the contrasts of Renaissance chiaroscuro. Moshinsky's iconographic method of preserving pastoral artifice may have been more sophisticated than Howell's reliance on the empty space, but we would do well to remember that both directors were, in a sense, responding to what was widely regarded as the failure of *As You Like It* and to Messina's belief that pastoral romance could be played "on location."

What was Coleman to do when Messina instructed him to translate the green world of pastoral into the great outdoors? The more realistic the setting, the more we are inclined to apply the criteria of naturalistic drama to the action. Thus, inevitably, we begin to question the logic of the play. How can callow Orlando beat the professional wrestler Charles? Why do Celia and Rosalind so gleefully decide to "waste" their time in a wilderness? Can't Orlando see through Ganymede's disguise? Isn't it absurd for a duke and his middle-aged courtiers to live like Robin Hood and his band of merry men? How can we credit the instantaneous conversions of Oliver and Duke Frederick? And where the hell does Hymen come from?

Before one attacks the BBC production for violating the spirit of the play, however, one must recall that *As You Like It* contains much mockery of the pastoral ethos within itself. Touchstone, for one, ridicules the excesses of pastoral romance by courting Audrey with barnyard manners, and Silvius himself stands as a ludicrous exhibit of such excess. Jaques chides the political presumption of pastoral retreat: for him, the courtiers have fled from one corrupt civilization only to corrupt another. Even Rosalind, in the voice of Ganymede, speaks of wedded love and fidelity with a seasoned skepticism. In these ways satire balances pastoral, just as it did in ancient Greece, and keeps us from being fully engaged with the artifice of the play. Shakespeare took pains to achieve a tonal balance that allows us both to participate in a celebration of love and, at the same time, to consider the more serious implications of pastoral. These pains were not wasted on Coleman, who praised *As You Like It* as "an anti-materialist play . . . about rediscovering Nature and our dependence on it. . . . It touches on our responsibility to the environment, questions the need for courts and armies and self-protection. It rediscovers natural freedom" (p. 26). These may sound suspiciously like the sentiments of a director straining to fit the fashion of the times; nonetheless, one should note his reluctance to mention the love, the romance, and all that makes the play a "festive" comedy.

Coleman, I suggest, made a virtue of necessity. Bound by Messina's decision to film on location and yet determined to have the play speak intelligently to a modern audience, he put quotation marks around the pastoral artifice. He played up the satire, he let us in on the game, he allowed "reality" to hold idealism at bay, as if assuming that only the skepticism inherent in the play could allow us to credit *As You Like It* as a serious exploration of love and society. Numerous examples illustrate how he used the camera's eye to catch a comic reality. It shows us Rosalind brushing away a fly that interrupts her first encounter with Orlando in Arden. It shows her straining to be heard over a very real wind. It shows us Orlando's verses hanging absurdly on real trees, and Orlando himself embracing an oak. As the duke's men carry off a bloody carcass in IV.ii, the camera reveals that buck season has come to Arden. And in response to Corin's question, "And how like you this shepherd's life, Master Touchstone?" (III.ii), Touchstone steps in sheep dung. There are indeed real sheep in this green world: Coleman insists on them.

The wooing of Ganymede by Orlando is likewise played to strain our belief in the pastoral fiction. Orlando, for one thing, is rather slight and understated: his defeat of the wrestler Charles is patently absurd. And Helen Mirren's Rosalind, buxom and beautiful, is clearly no male Ganymede. The camera does not disguise her femininity—indeed, exploits it when, in IV.iii, Ganymede faints at seeing Orlando's bloody handkerchief. As Oliver stoops to undo Ganymede's doublet, Aliena stops his hand and cries, "There is more in it!" The joke, made at the expense of preserving the artifice, glances wryly at the bosom that we, and perhaps Oliver, are meant to appreciate.

Ganymede's femininity is readily apparent to Orlando, too; and in the course of the wooing scene (IV.i), they both show through knowing smiles that they are playing a game, perpetuating a fiction, fully aware of the rules. At the outset, Rosalind is shown to feel real disappointment that Orlando is late: it is as clear to him as it is to us that she is not feigning a passion. A bit later, when she bids him to "woo me, woo me" in most seductive tones, he, who has been looking admiringly at her bosom, teasingly tries to steal a kiss from her on the line "I would kiss before I spoke." We assume either that he knows who she is or that he is gay, and the latter is unlikely. Further along, when he lounges suggestively on an old chestnut tree, she, "in a more coming-on disposition," kneels before him, fumbles with her hat, acts coy, and doesn't try to hide her true feelings; nor does he when, in the mock wedding scene, he seems to take his vows in earnest. The camera takes advantage of facial close-ups to indicate that these lovers know precisely what they are doing. They are playing with each other—and they play in a vein more knowing, more ironic than pastoral would ever allow. The effect of the scene finally is to detach us from the artifices of pastoral romance. Rosalind and Orlando indulge in a game that neither mistakes for reality; they see through one another's poses—and both are aware of that; they become self-conscious actors in a pastoral play. What Coleman achieves, I suggest, is a kind of alienation effect.

Coleman strains our belief in pastoral most comically in the appearance of Hymen. Stage productions have dealt with Hymen in a number of ways, ranging from the full-fledged theophanies of nineteenth-century productions to the more realistic accounts rendered by more recent productions, where, for example, as in the RSC's 1980 staging, Corin dresses as Hymen and enters atop a wagon bursting with the fruits of harvest. In either case, the pastoral fiction is preserved, either through the magic of *deus ex machina* or in the rustic celebration of harvest home. In Coleman's version, Hymen is neither god nor rustic. He is a fey figure dressed in gossamer—a ballet skirt, with a laurel wreath about his temples—who looks vaguely like a young man painted on a Greek vase. He is not a member of the Duke's entourage recruited by Rosalind to join her game, nor is he from Arden: his effete Oxbridge intonation and demeanor give the lie to that. And as he appears from atop a hill overlooking a beechwood grove, holding hands with Rosalind and Celia, we may well ask, Where did he come from? His appearance (and worse, his voice) is simply absurd. No one believes it is magic: the Duke's mystified look when ethereal music begins, and his greater astonishment when he sees the trio tripping down the hill, are deliberately funny. They confirm the idea that what we are watching is beyond belief. And that is just the point: Coleman bids us to laugh *at* pastoral artifice and *with* the characters who are themselves as detached from that artifice as we are.

If the pastoral romance is undercut by devices that alienate us from the action and prevent our suspension of disbelief, then the more serious pastoral plot involving the banished Duke is likewise darkened by the force of Jaques's cynicism. Coleman cast Richard Pasco, one of the RSC's finest tragic actors, as Jaques; and Pasco plays him as a melancholic, alcoholic, almost tragic visionary. This Jaques is alienated as much from the Duke as from the lovers, and his railing against the world has more bitterness in it than is usually the case. An examination of what I think is the strongest scene in this production, II.vii, will illustrate Coleman's bias.

The scene was filmed in a grove of yew trees at night. (Nighttime pastoral? The idea is as unconventional as it is sinister.) The Duke and his men sit around a blazing fire eating and drinking as Jaques, shrouded in smoke, delivers his seven ages of man speech. Cup of wine in hand, he speaks in a guttural voice and his face registers disgust. At his ultimate line about old age—"Sans teeth, sans eyes, sans taste"—his eyes light on old Adam, who enters with the aid of Orlando; and Jaques's disgust turns to sneer—"sans everything." To be sure, Adam cuts a silly and pathetic figure, his face (with apologies to Arthur Hewlett, who plays him) resembling nothing more than that of an aging basset hound. Once this venerable burden is set down, Amiens begins to sing in a rich baritone, "Blow, blow, thou winter wind;" but the melody and the singer alike are as melancholy as Jaques. There is no levity in them. But there *is* satire: as the camera backs away from Amiens, it reveals a whole consort surrounding him, viols and hautboys. We smile at the foolishness of a chamber orchestra in Arden; and as we do so, we join in Jaques's skepticism. The camera moves to him as the song continues, and there it lingers: he sits alone, still shrouded in smoke, drinking, and looking scornfully on the sentimental scene of Adam licking food from his master's fingers (and looking all the more basset-like for doing so). Lest we miss the satirical "angle" on such sentimentality, the camera keeps Jaques firmly in view, in the center background, during the final exchange between the Duke and Orlando. Their assurances of good will and familial love are mocked by Jaques's looking on. We see through his eyes, whose cynical vision clouds any optimism we may feel in this restoration of civility.

Jaques's satiric perspective sets the tone for much of the production. Take, as a final instance, his farewell in Act 5. The union of lovers there, as we have seen, is a bit too silly to be credited, and Coleman has allowed us to feel as alienated from the proceedings as Jaques does. With tragic sobriety, then, Jaques passes judgment on all the couples and, rejecting the Duke's entreaty to stay, vows to await him at his "abandon'd cave." He then begins a slow exit up the same hill that Hymen has earlier descended; and the camera, placed where the group of lovers stands, follows him up. But when the Duke bids the couples to "proceed, proceed" with their dance, the camera suddenly spies them from atop the hill—from the very position in which Jaques has just stood. We regard them as he does, looking down on them as they form a circle: we may note that the camera here repeats an earlier joke, when (in II.v) Amiens asks Jaques what "Ducdame" means, and, as the courtiers circle about him for an answer, Jaques explains that "'tis a Greek invocation, to call fools into a circle." As Jaques departs for the Duke's cave, he leaves behind him a circle of fools.

I do not suggest that Coleman's *As You Like It* is a successful production. Indeed, as most viewers agree, it is far too dark and self-conscious to do justice to the spirit of festive comedy. Other approaches to pastoral, such as Howell's and Moshinsky's, might better have preserved the play's balance between artifice and skepticism, belief and disbelief. I hope, however, that I have helped to rescue this *As You Like It* from accusations that it is naive or ill–considered, as if Coleman, like Messina, simply miscalculated in trying to equate pastoral with love in the woods. Coleman, it seems to me, knew what he was doing: his choices, even if we disagree with them, were both intelligent and consistent. Taking his cue from satirical qualifications of pastoral inherent in the play, he apparently decided that no television audience could swallow pastoral artifices straight, especially when they are played out in a "location" that by tradition demands realism. Thus he chose to alienate us from the fiction, to make the retreat to Arden seem a game that the players play only to keep from acknowledging the darker lessons of human nature that Jaques insists on. This is a peculiarly contemporary bias. As a response to Shakespeare's comedy, we may find it inadequate or discomforting. But if we find it so, we ought not to dismiss it before considering how it reflects, or speaks to, our age.

1. Quoted in Henry Fenwick's introduction to *The BBC TV Shakespeare* edition of the play, based on Peter Alexander's edition of 1951.

Why Measure for Measure?
H. R. Coursen

It is a puzzle for some viewers that the BBC *Measure for Measure*, one of the first productions in the Shakespeare Series, remains one of the best. I would suggest that it is not merely because subsequent productions, including Dr. Miller's *Taming of the Shrew* and *Antony and Cleopatra*, have been less than satisfactory. Assuming good casting and intelligent direction—warranted as-

Reprinted, with permission, from *Literature/Film Quarterly*, 12 (1984), 65–69.

sumptions in the case of Desmond Davis' BBC production—the script *per se* proves excellent for television. Before glancing at some of the excellencies of this particular version, I wish to examine some of the generic reasons why *Measure for Measure* seems almost to have been written for television.

Measure for Measure has been labelled a "problem play," of course, a convenient category that critics have invented to solve their problems. The problem play is unlike a comedy such as *As You Like It* in that the problems the problem play raises run deeper than the "folly" and myopia that get resolved at the end of the comedy. The problems of the problem play—in this case, illicit sexuality, radical abuse of political office, oath-breaking, and attempted murder—are potentially tragic issues. Yet at the end of *Measure for Measure*, no Hamlet dies (*Hamlet* has been called a problem play, of course), no Othello kills himself, no Macbeth is struck down by Macduff, no Octavius gives orders for the funeral of Antony and Cleopatra. The Duke has power to save. The play ends "happily," with the multiple marriages typical of the comic ending. Many feel, however, that nothing really has been solved beneath the imposition of Vincentio's politics, and that the comic ending is coerced, rather than springing from new awarenesses within characters, awarenesses that society is ready to incorporate within its widened frame. If society is a better place at the end of a Shakespearean comedy it is because most of the characters have learned something about themselves during the course of their dramatized careers. Is Vienna a better place as a result of all we have witnessed? Desmond Davis' BBC production might answer with a craftily qualified "yes." But one must be careful; for the production, like the script, invites the subjective response of the individual auditor, and *Measure for Measure* finds itself high on the list of plays that evoke radically divergent views, along with *Hamlet* and *Henry V*.

The problem play tends towards melodrama, a mode that may seem to raise profound issues but does not pretend to solve them. If it does pretend to solve them, the pretense shows through, as in the case, I would argue, of the celebrated *Equus* and, possibly, of *Measure for Measure*. Television is a medium for melodrama, and the best shows, "The Waltons," for example, are often the ones where the "solutions" are the most muted and ambiguous. While I do not believe that "ambiguity" works well on TV, as compared to the stage, the issues left unresolved at the end of a "Waltons" episode remained to be explored within a series whose theme was "growing up." But could Isabella, pressed against the closure of *Measure for Measure*, refuse the Duke's proposal *on television*? No.

It is true that the "situation comedy," a genre akin to farce, has been standard tube-fare for years. That means that *Love's Labour's Lost* and *The Taming of the Shrew* should be excellent on television. Our expectations for the medium form a large component of our response and also tell us something of the built-in limitations of the medium. It is a question, to paraphrase Robert Frost, of making the most of a diminished thing. Certainly television is not a medium for tragedy, nor is the "modern world." Nameless, faceless, sexless leaders, for all the world-shattering power at their fingertips, seem simply to have lost the stature of Oedipus, King Lear, or Mark Antony, whose fate is the world's fate. Perhaps that is a good thing. Derek Jacobi, a fine Hamlet a few seasons ago at the Old Vic, will be a very different Hamlet this fall on television. Not only must he accommodate himself to microphone and camera, but we will see a ten-inch figure mechanically reproduced within a frame. We will not be inhabiting the space where *Hamlet* is happening. The distinction between mechanical reproduction and living space is less important when we talk of melodrama: first, because melodrama accommodates itself so neatly to the dimensions of television, and second, because there is something mechanical about melodrama anyway, as in the way Duke Vincentio assigns parts to everyone at the end of the play, even designating a tiny cameo role to the head of the dead pirate, Ragozine.

One of my favorite melodramas from many years back was "Father Knows Best," with Robert Young and Jane Wyatt. One of the Anderson children would get trapped in an emotional dilemma—invariably chaste and usually through the sheer goodwill that welled within these three youngsters—and Robert Young would solve the problem with twinkly good humor during the final minute and a half of the show. The last scene of *Measure for Measure* consumes more than a minute and a half, but it is based on the "Father Knows Best" premise. Certainly that is the Duke's premise; whether it is Shakespeare's or not is debatable. But the problems the Duke solves are not just those of lukewarm youth or baffled adolescence. We have enormities here: the twin problems of sexuality and politics run amok. We do not expect, in America at least, anything of this magnitude from the tube. We turn ourselves off as we flip it on. *Measure for Measure* gives us unusual intensity, but it is momentary, because all issues seem to be resolved by ducal fiat and manipulation. We can, if we wish, comfort ourselves with the belief that while things looked pretty bad there for a while, it all turned out for the best.

Measure for Measure is super "soap." Although soaps do not end, they are melodramatic and episodic. In *Measure for Measure* we experience a sequence of one-on-one confrontations that only at the end come to be what the Duke wants them to be, or not to be, depending upon how we take this play and its shadowy chief character. Whatever we make of the Duke, he is a strangely passive protagonist, a disguised eavesdropper—a good character for melodrama. We do not get in this play the kind of linear progression of a comedy such as *As You Like It,* where banished Rosalind discovers that (*a*) her male disguise is a bad thing ("Alas the day! What shall I do with my doublet and hose?"), and (*b*) her disguise is an excellent thing in a woman. We observe, as she translates disguise into a dynamic device that sets most of her world into an androgynous harmony. Our sharing of Rosalind's evolving awareness of her own vibrant ability allows us to experience the comedy from the inside, with the feeling of participation that the comic form of dramatic irony permits. We derive similar benefits from the French Ladies in *Love's Labour's Lost* and Petruchio in *The Taming of the Shrew.* Viola's reversal of the process in *Twelfth Night* ("Disguise, I see thou art a wickedness!") neatly evokes our empathy for her. We can, however, only begin to second-guess Vincentio, and, then, only at the end of the play. Melodrama alienates us from the "participation mystique," except where we see a shadow looming behind the hero, or hear footsteps as Janet Leigh begins to take her shower. Melodrama makes us feel as helpless as Isabella feels just after her second meeting with Angelo. Our response to melodrama, like our response to so much within our own lives, is primarily that we "hope things will work out." Somehow we know they will in melodrama, at least. That Duke is there for a reason, even if only to force a happy ending on problems he himself has promoted. Assuming that the Duke is our moral focal point in this play, he is neither as attractive nor as seductive as, say, Rosalind or Hamlet. That Vincentio is not humanly appealing makes him useful, however, in *Measure for Measure*.

The play seems almost to have been written for television. Not only is it melodramatic and episodic, but, as episodic narratives often are, it is a series of vivid one-on-one confrontations. Such scenes work very well within the limited space of both a studio and a picture tube. Contrast *Measure for Measure* with, say, the rich and ambiguous second scene of *Hamlet*, or the multifaceted and climactic first scene of *King Lear*. *Measure for Measure* may resemble *King Lear* thematically in that a ruler absents himself from power, but Lear simply does not know what he is doing, and Vincentio, it would seem, does know. The jungle that Lear encourages ultimately swallows him. Vincentio, faced with something less than the explosion of Nature herself, is able to improvise his way towards the "happy ending" Lear intended to dictate in his first scene. Vincentio's "big scene" occurs at the end of his play, as he gathers all fragments together and labels them. We may not be satisfied with his labels—certainly Lucio is not—but they may be more satisfactory than those Lear applies in the first scene of his play, as he shatters his world into fragments left to find their own destinations. Until the last scene of *Measure for Measure*, we witness confrontations between Lucio and Claudio, Lucio and Isabella, Isabella and Angelo, Isabella and Claudio, Friar and Claudio, Friar and Juliet, Lucio and Friar; and even the large final scene is staged within the confrontational model.

Having argued that *Measure for Measure* is generically suited for television, I wish to suggest why Desmond Davis' production was a fine fulfillment of platonic form. First, consider the face of Kate Nelligan, a face figuring itself out. Miss Nelligan played an introverted and superficially self-possessed Isabella, at once ascetic and capable of that "prone and speechless dialect such as moves men." She made believable both Angelo's and Vincentio's response to her. Miss Nelligan portrayed ambivalence with a fine balance that Mr. Davis' cameras explored effectively. At the end, aware of the crowd pressure that Vincentio had brought to bear on her, Miss Nelligan's Isabella dismissed it as irrelevant, sought within herself for a response, found that being a duchess felt right to her, and took Vincentio's greatly relieved hand.

One felt the lack of a stage history behind this production—a point the Royal Shakespeare Company has driven home with a television version of its superb studio production of *Macbeth*. The relative stiffness of the two scenes between Angelo and Isabella, however, made a point. The ducal palace itself was a sober, almost Calvinistic zone of oaken furniture, inlaid flooring, and intricate leaded glass, a suitable setting for Tom Pigott-Smith's arrogant Angelo. But the arrogant facade soon melted in a flash of lust. The two scenes between Angelo and Isabella suggested profoundly how inner confusion can emerge as external absolutism, can become "that icy zealotry which is repressed passion," as Michael Long suggests of these two.[1]

Davis' camera was always alert to emotional nuance. Christopher Strauli's Claudio, with his weak and sensual mouth, agreed with the Friar's "Be absolute for death" because it was polite so to do. His superficial acceptance prepared us for the deep panic of his plea to Isabella. Yolanda Palfrey's Juliet, very much with child, accepted the Friar's condemnation of her transgression but resented his remorseless driving home of the point. The intimate effects achieved by Davis and his actors were nicely suited to the medium. Many of these grace-notes would have been swallowed up in large theatres. Davis' interpretation did not go as far, perhaps, as Long's indictment of Vincentio for believing "that the social world will be made beautiful if only nature can be stopped working."[2] Since some of the Friar's advice in the gaol does not really apply to the human issues involved—a young man facing beheading for premature consummation of his marriage, a young woman swelling with new life, but about to deliver a Posthumus—Davis' focus on the receivers of the advice allowed us to question the easy formulae.

Certainly Davis gave us a "studio production" at the end of the play, the obviousness of the setting reminiscent of Olivier's intentional reminders of artificiality in *Henry V*. And much to the same purpose: the war in France is a production staged by Henry V, and the long final scene of *Measure for Measure* is certainly Vincentio's production. The overt theatricality of that scene, as Davis rendered it, called attention to its function as a kind of "play within the play." Thus, as in so many of Shakespeare's plays, we were placed at a distance from the on-stage audience. Thus we were allowed to judge the Duke's production.

I have always found the Duke's manipulations distasteful. Davis allowed, I believe, for that interpretation, showing us only that Vincentio's elaborate mechanism works. But has the socio-political structure of Vienna's court widened to incorporate a vision of human possibility that it had formerly excluded? Or was the final scene merely an articulation of the Duke's egoneeds? While Davis gave us an image-conscious Duke, the production did not necessarily condemn him for that. Perhaps image-making is a necessity in politics, and perhaps Vincentio belongs in a triumvirate with Henry V and Octavius as Shakespeare's most successful public leaders. Davis' treatment probed the question of Vincentio effectively. The production did not coerce either script or spectator into any black-and-white interpretation.

Free of the "bright idea," the script was allowed to flow beyond the rigid demarcations Vincentio might have wished to impose on inchoate Vienna. And it was just that tension between individual energy and preconceived format that Davis captured, achieving a probing of our own energies that the usual television show does not attempt. The issues have not resolved themselves for us, obviously; nor will they merely because a Duke on the tube has dictated a comic ending to the tiny characters held within the colored rectangle.

The ending, then, whatever we make of it, goes well beyond melodrama. The term melodrama, in fact, is both inadequate for and unfair to *Measure for Measure*. The Duke may be a benevolent ruler, but with all Shakespearean rulers, including Prospero, ironies accrue. Angelo is hardly a conventional mustache-twisting villain; nor is he merely a typical hypocrite. Isabella is no Pearl Pureheart, roped to the railway tracks, awaiting the rescue of Mighty Mouse. Melodrama gives us characters both conventional and predictable, and that cannot be said of *Measure for Measure*. The issue of the play is a continuing evaluation by its spectator of the issues seemingly resolved on stage.

Television has an opportunity, via Shakespeare, to deepen its function. Some have argued that the tube, with its fantasies and wish-fulfillments, its vicarious experiences (where the housewife can substitute for the adulteress, somewhat as Mariana pinch-hits for Isabella), represents America's "unconscious." The tube, then, replaces the normal function of dreams, whether that function be to work off gastric upset in technicolor or recreate the previous few days' events via a newsreel that demonstrates the latent sexual content of those events. While I happen to believe that dreams are deeper than that, I find it interesting that television, if the unconscious, tends to reflect only the shallower versions of the psyche. Is such shallowness an absolute generic limitation of television, or is it merely a structural problem? Certainly such shallowness is a component of our crucially important expectation of what the tube will yield.

Suffice it that Davis' fine *Measure for Measure* opens our expectations for the medium towards the deeper definitions of the unconscious. Davis was not consciously attempting to do this, of course, but a good director's instincts take him and his play in directions that challenge the shallow one-dimensionality of a medium that can deal "in depth." This production proves the point. If our expectations of the medium incorporate only what it usually gives us, then we are as diminished as we would be were our expectations of our unconscious activity reduced only to the effects of those damned onions we had in the salad. Davis' production, based on a play already framed for a medium undreamt of in Shakespeare's philosophy, released the meaning latent in this ambiguous script. That meaning is, simply put, "With what measure ye mete, it shall be measured to you again, measure still for measure."

1. Michael Long, *The Unnatural Scene* (London: Methuen, 1976), p. 87.
2. Long, p. 92.

The BBC All's Well That Ends Well
G. K. Hunter

In choice of actors and actresses, the cutting of the text, the tempo of speech and action, the invention of stage business, the use of props—in all these respects the criticism of Shakespeare on television deals with the same matters as appear in theatrical or film criticism. To collapse television Shakespeare into this larger prospect is to lose what is unique or essential to it and to find material too rich and too divergent for treatment in this brief consideration of the BBC *All's Well That Ends Well*. I wish instead to focus on what television, as a unique medium with its own particular strengths, has brought to *All's Well*.

Before I reach that play, however, I must raise for inspection what I see as a basic problem about the presentation on television of plays designed to take advantage of the three-dimensionality of the stage. I use this clumsy locution to exclude some plays undoubtedly appropriate for the stage (I think of Beckett), part of whose hunger for renunciation expresses itself as a hankering for two-dimensionality. Stage dramatists who draw on conventional social life (as Shakespeare does) seem to expect us to see (in both the literal and the transferred senses) members of their stage society set before us on a series of planes of recession. Irony and sophistication derive in part from the mobility of these planes, their threat to collide or override one another. But television finds it difficult, if not impossible, to reproduce the visual component of this kind of structure, since it seems (technically?) incapable of showing us a convincing third dimension. What I take to be a *locus classicus* is television's apparent attempt, and total failure, to achieve the stage effects of the most celebrated passage of stage business in *Twelfth Night*—the gulling of Malvolio. In the BBC version of this scene the actors did what actors always do, and probably ought to do. They tried to make comedy out of the proximity of the two planes visible on the stage—the plane of the watchers (Andrew, Toby, Fabian) and the plane of the watched (Malvolio)—and the constant danger of their collision. They tried to show their superiority to Malvolio by running forward to stand (unseen) just behind him; and then, as he seemed about to turn around, they had to run back. But when there is no true third dimension in the scene, such movement by the actors is quite incapable of conveying the comic tension between achievement and loss, superiority and inferiority. On the small screen it was never entirely clear when the conspirators were really close to Malvolio or when they were safely distanced. For all the time, and of necessity, they were jammed against their victim inside the narrow confines of the camera's frame.

What we are given here is a dismal plastic reproduction of a brilliant theatrical object, stage-actors doing what they have every reason to suppose will work, inside a medium which ensures that it won't. My praise for *All's Well* in the BBC series is that it seems to accept the inevitable diminution in theatrical power that the translation involves, and tries to invent new relationships which will (to some degree) compensate for that loss. Of course it is only a spasmodic and half-cocked kind of compensation. There is still too much dependence on that kind of triangulation in which A faces B on the frontscreen position while C, slightly out of focus, contrives to keep his face always visible between the other two, until the camera finally rewards his persistence, unmists the focus, invites him into the foreground and sets up a new dialogue. But the opening scene, with its Dutch interior out of Vermeer and its open door through which characters come and go, and beyond which we see minuscule servants packing Bertram's tuck-box, gave us an excuse for thinking in painterly terms of artificial space instead of the theatrical vocabulary of real stage depth. Throughout the production, mirrors, windows, candlelight, firelight and deep shadow, obliquely angled shots, insisted on the "composed" quality of what we saw and so reduced our identification with the individual inside society and his movement through it.

That this did not work all the time was made evident in the second scene. Here we meet the French king, strongly lit and prostrate in bed. The scene reminded me of Rembrandt's "The Anatomy Lesson of Dr. Tulp." But where Rembrandt's composition is carefully balanced between the prostrate body, the elegant Dr. Tulp and the excited students, the *All's Well* scene was concentrated on the body. The court ("divers Attendants" in F_1) consisted of two persons, and they barely able to squeeze inside the frame. I do not know if the rather fruity performance by Donald Sinden was cause or effect of the absence of social diagram, but certainly the scene was one of the lapses in a usually cool and contained production, and seemed to be asking us for responses that were irrelevant to the rest of the play.

The production's capacity to think out visual coordinates for itself and not simply to follow the stage tradition may be discussed usefully in terms of the scene of the ambushing of Parolles (IV.i), which can be set against the scene of the gulling of Malvolio, already discussed. This time the relationship of watcher and watched was organized in terms of above and below rather than upstage and downstage. The watchers on a roof (or something such) look down on Parolles as he prepares to nap-out the time of his exploit. The viewpoint corresponds neatly to the pattern of dramatic advantage and disadvantage; but no attempt was made to exploit this further by suggesting the instability of the visual relationship (near or far). Much of the fun of to-and-fro that I seem to remember from Tyrone Guthrie's production was lost; and I suspect it has to be lost when we watch the play on television. It is worth noting that this scene came across more effectively than the more famous one which follows (IV.iii)—the scene of Parolles's interrogation, which seems, in reading, to offer many more possibilities. In this case the constant change of character-centre, the tripartite organisation, with the officers on one side, blindfolded Parolles on the other and the "Interpreter" going between them, was too complex to manage as a series of close-ups. As the camera swung from face to face we seemed to be given more disconnection and more distance than the scene could stand. The comic anticipation of answers was lost and the repeated shift in balance between different members of the group, as now one, now another, tried to take advantage, was hard to follow. Looking at Parolles on his own, one saw his terror rather than his social discomfiture; as commonly happens in television plays, psychology usurped the place of social reality.

I should like to finish with what seemed to me the best moment in the production. The last scene in *All's Well* is a famous set of puzzles, as Bertram tries to lie his way back into favour and actually succeeds. The scene sharpens intolerably the play's basic problem of horribly real people caught up in a fairy tale—a tale for which a single ending will cure everything, the resurrection of Helena being magically transformed from a trick (which is what *we* know it is) to a miracle (which is what *they* think it is). The play comes to rest, that is, on the magical transformation of *their* world, and to this the director in some way has to subordinate *our* knowledge. What they see is that the light that shone on them while Helena was alive is recoverable. On the stage, as the tension builds up through the intrigue, the reservation of Helena for a miraculous knot-cutting entry places an intolerable burden on that entry: can one simple step through the door cause all this? We see her as she is and not as she is received. The television production solved the problem, brilliantly I thought, by concealing the entry. The family and its supporters have lined up imperceptibly, facing the door through which Diana is being taken to prison. At the door she stops and pleads her final stay of execution: "Good mother, fetch my bail." As the cast looks through the door music begins to play. "Behold the meaning," says Diana. But the camera does not allow us to behold. Instead it does what the camera does best—it shows us a set of mouths and eyes. As it tracks along the line we are made witness to a series of inner sunrises, as face after face responds to the miracle and lights up with understanding and relief. I confess to finding it a very moving experience.

From "Television Shakespeare: Jonathan Miller and 'Director's Theatre' "

Stanley Wells

When we think about the performance of a play in the theatre, one of the most fundamental questions we ask ourselves is whether the director appears to have wished to convey a particular overall interpretation, and if so, what that interpretation is. We live in an age of what is often described as "director's theatre," or "director's Shakespeare," a movement which has been particularly, though not exclusively, forwarded by the work of the Royal Shakespeare Company. An early proponent of it with that company was Peter Hall; oddly enough, as director of the National Theatre he has seemed sometimes to be leading a reaction against it, with his own rather strenuously neutral productions of *Hamlet* and *Othello*, and with Peter Gill's *Much Ado About Nothing*. But even at the National there has recently been Michael Rudman's vivid, colorful, and joyous Caribbean *Measure for Measure*—a problem play with a happy ending. A few of the BBC television productions have similarly given the impression that the director was trying to convey ideas about the play during the course of its performance, and this impression is in part supported by the printed evidence. The textual abbreviation of *The Taming of the Shrew* clearly was carried out with interpretative intent. Dr. Miller has declared that "the great challenge" in directing this play "is to retrieve a humorous play from the wreckage of facetiousness, the accumulated tradition of horseplay." He has spoken very interestingly about the ideas of the play, suggesting that it "has overtones on a miniature scale of *King Lear*; the father's failure to recognise the truly valuable daughter; the importance of maintaining order; above all, the Calvinist issue of recognising that the virtue of your mind is all that matters, not the appearance of your body or your dress. 'To me she's married, not unto my clothes' and ''Tis the mind that makes the body rich.'" This is, he says, "one of [Shakespeare's] good, serious plays, cast in a comic mode."

Though I have no quarrel with Dr. Miller's comparison of the play with *King Lear*, I have to admit that I find some of his statements a touch portentous. More importantly, I feel that his interpretation resulted in a performance which denied some of the play's inherent comedy and reduced its complexity. It ended with the company singing "a Puritan hymn, a paraphrase of one of the psalms, in which marriage is celebrated not as a social convention but as a manifestation of the ideal relationship between man, woman, and God" (John Wilders, introducing the BBC edition). This may be apt enough as a symbol of "the importance of maintaining order," but it seemed to me a sad anticlimax. Cozy domesticism took over from the exhilaration, delight, and wonder at a transformation miraculously achieved, spiced with a hint of ironic skepticism, with which a good performance of the play leaves

Reprinted, with permission, from *Shakespeare Quarterly*, 33 (Fall 1982), 261–77.

me. I am all in favor of rescuing the play from bad traditions exemplified by Zeffirelli's film. I think it speaks to us on a serious as well as a comic level—or, more precisely, I think it speaks to us seriously because it speaks to us on a comic level—but I did not find that its comic seriousness was fully conveyed by Dr. Miller's production. In saying this I am simply disagreeing with Dr. Miller's interpretation, which is of course a subjective reaction and does not deny the possibility that Dr. Miller made of the play something that had its own validity. Because his interpretation consisted of an attempt to restore the play's Elizabethan-ness, not (as is common) to seek in it for modern relevance, the interpretation could be conveyed within the conventions of the series so far as costume was concerned. But undeniably it was achieved at the expense of textual authenticity. Henry Fenwick says as much, though he puts it rather differently, in his article in the BBC edition, where he writes: "The only cut Miller took was to remove the Induction—that odd and unresolved framework of the beggar Sly being duped and entertained by a wealthy lord. Its removal is by no means new, and not only did it tidy the play considerably, it also helped the seriousness of the approach." That amounts to an admission that we were offered an interpretation of the play's action which depended upon a denial of part of its text. In principle I do not object to this. As I have said, I think that adaptation is justifiable. It happens that I value the Induction rather highly, partly because it contains some very fine verse, partly because Sly is an excellent piece of characterization, partly because I think it is funny in a style of comedy that is grounded in reality, and most of all because I think that the framework, for all that it is, certainly, "unresolved," is nevertheless integral to the play in its portrayal of a beggar whose imagination is worked upon in ways that prefigure the way Petruchio is to work on Kate's imagination. So I think that its omission diminishes the play and therefore works against the declared aims of the series.

It also points, perhaps, to the fact that scenes in which some characters overlook or overhear others present particular problems on television, that the existence of an extra dimension which in the theatre may seem an enrichment may in television terms seem an untidiness. In the theatre we can be aware simultaneously of the presence on an upper stage level of Christopher Sly and others while we also watch the play that is being performed for their entertainment. This kind of simultaneity is much more difficult to achieve on the small, two-dimensional television screen; and I wonder if this may have been one of the reasons why it was eliminated. Certainly it seemed to be a problem in *Troilus and Cressida*, in the even more complex counterpoint of the scene in which Cressida and Diomedes are watched simultaneously by Troilus and Ulysses and also by Thersites. We saw some striking shots of Troilus and Ulysses watching the lovers' silhouettes cast as shadows on the wall of their tent; but Thersites was accommodated only by cutting to separate shots of him, and a number of his interjections were omitted. A different kind of simultaneity is needed in the last scene of *The Winter's Tale*, when it is important that we be made aware not just of Leontes' emotions at Hermione's apparent resurrection, but of the bystanders' feelings too. In the television production, I found, the focus on individuals denied us the sense of simultaneous involvement, the thrill of ritual participation as the stone is made flesh.

. . . The kind of interpretation which avowedly lay behind the production and adaptation of *The Taming of the Shrew* has not, I think, been common elsewhere in the series, where the style has tended to the neutral, towards an attempt to let the play speak for itself without directorial interposition. I was made particularly conscious of this by the fact that not long before seeing Jonathan Miller's television *Troilus and Cressida* I had seen Terry Hands's Royal Shakespeare Company production at the Aldwych Theatre. The stage version was very much the play as seen through the eyes of Thersites; many production devices were employed to guide the audience's reactions. The scene in which we see Helen of Troy was a virtual orgy: we were left in no doubt that we were to regard her as corrupt and decadent. The Greek heroes were caricatured; Achilles clearly intended to seduce Hector the night before the battle. Modern parallels were suggested: a mouth-organ played in the camp scenes, Pandarus ended the play virtually impaled on a barbed-wire fence.

The different approach of the television version was epitomized in the handling of the Prologue. In the printed text, the speaker of the Prologue has no other function in the play. Terry Hands gave the lines to Thersites, instantly setting a cynical tone. Jonathan Miller gave them to an anonymous voice—actually, I understand, and significantly, that of the actor who played Ulysses—which spoke them coolly, dispassionately. This objectivity characterized the entire production. A setting of broad, sunlit stone corridors and a circular, supposedly outdoor space, localized the action; the aim seemed to be simply to create a sense of reality, not to carry interpretative implications. There was no equivalent to Terry Hands's First World War analogies. The love-making of Paris and Helen was comparatively modest. The camera work was unobtrusive, often employing long takes with a static camera and no shift in perspective. There were few omissions, and most of these were in the complicated battle scenes. (It is clear from many statements in the BBC editions that the television directors dread battle scenes.) The action unfolded with exemplary clarity except in the difficult overhearing scene which I mentioned earlier. The result was an interesting and highly respect-worthy production, though not, I thought, one that plumbed the play's poetic depths.

If production styles have not on the whole been especially illuminating or penetrating, they have nevertheless had their originalities and even their brilliancies. There were interesting touches in the *Troilus*: Helen was present (though silent and virtually motionless) while her fate was debated by the Trojan leaders; Achilles clipped his beard before a looking-glass as he instructed his Myrmidons; Calchas was brought unexpectedly to vivid life as a slippery traitor. Still more of a director's success was Jonathan Miller's handling of the first part of *Timon of Athens*, a difficult because partially unrealized play. Dr. Miller skillfully filled in the crevices of the text, setting the opening scene at a lavish reception which made an appropriate background to Jonathan Pryce's portrayal of Timon's touchingly obsessive generosity. A realistic, and voraciously devoured, banquet reinforced the recurrent imagery of food and eating which is an essential part of Shakespeare's exploration of false and true values; and the masque was an admirable, genuinely and relevantly educational piece of period reconstruction. This seemed to me to be the kind of directorial brilliance which serves the play, realization rather than self-assertive interpretation. In the second part, however, eccentricity supervened, particularly in the decision to show nothing but Timon's head upside-down throughout his later speeches.

In looking for examples of interesting direction I find that I have unintentionally taken all of them from productions directed by Dr. Miller himself, which I hope is a tribute to the unfailing intelligence of his work. But his style of direction, along with that of all his colleagues, is one that throws a heavy burden of responsibility upon the actors. Neither in interpretation nor in technique of presentation is the director making things easy for them. In general, the conditions of acting are those of a theatre, but with no live audience and with cameras not far away. This presents problems especially of scale.

. . . The fact that one is conscious of such problems stresses the intimacy of television as a medium. Both this and the emphasis given by the series to the actors have encouraged a focus on individual character. I was made particularly conscious of this by reading the introductions to the BBC editions, where there is much talk about the characters as individuals. Of course, most actors need to believe in the reality of the character they are portraying; but Dr. Miller did not rebut Anne Pasternak Slater's comparison of him with "Bradley, with his painful detailing of character." To her remark "You're very interested in the fullness of character, too," Dr. Miller responded with an admission that he is "extremely interested in minute naturalistic detail" while stressing too that he has "a classicizing streak . . . which sees things as abstracted, reduced, and formalised." The interest in detail can lead to successes such as the vivid portrayal of so minor a character as Calchas. It can result in a kind of fragmentation which perhaps is particularly likely to occur with groups of actors who are brought together to act in a single production over a short period of time. There can be little opportunity in these circumstances to achieve stylistic cohesion. So in *The Taming of the Shrew* I felt at times too much of a sense that each actor was "doing his own thing" in a style that had not been tightly enough controlled. Anthony Pedley, as Tranio, deployed the full armory of the farce actor, with exaggerated facial expression and grotesque speech characteristics, while others—such as Frank Thornton in his unusually dignified and sympathetic presentation of Gremio—underplayed their comedy. A new departure for the series which we have not yet been able to assess is the use for the three parts of *Henry VI* and *Richard III* of a company of about forty actors, working under a single director, with a full-time fight director and choreographer, for all four plays. It will be interesting to see if this worthwhile experiment pays off in stylistic unity.

Nahum Tate Is Alive and Well
Elijah Moshinsky's BBC Shakespeare Productions
Gordon P. Jones

> I found . . . a heap of jewels, unstrung and unpolished, yet so dazzling in the disorder that I soon perceived I had seized a treasure. 'Twas my good fortune to light on one expedient to rectify what was wanting in the regularity and probability of the tale, which was to run through the whole a love betwixt Edgar and Cordelia that never changed a word with each other in the original.
>
> (Nahum Tate, "Dedication," *The History of King Lear*)[1]

Seventeenth- and eighteenth-century redactors of Shakespeare were inclined to revere and patronise Shakespeare at one and the same time. Here was treasure, but treasure that needed to be cut, reground, polished, and displayed in conformity with the styles, conventions and values of their age. Sir George Raynsford's Prologue to Nahum Tate's recension of *Coriolanus* explains the function of the author-reviser in these terms:

> He only ventures to make gold from ore,
> And turn to money what lay dead before.[2]

The adapter, in other words, processes otherwise valueless raw material to produce a profitable cultural commodity.

The most famous of these commodities, Nahum Tate's *History of King Lear*, is exemplary, not only for the manner in which it refines Shakespeare's play by simplifying and sentimentalising, but for the enthusiastic manner in which it was received. Unlike his adaptations of *Richard II* (*The Sicilian Usurper*) and *Coriolanus* (*The Ingratitude of a Commonwealth*), Tate's redaction of *King Lear* was enormously popular, so much so that "his version, and revisions of it, kept Shakespeare from the stage for a century and a half."[3]

Of course, Tate's adaptation of *King Lear* is much more fundamental than anything essayed in the BBC series. The BBC television versions may generally be abbreviated, and they may sometimes entail minor scenic rearrangement or redistribution of speech assignments, but they do not as a rule incorporate additional action or supplementary dialogue. Nevertheless, some of the BBC productions are much more severely truncated and much more radically adaptive than is generally appreciated. Indeed, a number of the productions are best understood as mild redactions, which labour, like Restoration adaptations of Shakespeare, to assimilate the text by reducing it to conventional formulas and popular levels of understanding.

The necessity of adjusting television productions of Shakespeare to the needs and expectations of a mass audience is articulated repeatedly in the prefatory material to the printed editions of the plays published by the BBC. One example will suffice:

> Under Jonathan Miller's rule as producer of the series, we have at all times tried to remain aware of the fact that every play will be seen by millions of people who have never seen, or indeed read, a Shakespeare play before; and that these people should therefore be given the chance to see a version of the play that sticks as faithfully as possible to the text. At the same time, however, such a ruling should never be enforced to the extent of possibly hampering a viewer's understanding, enjoyment and general involvement. . . . If omissions, and even rearrangements, have to be made in order to facilitate a director's attempt to tell the play's story, and to ensure an audience's involvement, then they have to be made.[4]

This draconian attitude to the expendability of dramatic material that may possibly hamper "a viewer's understanding, enjoyment and general involvement" is so prevalent that remaining close to the text becomes a matter for comment. In directing *The Winter's Tale*, Jane Howell "has chosen to remain largely faithful to the text as printed;"[5] Jonathan Miller's *Troilus and Cressida* is "allowed to run most of its curiously prolix course;"[6] in directing *Othello*, Miller "has chosen to remain reasonably faithful to the text as printed;"[7] and, in directing *The Merchant of Venice*, Jack Gold "has chosen to be entirely faithful" to the play as written.[8] Granted, these are the comments of the script editor, David Snodin, not the directors, but I take them to represent prevailing attitudes and assumptions.

I would submit that, mutatis mutandis, anxiety to temper the Shakespearean wind to the shorn lamb of the latter-day audience unites Restoration adapters and the more interventionist BBC Shakespeare directors, of whom Elijah Moshinsky is my example. Both deliberately reshape the text, more or less radically, to make plays "serve the stronger interests of moral clarity, of easily understandable motivation, of sharpened comparison and contrast, or simply of balance and unity."[9] This observation was made about Restoration adaptations of Shakespeare. It applies with equal force to the five plays Elijah Moshinsky directed for the BBC series: *All's Well That Ends Well* (1980), *A Midsummer Night's Dream* (1981), *Cymbeline* (1982), *Coriolanus* (1983), and *Love's Labour's Lost* (1984). As will be argued below, all five productions simplify action, dialogue, characterisation, and meaning, so as to make the plays more readily assimilable by a modern mass audience. Norman Rabkin's observation about Restoration adaptations applies equally to Moshinsky's television versions of Shakespeare—it is the ambiguities that are particularly excised.[10]

Restoration adaptations and television productions share another characteristic. They are alike in being responses to new technology. The new technology of our day is television; the new technology of the age of Nahum Tate was the proscenium stage.

> The picture stage had replaced the platform stage, and the picture stage necessitated the revision of plays, which were written for another method of presentation, but were now to be interpreted by another theatrical medium.[11]

Substitute "television" for "picture stage" in the preceding statement and you have the familiar theme that Shakespeare requires extensive textual modification in the passage from stage to television screen. The following account of editing A *Midsummer Night's Dream* for television is characteristic:

> There have been several cuts and changes in this production, some of which might seem quite savage to textual purists; but every such divergence from the text as printed has been made for a sound reason, very often simply in order to make this most theatrical of plays work more satisfactorily in what is after all the very different medium of television, and indeed to exploit to the utmost the advantages of the television medium over the theatre.[12]

The adjustments involved in this process of media transfer may be technical in origin; but they cannot remain simply technical in effect, even if no substantial textual modification is involved in a particular production. The low resolution and tight focus of the television image, the preselection of image and field of vision, the intimacy and immediacy of sight and sound, these all have interpretive consequences, which are amplified when the text is actively modified to accommodate features of the electronic medium or characteristics of the mass audience.

It is not surprising that Elijah Moshinsky's productions in the BBC Shakespeare series have been generally well received. They are attractive in design and polished in presentation. They utilise the medium intelligently and conform technically and stylistically to our experience as media consumers. They are also amongst the most heavily shaped and edited of the productions in the BBC series.

In modifying the plays for television, Moshinsky reduces running time quite drastically. In the process, he redefines the text, simplifying narrative, schematising structure and theme, and making dialogue and meaning more specific, more direct, and less multivalent. So, as a rule, without actually adding any material, Moshinsky may nevertheless be considered to be engaged in what Tate called "new-modelling" of a play,[13] or what Davenant referred to as "reforming" and "making fit" for a new generation of playgoers.[14]

The first of Moshinsky's BBC commissions was *All's Well That Ends Well* (1980). It is very attractive visually, with its Caroline costumes and Vermeer settings. Lighting, blocking, camera-work, switching and editing are imaginative and technically sophisticated. Despite Moshinsky's absence of previous television-directing experience, we are never in danger of feeling that the director does not understand the potential or relish the power of the medium in which he is working. However, the text of *All's Well* is very heavily cut, not only to reduce running time, but to simplify the narrative structure of one of Shakespeare's less familiar comedies. The director, we are informed, was "given the freedom to make several major omissions and even rearrangements in order to facilitate his attempt to tell the play's story and to guarantee his audience's involvement."[15]

The two brief and relatively unimportant scenes at the court of the Duke of Florence (III.i; III.iii) are omitted; the Epilogue is dropped; the Clown's part is halved; Lafeu's characteristic prolixity is trimmed; and many elaborative or generalising passages in various mouths are abbreviated or omitted. Material regarded as being "something of a divergence from the main thrust of the plot"[16] is sacrificed in the interest of clarity and directness of exposition. But this process of narrative simplification has direct implications for theme and character. The tangential comic commentary provided by the Clown is diminished, Lafeu's character is modified slightly, and the intellectual and philosophical fabric of the play is attenuated by reduction in the level of generalisation and abstraction. This doubtless makes the play easier to understand. It is easier to understand because its meaning has been diminished to meet the demands of the mass market and the technical requirements of the electronic medium.

Technical differences between stage and television as performance mediums are the rationale for textual changes in the second of Moshinsky's BBC productions, *A Midsummer Night's Dream* (1981). Many of the alterations involve dropping descriptive or recapitulatory material that can be directly shown or may be inferred, for example the dialogue between Puck and a Fairy about Puck's tricks (II.i.34–57), Puck's description of Titania falling in love with Bottom (III.ii.1–40), and much of the hunting-scene description (IV.i.100–123). Dialogue is made leaner, action is accelerated, and meaning is made more specific by abbreviating or omitting passages that are elaborative or generalising in effect. Speeches of Demetrius (II.i.188–94), Lysander (II.ii.137–42), and Helena (II.i.195–98, 229-34; III.ii.127ff.) are treated in this manner as a way of saving time as well as adjusting the text to a medium that specialises in discrete imagery and realistic speech and action.

Some cutting in *A Midsummer Night's Dream* combines technical and interpretive considerations. The asides and interjections from the Athenian audience in the Pyramus and Thisbe play-scene are reduced in number. This common Elizabethan dramatic device calls for precise editing and rapid switching in television production. It is avoided when possible in the BBC series, perhaps for technical, perhaps for stylistic reasons.

In the Pyramus and Thisbe scene, the script editor justifies dropping asides on interpretive grounds, "in order to allow the story . . . to unfold in a fundamentally serious and uninterrupted fashion."[17] Yet allowing the story of Pyramus and Thisbe as interpreted by Bottom and company "to unfold in a fundamentally serious and uninterrupted fashion" would seem to be precisely what Shakespeare does not intend. The truth of the matter is that, in the absence of a live theatrical or studio audience responding to the cumulative absurdity of the play-within-the-play, it is very difficult to make the scene work effectively and build to a comic climax. Removing some of the interjections and playing the episode straighter than usual is one way of making the best of a bad job.

The next of Moshinsky's productions was *Cymbeline* (1982), by which time, as Henry Fenwick rather bravely claims in the BBC edition of the text, "Moshinsky has already gained a reputation for his treatment of the texts. With an intense respect for them he nevertheless has no fear of altering them for purposes of the television screen."[18] As in Moshinsky's version of *All's Well That Ends Well*, narrative simplification was a major editorial consideration in preparing *Cymbeline* for the television screen:

> A good deal of fairly radical pruning and changing has occurred in this production. Much of this considerable abridgement and rearrangement has been the result of wanting to make a complex tale clearer by ridding it of comparative irrelevancies. . . .[19]

Another editorial criterion is also enunciated, that of maintaining "a peculiarly high level of emotional intensity."[20] In some scenes it was apparently "impossible to sustain the necessary energy without severe cutting . . . the prime victims of such surgery being the banished Belarius and his 'sons.' "[21] In addition to extensive curtailment of material in the vicinity of Belarius and sons, Cymbeline's defiance of Rome is abbreviated in III.i, as is Imogen's excitement in III.ii and the scene at Milford Haven between Imogen and Pisanio (III.iv). Also compressed or deleted are the brief scene of Roman war preparations (III.vii), the scene establishing the illness of the Queen (IV.iii), and Posthumus's dream of his ancestors (V.iv). Various scenes of military action are abbreviated, rearranged, relocated, or omitted. Asides are frequently deleted. The Second Lord's asides commenting on Cloten in I.ii are reduced in number from eight to two; Iachimo's aside on the rarity of Imogen is dropped (I.vi.13–21); and the scene involving Cloten and the two Lords (II.i) is abridged, including all six of the Second Lord's asides and his final monologue on Imogen's plight. However, the great sequence of revelations and recognitions in the final scene of *Cymbeline* is left more or less intact, except for a few questions, exclamations and recapitulations.

The effect of all this editorial intervention in *Cymbeline* is to simplify radically the baroque narrative structure of the play. One may wonder, however, whether narrative density and complexity may not have been a major feature of the dramatist's intention in this elaborate Romance.

The next of Moshinsky's BBC productions, *Coriolanus* (1983), is the production in which editing for television creates the most fundamental alteration in the structure and significance of the play. Like Moshinsky's other productions, it is visually interesting and technically adroit. It is also intellectually cogent; but the cogency is Moshinsky's, not Shakespeare's. The play is drastically cut, "in order to reveal the plot-line more starkly."²² "So quite a lot has gone," the script editor complacently observes; "we've cut from a run of three and a half hours to a play that's not much over two and a half."²³

The cutting of *Coriolanus* not only reveals the plot-line more starkly, it alters the shape and significance of the play. Henry Fenwick reports the convergent views of the script editor and the director:

> Many of the cuts were taken from scenes between servants or people of Rome, "not out of any elitist preference," Snodin laughs, "but because it does hold up the pure thrust of the story." "I really do think they're detachable," says Moshinsky. "You do want your plots on TV to become very intense and more close-up and you don't want suddenly to introduce by-play among the servants: it just wouldn't take it, I think."²⁴

Unfortunately for this rationale, in *Coriolanus* the servants and the people of Rome represent something more than simple "by-play." The plebeians are collectively a principal force in the play. Reducing their prominence fundamentally alters the structural and thematic balance of the work.

The initial exchange between Menenius and the Citizens, which does so much to establish the tone of the play, is cut by more than a third prior to the entry of Marcius (I.i). The subsequent manipulation of the plebeians by the Tribunes is edited out almost entirely (II.iii.173–96, 209–14, 216–60). The comic scene of Coriolanus among the servants in Aufidius's household (IV.v.1–52) and the later commentary by the same servants (IV.v.147–233) are discarded. The puncturing of the complacency of the Roman populace after the exile of Coriolanus (IV.vi.10–35) is also omitted.

Of a piece with these cuts is the disembowelling and decomicalising of Menenius. His initial exchange with the Citizens is compressed. His testy exchange with the Tribunes (II.i.42–60, 75–86) and his comic chuntering (II.i.176–85) are both cut. His quarrel with the Volscian Watch outside the walls of Rome is entirely omitted (V.ii.1–66), as is the subsequent commentary of the Watch (V.ii.91–105). In other words, the range and subtlety of human and political implication that Shakespeare introduces through the plebeians, the servants, the Watch, and Menenius are suppressed by Moshinsky, who is intent on producing a monochromatic political and psychological tract. It is not that a single dimension of the play has been neglected; the whole of the play is misrepresented by this treatment—as radically as *King Lear* is misrepresented by Nahum Tate's rewriting of Shakespeare's masterwork, or as radically as *Coriolanus* is misrepresented by *The Ingratitude of a Commonwealth*, in which Tate "purges *Coriolanus* of its central problematics."²⁵

Elijah Moshinsky's final production, *Love's Labour's Lost* (1984), is unique in the BBC series for its post-period costume and setting. Located in an eigh-teenth century evocative of the elegance of Mozart and the charm of Watteau, Moshinsky's production is an imaginative and stylish rendering of Shakes-peare's text for the visually insistent medium of television.

In adapting this most garrulous of plays, it is not surprising that Moshinsky should have found it necessary to drop some of the more obscure allusions and abbreviate some of the more elaborate displays of verbal virtuosity, "to allow a swifter narrative and lighter movement from scene to scene."[26] How-ever, what Moshinsky calls his "fairly radical pruning and changing of the text"[27] is by no means interpretively neutral. With few exceptions, the cuts underscore the production design, articulating a vision of an elegantly culti-vated society turning its back on the natural world. This vision is not untrue, it is simply partial. But it is elevated into the single design concept; counter-indications and alternative perspectives in the text are ignored or suppressed, and the full complexity and exuberance of the play are sacrificed on the altar of tonal consistency. The coarser perspectives and more patent behavioural absurdities of characters of less elevated social status are muted throughout the production. The distinctive if uncultivated voices of Armado, Moth, Holofernes, Costard, Dull, and Jaquenetta are all muffled by extensive cut-ting. The spontaneous, the natural, the vulgar, and the absurd are cut away to maintain the stylistic elegance that is the keynote of Moshinsky's adaptation of *Love's Labour's Lost*.

In I.ii approximately half of the badinage between Armado and Moth is omitted, and their comic discussion of love in III.i.7–44 is dropped. In IV.ii a little of the bantering amongst Jaquenetta, Holofernes, and Nathaniel is pruned; and the celebrated, if occasionally obscure, passage in which Moth, Armado, Costard, Holofernes, and Nathaniel debate language with more en-thusiasm than knowledge (V.i.39–72) is heavily abbreviated. Even ladies and gentlemen of social consequence are not safe from this gelding which drains so much energy out of the text. The brief exchange involving Maria, Boyet, and Costard in which Costard is rebuked for talking "greasily" (IV.i.122–34) is also absent from Moshinsky's version.

Other textual losses further reduce the vitality and blunt the cutting edge of *Love's Labour's Lost*. Some of Berowne's extravagant commentary on love is omitted or abbreviated (IV.iii.230–41, 253–61, 293–313, 379–82; V.iii.418–21), and three passages indicating a strain of sexual animosity be-tween Berowne and Boyet are dropped (V.ii.321–24, 462–67, 474–81). During the Masque of the Nine Worthies, the number of asides and inter-jections is reduced (as usual) and the episode is curtailed a little so that it ends before the horse-play between the "incensed worthies" develops (V.ii.676–95).

The general effect of the cuts is to diminish the human and stylistic range of *Love's Labour's Lost,* replacing the linguistic and behavioural diversity of Shakespeare's play with a single-faceted, designer-driven uniformity. The sub-stitution makes for a clean, precise production—one which translates Shakespeare's equations into visual and auditory formulae more immediately accessible to the modern mind; but in the process it necessarily misrepresents and over-schematises the play.

To be fair, it must be said that a sensitive and imaginative director, whether in the theatre or the television studio, will always modify a play to some extent, since he is engaged in a process of filtering the work through his own experience, values, and perceptions. The effect is likely to be accentuated by a shift of medium, with the substantive and accidental alterations required by that transfer. In preparing any stage play for television production, a director is caught in a bind. Compromises constantly have to be made between the nature of the text and the potential of the medium. If the requirements of the medium predominate, textual fidelity will inevitably suffer. If textual fidelity prevails, the production will fail to exploit the powerful potential of the medium. Not to put too fine a point on it: either the director betrays the text or he betrays the medium.

In the delicate and ultimately unstable balance between television medium and pre-television text that must be struck by every director, Moshinsky never betrays the medium. The corollary is that he too readily modifies, reinterprets, and sometimes misrepresents the literary text. He shapes productions which are interpretively imaginative, intellectually cogent, visually attractive, fast moving, and technically polished. By the same token, he shapes productions which are, in a fundamental sense, abbreviated, simplified, schematised, and vulgarised adaptations of the Shakespearean originals, tailored to the taste and understanding of the consumers of the modern mass medium.

1. Nahum Tate, *The History of King Lear,* ed. James Black (Lincoln: University of Nebraska Press, 1975), pp. 1–2.

2. Nahum Tate, *The Ingratitude of a Commonwealth* [1682] (London: Cornmarket Press Facsimile, 1969). Spelling modernised.

3. Black, p. xv.

4. *The Taming of the Shrew,* BBC edition, 1980; "The Text," p. 29.

5. *The Winter's Tale,* BBC edition, 1981; "The Text," p. 30.

6. *Troilus and Cressida,* BBC edition, 1981; "The Text," p. 31.

7. *Othello,* BBC edition, 1981; "The Text," p. 31.

8. *The Merchant of Venice,* BBC edition, 1980; "The Text," p. 29.

9. Christopher Spencer, ed., *Five Restoration Adaptations of Shakespeare* (Urbana: University of Illinois Press, 1965), p. 12.

10. Norman Rabkin, *Shakespeare and the Problem of Meaning* (Chicago: University of Chicago Press, 1981), p. 110.

11. Montague Summers, ed., *Shakespeare Adaptations* (London: Jonathan Cape, 1922), p. cvii.

12. *A Midsummer Night's Dream,* BBC edition, 1981; "The Text," p. 29.

13. Black, p. 1.

14. Spencer, p. 1.

15. *All's Well That Ends Well,* BBC edition, 1981; "The Text," p. 31.

16. *Ibid.*

17. *A Midsummer Night's Dream,* BBC edition, "The Text," p. 30.

18. *Cymbeline,* BBC edition, 1982; "The Production," p. 20.

19. *Ibid.,* "The Text," p. 29.

20. *Ibid.*

21. *Ibid.*

22. *Coriolanus,* BBC edition, 1983; "The Production," p. 20.

23. *Ibid.*, p. 21.
24. *Ibid.*
25. Rabkin, p. 112.
26. *Love's Labour's Lost*, BBC edition, 1986; "The Text," p. 28.
27. *Ibid.*

Cooling the Comedy
Television as a Medium for Shakespeare's Comedy of Errors
Robert E. Wood

Until the massive project of televising the Shakespearean canon was undertaken by the BBC, there had been little reason for examining the adaptation
of Shakespeare to television. But as the project reaches completion, we find
that its varied approaches to the plays often suggest a remarkable compatibility
between television and Shakespearean performance. In *Understanding Media*
(1964), Marshall McLuhan classified television as a "cool" medium, that is,
one which demands a high level of participation by the audience.[1] Despite
the growing sophistication of television technology, McLuhan's observation
remains true, in part because only a small proportion of television programming approaches the technical limits of the medium. In particular, the
presentation of stage drama on television makes little use of technology
which would invalidate McLuhan's system of classification. A television-
conditioned audience trained to complete "cool" images may thus, in its psychological response, more resemble a theater audience than does a film audience, which expects to be completely saturated by "hot" images. The BBC
production of *The Comedy of Errors*, a successful marriage of Shakespeare's
text to the medium of television, reflects both the general relationship of stage
drama to television and relationships particular to comedy, as well as some
characteristics unique to the theme of twins.

. . . The varied perspectives of the television camera offer new life to the
joke which results from mistaken identity in *The Comedy of Errors*.[2] For
much of the play we enjoy the distance from the joke which the theater grants
us and which comedy generally requires. But the camera also allows us to
look through the eyes of the characters. In so doing, it provides us with another dimension of the joke: the characters are emotionally distant from each
other, but operate at a proximity appropriate to social intimacy. We are intellectually distanced from their entanglement by our awareness of the existence
of the twins, while at the same time we view the confusion from the physical

Reprinted, with permission, from *Literature/Film Quarterly*, 14:4 (1986), 195–202.

perspectives of the characters. In effect, we move within the joke, although the joke is not on us. But in the last act the joke is distinctly on us as we become aware that the pairs of twins we see before us result from a split-screen reproduction of the actors, a phenomenon that we always experience, at least in part, as a technical tour de force. These variations of perspective provide the classic comic mechanisms with the requisite element of surprise within a framework of familiarity.

André Bazin once observed that the problem of filmed theater is to create a space with a "dramatic opaqueness while at the same time reflecting its natural realism."[3] Bazin deplores the traditional escape from the limitation of the stage, which consists of "opening up" the play by varying the scene and creating visual images of actions implied in the play. This technique runs a great risk of combating the devices of an art designed for a limited scene, in particular by denying the text the resonance appropriate to a closed space. *The Comedy of Errors*, however, does not tempt director James Cellan Jones to the perils of "opening up." Rather its classical unity of place suggests simple distinctions: inside and outside, above and below. His production choices preserve the stage of boundaries, yet he clearly uses the three dimensions of his set. In so doing he escapes a major danger of television drama, that of presenting its audience with "flatlanders," capable only of horizontal movement within an image of limited visual depth.

The set of this production is distinctly a playing area, representative rather than realistic, but it is a playing area to which the audience has extraordinary access through the camera. The intimacy which an actor achieved only at the foremost thrust of the Elizabethan stage can be achieved anywhere on the television stage. Proximity to the actors is thus not inevitably tied to the open spaces of the thrust stage. As a result, the bounded space of the stage becomes a greater resource and the concept of the stage as microcosm is invigorated. Shakespeare's equivalence of globe and theater is invoked by a stage floor which is a mosaic map on which a tale of misfortune at sea may be paced out as it is narrated. As the stage subsumes the map, the action of the play subsumes the broader narrative of travail, which it is ultimately able to resolve.

The original framework of Shakespeare's comedy is the peril of Egeon of Syracuse. Egeon has come to Ephesus in search of his son, one of twin sons, who was lost at sea in infancy together with his mother and a slave, the latter also one of a pair of twins. As a consequence of a standing feud between Syracuse and Ephesus, Egeon is condemned to die unless, within a day, he can find someone who will provide him with a thousand marks for ransom. His narration of the reason for his presence in Ephesus invokes sympathy from the onlookers but no present remedy for his plight. To this framework director Jones has added another, a group of mimes dressed in commedia dell'arte costume. The troupe's whirling capes represent storm winds on the mosaic map in an opening shot, and their subsequent clowning makes the Duke's entrance a kind of circus display. Egeon's narrative, a somewhat long-winded excursion for the modern audience, is mimed by the clown troupe, who produce a prop ship to present the sea voyage and travail to produce two sets of identically costumed clowns to represent the twin masters and servants.[4]

The effect of the clowns is to transform an ordeal from the past into a play in the making, to diminish the play's generic kinship to romance, extended in time, and thus to emphasize present confusion. In a stage play we would say that the clowns remain onstage for the course of the performance. In this television play they remain accessible to the camera throughout the play, visible on and around a mountebank's platform that occupies a part of the set. Together with a fortune-teller, they provide a set of images to support the contention of Antipholus of Syracuse that the city is inhabited by sorcerers and witches. When in Act V narrative revelations are necessary, their miming again serves to focus on the present processes of revelation and thus to preserve the moment-by-moment quality of the playing. Yet without being explicitly offstage, the clowns can remain off-camera for long periods of time. They serve as available images which do not intrude at moments when they are irrelevant. Because of the medium, we are prepared to accept this strong reference to a staging convention, the onstage ensemble, while experiencing a somewhat different form of dramatic narration.

McLuhan suggested that we are involved in depth with the cool medium of television, that we have a sense, which we do not have while watching a film, of being present in the action.[5] Certainly we watch a great deal of television programming which is not fiction and during which we are directly addressed by newscasters and sportscasters, by ministers and psychologists, by hosts and guests, by cooks and gardeners. We are satisfied by a television play that is not completely assimilated to the photographic medium because the production is in part an informative statement about how a stage play is performed, which preserves our sense of the jeopardy involved in live performance. The flexibility of our response to the television image has further advantages. We can distinguish by context between a close-up of a man speaking and that of a man speaking to us in our own persons. I would suggest that we are far more prepared to accept the Elizabethan stage conventions of direct address as members of a television audience than we would be as members of a film audience, accustomed as we are to direct address by the face on the small screen.

The invitation to intimacy implicitly offered by television is enhanced by the predominance of the close-up on the small screen. A single face frequently constitutes the television image. Moreover, although television often acknowledges the size of the audience it reaches, it primarily approaches them as individuals rather than collectively. The largest audience in history is, paradoxically, not a crowd, but a discontinuous collection of individuals who may be addressed with the vocal tone and eye contact appropriate to personal communication.

The BBC Comedy of Errors consistently evokes the power of intimacy. The viewer becomes the focus of the attempts of the characters to rationalize their situation. The world of comedy has been described as one in which logic cannot work because logical alternatives do not exhaust the realm of possibilities. In addition to A and Not-A there is a third alternative, realizable metaphor.[6] Identical twins who consistently cross paths without meeting constitute such a metaphor. In addition to being present or absent, a twin can appear to be present. If we accept the premise that a man searching for his twin deduces nothing from the observation that complete strangers appear to recognize him, we are left with the most logical collection of characters ever to inhabit a comedy. They are even logical in choosing to discuss the logic of their positions with us by directly addressing the camera; we are, after all, in a good position to assess their relationship. We know that Antipholus of Syracuse is not Antipholus of Ephesus, that Dromio of Syracuse is not Dromio of Ephesus. The effectiveness of the convention is further enhanced by the fact that characters off-camera are not offstage: the aside given in a close-up is thus easily assimilated into a scene dominated by dialogue. This production in fact takes a further step, transforming dialogue into direct address to the audience. It is not surprising that Antipholus of Syracuse is effective in addressing to the camera the soliloquy of self-definition which establishes the most serious implications of his quest.

> He that commends me to mine own content,
> Commends me to the thing I cannot get:
> I to the world am like a drop of water,
> That in the ocean seeks another drop,
> Who, falling there to find his fellow forth
> (Unseen, inquisitive), confounds himself.
> So I, to find a mother and a brother,
> In quest of them (unhappy), ah, lose myself.

(I.ii.33–40)

But it seems equally appropriate in this production that Adriana, discussing her unruly husband with her sister, turns aside to contemplate a mirror, and her image there addresses the camera with her lament.

> Hath homely age th'alluring beauty took
> From my poor cheek? then he hath wasted it.
> What ruins are in me that can be found,
> By him not ruin'd?

(II.i.89–90, 96–97)

Off-camera, her sister remains accessible when Adriana concludes her lament by addressing her directly. In an equally intimate style, the sister Luciana addresses the camera sympathetically with what might otherwise be merely a pompous remark, "How many fond fools serve mad jealousy?"

This increased intimacy, a product both of the medium of television and of the specific production choices, makes manifest the conceptual issue inherent in the joke of twins, the dependence of the self on the acknowledgement of others. Until the Abbess emerges to reconstitute the identities of

the twins in Act V, the viewer remains the locus in which the identity of the
characters is maintained. The viewer is the sane companion of each of
the confused twins. In the theater this contact is an appeal to a congregation
of people rather than an individual. Although the appeal is not mediated by
the camera in the theater, the individual's responsibility for response is nonetheless lessened because the burden is shared. Imposing a kind of conspiracy
on the viewer, the BBC production actually risks diminishing the distance
that most comic theorists have found essential to laughter.

. . . Although the BBC production extends the use of direct address beyond what the text would indicate as normal stage practice, there remains an
enormous quantity of debate reserved for the public forum. One Antipholus
has no house in Ephesus; the other is barred from the use of his house. All of
the explosive exchanges between master and servant take place in the mart or
public square as do arrests and accusations, trials and redemptions. And the
language of the public forum is the language of logic, "why and wherefore"
as Dromio would have it. Even without the disruption of rationality created
by the twins, the logic of debate exceeds its objective and a simple call to
dinner becomes a litany of cause and effect.

> The clock hath strucken twelve upon the bell:
> My mistress made it one upon my cheek:
> She is so hot, because the meat is cold:
> The meat is cold, because you come not home:
> You come not home, because you have no stomach:
> You have no stomach, having broke your fast;
> But we that know what 'tis to fast and pray,
> Are penitent for your default to-day.

(I.ii.45–52)

In more serious matters an excess of logic as law binds the Ephesian Duke,
who must sentence Egeon to death.

> Now trust me, were it not against our laws,
> Against my crown, my oath, my dignity
> Which princes, would they, may not disannul,
> My soul should sue as advocate for thee. . . .

(I.i.142–45)

If the self which is at risk in the confusion of Ephesus is the public self,
bound by social law into the response of an automaton, we have little interest
in seeing it preserved. The identity which we as viewers preserve for the twins
is their identity as twins. The untruth that they and the citizens of Ephesus
try to preserve by logic is the delusion that they are singlets. Our appreciation
of the joke of their discomfiture in the public forum is not diminished by our
knowledge of their secret, which is after all not a disaster but a "nativity."

But the greatest generator of comic distance, or perhaps restorer of comic
distance, is our awareness of the nesting of the medium of the performed play
within the medium of television. The hybrid energy (McLuhan's term) of the

intersection of media is in itself a source of interest.[7] The relation of the performed play to the televised play does not remain constant. At times a long shot clearly photographs a staged situation. At others, an actor directly addressing a camera establishes a relation to the viewer not possible on the stage. The hybrid medium revels both in the artificiality of its mosaic map on the stage floor and in its exuberant display of animals—a horse, a donkey, a monkey, doves—within that artificial setting. The camera's power of proximity is used to isolate objects—tarot cards, a pair of clasped hands—and in so doing it enhances the iconography of the production not by opening it up but by focussing within it, in effect reading the microcosm.

When the twins are finally united, we view shots which are pure television, composite shots in which a single actor appears as both twins. But we also view shots which suggest how the miracle is performed onstage—shots which shield the face of one or both of the twins and which might be performed by approximate doubles. The energy of hybridization enhances the play of the mind that accompanies comedy. McLuhan's paradoxical observation that television "involves us in depth, but it does not excite, agitate, or arouse," seems descriptive of our emotional reaction.[8]

When spectators are restricted to a single position in space by fixed seating, it is difficult to convey to them extreme contrasts in physical point of view. Viewing characters as being inside is not radically different from viewing them as being outside. But even the simplest television set which enables a director to distinguish convincingly between exterior and interior and to view the exterior from the interior intensifies the ability of an audience to contrast private and public space. In *The Comedy of Errors* the Syracusan Antipholus finds himself drawn into an interior, the house of his twin. There he is astonished at being treated as if he had come home to his own private space. In contrast, the Ephesian Antipholus finds himself exposed to a public forum which becomes increasingly strange to him. The Elizabethan stage is well suited to represent the openness of the forum but ill equipped to convey the intimacy of the private abode. The intimate space of the Elizabethan inner stage is achieved only at the expense of maximizing distance from the audience.

Shakespeare acknowledges the essential openness of his stage by placing most of the action in the mart, but the crucial action of excluding the Ephesian Antipholus from his home benefits greatly from the camera's freedom in point of view. As he has estrangement thrust on him, so his Syracusan twin has intimacy thrust on him. The camera intensifies our experience of intimacy and thus, by providing a clear contrast, intensifies our sense of estrangement as well.

The interior of Antipholus's house consists, for the purposes of the camera, of two parts: one, an entrance with a small staging area, a door, and a flight of stairs; the other, an upper chamber with windows overlooking the town. The first space constitutes a barrier between the house and the outer world. The door excludes strangers, among whom by mischance is numbered the master of the house. During this moment of confusion, the Syracusan

Dromio stands guard over the barrier space, mocking the outside world. Antipholus ascends the stairs with his brother's wife to reach an impenetrable private space where windows afford him a dominant perspective on the town but where he can neither be reached nor be seen against his will.

When Antipholus of Ephesus is excluded from his home, his servant clamors for admittance from outside a thick door. The camera can easily manifest one of the twin servants on either side of the door, but more importantly the space of the hallway isolates the upper chamber completely from the tumult below. The loud and conspicuous exclusion of one Antipholus is counterbalanced by the equally baffling inclusion of the other. Although stage rhetoric does not markedly distinguish between the language of the chamber and that of the forum, the private encounter is nonetheless more intimate because voice tone implies the relationship of the speakers. Luciana, pleading for the return to virtue of what she takes to be an erring brother-in-law, addresses him with the intimacy of a relative within the privacy of home. Her pleas to him, which we share through a close-up shot, prompt him only to declare his love for her. Of the noble twins, only the one who is a stranger enters private space or intimate conversation. In the mart he is again intimately addressed by a woman, the courtezan. She needs no privacy to assume an intimate manner and the camera captures in a close-up her presumption of intimacy. In radical contrast, the twin who is a citizen of Ephesus is excluded from intimate situations and even from private conversations. His wife and the courtezan join in accusing him of madness, but he converses privately with neither. His closest physical contact is to be bound face to face with Dromio, but the camera directs us to experience this encounter from without.

One space remains screened from the camera throughout the production, the interior of the convent where the Syracusans seek sanctuary. The television stage set permits the luxury of allowing the audience to become accustomed to the exterior of the convent (decorated with cherubs) as an occasional background during most of the play and then to center on the building when it becomes important at the climax of the plot. The spatial unity of the set which represents Ephesus is thus preserved without burdening the stage with a central and conspicuously unused housefront. The convent constitutes still another kind of space, sacred space, all the more so because its door provides a permanent barrier to the camera's eye. From this space emerges the only revelation which has been withheld from the audience, that the Abbess is the lost wife of the doomed Egeon. The Abbess stands at the threshold of the sacred space to resolve the mysteries of Ephesus. As the private interior defines by contrast the public mart, so our visual access to the house of Antipholus defines by contrast a mystery in the inaccessible interior of the convent.

Simultaneous to the exclusion of the audience from an interior and from a secret is a shift in visual style that plays a joke on the viewer. Although the viewer is aware that a single actor has been twinned by an editing process, he nonetheless experiences simultaneously two characters that he knows are derived from images of that single actor. And the more convincing the composite image the greater the viewer's delight. Reserving the most flamboyant use of the camera until the final moments of the play preserves the power of the visual image to surprise and releases it precisely where it can enhance a moment of grace.

The ultimate effect of this production is in some ways akin to that of environmental theater in multiplying the viewing perspectives of the audience while preserving a bounded playing area representative of reality yet obviously a stage. Camera angles allow us to share the perspective of the characters, but for the most part we share their emotions by being addressed as confidants in a manner more intimate than the stage aside. Because the questions of identity raised in the play are provoked by the outward appearance of the twins, the camera's capacity for purposeful looking becomes an asset. As an audience we look at images, mirror images, and duplicated images. Moreover, we look at how people look at each other when confusion begins to triumph. So much of the play is about being looked at that the simple close-up of an actor's face becomes an instrument of power.

Looks that imply suspicion of disloyalty, dishonor, and madness constitute a maze of funhouse mirrors from which the twins emerge into the bright sunlight of enhanced identity. To have a twin is to have more than ordinary significance as an individual. Thus the Duke marvels at the noble twins:

> One of these men is genius to the other:
> And so of these, which is the natural man,
> And which the spirit? Who deciphers them?

> (V.i.333–35)

Even the servant twins, who are left with the last word, are enhanced. The Ephesian observes to his brother, "I see by you I am a sweet-fac'd youth."

The techniques of television serve to sharpen the contrasts inherent in this Shakespearean text without distorting its natural rhythm. And having the implicit permission of its audience to contain another medium, television can preserve the element of play, deliberate unreality, which is of the essence of *The Comedy of Errors*.

1. *Understanding Media: The Extensions of Man* (New York: McGraw-Hill, 1964), pp. 308–37.

2. *The Riverside Shakespeare*, ed. G. Blakemore Evans and others (Boston: Houghton Mifflin Company, 1974). All references to *The Comedy of Errors* are to this edition.

3. *What Is Cinema?*, Vol. I, trans. Hugh Gray (Berkeley and Los Angeles: University of California Press, 1967), p. 111.

4. Jones in his deliberate theatricality follows the most successful modern stage production, that of Clifford Williams, which began at Stratford-upon-Avon in 1962, toured for several years, and was revived in 1972. See J. L. Styan, *The Shakespeare Revolution* (Cambridge and New York: Cambridge University Press, 1977).

5. McLuhan, p. 319.

6. Cedric H. Whitman, "Aristophanes: Discourse of Fantasy" in *Comedy: Meaning and Form*, ed. Robert W. Corrigan (2nd ed.; New York: Harper and Row, 1981), p. 234.

7. McLuhan, pp. 48–55.

8. McLuhan, p. 337.

Histories

The Historicity of the BBC History Plays
Peter Saccio

As so far videotaped by the BBC, the Shakespeare history plays do not attempt
to give us the sort of large-scale spectacle we frequently see in dramatized
history.[1] Neither at Shrewsbury nor at Agincourt do we get a bird's-eye view
or an organized sequence of shots displaying the battlefield in the manner of
Olivier's films. The coronation processions of Henry V and Anne Bullen are
pleasant little parades of a dozen or so people headed straight at the camera.
Crowd scenes are shot medium and close, so that we cannot tell how many
extras are present or determine the shape of the space they occupy. We see
people over other people's shoulders, not a whole composed array. Although
these practices play to the strengths of the small screen, we should recognize
that they are not dictated by the necessities of the small screen: the BBC has
plenty of experience in photographing the full panoply of royal occasions,
real as well as fictional. Cedric Messina and David Giles evidently decided to
sacrifice big historical display in favor of stress on individual persons and
relationships.

In other respects, these productions are deeply historical. Whether you
praise them for accuracy or find them "worthy" and "solid" to the point of
dullness, they are marked by their historicity.[2] They are more historical than
Shakespeare's scripts.

For one thing, they contain more historical fact. The chronicles report that
Henry IV suffered a disfiguring disease. Shakespeare omits this; the BBC uses
it, with a vengeance. Shakespeare is vague about the nature of Hal's wound
at Shrewsbury. The BBC has not only specified it, as any production must,
but accurately specified it as a facial wound and logically extended it as a
slowly fading scar.[3] A reader requires a footnote to know that Richard II really
was responsible for Woodstock's death, at least in the first scene of the text;
on the screen, a sudden cut to Derek Jacobi's face when Woodstock is first
mentioned settles the matter for all viewers.

Of course, any production striving to be in period will provide more historical facts than the script, and thus supply the audience with a deeper sense

of historicity. Appropriate architecture, props, and especially costumes (these are facts too) give us the impression of solid historical authenticity—authenticity to the period of the action, the early fifteenth century—whereas when we read, the language so dominates our impressions that we think more of the late sixteenth, of Elizabethans rather than Plantagenets. Such authenticity, as the BBC practices it, fortunately need not mean pedantry. Some costumes are theatricalized for the sake of characterization. Bardolph appears to be wearing every garment he owns, like a New York bag-lady, and the neckline and fitting of Doll Tearsheet's bodice are unmedieval (the modern effect diminishes in full-length shots). I cannot believe that, on an ordinary day, Henry IV's court ever sported so large a range of spiffy male headgear, but the elaboration of those hats contributes measurably to the individuation of the lesser characters. More importantly, historical accuracy is used for significant dramatic purposes, not just for its own sake. The design of their wimples underscores the likenesses and contrasts between two unhappy women in 2 *Henry IV*: young widow Percy, lyrically framed by a loving camera that stresses the dazzling white linen elaborately draped and gathered around her face, makes a moving cadenza solo of her elegy for Hotspur; while old widow Quickly, her plain wimple soiled and askew, is as jostled for space on the screen as her pleas are jostled by Falstaff's bullying.

Such use of visual detail, the selective employment of an unspectacular historical factualness, is very effective in the rejection of Falstaff. As taped, the point of this scene lies largely in the reduction of the royal party to walking dummies, their humanity and individuality reduced to stiff role-playing. It takes a moment to recognize the Lord Chief Justice: not only have coronation robes replaced his green garments, but the collar and cap muffle the distinguished figure we have come to know. It is even harder to recognize Hal's brothers, and that effect is clearly intended, since the most familiar of them, John of Lancaster, is placed farthest from the camera. For Hal himself, the historical fact of the soup-bowl haircut has been used trenchantly. With the locks of supposedly madcap youth shorn away, and with his plain open-throated jerkin replaced by a full ermine collar, his face appears as an unfamiliar mask through which emerge the obligatory words. The screen image of the newly crowned Henry V resembles the late portraits of Elizabeth I, where the face is but a stylized oval surrounded by emblems of monarchy. The king is an icon, and sweaty, quirky, living bystanders are given their orders and left to cope as best they may. The appearance of the king (an historical fact of one kind) is a visual metaphor for the powers and duties of kingship (historical and dramatic facts of another kind), and through it we see their effect upon human beings.

These productions are more historical than the scripts in another sense. History entails events arranged in a particular sequence and rhythm, and in some places the BBC has altered the Shakespearean arrangement so that the rhythm more closely resembles that of the sources. This occurs when a single scene is split up: in II.i of *Richard II*, when the colloquy of Northumberland, Willoughby and Ross is shot in a different location from the scene of Gaunt's death; in Richard's prison-soliloquy, which is interrupted by five ostentatious camera dissolves; and in *Henry VIII*, when Wolsey's fall is split into three scenes, the latter two separated by an act-break as well as a location change. In all three cases, Shakespeare's single written scene compresses historical time. The BBC's decompression allows more history—at least the fact and the sense of passing time—to peep through the interstices: Richard spent months in Pomfret, Wolsey's indictment followed his dismissal by a year. In the two latter cases, however, I suspect that the alteration arose only indirectly from a concern with historical accuracy: the more immediate cause lies in psychological plausibility. For a play, or a discourse of any kind, to be accepted as historical, it must conform to patterns that we regard (consciously or not) as guaranteeing plausibility. We assimilate facts within patterns, and when these patterns change, we rewrite the history.[4] In the case of Wolsey, the single scene entails a large shift in character from self-centered scheming to moral perceptiveness and prophetic insight, and a corresponding shift in audience sympathy. Such a shift did not strain an Elizabethan audience, accustomed as they were to sudden falls and consequent moral reflection. The demand on the audience was particularly small because their fundamental model for character change was religious conversion, the sudden descent of grace. A modern audience expects a slower process: our models for character change derive from the theories of Freud or Piaget or Erikson about childhood and maturation. For us these things just don't happen that fast. Richard and Wolsey are therefore given days (according to the convention of the camera), days of psychological time that we would consider necessary for self-examination, for the shifts in mood, for the changes and advances of thought that the words reveal. The assumption of a modern notion about psychic changes has made the material seem more historical.

Such alterations cohere with the BBC's heavy reliance on close-ups: reality in these productions is chiefly personal and psychological. The commanding power of the television camera to guide, edit, and comment here causes political and historical processes to be seen largely as a series of private interchanges and individual responses. No abstract critical formulation about the nature of history on the order of Tillyard's providentialism or Kernan's evolution toward Renaissance pragmatism, and no ceremonial or mythic notion of English history, appear to have influenced the producers. History takes place not in large-scale transformations or in public rituals of power and monarchy, but in backstairs maneuvers and subtextual pressures.

That it should do so does not violate my sense of period: here also the BBC shows historicity. The politics of Plantagenet England were the politics of a very small class, very nearly a family quarrel, as intimate as it was public. The politics of Shakespeare's time were heavily the politics of plot, of the conspiracies that interested Machiavelli, of Macbeth who kept a fee'd servant in every noble Scottish household, of Walsingham who did the same on a

European scale, of the younger Cecil who quietly and carefully paved the way for James I's accession. But equally, if not more so, this backstairs notion of politics is modern. In our age of public relations and image-building, we have good reason to suspect all public statements and to suppose that real political action takes place privately. Our public pronouncements have unstated objectives; our meetings have hidden agendas; our deeds are followed by rationalizing remarks from press secretaries; and the real action takes place backstage, in quiet and sometimes unspoken deals.

Whether period or modern (and the mere fact that modern technology reveals these intimacies to us makes it seem more modern), this notion of the political process saturates the BBC series. At the opening of *Henry V*, Canterbury and Ely quietly arrange their maneuvers while kneeling in apparent prayer. In the Archbishop's council in *2 Henry IV*, Lord Bardolph (despite heavy cuts in the lines) sets the tone of the scene by radiating anxiety and discontent with his allies' remarks. At one point he almost speaks in protest, but is quelled by a weighted glance from the Archbishop. He is left toying with a wine goblet, obviously dissatisfied with the plans. Although Shakespeare never bothered to explain, we may reasonably anticipate his failure to appear at Gaultree. When Northumberland plots with Willoughby and Ross in *Richard II*, the scene is controlled by the movements of his eyes, which not only cue the others to speak, but exert pressure on them to do so. Richard II's first entrance demonstrates his political technique: the first shot shows him coming down a corridor, pausing at a door, and drawing himself up to enter. That shot does nothing for the ceremonialism of the play—quite the opposite—it typifies Richard as actor. His pause is exactly that of a player preparing himself in the wings for a major entrance. We know that a charade will ensue. The televised *Henry VIII* is largely governed by a contrast between public scenes with the king and private colloquies among two or three lords or the two gentlemen who serve as semi-narrators. These private scenes are usually shot in passageways, on staircases, in tunnel-like arcades. The use of such locations may derive from immediate visual needs: a darkish location with an open archway to the rear gives the screen image a desirable depth. Such settings occur in most of the plays the BBC has so far filmed. In *Henry VIII* they are employed so consistently as to become metaphorical. These are the cunning corridors of history, to be punctuated occasionally by a public display.

One passage from the BBC *2 Henry IV* especially demonstrates two techniques of personal manipulation, two contrasting modes of gaining power: the accession scene, immediately preceded by Falstaff's soliloquy on Shallow. Throughout *Henry IV* Falstaff is the only character allowed to acknowledge the camera/audience. The visual power and emotional relationship with us that this acknowledgement gives him lends added strength to the subversion of values that is the content of his soliloquies. Here, we may think, is the ultimate intriguer, the one who can manipulate us. In his last soliloquy, his confidence is tremendous: his face gets redder the closer he gets; a raw, predatory note mingles with his laughter on the final line, "I *come*, Master Shallow, I *come*" (emphasis Quayle's). His presence is so overwhelming that he nearly leaves the screen and takes over one's living room. By deft employment of his talents, a man of this perception, this resourcefulness, this energy could take over the world. Visually, he certainly takes over the world of the play: it becomes what he makes it.

Hal's contrasting skill is demonstrated in the ensuing accession scene: he turns a group of grieving, fearful courtiers into a unified assembly that kneels to shout "God save the king!" (inserted line). Since the passage is not a soliloquy but an exchange among six speaking persons with many silent onlookers, the production technique naturally differs. More importantly, the production technique differs notably from that of other court scenes: it is almost a theatre scene, with an unusual number of full-length and distance shots, an unusual sense of the dimensions of the room, and three carefully staged entrances (the Lord Chief Justice, Hal's brothers, and Hal). But it is a theatre scene not because David Giles has irrationally changed his style. Giles retains some close-ups (including one very ill–chosen one[5]) to remind us of the subtext. It is a theatre scene because Hal makes it so. When nervously greeted by the Lord Chief Justice, Hal walks past him, turns, and pauses, standing in a posture of deliberate poise with hands clasped and feet together, framed by nearer bystanders, holding the court in suspense, making them wait for his response. After speaking to his brothers, he initiates his exchange with the Lord Chief Justice with a kind of muted pounce designed to sharpen anxiety ("You all look strangely at me . . . and *you most*"). Making his accusation, he collects the rest of the court with his eyes ("How might a prince of my great hopes") and spears the Lord Chief Justice with this collected gaze ("What! Rate, rebuke and roughly send to prison . . ."). During the Lord Chief Justice's long response, three close-up cuts to Hal's face show a very slight but increasing smile that reveals his satisfaction with the progress of the scene. He then exploits the ceremony with the sword, the handshake, the throne, the greater and lesser spaces between himself and others, and the variety of his own vocal tone, all to elicit the acclamation he receives at the end. Like a master actor playing an improvisation with sensitive but less experienced colleagues, he draws from them exactly the responses that he wants. He sets their roles and thereby solidifies his own. He achieves his political ends by manipulating the theatre of his relationships. Elizabeth I would have applauded—but not publicly.

1. Despite an ill-advised publicity flyer promising that "the Tudor pageantry of *Henry VIII* has been re-created in all its splendour."

2. Praise (with reservations) for accuracy occurs, for example, in Johannes A. Gaetner, "Notes on Costume Design: BBC Plays," *Shakespeare on Film Newsletter*, 5 (December 1980), 4. The charge of solid dullness is developed by Martin Banham, "BBC Television's Dull Shakespeares," *Critical Quarterly*, 22 (Spring 1980), 31–40.

3. David Gwillim's cheekbone scar actually looks more like a sword slash than the historical arrow wound. I know of no direct historical evidence for a lasting scar, although one historian has speculated that the unusual profile view in the official portrait of Henry V may have been intended to conceal such a scar.

4. I am of course only touching on issues that have been discussed by many philosophers of history. Hayden V. White, *Metahistory* (Baltimore and London: Johns Hopkins University Press, 1973), is especially germane.

5. The explicit adoption of the Lord Chief Justice as surrogate father, Hal's four lines beginning "You shall be as a father to my youth," is whispered in close-up with the two faces nose-to-nose, surely a mistaken choice for a formal act with manifest political content. The whisper is the major part of the problem. Variously in the BBC series the vocal levels are perplexing. Freed of the need for stage projection, the actors often make many points purely by diction and inflection, deploying a subtlety and speed not easily deployed in a large theatre, confident that the microphones will pick up anything. When more than two or three actors appear in a scene, however, it can be difficult to tell whether a character speaking in half- or quarter-voice intends to be heard by bystanders. I can perceive no consistent conventions at work equivalent to the theatrical conventions of aside, "aside to," and stage whisper. But in this case Hal clearly means to be heard by no one except the Lord Chief Justice.

BBC Television's Dull Shakespeares
Martin Banham

This essay, to be about as unoriginal as its subject matter, is written more in sorrow than anger—though some anger at the disservice the BBC's worthily intended production of the Shakespeare Canon is in fact doing must occasionally surface. It is a measure of my response that words such as "dull" and "worthy" are the ones that come to mind when trying to assess the series so far. We are offered fine actors working seriously, with no doubt equally fine directors, and with financial resources to match, plus the great enterprise of the presentation of thirty-seven of Shakespeare's plays, but all this leads us, in the end, only to something *dull*. Sadly we have to look on this venture, on the evidence to date, as the lost opportunity.

The evidence that I will offer centres on the productions in December 1979 of the two parts of *Henry IV* and *Henry V*. Here are three plays full of intrigue, power politics, broad and sharp comedy, excitement of the battlefield, poignant and sentimental relationships, and offering an opportunity to travel in history and scene in the company of some of Shakespeare's most famous characters. If, with such opportunities, we are eventually left disappointed and frustrated, where can the fault lie? Is it inherent in the medium? Is it that television cannot capture those qualities that make Shakespeare, at his best, such a marvelous experience in the theatre and an equally satisfying one in the imagination of the reader? When thinking of *Henry V* many of us think first of the play as a film—Laurence Olivier's famous version—and our memories of that (in contrast to the compressed scale of the television pro-

Reprinted, with permission, from *Critical Quarterly*, 22:1 (Spring 1980), 31–40.

duction) include the thrill of the splendidly recreated Globe Theatre for the opening sequences (architectural pedants apart!) and the essentially filmic reconstruction of the battle scenes. It may not have been pure, but it was fun. We *did* come out of the cinema playing at being our own Henrys, stimulated and delighted by the experience. We had been entranced and captured by the power of the language and the presence of the actor. We had laughed, and done so in the company of others. And this point seems to me to be important. In the theatre the experience of the play is a shared one—shared not only between the individual in the audience and the actors but by members of the audience among themselves. Theatre is a public medium; television, from a viewer's angle, a private one. Plays, it must be argued, and notably Shakespeare's, are written consciously for audience response and participation. The audience is invited, in creating the scene, to use the resources of its own imagination, and, in listening to the characters on stage, to offer them the feed-back and focus that is at the heart of the shared experience. Does television fall between two stools, being able to offer neither the visual scope and communal audience experience of film and the cinema, nor the total qualities of the act of theatre? To develop this point a little let us look at three particular problems that television seems to produce: those of settings, speech, and visual selection.

It is a cliché, but a perfectly respectable one, that, in a Shakespearean play, the best scenery is created in the mind of the audience, and that to dress the set in a realistic way may only serve to confuse the audience and edit the individual's response. We all know of the great Victorian stage productions of Shakespeare that allowed the spectacle to dominate and decimated the text to accommodate it; and though we might have enjoyed the effect, we cannot pretend that such productions served the plays or the playwright particularly well. If we allow that the film is likely to resort to some of the same literal reproductions of the scene, then we accept that as part of the nature of the beast, and sit back and enjoy it on its own terms. But television, certainly as evidenced by the Shakespeare series to date, too often aims between the spectacle of film and the simplicity and directness of theatre, giving settings that may in themselves be attractive, but which too often lack coherence and overall shape. They fail to contribute to the experience: prettiness is not enough.

The second problem is that of speech. The range and dimension of language in any Shakespeare play is considerable. We share the secret thoughts and the public squabbles, we participate in ritual and in rhetoric. The scale is always changing. Of course we find this particularly in the *Henry* plays, and part of our pleasurable anticipation of them is for the language that they offer. But the key words *are* range, scale, dimension, and it is arguable that television proves itself unable to cope with the full demands of Shakespeare's language. The quieter, private moments may succeed (thus Anthony Quayle's Falstaff could address us conspiratorially through the intimate window of the television screen) but the more robust, declamatory speeches often come perilously close to bluster—or, even worse, to petulance. Witness David Gwil-lim's uncomfortable handling of the famous "Once more unto the breach, dear friends" speech in *Henry* V. Deprived of the physical space in which to deliver this fine piece, he was diminished in scale and impact. A considerable part of this was also due to the fact that he didn't really have anyone to talk to. A few actors on a small set on a small screen do not a Harry make. Here, above all, the play (and the actor) needed *audience*.

The third related point is that of visual selection, and here I am concerned about the interference of the director in terms of what the viewer may see. Again it may be argued that Shakespeare, in writing and constructing his plays, always had in mind the fact that the audience could see all that was happening on stage at any given moment. The action off the ball may be as significant as that on it. We, the audience, make our own selection and that contributes essentially to our feeling for and sense of the complete drama in which we are participating. When a television (or, to be fair, a film) director cuts to a particular character, or comes into a close-up, or otherwise shapes our image of the action, he is intruding his own interpretation of what is significant between the action and the spectator. In so doing not only does he interfere with our imaginative liberties, he also runs the risk of destroying the sensitive integral framework of the play itself. One result of this, and of asso-ciated actions, has been to give these Shakespearean productions on television a linear feeling—a sense of being formed not with the circular, ultimately rounded and complete style of the "wooden O" (which is not merely a de-scription of a theatre but the whole embracing experience of the drama), but with an episodic, strung-out, single line of action. The television audience, not being allowed to stand at once within and beside the action, is pointed in various directions not by its own will and decision, and not by the logic of the play in its entirety, but by technical decisions in order to accommodate the workings of the medium. So, to return to an earlier question, are we in the wrong medium for Shakespeare?

Quite obviously the BBC does not think so. But it is worthwhile spending some time looking at the basis for the overall production style as it is revealed in the publicity handout accompanying the launching of the series. This rightly draws attention to the acting talent that has been employed by the series and to the generally high standards that may be expected from BBC television's scenic and costume designers. It reminds us, and fairly too, that "Since its foundation, the BBC has led the world in the production of classic drama. . . ." But it then goes on to make other claims which, if they have informed the general production style as they certainly appear to have done, could unkindly be referred to as wrong-headed, or more generously, as debat-able. Here is a sample:

> . . . it has been possible to record entire productions on location. . . . The settings are those the layman would expect to see when he hears the name of Julius Caesar or Richard II. The Forum belongs to ancient Rome. Italy of the high Renaissance, setting of many of the dramas, is brought to life in

squares and palaces that might well have been created by the artists of their time. *As You Like It* has been recorded in a real forest. The Tudor pageantry of *Henry VIII* has been re-created in all its splendour at Leeds Castle.

Shakespeare wrote to please an audience that was neither particularly so-phisticated nor literary. He wrote for people, not coteries. It is our intention to bring his plays on the same plain terms to a mass audience . . . we think he would have been delighted by the resources on which we have been able to draw.

There has been no attempt at stylisation; there are no gimmicks; no embel-lishments to confuse the student.

Now let it be said that I have quoted these extracts slightly out of context, but not in any way to alter their meaning. The first section deals with the settings, and emphasises the fact that the producers saw the re-creation of authentic settings as an advantage, indeed a virtue. Or did they see it as the only possible way for television to work and therefore set out to make it a virtue? Is it really supposed to be authenticising the play to have *As You Like It* in a real forest? To reiterate: prettiness is not enough. Another, and interesting, side issue becomes pertinent here. Much of the internal rhythm of a scene in Shake-speare, as with the Elizabethan drama in general, may be seen to be related to the physical dimensions of the stages of the period, as we understand them to have been. In other words, a scene and a sequence of scenes are con-structed in a way that is aware of the pacing and shaping implicit in the dimension of the acting area. Thus quick shifts of action may be especially sensitively contrived, the comings and goings may have been written to cover particular distances or to allow for moments of comedy or tension that are effected by subtle use of the specific playing area. This particular round peg will not fit comfortably into a square hole. In other words, change the staging conventions and you may destroy the integral rhythms of speech and action, and this brings us back again to observing the deadeningly linear experience of television. The further comment, in the quotation, about what the layman would expect to see, really does beg the question. The opportunity in this television series was to astonish and delight "the layman," not to confirm his prejudices that Shakespeare is wordy and dull or to seduce him with a scenic tour of Europe.

The second quotation challenges us with a question that is often raised—basically a sophistication of the "if Shakespeare had had TV he would have used it" argument. This may well be true, but again it seems to miss the point, which is that he didn't and that he wrote within the terms of his own world and his own stage, and that an acknowledgment and understanding of that is an essential *starting point* for any production of a Shakespeare play. The third quotation offers us "the student" (who, like the "layman," is not to be con-fused) who is to be given a gimmick-free production. The irony is that many of the most interesting, entertaining, thoughtful and revealing Shakespearean productions of the last twenty-five years have been the "gimmicky" ones—if one replaces the word with the alternative word "adventurous." The caution implicit in the third quotation is, perhaps, the downfall of the series—a lack of boldness, a lack of imagination, a cautious concern for the elusive idea of a straightforward definitive production. Good Shakespearean production has a base of scholarship and understanding and then a superstructure of ideas and ventures and risks. It is a living thing, full of embellishments, full of stylisation, full of intelligent, constructive "gimmicks."

Perhaps at this point it would be helpful to look at a number of scenes from the three *Henry* plays, as produced on television, and to see how and where the problems that I have been discussing in more general terms arise in specific scenes. After that, and in conclusion, I shall try to offer a more positive comment with some ideas towards the successful presentation of Shakespeare on television.

Henry IV, part 1, Act 2, scene 2. The battle at Gad's Hill. This is a comic scene, the basic comic business being at the expense of Falstaff who, being the robber, is himself "robbed" by Prince Hal and Poins. Various points make the comedy, amongst them, of course, the figure of Falstaff himself (admirably played in the TV production by Anthony Quayle) and the amiable trickery of the Prince. It is a scene full of hiding and seeking, set in the half-light of early dawn. This last fact is important, and the time is established quite clearly in the preceding scenes. But of course on Shakespeare's stage this scene would generally have been played in full daylight, and the illusion of semi-darkness would have been created by the comic action. Without that visual trickery (to which the audience is a party) the scene loses something of its fun. More important, though, is the implicit buffoonery of the action, with fat and foolish men hiding behind little pieces of cover on the stage in order to ambush others, and then themselves being ambushed by "thieves" whom the conventions of the comedy allow them to fail to recognise as their companions, and the audience to accept as disguised beyond recognition and covered by the mists of dawn. This is a big scene—and a lot is made of it a little later in the play. It should be riotous and ridiculous, and above all it should be clear. The essence of the humour is in the willing illusion that what everybody can clearly see is in fact invisible. In the television version this became a rather confused tumble, more of a giggle than a belly-laugh, and the realistic creation of the light of early morning and mists of dawn stole much of the wit from the scene. What should have been a memorable vehicle for the clowns became a rather hurried scuffle. I think we have an instance here of a scene that, unless treated in an entirely unrealistic way, fits most awkwardly into the medium.

Henry V, Prologue. The prologue, through the character Chorus, gives a fascinating impression of the Shakespearean stage, certainly of the early theatres, with his famous reference to "The flat unraised spirits that hath dared / On this unworthy scaffold to bring forth / So great an object. Can this cockpit hold / The vasty fields of France? Or may we cram / Within this wooden O the very casques / That did affright the air at Agincourt?" Even, a little later, the description "the girdle of these walls" reinforces the sense of being within a theatre where the audiences are *gathered around* the story-teller and the players. It is this intimacy, this gathering around, that invests the play with its extraordinary charm, its sense of oneness and companion-ship, of partisanship and patriotism. Chorus's comments are not an excuse, they are a carefully devised creation of a sense of unity and community— quite literally a statement, "We are all in this *together*." A challenge for any director and designer on a modern stage, which may not lend itself ar-chitecturally to this closeness between players and audience, is to find a solution that will capture this precious moment. It seemed particularly perverse, therefore, of the television production to play this scene with Chorus walking straight down towards the camera between two lines of gradu-ally revealed characters. The sense of the round was totally contradicted and replaced by visual signals which, far from drawing us into the action, placed us at a distance from it. Chorus thenceforth became a mannered and (spare the thought) gimmicky character, popping up from unexpected places, rather than the companion to our view and experience of the action as he should be.

Henry V, Act 3, *scene 1, and Henry IV, part 1, Act 5 (the battle scenes)*. I have referred earlier to the difficult circumstances in which David Gwillim was asked to deliver the "Once more unto the breach" speech, but it is worth looking in a little more detail at the scene. Battle scenes *are* difficult to stage, and we are all aware of productions where a few actors chasing each other over vast stages with pikes or swords have not exactly persuaded us of the reality of the conflict. Here we are firmly up against the possibilities and limitations of the Elizabethan stage. The battle scenes are peopled by a few actors at least to some extent because it didn't take many actors to look a crowd on a small stage, and certainly because the sense of a running battle, one that was passing in front of one's eyes but actually taking place on a wider battle-field, was more easily achieved within the confines of a small stage and the-atre, making full use of available exits and levels, and never allowing realism to take away the ability of the imagination to "Into a thousand parts divide one man." The battle scenes lacked focus in the television productions, offer-ing no clear sense of arena or direction, and compromising between the sim-plicity of the stage and the vast panoramas of the film with an indoor set dressed in unconvincing grass and shrub. And back at the breach itself, no one looked more lonely and embarrassed than poor King Henry urging on invisible troops to an indistinct objective via an improbable scaffold. Again we found ourselves in a kind of televisual limbo-land, half-way between the imagination and the reality.

Henry V, Act 3, *scene 4*. This is the scene where we are introduced to Katherine. It is an accurately placed scene, a moment of charm in the middle of turmoil, a hint of action to come, and a knowing moment for the audience to share in. In the BBC production the roles of Katherine and Alice were delightfully and wittily played by Jocelyne Boisseau and Anna Quayle, and the specific scene we are concerned with was a pleasure to watch and listen to in itself. But the problem was that it *was* in itself. It suddenly emerged on the screen, set in soft edges, like a dainty picture illustrating the text. In the sense that the director was presumably trying to capture the other world beyond the carnage and the politics the scene had its logic—but to divorce it from the action in quite such a way again runs the risk of upsetting the total rhythms of the action. It made the scene feel awkwardly placed, whereas in fact it is most subtly located.

Now I shall offer some more constructive comments. They are in the form of three possible and not entirely exclusive approaches to both the style and the philosophy of Shakespeare on television, and they are offered in the belief that my earlier question about the incompatibility between Shakespearean production and television has to be resisted. It has to be asserted that there are ways of presenting Shakespeare on television, most particularly because this is a great, developing and influential medium which must be able to take the classic drama into its repertoire.

The first concerns audiences. I have suggested earlier that the role of the audience in a Shakespeare production is an important one, and one understood and exploited by the playwright: Much of the power and impact of the action depends upon the presence of an audience. I have instanced Henry V's great rallying speeches, but equally one may think of his more introspective moments, when the audience is needed to give a full dimension to his words and thoughts. But a more urgent case has to be made out for the comic actors, in which our three history plays abound, and who, without the return of laughter and comment from the audience, have nothing to play to but the empty air. No wonder that on television their comedy falls flat, or survives at the level of self-indulgent posturing. This is not the fault of actors of the quality of Bryan Pringle or Gordon Gostelow, but rather the consequence of the dilemma in which they find themselves. It is a situation to which television would not expose its contemporary comics. It is no accident, surely, that Morecambe and Wise, Mike Yarwood and company perform on television with audiences. It enables their acts to work, and it enhances the enjoyment for the viewing audience. The audience provides the essential ingredient which brings the entertainment to life. It may be inappropriate and unnecessary for there to be an audience for a play specifically written for television, but is there any reason to deny an audience to one written for its living presence? It may not even be necessary for an audience to be in vision, but the fact of its being there could revitalise the experience of televised Shakespeare. I can see this suggestion being greeted with horror by television drama producers (and perhaps some television actors) to whom the live audience is often a strange experience and for whom it would merely conjure images of the early days of television when cameras entered the theatre and pointed themselves straight at the stage. But that is surely not the limit of the imagination and skill of contemporary television drama production. And which is more important, contemporary wisdom as to what television drama is, or the lifeblood of our greatest playwright?

My second suggestion concerns ways of giving a real unity and uniqueness to the series. I return to that opening sequence of the Olivier *Henry* V with the camera flying over "London" and settling on to the Globe stage. Given all the intriguing scholarship of this century which has gradually revealed for us the form and resources of the Elizabethan stage, what an opportunity there would have been for this series to have undertaken informed reconstruction of the various stages upon which Shakespeare's plays may have been performed, and to have brought them to life again in their finest setting. Here we might envisage a most fruitful blending of the simple imaginative arena of Shakespeare's own experience, and the ability of modern TV technology to bring this to the screen. A danger would certainly lie in mere historical pedantry, and museum Shakespeare is not what is intended. But one thing is certain: the present series will disappear rapidly from the mind, having nothing special to offer, whilst a lively reconstruction might have regenerated the thinking of our whole theatre towards Shakespearean production. It would only be pedantic in the hands of pedants, so let that not be used as an excuse.

Lastly, I offer what I would regard as probably the most realistic approach, and this takes us back to that self-satisfied but erroneous belief that in "no stylisation . . . no gimmicks . . . no embellishments of any sort" we have the recipe for excellence. What this series really demands is a number of individual productions that are strikingly original, daring, experimental—productions that exploit and explore the potential of television rather than sit sedately within the empty box. We should be content not with productions that simply confirm the layman's expectations, but with productions which stimulate, enrage, excite and delight us—and which make us keep coming back for more. Jacqueline Pearson concluded her review of the first television Shakespeares (*Critical Quarterly*, 21:1 [Spring 1979]) by saying that she remained "cautiously pessimistic" about the future of the series. The most recent evidence suggests that, like me, she should throw away her caution. But, dear BBC, for Shakespeare's sake, there is time (and life?) to change.

Jane Howell's First Tetralogy
Brechtian Break-Out or Just Good Television?
Dennis Bingham

During the first two seasons of the BBC Shakespeare series, critics charged
that producer and project originator Cedric Messina, in his desire for what
James C. Bulman refers to as "definitive productions" (572), had virtually
banished originality and creativity. A 1978 BBC press release flatly announced
that "There has been no attempt at stylization; there are no gimmicks; no
embellishments to confuse the student" (Banham 34). Pronouncements such
as these led the hearer to suspect that babies were being thrown out with the
stylized, gimmicky, embellished bathwater. If stylized visuals do not complement Shakespeare's stylized language; if "gimmick" is really a dirty word for
experimentation; and if "embellishments" refer to a director's own approach,
then the BBC has cast its vote—to borrow a phrase from Susan Sontag—
"against interpretation."

Many commentators, including Jonathan Miller, Messina's successor in
the series' third and fourth seasons, have dismissed the notion of the definitive
production. Indeed, one reason that Shakespeare continues to live is that the
plays elude definition; new generations see their own meanings in Shakespeare. This is why *Henry V* can be used, as it was in Laurence Olivier's 1945
film, as a nationalistic wartime rouser, but a generation later becomes troubling in its celebration of war and conquest. Messina and his corporate spon-
sors wanted to defy this changeability. Shakespeare's plays have been for the
ages, the thinking must have run, so why must a taped production bear the
unmistakable stamp of the era in which it was made? The definitive production, therefore, winds up being as close as the producer can come to a tran-
scription, or videotape, of a text, free of artistic concept, approach, or
interpretation.

Furthermore, the idea of definitive productions on television shows some
condescension toward the medium itself. Messina would never ask for a definitive production from the stage. Who knows exactly what such a production would be like? And film is too special and makes too many visual demands on a play script. But TV, a mere recording medium, notorious for
diminishing reality rather than enlarging it as film does, is seen as good only
for the straightforward photography of a play.

Many of the BBC plays show a fundamental misunderstanding of the television medium. Television, like theatre, is intimate. As H. R. Coursen writes,
the playing space in the shallow TV image would seem to be an approximation of the playing area on a stage (2). But most of the BBC shows reach for
naturalism. Detailed, realistic sets are used. Actors speak to each other as if
the heightened language of the stage were their everyday discourse. And in
their soliloquies, they emote to themselves, there being no getting through

the fourth wall in most of these productions. But even if naturalism were possible in a production which preserves Shakespeare's language—and I don't believe it is—unrealities rise up to head off naturalism once and for all. For instance, in John Gorrie's taping of *Twelfth Night*, Sir Toby Belch and Andrew Aguecheek leave a beautifully realistic set to cavort in front of a painted moon and the audience isn't supposed to notice. Disembodied close-ups and reaction shots clog the screen. Camera movements, when they are attempted, are obvious and awkward; when the director works hard to include a doorway in the composition, you just know that someone will walk through it. There is no unifying idea or style behind these "definitive productions." The recipe stipulates only what should be left out. No spice, no sauce, no seasoning. What's left in the pot is bland and indigestible, a queasy compromise between naturalism and artifice.

The feeling that Shakespeare had been imprisoned in a glass tube led many critics to suppose, around the end of the second season, that perhaps television was not the medium for the Bard. "Does television fall between two stools," asks Martin Banham, "being able to offer neither the visual scope and communal audience experience of film and the cinema, nor the total qualities of the art of theatre?" (32). There was, in fact, evidence inherent in the medium itself to confirm such suspicions. Social critic Jerry Mander wrote in 1977 that

> Programs concerned with the arts . . . are . . . distorted by television's inability to convey their several aspects. . . . Some people argue that television delivers a new world of art to people in, say, Omaha, who might otherwise never see the Stuttgart Ballet or the New York Philharmonic. They say this stimulates interest in the arts. I find this very unlikely. . . . On television the depths are flattened, the spaces edited, the movements distorted and fuzzed-up, the music thinned and the scale reduced. . . . Seeing the Stuttgart Ballet performing on television leaves one with such a reduced notion of ballet as to reduce the appeal of ballet itself. The result is likely to be boredom and switched channels. To say that such a program stimulates new interest in arts is to believe, as Howard Gossage put it, "that it's possible to convince an eight-year-old that making love is more fun than ice cream cones." (280–81.)

Despite the feeling at the end of the second season that perhaps objections such as Mander's were correct, no one was ready to give up on so promising and ambitious an undertaking as "The Shakespeare Plays." Critics dutifully, if not very convincingly, uttered optimistic phrases about "exploring the possibilities of the medium." But these well-meaning critics couldn't really predict what these possibilities would be, nor from whence would come the Admiral Peary who would explore them.

They couldn't have predicted Jane Howell's 1982 production of the *Henry VI-Richard III* tetralogy. Director Howell doesn't explore the possibilities of the medium. She masters the art of transforming theatre into television, and makes it all look easy. Her productions make Shakespeare immediate, startling, energetic, and finally deeply troubling. But her approach to the first tetralogy is idiosyncratic and specifically modern. It grows from a belief that television can indeed do many of the same things as theatre without necessarily looking "stagey." Howell insists that the viewer watch the plays on her terms, but once the spectator gets used to those terms, he/she finds that they are also Shakespeare's and television's. One comes away from these fourteen hours of televised Shakespearean history convinced that TV was practically made for the Bard, forgetting for a minute the twenty-odd productions that have suggested otherwise.

I have mentioned that viewers must look at Howell's productions on the director's terms. What this means is that the anti-naturalism of her approach requires that viewers be jolted out of their customarily passive roles as TV watchers. This is why, in Howell's 1 Henry VI, we are all but assaulted with audacious unreality. The action takes place entirely on a single, jerry-built set; the play's title comes unfurled on what looks like a paint tarp. Gloucester and Winchester joust at each other from hobby horses; characters make their private excuses and *apologias* directly to the camera. The tone, especially in the French scenes, is comic; the alarum and retreat of the French in I.ii, for instance, are cartoon-like. Charles impetuously leads his men out against the British, and about a second later they all come scurrying back in, unhurt but splattered with stage blood which the actors wipe off with handkerchiefs a few minutes later.

Actors begin showing up in multiple roles. The first character we see is a singer at the funeral of King Henry V. The actor who plays him, Peter Benson, will later appear as Henry VI and, in *Richard III*, he will turn up again in the brief role of a priest, a calling to which Henry might have been well suited. Similarly, Bernard Hill, who will play York, is first seen as the Master-Gunner of Orleans (I.iv) who schools his three sons (one son in the script) in the correct way to fire upon the English. This trio prefigures the three sons of York, who themselves will grow up to plague England.

Right at the start, Howell serves notice that this production will not be textbook Shakespeare. The early acts of Part I bubble with energy; it is exhilarating to see the rules broken with such abandon. However, the performance is calculated to steer us away from all expectations of representation, naturalism, and realism. As Stanley Wells wrote, "Jane Howell has dared to encourage us to remember that the action is taking place in a studio" ("The History of the Whole Contention," 105). Many of her startling techniques recall Bertolt Brecht's principle of "alienation," in which

> By breaking immersion in the fantasy the theater-goer becomes *self-aware* and attains a mental attitude that allows discernment, criticism, thought, and political understanding of the material on display. Without "alienation," involvement is at an unconscious level, the theater-goer absorbing rather than reflecting and reacting. . . . The goal was that each member of the audience became aware that he or she is in a theater, that actors are performing, that the characters are created on purpose to convey a message, and that the message applies directly to each person in the audience. (Mander, 311–12.)

The "alienation" tactics of Part I accomplish several things. Howell, in effect, sets up "diversions" to keep us from taking the French conflict—which will be more or less settled in Part I—too seriously. She points us instead to the overriding conflict of the tetralogy—the struggle for power between the houses of Lancaster and York. She also turns our attention to a style of performance which, after Part I, will surprise us not so much by its technique but by the contrasts it has opened our minds to.

Part I presents the modern director with special problems. First is the Elizabethan view—which the young Shakespeare seems to have shared—of Joan of Arc as a sluttish sorceress. Second is the depiction of the stalwart Talbot as some sort of militaristic hope of England. This latter may not sound like such a problem, but in a group of plays which sets an essentially pacifist king against the gross barbarity that surrounds him, Talbot, the manly champion of England, becomes an archaic, even foolish figure, and Howell presents him as such.

Joan la Pucelle, as played by Brenda Blethyn, is an ambivalent figure. The viewer gets the idea that Howell was glad to show us a human, sexual Joan, light-years removed from the transfixed, saintly figure we know from twentieth-century works, such as Carl Dreyer's 1928 silent film *The Passion of Joan of Arc*. But neither is she comfortable with Shakespeare's "she-devil of France." So Blethyn's Joan is a strong, confident woman who easily bests the puny men she comes up against; Talbot for one seems frankly nonplussed by her. Yet she speaks in an odd bumpkin-cockney dialect that certainly alienates us from the rapt mysticism of many of Joan's lines; a more earthbound Joan one will never see. This depiction avoids the two extremes of saint and witch, and this avoidance sometimes leads the director and her actress into some rather peculiar choices. For example, during the highly dramatic scene in which Joan calls on her spirits (V.iii.8–30), no spirits appear. Blethyn is left emoting to thin air, to the probable bafflement of viewers unfamiliar with the play. Howell must have longed to flout, just this once, the hard and fast BBC rule against cutting long passages.

Talbot is treated even more unconventionally. Played by Trevor Peacock, whom the BBC viewer may remember for his elegant Feste in *Twelfth Night*, Talbot is self-consciously macho. Everything seems too big for him—his sword, his armor which pads him out like a fullback, his heavy gait, and the deep, gravelly voice that the hearer would know was put on, even if he/she hadn't heard Peacock's natural voice elsewhere. Talbot is as ludicrous a figure in this tetralogy as John Wayne would be in a David Rabe play.

Talbot, Joan, and the French are nudged aside in order to focus attention on the "through-line" of the play, the conflict between the houses of Lancaster and York. The tone noticeably darkens for II.iv, the first scene between Richard Plantagenet (later, the Duke of York) and Somerset. Here formally begins the conflict that will fester into the Wars of the Roses. The lighting, which is light and high-key through most of Part I, becomes somber here, underlining the deadly earnestness of the conflict being set up. When Richard ends the scene with the line, "I dare say / This conflict will drink blood another day" (II.iv.133–34), he is to be taken seriously.

So the "defamiliarization" of much of Part I sends signals to the audience about what should and shouldn't be taken seriously for the purposes of the "superplay." (Terry Hands, who directed a 1978 Royal Shakespeare Company production of the three *Henry VI* plays, differentiates between the "superplay," featuring Henry, Queen Margaret, and York, and three "inner plays"— Part I, with Joan and Talbot, Part II, with Jack Cade, and Part III, with the three York sons [Swander, 149].) But Howell is also showing the audience how to watch her production. There are no better places to look for this "teaching" process than the numerous asides which become the most consistent characteristic of the entire production.

The first few times that a character, in effect, takes us aside and lets us in on something, we are surprised. Characters in the earlier, naturalism-obsessed productions certainly never looked out of their worlds to talk to us in ours; and when it is done here, our first reaction is that the aside is just one more "immersion-breaking" device. But its uses are much more varied and complicated. The aside becomes, as it would have been in the Elizabethan theatre, a way for a character to express a private motive. Shakespeare's way of writing a scene lends itself to—and some would say, demands—that characters "break out" into asides.

Before long, the direct addresses assume a fixed camera position. The camera moves just slightly to the side of a character, giving him or her approximately half the frame and leaving the other half open for the director to show something else. There are many interesting examples of this. In Part II, during the scene in which Jack Cade's followers are lured away from him by Buckingham and Old Clifford, who speak to them from a balcony, Cabe grouses to the camera—"Was ever feather so lightly blown to and fro as this multitude?" (IV.viii.58–59)—while behind him, the men scramble to gather coins that are being thrown down from above. In *Richard III*, Queen Margaret sneaks into the court during the speech of Queen Elizabeth which ends "Small joy have I in being England's queen" (I.iii.109): she slips in through a door at the very rear of the set, and it takes a sharp eye to notice her. But in time for her reply, which Shakespeare indicates as an aside—"And lessen'd be that small, God, I beseech him" (110–11)—Margaret is now seated *behind* Elizabeth's throne; only we know she's there, as we see a view of Margaret which aligns the audience with her as co-conspirators arrayed against the wretched court which goes about its business in the background. And in the scene in Part I in which Suffolk first woos Margaret (V.iii), the two of them address the audience so much that Shakespeare felt obliged to write Margaret a line acknowledging the device—"He talks at random; sure, the man is mad" (85). The twist in this scene is that the woman by whose beauty Suffolk is transfixed is not classically beautiful. This and his masculine presumption—"She's beautiful and therefore to be woo'd / She's a woman and therefore to be won" (78–79)—make Suffolk appear foolish and pigheaded.

A favorite Brechtian device is to have a character say something which is contradicted by what the audience sees. Here, Howell keeps us from living vicariously through the gazer, just as casting an attractive actress as Joan keeps us from agreeing with the characters who call her a hag; we end up, instead, wondering about *them*. So Margaret from the beginning becomes too interesting a person for us simply to categorize as Suffolk's courtly love interest, which, of course, is hardly how Shakespeare wrote her.

These foreground/background shots—and I have cited only three out of dozens—ingeniously solve several problems. First, they give television a neat approximation of theatrical upstage and downstage. On the stage, when an actor walks onto the apron to address the audience, he effectively breaks through the fourth wall and momentarily leaves the action of the play behind. The same is true here when the camera takes the foreground figure into a different dimension from the people in the background. As in the theatre, the audience has a choice of what to watch. The choice has not been made for us; and, indeed, sometimes what goes on in the background is at least as interesting as the foreground, especially since the two often comment on each other. Furthermore, the actors are encouraged to play to the camera in ways that could be seen only in the smallest theatre.

At the same time that the foreground/background composition is theatrical, it is also cinematic. With it, Howell comes as close as she can to cinematic *mise en scène*, or depth of field in a medium that is thought to be capable only of *montage*, as with all the cutting back and forth between disembodied close-ups in other BBC productions. Often the effect of the foreground/background composition is purely cinematic. For instance, Howell uses the composition for comic effect in III.i of Part I, the scene in which King Henry convinces Gloucester and Winchester to reconcile, which they do but very grudgingly. In the foreground are shown the two men's clasped hands, as Gloucester declares, "See here, my friends and loving countrymen, / This token serveth for a flag of truce" (137–38); through the hands are seen the men's brawling followers. This image shows up the reconciliation for the silly and ineffectual "token" that it is.

Directing characters to break out of the action by explaining themselves to the audience is a very "metatheatrical" thing to do, if one defines "metatheatre" as Lionel Abel does, focusing on our notion of the world as a stage, or, in Howell's case, a television studio (105). Metatheatre is dramatic narrative in which characters take responsibility for the telling of their own stories. York is handled in this way, and so certainly is his son Richard. In fact, Howell goes so far as to open *Richard III* with Richard hobbling across the set to a chalkboard on which he scrawls the name of the play that bears his name.

What the viewer comes to realize, however, by the time this style of performance has come to seem "normal" (about midway through Part II) is that direct address is perfect for television. It does not work on film; we in the audience are down in the dark, lost in this other world. For a character to break out of a narrative and talk to the audience would be to break the spell irrevocably. Besides, Warner Brothers cartoons and movie comedians like Hope and Crosby and the Marx Brothers beat Brecht to it.

On television, however, the audience is used to being addressed by newscasters, commercial pitchpeople, and talk show hosts, who routinely turn their attention back and forth between their guests and the camera. Johnny Carson's laugh lines during an interview are almost asides to the audience. As a child, I was confused by Fred MacMurray, the star of the naturalistic sitcom *My Three Sons*, because he always appeared before the theme music to say "Hi, welcome to our show for Hunt's Catsup." TV characters were not supposed to know, I was convinced, that they were on a "show." Former vaudevillians on TV were something else again. George Burns would leave the set of the sitcom in which he was involved, to wave his cigar at the audience and explain the plot. Red Skelton was enjoyable to watch because he could be depended upon to break the sanctity of a script in ways that appealed to children and adolescents: he would crack up in the middle of a line and try to crack up his usually more disciplined guest star as well. Sometimes he would ad lib a wisecrack to the camera, and then laugh at his own joke.

Similarly, television is far more conducive to stylization than Cedric Messina, Jonathan Miller and their various directors thought. It has only been in the all-videotape and all-color age that television producers have assumed that their shows had to look like movies and that only physical realism would do. The type of broadcast that relied most heavily upon stylization in the first decade of TV was children's programming. Shows like *Captain Kangaroo* took place on stylized sets with painted backdrops. The reasons for this were, of course, economic; these programs usually had very limited budgets, as indeed had "The Shakespeare Plays." But the sets allowed a child's imagination to complete the scene that the designer *suggested* but left unfinished. The same is true in the Howell productions. On TV, the theatrical sets feel childlike: the set designer builds, for example, a simple platform with a tall, red velvet-backed chair atop it—and leaves it to the viewers to complete the "throne room" in their imaginations.

Howell uses stylization, then, to put the viewer off guard up to the point where the stylization looks "normal" and the "realistic" looks strange. This is why the production's battle scenes seem so realistically brutal. If Howell had stylized all the violence as she does in the antic French scenes of Part I, the audience could watch the increasingly senseless carnage of the Wars of the Roses without feeling uneasy—could get accustomed to the killing. The convincingly real blood and gore in the midst of Howell's frankly unreal production, however, is much harder to tolerate. By Part III, the blood has virtually become the tetralogy's controlling motif. Soldiers have their throats cut in close-up; men are run through with lances. At the close of Part II—which ends in triumph for York and his partisans—Warwick proclaims, "Sound drums, and trumpets, and to London all: / And more such days as these to us befall" (V.iii.32–33). The camera moves from the elated Warwick to pan slowly over a pile of corpses, the war's casualties, until fade out. This ending gives a troubling and ghoulish feel to the thought of "more such days as these."

Part III opens with the same shot: a pair of hands places a dirty tarpaulin, on which is scrawled the title *Henry VI, Part III*, over the bodies; and the play—which begins with York literally seizing the throne—begins. Howell ends *Richard III* with an even more outrageous and ambiguous image: Queen Margaret, the only character who survives the entire tetralogy, laughs exultantly as she cradles the body of Richard atop a veritable mountain of corpses. Margaret's long, flowing blonde hair is down for the first time since she was presented to King Henry. She looks young; her laughter is not harsh, but warm; she is sibyl, victim, and weird sister rolled into one.

The excess of blood and death that drives Margaret to this enigmatic laughter in fact aligns us with Henry, who, viewing the carnage in *3 Henry VI*, asks despondently, "What is there in this world but grief and woe?" (II.v.20). Howell has been careful to keep Henry far removed from the hurly-burly of power politics and, through him, to question whether power is worth such sacrifices. Henry is never in the foreground in a foreground/background shot because he never says anything that he would not say for all to hear. He is sometimes shown as a figure marooned in the middle of the set, crazed warriors racing past him. His bewilderment becomes immensely sympathetic by Part III; and the camera, which focuses on corpses while ignoring the victors, becomes his ally—an instrument of moral judgment.

Thus the stylization works on many levels. The half-accomplished, chaotic set reflects the half-accomplished, chaotic rule of King Henry VI. As on the stage, lighting changes with the mood of the scene. In the last two plays of the tetralogy, the bright pastels of Part I fade to a monochrome; and in fact, the visual dankness risks growing monotonous. *Richard III* probably contains less drama and variety than independent productions of that play because Howell has painted herself into a corner with her concept: the four parts are designed to grow as increasingly grim as their moral tone. *Richard III* thus seems unfortunately anticlimactic; the kingdom has been so sapped of vigor that Richard's downfall comes mercifully as a relief. The resultant loss of theatrical energy is the price Howell pays for the concept, but the concept is well worth the cost.

Howell serves Shakespeare extraordinarily well by adapting him to a modern and often troublesome medium in ways untested by previous directors. One reason she could be so free with the first tetralogy is that the plays have been seldom performed. Giving them a radical twist, therefore, does not upset a defined, traditional interpretation. However daring—however Brechtian in strategy—her productions may be, they do not alienate the television viewer. Rather, Howell has figured out how to engage the viewer by appropriating some of television's least artistically respectable, but most characteristic, techniques. Her productions are startling because they are not what we expect from cultural programming: they are playfully, irreverently self-conscious.

The ease with which they settle into television, once Howell has accustomed us to their unreality, proves the validity of her concept for the medium.

Abel, Lionel. *Metatheatre*. New York: Hill and Wang, 1963.

Banham, Martin. "BBC Television's Dull Shakespeares." *Critical Quarterly*, 22 (1980), 31–40.

Brecht, Bertolt. *Brecht on Theatre*, ed. and trans. John Willett. New York: Hill and Wang, 1964.

Bulman, James C. "The BBC Shakespeare and 'House Style,'" *Shakespeare Quarterly*, 35 (1984), 571–81.

Calderwood, James L. *Shakespearean Metadrama*. Minneapolis: Univ. of Minnesota Press, 1971.

Charney, Maurice. "Shakespearean Anglophilia: The BBC Series and American Audiences," *Shakespeare Quarterly*, 31 (1980), 287–92.

Coursen, H. R. "The Bard and the Tube." Paper presented to the 1986 conference of The Shakespeare Association of America.

Hallinan, Tim. "Jonathan Miller on *The Shakespeare Plays*," *Shakespeare Quarterly*, 32 (1981), 134–45.

Holderness, Graham. "Radical Potentiality and Institutional Closure: Shakespeare in Film and Television," in *Political Shakespeare*, ed. Jonathan Dollimore and Alan Sinfield (Manchester Univ. Press, 1985), pp. 182–201.

Jones, Gordon P. "Long-Distance Shakespeare," *Shakespeare Quarterly*, 35 (1984), 591–97.

Mander, Jerry. *Four Arguments for the Elimination of Television*. New York: Morrow, 1978.

Manheim, Michael. "The Shakespeare Plays on TV: The *Henry VI-Richard III* Tetralogy," *Shakespeare on Film Newsletter*, 8:2 (April 1984), 2.

Rothwell, Kenneth S. "*The Shakespeare Plays: Hamlet* and the Five Plays of Season Three," *Shakespeare Quarterly*, 32 (1981), 401–08.

Swander, Homer D. "The Rediscovery of *Henry VI*," *Shakespeare Quarterly*, 29 (1978), 146–63.

Wells, Stanley. "The History of the Whole Contention," *Times Literary Supplement*, 4 February 1983, p. 105.

Wells, Stanley. "Television Shakespeare," *Shakespeare Quarterly*, 33 (1982), 261–77.

Part Three
SHORT SUBJECTS

III Reviewing Shakespeare: An Introduction

The reviewer is a privileged interpreter, a mediator between production and audience. The review may be a retrospective analysis or a guide for an audience about to view a production. The differences between reviewers and reviews are often dictated by the differences in audiences, from the readers of a daily newspaper deciding what to watch on television that night, to the much smaller group of Shakespeare scholars reading what one of their colleagues has to say about a production they have already watched.

The reviewer for a daily newspaper must consider a Shakespeare production in light of the expectations his audience has for television programming in general—an audience for whom Shakespeare would be exceptional, perhaps even someone for whom a favorite show must be sacrificed. Some reviewers feel compelled to summarize the plot to make the play accessible to a mass audience, to explain its affinities with other programs. Others point out that a Shakespearean production is really different from its competition on the other channels. Regardless of the reviewer's approach—whether to compare the Shakespeare play with "Dallas" or "Hill Street Blues," or to set it in a zone of its own—the best of the dailies pay serious attention to Shakespeare on television.

Reviewers for the popular press can give only an instant response. They are watching Shakespeare even as they review the sit-coms, documentaries, and made-for-TV films that may also consume a given evening. Because their response is immediate, however, the reviewers are likely to provide a strong pro or con critique and thus to approximate our own initial, gut reaction to what we watch. The value of the review in the popular press derives precisely from its freedom from erudition and from a lengthy period of evaluation. The excerpts we have included in this section represent a spectrum of response from absolute praise to downright condemnation.

John J. O'Connor of the *New York Times* gives an amusing account of the outrage heaped upon his desk after his rave pre-review of the Trevor Nunn *Antony and Cleopatra*, which appeared on ABC in January 1975.[1] It was, O'Connor claimed, a "marvelously imaginative interpretation, beautifully performed." It was also, however, constantly interrupted by commercials, as one viewer complained:

> At the end of the play, the split-second cut from the dead Queen of Egypt in robes of state to a middle-aged man in pyjamas announcing "That's my last cough" would have been incredible, except by then, after three hours of similarly ludicrous hi-jinks, not even a plug for an asp antidote would have been surprising.

O'Connor explains that many of the angry writers "had canceled dinner invitations, rushed home from theatre matinees or given up an evening at the movies on the basis of my enthusiastic endorsement. . . . Most assumed that I had seen the production without commercials. They were right."

O'Connor thus broaches the crucial question—the circumstances within which Shakespeare is experienced: "the reviewer has to assume that the mass public fully understands commercial TV means commercial interruptions." It must be added that "pure" Shakespeare, too, such as the BBC series has offered recently on PBS, has its problems. Relatively complete scripts that provide two one-minute breaks during a three-hour period quite simply strain the attention-span of even the best-willed of viewers. But PBS cannot say, "We will now have a fifteen-minute interval." The airwaves must be peopled. Suffice it, then, that the conditions in which a viewer or reviewer experiences a Shakespeare production are a vital component of response. As a new, popular medium, television reflects its age in the assumption that the medium's purpose is to sell merchandise. The medium itself embodies that oxymoron called "popular culture." Our expectations of the medium become a significant, if often unperceived, component of our evaluation of what has appeared on the small screen.

The academic reviewer has several advantages over the reviewer working for a daily newspaper. His deadline is often measured in months, not hours. He can study a tape of a production, can pause, reflect, revise. He writes towards a permanent record, and his field is Shakespeare (and, even more narrowly, Shakespeare-in-performance), not television. He probably does not know "what else is on" on a given evening, but he does bring to a specific production a knowledge of other productions of the same play. This reviewer, whether for a journal like the *Shakespeare Quarterly* or a weekly like the *Times Literary Supplement*, will assume a reader's familiarity with Shakespeare's play, will draw without apology on his knowledge of production history and scholarly tradition, and will inevitably examine the production's handling of problems inherent in the script. While such matters are of little concern to a mass audience, they are crucial to anyone studying the script as a source of the play's setting, psychology, and meaning. The academic reviewer usually has a lively and complete knowledge of the script and will respond on that basis, playing his evaluation against his memory of other manifestations of that script.

Yet all types of reviews, from the popular to the academic, have more in common with each other than with the essays in Parts I and II. Part I concentrates on how, or whether, Shakespeare's plays can be translated to television. Some essays examine the history and evolution of televised Shakespeare. Others probe the aesthetic, moral, and political issues inherent in such translation. The essays in Part II narrow from the general to the particular; they consider camera techniques, settings and costumes, directorial biases, and problems of anachronism, of genre, and of cultural orientation. Often they study productions comparatively. These essays benefit from periods of reflection. They neither judge all aspects of a given production nor provide an assessment for an audience, except possibly as induced from their explorations. The writers of these essays would be surprised if their work were labelled "reviews."

A good review, on the other hand, will usually assess four elements of a televised Shakespeare production:

1) The presentation of the script. Is the story made clear for an audience unfamiliar with the play? (The reviewer who is familiar with the play must place himself in the position of the "naive spectator.")

2) The quality of the acting. Does it seem "natural," as our expectations of television and the scaled-down nature of the medium seem to demand, or is it histrionic and stagey, confirming a viewer's worst preconceptions of "how Shakespeare is done?"

3) The "mounting" of the production: sets, costumes and camera work. Does the production "fit" the tube? Is it scaled down sufficiently for a smaller medium but nevertheless adequate to express—with its images and its shifting from close-ups to wider purview—the issues the script is working out?

4) The production's overall success in translating the play onto the television screen. Is it good or boring? Would the reviewer recommend it to a wider audience? If so, under what conditions?

The reviews we include should allow students to measure their own response to a specific production against that of the "expert," to identify the often unstated premises underlying a review, and to discover that his own psychology of perception is just as accurate as that of any reviewer, even if the latter has more practice and expertise in expressing his perceptions.

Shakespeare has always been a function of the "ideas of an age." Just as the preconceptions, biases, and clichés of the times flow into a specific production and condition our response to that production, so they creep into reviews themselves. The reviewer who claims to be objective finds that his subjectivity has slipped in the back door. The reviewer who befriends his subjectivity, however, and lets it work for him, makes a modest and accurate statement—not "here is how the production was," but "here is how I found it on this particular evening." A review often says as much about a reviewer and the times he lives in as it does about a particular production; and in this way, reviews for the popular press are no less accurate than those written for the scholarly journals.

Part III is also "for the record." We include responses to early televised Shakespeare that are themselves illuminating and that will be of value to historians of performance as well. We have also tried to create some balance between Parts II and III. Where specific productions are not treated in detail in Part II, we have included more substantial reviews of those productions in Part III to provide a fuller context for judging them. The reviews themselves may suggest why more considered or scholarly evaluation of certain productions has not been forthcoming.

Finally, Shakespeare wrote for live audiences, who could help shape a production as it was acted. Often Shakespeare's plays invite a response directly. Beyond that direct invitation, however, the plays are "metadramatic." They know they are plays, and they presuppose a vital reciprocity between actor and audience that can build a profound continuum between stage and spectator over the course of a performance. The laughter behind Archie Bunker is not the same as what Virginia Carr calls "the communal laughter of the theatre audience."[2] Television directors must tailor their productions towards the *absence* of an audience when the script presupposes its presence.

Some of the productions reviewed below, however, represent live performances taped for television. The audience is there and is sometimes used as part of the texture of the television show. The audience for "All in the Family" is seen but not heard. Archie and Edith play to a "fourth wall," as if no one is observing. Television drama tends to be a "fourth wall" medium. Shakespeare's plays, however, incorporate the soliloquy, the aside, the chorus, and the epilogue, plenty of eavesdroppers that we see, and inner audiences for what we at the outer dramatic circumference call "plays-within-plays." The genre of "live Shakespeare on television" thus requires a subtle evaluation of a play designed for a live audience but redesigned and redirected for viewers sitting at home. The true test of Shakespeare, after all, is how it plays to us.

The reviewer's question, therefore, is "How does one best translate scripts designed for the stage, and for a stage with conventions very different from ours, to television?" The medium is ours within what McLuhan terms a "global village." Shakespeare has no problems in that village, as Kozintsev's *Lear* and Kurosawa's *Throne of Blood* and *Ran* attest. But Shakespeare on television has his problems: the debates carried out in these reviews clearly demonstrate that.

We apologize to those reviewers whose work has been condensed because of space limitations. We urge readers to seek out the full reviews.

JCB
HRC

1. John J. O'Connor, "And Now a Few Words from Irate Viewers," *New York Times*, 22 January 1975, sec. D, p. 29.

2. Virginia Carr, "Review of *Measure for Measure*," *Shakespeare on Film Newsletter*, 4:1 (Dec. 1979), 5.

The Productions

This section presents only a sampling of responses to more than seventy productions of Shakespeare's plays broadcast in America, Canada, and Great Britain over the past forty years. For a more complete bibliography, see Annabelle Melzer and Kenneth Rothwell, *Shakespeare on Screen: A Filmography/ Videography* (Neil Schuman, forthcoming); and, for a list that focuses largely on British productions, Graham Holderness and Christopher McCullough, "Shakespeare on the Screen: A Selective Filmography," *Shakespeare Survey*, 39 (1987), 13–37.

Twelfth Night (NBC, 20 February 1949)

Andrew: Vaughan Taylor. *Feste*: John McQuade. *Malvolio*: John Carradine. *Toby*: Richard Goode. *Viola*: Marsha Hunt.
     Director: Fred Coe.
     Jack Gould, *NY Times* (27 Feb. 1949). "Cohesion of the comedy . . . sacrificed to the demands of the studio clock, making the play a succession of episodes. . . . [Production] had a static and chopped-up quality. . . . [Comedy] pared down to a bare narrative." Marsha Hunt, as Viola, "switched deftly . . . from the radiant image of the girl in love with Orsino to the detached and humorous messenger [to] Olivia."

Julius Caesar (CBS, 6 March 1949)

Antony: Philip Borneuf. *Brutus*: Robert Keith. *Caesar*: William Post. *Cassius*: John O'Shaughnessy. *Casca*: Vaughan Taylor. *Portia*: Ruth Ford.
     Producer: Worthington Miner. Director: Paul Nickell.
     Jack Gould, *NY Times* (13 Mar. 1949). "The most exciting television yet seen on the home screen—a magnificently bold, imaginative, and independent achievement." While the production's modern dress invites some superficial comparisons with the Welles 1937 version, this one "went to the heart of video's needs, which is to make a picture not to take one." After Antony's final eulogy, he pushes Brutus into the gutter. Camera techniques and conception praised unreservedly.

Julius Caesar (NBC, 3 April 1949)

Amherst College Masquers. Inaugural Performance, Folger Shakespeare Library Theatre.
     Director: F. Curtis Canfield.
     Jack Gould, *NY Times* (10 Apr. 1949). "Ill-advised . . . camera work awkward and indistinct." Not up to professional standards. Arch Taylor praised as Brutus.

Macbeth (NBC, 1 May 1949)

Lady Macbeth: Joyce Redman. *Macbeth*: Walter Hampden. Others in the cast: Walter Abel, Sidney Blackmer, John Carradine, Leo G. Carroll, David Wayne.
     Directors: Anthony Brown and Gerry Simpson.
     Jack Gould, *NY Times* (22 May 1949). "Trying and awkward."

Romeo and Juliet (NBC, 15 May 1949)

Juliet: Pat Breslin. *Romeo*: Kevin McCarthy.
     Director: Albert McCleery.
     Jack Gould, *NY Times* (22 May 1949). The "technique of arena theatre . . . made for a static sixty minutes. [Production] emphasized the limitations of the medium." Horrible taste demonstrated when, after the camera viewed corpses of Juliet and Romeo, it fixed upon a "floral wreath" with "The End" across it. "Sheer elaborateness of the dress, which can be very eye-catching on stage, was only disconcerting on the small screen. . . . As in so many phases of television production, simplicity is all-important in costuming. . . . Except for Kevin McCarthy . . . the cast . . . seemed . . . at loose ends."

Othello (NBC, 27 September 1950)

Cast included Edward Cullen, Olive Deering, Muriel Hutchinson, George Reane, Alfred Ryder, John Seymour, Alan Shayne, Torin Thatcher.
     Producer: Fred Coe. Director: Delbert Mann.

Coriolanus (CBS, 11 June 1951)

Coriolanus: Richard Greene. *Volumnia*: Judith Evelyn.
     Producer: Worthington Miner. Director: Paul Nickell.
     Jack Gould, *NY Times* (17 June 1951). "A constructive evening, albeit not a very exciting one." Coriolanus "seen as a type, rather than a dominant

personality. [The production thus] lost . . . dramatic unity [that can be] built around a forceful, mature and arresting figure." Richard Greene "was no Coriolanus . . . virtually expressionless." Judith Evelyn's Volumnia "almost alone carried the climactic scene."

Macbeth (CBS, 22 October 1951)

Lady Macbeth: Judith Evelyn. *Macbeth*: Charlton Heston.

Producer: Worthington Miner. *Director*: Paul Nickell.

Jack Gould, NY *Times* (24 Oct. 1951). "A striving for unique pictorial composition which largely defeated its own ends because the viewer was so abundantly conscious of the camera movement. . . . Judith Evelyn . . . superb . . . as Lady Macbeth. . . . Charlton Heston brought the animation more of a personal appearance than of a performance [and was] handicapped by very poor enunciation and little versatility in interpretation. . . . The program's extreme reliance on . . . the stream-of-consciousness technique . . . made it hard to tell whether Mr. Heston was himself or only an automaton."

Othello (CBC, 1952)

Cassio: Patrick McNee. *Desdemona*: Peggi Loder. *Emilia*: Katherine Blake. *Iago*: Josef Furst. *Othello*: Lorne Greene. *Roderigo*: Richard Easton.

Director: David Greene. *Designer*: Nicolai Soloviov.

Alice V. Griffin, *SQ*, 4 (1953). "The production was marked by imagination, dramatic unity, and ensemble acting. . . . " Greene's Othello "with his simple nobility . . . was impressive. . . . Furst's Iago emerged as a character of intense, cold cruelty, without the subtlety or complexity of Jose Ferrer's [Iago]."

Hamlet (NBC, 26 April 1953)

Claudius: Joseph Schildkraut. *Gertrude*: Ruth Chatterton. *Hamlet*: Maurice Evans. *Horatio*: Wesley Addy. *Ophelia*: Sarah Churchill. *Polonius*: Barry Jones.

Directors: George Schaefer and Albert McCleery. *Designer*: Richard Sylbert.

Maurice Evans, "An Actor Discusses His TV Debut," NY *Times* (26 Apr. 1953). Then as now—"TV? Any 6-year-old in the living room can obliterate actor and play with a flick of the wrist and go on to more tonic pursuits."

Philip Hamburger, "The Dane," *New Yorker* (9 May 1953). "So splendid, mobile, imaginative, and graceful that [I am] almost speechless with admiration. . . . [Evans's] performance was a triumph of intelligence and talent. . . . Tom Hughes

Sand's adaptation seemed to me poetic editing of the highest sort."

Jack Gould, "Maurice Evans Makes an Exciting Debut in Medium with His Capsule Version of 'Hamlet,'" *New York Times* (27 Apr. 1953).

Maurice Evans brought his short version of "Hamlet" to television yesterday afternoon over the N.B.C. network, and it made for memorable and exciting viewing. Edited down to slightly more than an hour and a half, the tragedy was played for its sheer dramatic value and proved superbly arresting theatre. Mr. Evans' debut before the video cameras will not be soon forgotten; the home screen has not seen anything quite like it.

In the main, the production adhered to the medium "shots" that minimized abrupt changes. Some of the scenes admittedly were a trifle cluttered and overcrowded, but considering the magnitude of the assignment—the longest drama ever done on American television—the direction was a superior job.

Alice V. Griffin, "Shakespeare Through the Camera's Eye—*Hamlet* on Television," *Shakespeare Quarterly*, 4 (1953), 333–35.

As he has played it on the stage, Evans' Hamlet is a vigorous young man, an interpretation not unfamiliar to modern scholars and stagers. Evans says of his portrayal: "too often Hamlet has been played as a study in dyspepsia rather than as the inner conflict of a man who was a very normal human being caught up in a web of circumstance which sets him to questioning the values and standards by which he has lived. Hamlet has been called a psychopath. I think he just has a universal reaction to a pretty staggering problem."

As in Olivier's film, the "To be or not to be" was transposed, and the television version also transposed the first and second scenes of Act I. Closeups were generally confined to objects rather than characters, most of the scenes being medium shots. One effective closeup showed Gertrude's hand on Hamlet's in I.i, and then the King's hand withdrawing hers.

Richard Sylbert's set, covering an area 60 by 70 feet, was visually helpful and generally uncluttered, depicting various Victorian interiors. The costumes were of this period too. In these trappings, the King and Queen seemed more like upper-class Victorians, however, than the rulers of Denmark. The Player King and Queen were attired, as in Evans' stage productions, like playing-card royalty.

King Lear (CBS, 8 October 1953)

Albany: Arnold Moss. *Cordelia*: Natasha Parry. *Goneril*: Beatrice Straight. *Lear*: Orson Welles. *Regan*: Margaret Phillips.

Producer: Fred Rickey. *Directors*: Andrew McCullough and Peter Brook. *Designer*: Georges Wakhevitch.

Val Adams, "Random Notes on a Shakespearean Rehearsal," *NY Times* (18 Oct. 1953). An interview with Orson Welles. Welles on "attention span:" "If we did a full length version [of *King Lear*], it would be too long for television. I've seen two-hour dramas on the B.B.C. and they got tiresome."

Alice Griffin, "Shakespeare Through the Camera's Eye 1953–1954," *Shakespeare Quarterly*, 6 (1955), 63–66.

Between October 1953 and November 1954, three major television productions of Shakespeare's plays have been offered, *King Lear* on the CBS Omnibus program and *Richard II* and *Macbeth* by the Hallmark Hall of Fame on NBC. Although these marked a technical improvement over the *Hamlet* and *Othello* reported in an earlier issue of the *Quarterly*, they revealed no artistic advance.

In general, although the medium could contribute much to a fluid presentation, the productions are static; with some exceptions they are not well cast or convincingly acted or spoken; the cameras are still too "busy," roving during the major speeches as if the producers were fearful to let Shakespeare's words speak for themselves, and, finally, there is lacking an over-all artistic unity of spirit or style.

The ninety-minute *King Lear* presented on the CBS Omnibus program in October of 1953 had, to at least one viewer, the greatest merit, although it also had the greatest faults, of the three productions to be discussed here. Its most important achievement is that it did evoke the grandeur and tragedy of *Lear*, whereas when *Richard II* and *Macbeth* were presented, the medium reduced the stature of the plays to that of the "action-packed" television script rather than living up to the greatness of the works. . . .

Peter Brook did not seem to realize that three's a crowd on the video screen, and his large cast, as in the scene of Lear's boisterous companions, did not make the screen seem expansive, but rather accentuated its limited size.

Mr. Welles' best acting, and indeed one of the best scenes in the production, came in his meeting with the blinded Gloucester (IV. vi), when Welles excellently conveyed both the tragic ruin of the character and his realization, in his madness, of his own former blindness of spirit. Simply and movingly done, without the distracting properties and trick camera shots that characterized other parts of the production, this was a most impressive scene.

The adaptation by Mr. Brook was unforgivably bad; granted that time had to be cut, many precious minutes were spent on visual effects which contributed little to the play, while important speeches were omitted or reduced to a line or two.

Richard II was presented early in 1954, and *Macbeth* in November. While the viewing public cannot but be grateful to the producers for making the plays in performance available to such a large audience, it is too bad that these costly programs could not have been better in their conception and presentation. The acting of the major roles as well as the minor ones generally left something to be desired, and the direction by Mr. George Schaefer approached the nonrealistic plays realistically, reducing them in stature, and it failed to provide any over-all style or unity.

The main impression of *Richard II* was that it was too cluttered, and like the *Macbeth* it substituted the literal for the imaginative. The setting consisted of an over-abundance of towers and turrets, massive but unconvincing, while the garden set was so filled with flowers and leaves that one had trouble distinguishing the actors.

Richard II is Maurice Evans' best role, and he was especially effective in the first half of the play, though the total character lacked the electricity and depth which Michael Redgrave brought to it at Stratford-on-Avon in 1951. Mr. Evans conveyed well the self-indulgent, sentimental side of Richard; the passage "What must the King do now?" (III. iii) was very well spoken, as is true of all Mr. Evans' lines. But sometimes he seems to "speechify" rather than act, and at other times seems to employ the facile and the obvious in his interpretation.

The trimming of the script was well done, and the chief merit of this presentation was its clarity, being far more easy to follow for the new viewer of Shakespeare than was the *King Lear*. The conclusion of the play was in questionable taste, sacrificing the dignity of the funeral procession for a closeup of the dead Richard.

Presented last November by Hallmark in color, *Macbeth* was the most ambitious of the three programs, and in the acting of Judith Anderson the NBC Shakespearean series achieved for the first time the sense of high tragedy. It will be recalled that Miss Anderson and Mr. Evans acted Lady Macbeth and Macbeth together on the legitimate stage in 1941, and the parts as interpreted on television were substantially the same, that of a weak Macbeth who is driven to murder not so much by his own "vaulting ambition" as by his wife's. In the cut television version this approach, perhaps because Miss Anderson was so effective, seemed to shift the central focus to Lady Macbeth, and the hero of the play seemed more pathetic than tragic. Nor did he seem very heroic, the lines of the bloody sergeant about Macbeth's brave deeds in battle perhaps having been cut intentionally by Mr. Evans in his adaptation of the play.

In the banquet scene the depiction of Banquo's presence by a disembodied head, shining with red blood and bouncing about like a tennis ball, was just short of ludicrous.

Except for Miss Anderson there was no grandeur and little poetry in this production. Her interpretation moved steadily to a climax, from the reading of the letter and realization of what it could mean; then her steeling herself, in a magnificently rendered delivery of the soliloquy "The raven himself is hoarse;" and later her concern for her husband and mounting apprehensions about their deed; until finally the truly terrifying sleepwalking scene.

Mr. Evans' Macbeth was less successful, because in the close range of television he did not seem to convey the stature or the complexity of this character. And again, as in the *Richard II*, a number of his passages seemed recited rather than acted.

Richard II (NBC, 24 January 1954)

Bolingbroke: Kent Smith. *Gaunt*: Frederick Worlock. *Queen Isabel*: Sarah Churchill. *Richard*: Maurice Evans. *York*: Richard Purdy.

Time (1 Feb. 1954). "Evans brilliantly played Richard as a posturing, unsettled man, forever wavering between false triumph and real despair."

Life, "Video Rushes In Where Angels Fear . . ." (8 Feb. 1954). Photos of "By far TV's most successful Shakespeare . . . also TV's best acted and most sumptuous."

Jack Gould, "Television Review: Evans' *Richard II*," *New York Times* (25 Jan. 1954).

Maurice Evans brought to television his greatest stage success, *King Richard II*. His interpretation of the unhappy monarch was a stirring and lucid performance that finally managed to overcome an often disappointing production.

In the third act of the televised *Richard*, wherein a viewer saw a measure of the monarch as a man and not a king, there was superb and fluid theatre on the home screen. But in the first two acts the tragedy of the playboy ruler was all but lost amid a bewildering preoccupation with settings, props and effects. Too often the camera and not the play was the thing.

The grouping of the supporting players was especially static and repetitious, and the pursuit of tricky camera angles intruded on the meaning of the play. The excessive emphasis on spectacle and pageantry in particular tended to becloud the human values essential to a coherent telling of the fall of Richard and the rise of Bolingbroke. Elaborate physical production can be very impressive in the studio; it is usually much less so on the home screen, where the proscenium arch is only twenty-one inches.

Macbeth (NBC, 28 November 1954)

Banquo: Staats Cotsworth. *Duncan*: House Jameson. *Lady Macbeth*: Judith Anderson. *Macbeth*: Maurice Evans. *Macduff*: Richard Waring.
    Director: George Schaefer.

Jack Gould, "Adaptation of *Macbeth* Shown on N.B.C.," *New York Times* (29 Nov. 1954).

This production of *Macbeth*, starring Maurice Evans and Judith Anderson, was two hours of television theatre at once extremely interesting yet, to this corner at least, strangely disappointing. By video's standards it was assuredly an event not to have been missed, but it also seemed a *Macbeth* regrettably often out of joint.

There were quite real rewards, to be sure. Miss Anderson's diabolical and earthy persuasiveness as a conspirator and her interpretation of Lady Macbeth's sleepwalking scene are acting treasures that transcend mere media. In the "sound and fury" soliloquy, Mr. Evans was tragic and moving. Television earnestly needs such moments.

But in adapting *Macbeth* as a whole to the requirements of television something intangible but none the less vital was lost. Call it the underlying excitement, the sense of ambitious urgency, that drives Macbeth toward evil and doom. The compelling sweep of the unified whole appeared sacrificed to the demanding technical gods of TV.

For their presentation, Mr. Evans and George Schaefer had at their disposal massive detailed settings and apparently limitless cameras. With a commendable willingness to experiment, they sought to resolve by TV's personalization and intimacy the awkwardness of *Macbeth*.

In execution, however, their approach became a prisoner of their technique. A protracted series of capsule scenes and close-ups made the play, however inadvertently, seem excessively episodic. The tricky camera angles, the overly studied visual perspectives and superimpositions and the confusion of entrances and exits gave too much emphasis to the players and not enough to the dominance of the play.

By eliminating the physical proscenium arch, the televised *Macbeth* also lost the play's unifying arch of tragic human greed. On the home screen *Macbeth* was too much the story of man against man rather than man against fate. The realism of modern television sometimes is less to be preferred than the stark emotionalism of Elizabethan drama.

Macbeth was televised in both black and white and color. The monochrome version was the better of the two; the restless camera work imposed lighting problems beyond color TV's grasp at the moment. In the murder scenes, the hands of Mr. Evans and Miss Anderson were covered with the most vivid of red liquids, as was the face of Banquo in the famous ghost scene. Shown in an extreme television close-up, these interludes represented a lamentable slip in theatrical judgment. There is a difference between horror and the horrible.

See also the review by Alice Griffin reprinted in this volume, pp. 239–40.

The Taming of the Shrew (NBC, 18 March 1956)

Baptista: Philip Bourneuf. *Bianca*: Diane Cilento. *Kate*: Lilli Palmer. *Petruchio*: Maurice Evans.

Producer: William Nichols. Director: George Schaefer. Designer: Rouben Ter-Aruntunian.

Jack Gould, NY Times (19 Mar. 1956). "Maurice Evans frolicked through The Taming of the Shrew in a most infectiously inventive production. Done in the style of commedia dell'arte, the Shakespearean comedy emerged as a free-wheeling lark, replete to the appearance of Kate and Petruchio in a boxing ring. It was delightful fun."

Twelfth Night (NBC, 15 December 1957)

Andrew: Max Adrian. Feste: Howard Morris. Malvolio: Maurice Evans. Orsino: Lloyd Bochner. Toby: Dennis King. Viola: Rosemary Harris.
Director: William Nichols.

NY Times (15 Dec. 1957). A picture of Evans and a program note: "William Nichols . . . concept of the comedy is that of a dream as seen through the eyes of . . . Feste."

Jack Gould, NY Times (16 Dec. 1957). "Tricks and embellishments galore . . . only compounded the confusion. . . . A delicate illusion is not always enhanced by microscopic scrutiny of how it is created." Concept and camera technique hampered all the actors, except for Rosemary Harris, "charmingly believable" as Viola.

Hamlet (Old Vic Production. CBS Dupont Show of the Month, 24 February 1959)

Claudius: Oliver Neville. Gertrude: Margaret Courtenay. Hamlet: John Neville. Laertes: John Humphrey. Ophelia: Barbara Jefford. Polonius: Joseph O'Conor.
Directors: Michael Benthall and Ralph Nelson.

John P. Shanley, NY Times (22 Feb. 1959). [Picture of Duel Scene]. Ralph Nelson explains his editing. He wanted to cut "To be or not to be"—a "show-stopper. . . . We finally kept it in, though [Michael] Benthall still bemoans the time lost that could have been used to such advantage elsewhere." For parapet scenes, actors will wear a "small piece of dry ice . . . secured to their faces by invisible bands. As they breathe, the wintry vapors will be visible even though the scene was taped in a studio where the temperature was about 70 degrees."

Jack Gould, NY Times (25 Feb. 1959). "Cumbersome staging . . . a frightful bore . . . skeletonized to 78 minutes." John Neville "gave little more than ecstatic recitation. . . . In Ophelia's mad scene, Barbara Jefford contributed the evening's only fleeting moment of gripping characterization." This production was not "anywhere near [the] class of [Maurice Evans' 1953 production]."

H. R. Coursen remembers the sheer rush of this production. Hamlet's first soliloquy was superimposed via a sudden close-up over the opening business of the court (I.ii), thus before the premises of Hamlet's anguish had really been established.

The Tempest (NBC, 3 February 1960)

Ariel: Roddy McDowall. Caliban: Richard Burton. Miranda: Lee Remick. Prospero: Maurice Evans.
Director: George Schaefer.

Jack Gould, NY Times (4 Feb. 1960). The play "poses a severe traffic problem" for the small screen. The settings "overshadowed the fragility of the narrative." "Closeups" not helpful with a play that "requires reporting that is fanciful not factual."

Virginia M. Vaughan, "The Forgotten Television Tempest," Shakespeare on Film Newsletter, 9 (Dec. 1984).

Schaefer was imaginative in casting various celebrities in the major roles. Maurice Evans starred as Prospero, with Roddy McDowall as Ariel, Richard Burton as Caliban, and Lee Remick as Miranda. Evans' Prospero was dignified, old, but loving toward his daughter and influenced by Ariel's sensitivities. Lee Remick's Miranda was the best I've seen. Burton's resonant voice did wonders for Caliban's poetic passages, particularly in the close-up in III.iii (his description of the island's music). Despite our awareness of the performers as celebrities, they're so obviously having a good time that we become involved. There's nothing pompous or self-important about this production.

Hamlet (Austrian Television, 1960. English dubbed.)

Claudius: Hans Caninenberg. Gertrude: Wanda Rotha. Hamlet: Maximilian Schell. Ophelia: Dunja Movar.
Producer: Hans Gottschalk. Director: Franz Peter Wirth.

Lillian Wilds, "Maximilian Schell's Most Royal Hamlet," Literature/Film Quarterly, 4:2 (1976). Wilds finds much to praise in this production. Hamlet's "disturbed state, its cause, and his relationship to his mother, his uncle, Ophelia, and the court are all established economically . . . in our first introduction to him . . . by the use of the close-up, intercutting point-of-view shots, and the voiceover." Students of the production qua film will wish to read this detailed and perceptive study.

Hamlet at Elsinore (BBC/Danmarks Radio, 1964. Taped at Elsinore Castle, Denmark.)

Claudius: Robert Shaw. Gertrude: June Tobin. Hamlet: Christopher Plummer. Horatio: Michael Caine. Ophelia: Jo Muller. Polonius: Alec Clunes.
Producer: Peter Luke. Director: Philip Saville.
Designer: Paul Arnt Thomsen.

"Gentle Spirit of Hamlet in Its Native Setting," London Times (20 Apr. 1964). Plummer's Hamlet "is a romantic. . . . Having killed Polonius, he is momentarily appalled by the deed. He has wit and elegance; his pretended madness is a clever game. . . . He is the Hamlet of Goethe and Coleridge, the gentle spirit broken by a burden too heavy for him to bear."

An Age of Kings (BBC, 1960)

A fifteen-part series comprising Shakespeare's two tetralogies—English histories from *Richard II* through *Richard III*.

Chorus: William Squire. *Falstaff*: Frank Pettingell. *Henry IV*: Tom Fleming. *Henry V (Hal)*: Robert Hardy. *Henry VI*: Terry Scully. *Hotspur*: Sean Connery. *Joan la Pucelle*: Eileen Atkins. *Katherine*: Judi Dench. *Margaret*: Mary Morris. *Mistress Quickly*: Angela Baddeley. *Richard II*: David William. *Richard III*: Paul Daneman.

Producer: Peter Dews. *Director*: Michael Hays. *Designer*: Stanley Morris.

The Spread of the Eagle (BBC, 1963)

A nine-part series comprising three of Shakespeare's Roman plays—*Coriolanus, Julius Caesar,* and *Antony and Cleopatra*, in that order.

Antony: Keith Michell. *Caesar*: Barry Jones. *Cassius*: Peter Cushing. *Cleopatra*: Mary Morris. *Coriolanus*: Robert Hardy. *Menenius*: Roland Culver. *Volumnia*: Beatrix Lehmann.

Producer/Director: Peter Dews. *Designer*: Clifford Hatts.

London *Times* (4 May 1963). Review of *Coriolanus* suggests that "the problem [with this series], compared with the earlier 'An Age of Kings,' will be continuity" in linking the plays together.

The Wars of the Roses (BBC, 1964)

A three-part series of Shakespeare's first history tetralogy, adapted from the Royal Shakespeare Company productions.

Cade/Edward IV: Roy Dotrice. *Gloucester/Richard III*: Ian Holm. *Henry VI*: David Warner. *Joan la Pucelle/Lady Anne*: Janet Suzman. *Margaret*: Peggy Ashcroft. *Richmond*: Eric Porter. *Talbot*: Clive Morton. *Winchester*: Nicholas Selby. *York*: Donald Sinden.

Producer: Michael Barry. *Directors*: Peter Hall, John Barton (RSC); Robin Midgley, Michael Hayes (BBC). *Designer*: John Bury.

Alice V. Griffin, "Shakespeare Through the Camera's Eye: IV," *Shakespeare Quarterly*, 17 (Autumn 1966).

A second seeing of the British Broadcasting Company's television films of the Royal Shakespeare Company's *Henry IV, Edward IV,* and *Richard III* convinced the writer (who had seen both the stage productions and the television films previously in England) that these are the best television productions of Shakespeare's plays.

Although the execution was highly complex, the idea was simplicity itself. At the end of 1964, at

the conclusion of the Stratford season, three of the plays were re-staged and filmed for television in the Stratford theater itself, which was transformed into a huge television studio. Seats on the orchestra floor were boarded over and the stage extended by forty feet to accommodate crowd and battle scenes with the original cast of nearly seventy performers. Peter Hall, who directed the plays, and John Barton, who did the adaptation of the three parts of *Henry VI*, worked closely with the television producers "to make sure that the television production preserved everything of the stage version, was not distorted but was indeed expanded," explained producer Michael Barry.

Although all of the parts were well played, it was a boon for the viewer to see in close-up the faces of the principals, with all of the subtleties revealed which these actors brought to their parts: Peggy Ashcroft as Margaret, David Warner as Henry VI, and Ian Holm as Richard III. Dame Peggy is undisputedly the finest Shakespearian actress on the English-speaking stage, and it is an unforgettable experience to witness at such close range her portrayal of Margaret from the coquettish French princess in the first play to the vengeful crone of the third.

Another way in which the directors used their twelve cameras to achieve clarity was in focusing and directing the eye of the audience, much as a spotlight would on stage, as when picking out the faces around the council table in *Richard III*, III.iv, especially that of the ill-fated Hastings. Asides and soliloquies were spoken directly into the camera, as Richard's "So wise, so young, they say do never live long," in III.i, or his soliloquy which begins the play, in which the camera moved slowly back to reveal Richard's deformity.

When depicting a group, the camera wisely concentrated on a few, usually two, the speaker and the reactor. This was done with variety, with over-the-shoulder shots, or two actors in the foreground with others in the back (as Richard and Buckingham plotting at the end of III.i, while seeming to be engaged in exchanging pleasantries). Often, rather than cutting from speaker to speaker, the camera moved as the eye would move, across the group, coming to rest on the new speaker. Sometimes, with telling effect, the camera stayed on the listener rather than the speaker, as when Henry VI hears the members of this council accusing Humphrey, Duke of Gloucester.

When there was a large crowd to depict, as in the Jack Cade episode or the battles, the camera, after giving the impression of a crowd, concentrated on small groups, panning, for instance, the reactions on the faces of Cade's followers when they are promised leniency by the King. The battle scenes were effective, though by the time Richard got to Bosworth Field, there seemed to be a sameness about the battles. Generally, the camera concentrated, as Shakespeare did, on a few skirmishes between individual soldiers, to achieve a representational effect of battle. Smoke and the various appurtenances of war added a sense of realism, although one wonders why all the battles were fought, or seemed to have been fought, at night.

Hamlet (NBC, 17 November 1970)

Claudius: Richard Johnson. *Gertrude*: Margaret Leighton. *Ghost*: John Gielgud. *Hamlet*: Richard Chamberlain. *Ophelia*: Ciaran Madden. *Polonius*: Michael Redgrave.

Producer: George LeMaire. *Director*: Peter Wood. Adapted for television by John Barton.

Richard Chamberlain, "Why Does An Actor Agree to Do *Hamlet*," *NY Times* (15 Nov. 1970). "Often I found that my own experience as an actor contradicted the value judgments offered by critics. . . . Hamlet . . . is not king material. He lacks the blinkered qualities of mind that make the best of bureaucrats. He understands too much. . . ."

Jack Gould, *NY Times* (16 Nov. 1970). Chamberlain "held his own remarkably well [with a] straightforward Hamlet . . . in the heroic and romanticized tradition. [Otherwise, the experienced British actors] virtually acted him right off the stage." A "star was born in the beautiful Ciaran Madden as the rejected Ophelia."

The Merchant of Venice (BBC, 1972)

Antonio: Charles Gray. *Bassanio*: Christopher Gable. *Portia*: Maggie Smith. *Shylock*: Frank Finlay.

Producer: Gerald Savory. *Director*: Cedric Messina. *Designer*: Tony Abbott.

Stanley Reynolds, London *Times* (17 Apr. 1972). The production "lay as easy on the eye as a set of exquisite transparencies."

Much Ado About Nothing (CBS, 2 February 1973)

Beatrice: Kathleen Widdoes. *Benedick*: Sam Waterston. *Don Pedro*: Douglass Watson.

Producer: Joseph Papp. *Director*: A. J. Antoon.

Gerald Clarke, *Time* (12 Feb. 1973). "Happy incongruity . . . proved ideal for the small screen . . . telling close-ups, like Fabergé-crafted peekaboo Easter eggs . . . created an almost 3-dimensional illusion of depth. . . . Papp scores a clear triumph."

Day Thorpe, "Too Much Ado," Washington *Evening Star and Daily News* (8 Feb. 1973). The commercials of IBM's . . . three hour show featuring *Much Ado About Nothing* were the most entertaining aspects of the evening's entertainment. . . . When it comes to theater . . . IBM should spend its money far more wisely, for Joseph Papp's travesty of Shakespeare has no wit, no pace, no point. . . .

Beatrice and Benedick can never stop talking, and the ceaseless torrent of invective with which they amuse each other is the rushing water on which the whole play floats. In the television production this wonderful stream of witticisms, puns, double meanings and cherished insults turns into a stagnant pond of tedious, pointless and embarrassing bad-mouthing . . . pointless, dim-witted misunderstandings of the original. . . . The revisers are so unaware of their material that in adapting the witticisms of the two loquacious lovers they frequently set up a joke and expunge the punch-line or leave a punch-line of a deleted joke.

In a way it really doesn't matter very much. The direction drags to the point of complete somnolence, the script writers finally become so drowsy that they forget their own modernizations. . . .

To say that the acting is amateurish is to insult many non-professionals. The actors stumble through their lines, forgetting the order of the words, the meaning of which they seem never to have been told. Moreover, everybody is continually guffawing or chuckling in imitation of cued-in laughter in soap operas. . . .

One does not have to enjoy shows like "Ironside" and "Mannix" to be aware that there is a great deal of professional competence in the treatment of their clichés, which have become the accepted basis of TV dramatic entertainment. . . . If there is a re-run of *Much Ado* it should be scheduled for 4 o'clock in the morning, so that it will not pre-empt legitimate TV.

"Sedulus on TV: Two for the Price of One," *New Republic* (10 Feb. 1973). Papp is one of the great anybody-can-appreciate-it practitioners, but ironically his practice shows he doesn't believe anybody can appreciate it. He acknowledges a wide cultural gap between Shakespeare and us by making great stage efforts to bridge it [but] his method of bridging seems to me the least promising . . . rather than revising the original he puts a second play on top of it. In the present TV production . . . Papp provides setting and clothing out of the Gay '90s—this being a temporal removal the audience *has* been educated up to—and imports music and conventions from early film melodrama; but he leaves Shakespeare's script intact. . . . The result is two plays, with the Shakespearean play rendered hysterical by its competitor.

Shakespeare's medium was words. Here the words compete with bright busy images and a sophisticated musical score. The Shakespeare part of the play would have been more "visible," I submit, on radio. Only when the screen medium achieves a rare quiet moment do the words manage to dominate the pictures. Such domination occurred chiefly in Act III, the play's high moment, when

Benedick soliloquizes comically in a canoe, and listens in on comments about himself and Beatrice. Here the words matter; they are audible and well-paced, and are effectively reinforced but not supplanted by the clever canoe business. . . .

The hysteria I refer to comes from having both the plays—or perhaps I should say both the media—going at full speed at once. Instead of a light comedy and the appropriate emotional levels for light comedy, we are treated to a big, loud, indiscriminate bundle of farce, tragedy, melodrama and fairy tale.

Edward T. Jones, "Another Noting of the Papp/Antoon *Much Ado About Nothing,*" *Shakespeare on Film Newsletter,* 3:1 (Dec. 1978).

A. J. Antoon's 1910 setting permits a recognition of ordinary behavior beneath the theatricality and acting that forever rise to the surface in this play. The world of carousels, bandstands, Victorian Gothic houses and gazebos, rustic bridges and player pianos, barber shops and village squares, has at once nostalgic distance and familiarity. This ambience further offers the necessary nooks, crannies, and conservatories where characters may be concealed in order to overhear—perhaps the principal action of *Much Ado.*

A brilliant and plausible example of this requirement finds Benedick hiding behind the upturned canoe that Don Pedro knowingly addresses. Benedick is literally a fisherman, a fact that makes concrete Claudio's aside—"Bait the hook well; this fish will bite," as the good conspirators plot the love match between Beatrice and Benedick. When Beatrice speaks "in the sick tune," during Hero's preparation for her nuptials, the immediate cause is the cold she has contracted while hiding in the conservatory overhearing Margaret and Hero discuss Benedick's supposed love for her. At that time the conspirators by turning on the conservatory's sprinkler system had drenched the concealed Beatrice.

What emerges is a romantic *Much Ado,* impressive for its *eros* of wit, good nature, and richness of texture, all of which seem implicit in the text but in performance too often yield to brittle sarcasm.

The Merchant of Venice (BBC, 1973 [ABC, 16 March 1974])

Antonio: Anthony Nicholls. *Bassanio:* Jeremy Brett. *Portia:* Joan Plowright. *Shylock:* Laurence Olivier.

Director: Jonathan Miller. *Designer:* Julia Trevelyan Oman.

A National Theatre stage production of 1970.

John J. O'Connor, *NY Times* (15 Mar. 1974). "The [Rothschild] conception is consistently fascinating and beautifully mounted, but finally . . . fails. . . . Shylock is Shakespeare's villain . . . Olivier is superb."

John J. O'Connor, "If Shylock Were Not Jewish," *NY Times* (17 Mar. 1974). The anti-Semitic debate. "The [effort to make Shylock sympathetic] was persuasive up to a point. [His] revenge was securely tied to the loss of his daughter, Jessica. . . . But, in the end, it did not work, for, of course, this is not [as Olivier claims] 'a harsh portrayal of prejudice.' " The debate continues in subsequent issues of the *NY Times* (18 March, 3 April, and 28 April, 1974).

Robert Waterhouse, "*The Merchant of Venice,*" London *Times* (28 July 1970). (Stage.) Shylock "is not a role which stretches [Olivier], or one for which he will be particularly remembered."

Irving Wardle, "Merchants All, Old Vic, *The Merchant of Venice,*" London *Times* (29 Apr. 1970).

Modern dress Shakespeare has been tried and found useless as our own society is too close to serve as a lens to bring the past into focus. But periods other than our own, midway between ourselves and Shakespeare and possessing strongly defined characteristics, are one of the strongest interpretive mediums at the director's disposal as Jonathan Miller reconfirms in this late nineteenth century production of what might better be called *The Merchants of Venice.*

It is, notoriously, a divided piece: part insipid fairy tale, part a pioneering masterpiece in Christian-Semitic relationships. Tenuously holding the two parts together is the theme of money; and in Dr. Miller's version this thread has thickened into a steel cable.

From our first view of Julia Trevelyan Oman's set, a bare businesslike square with a couple of curtain upstage houses that open like jewel caskets, this is clearly not a romantic Venice but a Tuscan centre of private bankers and merchant venturers. And our first view of Anthony Nicholls's Antonio is of a sombre top-hatted figure, arriving preoccupied as if from a company meeting, hardly attending to the surrounding chatter until he is left alone with Bassanio over a cafe table, to whom he then addresses a curt, "Well?" Jeremy Brett's Bassanio, squirming and ill-at-ease in leading up to his plea for yet another loan, grows lyrical when he gets to the point. "In Belmont is a lady *richly* left," at which an off-stage violin strikes up.

The setting, in other words, works in two ways. It emphasizes the obvious financial element of the play: and it also unmasks the romantic element as so much flimsy sentimental decoration. The whole apparatus of treacly late-Victorian sensibility is wheeled into position to reduce the love affairs to so much beribboned marzipan. Pastiche Mendelssohn, Portia's boudoir bursting with tastelessly ornate furnishings and status-affirming dresses, all bespeak a greedy philistine society whose real life goes on in counting houses and legal chambers like the sober leather-seated room where Shylock comes to judgment.

This, of course, is not exactly the play that Shakespeare wrote. One should be more charmed by Portia than one is by Joan Plowright's auburn frizzed homebuilder, not to mention Mr. Brett's caddish adventurer (who takes a distinctly arrogant line with his social inferiors). If the production is perverse, it shows this most in the nocturne for Jessica and Lorenzo: this Shakespearean hymn to the power of music is played indoors by a couple of householders—a stolid pipe-smoking Lorenzo who spreads a handkerchief before exposing his natty suit to the floor, and a Jessica (Jane Lapotaire) who drops off to sleep during his speech. It fits the production, but it creaks.

However, to come to the main business of the evening, it forms a necessary framework for Laurence Olivier's Shylock which marks a total departure from stage tradition. Olivier jettisons altogether the rabbinically bearded tribal figure (on his lips the very word "tribe" approaches a sneer). He is not a Jew of the Renaissance ghetto, but one who has come into his own in a mercantile age and can almost pass for a Christian merchant; in his morning suit, gold spectacles, and top hat he is indistinguishable from Antonio.

Within, however, he has been incurably maimed by the process of assimilation. His delivery is a ghastly compound of speech tricks picked up from the Christian rich: posh vowels and the slipshod terminations of the hunting counties. "I am debatin' of my present state," he spits out, fingering a silver-topped cane: and then spoils the gesture by dissolving into paroxysms of silent, slack-jawed laughter. Olivier's face has exchanged its familiar contours for a fleshy apoplectic countenance whose very lips have somehow grown thick and flabby. The voice is thin and nasal, except when it hits those ringing top notes: and altogether the performance disdains the easy process of making Shylock "sympathetic;" instead it shows the kind of monster into which Christian societies transform their shame.

Peter Ansorge, *Plays and Players*, 17:9 (June 1970). (Stage.)

Olivier "adds very little to the inner life of Shylock. We first see him as a relaxed businessman who occasionally grimaces when uttering a mistimed vowel, a quiet cackle, a swallowed insult. [Then] his animal nature usurps his reason and we watch another version of Othello falling back into the dark, tribal blood rites. The Venetian setting dwindles into a cardboard background for an 'heroic' performance. Olivier's Shylock isn't a Jew, but an actor with a Jewish director up his sleeve. . . . Joan Plowright's Portia was an original creation: a new rich, snobby spinster who, apart from a determination to buy a husband (preferably with a lower income than herself), was utterly indifferent to the events taking place around her. . . . [But] her appearance at the trial scene . . . undercut much of

the originality that had fired [her] performance in the earlier scenes." Miller's version "doesn't easily absorb the violent, quick-changing rhythms of the Elizabethan drama—which were designed to portray human experience in an open context, as opposed to the closed, private world of the nineteenth-century novel. . . . The Prince of Arragon crawled towards the silver casket as senility personified (wrecking the sense that we were watching a Jamesian choice of spouse and income on the part of Portia)."

King Lear (PBS, February 1974)

Cordelia: Lee Chamberlin. *Edgar*: Rene Auberjonois. *Edmund*: Raul Julia. *Fool*: Tom Aldredge. *Gloucester*: Paul Sorvino. *Goneril*: Rosalind Cash. *Kent*: Douglass Watson. *Lear*: James Earl Jones. *Regan*: Ellen Holly.

Producer: Joseph Papp. *Director*: Edwin Sherin.

A New York Shakespeare Festival production of 1973.

Jack Jorgens, "The New York Shakespeare Festival: 1973," *Shakespeare Quarterly*, 24 (Fall 1973). "Jones restrained his power altogether too much [but] was interesting and at times moving." A detailed and incisive analysis of the stage version.

Alan M. Kriegsman, *Washington Post* (20 Feb. 1974). "Jones' Lear sets standards that his fellow actors . . . can only sporadically approach. Jones' performance tends to set to rest all the old bugaboos about 'Lear' not being actable. The rest of the production digs them."

H. R. Coursen, "A Review: The Papp-Sherin *King Lear*," Pulse (Apr. 1974).

Papp's *Lear*, unlike his *Much Ado*, was ungimmicky, coherent, often powerful, projecting some of Shakespeare's most difficult language articulately to our ears. The performance was enhanced by the presence of a live audience in Central Park, an effect employed originally by Olivier in his superb film version of *Henry V*. The TV camera made no effort to hide the audience, which became part of the texture of the production, along with the huge apron of a stage and the versatile columns behind it. Camera work allowed both for effective close-ups and for an appreciation of Director Sherin's excellent blocking. Elements which might clash were blended into a cohesion I have never before seen on the tube.

James Earl Jones underplayed Lear's often violent rhetoric, creating the effect of an internal monologue lapsing towards internal chaos. His eyes rolled ceaselessly from face to face, seeking the answer he had to find within himself. Jones was particularly brilliant in his efforts to keep Lear from weeping, and in his dialogue with blinded Gloucester, where Jones was at once pathetic and amusing. He was weakest in his understated ending. He had created a launching pad for the release of the pent-up power of his physique and voice, but he didn't use it. His "howl" and "never" were needlessly muted. I had the strange feeling that I would have found his performance disappointing had I witnessed it in Central Park. For the most part, however, it was just right for the narrower dimensions of television.

From "Shakespeare and the People: Elizabethan Drama on Video," *Shakespeare on Film Newsletter*, 1:2 (Apr. 1977).

James Earl Jones starring in the title role, like Morris Carnovsky but differently, teaches us about the range of Shakespeare's most dynamic character. Carnovsky projected a once powerful king now old and fragile; Jones reveals a king newly conscious of senescence.

Weary but strong, with the slow movements of old age, Jones still displays an astonishing array of emotions. His acting makes the production memorable.

Antony and Cleopatra (RSC/Audio-Visual Productions, 1974 [ABC, 1 January 1975])

Antony: Richard Johnson. *Cleopatra*: Janet Suzman. *Enobarbus*: Patrick Stewart. *Octavius*: Corin Redgrave.

Producer: Jon Scofield (AVP). *Directors*: Trevor Nunn, Buzz Goodbody, Euan Smith (RSC). *Designer*: Christopher Morley.

A Royal Shakespeare Company stage production of 1972.

Benedict Nightingale, "Decline and Growth," *New Statesman* (25 Aug. 1972). (Stage.) "The bias of Miss Suzman's performance is always towards intelligence and cunning. [Would] such a Cleopatra kill herself rather than continue matching wits with Octavius?"

Leonard Buckley, London *Times* (29 July 1974). "Television lifted the production off the stage into its own ethereal element . . . superb."

John J. O'Connor, *NY Times* (3 Jan. 1975). "The visual structure, relying more on suggestion than literal definition, provides an unusually effective vehicle for the [many] brief scenes flowing between Egypt and Rome. . . ." Johnson and Suzman "are splendid."

"Shakespeare Loses Out to Archie Bunker," *NY Times* (9 Jan. 1975). The ABC *Antony and Cleopatra* hit an all-time prime-time low rating, losing out to "All in the Family," "Emergency," "Mary Tyler Moore," and "The Log of the Black Pearl"— and overwhelmingly in each case.

John J. O'Connor, "Irate Viewers," *NY Times* (19 Jan. 1975). O'Connor says that "few programs have generated more letters of protest and outrage" to his desk. Primary outrage directed at the plethora of tasteless commercials.

Robert Speaight, "Shakespeare in Britain," *Shakespeare Quarterly*, 23 (Fall 1972).

Antony and Cleopatra—directed by Trevor Nunn, with the assistance of Buzz Goodbody and Euan Smith—was the best production of the play I have seen. The work—in some ways the most wonderful of Shakespeare's tragedies and the summit of poetry—is a Matterhorn that Stratford has been reluctant to climb since 1953. The difficulty is always the same; where to find an actor and actress capable of sustaining the principal parts. The "serpent of old Nile" does not slither easily on the banks of the Thames or the Avon. Competence, or even genius, is not enough. Physical beauty will not compensate for the lack of that hardly definable essence which is the secret of Cleopatra. Intelligence will take an actress no further than the lower slopes of the mountain. But Janet Suzman succeeded where Peggy Ashcroft and Edith Evans had both failed, the latter somewhat ignominiously. To begin with, Miss Suzman has the breadth of style which the part, and this particular theater, demands. She enchants the eye and ear, and satisfies the mind. She is naturally royal without being affectedly regal. She can scold like a fishwife, and sulk like a naughty child. Devious and devoted, seductive and sincere, she has the quicksilver of Egypt in her veins as well as in her voice. She is noble to the heights of heroism, and ignoble to the depths of depravity. Above all and beyond all, she is lovable—so that "Husband, I come" transports one suddenly to a matrimonial couch, if not to a domestic hearth. To have realized this paradox so completely was a considerable achievement. I was taken back nearly fifty years to the night when I saw Lotte Medelsky in the part at the Burg-theater in Vienna. That is an abiding memory, although time has dimmed its detail. Miss Suzman's Cleopatra will stand beside it.

She was better partnered than Lotte Medelsky. Richard Johnson's Antony—the black beard now appropriately grizzled—had matured in exactly the right way, so that one asked oneself whether Shakespeare would not finally have shared the belief of his protagonist that kingdoms were not worth a kiss from Cleopatra's lips. There was a soft center in Mr. Johnson's Antony, but no trace of the actor's craving for unmerited sympathy. This Antony had a careless grandeur and irresistible largesse; you realized that he was beaten by Octavius because Octavius was a political animal and Antony was not—or was not any longer. There was no trace of the diplomacy which had carried him to victory in the Forum, and one liked him the better for it.

Here was simply the *homme moyen sensuel*, but raised through intensity of feeling and sublimity of speech a Matterhorn's height above mediocrity.

In support of these splendid performances Patrick Stewart's Enobarbus looked on in smiling admiration of what he reluctantly disapproved. The "barge" speech was perfectly delivered, more to himself than to the audience or his interlocutors—a memory, not an aria.

H. R. Coursen, "Trevor Nunn's TV *Antony and Cleopatra*," *Maine Times* (Apr. 1975).

Visually, this production was hardly as arresting as Zeffirelli's *Romeo and Juliet*, but it did not try to be. It was television, not film, and was scaled down to its 19 diagonal inches, not expanded towards the unavailable amplitude and depth of the wide screen. It allowed Antony and Cleopatra to grow, as they do in the play, through a series of ebbings and flowings, until Suzman convinces us that she is both the serpent of Old Nile and a woman, rising on her arias to reunion with her Antony. Johnson, only semiconvincing most of the way, reached his peak in the whipping of Thidias, superbly played by a young actor named Ben Kingsley.

As can happen with this script, minor roles almost captured the production. Patrick Stewart played Enobarbus, perhaps the greatest supporting role in Shakespeare, with a Scots accent which somehow worked. Stewart's description of Cleopatra on Cydnus, nicely counterpointed by ironic Agrippa, was magnificent. His was a powerful depiction of a good soldier ripped between reason and loyalty. Stewart's last speech, unfortunately, was delivered from a prone position and was virtually lost in his beard. Corin Redgrave's Octavius was so brilliant that, from the first, we knew it was no contest between him and Antony for sole possession of the earth. But then Johnson's Antony seldom projected a sense of even former greatness. Mary Rutherford was fine as the pathetic Octavia, particularly in the scene where Antony rebuffs her timid sexual advances, and on her forlorn return to Rome, which Redgrave played beautifully, scoring political points from his sister's rejection. Morgan Shepherd was excellent as scar-faced Scarus.

This is the first *Antony and Cleopatra* ever to be projected to an audience by electronic or filmic means. It is an auspicious first. While I regret the omission of the Menas-Pompey plot, and of the wonderful scene where Hercules deserts Antony, Nunn's production stands with Olivier's *Merchant of Venice* as the finest Shakespeare television has ever offered. The production deserves a mounting free of the seductions of Lysol, Noxzema, Right Guard, Prell, Wizard, Cascade, Geritol, and Grecian Formula. Janet Suzman's throaty Cleopatra needed a little more support from Johnson's Antony, but she needed none from Madison Avenue. I look forward to viewing this production free of twentieth century sponsorship.

Macbeth (BBC, 1975 [PBS, 27 September 1975]).

Banquo: John Thaw. *Duncan*: Michael Goodliffe. *Lady Macbeth*: Janet Suzman. *Macbeth*: Eric Porter. *Macduff*: John Woodvine. *Malcolm*: John Alderton.

Producer: Cedric Messina. *Director*: John Gorrie.

"Shakespeare and the People: Elizabethan Drama on Video," *Shakespeare on Film Newsletter*, 1:2 (Apr. 1977).

In outward beauty and inner degradation Eric Porter's Macbeth and Janet Suzman's Lady Macbeth suggest the fairness of the foul and the foulness of the fair. That equivocal condition, deeply embedded in the play's language, gets visual support from camera angles forcing the audience to look down, not up, at these two gorgeous but treacherous creatures.

Especially subtle is Janet Suzman's portrayal of Lady Macbeth's disastrous misreading of her husband's character. Despite these virtues, it is also a production that does not quite seem to have found its own vision of the play's "metaphysical core."

H. R. Coursen, "The Classic Theatre: *Macbeth* directed by John Gorrie," *Pulse* (Oct. 1976).

Channel Ten's "Classic Theatre" began auspiciously with the BBC's production of *Macbeth*. Eric Porter and Janet Suzman played the thane and lady who kill a king, gain a crown, and reap torment, nightmare, insanity and damnation for their effort.

This *Macbeth*, produced for television, understands its medium, as cluttered productions like Joseph Papp's *Much Ado About Nothing* of a few seasons ago did not. Backgrounds—gray walls and trails of fog—are suggestive rather than explicit, allowing faces and voices to focus our attention. The faces and voices are worth attending.

Suzman, fresh from her fine Cleopatra on ABC last year, brings a sexual vitality to Lady Macbeth which the script demands but which the role seldom receives. The weapons of Eve she employs against her husband's reluctance are powerfully conveyed. Lady Macbeth's gradual descent from souped-up strength to enervated madness, from a clenched control to a relapse of recognition is superbly articulated.

Porter's Macbeth grows as his character descends to evil. One does not feel vividly enough Macbeth's early struggle between his corrupt will and his virtuous understanding. Perhaps the conviction and sensuality of Suzman's Lady simply overpower Macbeth's subtle debate with himself, but Porter's early Macbeth lacks the tug-of-war ambivalence for which the role calls. As he descends to explore the wrong side of nature which becomes his kingdom, however, this Macbeth reaches the full dimensions of tragedy. Porter gives a sudden vitality to the too-well-known "Tomorrow . . ." speech. Macbeth's nihilism shouts out at the sky, as the camera rises above him to receive his words.

An index within the play of Macbeth's evil power is the fear the Weird Sisters display when this mortal threatens to curse them. They are already cursed eternally, yet perceive in Macbeth an evil even greater than their own. The student has outgrown his tutors.

One of the great virtues of this production is its simplicity. It is nicely measured to its medium, and its limited cast and unspectacular special effects allow the language—the poetry—to be the message. The Weird Sisters are old women with filmy beards, like those one sees in London or in Lewiston on side streets, carrying shopping bags which one would hesitate to explore. The Witches' preparation of the caldron is simple, explicit, and horrifying, as each element plops into the stew. Macbeth is the final ingredient, his head dropping into the foul puddle after Macduff has slain him.

Surprisingly, one of this production's strongest scenes is the one in England, usually heavily cut. This production does cut the line about Edward the Confessor, an understandable deletion but unfortunate, in that those lines establish Edward as Macbeth's spiritual antithesis, healer rather than killer. But Malcolm's detractions of himself are retained with unusual power. The young and future king goes through a psychic struggle, naming all the evil things he is not, but facing in the process the ultimate challenge kingship represents. Malcolm's struggle with himself explains, one infers, his strangely muted final speech. Not much triumph there—instead, a calm assumption of the role he has anticipated. His character comes through with a clarity of conception seldom, if ever, realized in this script.

This Macbeth deserves another showing, perhaps at an earlier hour, when younger students who will find the production exciting will be able to watch without violating their bedtimes.

The Taming of the Shrew (PBS, 1977)

Kate: Fredi Olster. Petruchio: Marc Singer.
  Directors: William Ball, Kirk Browning.
  An American Conservatory Theatre stage production.
  Edward T. Jones, Shakespeare on Film Newsletter, 2:1 (1977). "Kate appears as a forceful, intelligent, single woman." Looks at the play in light of feminist criticism, particularly that of Coppélia Kahn. "Male stereotyping of women leaves Kate a pariah until Petruchio marries her. . . . So the audience will catch the ironic overtones of Kate's last stand, Olster provides a definitive wink right to the camera."

Macbeth (ITV, 1979 [PBS, February 1980])

Banquo: John Woodvine. Duncan: Griffith Jones.
Lady Macbeth: Judi Dench. Macbeth: Ian McKellen. Macduff: Bob Peck. Malcolm: Roger Rees.

Producer: Philip Casson. Director: Trevor Nunn (RSC). Designer: John Napier.
  A Royal Shakespeare Company stage production of 1976.
  Peter Fiddick, Guardian (5 Jan. 1979). McKellen and Dench "come to the screen with all the weight of [stage] experience behind them . . . it showed from the first word to the last."
  Sean Day Lewis, Daily Telegraph (5 Jan. 1979). "The lines and faces are enough. . . . [Lady Macbeth's] sleep-walking scene was the most agonizing I can remember."
  Benedict Nightingale, "TV or Not TV," NY Times (24 Feb. 1980). "Nunn's production demonstrated how much could be achieved with how very little in the way of visual effects [and] how Shakespeare could work well if the actors themselves were the set."

Marvin Rosenberg, "Trevor Nunn's Macbeth," Shakespeare Quarterly, 28 (1977). (Stage.)
  The staging was as stark and simple as the bare walls. Just £250 was allotted to the show, Ian McKellen (Macbeth) told us. The single gorgeous ornament was a royal robe for the three kings, beginning with a saintly Duncan; the garment and the Duncan characterization were holdovers from an elaborate Macbeth Nunn had staged the year before, and both could easily have been dispensed with.
  The other costumes were of the simplest: the men mainly wore dark, functional uniforms, vaguely suggestive of the American Civil War. Lady Macbeth was dressed throughout in unornamented black. Lady Macduff wore white. The furniture consisted of boxes, including a few placed before the first rows of spectators, and there the actors sometimes sat before entering the round, lighted acting area.
  In that cribb'd, cabin'd, confin'd space, the tragedy, already so compressed, seemed to strain against the walls. Only at the extra-textual beginning, when Duncan, excessively benevolent, doddering, half-blind, was ritualistically guided to and from a prayer altar, was the rush that Shakespeare designed hobbled. Once the Sisters—two hags and an unkempt blonde girl in a half-trance—weirded their way to the rendezvous with Macbeth, the white circle on the stage floor became a pit of continuous tension.
  McKellen, as Macbeth, drove the play on with an energy that grew manic as he was frustrated by forces inward and outward. The actor said he saw Macbeth as a "superstar," an overreacher formed to grasp beyond what most men dared not try to reach. A capacious sense of humor went with the design: to this Macbeth, the world was an ironic place, and his laughter became more shrill as he saw the cosmic joke turned on him; or it was edged with pain when the cut was deep, as at Lady Macbeth's death.

Judi Dench's marvelous Lady Macbeth accentuated the drive of the play by the intense emotion she brought to every moment she was onstage. When she first rushed in, she hardly needed to consult Macbeth's letter in her hand: she had already greedily memorized it, and was excitedly saying the crucial phrases over. There grew on her, this gracious woman, deeply in love with her husband, a vision of the future that at once exalted and frightened her. She summoned the strength to invoke the murd'ring ministers; but halfway through she was so scared she stopped and ran back from where she had knelt; only slowly could she bring herself to return and finish. The dread underlay her persuasions of Macbeth to the murder; and thereafter she was whipsawed between resolution and terror, until the sleepwalk. There she seemed unmistakably a wretched queen whose sleep had given her no rest for so long that she might indeed be better with the dead.

To Dench, Lady Macbeth was not inherently wicked: loving her husband, wanting him to realize a dream, she thought, fearfully, "Perhaps to kill—once. This *once*." It was then she realized that the "once" was endless, and only a beginning—that the husband she had to incite to murder, and then support and mother in his fear and remorse, was suddenly let loose to a violence she could not have imagined, and could not bear.

I felt the intensity of Dench's emotional involvement the more as we sat in her dressing room while she finished making up for Beatrice in *Much Ado*—a characterization dazzling with lights and darks of comedic feeling—and heard her intuitions about Lady Macbeth. To see one role played after the other was a special experience of the versatility of the distinguished repertory actor's art, and of Shakespeare's provision for it.

John Woodvine, an exquisitely solemn Dogberry, was also a remarkable Banquo: Macbeth's equal in force, but brilliantly contrasting in design—lean, shrewd, hardheaded, observant of all around him. He protected the ambiguity in the role: to his untimely end, he was not committed either to an unqualified moral repugnance to Macbeth's act, or to an exclusively self-serving policy of accommodation. "Did Banquo have any plan, after Duncan's murder, for dealing with Macbeth?" we asked him. Woodvine smiled: "Who knows what he would have done—if he had lived."

The acting was uniformly excellent. I was troubled, though, that when Ian McDiarmid turned from his Ross—a brilliantly conceived politician-courtier—to double as the Porter, he did a music hall turn. It evoked the wrong kind of laughter, and momentarily dispelled the reality of the *Macbeth* experience. Shakespeare's cunning drunk is a proper doorkeeper for Inverness—not a stand-up comic, but a true Fool. His joking is not to be easy on us; it has bite.

In the small barn only considerable theatrical ingenuity could have managed the marches and countermarches of Act V. Here the play was edited: an increasingly hysterical Macbeth was left spotlighted in stage center while the thanes, standing in the encircling dark, spoke the lines about his anguish and the Birnam Wood strategy. Their choral accompaniment to his growing despair paced him to the climax, a fierce swordfight with Macduff that seemed genuinely dangerous not only to the combatants but also to the spectators only inches away. After the intensity of this battle, the final mood of the tragedy was exhaustion and disillusion. The "Hails" to Malcolm were lifeless; the new king's final exhortation did nothing to lift the spirits of the thanes, sitting dejected on their boxes, and it trailed off to a drear blackout.

On the other hand, on both nights I attended, the final mood of the audience—held in a spell during the two hours' traffic (without intermission)—was exhilaration. The production demonstrated once again that Shakespeare's drama does not need elaborate setting, lavish costuming, complicated lighting plans. In that austere room, the play, left to itself, worked: the play was the thing.

Herbert Kretzmet, "The Mail TV Critic," London *Daily Mail* (5 Jan. 1979).

Macbeth might have been written for television. The world it describes is confined and suffocating. Most of its action takes place at night, and seldom outdoors. Its true landscape is the human mind obsessed by violent death. It is a play of close-up and shadow.

Philip Casson's miraculous production, swallowing two hours of ITV prime time last night, recognises and cannily exploits the claustrophobic nature of a play composed exclusively of nightmare and darkness.

There are no sets to speak of, few props, no blasted heaths or battlefields. Sudden squares of light indicate doors opening elsewhere, unseen. Soliloquies and suspicions are confided directly into cameras which keep moving into unblinking, alarming mouth-to-eyebrow enlargements of the human face.

Casson's TV version, based on Trevor Nunn's parent production at Stratford, pulls the viewer into the soul of the play, just as Lady Macbeth (Judi Dench), when she welcomes Duncan, seems literally to pull the doomed king into an unlit world he will never leave alive.

Television is honoured by this *Macbeth*.

Julius Caesar (BBC, 1979 [PBS, 14 February 1979])

Antony: Keith Michell. *Brutus*: Richard Pasco. *Caesar*: Charles Gray. *Calpurnia*: Elizabeth Spriggs. *Cassius*: David Collings. *Portia*: Virginia McKenna.

Producer: Cedric Messina. *Director:* Herbert Wise. *Designer:* Tony Abbott.

Tom Shales, *Washington Post* (14 Feb. 1979). "Glorious . . . a magnificent start . . . [shows] how powerful television can be . . . spellbinding immediacy and urgency. . . . Only television could make this great tragedy as accessible as it is eloquent."

Arthur Unger, *Christian Science Monitor* (12 Feb. 1979). "A scholarly, peculiarly bloodless rendition of a passionate play . . . lacks bravura sweep . . . lots of tight close-ups, featuring superb enunciation without declamation."

Gerald Clarke, "Longest Run," *Time* (12 Feb. 1979). Praises Gray's Caesar. The murder is "shockingly intense." Michell "too old and fleshy to be a vigorous and virile Antony."

Cecil Smith, *Los Angeles Times* (14 Feb. 1979). "Never have I seen [the assassination scene] more movingly played. . . . Pasco endows [Brutus] with enormous complexity. . . . The play comes through splendidly."

G. M. Pearce, *Cahiers Elisabéthains*, 16 (1979), 83–84. "It seemed a pity in the battle scenes . . . that television could not have shown its superiority over the stage . . . and used an outdoor location."

Janet Maslin, "TV: *Caesar* Tailored to Small Screen," *NY Times* (14 Feb. 1979).

It takes special tricks to hold a television audience's attention, even in the most edifying circumstances. So there are very few long shots in *Julius Caesar* for television, even though a theatrical film version of the play could well employ long shots for comprehensiveness. Instead, the camera does a great deal of tracking, moving after the actors with very few cuts, to give the program a momentum that compensates for its small scope.

Instead of pausing for reaction shots or close-ups of individual players, the camera swoops in upon them, or remains fixed on an actor who's listening while the actor who's speaking strides in and out of the frame. This may look sloppy at times, especially when someone in the foreground stands with his back to the camera for any length of time. But it's also exhilarating, introducing an element of visual suspense and holding the viewer at close dangerous range. . . .

The performances are geared to television, too. The actors work in a slightly exaggerated manner, establishing character independent of the particulars of the play. Soliloquies are delivered as voice-overs, which tones them down somewhat but also makes them plausible, considering the proximity of the camera. The performances are so dependent upon facial details that it's hard to imagine how they might work on stage. But for television, the resemblance and physical affinity between Keith Michell as Mark Antony and Charles Gray as Caesar becomes both immediate and useful. And Richard Pasco, as Brutus, has a heavy-lidded look

and grave demeanor that makes his performance a success even before he speaks.

Not all of the actors are as well suited to the television. Mr. Michell's stolid Antony is this production's principal disappointment, if only because he fails to be sufficiently spell-binding during the "Friends, Romans, countrymen . . ." speech, which is further marred by the Cockney accents of the "Roman" rabble. And Virginia McKenna as Portia is so tremulous and hysterical to begin with that the camera can only magnify her excesses. But David Collings as Cassius is ideally shifty-eyed and spiky. And Mr. Gray so expertly typifies the politician as performer that his scenes, as Caesar, are the most affecting portion of this production.

Though much of the play is delivered conversationally or in whispers, Mr. Gray's oratorical manner is so welcome that it casts . . . doubt about the idea of scaling-down Shakespeare for television at all.

Jack Jorgens, "The BBC-TV Shakespeare Series," *Shakespeare Quarterly*, 30 (Summer 1979).

When a chatty epilogue with an announcer and shots of the Thames proves more interesting than the play it follows, you know you are in trouble. The performances in *Julius Caesar* were silly, affected, awkward, wooden, or misguided. The production was a curious mixture of the grimly conservative and the eccentric.

Director Herbert Wise seems attuned to the ironies of the play, noting that Shakespeare is saying, "It's possible to do exactly the wrong thing for all the right reasons." But what is one to make of the strong homosexual cast to the work, in which a murderous male game is afoot, in which Caesar and Brutus are seduced away from their wives and destroyed, in which political players strut and simper and orate themselves to climaxes in which they plunge daggers into themselves or some other male?

Despite some ingenious and complicated shotmaking, this *Julius Caesar* is a mediocre piece of television, full of disorganized, banal, ugly images which are the antithesis of the lucid structures of Shakespeare's language and dramatic action. The camera fails to keep up with the action, moves pointlessly, or has an uncanny knack for being in the wrong place. Extensive use of "voice-over" makes it seem that Romans orate even in their thoughts.

Robert E. Knoll, "The Shakespeare Plays: The First Season," *Shakespeare on Film Newsletter*, 3:2 (Apr. 1979).

The BBC production of *Julius Caesar* is notable for a number of reasons. First, the quality of the acting is uniformly high. One is not likely to see a more subtle Cassius than David Collings, a slower-witted Brutus than Richard Pasco, or a more eloquent Antony than Keith Michell.

The production is interesting for additional reasons. We are not likely ever to see a better *television* version of this play. Constantly the cameras give us close-ups of the conspirators, and we look into their eyes with an intimacy not possible on the stage or in the cinema. Still, we rarely if ever hear one person talking without seeing the reactions of others.

We constantly peer over the shoulder to perceive social relationships. Sometimes the backs of listeners' heads appear in the foreground, blurred because they are so close to the camera's eye; and as a result of these shots we are drawn into intimacy with these characters. We get involved in their motives and responses. Aesthetic distance is minimized. The long continuous shots of the first-act conversation between Cassius and Brutus are especially notable in this respect. The play becomes very intense. The viewer is exhausted by all this insistent, fascinating, uninterrupted eavesdropping.

Sometimes the close-ups provide a curious effect. In the garden scene of Act II, the camera makes the conspirators, who are sitting and standing in rows, look like animated Roman busts. Grouped around a marble statue of one of Brutus' ancestors, they are made to resemble the marble.

It is important that Brutus and Cassius and the others all talk as though they were on soap boxes, even in their private dialogues. They *have* no private lives. Even Portia and Brutus, in their bed chamber, indulge in the same rhetorical apostrophes, the same stentorian modes of address, that Senators use in the Roman Forum. (The disproportion of language and situation may be a bit funny—but that is a matter never exploited in any production that I have ever seen.) In the fourth-act quarrel between Brutus and Cassius, the mode of speech remains Ciceronian rhetoric. This is part of their problem: the private man can find no ready agency for conveying human relationships.

Though the center of the play is not psychology but stagecraft, the television production takes us into psychology. One does not object to this reading of the play. Indeed one is pleased to see that the director understands what his medium can do—and what it cannot do. It can give subtle variations of individual personality. It can not as easily give the sweep of history. And when this play calls for the sweep of history, as in Act Five, the play falls off. The battles of Philippi are not clearly presented nor is Cassius' relationship to them as lucid as it needs to be. This television camera is not set for heroic shots. It concentrates on one person and then one person and then one person.

But by the time we get to Act V, we are so interested in Brutus and Cassius and the others that we hardly mind. It is true, Keith Michell's marvelous rendition of the third-act address in the Forum seems strangely truncated by the size of the Roman crowds—tens are made to represent thousands. As a result we concentrate on Michell's reading rather than on the total dramatic situation of which Antony's speech is the manipulating center. This production breaks this wonderful scene into its component elements. Nobody minds because Michell so cleverly suggests Antony's multiple purposes and develops them right before our eyes. But this is not the Roman spectacle that the text seems to call for and against which the quarrel scene (Act IV) develops. This is an *intimate* production of a *public* play.

As You Like It (BBC, 1978 [PBS, 28 February 1979])

Celia: Angharad Rees. *Duke Senior*: Tony Church. *Jaques*: Richard Pasco. *Orlando*: Brian Stirner. *Phebe*: Victoria Plucknett. *Rosalind*: Helen Mirren. *Touchstone*: James Bolam.
    Producer: Cedric Messina. *Director*: Basil Coleman. *Designer*: Don Taylor.

Don Shirley, *Washington Post* (28 Feb. 1979). "It's too bad the whole canon can't be moved to the great outdoors, if *As You Like It* is any indication . . . away from the cold studio that constricted *Julius Caesar*. . . . This colorful production is escapist entertainment at its most sublime."

John J. O'Connor, *NY Times* (28 Feb. 1979). "The play reads beautifully [but] it was a mistake [to place it] in the relentlessly realistic setting of Glamis Castle and its environs. . . . The sunny hills of Scotland . . . throw a curious shadow over the play's magical aspects."

Sally O. Davis, "Helen Mirren," *Chicago Tribune* (20 Feb. 1979). An interview with Helen Mirren, Rosalind in BBC-TV's *As You Like It*.

Jack Jorgens, "The BBC-TV Series," *Shakespeare Quarterly*, 30 (1979). "Seldom have natural settings been used to less effect. . . . The blocking and framing are often awkward, the compositions ungainly, and the cutting poorly timed."

Cecil Smith, *Los Angeles Times* (28 Feb. 1979). "A marvelous production. . . . The springtime colors of the Scottish countryside match the springtime lilt of the romantic play. . . . The clarity of Mirren, Rees, Pasco and the rest . . . is almost music.

Cecil Smith, "Richard Pasco," *Los Angeles Times* (28 Feb. 1979). Pasco discusses his career, and the roles of Brutus and Jaques for BBC-TV.

Maurice Charney, *Shakespeare Quarterly*, 31 (1980). "Visually appealing . . . evoked all the wish-fulfillment images of pastoral. . . . The smaller scope of [the comedies] is . . . suited to television."

Jacqueline Pearson, "Shadows on the Shadow-Box: The BBC Shakespeare," *Critical Quarterly*, 21 (1979).
    Of the first group of three plays in this extended series, the most successful was *As You Like It*. Several reasons for this suggest themselves. Perhaps the

fantasy-world of comedy transfers best to the fantasy-world of television. More important, three key actors, Helen Mirren (Rosalind), Tony Church (Duke Senior) and Richard Pasco (Jaques), learned ensemble acting in the best school, the Royal Shakespeare Company, and brought a coherence and an intelligence to the production that neither of the others attained. Perhaps the greatest achievements of this series are to be in comedy. *As You Like It*, with its stress on ensemble acting and on a delicate balance between comic and serious statements, raises some hopes for the future. For the remainder of the tragedies and histories, I remain cautiously pessimistic.

R. Alan Kimbrough, "The Shakespeare Plays: The First Season," *Shakespeare on Film Newsletter*, 3:2 (Apr. 1979).

As You Like It [?], the second in The Shakespeare Plays series, strikingly contrasts with the premiere production, *Julius Caesar*, and demonstrates the range of television's potential. The central feature of this production was the decision to tape on location (Glamis Castle in Scotland) rather than in a studio. Many of the production's visual delights and many of its visual disasters derive from that decision.

Those delights strike immediately: the elegant yet sufficiently forbidding fairy-tale castle, its gracious gardens, the splendidly pastoral forest, and the bucolic patches of meadowland. Costume designer Robin Fraser-Paye manages some notable successes in the contrasting blacks and whites for the romance villains and heroes in their court settings and the muted colors that work well against the background of the gray-green forest. Some may cavil about the enormous headdresses he gives Rosalind and Celia at court and about the gauzy outfit in which Hymen flutters over the hill, but those who like will be able to defend those choices as well. The location shooting also fosters the success of the two moments in the play when physical action becomes possible: the close-range wrestling match of I.ii and the dizzying eviction of Oliver down the spiral stone staircase and out the door of the castle at the beginning of Act III.

Some, however, may find that those visual treasures are purchased at too great a price. For the location shooting limits severely and forces some disquieting contradictions between what the characters say and what we see. Those manicured, symmetrical gardens at court belie the moral disorder those courts harbor. And the early summer lushness of the woods makes the characters' complaints against wintry discomfort in their "desert" of banishment seem disturbingly self-indulgent. No "icy fang . . . of the winter's wind" has assailed anyone in this Arden for some time. Moreover, although producer Cedric Messina is on record as rejoicing in this location's freedom from the noise of planes and motorways, the nearly ceaseless chirping chatter of birds as the only background noise blurs distinctions (court/forest, nobles/rustics) between scenes.

Several other incongruities between what we see on screen and what we hear from the text may disconcert. Duke Frederick says—with apparent reason—that Rosalind's graces steal public favor from Celia. Yet surely the vivacious and stunningly beautiful Celia of Angharad Rees needs feel no threat from the sullen Rosalind we see in the opening act. Only after she falls in love, and even more after she adopts her Ganymede identity, does Helen Mirren make Rosalind become captivatingly alive and dominant.

The shepherd Corin—again with apparent reason—tells Touchstone (James Bolam), "Those that are good manners at the court are as ridiculous in the country as the behaviour of the country is most mockable at the court" (III.ii; Scene 16). But Coleman's cameras tell us something very different, for Bolam never seems ridiculous in Arden, whereas the behaviour most open to mockery at court is scarcely that of a rude rustic but rather that of the foppish Le Beau (John Quentin), whose mincing manner suggests a stock Oswald or Osric out of a *Lear* or *Hamlet* company.

Touchstone—again with an apparently trustworthy eye—tells us repeatedly how ill-favored his Audrey is, and she admits as much. But Marilyn Le Conte is far more comely than homely, making Touchstone's predictions of being cuckolded in the future (emphasized in lines cut from this production) far more convincing than his deprecations of Audrey's attractiveness.

Voices, too, ring wrong in this production. It is something of a shock when "Monsieur Charles" first opens his mouth and a thick Scottish burr *pourrrs forrrth*. Much of the play's system of contrasts and complements depends upon the social heterogeneity of the couples in Arden. Yet—with the exceptions of Victoria Plucknett's Phebe, who has curiously managed to emigrate from Ireland to Arden, and Jeffrey Holland's doltish William—the voices we hear are remarkably similar in accent. Much sharper (and more effective) distinctions in accents characterized *Julius Caesar*.

Apart from the considerable triumphs of Helen Mirren's Ganymede-Rosalind, the acting interest in this *As You Like It* is generated by Richard Pasco (*Julius Caesar*'s Brutus) as Jaques. Pasco's alienating facial features—heavy eyelids, bulging eyes, pronounced bags under those eyes, and minimal change in expression—work as well for this cynical Jaques as they did for the priggish Brutus. Pasco effectively demands attention yet does not command assent. He strikes a balance as right for the malcontent (whom Shakespeare here gives the most famous lines but yet excludes from the ending comic celebration) as it is for the humorless "noble" ideologue, Brutus.

Romeo and Juliet (BBC, 1978 [PBS, 14 March 1979])

Capulet: Michael Hordern. *Chorus*: John Gielgud. *Juliet*: Rebecca Saire. *Mercutio*: Anthony Andrews. *Nurse*: Celia Johnson. *Romeo*: Patrick Ryecart. *Tybalt*: Alan Rickman.

Producer: Cedric Messina. Director: Alvin Rakoff. Designer: Stuart Walker.

John J. O'Connor, *NY Times* (14 Mar. 1979). "Rebecca Saire and Patrick Ryecart are never less than appealing and nearly always touching. . . . Miss Saire beautifully embodies the innocence and natural sophistication of Juliet. . . . This . . . production concentrates on Shakespeare, his play, and his poetry. And it succeeds in delivering them admirably. . . . The supporting cast . . . is incredibly good."

Tom Shales, *Washington Post* (14 Mar. 1979). "The casting of the two leads is a disappointment. . . . The language and speeches . . . often become sing-songy and cantish. . . . Saire's Juliet . . . persuasively youthful and eager, nevertheless lacks passion."

Howard Rosenberg, *Los Angeles Times* (14 Mar. 1979). "Romeo's revenge [against Tybalt] is savage and the staging of it superb. . . . The sets are beautifully done. . . . Saire is appropriately fresh as dew, fragile and innocent . . . if not the pure . . . beauty that might entrance [Romeo]."

Mike Silverman, New Orleans *Times-Picayune* (14 Mar. 1979). Director Rakoff explains his rationale for casting Rebecca Saire as Juliet. Silverman calls it "a gamble that did not pay off . . . Miss Saire . . . seems more a petulant child than a passionate young woman . . . Especially gripping is the fight."

Charles Lower, *Shakespeare on Film Newsletter*, 3:2 (Apr. 1979). Contrasts Zeffirelli's film with the TV version: "unlike a movie, television—its small screen viewed in the home—greatly restricts both style and camera-work."

Jacqueline Pearson, "Shadows on the Shadow-Box: the BBC Shakespeare," *Critical Quarterly*, 21 (1979).

In [*Romeo and Juliet*] the cutting seemed odd and even inconsistent. . . . [M]ost of the long last speech of Friar Laurence [was cut] at precisely that moment in the play when, as we are about to leave it, we need most help in assessing the relationship between the play-world and our own. More seriously, most of Laurence's warning speech to Romeo (II.vi.10–13) was cut: 'The sweetest honey / Is loathsome in its own deliciousness.' This omission is revealing of the quality of the production. *Romeo and Juliet* is not simply a play in praise of young love. The central relationship is surrounded by teasing ambiguities. The world of Verona is marked by extreme, irrational and destructive emotions, by the unexplained feud between Montagues and Capulets, by Romeo's paralysing infatuation with Ro-

saline. Even Friar Laurence's herbs illustrate a cosmic battle between 'grace and rude will' (II.iii.28). In this context, what kind of judgments are we to make on the extreme, irrational and destructive emotions of the lovers? The play is deliberately ambiguous. Affirmative images of sun, light and growing plants balance negative images of darkness, death, sweet things so sweet that they become disgusting. The BBC rather sentimentalised the relationship by cutting out these antithetical images or minimising their dramatic impact.

Jack Jorgens, "The BBC-TV Shakespeare Series," *Shakespeare Quarterly*, 30 (Summer 1979).

The chief of many flaws in Alvin Rakoff's production of *Romeo and Juliet* is in the lead roles. Patrick Ryecart's rouged, pretty Romeo and Rebecca Saire's rather plain Juliet never arouse our interest, never mesh either as actors or as characters supposed to be lovers. Nor is it just a matter of weak screen presences and inadequate rehearsals. The greater problem is that it simply seems incredible that so experienced a Romeo could be so taken with such a simple, pale young girl. This rather soggy production of *Romeo and Juliet* demonstrates once again how important the speed and energy of Zeffirelli's film are to Shakespeare's play. A marriage of the violence, humor, and color of that film with the verbal skills of the BBC actors would give us a really startling aesthetic experience; but given the current segregation between the creative talents of stage and screen, such a union is unlikely.

Richard II (BBC, 1978 [PBS, 28 March 1979])

Bolingbroke: Jon Finch. *Duchess of York*: Wendy Hiller. *Duke of York*: Charles Gray. *John of Gaunt*: John Gielgud. *Richard*: Derek Jacobi.

Producer: Cedric Messina. Director: David Giles. Designer: Tony Abbott.

Gerald Clarke, "Longest Run," *Time* (12 Feb. 1979). Play becomes "an almost contemporary story of power used and abused." Jacobi praised in title role.

Henry Fenwick, "Gielgud Approaches Shakespeare on TV, Warily," *NY Times* (25 Mar. 1979). Interview with Sir John: "the least flicker of an eyelash . . . will carry for television where it couldn't for stage." Discusses BBC *Richard II*.

Howard Rosenberg, *Los Angeles Times* (28 Mar. 1979). "Extraordinarily fine, fully realized production. . . . Jacobi . . . is a glorious Richard. . . . Charles Gray is superb as the poor old Duke of York. . . . Richard's last hours . . . alone and introspective, are beautifully directed . . . as Giles rearranges time and space."

Joseph McLellan, *Washington Post* (28 Mar. 1979). Jacobi's "Richard is both believable and kingly, with a nicely calibrated sense of the differences between the public and the private personality. . . . [Richard is] a fine, royal figure on ceremonial occasions . . . but foppish among his friends, weak and indecisive when he is not supported by the strength of armies and pageantry, and utterly desolate after losing his throne. . . ."

John J. O'Connor, *NY Times* (28 Mar. 1979). "Television proves a distinct advantage for the brief but crucial scenes that serve as connecting points for the plot. Often lost on the expanses of a large stage, they received their proper weight in the intimacy of the small screen."

Arthur Unger, *Christian Science Monitor* (26 Mar. 1979). "Sir John [Gielgud] and Dame Wendy [Hiller] . . . bring warmth and humor to their parts, playing them with a kind of gutsy enthusiasm balanced with irony. . . . Jacobi excels . . . in the isolation of his imprisonment. . . . [This production] is a total experience."

Jack Jorgens, "The BBC-TV Shakespeare Series," *Shakespeare Quarterly*, 30 (Summer 1979).

The first three productions hardly gave us warning of such a solid production of *Richard II*, directed by David Giles. Derek Jacobi was superb at rendering the arc of Richard's development—from vanity, to hope, to despair, and finally to wisdom and courage as he kills several of his assailants before being cut down. Jon Finch [as Bolingbroke], who brought his tough, terse manner from his performance in Polanski's *Macbeth*, was a perfect foil for Jacobi's quixotic softness, and they enjoyed a fine supporting cast including a feisty, touching Gaunt by John Gielgud, Wendy Hiller as a motherly Duchess of York, and Charles Gray as a fussy, well-meaning Duke of York.

In the earlier efforts, one feels the pressures of time and money as directors rush past "small" scenes in order to spend more effort on the big ones. But some of Shakespeare's best work is in those "small" scenes, and it is in their quality that this production really shines. To take but one example, in the scene where Bolingbroke sentences Bushy and Green to death, we get all three perspectives: (1) Bolingbroke's righteous indignation at being stripped of his lands and title, his straight-faced lies, and his casual indifference to the beheadings; (2) York's silent protests as Bolingbroke accuses the prisoners of causing not only the rift between Richard and the Queen but that between Richard and Bolingbroke, and his shock at the sound of the beheadings off-frame as Bolingbroke calmly instructs him to send "fair entreaties" and "kind commends;" and (3) Bushy and Green's vulnerability, their shirts and bare chests contrasting with the armor of their captors, and their Richard-like impotence as they insult Bolingbroke before being taken away. The confident use of the camera, which includes and excludes characters with precision and moves when Bolingbroke motivates it to move, provides a striking contrast with the randomness of earlier productions.

Jacqueline Pearson, "Shadows on the Shadow-Box," *Critical Inquiry*, 21 (1979).

Cutting was damaging in *Richard II*. The play itself is an intricate web of repetitions, contrasts and parallels. Bolingbroke's bidding farewell to the English soil (I.iii.306–7) parallels Richard's greeting of the English earth on his return from Ireland (III.ii.6–7). The opening scene asks difficult questions about treason. Is Mowbray a traitor because he has instigated a murder when commanded by his king, or is Bolingbroke a traitor for opposing this royal murder? Later the play provides a direct parallel in the scene (V.iii) in which York begs for the death of his son Aumerle. Is Aumerle a traitor because he has plotted to kill the usurper Bolingbroke, or is his father York the traitor because he has supported that usurper? The BBC captured some of these parallels, but some equally significant ones were jettisoned. The scene (IV.i) where Bagot and Aumerle quarrel shows how authoritatively Bolingbroke handles exactly the same kind of 'home alarms' that defeated Richard earlier in the play. This scene is cut completely, and the delicately poised structure of parallels collapses. Again, the Queen's sense of impending doom when Richard is in Ireland, and the complex image of 'perspectives' (II.i.14–27) which is used to explain it, are also cut. . . . Some of these cuts seem seriously to menace the unity and the meaning of the play.

Michael Manheim, "The Shakespeare Plays on TV: Season One," *Shakespeare on Film Newsletter*, 4:1 (Dec. 1979).

Television, which is highly dependent on close-ups to achieve its effects, might seem less effective for the histories, which demand the magnificence and broad, sweeping action of the long shot, than for other Shakespearean genres. This production achieves the magnificence and broad sweep with texture rather than distance. Even the lists at Coventry are shown in close-up—the screen overwhelmed with bright colors, precise heraldry, and the flash of sunlit metal that more than make up for the absent rows of horses or sprawling meadows. At one point, however, distance is used most meaningfully. There are few close-ups as the defeated Richard high upon the walls of Flint Castle has his first meeting with Northumberland below. That both Richard and Northumberland are seen at a distance establishes the highly political, patently insincere nature of their exchange. The more familiar close-ups take over, then, as Richard speaks his real feelings to his entourage.

This production is outstanding in other ways. David Giles has served as teacher as well as director. He teaches us history we might not know when, following Bolingbroke's accusation that Norfolk has murdered the Duke of Gloucester, Giles has the camera switch not to Norfolk but to Richard, the real culprit in Gloucester's death. Thus we realize that what seems a confrontation between two knights in the opening scene is really the first skirmish between a would-be usurper and his king. Another instance of Giles's direct orial intelligence is his treatment of Richard's last-act soliloquy. Both because that long, late soliloquy tends to lose modern audiences and because Richard's theme is time, Giles breaks the speech up, having it shot against a variety of backgrounds within the prison. This has the effect of both holding audience attention and suggesting the length and tediousness of Richard's incarceration. Early in the play, we saw Richard waste time; here we literally see time waste him.

The transition from arrogant prince to tragic hero is difficult for any Richard, but Jacobi is up to the task. His Richard returns from Ireland already chastened by the storm at sea and the news of Bolingbroke's successes. From the moment he returns to his beloved English soil, he is and remains to the end a political victim unique in his ability to give full and original poetic utterance to the pain of what is happening to him. His sharp intelligence never at rest, Jacobi's Richard realizes that he possesses the eloquence to make his deposition scene a personal triumph. Despite the sincerity of his tearful outbursts, he manipulates Northumberland and Bolingbroke into revealing themselves as the power grabbers they are. Contrary to earlier appearances, he is not in the least infirm of purpose or cowardly in this scene or in the final act, where Jacobi's courage and agility are convincing as Richard kills two of his intended murderers before receiving Exton's fatal blow.

Measure for Measure (BBC, 1979 [PBS, 11 April 1979])

Angelo: Tim Pigott-Smith. *Isabella*: Kate Nelligan. *Lucio*: John McEnery. *Pompey*: Frank Middlemass. *Vincentio*: Kenneth Colley.

Producer: Cedric Messina. *Director*: Desmond Davis. *Designer*: Odette Barrow.

Robert Last, London *Times* (19 Feb. 1979). "A vital contemporary performance, full of irony and black humour. . . . Kenneth Colley seemed strangely miscast [as the Duke]."

G. M. Pearce, *Cahiers Elisabéthains*, 16 (Apr. 1979). "With Kate Nelligan's immensely serious Isabella, the tragic side of this problem play was predominant."

Cecil Smith, *Los Angeles Times* (11 Apr. 1979). "Dazzling . . . acting is wonderful, particularly Kate Nelligan's performance as [Isabella]."

Tom Shales, *Washington Post* (11 Apr. 1979). "*Measure for Measure* benefits immeasurably from the key performances of two women. Kate Nelligan is the image of idealized faultlessness as Isabella. . . . Jacqueline Pearce [Mariana], mean-

while, voluptuously and charismatically represents another aspect of womanhood. . . . *Measure* works splendidly and gladdeningly, and the fluid touch of director Desmond Davis serves it well."

Virginia M. Carr, *Shakespeare on Film Newsletter*, 4:1 (Dec. 1979). "In Isabella's two visits to Angelo, the confrontations are especially intense, and here television may be the best vehicle available for Shakespeare's art. But with the street scenes, with Elbow's mock justice, even with Lucio's slanders against the Duke, television cannot provide the same response as the theatre. Still *Measure for Measure* . . . is especially suited to the small screen."

Maurice Charney, "Shakespearean Anglophilia: The BBC-TV Series and American Audiences," *Shakespeare Quarterly*, 31 (1980). Whatever the producer and the directors tell us about the special opportunities and limitations of the television medium, the success or failure of the plays seems to depend most powerfully on the acting. That is what made *Measure for Measure* the most brilliant success of the series so far: the incredibly charged confrontations between Tim Pigott-Smith's Angelo and Kate Nelligan's Isabella. (Tim Pigott-Smith was also a memorable Hotspur.) For once we lost all sense of camera placements, settings, costumes, color coordination, and other technological details of the television medium. We were conscious only of the tremendous sexual and moral conflict between two overweening characters, in many ways mirror images of each other. We were pleased to see the play finally cohere as a bitter comedy, and especially to find the Duke displaced from his manipulative role at the center of the action. Desmond Davis' *Measure for Measure* succeeded by the intelligence of its conception, beautifully rendered by the actors. It is the only production of the series so far that one wants to compare to memorable performances in the theatre—though as single performances one should perhaps add Derek Jacobi's Richard II and Charles Gray's Julius Caesar.

Henry VIII (BBC, 1979 [PBS, 25 April 1979])

Cranmer: Ronald Pickup. *Henry*: John Stride. *Katherine*: Claire Bloom. *Wolsey*: Timothy West.

Producer: Cedric Messina. *Director*: Kevin Billington. *Designer*: Alun Hughes.

Benedict Nightingale, "TV or Not TV?" *New York Times* (24 Feb. 1980). "Henry VIII was well-suited to the halls and passages, nooks and crannies of such Kent castles as Hever, Leeds, and Penshurst. [Directors other than Kevin Billington] have admitted themselves somewhat baffled by the problem of reconciling Elizabethan verse with a medium whose drama is usually naturalistic, even documentary."

Sylvia Clayton, London *Times* (26 Feb. 1979). "The magnificent velvets, furs, and jewels of Tudor costume . . . glowed in the kind of gray-stone setting for which they were intended."

Arthur Unger, *Christian Science Monitor* (23 Apr. 1979). "A brave and bravura production . . . lush processions, songs, and dances. . . . Claire Bloom is hauntingly vulnerable . . . as Katherine. . . . John Stride and Timothy West create fascinatingly complex portraits of Henry and Wolsey and Ronald Pickup a shrewd and manipulative Cranmer."

G. M. Pearce, *Cahiers Elisabéthains*, 16 (Apr. 1979). The "production would have been worth watching for design and set alone." Bloom's Katherine is "moving."

John J. O'Connor, *NY Times* (25 Apr. 1979). "The production was [taped] attractively in authentic castles. Unfortunately, the weather was obviously damp and cold, leading to a seeming epidemic of vocal nasality among many of the actors."

James Lardner, *Washington Post* (25 Apr. 1979). Indicts the actors for overly "low-keyed" performances, warns parents to keep their children away that night.

Maurice Charney, *Shakespeare Quarterly*, 31 (1980). "Close-ups . . . used . . . monotonously to represent conflict and intense emotion."

Jack Jorgens, "The BBC-TV Shakespeare Series," *Shakespeare Quarterly*, 30 (Summer 1979).

If the final production, *Henry VIII*, was less successful [than previous productions of Season One], it was not the fault of the director and actors, who did a creditable job, but of the script, which has pronounced weaknesses—weaknesses all too apparent to a television public which has seen other versions of the story of Henry and his wives, versions that take much better advantage of the historical material. Shifting its emphasis from Buckingham, to Katherine, to Wolsey, to Cranmer, to the baby Elizabeth—over whom Cranmer prophesies a peace and prosperity eloquently recalled by a nostalgic Shakespeare in 1613—and providing an enigmatic Henry who pops in and out of focus, the play simply fails to sustain interest for three hours. In the theatre, directors have traditionally resorted to spectacle, but small budgets and a smaller screen do not lend themselves to such a treatment. In spite of the weight placed on them, the actors bore it very well, especially Timothy West as a superb, brooding, villain Cardinal Wolsey with the same lumpy face and menacing eyes that Orson Welles brought to the role in *A Man for All Seasons*. The elegance of design and the control of camera and editing in this production seem to indicate that the BBC has hit its stride. It may even be able to take a few risks now, with some solid accomplishments under its belt.

R. Scott Colley, "The Shakespeare Plays on TV: Season One," *Shakespeare on Film Newsletter*, 4:1 (Dec. 1979).

The domestic activities of Henry VIII have insured his continued presence in the popular imagination: his character has come to life in various films as well as in a television series. Now Henry reappears as Shakespeare conceived him. When the first season of the BBC Shakespeare plays was announced, *Henry VIII* seemed an eccentric companion to *Richard II*, *Romeo and Juliet* and the others. Shakespeare's odd, late history turns out to have been a good choice. It also turns out to have been one of the best productions so far in the series.

Kevin Billington's interpretation of the play demonstrates how certain Shakespearean plays can come alive on the small screen, and how some of these plays can merit popular attention as melodramatic adventure stories. There has been much discussion about who was chosen to perform and direct the BBC Shakespeare plays: the British Shakespeare establishment was left out. Experienced television directors and actors were in. Now, the people who brought you *Upstairs, Downstairs* are bringing you Shakespeare. And they brought *Henry VIII* to television with great skill indeed.

Shakespeare conceived of Henry's reign as a succession of revolutions of the wheel of Fortune. Buckingham's fall marks the period of Wolsey's greatest power and influence. Anne Bullen's rise is in counterpoint to Wolsey's fall. Good Queen Katherine is out. Good Archbishop Cranmer is in.

Sentimentality works well on television, and it works particularly well when it is a part of the atmosphere Shakespeare created. For instance, Buckingham's, or Wolsey's, or Katherine's faces fill the screen as they speak their respective farewells: their speeches seem to be directed as much to themselves as to others, and television captures that half-musing quality of the several monologues. The screen brings us close to their suffering and to their transcendence.

Shakespeare's *Henry VIII* pretties up some nasty business. Billington and Stride decide to pretty up Shakespeare. The only hint of the Henry most of us remember is that old figure who slumps on the throne during the prologue. The production itself is a kind of nationalistic romance in which time stops at a moment of birth and reconciliation. It is good melodrama and excellent television.

Twelfth Night (BBC, 1980 [PBS, 27 February 1980])

Feste: Trevor Peacock. *Malvolio*: Alec McCowen. *Olivia*: Sinead Cusack. *Orsino*: Clive Arrindell. *Toby*: Robert Hardy. *Viola*: Felicity Kendal.
    Producer: Cedric Messina. *Director*: John Gorrie. *Designer*: Don Taylor.

John J. O'Connor, *NY Times* (27 Feb. 1980). "[N]ot dazzlingly brilliant . . . solid . . . admirable. . . . Many of the performances are masterful . . . some . . . inadequate. . . . Clive Arrindell [Orsino] looks pretty but is naggingly insubstantial . . . Alec McCowen [Malvolio] remains a stranger among the other characters. Perhaps the impression is intentional . . . but, in the end, it remains a failed curiosity."

G. M. Pearce, *Cahiers Elisabéthains*, 17 (Apr. 1980). "Cheerful, vigorous . . . made one far more aware of the relative social positions of all the characters than [does the usual] stage production."

Cecil Smith, "A BBC Delight," *Los Angeles Times* (27 Feb. 1980). "A spirited, joyful romp."

Virginia Carr, *Shakespeare on Film Newsletter*, 4:2 (Apr. 1980)."The subtext's darker elements are not emphasized. But . . . the themes of madness and lost identity strike home. . . . Those who know the play accept its conventions [identical twins, for example]. But does the play make sense to those who have never read Shakespeare? . . . Feste's final song . . . is a recapitulation of the play, rather than a comment on the human condition."

Larry Kart, "The Bard Too Talky for a Medium in Which the Message Must Show," *Chicago Tribune* (22 Feb. 1980).

One great advantage the movies have over television is that they once were silent. . . . Every movie and every TV show that works does so in part because the lessons of the silent era have been absorbed: show me first and tell me later. . . . If you can't show me, no amount of high-class or low-class verbiage is going to make up for it. . . .

Shakespeare is as much about language as anything else. . . . In the comedies, the language is the high-speed, punning verbal wit of a society in which a well-turned retort was only a step removed from a sword thrust. . . .

Thus, I suspect that even an audience steeped in Shakespearean lore will have trouble taking in the BBC-TV production of *Twelfth Night*. . . . The "low plot" is almost a complete dud. [But] the more sentimental humor of the "high plot" comes through with considerable clarity. . . . The verse [these characters] speak is less rapid-fire than that used by the "low" characters, giving us a chance to absorb the sense and the beauty of the words and look—I repeat "look"—at the effects these words have on the people who speak then and listen to them.

When, for example, Viola tells Orsino, who has been kvetching about how hard love is for men, that she knows a woman (herself, of course) who "never told her love," everything comes through, the verbal music, its meaning in the plot, and the pathos of a woman confessing her love to a man who can't understand what she's talking about.

Maurice Charney, "Shakespearean Anglophilia: The BBC-TV Series and American Audiences," *Shakespeare Quarterly*, 31 (Summer 1980).

In the modest but very satisfying *Twelfth Night* that opened the second season, Alec McCowen's Malvolio is wonderfully restrained and intelligent. A natural butt because he is so egregiously filled with petty pretension, the Steward comes to grief because once in his life he lets his ambitious imagination wander. Robert Hardy plays Sir Toby very much in the tradition of a lesser Falstaff, which prepared us surprisingly well for the kind of Falstaff represented by Anthony Quayle. In *Twelfth Night* the Cavalier sets of Don Taylor have their own country charm, contributing not a little to a feeling of domestic reality: "The effect of this massive set [Taylor says], with its nooks and surprising new vistas, is to create a very strong sense of a household going about its business." As Cedric Messina puts it, *Twelfth Night* is "the *Upstairs, Downstairs* of the Shakespearean canon." We feel at home in the play, whose events unfold with a believable authenticity.

1 Henry IV (BBC, 1979 [PBS, 26 March 1980])

Falstaff: Anthony Quayle. *Hal*: David Gwillim. *Henry*: Jon Finch. *Hotspur*: Tim Pigott-Smith. *Mistress Quickly*: Brenda Bruce.

Producer: Cedric Messina. *Director*: David Giles. *Designer*: Don Homfray.

Russell Davies, London *Times* (16 Dec. 1979). "Quayle . . . perfectly caught . . . Falstaff's insecurity—the moment of facial panic after the uttering of a joke before the reaction sets in around him. . . . Finch's King [was] starchily declamatory beyond the call of regal duty. His lecture to the Prince was a rant."

Christian Williams, *Washington Post* (26 Mar. 1980). "This understated production . . . takes about half an hour to build [but] brings out everything that need be hoped for—tender moments between man and wife; a lovely song in impenetrable but hypnotic Welsh; vast edifices of hilarity that crumble into death and moral ambiguity; the elusive characterizations in which lie the playwright's genius, and battlefield scenes of majestic slaughter and crushing impact. . . ."

Michael Kernan, "Actor Jon Finch," *Washington Post* (26 Mar. 1980). An interview of the Bolingbroke of the *Richard II*-*Henry IV* sequence, in which we learn the meaning of "Roll back the burner to its full extent."

John J. O'Connor, *NY Times* (26 Mar. 1980). . . . Picking up with the final death scene from *Richard II*, this *Henry IV, Part I* is characteristic of the overall series so far. These are not brilliant, dazzling productions, stuffed with pyrotechnical turns. They are certainly not "experimental" in any way. Instead, these are careful, almost primerlike interpretations, rarely less than competent, frequently shot through with marvelous displays of acting. . . . In the notorious scene-stealing role of Falstaff, it is Anthony Quayle, who played the old boy on stage 25 years ago but now admits that he was really much too young for him. His Falstaff here is still the insinuating scalawag, never at a loss for a scheme or an excuse.

But Mr. Quayle taps an intriguing vein of melancholy in the character, an awareness that he can be, and eventually will be, rejected by Sweet Prince Hal. When Hal calls him a "villainous, abominable misleader of youth," this deeply wounded Falstaff is curiously moving. Mr. Quayle's performance is, as usual, intelligent and splendidly theatrical.

Samuel Crowl, "The Shakespeare Plays on TV: Season Two," *Shakespeare on Film Newsletter*, 5:1 (Dec. 1980).

Henry IV, Part One represents Shakespeare at his most dazzling: epic in sweep, ironic in structure, festive in spirit. The small screen just can't contain or capture its massive energies. Director David Giles employs several of the strategies which worked well for him in last season's claustrophobic *Richard II*, but 1H4 can't be squeezed into a series of medium close-ups. Such an approach places a premium on the control and command of the actor's face, and unfortunately Jon Finch's range of expression appears to extend from dread to dead.

To compensate, Finch gives his king an embarrassing and irritating series of hand gestures as his sole means of displaying Henry's care, concern, guilt and insecurity. Finch cannot refrain, in his every scene, from indulging in the most amateurish sign language: he rubs his hands together, strokes the left with the right, plays nervously with his gloves and his signet ring, massages his forehead, and goes through an elaborate ritual cleansing of those busy hands in the scene (III.iii) where ironically he accuses his son of misbehavior. The stain of Henry's usurpation becomes such an overpowering image that it subverts Shakespeare's certain intention to create in 1H4 not an embryonic *Macbeth*, but a far more generous and optimistic work about the rewards and risks of power politics.

Fortunately 1H4 is such a rich and resonant play that it cannot be flawed fatally by a limiting approach or by a single inadequate performance. In fact, the close-ups that expose the shallowness of Finch's performance are turned to advantage by David Gwillim's Prince Hal and Anthony Quayle's Falstaff. Gwillim is an inventive actor blessed with a remarkably wide and expressive mouth which he uses most effectively—by playing his lips into a series of carefully modulated mischievous smiles—to capture Hal's essence as mimic and mocker. The edges of that smile almost seem to twinkle as Hal dances his way along the narrow path weaving among playboy, pariah, and prince. Gwillim's Hal genuinely seems to discover himself—and the political advantages to be reaped from his riotous living—as he thinks his way through the notoriously dangerous "I know you all" soliloquy. The lines seem immediate and fresh as Gwillim plays with the seeming contradictions involved in fault and reformation, holiday and everyday, sport and work, offense and redemption.

Anthony Quayle's Falstaff is conceived—through costume, out of beard, and posture—as though he had waddled straight out of George Cruikshank's somewhat melancholy ink and water-color sketch (1858) of the fabled fat knight. Quayle's performance is most interesting when director Giles has him identify and confront the camera-as-audience and to share his anti-establishment jests as a series of private confidences directly with us. He is less effective in action with Hal because he repeatedly slows the pace of their nimble exchanges by unnecessary interjections ("ah . . . er . . . oh-ho . . . harumph . . . hmmmm") as though the quickest mind in the west needs to fumble for words in repartee with his own student.

Tim Pigott-Smith's Hotspur is appropriately red-headed and fiery but fails to rival our affection for Hal. The production's battle scenes are studio-stilted, but the play does emerge with more of its life intact than many of the other productions completed under the general direction of Cedric Messina.

2 Henry IV (BBC, 1979 [PBS, 9 April 1980])

Chief Justice: Ralph Michael. *Doll*: Frances Cuka. *Falstaff*: Anthony Quayle. *Hal*: David Gwillim. *Henry*: Jon Finch. *Pistol*: Bryan Pringle. *Mistress Quickly*: Brenda Bruce. *Shallow*: Robert Eddison.

Producer: Cedric Messina. *Director*: David Giles. *Designer*: Don Homfray.

Laurence Christon, *Los Angeles Times* (9 Apr. 1980). "Very long and very dull. . . . The single camera shots between Henry [V] and Falstaff at the moment of Falstaff's repudiation fail to give us the poignant sense of their doomed relationship. . . . This is the worst kind of Shakespeare in its deadly reverence for the word and its mediocre response to the spirit."

Gerald Clarke, "Fathers and Sons," *Time* (31 Mar. 1980). "Gwillim adroitly captures all Hal's contradictions. . . . Anthony Quayle makes [the part of Falstaff] not only simple, but natural. . . . Jon Finch is also good as Henry IV."

Michael Kernan, *Washington Post* (9 Apr. 1980). "Quayle brings the play to life. . . . [Then] Finch takes hold of the play with complete authority and never lets it go."

John J. O'Connor, *NY Times* (9 Apr. 1980). "Some of the plays may not deserve a full-scale production. . . . Even Shakespeare had his weak artistic moments. . . . *Henry IV, Part II* [is] a mere link in the play cycle, an episodic necessity connecting two vibrant points. . . . Jon Finch . . . Anthony Quayle . . . and David Gwillim . . . strive mightily, but the thing is generally reluctant to move at more than a snail's pace."

G. M. Pearce, *Cahiers Elisabéthains*, 17 (Apr. 1980). "Shallow's orchard, for which they appeared to use the mellow grounds of Chipping Camden church, made a more natural setting [than the other "studio-bound" scenes] and gave these delightful scenes an added feeling of authenticity."

Maurice Charney, "Shakespearean Anglophilia," *Shakespeare Quarterly*, 31 (1980). "Quayle . . . convincingly expresses [Falstaff's] doubleness and ironic conception of himself. . . . " Michele Dotrice's Lady Percy makes Act II, scene iii "unforgettable."

William A. Henry, *Boston Globe* (9 Apr. 1980).

William Shakespeare's *Henry IV, Part 2* is rarely produced or discussed except as the least glorious play in the four-part Henriad, the inconvenient explanatory bit required to get the action from the insurrections in *Richard II* and *Henry IV, Part I* to the glorious and bloody victories of *Henry V*. In comparison, *Richard II* is revered for language, *Henry IV, Part 1* for comic verve, *Henry V* for action and valor. But for a war-weary generation—and that, alas, is practically every generation in the history of mankind—*Henry IV, Part 2* is a more mature and moving play.

Henry IV, Part 1 is a story of impetuous youth, of playful Prince Hal and valiant, excitable Hotspur. *Henry IV, Part 2* is a story of regretful age, of fat Falstaff and the prematurely careworn king and addled Justice Shallow. War ages a man before his time, and ages a country, too. It demands ultimate faith and it destroys faith. The central characters of *Henry IV, Part 2* are old and bitter and lonely. The best scenes are scenes of clowns crying—Falstaff, Justice Shallow—or kings bemoaning power, telling us, "Uneasy lies the head that wears a crown." The themes of the play are betrayal, contradiction, reversal of expectations, disloyalty of the kingdom, of rumor, of friends, of one's own body. It ends with one of the coldest betrayals in literature, Prince Hal's of Falstaff, and it takes just six unexpected words: "I know thee not, old man."

Director David Giles, who made a brilliant *Richard II* last year and added the best *Henry IV, Part 1* we are likely to see, has surpassed himself in finding the maundering intimacy and pathos of *Henry IV, Part 2* without muting any of the roaring laughter. Anthony Quayle as Falstaff, with the craft accumulated over a lifetime, treats the richest moments with the utmost simplicity, especially

when he tells the whore Doll Tearsheet, "Do not speak like a death's head. Do not bid me remember my end." In his big comic turn, the recruitment of soldiers in Justice Shallow's garden, he reduces each draftee to a mere figure of speech, yet hints just enough in his manner that he knows his choices are going off to die.

At moments Quayle is matched by Robert Eddison, whose portrait of Justice Shallow carries the audience from envy to mockery to pity and back to envy for the old rake whose stories about his wanton youth prove all pathetic lies—yet who has, by turns of fate, become a man of wealth and power, and who richly enjoys the pleasures that time one by one strips away.

Jon Finch is too histrionic in his madness as the king, and David Gwillim is blandly pretty as Prince Hal, but a wonderful supporting cast lets us feel all the emotion in this unappreciated masterpiece, from Michele Dotrice's sobbing about war and honor as Hotspur's widow, to Brenda Bruce's half-rage, half-forgiveness at Falstaff's string of broken marriage promises, to the weedy recruits in Shallow's garden, some bribing, some lying, some desperately persuading themselves it doesn't matter whether they die.

Peter Saccio, "The Shakespeare Plays on TV," *Shakespeare on Film Newsletter*, 6:1 (Jan. 1982).

In the BBC Lancastrian tetralogy, the small screen has diminished some important things: the pageantry of *R2*, the range of bustling life in *1H4*, the battles and public oratory of *H5*. Despite a 25% cut in the text, *2H4* has lost least, and emerges for me as the most absorbing of the four productions. For politics takes place not only in public display, oratory, battles, and crowds, but also in tense private conversations, and these are the heart of *2H4*. What happens in this play occurs largely in the personal struggle of two or three individuals. The small camera can catch that superbly in the juxtaposition of faces.

The production offers a fine gallery of old faces. Falstaff and the Lord Chief Justice strongly establish the motif: Anthony Quayle, flushed, puffy, bearded, hoarse, clad in rough browns, confronting Ralph Michael, a distinguished gent, clean-shaven, clear-voiced, robed in green damasked silk. The Archbishop has a sharp asceticism, verging on the fanatical in his prominent facial bones and deeply incised facial lines. Shallow, with a pursed, twitchy, blinking face and wispy beard, contrasts with the placid idiocy of a nightcapped Silence. Mowbray has been changed from a youngster into a stout graybeard. With the King, a long-suspended obscurity is at last clarified. Jon Finch's obsessive hand-rubbing in *1H4* was emphasized but ambiguous: was it nervousness? calculation? Pilate-like guilt? the leprosy legend? All are appropriate, of course. In *2H4*, the leprosy takes over, scarring his handsome face. The lesions, together with his restless eyes and disordered hair, give us a hagridden king epitomizing his sick realm.

These old faces confront each other, and confront the young. The Archbishop's fierce sincerity can make no dent on the plastic smoothness of Prince John. Young widow Percy, red-eyed with grief and wimpled in dazzling white, makes a moving solo cadenza of her elegy for Hotspur, only to be succeeded by old widow Quickly, her wimple soiled, as jostled for space on the screen as her pleas are jostled by Falstaff's bullying. In one disturbing scene, two young faces confront each other. Hal and Poins, dicing alone, probe each other's masks, and each has several. Critics have written much on Hal's condescension and anxiety here. New and painful to me are Poins's edginess, his hinted bitterness, his momentary triumphs, his discomfort about the rumor of his sister Nell: a fine cameo of the awkwardness entailed in being Hal's semi-confidant. Although slightly flawed by a badly placed act-break, the King's deathbed satisfyingly climaxes these encounters. For those three long speeches, Finch's ravaged face confronts the grieving David Gwillim (who has an extraordinarily expressive mouth) with the crown frequently in view. Father and son, the crown as glory and as burden, anger and repentance and relief and determination: the passage powerfully captures what kingship does to kings and heirs.

All these faces reflect political anxiety. The BBC 1H4 was, I think, too deeply political: Hotspur's dash never really competed with Hal's deep-revolving thoughts, and Hal seemed to be thinking so often of Westminster that I wondered why he'd gone to Eastcheap at all. But 2H4 is a more anxious play, in which men maneuver for position with increasing wariness and weariness. This production images with resourceful variety the sheer strain of politics. And I do mean images: the deepest cuts come from the rebels' reminiscences, and these lines are effectually replaced by shots from R2 and 1H4 accompanying the opening credits.

It is not all tense duos and trios. Larger confrontations have screen actions crystallizing the pressures. In V.ii, the camera cleverly manipulates the spaces between the superbly poised Gwillim and his worried courtiers. At Gaultree, John greets the Archbishop by kneeling to kiss his ring, but ends the scene by ripping the cross from the Archbishop's neck. (The snare motif immediately carries over into the Colville episode: the Boy stakes down a trip-rope to allow Falstaff his capture.) In the tavern, Doll suddenly lifts her sleazy ruby dress and whips a knife from her garter to attack Pistol. Although her later arrest is cut, Frances Cuka needs only the one scene to create a Doll who is not only boozy, sentimental, and genuinely fond of Falstaff, but also temperamental and very dangerous. Whores have hearts of alloy—gold and steel.

At the end, in the rejection, this rich array of humanity is deliberately reduced to stiff role-playing. The coronation procession is a parade of walking dummies, shot so as to avoid any real splendor, and Gwillim, his long hair shorn so that none shows beneath the crown, is a mask of kingship saying the obligatory words. Sweaty, quirky, living people (Falstaff and his crew, the crowd) are given their orders and left behind. What kingship does to everyone who comes near it is dryly clear.

Henry V (BBC, 1979 [PBS, 23 April 1980])

Chorus: Alec McCowen. Fluellen: Tim Wylton. Gower: Brian Poyser. Henry: David Gwillim. Katharine: Jocelyne Boisseau. Mistress Quickly: Brenda Bruce. Pistol: Bryan Pringle. Williams: David Pinner.

Producer: Cedric Messina. Director: David Giles. Designer: Don Homfray.

Diana Loercher, Christian Science Monitor (19 Mar. 1980). "Henry V is the most chauvinistic and least interesting of [this tetralogy]. . . . The attrition of characters has resulted in an attrition of substances as well, and Henry in his public moments seems a great king but a hollow man."

G. M. Pearce, Cahiers Elisabéthains, 17 (Apr. 1980). "Alec McCowen gave to the marvelous verse of the Chorus an intensity and suppressed excitement. . . . The steely interior which had been glimpsed in David Gwillim's playing of Prince Hal was not fulfilled in Henry V, who inclined more to compassion and understanding for his men. . . . Jocelyne Boisseau['s] authentic French and delightful broken English added great charm to the regrettably few scenes in which she appeared."

John J. O'Connor, NY Times (23 Apr. 1980). "Solid, unfussy, intelligent. . . . As Katharine, Jocelyne Boisseau is a model of captivating innocence."

Cecil Smith, Los Angeles Times (23 Apr. 1980). "Solidly professional. Rather academic in approach, and a bit too stage-bound. . . . Director Giles has noted that the chorus gives us the idealized Henry, while the play brings us the real king, who is quite different. . . . Henry V is a warrior king if there ever was one. . . . Gwillim's is underplayed and rather soft of tone and manner."

Paul M. Cubeta, "The Shakespeare Plays on TV: Season Two," Shakespeare on Film Newsletter, 5:1 (Dec. 1980).

David Gwillim's Henry V seems happily to have grown accustomed to "this new and gorgeous garment, majesty" that at the end of 2 Henry IV "sits not as easy on me as you think." Gwillim's Henry thoroughly enjoys his performance as king. His face reveals Henry as an actor playing a king with a political conscience as he listens to the conniving Archbishop of Canterbury affirm their agreed-upon claim to the French throne.

But for Henry, public role is always character. Although without showing the relish of his practical jokes on Francis the tapster in Eastcheap, Hal can still set up his betraying friends Scroop, Cambridge, and Grey so that they condemn themselves. He is moved by their treason, pleased with his manipulation. Gwillim is splendid playing a king whose inscrutable surfaces force his audience to judge whether his prayers before Agincourt are pieties or devotion, whether his self-pity as a man can exist without equivocation along with his tormented Lancastrian guilt. The tears for gallant York are as genuine as the ruthless command to kill all French prisoners. His self-mockery as a lover is portrayed without contradicting the hearty bravado of a king who knows that the woman he courts by urging that she "clap hands" in a bargain is herself article one of the peace treaty being ratified during the courtship.

Gwillim is most persuasive in creating a unity of the double reflecting self of Henry as king and man, in a play that holds all contradictions in calculated equipoise. His scenes move between those of the regal figure of king in encompassing royal robes, fully encased armor, or concealing cloak of Sir Thomas Erpingham and those focusing on close-ups of Gwillim's expressive features, with their wry good humor, confidence and exhilaration.

David Giles, the distinguished director of the Second Tetralogy, skillfully engages the problem of the unreliable Chorus to move as a bridge between the loose episodic scenes of the play. The Chorus plays an Alistair Cooke smugly providing exposition as though we couldn't enjoy the play without his presumably indispensable commentary. At the outset he stresses we are at a play as he walks through the set of immobile figures to address us and then turns his back to activate the performance. He can appear with little intrusion at the Southampton docks or at the French court or in the French camp that dissolves into the English encampment. When at the end he tells us there simply isn't time enough and that his story must "brook abridgement," we understand as a television audience that cuts must be made in Shakespeare's text.

Giles is never intimidated by the Olivier movie, his monumental predecessor. He succeeds as Olivier did by making the medium express in its best mode what is available to each in Shakespeare's text. There is no army here with crossbows whirring across the screen, yet entrances from various angles skillfully create the sense of larger spaces. The one stunning, silently focused close-up of Boy, the play's delightful and perceptive junior chorus, bleeding at the mouth and lying dead, says more about the victory of Agincourt and its "spotless cause" and "spotted men" than all the absurd exaggeration of the French body count. The fine performances by the members of the French court,

like the comic counterspectives of Fluellen, Macmorris and Pistol, create the ironic balances that prevent Henry's jingoistic rhetoric and strenuous exhortations from undermining themselves. Although Williams' moral questions about royal responsibility may be sidestepped by Henry cagily or indifferently, the production presents the dubious confrontation with theatrical integrity.

The troubled vision of the "French Chorus" Duke of Burgundy in showing a France suffering the horrors of war is somehow more effective than the chauvinistic pronouncements of the English Chorus. The suggestive close-ups of Canterbury and Ely ostensibly kneeling in prayer while they plot political advantage bring the thematic paradoxes of the play theatrically alive in the opening moments. At the end, the static formal tableau of the Archbishop's blessing of the royal couple freezes the marriage in figurines of unusual beauty, as though for eternity, while the Chorus tells us of what "small time" is left this star of England.

Mark Crispin Miller, "The Shakespeare Plays," *The Nation* (12 July 1980).

What prompted the BBC and those other corporations [Exxon, Metropolitan Life, and Morgan Guaranty] to embalm Shakespeare's entire corpus, at a cost of $13.6 million? Surely not love of drama, since there is little that's either loving or dramatic in this enterprise. We can also rule out any longing to "bring Shakespeare to the masses," since the project's relentlessly pedantic approach has made the plays incomprehensible, and therefore inaccessible. These adaptations are desperately "Shakespearean" and entirely meaningless, turning the plays into empty antiquarian spectacles.

Their emphasis, in other words, is the opposite of Shakespeare's. The actors at the Globe performed on an empty stage, expecting their audience to listen with imagination: "Think, when we talk of horses, that you see them / Printing their proud hoofs i' th' receiving earth." Shakespeare's language was evocative enough to make backdrops and props redundant. In order to let that language do its work, the best directors of Shakespearean film and television—Olivier, Brook, Welles, Kozintsev, Hall—have tried to stylize their productions. Each has avoided historical literalism, using his medium not to bolster vulgar notions of the past but to convey a certain set of meanings derived from personal study of the text. "The Shakespeare Plays," on the other hand, reflects the corporate approach, hiring lots of "experts," spending too much money and making something deadly out of something good. Each play is just another useless product, meant for quick consumption.

Struggling to create the proper aura, the BBC has blown a wad on late medieval bric-a-brac; hogsheads, cross-bows, goblets, scrolls—everything but ye kitchen sink. These irrelevant items clutter irrelevant sets, all those dungeons and taverns and banquet halls which Shakespeare only mentions, but which the BBC has meticulously reconstructed. Such "realism" is supposed to lend these shows an atmosphere at once authentic and colorful, but it only distracts us from the verse, and has the further ill effect of implying a certain condescension, both to the plays and to the past. This literalism becomes hilarious when the action moves "outdoors," that is, onto a studio set covered with fake knolls and plastic trees. While the film studio can present a credible illusion of the natural world, the nails and plaster are always obvious on television. (Using the real thing is no less of an error, as last year's As You Like It, set disconcertingly amid actual woods, made very clear.) This fact of video adds a touch of humor to the BBC's battle scenes, in which small groups of uneasy men try to roughhouse on fields of Astroturf.

But the text suffers most, paradoxically, from the BBC's pedantic treatment of it. If Shakespeare were still alive, he would delete the dead puns and topical references which only his contemporaries could grasp at first hearing. The BBC has left it all intact, cutting only to save a little time, but never to interpret or illuminate the plays. This indiscriminate retention is an expression of contempt, rather than "reverence," for Shakespeare. The BBC retained both good and bad, lasting and archaic, evidently figuring that the plays are all so great and hard and meaningless that it really doesn't matter if nobody understands them, as long as everybody buys them.

"Can this cockpit hold / The vasty fields of France?" the Chorus (Alec McCowen) asks us at the start of Henry V, "Or may we cram / Within this wooden O the very casques / That did affright the air at Agincourt?" What "cockpit?" What "wooden O?" All we see is some guy on television, whereas these terms refer to Shakespeare's circular theater; and the question, furthermore, is irrelevant on an electronic medium, which can "hold the vasty fields of France." If the adapters at the BBC were intent on keeping these famous lines, they ought to have staged them in some meaningful way, but that would have required an understanding of the verse, an awareness of television's possibilities and a little thought.

Prince Hal is the hero of this tetralogy although he never appears in Richard II, which only sets the stage (so to speak) for his ascent. He is not a sympathetic sort of hero. At the outset of Henry IV, Part I, he tells us frankly that he is only using Falstaff and the other rogues to make his eventual acceptance of responsibility seem sudden and miraculous: he is confident that, when he finally gives up such bad company, "My reformation, glitt'ring o'er my fault, / Shall show more goodly and attract more eyes / Than that which hath no foil to set it off." Hal understands that power is based on an ability to perform convincingly; throughout his life on stage, he observes this Machiavellian principle

with spectacular efficiency, putting on the attributes of those whom he surpasses and destroys. At the right time, he humiliates Falstaff with a public rejection, yet retains that facility with the lowly which he had been able to perfect in Falstaff's world; in Henry V, he converses easily with the common soldiers. Later in that play, he courts Katharine of France with a rough, soldierly humor that recalls his enemy, Hotspur, dallying with another Katherine in Henry IV, Part I. And, when necessary, he can overwhelm his opponents with "hard-favour'd rage," as his father, beset by conspirators, had tried and failed to do. Hal can redeem England from its fallen state because he is a flexible and rousing actor. The war in France, begun on the flimsiest of legal pretexts, is only a theatrical occasion, offering Henry V a chance to play his greatest role.

Whether or not Shakespeare treats Hal's heroism ironically is a subject of much critical debate. The fact remains that Hal's power depends on pretense, violating what we cherish today as "sincerity." It is doubtful, however, that a group of corporations can produce a work critical of, or even objective about, the mighty. Moreover, the profit-making habit is hard to shake: Exxon would surely prefer a hero with broad and immediate appeal. The BBC has therefore bowdlerized this difficult character, turning "the warlike Harry" into a really nice person.

This revision owes something to the casting, which, like everything else in these productions, entailed much pointless research: David Gwillim was apparently chosen for the lead because he looks something like the real Henry V as represented in contemporary portraits.

This Henry is a peach. Telling us that he will dump his companions when the time comes, Gwillim makes it sound not like a calculated step but like a cute idea that's just occurring to him. His relationship with Falstaff is without tension, reminding us less of Shakespeare than of Neil Simon: a slob and a prig, sharing a place, bicker adorably. And, in Henry V, when the king condemns to death three would-be assassins, Gwillim's Henry's diatribe is a long passage of exalted wrath, but Gwillim makes it mawkish, choking back the tears and sinking to a bitter whisper. His rejection of Falstaff at the end of Henry IV, Part II is also played weepily, with Henry doing what he must despite his breaking heart.

This tearful moment depends on the complete neutralization of Falstaff's character, which is, in fact, no longer funny in Henry IV, Part II. His banishment is necessary, and no tragedy. The BBC Falstaff, however, does not go from merriment to melancholy, or from any particular mood to any other, since Anthony Quayle's performance is one long coy wheeze. He plays it fat and phlegmy, upstaging the gentle Gwillim with a moist selection of respiratory sound effects. Of all the unfortunate actors in this series, only Jon Finch does credit to the playwright, achieving a performance of isolated brilliance as the bitter and guilt-ridden Henry IV.

The Tempest (BBC, 1980 [PBS, 7 May 1980])

Antonio: Derek Godfrey. *Ariel*: David Dixon. *Caliban*: Warren Clarke. *Ferdinand*: Christopher Guard. *Gonzalo*: John Nettleton. *Miranda*: Pippa Guard. *Prospero*: Michael Hordern. *Stephano*: Nigel Hawthorne. *Trinculo*: Andrew Sachs.

Producer: Cedric Messina. *Director*: John Gorrie. *Designer*: Paul Joel.

Maurice Charney, "Shakespearean Anglophilia," *Shakespeare Quarterly*, 31 (1980). "Everything goes wrong here. . . . As Prospero [Hordern] is so droningly grandfatherish that he puts everyone to sleep as effectively as he does Miranda."

New Orleans *Times-Picayune*, "The Play Isn't the Thing—Hordern Is!" (4 May 1980). Hordern "saves the day with his marvelous performance as Prospero." Also, an interview with Hordern about playing Prospero.

Cecil Smith, *Los Angeles Times* (7 May 1980). "Horrendous . . . a lead-footed, tedious disaster. . . . The play hits bottom when Prospero conjures forth a ballet of dancing elves and fairies [whose clumsiness] is quite embarrassing in a professional production."

Stanley Reynolds, "*The Tempest*," London *Times* (28 Feb. 1980)

There was very little for purists to find fault with in the BBC's new prestige production of *The Tempest* but that perhaps may be the most damning thing you could say about it. An adventurous production might have had them spluttering with rage this morning, and critics scratching their heads trying to make up their minds as to what they really thought. Such, you will recall, was the reaction to Mr. Peter Brook's circus-ring *Midsummer Night's Dream*, which is now remembered as a masterpiece which gave audiences a totally new look at a much-loved play. Alas with *The Tempest*, there was nothing to stir the blood either to hot flashes of anger or to the electric joy of a new experience. What we got was some more of the BBC's ghastly middle taste.

This was yet another stiff production aimed at the archives, and one can certainly see it gathering a lot of dust there in years to come.

John J. O'Connor, *NY Times* (7 May 1980).

The Tempest is one of those dramatic masterpieces that usually read[s] better than [it plays]. The poetry soars, but the elements of magical fantasy tend to get trapped in a kind of gauzy pretentiousness. [This] version is hardly unflawed but, using its own electronic magic, manages to avoid some of the more familiar pitfalls. . . .

Mr. Gorrie's . . . approach . . . is clean and unfussy. Paul Joel's designs are generally uncluttered,

relying on limitless horizons for a sense of almost overwhelming space that subtly reduces mere mortals to the stuff that dreams are made of. . . .

Ariel . . . is out of the flitty-flighty school of stage spirits. But with the help of trick photography, his appearances and disappearances do indeed become magical.

When Ariel is joined at a banquet by several "strange shapes," also stuffed into bikinis, the scene begins to suggest an especially busy weekend at Fire Island. . . . "Heavens, what were these! Such Islanders!"

Dominick Grundy, "The Shakespeare Plays on TV," *Shakespeare on Film Newsletter*, 5:2 (May 1981).

The popular poetic charm of *The Tempest* rests paradoxically on assumptions about authority which a contemporary audience would probably prefer to gloss over. Prospero's magical art of rendering people unable to oppose him, expressed through storm, hypnosis or ague, is power made legitimate by its aim, *his* dukedom. When this is regained his renunciation of the magic is logical, *pace* those who would see him as the artist or hear his epilogue as Shakespeare's.

It is our upside-down fate to watch Shakespearean actors shine in the hierarchically inferior roles. The Stephano-Trinculo-Caliban scenes are well played (Nigel Hawthorne, Andrew Sachs, Warren Clarke), and of the courtiers in the wood, Sebastian and Antonio (Alan Rowe, Derek Godfrey) come off as the most convincing, though they are not as edged and tough as they could be. His Majesty Alonso (David Waller) does a good imitation of a Polish commissar hearing of yet another workers' strike; stolid, well-spoken, yielding not an inch to despair, contrition, or the possible dimensions of his role, he finds himself just "being there."

Thus the best lack all conviction and intensity, and the attractions of this *Tempest* tend either to be negative—there are no gross excesses—or external.

Hamlet (BBC, 1980 [PBS, 10 November 1980])

Claudius: Patrick Stewart. *First Player*: Emrys James. *Fortinbras*: Ian Charleson. *Gertrude*: Claire Bloom. *Hamlet*: Derek Jacobi. *Laertes*: David Robb. *Ophelia*: Lalla Ward. *Polonius*: Eric Porter.

Producer: Cedric Messina. *Director*: Rodney Bennett. *Designer*: Don Homfray.

Russell Davies, London *Times* (1 June 1980). "Patrick Stewart's performance as the King was typical: when in scheming mood and forced by the words to appear to devise something as he went along, he was guileful and fine; but left alone with his conscience, he rambled and gabbled alternately. . . . Derek Jacobi's . . . performance . . . seemed set out as plea rather than protest."

John Lardner, "Changing of the Bard," *Wash-*

ington Post (10 Nov. 1980). "Jacobi told [an interviewer] recently that he had hoped to deliver 'To be or not to be' not as a soliloquy at all, but as an address to Ophelia—perhaps a gloomy form of flirtation. Unfortunately, Director Rodney Bennett would have none of it. . . . But otherwise this is a bold and venturesome production, full of memorable images. . . . The climactic sword fight, instead of degenerating into the usual incomprehensible hodge-podge of blows and blood, is played with unexpected vigor, so that the story gets more involving when it might get less."

John J. O'Connor, *NY Times* (10 Nov. 1980). "This Dane is less melancholy or hesitant than passionate and impetuous. . . . The director sticks largely to a practical conception of *Hamlet* as thriller, as a model of the traditional revenge play. . . . The BBC has fastened upon the hypnotic mood of the play. . . . Claire Bloom here offers a lovely, intelligent, and sympathetic Gertrude. . . . [Jacobi's] is a Hamlet that demands attention and acclaim. . . . Occasionally, [the] bare-bones approach [to the setting] falters. In the graveyard scene, there is just about no place for Hamlet and Horatio to hide from the mourners at Ophelia's funeral."

Cecil Smith, *Los Angeles Times* (10 Nov. 1980). "Shaw once said that Hamlet, born to military barbarism and heir to a blood feud, was incapable of conventional revenge because 'he had evolved into a Christian without knowing it.' . . . Jacobi's Hamlet . . . seems to bear this out . . . his soldier's militancy in deadly battle with his student philosophy." Hamlet and Ophelia "have been lovers; this is unmistakable in the intimate gesture he makes to her in the 'nunnery scene.' . . . The production [is] very stage-bound . . . but the stage belongs to Jacobi . . . a Hamlet you will not soon forget."

NY Times (16 Nov. 1980). "Derek Jacobi . . . portrayed Hamlet with freshness and understaged conviction; we sensed in him a new kind of acting skill, tailored to the tiny screen. Micro-acting. . . . His face, not movie-star handsome but amiable and ordinary, is suited to the micromedium."

Kenneth Rothwell, "The Shakespeare Plays: *Hamlet* and the Five Plays of Season Three," *Shakespeare Quarterly*, 32 (Autumn 1981).

Whatever the reason, the experience of watching Rodney Bennett's *Hamlet* was not entirely satisfactory. Perhaps it should have been presented in two parts; just the physical discomfort of sitting for several hours with no real opportunity to attend to personal needs provides a stumbling block. What appeared on the small screen were a dozen or so talented actors auditioning for roles in *Hamlet* but not performing *Hamlet*. This was Hamlet without a *Hamlet*.

After a splurge of crude Hamlets, hippie Hamlets, boorish Hamlets, and rebellious Hamlets, Jacobi returns to the old-fashioned neurotic Hamlet

of the nineteenth century. The neuroticism, however, includes a tinge of feline hostility not always pleasant to contemplate.

The production works best when Hamlet is closely integrated into the emotional orbit of other characters. The Mousetrap sequences add a novelty when the Prince, like the drama critic Birdboot in Tom Stoppard's *The Real Inspector Hound*, suddenly leaps on stage and gets into the action alongside the player nephew. The subdued tone of Claudius' "Give me some light," however, by making Hamlet look foolish in the eyes of the court, robs him of strength he badly needs to preserve the play's equilibrium. This moment of recognition should be Hamlet's as much as Claudius'. The bed-chamber scene with Gertrude, which seems to borrow abruptly from the Freudian coloration of the old Olivier film, provides splendid histrionics as Hamlet and Gertrude (Claire Bloom) quarrel on and around the royal bed of Denmark.

A word needs to be said about the settings: they suffer from some kind of identity crisis, suggesting that the designer was unable to decide whether to aim for the real or the illusory. In the graveyard scene a stylized funeral procession across an empty space plainly declares that one must imagine a graveyard since none will be supplied at BBC expense. Suddenly, however, a botched attempt is made at providing a real grave, complete with dirt, for Ophelia, whose poor corpse rests on a litter thriftily borrowed, it would seem, from the civil defense people down the hallway. Unaccountably the graveyard is also lit up like the strip at Las Vegas, a lighting effect also thought appropriate for Hamlet's "'Tis now the very witching time of night" speech. Perhaps the real villain is not technology but parsimony. There is no Pentagon budget behind this series, and all too often it shows.

Bernice W. Kliman, "The BBC *Hamlet*, a Television Production," *Hamlet Studies*, 4 (1982).

With *Hamlet*, the producers of the BBC Shakespeare Plays have finally met the demands of Shakespeare-on-television by choosing a relatively bare set, conceding only a few richly detailed movable panels and props to shape key locales. By avoiding both location and realistic settings, they point up the natural affinity between Shakespeare's stage and the undisguised sound set. This starkness of setting admits poetry, heightened intensity—and "what not that's sweet and happy."

The producers have thus made a valid choice from among television's three faces: one, broadcast films, whether made for television or not, which exploit location settings, long shots, and all the clichés we associate with movies, including sudden shifts of space and time and full use of distance, from the most extreme long shots to "eyes only" closeups; two, studio-shot television drama with naturalistic settings, such as the hospital corridors and middle-class living rooms of sit-coms and soap operas, mostly in mid- to close-shots, often interspersed, to be sure, with a bit of stock footage of highways and skylines to establish a realistic environment. This second style varies from a close representation of real action to frankly staged action, where canned laughter or even shadowy glimpses of the studio audience can heighten the staged effect. Three, there is bare space with little or no effort made to disguise that this is a televised activity with a television crew out of sight but nearby. News broadcasts, talk shows and some television drama fit into this third category. Because of its patently unrepresentational quality, this last type offers the most freedom in shooting style. To all three kinds of settings we bring particular expectations in response to their conventions.

Shakespeare's plays work best in the last kind of television space, I believe, because it avoids the clash between realism and poetry, between the unity often expected in realistic media and the disunity and ambiguity of many of the plays, especially *Hamlet*. Yet, while closest to the kind of stage Shakespeare wrote for, the bare television set can be stretched through creative camera work. For example, when Hamlet follows the ghost in the BBC play, the two repeatedly walk across the frame and out of it, first from one direction, then from another; framing fosters the illusion of extended space. Freeing this *Hamlet* from location (as in the BBC *As You Like It*) and from realistic sets (as in the BBC *Measure for Measure*—however well those sets worked for that play) allows the play to be as inconsistent as it is, with, as Bernard Beckerman has so brilliantly explained in *Shakespeare at the Globe, 1599–1609*, a rising and falling action in each individual scene rather than through the course of the drama as a whole. It also allows for acting, the bravura kind that Derek Jacobi is so capable of.

Although gradually coalescing like the pointillism of impressionistic paintings into a subtly textured portrait, at first his mannerisms suggesting madness seem excessive. It is to be expected, perhaps, that Hamlet is a bit unhinged after the ghost scene, but Jacobi's rapid, hard blows to his forehead with the flat of his hand as he says "My tables" recall the desperation of Lear's cry: "O, let me not be mad, not mad, sweet heaven." And soon after, following the last couplet of the scene, Hamlet, maniacally playful, widens his eyes and points, pretending to see the ghost again, then guffaws at Marcellus's fears. Even more unsettling is his laughter when he is alone, as while he is saying "The play's the thing / Wherein I'll catch the conscience of the King." More significantly, he breaks up his own "Mousetrap" by getting right into the play, destroying the distance between audience and stage (a very real raked proscenium-arch stage), spoiling it as a test, because Claudius has a right to be incensed at Hamlet's behavior. Of course, Ham-

let does so because Claudius never gives himself away, an unusual and provocative but not impossible interpretation. Thus, Claudius can only have the court's sympathy as he calmly calls for light and uses it to examine Hamlet closely. Hamlet, in response, covers his face, then laughs.

Hamlet himself thinks he is mad. To Ophelia he says, as if the realization had suddenly struck him, "It *hath* made me mad [emphasis his]" (III.i.147). To his mother he stresses the word "essentially" in "I *essentially* am not in madness" (III.iv.187). That is, in all essential matters he can be considered sane, though mad around the edges. This indeed turns out to be the explanation.

However doubtful about Hamlet's sanity Jacobi's acting leaves us, in this production this question does not seem to make a difference because it does not have a bearing on the tragedy, and this is true at least partly because in each scene on this nonrealistic set we seem to start anew, ready to let Hamlet's behavior tell us if he is mad or not. Moreover, if Hamlet is mad, it is not so totally as to obscure reason or sensibility. Far from it. It is more as if exacerbated reason and sensibility sometimes tip him into madness. This madness is no excuse for action or delay; it is simply part of the suffering that Hamlet is heir to.

Hamlet, then, is left to struggle against himself—surely where Shakespeare intended the struggle to abide. One of the conflicts in this Hamlet results from his affinity, perhaps, more to the bureaucratic Claudius who handles war-scares with diplomacy and who sits at a desk while brooding over his sins than to the warlike King Hamlet who comes in full armor. Hamlet may admire Fortinbras but is himself more like the bookish Horatio. Through nuance of gesture, through body movement, through a face that is indeed a map of all emotions, Jacobi shapes a Hamlet who loves his father too much to disregard his command, yet who cannot hate his step-father enough to attend to it. Because Jacobi conveys so fully Hamlet's aloneness and vulnerability, one could be struck, for the first time, by the ghost's silence about his son. There is no declaration of love, no concern about Hamlet's ascension to the throne. Hamlet is doomed, it seems, to care about those who consistently care more for others than for him.

All of this production's richness and suggestiveness was realized not only because Jacobi is a marvelous actor—as indeed he is—but also because within the set's spareness that acting could unfold, an acting style that subsumes and transcends the "real." This production's space tells us what is possible for television presentations of Shakespeare. The more bare the set, it seems, the more glowing the words, the more immediate our apprehension of the enacted emotion.

The Taming of the Shrew (BBC, 1980 [PBS, 16 January 1981])

Baptista: John Franklyn-Robbins. *Bianca*: Susan Penhagilon. *Grumio*: David Kincaid. *Katherina*: Sarah Badel. *Petruchio*: John Cleese. *Tranio*: Anthony Pedley.
Producer/Director: Jonathan Miller. *Designer*: Colin Lowrey.

Michael Ratcliffe, London *Times* (28 Oct. 1980). Cleese's restraint "gave the show a fine dangerous edge." Badel's Kate was "a nervous hysteric anxious for attention. . . . When she insisted on wearing the trampled little red hat . . . you knew she had got [Petruchio's] measure."

Andrew Sinclair, *The Listener* (30 Oct. 1980). "As fresh and appealing as Shakespeare could possibly be. The casting was inspired. John Cleese had the authority and boorishness of a good Petruchio, yet added his own brand of comic malice . . . And Sarah Badel's Katherina certainly convinced me that she was the ultimate terror tactic against the conspiracy of men. . . . "

Benny Green, *Punch* (5 Nov. 1980). "John Cleese turned up with the best-written part of the week. . . . The upshot was a brooding Petruchio of fitful brilliance, comic rages mingled with genuine despair. . . . His Petruchio [had] seemed at times to be in danger of becoming obscured by the teeth-picking and the beard-tugging. . . . When Sarah Badel delivered that last speech about thy husband being thy lord, thy life, thy keeper, I thought I heard the ghostly laughter of Anne Hathaway floating on the night air."

David Sterritt, *Christian Science Monitor* (23 Jan. 1981). "I've always thought of [Cleese] as an able buffoon . . . but not an actor of Shakespearean range. He proves otherwise here, with a performance that is at once precise, carefully modulated, and ever-so-slightly insane. . . . [He] is capably supported by Sarah Badel as a fiery yet somehow subtle Kate. . . . While TV is far from ideal at conveying dramatic works—lacking the immediacy of the stage and the pictorialism of cinema—its possibilities are richly exploited in this cheerfully untamed Miller production."

David Cuthbert, New Orleans *Times-Picayune* (25 Jan. 1981). "Beautifully done and wonderful fun. . . . Cleese ambles into the play easily, his speech casual and ironic. . . . Badel is an understandable, clearly developed Kate. . . . Miller's staging is quietly, unfailingly ingenious. . . . " Miller sees it " 'as the way the Elizabethans viewed marriage.' "

Tom Shales, *Washington Post* (26 Jan. 1981). "An Elizabethan view of marriage from a time when people reveled in obedience to authority figures. . . . The warfare is mainly psychological between [Cleese] and Sarah Badel's Katherina, a highly enigmatic figure who proves not so much

troublesome as intensely proud of herself and her sex. . . . They make an unspoken bond from early on to go through the sexual roles assigned them even while quietly admiring each other's individuality. . . . Unfortunately, most of the other scenes, while beautifully lit and artfully designed, tend towards antic dullness. Miller . . . chose often to hold a single shot for long, long minutes; characters come forward to the camera to make their speeches, then recede into the background to be replaced by others. It's . . . a Macy's window approach, and not a particularly telegenic one."

G. M. Pearce, *Cahiers Elisabéthains*, 19 (Apr. 1981). "Badel was not subdued and resentful [at the end], but glowed . . . with warmth and contentment, happy to be dominated by such a man. . . . Between the starvation and the degradation she found it quite natural to obey [Petruchio] by the time they set forth back to see her father. Once home again, however, with a husband she could love and respect . . . she realized that she was the winner in the contest and manifestly better off than Bianca. . . . The final scene was far more convincing than usual."

Stanley Wells, "A Prosaic Transformation," *Times Literary Supplement* (31 Oct. 1980).
Jonathan Miller—acting, we must hope, in defiance of his literary consultant John Wilders—offered a simplified version of *The Taming of the Shrew* in this BBC production. To omit the Christopher Sly episodes is to suppress one of Shakespeare's most volatile lesser characters, to jettison most of the play's best poetry, and to strip it of an entire dramatic dimension. In a series announcing itself as "The Complete Dramatic Works of William Shakespeare," this leaves a serious gap.

The consequent reduction of the play's imaginative complexity was reflected in a generally prosaic, literalistic mode of presentation. We opened on a stagy Italianate market place, peripheral touches of local colour being provided by a dwarf, a juggler, an apple-eater and basket-weavers. Baptista's house had lovely interiors reminiscent of Vermeer, sunlit, uncluttered rooms opening into one another through elegant arches with some ingenious mirror effects. The peaceful setting provided an ironic contrast to Kate's fits of temperament. Later, staginess returned, particularly in the closing feast, at which nothing was eaten and precious little drunk.

If a merit of this was to throw emphasis on the actors, Miller could not be said to have evoked a consistent acting style. Some of his performers elected for a stylized, consciously comic mode. Jonathan Cecil endowed Hortensio with a sweetly naive simple-mindedness, an eager, dim-witted charm. One of the production's few genuinely funny sequences was provided by the increasing self-absorption with which he expounded his plot to win Bianca, initially addressing himself to Petruchio but gradually losing all consciousness of his hearer, who looked on with that fascinated, if slightly abstracted, contemplation of folly of which John Cleese is a master.

As Tranio, Anthony Pedley deployed the full armoury of the farce actor, with exaggerated facial expressions and grotesque speech characteristics—dropped and misplaced aspirates, impure vowels, glottal stops, affectations of gentility. If all around him had been playing in the same mode, we might have admired; as they were not, we remained unconvinced. Actors in lesser roles descended to the kind of half-hearted improvisation which may be useful in rehearsal but should be expunged in performance; "*cum privilegio ad imprimendum solum,* i'n it, eh?" said Biondello; and the Pedant added "Was that all right?" to one of his inventions.

By contrast, other performers underplayed their comedy. But the production's main strength lay, fortunately, in the leading actors. John Cleese's splendid physical presence helps him to create strong effects with little apparent effort. We saw the taming process, properly enough, through his eyes. Apart from a few necessary moments of flamboyance and a tendency to cluck amiably from time to time, it was a deeply thoughtful performance, convincing us of the seriousness of Petruchio's intentions. He clearly but unobtrusively established his strong physical attraction to Kate, and their relationship became a wholly credible process of mutual adjustment. Cleese's comic talent came into its own in the scenes following the wedding, in which he works on Kate's body, intellect, and imagination through a series of trials.

Sarah Badel, a comely, bosomy Kate, strong in physique and voice, matched him well. As their relationship developed and matured, we sensed, in her enjoyment of complicity, an inner understanding between the pair which robbed Kate's advice to the other wives of offensiveness and contributed to the deep satisfaction with which Petruchio spoke "Why, there's a wench. . . . "

This was not an inventively funny production, nor a deeply imaginative one. Jonathan Miller had little success in finding the play's natural rhythms and adapting them to the small screen. He ended in anti-climax with Baptista's entire household, directed by Gremio, joining in an added part-song. Domestic cosiness took over from the sense of wonder at a transformation miraculously achieved with which Shakespeare leaves us. Still, we had seen the transformation take place; and in this at least the production justified itself.

Kenneth Rothwell, "The Shakespeare Plays: *Hamlet* and the Five Plays of Season Three," *Shakespeare Quarterly,* 32 (Autumn 1981).

In *The Taming of the Shrew,* which ushered in the third season on 26 January 1981, Director Jonathan Miller filled the screen with witty surprises. Our amazement, however, stemmed not from Artaud-like effects like having Petruchio flying

through the air on a rope over Kate, but rather in the simple audacity with which Miller reversed our normal expectations. The sly joke began with the casting of John Cleese of Monty Python fame as a sober, puritanical Petruchio. By "supposing" that an actor so zany as Cleese could play a Petruchio so sober as this one, Miller at once echoed a major theme of the play, even though he jettisoned the Sly Induction scene. This Petruchio completely overturns the image projected in past flamboyant portrayals by Douglas Fairbanks and Richard Burton.

Sarah Badel's Katherina is full of surprises, too, though the innovation is primarily that there is no innovation. This healthy, aggressive woman, who can throw as stormy a temper tantrum as anyone in Padua, ultimately supports traditional values as set forth in the Anglican wedding vows, which in turn reflect St. Paul's opinions on the authority of the husband. The part-song the banquet guests sing at the close of Act V (Psalm 128, "O blest is he that fears the Lord") signals Miller's view that in Shakespeare's lifetime neither man nor woman was liberated, but each was bound (presumably in love) to the other.

Long after the tube cools off, one recollects with pleasure visually arresting bits of business: Cleese's soliloquy at IV.i, when he shatters the monotony of the talking head with an inventive catalog of yawning, scratching, rubbing of temples and nose, etc.; the sweeping servant at the opening of II.i who establishes the social framework for the Minola household at the same time that she adds a needed third dimension to the Vermeer-like *mise en scène;* the incredible whimpering of Leslie Sarony as Gregory, whose blatant scene-stealing in this energy-charged atmosphere simply adds to the general fun.

Some of this activity can as well be said to be good theatre as good television. For example, Grumio's response to Petruchio's "Villain, I say, knock me at this gate / And rap me well," by exposing the literal sense of the construction, offers an instant lesson in Elizabethan grammar for people whose only knowledge of the ethical dative stems from occasional encounters with a passing redneck. Petruchio's stress on the imperative mood with Grumio foreshadows the domestic imperialism with which he later subdues Kate. Other brilliant theatrical touches include Anthony Pedley's Tranio affecting an upper-class accent while disguised as Lucentio; and Grumio's explication of the meaning of "Lend thine ear" to Curtis, which, it develops, is intended as much to attract the audience's as Curtis' attention. Shakespeare knew how to teach actors the tricks of their trade.

In other respects, this *Shrew* is not only good theatre but adroit television. The problem of ensemble acting has been solved by getting the actors, not the camera, to move. Choreographed blocking allows as many as six actors to whirl their way through a frame, each one getting his share of proper attention. A good example occurs immediately after Kate's wedding. Against a backdrop of doorways and loggias, Baptista, Tranio, Bianca, Lucentio, Gremio, and Biondello chatter about the forthcoming feast. Almost subliminally a bouquet removed from a public fountain is handed from Baptista to Tranio to Bianca to Lucentio to Gremio to Biondello and then back to Baptista. Acting as a bond holding the scene together, it is only one of many cunning touches that make this performance so rewarding to watch. Elsewhere this same setting of doorways and loggias plausibly represents an Italian street with a juggler in the background on the church steps and transients passing by. Rather than offering a barrier to Shakespeare's language— through intelligent editing and camera work, which knows when to hold and when to move on—this realism supports rather than detracts from the spoken word.

Irene G. Dash, "The Shakespeare Plays on TV," *Shakespeare on Film Newsletter*, 6:2 (Dec. 1982).

Enlivened by some fine moments and crushed by some dull ones, this televised *Taming of the Shrew* fails because of the director's culture-bound vision of women.

Discarding the incomplete frame of Shakespeare's text—the appearance of Christopher Sly at the start and his absence at the close—the TV offering substitutes another frame: the producer's discussion of the play's meaning. So infrequently do we hear a producer's voice—except as we exhume his correspondence after his death or note the excisions and transpositions of scenes in prompt-books— that this new "frame" offers valuable insights into readings and misreadings of Shakespeare's comedy. For, though Jonathan Miller believes he is presenting a "liberated" *Taming of the Shrew*, he is still bound by the old clichés. His own words—in conversation with John Cleese, the actor playing Petruchio—betray him. For Miller describes Petruchio's actions as "bringing a spirited steed under control" (!) This inability to see Kate as a whole person informs and mars the work.

Miller presents [Kate] as a compliant woman who delivers that last speech with neither humor nor irony. In the interview following the production, Cleese comes close to understanding Kate. He seems to suspect that she remains "untamed," retaining her self-respect and independent spirit. Cleese notes, and wonders at, the hostility, sharpness, and intellectual vigor in her exchanges with the other women. Miller, however, dismisses these indications of character, explaining that Shakespeare wrote these lines as banter for audience enjoyment. To further support his thesis, Miller alters the ending. Instead of being absent when the foolish Hortensio proclaims her a tamed shrew, Petruchio and Kate are kept onstage. Their presence indicates silent assent. Thus Miller joins a long line

of misogynistic producers who could not accept a strong, attractive Kate.

The Merchant of Venice (BBC, 1980 [PBS, 23 February 1981])

Antonio: John Franklyn-Robbins. *Bassanio*: John Nettles. *Nerissa*: Susan Jameson. *Portia*: Gemma Jones. *Shylock*: Warren Mitchell.
Producer: Jonathan Miller. *Director*: Jack Gold. *Designer*: Oliver Bayldon.

Mervyn Jones, *The Listener* (Dec. 1980). The production "declines to take a stance on the vexed question of whether the play is anti-Semitic. . . . The whole action is presented amid studio sets . . . [that] suggest that the characters are camping out in the ruins of a Roman forum. . . . The sky is permanently lurid and murky. . . . The cast . . . did as little with the characters as they reasonably could. . . . Fatuous laughter . . . is used far too often in the production."

Christian Science Monitor (20 Feb. 1982). "It is a fast-moving, challenging tragicomedic production which loads itself down with stereotypical but believable characters—especially that of Shylock, played with an incessant series of bromidic Jewish mannerisms by Warren Mitchell. Gemma Jones . . . plays Portia with utterly believable intensity. . . . According to Miller and Mitchell, it is indeed a play about anti-Semitism but also about oath vs. obligation, law vs. grace, Old Testament vs. New."

Michiko Kakutani, "Debate over Shylock Simmers Once Again," *NY Times* (22 Feb. 1981). An historical survey of Shylock and the anti-Semitic issue, followed by the usual Big Apple flap—letters in subsequent issues from Thomas Pendleton, Morris U. Schappes, and Karen Takach.

John J. O'Connor, *NY Times* (23 Feb. 1981).

Obviously, a series intended to cover the complete works of Shakespeare can hardly eliminate *The Merchant of Venice*. We are then left with the matter of interpretation. Will Shylock be noble or sentimental or outrageously victimized? Jonathan Miller, the producer, and Jack Gold, the director, both Jewish, have decided to be audacious. This Shylock, portrayed by Warren Mitchell, is something of a seedy pawnbroker, whose Jewishness is unmistakable.

. . . Shylock is firmly established as the "outsider." He is fierce and unapologetic, he believes in himself and his religion. With an absolutely riveting performance from Mr. Mitchell, also Jewish, he is a most worthy protagonist. Oddly enough, he appears in only a handful of scenes but the role dominates the play. . . . This production is splendid, helped immeasurably by the performances of Gemma Jones as Portia, John Nettles as Bassanio and John Franklyn-Robbins as Antonio.

Michael Manheim, "The Shakespeare Plays on TV," *Shakespeare on Film Newsletter*, 5:2 (May 1981)

I had, naturally enough, reservations about the production. The director made a serious error in having Shylock speak his "Hath not a Jew eyes" speech while his tormentors are volubly abusing him. This action draws one's attention away from the important irony that cruel money-lenders may have human feelings. I was also put off by the interpretation of Jessica. Played competently enough by Leslie Udwin, she is seen here as a scheming hussy whose lust for a dissolute Venetian boy is a far cry from the intended innocent Jewish maid responding to the (for her) novel appeals of Petrarchan and Christian love.

G. M. Pearce, "*The Merchant of Venice*," *Cahiers Elisabéthains*, 19 (Apr. 1981).

This production of *The Merchant of Venice* was unusual in having a Jewish producer and director and Jews playing the roles of Shylock and Jessica. . . .

. . . One had been prepared for the emphasis on the Jewish aspect of this *Merchant of Venice*. Unfortunately, this proved to be at the expense of other attributes which were not brought out by the director. The greatest loss was perhaps the casket scenes where Marc Zuber as the Prince of Morocco and Peter Gale as the Prince of Arragon delivered their speeches directly to the camera, while Portia and her retinue remained half hidden in a haze in the background. Not only was all the comedy of the scenes lost, but much of the significance as well.

Elsewhere, Dennis Channon's use of chiaroscuro and hazy lighting enhanced the sets, being particularly attractive in the final scene. The sets (by designer Oliver Bayldon) were, apart from the courtroom scene, mostly outdoor, with a gazebo as the focal point of Portia's garden, flanked by formally shaped shrubs and classical pillars. When the scene shifted inside Portia's house for the caskets, there was still an illusion of space and light. The streets of Venice were tinged with pink and there was very effective use of back-lighting to dramatize Shylock's first appearance as he emerged suddenly from the obscurity of an archway. This technique was used again later.

The costumes were contemporary, in rich colours and fabrics with extravagant hats. Even the downtrodden Jessica, before her elopement, wore a most opulent gown. The careful grouping of the elegantly dressed crowd amongst pink marble pillars evoked many memories of Renaissance paintings.

The outstanding performance of the evening came from Warren Mitchell as Shylock. His comic stock Jewish accent and frequently undignified behaviour were allowed now and again to slip in order to reveal the intensity of passion and pain beneath. This was most striking in the trial scene at the moment when he was forced to adopt Christianity, which was portrayed here as a far greater punishment than the loss of his money. Most original was his rendering of the "Hath not a Jew" speech, which he did with many gestures in rib-tickling proximity to Salerio and Salanio up to the words "Shall we not revenge," where the sudden silence and switch in mood added greatly to the sinister implications of the speech.

Although the audience was allowed to feel sympathy for Shylock, there was nothing but hatred for him from daughter Jessica, played, not with the usual modesty associated with this role, but with vehemence and venom by Leslie Udwin. She even mouthed Shylock's stock proverb with an expression of extreme hatred behind his back in their scene together. The good-looking black-bearded Lorenzo of Richard Morant would have no easy task keeping this "gentle Jessica" under control. The Nerissa of Susan Jameson was more an accomplice and no mere follower of her mistress Portia, played by Gemma Jones. Her Portia was brisk, efficient, cool and business-like, rather than romantic. She was at her best in the trial scene with her wispy blonde hair concealed under the severe head-gear and her ascetic features suited to the masculine and legal disguise. Despite her evident command of the situation, the compassion whose cause she pleads so eloquently showed in her face both for Antonio and for Shylock in his total defeat. This same compassion was manifest at the end towards Antonio (John Franklyn-Robbins), who was utterly downcast by the transfer of Bassanio's affection to Portia and whose evident infatuation with Bassanio gave additional meaning and coherence to this aspect of the plot. John Nettles, whose speaking of the verse was impeccable, was perhaps too noble as Bassanio and did not give much evidence of the self-seeking side of this character.

The casual cruelty of society was underlined by the pathetic portrayal of Old Gobbo by Joe Gladwin in his reunion with Launcelot Gobbo (Enn Reitel in an energetic performance). This cruelty was echoed in the extreme venom of Gratiano (Kenneth Cranham) towards Shylock at the trial. Salerio (John Rhys-Davies with a rich mellifluous Welsh accent) and Salanio (a sardonic Alan David) had merely mocked Shylock up till now and it was left to Gratiano to demonstrate the full force of anti-Semitic feeling.

Warren Mitchell will surely be remembered as one of the great Shylocks and it is a pity that other important aspects of the plot were not given equal weight. While Shylock's fate may be the dominant theme, Portia's destiny has at least as much of the text devoted to it, and by underplaying this, much of the comedy was lost. Apart from this, however, it was a pleasing production visually and a stimulating evening's entertainment.

The Merry Wives of Windsor (Bard Productions, Ltd., 1981)

Doctor Caius: Joel Asher. *Falstaff*: Leon Charles. *Mistress Ford*: Valerie Seelie-Snyder. *Mistress Page*: Gloria Grahame. *Mistress Quickly*: Dixie Tymitz.

Producer: R. Thad Taylor. *Director*: Jack Manning.

Staged by the Globe Playhouse in Los Angeles for the Shakespeare Society of America.

John H. Stodder and Lillian Wilds, *Shakespeare Quarterly*, 31 (Summer 1980). (Stage.) A positive review that says that "Taylor's videotaped version [maintained] the . . . polish and flair."

Jeanne Addison Roberts, "*The Merry Wives of Windsor*," *Shakespeare on Film Newsletter*, 6:2 (Mar. 1982).

The Bard Productions videocassette of a performance of *The Merry Wives of Windsor* staged at the Globe Playhouse in Los Angeles for the Shakespeare Society of America is a welcome addition to Shakespeare on screen.

The production itself is marked by fine performances by key characters. Leon Charles is a Falstaff of convincing corpulency, with strongly marked features and a forceful presence which makes him genuinely reminiscent of the Falstaff of the Boar's Head Tavern. When he says in the last scene, "I was three or four times in thought that they were not fairies," one fancies for a breathless second that he may recover from deception as miraculously as he did at Gad's Hill. Gloria Grahame's Mistress Page is also unusually effective. Her resonant voice and beautiful articulation work splendidly to signal a sudden shift from realism to myth as she intones her key speech in IV.iv about the old tale of Herne the Hunter, while her cohorts line up ritualistically to recite their parts, and a mysterious black-cloaked figure emerges to dance about them.

The set, in spite of the vaunted Elizabethan authenticity of the stage, seems in the filming rigid and confining. A busy backdrop intended to suggest Tudor architecture in a rural village distracts from central images throughout and is particularly annoying in the last scene when it is only partially covered by a painted "forest." Having gone so far with scenery, the designers might well have provided a more reasonable facsimile of Herne's Oak. Costume design, generally conventional Renaissance style and quite acceptable, also fails in the last scene with Falstaff's horns, which are disappointingly unbestial and are never doffed for his return to social reconciliation.

At several points the staging is particularly striking. In his first assignation with Mistress Ford, Falstaff kneels before her melodramatically, then suddenly grabs her ankle and wrestles her to the floor before the timely arrival of Mistress Page. At his second assignation a cuckoo clock appropriately tolls the hour. The generation of the magical quality of the final scene by intoned lines, mysterious shapes, and strange noises, convincing as it is, probably worked better on the stage, because the spell is broken in the videotape by a distance shot which features a large meaningless expanse of bare stage with indistinct figures clustered at its fringe. At other times the taped version solves stage problems with close-ups showing masks and costumes which both conceal and reveal. The Fairy Queen is unmistakably Quickly, and Evans can be sorted out by shape as well as accent. The "pinching" however, looks more like tossing in a blanket, and the proximity of the camera adds to the difficulty of accepting this part of the scene as ritual. On balance the confusion frequently engendered on the stage seems preferable to the explicitness of a close view.

Antony and Cleopatra (BBC, 1981 [PBS, 20 April 1981])

Antony: Colin Blakely. *Caesar*: Ian Charleson. *Cleopatra*: Jane Lapotaire. *Enobarbus*: Emrys James.

Producer/Director: Jonathan Miller. *Designer*: Colin Lowrey.

Michael Ratcliffe, London *Times* (8 May 1981). "Miller's first triumph [is] the verse-speaking . . . neither numbingly 'musical' nor mindlessly modern; it simply makes sense. The second is the casting. . . . Colin Blakely's marvellous and moving performance restores the warm-blooded, witty and gentle soldier of huge capacity for loving and attracting love . . . Lapotaire's Queen radiates nervous high spirits and mischief. . . . Through . . . an overall use of intelligence and scale, a great play is brought to life."

Miles Kington, London *Times* (8 May 1981). A review of a television show featuring Jonathan Miller's direction of the production.

Henry Mitchell, *Washington Post* (20 Apr. 1981). "Gorgeous . . . handsomely, even superbly mounted—it is hard to ask more of the jiggly medium."

John J. O'Connor, *NY Times* (20 Apr. 1981). "In the end . . . Mr. Miller's grand scheme fails. Too much of the romance and glamour is eliminated. . . . The sight of Cleopatra and her servants sitting around in elaborate upswept hairdos and wearing ornate necklaces and earrings is simply ludicrous. In fact, Mr. Miller has created what he professes to loathe. The scene suggests nothing more than a suburban tea at which the beautiful ladies have decided to mount an afternoon theatrical. Even Hollywood glamour is preferable."

Cecil Smith, *Los Angeles Times* (20 Apr. 1981). Blakely "marvelous." Lapotaire "a bright and witty suburban housewife with whom a soldier like Antony might dally but hardly one for whom he would give up being one of the rulers of the Roman world. . . ." Enobarbus's description of her and her barge, then, obviously a put-on of the Roman staff officers. Production "has vigor . . . brawn . . . wit . . . and clarity."

Jack Kroll, "Dr. Miller's Shakespeare," *Newsweek* (27 Apr. 1981). "In *Antony* [Miller] galvanizes the screen with the canted angles, pleated draperies and sensual tints of a . . . Veronese. But in his zeal to cut the fat out of Shakespeare, he has undercut the tragic dimension. . . . Much of the time Miller's Antony and Cleopatra behave more like Wilbur Mills and Fanne Foxe than Shakespeare's world figures deeply divided between grandeur and meanness of spirit."

Charles Lower, *Shakespeare on Film Newsletter*, 6:2 (Mar. 1982). The production is "smallish, almost domestic. . . . The title pair capture and sustain viewer attention, minor characters such as Emrys James' Enobarbus are distinctive and memorable, and the richly costumed production has lively pacing."

G. M. Pearce, *Cahiers Elisabéthains*, 20 (Oct. 1981). "A satisfying experience. . . . The rich costumes were a visual treat and the uncluttered set and use of close-ups allowed us to concentrate on the actors. . . . Jane Lapotaire . . . not only displayed her quicksilver temperament with Antony, but with all her entourage, and all were aware of her magnetic attraction. . . . Colin Blakely gave her a virile and hot-tempered Antony to love . . . a soldier first and foremost, with an expansive personality which tended to a laissez-faire attitude towards life."

Nicholas Shrimpton, "Shakespeare: In Miniature . . . ," *Times Literary Supplement* (15 May 1981). Jonathan Miller's production of *Antony and Cleopatra* proves to be an extended pun on the word "composed." His Egypt is the Orient of Veronese's "The Family of Darius before Alexander," where Renaissance ladies in satin and ringlets meet Roman heroes in shapely cuirasses and greaves. And, like Veronese, Miller chooses to arrange these characters into expressive tableaux before unashamedly one-dimensional settings. On occasion such painterly conceptions produce a ravishing interplay of foreground and background. A wordlessly fretful Cleopatra, for example, is glimpsed between Charmian and the Soothsayer. The mourning Caesar is framed by his officers as he weeps in the depths of his tent. But on the whole it is the surface plane with which we are concerned. Actors play, seemingly, inches from the lens. Inches behind them stand backdrops. The predominant effect is of complicated events in a crowded corridor.

The reason why this elegant constriction does not produce mere fuss and bother is the other point of the pun. Miller's *Antony and Cleopatra* is composed in the emotional as well as in the artistic sense. Colin Blakely's jaunty gamecock of an An-

tony is an anomalously noisy man in a quiet world. Caesar speaks in a dour Scots whisper, Pompey with the calculating murmur of a thug on the make. Even Cleopatra, though she allows herself moments of aristocratic sprightliness, is a model of elegant manners and fills the play with uncustomary calm.

The joint effect of visual and verbal serenity is, of course, evidence of how deeply Jonathan Miller has pondered his medium. Television is both flat and intimate. Shakespeare's theatre was neither, and the director who seeks to transfer its texts to the screen must come to terms with the disparity. After the echoing halls and lengthy vistas of *Timon of Athens*, the BBC Shakespeare has now turned to a kind of theatrical bas-relief, designing static and shallow pictures which are studied with unblinking care. Pompey, Menas and Menecrates discuss tactics in a rigid, full-frontal line. Enobarbus outstares the viewer as he button-holes us with his shame. And when this insinuating camera is not putting us into bed with Cleopatra, it is giving us a beautician's view of Iras's pimples.

Hand in hand with this steady intimacy goes a necessary elimination of the heroic gesture. The clutter of entrance and exit lines ("From Sicyon, ho, the news? Speak there!") is an obvious choice when a director is obliged to cut. In theory such material is redundant as soon as an actor can sidle into shot rather than stride on from a tiring house. And its absence undoubtedly helps to reduce the clangour and remoteness of the play.

In practice, however, it is the persistent omission of this trivial material which first prompts doubts about the susceptibility of *Antony and Cleopatra* to intelligent miniaturization. It is arguable that Shakespeare gave his Antony too few heroic lines in the first place. Take away the opportunity to be imperious even to his messengers and his status as a triple pillar of the world becomes incredible. Despite his lack of inches, Blakely resists the idea that Antony is fallen from the first, and does his best to project a commanding manner. But the production's stillness restricts his finest effects to private life and turns his martial mode to bluster.

All about him people behave as if they already knew that there was to be a death in the house. At one point I even began to wonder whether Dolabella might not appropriately be replaced by a new character called Decibella, round from the Tribunate of the Environment to monitor a noise abatement order. In such circumstances he prospers best who whispers best, and the triumphs of the production are Emrys James's Enobarbus and Ian Charleson's Caesar. The latter somehow combines a stony inhibition with a naked itch for power, and caps them with a splendid account of the repressed man breaking down once his ends are finally achieved. James senses the opportunities which an intimate stage style gives to the playing of Enobarbus and exploits them greedily. His back-stairs manner and his secret crisis of conscience are both delightful; his delivery of "The barge she sat in" as lascivious male gossip over the after-dinner port casts real new light into the play. Both men benefit mightily from Miller's distinctive combination of visual invention and psychological aptness.

In their best moments Colin Blakely and his Cleopatra, Jane Lapotaire, benefit from these things too. Breaking the news of Fulvia's death, or achieving the difficult reconciliation after the sea-battle, they generate an authentic emotion. But their inhibiting context works constantly against them. Jane Lapotaire's early endeavours to suggest the wanton are stifled by the chilly elegance of her dress. By the final act, when the same costume might help the regal dignity of her dying, the visual style has shifted and she chokes out her final speeches, very much an ordinary woman, in a voluminous nightie. Within its careful limits this *Antony and Cleopatra* moves very surely. But it is a smaller thing than Shakespeare.

H. R. Coursen, "The BBC-TV *Antony and Cleopatra*: Far More Harm Than Good."

In addressing a disaster as unmitigated and as monumental as Dr. Miller's *Antony and Cleopatra*, one is at a loss as to where to begin. I begin by saying that this production is bound to contaminate the attitudes of thousands of students towards this magnificent script. I hope that it is only thousands—it may be millions who will reject Shakespeare on the basis of their dismal experience of one of his masterworks. Faced with this production, we teachers can only claim "Believe it or not, this is a great play!" Students, however, tend to believe what the tube shows them, not what we teachers tell them.

Miller insists on coming out in advance of his productions to chat with us. The chatter is arrogant, patronizing, and reductive. We learn that *Shrew* will be hollowed-out to conform with Miller's conceptions of late sixteenth-century male-female norms. Thus is Sarah Badel robbed of her role at the outset by directorial fiat. We learn that *Merchant* should not even be produced, since it is anti-Semitic. We are told that Cleopatra is a "treacherous slut," even as the actress playing the part asserts that Cleopatra is "fun to be with." I have encountered treacherous sluts in my time, but I seldom found it fun.

Miller's approach is all wrong from the outset. Instead of an imaginative entrance to the production, we are subjected to opinion, a quasi-ideational format, delivered, literally, off-the-cuff, a revelation of directorial intention that defeats whatever dramatic intentions the production might reveal. Framing is vital, as Shakespeare shows so often *via* choruses, misdirected challenges, Weird Sisters, and apparent shipwrecks, and as Olivier

demonstrated in that superb approach to the Globe Theater at the beginning of his *Henry V*, and in his return to it at the end. Miller might have employed an old map of the world—Italy's boot separated from tropic Alexandria by "our sea." The world is the issue, and divisions within it the drama. The map might absorb color, and the camera might zoom in towards Egypt, where, perhaps unexpectedly, Philo's Roman thought might strike us. The framing I suggest might have prepared us for Miller's awkward and confusing treatment of Actium. Ah, but I am designing an alternative production, as I did with increasing impatience throughout Miller's version.

By imposing the "old masters"—Veronese, in this case—upon his production, Miller erased the distinction the play makes between Rome and Egypt. Thus Miller also erases the conflict suffered by the play's hero, Mark Antony. Cleopatra and her court—with the exception of dusky Iras—could have been in Rome. Octavia could have been Cleopatra. Rome is of swords and columns, of the eagle, of consciousness, sobriety, and control, of precise measurement and efficient logistics, of military intelligence, and of power in this world. Its complete figure is cool Octavius. Rome is yang. Egypt is of recumbent pleasure, fertility, excess, of Keats's bursting grape against the palate, it is the zone of the serpent. It is warm and sensuous, a place where men lose their swords and soldiership, where Roman phallicism yields to liquidity, to ooze and slime. It is yin. Cleopatra. Torn between these extremes is Antony, who would remain a triumvir, who would retain Cleopatra. He can find no midway between these extremes.

Miller showed us none of this. In his effort to escape the Hollywood, Elizabeth Taylor vision of Egypt, Miller forgets that Cleopatra's production on the River Cydnus—if Enobarbus be accurate—outworks even the fancies of C. B. DeMille. Miller, it would seem, was simply not up to his own imaginative re-creation of a central contrast which defines the central conflict.

In his effort to create the patina of an old master, Miller forgets that he is working with drama. Not painting. It is as if he took his scene designer and lighting director to the National Gallery, pointed at a canvas, and said, "There! That's what I want." Such an approach *can* work in some of the static set-piece scenes of *Merchant*, a play that offers, after all, a "High Renaissance" setting and style. But the approach failed in *Antony and Cleopatra*. Drama was stifled beneath canvas. The confrontation between Caesar and Antony (II.ii), for example, *was* pictorially beautiful, ornate goblets and bowls of fruit glinting and glowing in the foreground. But what happens in the scene? One could argue that Caesar manipulates Antony adroitly into condemning Egypt's "poisoned hours," then, via

Agrippa, springs the trap of marriage to Octavia. Caesar draws his great competitor into the "double bind" that typifies poor Antony's conflict.

I maintain not that this reading is the only one the scene will bear but that *any* sense of anything dramatic happening was trapped behind the beautiful picture. We were given a tour through a museum, not a play, and certainly not *this* play.

While good acting could not have struggled free from ancient oil, the casting for this production was egregious. A short, pathetic Antony, who, never having been on the hill, could not be over it. A sexless Cleopatra. Whatever the field of her infinite variety, a depth of female sensuality lies close to the heart of her mystery, as Janet Suzman demonstrated in her successful Cleopatra some years ago. Whatever ironies abound within and around each character, they must convince us that one is a "Herculean Roman," the other suited to "the habiliments of the goddess Isis." Since neither tried to touch mythology, we could not believe that such diminished beings were capable of the grand passion the play explores. At their best they were, as Jack Kroll suggested, "like Wilbur Mills and Fanne Fox" (*Newsweek*, 27 April 1981). At their worst, they bickered petulantly, this treacherous slut and this sad old man. It was Edward Albee, not William Shakespeare. We were subjected again, as in *Shrew*, to the "bright idea" that glows dimly from directorial ego, and that casts Shakespeare into the outer darkness.

If we cannot believe that something other than game-playing and manipulation lies below the surface, if we cannot believe in the love, or passion at least, of these two great figures—however destructive and self-destructive—we cannot believe the play itself. Cleopatra's arias to and about Antony in Act V become, then, efforts to create what was never there in the first place—self-refuting rationalizations. She becomes as pathetic in her hyperbole as was the silly, self-deluded drunk she claims to have loved. The "god, Hercules" never leaves Antony in this production—that wonderful scene (IV.iii) was cut. Wisely was it cut, for Hercules had never visited this Antony, except perhaps in his fantasies.

Beautiful pictures cannot compensate for bad casting, obvious under-rehearsal, or for the director's unwillingness to seek the tensions and conflicts of the play and its every scene. As Kroll says, "Miller, like many modern skeptics, is suspicious of the very idea of greatness and passion." Well, so am I, existentially. But our own narrowness meets its compensatory energy in a great and passionate play like *Antony and Cleopatra*. Miller's defense against what Shakespeare understood is to filter the play to us via Veronese, thereby rendering the play static, passionless, undramatic, and frozen in a time that Shakespeare should be allowed to transcend.

All's Well that Ends Well (BBC, 1981 [PBS, 18 May 1981])

Bertram: Ian Charleson. *Countess*: Celia Johnson. *Diana*: Pippa Guard. *Helena*: Angela Down. *King*: Donald Sinden. *Lavache*: Paul Brooke. *Lafeu*: Michael Hordern. *Parolles*: Peter Jeffrey. *Producer*: Jonathan Miller. *Director*: Elijah Moshinsky. *Designer*: David Myerscough-Jones.

Corinna Adam, *The Listener* (8 Jan. 1981). "Miller knows how to make people speak."

Russell Davies, London *Times* (11 Jan. 1981). "A memorably brainy performance from Angela Down."

Benny Green, *Punch* (14 Jan. 1981). "The programme was elegantly mounted and intelligently acted, with Miss Johnson and Angela Down taking the honours and Donald Sinden conveying regal authority with a voice redolent of adhesive fruitcake."

John J. O'Connor, *NY Times* (18 May 1981). "It works surprisingly well on television. . . . Donald Sinden is masterfully authoritative and convincing. . . . Pippa Guard . . . just about steals every scene she's in. . . . Too much of the dialogue is delivered in a kind of ominous hush."

Cecil Smith, *Los Angeles Times* (18 May 1981). "A beautiful production . . . admirably played."

Lon Tuck, *Washington Post* (18 May 1981). "The lights and setting make the most of [Angela] Down's ephemeral fragility [as Helena]. . . . Celia Johnson, one of the finest actresses of the Olivier-Gielgud generation [gives] a performance of real distinction [as the Countess of Rousillon]."

G. M. Pearce, *Cahiers Elisabéthains*, 19 (Apr. 1981). "An impressive cast. . . . The only discordant note was Ian Charleson's Bertram, played as a sullen angry young man, only believable in the naked lust he portrayed for Diana. . . . Angela Down was a very cerebral Helena with just sufficient invitation in her behaviour to justify the King of France's submission and attraction to her. . . ."

Kenneth Rothwell, "The Shakespeare Plays: *Hamlet* and the Five Plays of Season Three," *Shakespeare Quarterly*, 32 (Autumn 1981).

For a variety of reasons, some of them having to do with the play itself, Elijah Moshinsky's *All's Well that Ends Well* turned out to be the hit of the season. A major cause, I would suggest, was the director's willingness to collaborate actively with technical people like lighting designer John Summers, whose resourcefulness makes the cloning of seventeenth-century Dutch art possible on the television screen. This visual energy, with inspiration from both Rembrandt and Vermeer, strongly supports the verbal wizardry of the Shakespearean text: light [spilling] from a window silhouettes Angela Down as Helena in profile before her spinet; a high-angle shot of the King of France in bed silently comments on the plight of a fallen monarch;

women at domestic tasks come alive in rich vibrant hues of Flemish masters; doctors peer at the King of France in a grouping borrowed from Rembrandt's "The Anatomy Lesson;" courtiers move through the baroque splendor of a hall of mirrors; and a fire glows richly and warmly in a room occupied by Bertram and Helena. This is a visual feast.

A controlling metaphor is the mirror, used much the same way as in Miller's *Shrew*. It expands the tiny world of the *mise en scène*, gives it a third dimension, and at the same time suggests the conflicting planes of perception and reality that make up Helena's and Bertram's fractured worlds. Parolles, for example, is glimpsed in the mirror above Helena's spinet, as though to underscore the fictitiousness of his essential being. The mirror also reminds us that Parolles' willingness to sacrifice any principle to achieve doubtful ends applies as well to Bertram and Helena. Helena pursues Bertram as ruthlessly as Bertram spurns Helena. In this unforgiving city comedy, there is no magic forest where an Oberon can restore a Helena to harmony through the agency of a love potion. In their lying and deceit, Helena and Bertram can match Parolles in craft. These bitter truths, too painful for firsthand viewing, are best but glimpsed in a mirror.

Angela Down plays Helena as though she were possessed, a witch in fact. The plain, spinsterish, puritanical face with the unruly strands of hair conceals a volcanic disposition, a point nicely punctuated when Down's Helena exchanges an erotic kiss with the King of France. Ian Charleson, superb as the snotty Bertram, returns her proffers of affection with the arrogance of a Guards officer bawling out orders to the troops at Buckingham Palace. The veteran Michael Hordern turns in his usually polished performance, this time as Lafeu, the scourge of Peter Jeffrey's pathetic Parolles. Generous portions of the text, mostly prose passages steeped in the inimitable scurrilities of Jacobean satire, have been deleted. The sacrifice of such details as Lavache's learned commentary on the "pin" and "quatch" buttocks seems a reasonable trade-off for the pace and energy generated in this memorable performance.

Herbert Weil, Jr., "The Shakespeare Plays on TV," *Shakespeare on Film Newsletter*, 7:1 (Dec. 1982).

Elijah Moshinsky's *All's Well* impresses us as one of the best BBC productions because of fine casting and extremely intelligent and sensitive performing and editing. One admires this director's close attention to the lines and feels that, despite the extensive cutting, he faces rather than evades the basic problems of the play. Angela Down, cool, troubled, flexible, and restrained, complements particularly well the exceptional pictorial settings that skillfully evoke the lighting, the casements, mirrors, and drapery of Vermeer.

Even those pleased with this production could hardly have expected its brilliant consummation in the notorious conclusion which so infrequently has convinced readers and spectators that Bertram has become worthy. In the film, Bertram seems to repent until, confronted by the ring, he lies and slanders Diana outrageously. Diana playfully riddles, seems to insult the King, and with a superbly shot eye movement, suggesting both magic and seduction, as a new soft musical theme begins, declares, "Behold the meaning." With a technique impossible on stage but finely suited to the screen, the camera very slowly pans from right to left (probably recalling Helena's choice), finding first Parolles, then the smiling Diana, then Lafeu, the King, the Countess, and finally Bertram. We see their eyes and mouths express their wonder as they see Helena—before we finally see her.

The scene is strikingly effective and some of us can now believe in the sincerity of this Bertram's brief promise to "love her dearly, ever, ever dearly." The production omits the Epilogue and fittingly concludes with Lafeu requesting from Parolles his dirty, smelly handkerchief—but then declining to use it. The music continues and the camera circles, pauses, and finds the King for his concluding couplet.

Macbeth (ARTS, 3 March 1982)

Banquo: Fritz Sperberg. *Duncan*: Neil Vipond. *Lady Macbeth*: Maureen Anderman. *Macbeth*: Phil Anglim. *Macduff*: J. K. Campbell. *Malcolm*: John Vickery.

Producers: Richmond Crinkley, John Goberman. *Directors*: Sarah Caldwell (Lincoln Center Repertory Company), Kirk Browning (ARTS). A Lincoln Center for the Performing Arts stage production of 1981.

Maurice Charney and Arthur Ganz, "Shakespeare in New York City," *Shakespeare Quarterly*, 33 (1982). (Stage.) Caldwell "chose to remove the forestage and work within a conventional proscenium opening. This curious decision meant that for the verse . . . to be heard almost all the action had to be played along the curtain line with the murky reaches of the Beaumont stage stretching, visible but largely unused, behind it. . . . A great spindly catwalk . . . made a striking effect at moments . . . but was sometimes a disastrous impediment. . . . Maureen Anderman did not entirely escape the familiar Dragon Lady mode [but] did manage an excellent sleepwalking scene."

H. R. Coursen, "*Macbeth*. Lincoln Center for the Performing Arts. Directed by Sarah Caldwell."

This is a solid production, a good one for students. It delivers the script without gimmicks or "bright ideas." It does not have the luminous Janet Suzman as Lady Macbeth, but it does not have the ludicrous Nicol Williamson as Macbeth either.

This is a television version of a live stage production. Indeed, as Macbeth talks of a "sure and firm set earth," a bald head sits surely in the firm-set first row.

While the audience is permitted to applaud and the actors to take curtain calls, the sense of "theatrical event" is uneven. The Papp-Jones *King Lear* of 1974 used its Central Park audience as part of the "texture" of the TV experience. The Stratford, Canada, *Shrew* of 1982 employed the audience as an outer component of a highly "meta-theatrical" event. Here the audience was seen, it seems, simply because long shots could not avoid including the first few rows. So the two media, stage and television, are uneasy with each other. The camera angles are very conventional, but they incorporate backstage spotlights, which make the torches carried by some of the characters anachronistic and unnecessary. The TV production used titles between the scenes, a "silent screen" technique that further confused the generic issue and slowed the pell-mell pace of this play.

But, as with many productions of "The Scottish Play," this one got better as it went along. Anglim was unconvincing at first, having studied his lines carefully but not having settled on a style that worked either for stage or TV. The lines, while well-articulated, had no subtextual energy or intention working through them. But Anglim improved as he descended from his coronation for the chilling catechism for Banquo. Macbeth's final question was cued by Fleance's appearance at his father's side. Macbeth's "Tomorrow" speech was a moving expression of grief, accented by a tear. At the end, he tossed his shield aside, refused his sword, crossed himself vaguely, accepted Macduff's sword, and sighed "enough" after the fatal thrust. This was an interesting reading, in which Macbeth becomes more sympathetic as he becomes a victim of the negative world he chooses to explore.

Anderman's Lady, at the outset, was cold and commanding, but not overpowering. She didn't pull the silly sexual stunts that so diminished the Ladys of Lapotaire and Laurie, each attempting hysterically to compensate for opposite deficiencies: starveling scrawniness in the one, thick rotundity in the other. Anderman became more sensuous as the production progressed, kissing Macbeth at the Banquet Scene, for example, as if to say, "There—it's all right now!" Her mad scene, hair down around a chalky face, one hand stretched upward, was grippingly good. Since Macbeth seemed such a paltry object for her affection and ambition, her early scenes with him were flat. The Murder Scene was splendid, however, and achieved the power that is in the scene but not often realized in production. Anderman showed that this is Lady Macbeth's scene (for all of Macbeth's frenzy) by nerving herself up for the long walk back to Duncan's chamber with the daggers and by returning with almost hys-

terical good humor. She convinced us that she had been in that room only seconds before. The sense of a failed relationship between thane and wife came through more strongly as the play developed than I would have thought possible, since Anglim and Anderman hadn't established a relationship at the outset, as Ian McKellen and Judi Dench had, for example, in the Trevor Nunn 1979 version.

Of several good moments in this production, a few are worth special noting: Fleance playing at soldier with his father's sword: Macbeth's sudden and reluctant knee as Duncan named Malcolm Prince of Cumberland; Macbeth's exit from the upstage banquet for Duncan, Lady Macbeth's pursuit a moment later, and their return in resolution to kill the happy guest; Banquo's first appearance as a silver-gray corpse along the catwalk that rode over the stage, and the later line of spectral kings along the same slender bridge; the Weird Sisters' delight at Macbeth's threat to curse them eternally ("the curse is on *you!*"). While I feel that the lines in IV.iii about Edward the Confessor are important and should not be cut, as they were here, the scene in England was splendid. The point was that Scotland (represented by Macduff) does not know Malcolm. Nor is Malcolm certain that Scotland wants the "king-becoming graces" he represents. He will not return unless Macduff confirms the need for the spiritual antithesis to Macbeth. (And that is one reason why Malcolm's sponsor, Edward, should be given his encomia.) The Malcolm-Macduff exchange worked brilliantly here, as it did in the 1976 Gorrie production. We, like Macduff, must learn who this prince and future king is (and is not), if we are to believe in his crusade. We have no problems, moments later, in believing in Macduff's vehement role in that crusade. Malcolm's final speech was potently rendered, from the commanding position of the catwalk. Gorrie's Malcolm let no one get near him ("I remember what happened to my father!"). Nunn's Malcolm was exhausted—a great force has left us, however malign, and we have little to replace it with. Gold's Malcolm was upstaged by Fleance (in the BBC version), a confusing and needless borrowing from the pernicious Polanski, where Donalbain sought out those wired sisters at the end of that clattering film. The ending here carried not just Malcolm's conviction, but the sense of the script as well.

I question the production on a point or two. The Weird Sisters were two out-of-work strippers and a soldier. No beards, but Banquo's line was there. What do modern directors think the line means? While the sisters and brother sang some of the opening rhymes, this Verdian effect was not carried through by Miss Caldwell, whose genre is opera. Why did she cut the ingredients of the witches' stew later on? Now that might have made a little night music! Macbeth at the Banquet "woke up" after Banquo's second visitation and found himself standing on his own festive board. He jumped off and got a laugh from the outer audience, even as the inner audience remained appalled. At any rate, the scene did not crack the outer audience up into that helpless, tear-stained, roll-in-the-aisle hilarity that it can induce. The Porter got some necessary laughs as he sparred with his straight-man, Macduff, but his soliloquy was cut. Too bawdy for sober yuppies? The sureness of Shakespeare's dramaturgy is only emphasised by such omissions.

And, finally, the stage amplification was not suited to the tube. The sound was not balanced in volume and, at moments, the television auditor trembled on the brink of his decibel-limit. Aside from some minor negatives, I find this a good production that educates us about its conventions and its characters as it goes along. It deserves a place on our video shelves alongside the Gorrie and Nunn versions.

The Winter's Tale (BBC, 1980 [PBS, 8 June 1981])

Autolycus: Rikki Fulton. *Florizel*: Robin Kermode. *Hermione*: Anna Calder-Marshall. *Leontes*: Jeremy Kemp. *Paulina*: Margaret Tyzack. *Perdita*: Debbie Farrington. *Polixenes*: Robert Stephens.

Producer: Jonathan Miller. *Director*: Jane Howell. *Designer*: Don Homfray.

Anthony Masters, London *Times* (9 Feb. 1981). Criticizes pace and settings, praises Anna Calder-Marshall ("an unusually petite, feminine Hermione"), Jeremy Kemp's "effectively underplayed Leontes," and Margaret Tyzack's "Paulina of regal tremendousness whose 'What studied torments' speech was truly thrilling."

Joseph McLellan, *Washington Post* (8 June 1981). "The essential unreality of the play has been warmly embraced. [The] scanty, semi-abstract scenery [is] appropriate for a story whose true location is never-never land, and the cameras spend little of their time on background and much on close-ups—a device that Shakespeare would have loved. . . . Particularly notable in a fine cast are Jeremy Kemp, who makes the madness of Leontes believable, Margaret Tyzack . . . and Rikki Fulton playing the rogue Autolycus."

John J. O'Connor, *NY Times* (8 June 1981). "Once again . . . a less-known work proves to be the most successful [on] television. . . . The language emerges brilliantly, even as the actors are giving solid, at times superb performances. . . . Unburdened by the exhausting baggage of familiarity, *The Winter's Tale* will prove a delightful surprise to anyone pretending to a keen interest in Shakespeare."

G. M. Pearce, *Cahiers Elisabéthains*, 20 (Oct. 1981). Discusses setting, the increasing fur on Leontes' costume which, as he sinks deeper into

jealousy, links him "with the black bear who filled the small screen. . . . Before dispatching Antigonus. . . . Leontes [had little] to fuel his suspicions because of the innocence and purity which surrounded . . . Hermione like an aura. . . . The delightful playing of . . . Jeremy Dimmick, as Mamillius . . . provided a fitting link with the celebration of youth in the second half. . . . There was little attempt to age the characters between the first and second half."

Donald Hedrick, *Shakespeare on Film Newsletter*, 6:1 (Jan. 1982). "The production is characterized by elegance and clarity. . . . We see brief, ambiguous distant shots of Hermione's initial joking with Polixenes, during Leontes' jealous soliloquy—an emotional perspective from the husband's mind. . . . But in general the actors . . . have too little to do."

Stanley Wells, "Goes Out, Followed by a Furry Animal," *Times Literary Supplement* (20 Feb. 1981).

A permanent set of angled, wedge-shaped blocks, like great lumps of cheese, defines the playing area. For the first half, the blocks are granite-grey, the floor is patterned in black and white. It's a chilly winter in Sicily, the furry costumes tell us. For Bohemia, the wedges turn double-Gloucester yellow, the floor green; stooks of corn and potted plants replace skeletal trees. Nature is art; symbolism is enhanced; but the set's limitations in Jane Howell's production—the latest in the BBC Shakespeare series—deny the romantic liberties of the tale.

The small screen all too easily circumscribes, concentrating attention, reducing perspective, diminishing stature. Frequent head-and-shoulder shots addressing us directly through the perspex, fine for Rikki Fulton's Irishly plausible Autolycus, at other points make too explicit a distinction between private and public utterance. Rhetoric is inhibited. Anna Calder-Marshall is a sympathetic Hermione, but too confidential at her trial. Why should only we learn that the Emperor of Russia is her father? She should be pleading to the whole court, not just to Leontes and to us. Jeremy Kemp's Leontes, introverted, properly humourless, seems understated. His anguished utterances need air. He avoids embarrassment but sacrifices range. He contrasts with Robert Stephens's Polixenes, never dull, but mannered, visually and vocally, with no respect for the pentameter line.

Individual performances are well characterized— a powerful, deeply felt Paulina from Margaret Tyzack, Cyril Luckham endearing as her ill-fated husband, Arthur Hewlett an earnest and sincere Old Shepherd. Debbie Farrington as Perdita is pretty, innocent but amused, a country lass to be reckoned with. George Howe brings style to Paulina's steward, and television can give us a real baby as the infant Perdita.

Jane Howell's direction is sensible and fluent. Some pitfalls are avoided. If Robin Kermode's pleasant Florizel does not make time stand still with his praises of Perdita in the pastoral scene, at least the jollity seems reasonably unforced. The set-piece dances are cut, with some justification. But the play seems smaller, flatter than in the theatre. There is less sense of interaction among the characters, and so less comedy, less drama. The bear looms and Antigonus cowers, but our withers are unwrung. Though the statue scene is moving, the focus on individuals denies us the sense of simultaneous involvement, the thrill of ritual participation as the stone is made flesh. The approach is intelligent and honest, the acting accomplished, but the medium has reduced the message.

Kenneth Rothwell, "The Shakespeare Plays: *Hamlet* and the Five Plays of Season Three," *Shakespeare Quarterly*, 32 (Autumn 1981).

Since there never was a seacoast in Bohemia, director Jane Howell showed good judgment in abstracting the Sicily and Bohemia of *The Winter's Tale* into places, as Jonathan Miller has noted, that are not particularly anywhere except in the "climate" of the human heart. To capture the "woe" and "wonder," the "numinous" and "miraculous" aura of this late romance, Ms. Howell has encoded "things dying" and "things reborn" in contrasts of stark white and subtle greens and pinks. Leontes' "winter of discontent" yields to the summertime of Perdita's sheep-shearing festival. Profiting from earlier experience with ramps and open space in the Messina *Henry V* and *Hamlet*, designer Don Homfray remains unequivocally non-representational in rendering this tragicomedy as a dream play set against a symbolic world of pyramids and cones, though in interior sequences a vast hall is sometimes introduced. Actors make exits and entrances through a vomitory, so to speak, piercing the stylized geometrical shapes. A shrewd touch has little Mamillius' vagrant ball come bouncing on stage before anyone else enters. As a pathetic symbol of the havoc about to descend on this family because of the tyrannical and crazy Leontes, it works very well. Indeed, everything about Leontes in the first act confirms the darkest feminist visions of male aggression leading to the "battered-wives" syndrome.

There is, however, a drawback, an incongruity, in this symbolic treatment of the play's geography. To make it work, the King of Sicily appears outfitted in a Muscovite-style heavy black fur coat and hat, and the Sicilian landscape resembles Vermont in January. Worse, Leontes cannot even manage to doff his hat and coat in the "interior" trial scene. While the director was doubtless clever to suggest a kinship between Leontes and the bear that slew Antigonus, her decision creates a confusion about setting. If one is interested in reconstructing the Elizabethan world picture (as Miller seems to be),

it is worth remembering that sexual jealousy was often equated with the heat of southern climates. In Howell's conception of Leontes as a bear, the King must fan himself into a jealous rage in a refrigerator.

Jeremy Kemp's Leontes is very understated. Kemp behaves nothing like the spitting, venomous Leontes of Daniel Seltzer, for example, in a Loeb Theatre production of some seventeen years ago at Harvard. He is moody, meditative, contained, content to express the inner turmoil with an outer tension. The "staring, frowning, grinning, rolling of eyes, menacing, ghastly looks, broken pace" that Robert Burton associates with jealous husbands do not figure in this method of acting. Kemp's laid-back style may be best for the intimacy of television. At times, however, I would have liked to see the camera pull back so that from a suitable distance I could behold Leontes properly rave and rant. Like Titus and Lear, he should fly off the handle.

Othello (BBC, 1981 [PBS, 12 October 1981])

Desdemona: Penelope Wilton. *Emilia*: Rosemary Leach. *Iago*: Bob Hoskins. *Othello*: Anthony Hopkins.

Producer/Director: Jonathan Miller. *Designer*: Colin Lowrey.

Sean French, London *Times* (28 Apr. 1985). "Magnificently conceived for television . . . almost all in closeup, the dialogue conducted in whispers, a style that could never have worked on stage, but . . . appropriate for [this] cloistered drama."

Choice (Feb. 1982). "Mediocre . . . lacking [in] verbal music, passion, and epic tragic scale. . . . Hopkins [is] miscast as Othello. . . . Iago and Desdemona have been more interestingly and movingly played in dozens of regional theater productions in the U.S. . . . It is certain to alienate the public and students from . . . Shakespeare." Olivier film [is] "far superior," Welles film "far more interesting."

Russell Davies, London *Times* (11 Oct. 1981). "Hoskins . . . was nasty, brutish, and short. . . . Making Iago a giggling psychopath reduces the tragedy to victimisation. Nothing really matched until the final scene, nobly hauled together by Rosemary Leach's Emilia."

Nancy Banks-Smith, *The Guardian* (18 Oct. 1981). "For someone with Penelope Wilton's decided chin to behave like Desdemona suggests she must have been dropped on her head at an early age."

John Naughton, *The Listener* (8 Oct. 1981). "Every time Miller's cast moved, they moved into another still life. . . . Quite, quite ravishing to watch."

G. M. Pearce, *Cahiers Elisabéthains*, 21 (Apr. 1982). "Anthony Hopkins would not have been everyone's idea of Othello, being too slight and pale. . . . The small, powerfully built mastiff-like Iago of Bob Hoskins was at his most venomous [in the epileptic scene] and . . . was by turns disturbing and magnetic throughout. . . . Overall, it was not one of the most successful of the plays so far produced by . . . Miller, although often visually very beautiful and with some striking individual performances."

John J. O'Connor, *NY Times* (12 Oct. 1981).

The director argues that Othello's blackness has "assumed an importance out of all proportion to its role in the play." Mr. Hopkins . . . plays Othello, the noble Moor, as an Arab, an exotic figure plucked from a painting by Velazquez. . . .

Mr. Miller works incessantly against what is perhaps the most familiar interpretation of the play: the Noble Savage booming out his lines sonorously, the scheming aide worming his way into total confidence and the victimized wife, delicate and helpless. Mr. Miller offers an Othello who is almost conversational within the cramped confines of a television screen. Mr. Hoskins . . . turns Iago into a hysterically giggling, crackling psychopath. And Miss Wilton's Desdemona, anything but passive, is an outgoing woman incensed at being wrongfully accused. . . . Mr. Hoskins has said that Iago "just gets a kick out of causing pain, anarchy, and chaos." But [Iago] seemingly had good reason for resenting the promotion of the less capable Cassio to a position he himself coveted. Further, as he reveals . . . he suspects Othello of having seduced his wife, Emilia. . . . These explicit details put a decided crimp in the utter-anarchy theories.

The performances in this production are, at the very least, distinctive, if not distinguished. Mr. Hopkins's speech mannerisms seem to have settled into a pattern of delivering the lines in somewhat punchy phrases and momentary pauses. This can often produce a remarkable clarity of meaning. . . . When Mr. Hopkins explodes emotionally, he seems to slide incomprehensibly into the accents of his native Wales.

Mr. Hoskins['] Iago is . . . very much in the mode of a sadistic gangster, an interpretation that works to a surprising degree. Miss Wilton's skill and assurance transform Desdemona into a figure of unusual strength. And as Emilia, Rosemary Leach is superb, very nearly stealing one of the key final scenes from the rest of the cast.

Conceiving of *Othello* as a closet drama, encompassing a relatively small number of major characters within the confines of a household tragedy, Mr. Miller has restricted most of the action to close, almost cramped quarters. . . .

David Richards, *Washington Post* (12 Oct. 1981).

Miller clearly wishes to impart the impression that the viewer is eavesdropping on the tragedy. To that end, the cast mumbles and whispers most of the great speeches. Indeed, things get so confidential at times that the viewer may well consider himself expendable. . . .

Hopkins's Othello cannot even be described as vaguely swarthy, which makes all the references to the character's dark look and exotic demeanor patently ridiculous. Hopkins is, in fact, an exceedingly controlled, well-spoken gentleman for most of the play's duration. . . . What rage Hopkins does bring to the part is peevish and snarling, thereby fostering the notion that what Othello really needs is a good spanking. . . . Bob Hoskins['] Iago is obviously of the lower classes—loutish, vulgar . . . appear[ing] to have no neck and a dumpy body, which suggests . . . [along with] his sniggering laugh, that Iago is the eighth dwarf—Nasty.

If the overall production had more drive, it is possible that the viewer might feel more charitable toward the performances. But Miller, in his efforts to bestow a quiet intimacy on the text, has merely succeeded in slowing the tragic events to a near standstill. The camera lingers on pensive faces. The actors brood, whisper to themselves, and brood some more. And still the camera lingers.

And when Desdemona retreats to her chamber and prepares for her fateful night in bed, what does Miller place conspicuously on her dressing table? A skull! Desdemona gazes at the skull. The skull stares back. Meanwhile, the isle of Cyprus dozes off. So may the home audience.

R. Thomas Simone, "Jonathan Miller's Iago," *Shakespeare on Film Newsletter*, 6:2 (Mar. 1982).

When Verdi was writing his opera based on *Othello*, he seriously considered naming his work after the villain, but the old man ultimately decided both in emotional weight and in title on the primacy of Othello. Jonathan Miller in his BBC production came to other conclusions. He wanted a play called *Iago*.

From the director's opening apologia to the final shot of the ancient being led off to torments, the figure of Iago dominates this production. Miller discounts the importance of Othello's blackness, which he terms the "myth of performance over the text"—this in spite of the repeated allusion in the text to Othello's race. Consequently, we get a slightly dusky Moor dressed in dandified Venetian clothing, a vision much closer to Ronald Colman than to Laurence Olivier.

The essential point, says Miller, is "the appalling power of the insatiably envious and of the horrible effects of the trickster and the practical joker." The concluding tableau of the production is typical of the emphasis on Iago.

In the last sequence Miller's bedchamber is cramped, indeed, with the bed and Desdemona's body scarcely visible. As Othello bends to kiss his dead wife, he drops out of the frame and the camera pans to the deranged, laughing Iago. Our sight is deprived of the "tragic loading of this bed" and made to follow the arrested Iago as he is led down a corridor. His laughter continues from the distance.

To give the devil his due, it must be admitted that television plays to the intimate scurrilousness of Iago and against the rhetoric and passion of Othello. Also, Miller may have been deprived of his real choice for an actor of the title part. Mel Gussow reported in *The New York Times* of August 22, 1981, that James Earl Jones had been invited to do Othello in this production but was barred from participation by the British actors' union. If so, Miller may have had to adopt an Iago-like guile for the entire enterprise.

The domestication of Othello echoes in the settings and costuming of the production. Almost all of the scenes take place in confining rooms and corridors, with the senate council scene and the drunken uproar in Cyprus suffering notably from cramped quarters. For me it was almost impossible to believe that Hopkins' Othello appears in shining breastplate, holding a plumed helmet that was far too unruffled to have seen military service. In this arrival at Cyprus, a country hardly distinguished in setting from the Venice of Act I, Hopkins first appears in his unfortunate pants with the boldly striped legs and codpiece, pants that cling to his character for the rest of the production.

The BBC's *Othello* shows flashes of brilliance, particularly in the acting of Bob Hoskins and in the support of Penelope Wilton and Rosemary Leach. Anthony Hopkins' portrayal and Jonathan Miller's confining of Othello, however, limit the achievement of the production. A valid debate about the relative weight and worth of the two main figures continues, but Miller so prejudices the argument that the dialectic of the play is lost. The largeness of the character of Othello is thrown away like the pearl "richer than all his tribe." We may well sympathize with Othello's cry: "every puny whipster gets my sword."

Timon of Athens (BBC, 1981 [PBS, 14 December 1981])

Alcibiades: John Shrapnel. *Apemantus*: Norman Rodway. *Flavius*: John Welsh. *Lucius*: Hugh Thomas. *Timandra*: Diana Dors. *Timon*: Jonathan Pryce.

Producer/Director: Jonathan Miller. *Designer*: Tony Abbott.

Anthony Masters, London *Times* (16 Apr. 1981). "Mr. Pryce's Timon needs friendship like a drug and will pay anything just for a counterfeit. That explains not only his insane largesse but the violence of his reaction when his toadies abandon him. . . . In these latter scenes . . . Timon comes briefly within touching distance of *Lear*."

Michael Ratcliffe, "Drama on Television," *Drama*, 139 (1981). This production "did little

more for a difficult and linguistically spare play than earlier directors have done. . . . Timon dying was like an image from Goya or Odilon Redon; the words came out of the top of his head."

Corinna Adam, *The Listener* (23 Apr. 1981). "My picture will remain . . . Miller's: a court of black-velveted Tudor lords . . . piggy-eyed and whispering nervously . . . hangers-on . . . barely listening to each other's conversation as they watch for someone more important. . . . Above all, Jonathan Pryce . . . his enormous eyes first melting with delight at his own generosity, then hurt and sly, finally the bitterest man on earth."

John N. Gundas, "This Doctor is 'In,'" New Orleans *Times-Picayune* (25 Jan. 1981). Interview with Jonathan Miller, who discusses the then upcoming *Timon of Athens*.

John J. O'Connor, *NY Times* (14 Dec. 1981). Pryce "is remarkably in control as Timon . . . especially . . . in the first acts because their 'innocence' is more difficult to make believable than the latter bitterness." Rest of cast: "uniformly splendid."

G. M. Pearce, *Cahiers Elisabéthains*, 20 (Oct. 1981). Pryce "was well suited to [Timon], his excessive leanness suggesting one who consumes himself from within."

David Richards, *Washington Post* (14 Dec. 1981). "Pryce, dewy-eyed and gentle while his money holds out, makes a bold metamorphosis into the bitter, rancid misanthrope. . . . Timandra, a bloated, pox-infected camp-follower . . . is actually Diana Dors, Britain's answer in the 1950s to Marilyn Monroe. Timon himself would have appreciated the irony."

Cecil Smith, *Los Angeles Times* (14 Dec. 1981). Timon is "a satiric comedy linked to a tragedy. . . . Yet . . . Pryce plays Timon so skillfully in [this] impeccable production . . . that you accept both sides of the man willingly. . . . For a play once dismissed as unplayable . . . Miller and Pryce have turned in an absorbing work of television."

Stanley Wells, "Living Both Ends," *Times Literary Supplement* (24 Apr. 1981).

The play survives only in a text with serious loose ends and much unpolished dialogue, seemingly laid aside without being brought to completion. Editors have struggled to create a coherence acceptable to readers. Invariably, and justifiably, directors brave enough to grapple with it make changes to lick it into shape.

It is problematical to critics as well as to textual scholars; but for all its imperfections it fascinates in its satire—uncharacteristic enough to support the theory that Shakespeare had Middleton as a collaborator—its invective, its pathos, and the imaginative intensity underlying its portrayal of Timon, who, as his keenest critic the cynic Apemantus puts it, never knew "the middle of humanity . . . but the extremity of both ends."

Jonathan Miller's direction emphasizes the similar polarity in the play's structure. He intensifies the first of the two parts into which it is divided—up to Timon's self-banishment—partly by textual manipulation, partly by skillful use of Tony Abbott's flexible set, which concentrates the action on Timon's palace, a grand establishment of massive, sunlit stone walls and columns. Costumes are Jacobean; Athens is not visually evoked, nor is the corruption of its society suggested except through individual characterization.

Odd direction does not help. For Timon to burrow into the shingle beneath a block of marble which becomes his tomb, and to address all his speeches to the Senators thence, is interesting enough as a symbol of withdrawal—anorexia is perhaps as good an explanation as any for his death—but to show nothing but his head upside-down throughout his later speeches seems willful and constricting. More important (though understandable in the circumstances), the actor does not find the strange music which suggests in Timon an awareness of a world elsewhere, a dying vision beyond the ordinary. We cannot see why this Timon should say "nothing brings me all things," should be lamented as "noble Timon" in the elegiac closing scene (dignified by John Shrapnel, a sympathetic and strongly-spoken Alcibiades). So the final image, of a heartbroken Flavius musing over Timon's epitaph, seems a sentimental ending to a gallant and largely successful production.

Miriam Gilbert, "The Empty Table . . . ," *Shakespeare on Film Newsletter*, 6:2 (Mar. 1982).

The BBC Shakespeare series has often seemed more successful with the less frequently performed plays. Thus I looked forward to Jonathan Miller's production of *Timon of Athens*, especially since I had seen Ron Daniels' production for The Other Place (Stratford) early in January, 1981. But though both productions provided moments of satisfaction, eventually they offered us, like Timon's guests, an empty table.

The opening scene in the BBC production created a promising ambience: overheard conversations between characters nearly indistinguishable (and so, by implication, superficial) in tones of polite gossip. Though Timon (Jonathan Pryce), like everyone else, wore black, he seemed noticeably younger; did his generosity, casually manifested in the encounter with the old Athenian and Lucilius, spring from naiveté? He joked with the Jeweler and, just as easily, with the white-haired, white-bearded Apemantus (Norman Rodway). But the first banquet scene showed us the tension beneath the social graces. While all the guests seated at the long table ate with relish, Timon fingered his napkin; his plate was empty; he refused the fruit offered to him. These details hinted at a strain not seen before—and when he called for his steward in the middle of the dancing and began giving out jewels,

we saw that the generosity was not merely naive but compulsive.

Pryce carefully balanced that inner strain with optimistic tones, especially in his conversation with the Steward (II.ii). His assertion, "I am wealthy in my friends," was confident while he sent a servant off to Lucullus with the remark, "I hunted with his honor today," thereby implying that everything would turn out for the best. Only the news that the senators had already rejected the Steward's entreaties caught him by surprise.

The hysterical moments finally began in III.iv. When bill collectors surrounded Timon, he threw down his jacket, hit the men who were trying to force papers at him, and, almost weeping, tossed the papers in the air. His hysteria contrasted with the control of Alcibiades (John Shrapnel) in II.v, while Alcibiades' white shirt linked him visually to the white-shirted Timon we had just seen. Perhaps the details for callousness went too far; would a senator really cut out paper figures during a state discussion, or would another clean his nails? The persistent long shots in the scene created a distance which also controlled Alcibiades' anger. Even his defiant reply, "Banish me / Banish your dotage, banish usury, / That makes the Senate ugly," was spoken to a distant camera. Only at the scene's end, when Alcibiades was left alone, did the camera finally move to him—and he, like Timon, stood by an empty table.

As the guests waited awkwardly for the second banquet, Lucullus' twitching mouth re-emphasized the play's focus on eating. Timon's attack progressed from washing his hands in the warm water to sprinkling it with a flick of his fingers, and then finally ladling it out onto someone's head; the guests' nervous laughter suggested that they thought/hoped this was all a joke. Once more hysteria struck (this time making Timon's lines unintelligible) until, after smashing of pots and overturning of tables, Timon left, in chilling silence.

However, once Timon has left Athens, the play seems to come unglued. Jonathan Pryce commented revealingly, in the post-production interview, that he had originally seen the difficulty as being the first half of the play, but found it much easier than he had imagined to play the "outgoing, giving person" of the first half. The famous poetry comes in the second half, but the scenes aren't easier to play—or to vary in tone. In Stratford, the geometrically neat set of the beginning was disarranged, hung with net, strewn with debris, and the Japanese-style costumes gave way to rags. On television the original set was "changed" from indoors to outdoors by the addition of a small cave and many loudly scrunching rocks. Anyone who came to see Timon announced his or her entrance with strange noises. Only Apemantus, against his setting, looked neater, and his manner became genial. It was the production's strongest indication of

Timon's change; if Apemantus was normal, what should we make of Timon?

Yet the play's structural problems weren't solved by the setting, or the acting. What is the progression—of emotion, of action, of thought—in the sequence of visitors and soliloquies? What leads to Timon's death? The production showed him turning into a kind of living head of John the Baptist—body inside the cave, grotesque upside-down face talking to the Senators. And what does that death mean? The final images were the despair of the Old Steward, Alcibiades' attempt to comfort him, and then a hand tracing Timon's epitaph, but the connections made so clearly in the first half between the two plot lines were absent here. It seems only fair to say that I'm not sure the problem can be solved—Richard Pasco and Ron Daniels weren't that much more successful at Stratford. But surely the lack of variety—little movement, few changes of tone, the absence of feeling—seemed to offer us lukewarm water for the second half of the BBC production.

Troilus and Cressida (BBC, 1981 [PBS, 17 May 1982])

Achilles: Kenneth Haigh. *Ajax*: Anthony Pedley. *Cressida*: Suzanne Burden. *Hector*: John Shrapnel. *Helen*: Ann Pennington. *Pandarus*: Charles Gray. *Thersites*: The Incredible Orlando. *Troilus*: Anton Lesser. *Ulysses*: Benjamin Whitrow.

Producer/Director: Jonathan Miller. *Designer*: Colin Lowrey

Michael Ratcliffe, London *Times* (9 Nov. 1981). Miller's *Troilus* "was sadly lacking on . . . good casting, clarity of argument and a single, dazzling visual key . . . yet both love scenes were first rate, and the farewell very moving."

John J. O'Connor, *NY Times* (17 May 1982). "For much of the production there is a confusion about who is who and who is on which side. Perhaps there is some calculation in this, the point being that it doesn't matter who wins or loses. But anybody not familiar with the play is only likely to be puzzled."

G. M. Pearce, *Cahiers Elisabéthains*, 21 (Apr. 1982). Pearce questions the strengths and weaknesses in the casting; Gray as Pandarus "overwhelmed" Anton Lesser as Troilus. Production "stronger in scenes of war than of love . . . confusion was often allowed to reign."

Stanley Wells, "Speaking for Themselves," *Times Literary Supplement* (20 Nov. 1981).

Terry Hands's production of *Troilus and Cressida* at the Aldwych earlier this year was accused, with some justice, of interpretative excess. The charge is not likely to be brought against Jonathan Miller's television version. The difference in approach is typified in the treatment of the Prologue. At the Aldwych it was spoken, in character, by Thersites, thus setting the tone for a production which took a generally satirical view of the play's characters and events. On television it is delivered by an unseen speaker, courteously, anonymously, with neither rhetoric nor passion.

Jonathan Miller's whole production is similarly dispassionate. It is set in those broad, sunlit stone corridors, and on that circular outdoor space, to which familiarity is endearing us. Though scenes are given a local habitation, the aim seems to be to create a sense of reality rather than to carry interpretative implications. There is no equivalent to Terry Hands's First-World-War analogies, no emphasis on the fact that the siege of Troy has been going on for a long time; the Greek commanders are poised, well dressed, barbered and fed. Paris and Helen's lovemaking during Pandarus' song is modest, especially by comparison with the Aldwych orgy. Only occasionally is there a surprise: Helen is present (though silent and virtually motionless) while her fate is debated by the Trojan leaders; Achilles clips his beard before a looking-glass as he instructs his myrmidons.

The camera work is unobtrusive, with some beautifully lit close-ups; long stretches are played with no shift in perspective. The action unfolds with exemplary clarity, except in the difficult scene in which on the one hand Troilus and Ulysses, on the other hand Thersites, oversee, overhear and comment upon Diomedes and Cressida; in spite of some striking shots of Troilus and Ulysses in the foreground, observing the lovers' shadows on the wall of their tent, the scene's complex counterpoint is not fully realized. Except for a few cuts, mostly in the complicated battle scenes, the text is pure (it is a misplaced pedantry that insists on the pronunciation "Troyan" for "Trojan"). There is an implicit acknowledgment that this is a play in which what is said is of paramount importance.

I watched this production with interest and respect, but for me it does not convey that sense of the desolating futility of war, the pathetic grandeur of the human challenge to oblivion through heroism and love, of which (as Peter Hall's 1960 production supremely showed) the play is capable.

Barbara Hodgdon, "Mostly About Cressida?," *Shakespeare on Film Newsletter*, 7:1 (Dec. 1982).

We are, by now, familiar with the first images of BBC-TV Bard-ing: that glossy, slowly rotating bust of Shakespeare replaced by the open countenance of Jonathan Miller and his condescending program notes. I tire of these prologues just as I tire of watching three talking heads, two in three-quarter profile, one slightly backgrounded—much as that shot setup suits the voyeurism of *Troilus and Cressida*. That introductory railing aside, I much admire the clarity and generosity of this production. Rather than imposing an "aboutness" on the play, Miller's version works from the inside out, seeming to convey the points of view of the characters themselves; rather than showing us (as in Terry Hands's 1981 RSC production) a handful of moral idiots, caricatures of the great persons of our expectations who wrangle at their empty causes in vain, this version keeps all options open, treating the characters with care and respect, as persons who believe that what they say and do has value.

A Midsummer Night's Dream (BBC, 1981 [PBS, 19 June 1982])

Bottom: Brian Glover. Demetrius: Nicky Henson. Helena: Cherith Mellor. Hermia: Pippa Guard. Hippolyta: Estelle Kohler. Lysander: Robert Lindsay. Oberon: Peter McEnery. Puck: Phil Daniels. Theseus: Nigel Davenport. Titania: Helen Mirren. Producer: Jonathan Miller. Director: Elijah Moshinsky. Designer: David Myerscough-Jones.

John J. O'Connor, NY Times (19 Apr. 1982). "Magically . . . Moshinsky's conception weaves its spell from beginning to end. . . . The typically strong and impressive cast [is used] brilliantly in terms of television. . . . Mr. Brook may have given us a production for the last decade. Mr. Moshinsky has given us an equally splendid one for the 80's. It, too, will be a hard act to follow."

G. M. Pearce, Cahiers Elisabéthains, 21 (Apr. 1982). "Sexuality was strongly present in Helen Mirren's lush Titania . . . perhaps more . . . an earth goddess than a fairy queen. . . . Pippa Guard [was] a demurely pretty Hermia, particularly when instructing Lysande lie further off yet. . . . Moshinsky had said, 'Let's set it in water.' . . . The fluid movement that this gave to the production is its most memorable feature, together with Helen Mirren's sensitive and seductive Titania."

Nicholas Shrimpton, "Hot Ice and Wondrous Strange Snow," Times Literary Supplement (25 Dec. 1981).

A midwinter night's snow outside the window and A Midsummer Night's Dream inside—a bizarre conjunction of climate and programme-schedule seemed determined to allow the maximum effect to the latest instalment of the BBC Shakespeare. With old Hiems' thin and icy crown firmly in place, the viewing public must have settled down to warm the cockles of their hearts on the glowing limbs of Helen Mirren with unusual relish. It is hard to believe that they were not disappointed. Elijah Moshinsky's production of Shakespeare's most fool-proof comedy was the nearest this series has come to disaster since Jonathan Miller first stepped in to rescue it from banality.

What was wrong was simply incoherence. The house-style of the BBC Shakespeare is a Jacobean reference in sets and costumes, interpreted with greater or lesser freedom according to the imagination of the individual director. At the court of Athens, Moshinsky observed the convention punctiliously. Egeus complained about the alienation of his daughter's affections at a Puritan council of state. Helena denounced the iniquities of Cupid while pacing a long gallery. Theseus and Hippolyta discussed the imagination in a seventeenth-century library complete with book-presses, leaded lights and chequered stone floor.

But the director's heart was not in it. What he wanted to do was turn the clock back in a quite different way, to the Romantic account of A Midsummer Night's Dream which established itself in the 1840s with the help of gas-light and Mendelssohn, reached its apogee in the hands of Herbert Beerbohm Tree, and finally disappeared from the stage in the mid-twentieth century. As soon as we entered the wood, therefore, we found ourselves abruptly plunged into the world of the spectacular theatre. The allusion was perhaps meant to be even more specific. For the settings bore an uncanny resemblance to the work which provides our most illuminating record of the grand Edwardian manner, the film of A Midsummer Night's Dream which William Dieterle and Max Reinhardt made in Hollywood in 1935. Glimmering moons, massed child-fairies and pools of still water are the keynotes of both productions. Substitute a Cockney Puck (Phil Daniels) for Mickey Rooney's Bronx imp, and an earth-goddess Titania for her more fragile predecessor, and you are still left with a substantial overlap.

Moshinsky's problem was to reconcile such reckless fantasy with the austere historicism of his Athenian scenes. Stephen Oliver's uncharacteristically nervous score was an index of how little the production succeeded. Sub-Mendelssohn at one moment, sub-Gibbons at the next, the music swung vertiginously from one period to another without ever establishing an identity. The acting was every bit as uncertain. Lovers who at Athens conversed in portentous whispers suited to their unusually advanced years were obliged to treat the wood as a species of adventure playground, ducking and bedraggling each other with coltish abandon. Even a player as gifted as Nicky Henson looked lost in these circumstances, and the director's modish willingness to allow several characters to speak at once reduced the quarrel scene to an incomprehensible gabble.

The trouble with this inconsistency of manner was not that it offended some pedantic conception of the chastity of styles. Productions which wish to establish a deliberate contrast between courtly and natural, or even waking and sleeping experiences can very properly adopt different modes of performance in different sections of the play. But in this case the disparity suggested merely indecision, an indecision which infected every corner of the interpretation. Estelle Kohler's Hippolyta, for example, was initially a resentful prisoner of war. By the time

of her second appearance that idea had been quietly dropped and she appeared instead as a bub-
blingly enthusiastic fiancée.

The worst uncertainty, because the most important, involved the mechanicals. First seen as a
huddle of matey drinkers, they appeared to have
been assembled for the purposes of an academic
dialect study, so various were their voices. What a
Home Counties Quince was doing with a Cockney
Flute and a Northern Bottom, however, rapidly
ceased to matter. What did matter was that they
were not allowed to be funny. "Pyramus and
Thisbe," the most sure-fire fifth act ever written for
the comic stage, became a strange sequence of individual party pieces (including an operatic Moon-
shine), provoking almost everything but laughter. A
few good deeds shone out amidst this gloom, above
all Helen Mirren who, though so hung about with
infant fairies that it was hard not to think of her as
a harassed nursery-school teacher, gave a spirited
account of Titania. Elsewhere the rewards were
desperately few. Puck, for once, drawled the apolo-
getic epilogue altogether too casually. His company
was scaping the serpent's tongue by a narrower
margin than he realized.

David Richards, *Washington Post* (19 June 1981).

Until English director Peter Brook came along
in the mid-1960s to alter our vision of it, *A Midsummer Night's Dream* was customarily staged as a
lavish slice of romanticism, drenched with flowers
and bombarded by moonbeams.

Brook swept away the foliage and the moonlight
and shut the action up in a tight, whitewashed box
with trapezes for trees.

As producer Jonathan Miller says, Brook's "for-
biddingly excellent" production, inspired by the
nonrealistic traditions of Persian theater, constituted "a preemptive strike." Any subsequent *Mid-
summers* were likely to pale in comparison.

Hence the problem faced by Miller and the
BBC, which is taping all of Shakespeare's plays for
television. What to do, in this post-Brook age, with
Titania and Oberon, Puck, Bottom and those misguided lovers who end up loving at cross-purposes
in a wood outside Athens? Tonight's production
simply goes back to the old silvery ways and—
God's bodkin!—it is something of an enchantment.

Director Elijah Moshinsky sets the action in a
lush and brooding landscape. The trees hang heavy
with vines. The night sky is purply black. Owls
hoot and crickets chirp in the distance. Around an
inky black pond the lovers sigh and splash, and
sometimes they tumble over backwards right into
the water. His shirt open to the navel, his black
hair falling to his shoulders, Oberon first appears
on horseback. Titania, looking as if she stepped
from a Pre-Raphaelite canvas, shows up with a
cluster of angelic children equipped with diaphanous wings. Even the faces of the bumbling rus-
tics, who are rehearsing "the most lamentable

comedy, and cruel death of Pyramus and Thisbe,"
are lit in the golden tones of an Old Master.

Not without justification does Moshinsky refer
to his version as an "homage to Max Reinhardt,"
the turn-of-the-century German director whose
sumptuous stagings of *Midsummer* established the
very tradition that Brook shattered with his lean
and mean innovations. While a case can be made
for the cruelty lurking in the hearts of Shakespeare's
mortals and in the mischievous imaginations of his
sprites, *Midsummer* really is more fun when the
consequences are less grave. Puck in this production has a touch of punk and it still is a bit unsettling to see Titania snuggle into bed with an ass.
But otherwise, Moshinsky is not about to dwell on
the darker aspects of the fable.

It's a dream, not a nightmare, after all. And the
cast plays it so—with grace and poetry and the
slightly dazed look of any moonstruck lover who
happens to spot his lady fair on the far side of the
pond and promptly wades into the water to reach
her. Cherith Mellor is especially appealing as Helena, that self-described "spaniel" who is admired
by no one at the start of the play and then, through
the magic of Oberon, suddenly has two ardent
swains alternately throwing themselves at her feet
and caressing her frazzled red hair.

Mellor's jaw drops in disbelief. Wide-eyed, she
gazes at her unexpected beaus through wire-
rimmed glasses. Then she takes off her glasses and
squints at them, as if to get a better focus on
events. Pure wonder and amazement are her fate.
By allowing itself to indulge in similar sentiments,
this *Midsummer* turns back the clock and turns up
a good measure of bewitchment. Tradition, it appears, is not without defense.

Scott Colley, "The Shakespeare Plays on TV,"
Shakespeare on Film Newsletter, 8:1 (Dec. 1983).

Elijah Moshinsky's BBC version of *A Midsummer Night's Dream* is neither as misty and pretty as
the Reinhardt/Dieterle black-and-white 1935 film
version, nor as erotic as Peter Hall's lush, colorful
1969 RSC production. In contrast with the cavernous sets of the Hollywood extravaganza and the
echoing neoclassical mansion of the Hall film,
Moshinsky's video version encloses the players in
tight interiors.

If the Reinhardt/Dieterle film recalls Inigo
Jones, and the Hall the exotic flora and fauna of
Richard Dadd, then Moshinsky's *MND* comes
straight out of the seventeenth-century Dutch
school of de Hooch, Hals, and Rembrandt. He
learns well from his Dutch models, even down to
the chiaroscuro of many interior shots.

His problem is that moving images require spatial arrangements different from those of the Dutch
masters. Once Bols arranges his "Members of the
Wine Merchants Guild," he can sustain that
grouping forever. A TV camera, however, demands

movement, and a tight frame can become a noose that chokes the actors.

The rigid settings were intended to catch the tensions of the daylight Athenian milieu, a place of constraints. The early shot of Hippolyta nervously pacing amidst courtiers and pages deftly suggests her residual tension. She has been defeated but not conquered.

Egeus's complaint to the Duke takes place with Hermia, Lysander, and Demetrius stiffly seated at a table after the manner of Bols's wine merchants. Likewise the rude mechanicals are discovered ranked along a table at a pub, with poor Flute perched high on the back of the bench. No one in Moshinsky's Athens seems to have room to stretch.

Even the forest seems cramped: few characters can find their way through the woods without falling into a giant mud puddle, giving the impression that there is only one damp path to follow.

In that one sense, however, Moshinsky follows Hall, who made certain his characters were soaked before being led "thorough bush, thorough brier."

Helen Mirren (who had played Hermia for Hall in 1969) is the star of the show. Her Titania is regal, imperious, a fairy queen whose white gown seems the source of all the light in scenes in which she appears. Backgrounds fade into umber only a short distance from her. She alone seems languidly self-confident and at ease with her universe.

Cherith Mellor as Helena is another bright spot, tall, spindly, bespectacled, her hair awry, looking for all the world like a woman who has been jilted and who would expect a practical joke in poor taste at the hands of Lysander and Demetrius.

A Midsummer Night's Dream (ABC Video, 1982)

Bottom: Jeffrey DeMunn. Demetrius: Rich Leiberman. Helena: Christine Baranski. Hermia: Deborah Rush. Hippolyta: Diane Venora. Lysander: Kevin Conroy. Oberon: William Hurt. Puck: Marcel Rosenblatt. Theseus: James Hurdle. Titania: Michele Shay.

Producer: Joseph Papp. Directors: James Lapine (stage), Emile Ardolino (ABC). Designer: Heidi Landesman.

Staged at the Delacorte Theatre, Central Park, by the New York Shakespeare Festival, summer 1982.

Arthur Ganz, "Shakespeare in New York City," Shakespeare Quarterly, 34 (Spring 1983). "The costume allotted to Oberon [was] a loose vest and a pair of trousers made of what appeared to be a cross between feathers and new-mown hay. . . . As Mr. Hurt—with a raspy, high-pitched voice and poor phrasing—is not a very successful classical actor, he failed, even with his blond good looks, to make the image work. . . . But by far the most annoying element of the production was the Puck of . . .

Marcell Rosenblatt, who shrieked most of her speeches while hurling across the stage in an all-out sprint and regularly interspersed her lines with a series of manic giggles. This grisly miscalculation was balanced, fortunately, by the delightful Helena of Christine Baranski, a tall, willowy blonde who added to her charms the impeccable timing, adroit handling of stage business, and wryly self-deprecating humor of a youthful Carol Burnett."

H. R. Coursen, "Joseph Papp's A Midsummer Night's Dream."

This is a televised version of a stage production, like Papp's 1974 King Lear, Sarah Caldwell's 1981 Macbeth, and the 1982 Stratford, Canada, Shrew. Papp's Lear wove its Central Park audience into the fabric of the production. Its faults were not a product of the mechanical reproduction of live theatre. The Lincoln Center Macbeth seemed uneasy with its audience, while the Stratford Shrew made the outer spectators part of a meta-dramatic event that was a play-within-a-play to begin (and end) with. This Dream began with wildflowers, musicians, and a splendid "establishing shot" in which the camera roved down across the settling audience towards the stage.

While the audience was seen a few more times (behind Egeus's angry entrance, for example), it was mostly merely heard now and then as the play progressed. Since Dream is as meta-dramatic as Shrew, the erasure of the outer audience—the god to whom Prospero prays at the end of Tempest—was disappointing. Some way must exist to employ all those people watching a play, even when we see them watching a play on television. They represent an energy beyond that of the "canned laughter" to which they tended to be reduced here.

The setting was superb. A bronze Cupid rose above a pool. A mossy old tennis court created a central platform. Birch trees bent to left and right against the straighter lines of New York City. The set alone makes this production a joy to watch. It can be usefully compared with Moshinsky's "homage to Max Reinhardt" for BBC-TV, but it is really a stage set, like that one encounters at London's Regent's Park. This one was as enchanting in its way as was the beautiful set for John Barton's RSC Dream of the late 1970s, based on the illustrations of Arthur Rackham.

The weaknesses of this production, however, are glaring. The costumes were eclectic, either bizarre or drab, and contributed nothing to the texture of the production. The artisans were a group of types apparently instantly recognizable to the audience but in no way coherently blended in with whoever the other groupings were supposed to be. "Pyramus and Thisbe," however, was done in a quasi-Elizabethan mode which did make some sense. Any play done in relatively modern dress that has a play-within can do some stunning things when the play-within is "Shakespearean," as was "Gonzago" in the Prussian Cuilei *Hamlet* at the Arena in Washington some years ago.

Marcel Rosenblatt's Puck was awful. She was allowed to upstage Quince's rehearsal, to bray stage-laughter against the delicate sway of leaves in a summer-night's breeze and, in sum, to destroy those moments in which she participated. For this the Director is to blame. Bottom's head was a huge set of ear muffs and a smudge on the nose. All that stuff about transformation and monstrosity was simply ludicrous. There was Bottom all along! The lighting had not accommodated to the close vision of the TV cameras and was often blatant. The exception was an intentional calling attention-to-itself when a spot switched off as Oberon said, "I am invisible." That moment earned its laughter. Well known film actor William Hurt's Oberon was not helped by his "Son of Sitting Bull" outfit, but he wrecked a rich role by running past the signals in Oberon's poetry and, perversely, by pausing to sing out irrelevant vowel sounds. He did get music behind "I know a bank . . ." and he probably laughed all the way to it. Michele Shay got a sense of vicarious pregnancy into her description of the changeling's origin, but otherwise concentrated on looking beautiful. In that she succeeded.

The cutting was standard—Theseus's lecture on magnanimity was gone as was much of the raillery during "Pyramus and Thisbe." One sequence, however, may have disturbed those who know the script. While Puck led Demetrius and Lysander through the fog, Oberon was rebuffed at the edge of Titania's grotto. She, feeling guilty it seemed, and doing the only thing she could, slipped out with her Indian boy. Finding Oberon prostrate in pretended grief, she placed the boy in his arms. Oberon reported to Puck, "While I in this affair did thee employ, / I've been to my Queen to beg her Indian boy." His later speech cut from "Her dotage now I do begin to pity" to "And now I have the boy again." This editing does not alter the "masculine control" Oberon asserts over Titania but it does qualify sympathy for her distress within a bad dream she knows she is having. I leave it to other auditors to assess the impact of a changing of the script seemingly dictated by the values the production was finding within its setting.

While Deborah Rush's Hermia had a baby-voice just this side of Helen Kane's, Christine Baranski's Helena had an aristocratic and self-mocking tonality that wonderfully fulfilled one of the great roles in the canon. Ms. Baranski's pulling on her gloves—a la Oscar Wilde—as she chose to leave an unsatisfactory social scene in the forest was hilarious.

Another good moment occurred when Bottom, preparing for Pyramus's elongated death, spied Titania tripping past the storm-soak of an oak bole.

His final words pressed their silliness towards the quality of the lines they parody—Romeo's in the tomb. Pyramus's lines will not support tragedy, of course, but it was a brilliant directorial touch to have Bottom reminded of his love in the middle of his equally fictional love affair with Thisbe. Bottom's "what I had" alluded not to his ears but to where he had had Titania. He recognized at the end of the play-within that his woodland experience had been more than a dream.

For all of the unevenness and remarkable lapses of taste of this production ("Ay, that left Papp!"), this one is worth watching.

The Taming of the Shrew (CBC, 1982)

Bianca: Lynne Griffin. *Katherina*: Sharry Flett. *Petruchio*: Len Cariou. *Sly*: Desmond Ellis.

Directors: Peter Dews (stage), Norman Campbell (CBC).

Staged by the Stratford Festival, Canada, summer 1981.

Ralph Berry, "Stratford Festival: Canada," *Shakespeare Quarterly*, 33:2 (Summer 1982). (Stage.)

Initially, Katherina appears trapped within her shrewish role, a defensive posture she has adopted toward a society which insults her intelligence and constrains her energy. . . . Petruchio frees her from this role by enacting a calculated plan of behaviour modification: he imitates her conduct with a vengeance, revealing its absurdity in full-blown caricature, and he complements the qualities masked by the role, offering her another model." Thus the Festival program, at which my heart sank. It is all very well for such sentiments to be circulated in the academic trade press. We are used to them there, and they do no harm. They can be dangerous when allowed to fall into the hands of actors. Len Cariou, unfortunately, had seen the program; and he offered a Petruchio in the current Social Worker mode. On this reading, Petruchio is primarily concerned to save Katherina from herself, and he imparts to her the correct role model. To see the *Shrew* assimilated into homiletic drama is hard for those of us who regard its vital essences as brutality and sexuality. Sharry Flett, after some initial incredulity, acquiesced in this view of matters. She seemed ill-suited to the coarse exchanges of II.i, and conveyed that she was placed in the wrong genre. ("I'm really a comedy of manners specialist," and indeed she played Célimène in the Festival.) The opening scenes with her lacked fire. Had I been refereeing in II.i, I should have stopped the contest, warned Katherina to show more action, and reprimanded Petruchio for gentlemanly conduct. Things moved on to a more believable level in the second half, when the protagonists agreed to be civilized at everyone else's expense. The suburban bickering of Act V was convincing enough, and the great final speech came over with entire conviction, as why should it not? Naturally, it can be delivered with the irony it asks for (and got, from Paola Dionisotti in Bogdanov's RSC production). On the other hand, there's no reason why Katherina shouldn't mean every word, in context. The key is that Petruchio has won a bet, and Katherina knows it:

LUCENTIO The wisdom of your duty, fair Bianca, Hath cost me an hundred crowns since supper time.
BIANCA The more fool you, for laying on my duty.

The glance that Sharry Flett shot at her groom registered the point fully. ("Did you? Good for you! And now you can buy me another gown.") I see no reason why Katherina, alone in Padua, should be untouched by the economic drives sustaining her community. So Kate sang for her supper, and very prettily too.

The other side of Katherina's motivation is Bianca, very plausibly presented by Lynne Griffin. This was an intolerable minx, twirling a tassel and poking her tongue out at Katherina behind Daddy's back. She looked a much better candidate for Northrop Frye's Tyrant category than her sister. Her provocations met a deserved fine in Act V, and one gleaned that Katherina's sweetest satisfaction lay in upstaging her open-mouthed sister.

Over all this presided Sly—literally so, for he sat in a commanding balcony seat overlooking the stage. I was happy to see the drunken humors of Sly restored to the play, unaccompanied, be it said, by program allusions to the Theme of Appearance and Reality. Sly (Desmond Ellis) helped make the party go. So did the Lord (well played by Shaun Austin-Olsen), who leapt down from his balcony seat to participate in the general action. I speculated hopefully on the ultimate Pirandellian happening, a stage accident leading to a groaning Cariou being carried off, and the Lord (Petruchio's understudy, as it happened) taking over. But no such luck. Peter Dews retained the ending of A Shrew, with Sly waking up to carry his dream back home. Though lacking intensity at its core, this Shrew was a genial romp that improved as it went along.

H. R. Coursen, "The Stratford, Canada, Shrew on TV."

I saw this production on the Arts & Entertainment cable network in the summer of 1986. It had been directed by Norman Campbell for CBC. While the production was not redesigned for television, it did incorporate a number of camera angles and shots—a zoom-in on Biondello's "Where have I been?," some shots from upstage, as in Kate's complaint outside the church, and an over-the-shoulder "reaction shot" when the Pedant reacted to Tranio's horror at the former's Mantuan origin.

Campbell's camera was alert to the rhythms of the theatre, as in its instant grasp of Lucentio's and Biondello's entrance, stage right, only a moment after their exit, stage left, in IV.iv.

The production's outstanding quality was its theatricality. The Sly frame was retained. The ending of A Shrew completed the framing. Sly sat on a balcony—a kind of tree-house—upstage center. The actors bowed to him. He applauded, even interrupting at times. Petruchio had to re-position himself for his opening speech as he waited for Sly to quiet down. Messages were delivered between Sly and Bartholomew. Kate blundered into the balcony, thinking it her "bridal chamber." When Petruchio appeared a moment later, Sly gave him a high-sign, Sly enjoying a vicarious concupiscence. Petruchio delivered his "Falcon Soliloquy" from the balcony. When Sly objected to Vincentio's incarceration, Sly was reminded that "this is but a play." This interpolation reminded us, as the Induction does, that this all is an illusion. The Pedant appeared through a door in the roof of the theatre for his rebuff of Vincentio in V.i, thus incorporating Sly, in his balcony below, within the space of the "play-within." The Lord's decision to place Sly once more under the ale house sign preceded the final scene of the inner play. At the very end, Sly tried to brush away the cock's crowing, then rose and exited to laughter, as he promised to tame his own froward wife.

In addition to the skillful integration of frame and inner play, which is itself a theatrical tour-de-force featuring Petruchio and an initially reluctant Katherina, Campbell exploited the production's concept of "audience." The Lord and his attendants became the spectators for the play-within, ranging themselves stage left and right, and on the steps at the sides of the thrust stage. They became stage-hands and servants. Characters arriving at Padua—Pedant, Kate and Petruchio—came up from the aisles, thus pulling the audience into the illusion being framed for them. At times, as in the TV version of the Joseph Papp King Lear, that outer audience was visible. This was a production which, like the play, was consistently and delightedly aware of its premises as theatre.

Yet theatricality was also a problem on television. The subtle nuances that can be captured in a studio were lost amid the broad gestures and amplification demanded by the auditorium. Bartholomew's efforts to control his voice were just plain silly, even if they did draw laughs from audiences conditioned to laughter by Lucy. And while Petruchio's bravura performance can succeed in such a context, Katherina tended to be lost in it. Sharry Flett screamed too much, drowning in decibels the end of her first confrontation with Petruchio and his "rescue" of her from the wedding guests. If, as Mr. Berry argues, Ms. Flett, with her slender build and haughty tonality, is better suited to conquer by wit, she stooped to yelling here. While Lynne Griffin played Bianca as a nasty, finger-thumbing little tease, she too had been directed to scream her silly head off at Katherina's mischief. Rod Beattie's Gremio was often effective. He delivered his line, "Yea, leave that labor to great Hercules" to Grumio, and through him to that outer audience. But when he recounted the events in the church, he pulled a long pseudo-"corpse" that may have moved some quantity of barren spectators to laughter, but that proved a tedious interruption to the pace of this production. The narrative itself, if well rendered, is amusing enough. Zeffirelli, in his film, showed us Burton and Taylor, with a hilariously hapless priest between.

Perhaps in a large auditorium all of this must be played as farce. Perhaps Kate must kick a chair to set up Petruchio's, "Why doth the world report that Kate doth limp?" Perhaps Petruchio must pull out a string of sausages when he asks, "What dogs are these?" Perhaps. But over-playing and playing to the least common denominator of the audience seemed to me to be the chief flaws of this production.

And here I take issue with Mr. Berry. While I am no fan of a director's program notes, good actors overcome concepts. And this concept does have textual support. Petruchio is holding a mirror up to Kate. Tranio's "Curster than she?," Curtis's "By this reck'ning he is more shrew than she," and Peter's "He kills her in her own humor," show the servants' sharp perception of Petruchio's behavioral strategy.

The concept worked well enough within the abundance of space to be included. Kate responded to Petruchio's praise of her beauty. She had not heard that one before! We got the comic analogue to Richard's wooing of Lady Anne—a scene played at about the same time by the same Richard Burbage and his boy actor. We saw Kate choke on her "Thank you, sir," begin to get the point even as she resisted it, then fall into step on the road to Padua. She kissed Petruchio for the first time with sudden fervor, having been denied that too by his "conditioning program." She did read her last speech straight. She was a winner—"too little payment for so great a debt," she emphasized. She spoke as a woman whose body had been discovered by someone else, thus rediscovered by herself. She spoke from her secure status as wife of the best man in the house. Petruchio interrupted her move to place her hand beneath his foot with his own hand. It brought her up to his level. She laughed at his publicly necessary, "Why, there's a wench!" She hugged her father as she exited towards a well-deserved bed. Once freed of her compulsion to scream, Ms. Flett's Katherina modulated towards an effective finale. This *Shrew*, though broadly played, and thus neglectful of the emotional en-

lightenment that comedy tends to show us and encourage in us, earned some of its laughs and most of its applause. It would seem to be the best television version of the play currently available.

King Lear (BBC, 1982 [PBS, 18 October 1982])

Albany: John Bird. *Cordelia*: Brenda Blethyn. *Edgar*: Anton Lesser. *Edmund*: Michael Kitchen. *Fool*: Frank Middlemass. *Gloucester*: Norman Rodway. *Goneril*: Gillian Barge. *Kent*: John Shrapnel. *Lear*: Michael Hordern. *Regan*: Penelope Wilton.

Producer: Shaun Sutton. *Director*: Jonathan Miller. *Designer*: Colin Lowrey.

Cecil Smith, *Los Angeles Times* (18 Oct. 1982). "Stark, clean, chilling . . . utterly compelling. . . . Miller caught the fairy tale aura to *Lear*. . . ." The Storm Scene is "brilliant."

Megan Rosenfeld, *Washington Post* (18 Oct. 1982). "The main problem with Hordern's otherwise graphic performance [as Lear] is that there is too much self-pity in his madness . . . not enough sense of his redeemed social conscience. The conception of Anton Lesser's Edgar's feigned madness as a gibbering, drooling idiot was also a mistake, overkill for the small screen, particularly as he is costumed as Jesus Christ on the cross, complete with holes in his palms. But the essential drama is developed clearly. . . . Gillian Barge and Penelope Wilton as Goneril and Regan are thoroughly evil, and John Shrapnel's . . . Kent . . . is the essence of compassion. . . . A clearly conceived and well realized *Lear*."

Dennis Hackett, "Pride and Pathos," London *Times* (20 Sept. 1982).

It says much for Jonathan Miller's direction of *King Lear*, which began BBC2's fifth season of the complete dramatic works of Shakespeare last night, that the play seemed to last far less than the three hours and ten minutes allotted to it.

The combination of Miller, as director, Michael Hordern, as Lear, and Frank Middlemass, as the Fool, has been seen twice before—more recently as Play of the Month in 1975—but never previously has there been time for the full text. This third essay enabled them to achieve a memorable reconciliation of reflective experience with opportunity that must have been as satisfying to them as to the producer, Shaun Sutton, and the viewers.

It is said that Hordern, one of those actors whose appearance never fails to make me optimistic about any production where he unpacks his skills, felt that in previous Lears he had over-emphasized familial relations at the expense of regality. If that is so, then he has put it to rights. He produced a Lear of kingly hubris and destructive vanity but with a pathos that constrained us from assigning blame. Middlemass was an older Fool than we are used to but the device worked wonderfully, giving the worn wit of an aging jester a sharpened edge and heightening the intimacy between man and master.

The cast were splendid. John Shrapnel restrained his almost acrobatic vigour in the course of giving us a passionately dutiful Kent. Penelope Wilton and Gillian Barge were evilly though attractively assertive as Regan and Goneril respectively. Brenda Blethyn made Cordelia shine with virtue; Michael Kitchen's exercise in moral depravity as Edmund was counterpointed by the fine playing of Anton Lesser as Edgar; and Norman Rodway was excellent as the hapless Gloucester.

H. R. Woudhuysen, "An Interest in Evil," *Times Literary Supplement* (1 Oct. 1982).

Bradley told us, a long time ago, that "*King Lear* is too huge for the stage." How is it to be squeezed into the "Little Easel" of the television screen? Jonathan Miller, in the first of the new season of the BBC television Shakespeare, gives us a relatively full version lasting a little over three hours. The actors are placed in large unparticularized, floor-boarded rooms, with bare rock and rectangular, massive shafts, or plain stone for walls. As the play goes on the sets become even starker. When Gloucester thinks he is on Dover Cliffs, he is standing on what appears to be ploughed up matting. Poor Tom's hovel is a large drain-pipe. The production's visual bareness extends to the flat grayness of the lighting, closer to black and white than colour television. The actors wear black costumes, and all the men seem to have beards, except for the white-faced Fool, and the shaven-headed, ear-ringed Kent, when in his "razed" disguise.

No doubt this is all intentional, along with the simplicity of some of the camera work: one long-held shot of Lear's and Gloucester's painful re-encounter in Act IV, and some badly composed groupings, with unfocused figures in the background, as well as some very knowing looks given directly to the camera. Our attention is directed to watch all this intently, to concentrate our minds wonderfully on what is going on. Jonathan Miller's major ambition in his *Lear* is to do just this. The play's story is clearly put forward, and despite its length never drags. This in itself is quite an achievement, but there is still too much of the unexplained and the unnecessary which distracts the viewer from the action.

In his plain black, and with no train of knights in evidence, Lear is not sufficiently regal; there is no apparent majesty in him. As a result of this the tragedy, inevitably, becomes a domestic, not a national and universal one. The real interest throughout the play seems to be not in Lear's suffering, but in the character of his enemies. Perhaps this is inevitable with a medium which finds that evil makes good television, but there is a feeling that we are meant to find the play's cruelty more interesting and compelling than its depiction of human frailty.

Above all it is puzzling why so much weight is placed on the first two acts, which run for nearly an hour and a half. The play's interval usually comes at the end of the third act, after Gloucester's blinding. Here, at the end of the second, it has the effect of breaking up the continuous action of the first three acts, and the second half of the play is rather rushed, with more cuts, and a distinctly episodic feeling about it, as against the much fuller and better integrated first half.

In spite of this, Michael Hordern's Lear is quite astonishingly good. His movements and expressions, his eyebrows, his nail-biting and puckering forehead never distract from his growling and worried delivery, and astonishing range of inarticulate noises. Consistently intelligent and moving, he carries effortlessly the weight of his part, and also much of Frank Middlemass's aggressive and similarly aged Fool. This is a tiresome and unwitty, miscast Fool. An equally odd conception must have been behind the choice of John Bird as Albany, puzzled and quite out of his depth against Gillian Barge's Goneril. Apart from his unfetching appearance, and predictable yokel's accent, Kent (John Shrapnel) is convincing, but there is much stumbling and mumbling elsewhere in the cast.

Jonathan Miller's *Lear* demands close attention. In the title-role's part it deserves this; but there is still too much intrusive, directorial heavy-handedness to allow us to concentrate on the words themselves, or to feel that we are getting beyond a messy set of domestic and family squabbles.

Steven Urkowitz, "*King Lear* Without Tears," *Shakespeare on Film Newsletter*, 7:2 (Apr. 1983).

During seasons three and four, as executive producer and sometime director, Jonathan Miller supervised productions of memorable and important televised Shakespeare, particularly *Troilus and Cressida* and *Timon of Athens*. His direction of the fifth season's *King Lear*, however, is best quickly forgotten as a hasty and inconsistent effort. We never feel the tragic paradoxes of family love and conflict worked out in Shakespeare's magnificent design.

Problems in this *Lear* begin with a basic isolation of the actors from the emotional life implied by the words they speak. For example, Shakespeare's actors should weep when they say they are weeping. But when Cordelia bids farewell to her sisters "with washed eyes," when the king complains of "these hot tears" forced from him by Goneril, and when he tells Cordelia "mine own tears do scald like molten lead," the actors' eyes are dry. They don't even pretend to wipe away a tear. Their words are unconnected to what we see happening on the screen.

Many large-scale stage actions called for in the dialogue also fail to appear in this production. Goneril's steward, Oswald, should be hit by Lear and then tripped or knocked down by Kent when he brazenly offends the king (I.iv). Later lines depend on these events, as Kent asks Oswald, "Is it two days since I tripp'd up thy heels and beat thee before the King?" and as Oswald reports these same actions to the Duke of Cornwall: "It pleas'd the King his master very late To strike at me . . ." and he "Tripp'd me behind" (II.ii). Neither the blow nor the fall happens in the scene we witnessed.

Most of the vigorous movement that makes Shakespeare's scripts so dramatic seems to have been suppressed, and only action that wouldn't move out of the fixed camera frame remains. Early in the history of motion pictures, film directors learned that they could move their cameras. By shifting their points of view they could concentrate on specific details and control the pace or rhythm not only of the action but also of the audience's perception of the action. Miller rejects conventional film and video technique and relies instead on the unmoving frame into which he brings more and more actors, usually at very close range. Many scenes resemble football huddles as three, four or even five speakers stand cheek to cheek and nose to nose for minutes on end.

The undifferentiated black-and-white costumes generally serve to reduce the variety and complexity of characters in this *Lear*. At the outset, everyone seems to have dressed out of the same costume box—King, courtier, and servant handsomely turned out. This may imply an interesting failure of distinction in Lear's kingdom.

Two images stick in my memory: first, while Cornwall gouges Gloucester's eyes our attention is drawn away from the horror of the moment towards an out-of-focus figure of a bearded old man in the background. He hops up and down while patting himself on the top of his head in a gesture of impotent concern. Second, when Lear meets blind Gloucester after the storm, instead of sharing wild wisdom and sympathy, during his lines Lear buffets Gloucester on the head, pushes his fingers roughly against Gloucester's ruined eyes, and shouts harshly in his ears. We wince at these scenes.

But what prompts them? We can't tell from the words being said, and we can't tell from any chain of consistent actions or meanings presented earlier in the play. We lose sympathy for the characters because they've become like those victims glimpsed in the evening news. We recognize their shapes and acknowledge the event of their suffering, but because the presentation makes no demand of involvement or sympathy, we know we'll swiftly turn to the commercial and tomorrow's weather.

Cymbeline (BBC, 1982 [PBS, 20 December 1982])

Cloten: Paul Jesson. *Cymbeline*: Richard Johnson. *Iachimo*: Robert Lindsay. *Imogen*: Helen Mirren.

Posthumus: Michael Pennington. *Queen*: Claire Bloom.
Producer: Shaun Sutton. *Director*: Elijah Moshinsky. *Designer*: Barbara Gosnold.

G. M. Pearce, *Cahiers Elisabéthains*, 24 (Oct. 1983). For a moment "one feels [that] Imogen [Helen Mirren] is drawn towards" Iachimo—"a portrayal of pure evil by Robert Lindsay. . . . Claire Bloom . . . played [the Queen] with . . . restrained venom."

Katherine Duncan-Jones, "Sitting Pretty," *Times Literary Supplement* (22 July 1983).
While few modern readers of *Cymbeline* would go the whole way with Johnson in his refusal to "waste criticism upon unresisting imbecility," it is undeniable that any modern director of the play must make some positive decision about how to deal with this clogged, often obscure, and highly complicated romance. What Elijah Moshinsky decides to do is to impose on the cluttered world of Shakespeare's Ancient Britain the lucid visual images of the great Dutch Masters. This produces some delightful effects, especially in the opening scenes of the play. The Second Gentleman, who asks all those helpful questions about the status quo in Cymbeline's court, becomes a dignified Rembrandt old lady in a ruff (Aimee Delamain). Claire Bloom makes an icily beautiful Queen, especially when proposing experiments on live animals to her leather-bonneted Doctor (Hugh Thomas). Imogen sitting alone waiting for news of her exiled husband is a Van Dyck beauty in a Vermeer interior. These images, and many more, are what is gained. What is lost, however, is almost all the poetry, a good deal of the action, and all the sweet poignancy which made this a favourite play of Keats, Swinburne and Tennyson. Exterior scenes are kept to a minimum, though the text would seem to call for many. The mountains of Wales are for some reason presented as the steppes of Russia. Instead of a cave, the Welsh exiles inhabit a comfortable if plain dacha, so the vital contrast between the court and the pastoral world is lost. The most painful casualty is Fidele's funeral, which happens inside the dacha with the princes squatting uncomfortably over the corpse. Instead of promising a perpetual strewing of "fairest flowers / Whilst summer lasts," the boys thrust two dusty-looking dried flowers into Imogen's hands, and leave it at that. The Snow White-like domesticity of the pastoral episode is also eliminated; here is no "neat cookery," with Fidele cutting the vegetables into "characters." Helen Mirren's Imogen, more at ease as distressed boy than as chaste wife, is clearly no home-maker.

Because of its emphasis on painterly tableaux, this production is overwhelmingly static. Characters seem loath to rise from their high-backed chairs, and with a few exceptions, such as Cymbeline (Richard Johnson, looking like George V) and Belarius (Michael Gough), are apt to converse in whispers. Posthumus (Michael Pennington), sitting at a still-life breakfast in Philario's elegant palazzo, scarcely looks up to receive Imogen's letter and Iachimo's report on the outcome of the wager. The dignified Lucius (Graham Crowden) declares war on Britain without rising from his seat at table. That useful messenger Pisanio, instead of being constantly on the move between Wales and Lud's Town, is often seen seated as he reads vital letters. Cloten (Paul Jesson), here presented as lisping and foppish, meditates rape and murder while lolling on his bed in the firelight. This immobility cannot be entirely explained by the constraints of the medium. Opportunities for close-up are often missed. We have no detailed view of the diamond ring and bracelet exchanged by Imogen and Posthumus and surprisingly we are not allowed to see either the "mole cinque-spotted" on Imogen's left breast or the "sanguine star" on Guiderius's shoulder.

Overall, the gentle, almost sentimental texture of the play is denied, in favour of an attempted intensity which becomes rather wearisome. The play offers repeated softenings of Shakespeare's earlier work. Iachimo, for instance, is a Tarquin who makes an inventory of Lucrece's bedroom furniture, rather than raping her—an Iago whose provocation of jealousy is bantering rather than malign. But here Robert Lindsay's Iachimo, in a black leather traveling outfit which makes it appear that he has left his Jacobean motor bike parked outside Cymbeline's palace, is clearly intended to present real menace; and what is more, it is by no means clear that Imogen dislikes his attentions. Her "What ho, Pisanio" in the attempted seduction scene is so *sotto voce* that the lady scarcely protests at all, and her restless slumbers in the bedchamber scene are, the *Radio Times* preview suggested, intended to make us see Iachimo's visit as an enactment of her sexual fantasies. It is odd, though, that we see so much of Iachimo's nakedness, and so little of hers; odd, too, that Posthumus suddenly plants a kiss on the cheek of the British Lord to whom he has described the outcome of the battle with the Romans. Moshinsky seems at times intent on adding more puzzles to an already puzzling text. The cutting and rearranging of scenes in Act V does not make the story any plainer. Posthumus's vision comes over as a fragment from *Ruddigore*; Jove (Michael Hordern) has no eagle and looks like a shabby old clergyman; the comic Jailer, whom Shaw called "just the thing to save the last act," is so cut as to waste an excellent little performance by Ray Mort. Patricia Hayes does very well as the Soothsayer in the closing minutes, expounding the prophecy with compelling authority. But boredom often threatens, and there might have been a case for using Shaw's *Cymbeline Refinished*, which gets Shakespeare's 485 lines in the final scene down to 89.

Henry E. Jacobs, "The Shakespeare Plays on TV," *Shakespeare on Film Newsletter*, 7:2 (Apr. 1983).

Cymbeline is a very difficult play to produce in any medium for several reasons. A surfeit of names, characters, places, and plots creates an unusually tricky situation for the director. Although some of the play's problems proved to be as problematic on television as they can be on the stage, Elijah Moshinsky breaks new ground with his videotape of the play.

Moshinsky was less than successful with his solution to the problem of place and culture. The choice of a generalized eighteenth-century milieu as the "ground" for the BBC tape blurred the essential distinctions between the worlds of the play: prehistoric Britain and Wales, Augustan Rome, and Renaissance Italy. He more clearly established and sustained the distinction between urban settings and the hard pastoral world of Wales with the contrasting blacks and whites for Wales's stark winterscape.

The great strength of this production may be found in Moshinsky's treatment of the characters and the superb performances that he elicited from most of the actors. Richard Johnson's Cymbeline was a man whose judgment and moods were controlled by his own changeability and his wife's manipulations rather than by age or sickness. Indeed, this Cymbeline never does change very much; he is as mercurial in the catastrophe as he was at the play's opening.

Claire Bloom's portrayal of the Queen was a model of subtle and cold malevolence. Moshinsky avoided the excess of turning the Queen into an archetypal witch/stepmother.

This production manages to make a rarely produced and very difficult play work very well indeed. The denouement was a theatrical *tour de force* that succeeded in manipulating our emotions backwards and forwards between the joy and anguish of the characters. In the true spirit of the tragicomic mode, we leave this production with a mixture of smiles and tears.

The Merry Wives of Windsor (BBC, 1982 [PBS, 31 January 1983])

Doctor Caius: Michael Bryant. *Falstaff*: Richard Griffiths. *Ford*: Ben Kingsley. *Mistress Ford*: Judy Davis. *Mistress Page*: Prunella Scales. *Mistress Quickly*: Elizabeth Spriggs.

Producer: Shaun Sutton. Director: David Jones. Designer: Don Homfray.

D. A. N. Jones, *The Listener* (6 Jan. 1983). "As Falstaff, Richard Griffiths—with his dark, predatory eyes asking for trouble—easily persuaded us that he could win a woman, despite his age and size; the flaw in his stratagem was only his sheer cheek in courting two wives at once—and bosom friends, at that."

John Engstrom, *Boston Globe* (31 Jan. 1983). "A very funny production, filled with imaginative comic performances and bright splashes of slapstick . . . a virtuoso performance by Ben Kingsley [as] an Elizabethan Charlie Chaplin."

Walter Goodman, *NY Times* (31 Jan. 1983). "Richard Griffiths gives us a grizzled [Falstaff], clinging shakily to faith in his own 'charms.' Although this interpretation loses that inimitable Falstaffian quality, Griffiths creates a consistent character who rises as required to moments of high farce."

G. M. Pearce, *Cahiers Elisabéthains*, 24 (Oct. 1983). "Griffiths . . . certainly had the required figure for Falstaff, but spent the entire time . . . looking grim-faced and worried. . . . The real star . . . was Elizabeth Spriggs as Mistress Quickly, a wonderfully observed portrait of a stout aging gossip and busybody . . . not above an enthusiastic cuddle with the lusty Pistol (Nigel Terry). . . . The scenes in the sunlit orchard contrasted pleasantly with the dark interiors of the Elizabethan houses and taverns. There were also bustling street scenes, as when Mistress Page consults Sir Hugh Evans (a nice cameo . . . by Tenniel Evans) on her son's progress in Latin."

Dan Sullivan, *Los Angeles Times* (31 Jan. 1983). "Scenes obviously meant to be played robustly and with a wink are interiorized and lingered over, losing the play's theatrical rhythm and the fun of the plot. . . . It's Shakespeare-for-the-record."

Stanley Wells, "A Picturesque Comedy of Character," *Times Literary Supplement* (14 Jan. 1983).

Because *The Merry Wives of Windsor* has a skillfully plotted intrigue and contains a higher proportion of prose over verse than any other of Shakespeare's plays, it is often treated as farce. But the prose is supple, colourful, and idiosyncratic, and though some of the characters are recycled from other plays, Shakespeare establishes for them individual identities in their new context. Admittedly this is the least aristocratic of his comedies, but the values that it endorses as it moves into the verse of the final episodes are those of romantic comedy. The manically jealous Ford is cured of his obsession, begs forgiveness of his wronged wife, and joins in the plot to trick Falstaff. Anne Page elopes with her handsome young lover, not with either of the less attractive suitors favoured by her parents; her new husband, unabashed by their dismay, preaches a brief but pithy sermon on the miseries of enforced marriage and is forthwith welcomed into the family circle. Falstaff himself is led to see the error of his ways and is invited to the celebratory feast. The play ends, not in the disintegration of farce but in a comic harmony in which the outsider joins the society whose moral values he has been trying to subvert.

David Jones, directing the play for the BBC Shakespeare series, places more emphasis on the characters than on the society. Sensibly, he scarcely reminds us of the worlds elsewhere with which some of them are associated: only as Pistol kisses Mistress Quickly in the shadows does the direction invite us to remember the plays of the French wars. Less happily, little is done to establish a social context. Though naturalistic settings may seem to demand some kind of social perspective, in this production scarcely anything happens on the fringes of the action, played against and in a pretty setting of half-timbered buildings. It is all more like an underpopulated travelogue on behalf of the Shakespeare Birthplace Trust than an evocation of Tudor Windsor. Elizabethan costumes admirably complement the period setting, but Slender's folly might usefully have been set off by stronger visual reminders of his wealth, inadequately conveyed to a modern audience by the information that he has "three hundred pounds a year."

The text is played with little alteration—omissions of a few obscurities, classical references, and the allusions to the Garter ceremony; minor adjustments to take advantage of the fact that, for instance, the camera can show Falstaff lolloping away from Ford's house in his guise as the old woman of Brentford; and occasional, harmless modernizations—"kidneys" for "reins," "protected" for "delivered." The production style is gently comic rather than uproariously farcical, while admitting mildly amusing comic business involving the problems of negotiating a low beam in Falstaff's attic bedroom along with more robust horseplay in the climactic scenes of Ford and the buckbasket. David Jones seeks comedy of character rather than of action, sometimes at a sacrifice of complexity. The final scene gives us the mischievous geniality of the tricksters but fails to counterpoint it with a sense that Falstaff may truly take them to be emanations of the supernatural.

Jeanne Addison Roberts, "The Shakespeare Plays on TV," *Shakespeare on Film Newsletter*, 7:2 (Apr. 1983).

Rather reluctantly we must add *The Merry Wives* to the debit side of the ledger in accounting for the plays produced so far by the BBC. In spite of a few inspired moments, intelligent editing, and some creditable acting, the production simply never cohered into an exciting whole.

Unfortunately the very first scene was enough to send most viewers back to the rerun of *Shogun*, where unintelligibility could be clearly accounted for by foreign land and language. Admittedly the scene is a hard one. Ten characters must be identified and the threads of some rather nebulous previous action must be at least faintly grasped. It helps if the play follows a production of $1H4$ so that audiences may at least recognize Falstaff, and Bardolph, and later Mistress Quickly; but failing that the eccentrics of the play must be really eccentric. And the lines, even the obscure ones, must be crystal clear. Here Shallow and Evans were distinguished chiefly by length of beard, and Pistol, Nym, and Bardolph were fuzzily merging types. Even the Host, who has enough lines to shape a character, was low-keyed and colorless. And here, as so often in the TV productions, lines and whole speeches were thrown away in a futile approximation of verisimilitude.

Later scenes, though handsomely costumed and set largely in lush pastoral surrounding, could not reverse the effects of the unpromising start. When the wives shared their outrageous letters from Falstaff in a scene which ought to be one of the funniest in the play, the effect was again marred by an intimate conversational style which downplayed theatrical impact and wasted some of the best lines. Elizabeth Spriggs as Mistress Quickly gave the one truly distinguished performance of the piece, bringing wonderful life to her all-too-brief scenes; but it was not enough.

The two characters who ought to be the stars of the show, Falstaff and Ford, were strangely mismatched. Richard Griffiths as Falstaff was subdued, with an undertone of melancholy which turned his second love scene with Mistress Ford into a pensive romantic interlude reminiscent of *Chimes at Midnight*. By contrast, Ben Kingsley, fresh in the minds of American audiences from his performance as Gandhi, clearly thought he was playing in a farce. His Ford was not only choleric but frequently hysterical; he was a short man frantically insecure in his marital role. Either style might have been the basis for a consistent interpretation, but together they worked at cross purposes. Similarly the lower-class accent, affected determinedly by Mistress Page but much less reliably by Mistress Ford and the husbands, proved distracting, perhaps even confusing, since Mistress Page sounded to an American ear like a downstairs character from *Upstairs Downstairs* rather than a prosperous village landowner.

The final scenes were extremely well done. The lighting conveyed a mysteriously moonlit midnight landscape without obscuring the identities or actions of characters. Falstaff and Sir Hugh Evans were intriguingly linked by lifelike animal masks. Falstaff's buck's head was raised off his face, but he bent his head to reveal it and for a moment became a deer. When Sir Hugh appeared suddenly over the horizon with his horned goat's head over his face, a spine-tingling chill convinced an audience that Falstaff might indeed be struck dumb with terror. The pinching and burning were accompanied by ritual chants and dances which removed us from the realm of reality and made us feel part of some strange pagan ceremony. The final unmasking and reconciliation were accomplished with grace and dispatch; and the last image was of the newly purged community marching with a song back over the hill to Windsor. If the whole videotape had been carried out with the unity of vision and imaginative detail of the conclusion, it would have been a notable success instead of a mediocre near-failure.

Henry VI (3 parts) and *Richard III* (BBC, 1983 [PBS, March-May 1983])

Lady Anne: Zoe Wanamaker. *Jack Cade/Talbot*: Trevor Peacock. *Henry VI*: Peter Benson. *Joan la Pucelle*: Brenda Blethyn. *Queen Margaret*: Julia Foster. *Richard III*: Ron Cook. *Winchester*: Frank Middlemass. *York*: Bernard Hill.

Producers: Jonathan Miller (Parts I and II), Shaun Sutton (Part III and *Richard III*). *Director*: Jane Howell. *Designer*: Oliver Bayldon.

Peter Ackroyd, London *Times* (3 Jan. 1983). (On 1 *Henry VI*.) "The paradox was that of television accommodating a self-consciously staged production, rougher and more pantomimic than anything to be found in the theatre itself. . . . And yet it worked: it extracted enjoyment from a play which otherwise would have been sheer torture to watch."

D. A. N. Jones, *The Listener* (6 Jan. 1983). (On 1 *Henry VI*.) "It is primitive, naive and, sometimes, almost Homeric. . . . I much admired the way the production and setting managed to contain both the kindergarten babyishness and the noble savagery of the work."

Russell Davies, London *Times* (30 Jan. 1983). (On *Richard III*.) "It was the women who came out of the production best. Queen Margaret . . . by Julia Foster . . . cracklingly consumed by [age]. Rowena Cooper's pinch-faced Elizabeth was similarly strong. But Mr. Cook . . . was not so much a lump of foul deformity, more a disaffected pensionee of the Injured Jockeys' Fund."

Stanley Wells, "The History of the Whole Contention," *Times Literary Supplement* (4 Feb. 1983).

Shakespeare's three long plays on the reign of King Henry VI, with their climactic sequel *Richard III*, all written early in his career, form a more ambitious dramatic structure than had been attempted by an English playwright up to the time of their composition: nor was Shakespeare himself ever again to work on such a scale. Admittedly, the plays do not add up to an artistic unity of the order of, say, Wagner's *Ring*. The first play, 1 *Henry VI*, does not look forward to the last, *Richard III*, in the way that *Richard III* looks back to its predecessors. Individual works in the series employ somewhat different theatrical conventions; their verbal styles vary, a development in poetic mastery is evident from one to another. *Richard III* is a more confidently rounded whole than the three earlier plays.

Nevertheless, their narrative links are stronger than those within any other group of Shakespeare's plays; they are far more uniform in style than his later composed sequence, also of four plays (*Richard II*, *Henry IV*, Parts I and II, and *Henry V*, dramatizing the immediately preceding period of English history); and *Richard III*, in particular, gains greatly in resonance when experienced in conjunction with its predecessors. The enormous success of Colley Cibber's adaptation, for two centuries perhaps the most popular play on the English stage, bears witness to this, for Cibber had the wit to provide some of the background that Shakespeare's play, acted alone, lacks. The theatre's abandonment, during the late nineteenth century, of his adaptation, lamentably though it coarsens some aspects of its original, has not given to the unadulterated text a comparable pre-eminence; and the most successful version to be performed during the twentieth century, with Laurence Olivier at its centre, adopted some of Cibber's structural changes and even retained a few of his verbal additions.

Jane Howell has accepted the challenge of making the plays work in very much the terms in which they were originally composed, and has displayed great cunning in effecting the transition from the wooden O to the celluloid rectangle.

In some respects she embraces the plays' theatricality. Her basic set (designed by Oliver Bayldon) is constant throughout. Most of the earlier plays in this series have been quasi-naturalistic in their settings; a few have been filmed on location. But Jane Howell has dared to encourage us to remember that the action is taking place in a studio—or, more precisely, in a warehouse that was converted into a studio for the six months during which a single company of actors rehearsed and filmed the sequence. The wooden structure of palisades, steps, platforms, alcoves, walkways, gates, and swinging doors on, around and within which the actors work has been described as "a medieval adventure playground," and the director, in a radio broadcast, remarked that it accidentally resembled "an Elizabethan theatre-in-the-round." In the first play, particularly, we are very conscious of the conventionalized setting, and it becomes a way of helping us to accept the play's artificiality of language and action. In the Countess of Auvergne episode, for instance, Talbot has only to blow his horn for his army to materialize in the countess's chamber. To play this naturalistically would make it seem absurd; to accept its unreality allows us to concentrate undistractedly on the action's significance. As the sequence progresses, however, a sense of reality increases, until in *Richard III* many of the scenes seem to take place in virtually real interiors.

Acceptance of unreality is apparent, too, in the fact that about thirty actors share roughly 200 speaking parts among them; nor is any great effort made to alter their appearance from one role to another. Casting has been careful and intelligent,

with an eye both to making the characters' appearances conform to what is said about them and to clarifying the actions. There is no escaping the fact that even those who know their Shakespeare well may have problems in keeping track of who is who in these plays, in which Shakespeare's powers of characterization are relatively undeveloped. Jane Howell does what she can to help by providing a wide range of physical types and, more questionably, by endowing them with a variety of regional accents. All members of the cast speak with skill and understanding; some of them handle verse mellifluously in voices whose beauty is unimpaired by regional characteristics. The director is remarkably successful in encouraging her performers to invest with personal significance countless lines which might be ranted or treated as generalized sententiousness—the death scene of Warwick (played by Mark Wing-Davey) is a notable example. But most local accents inevitably create something of a plebeian impression which may seem at odds with the dignity and status of the aristocratic and royal protagonists.

The commitment of a relatively small number of actors to these plays over a long period of time has resulted in a unity of approach that has been sadly lacking in some other components of the series. The unfamiliarity of the plays is perhaps a help. Responses are fresh; there is no sense of famous actors dropping in between engagements to repeat performances that are well known in other contexts, no need to scale down effects that were originally conceived for the stage. The company has few weak links, and almost all the actors find the right scale of projection. Soliloquies and asides are frequently and effectively spoken directly to camera; rhetoric is given with inward force rather than with theatrical expansiveness. Playing is unselfish, but inevitably some roles stand out.

Peter Benson opens the first play singing beautifully in an episode of mourning for Henry V, and later takes on the role of Henry VI, anorexically thin, whey-faced, innocent-eyed, puffin-nosed, befringed. He succeeds in making Henry both pathetically ineffectual and truly saintly. It is a delicate performance, at times permitting an amused response but never cheapening the role. One remembers, for instance, his first meeting with Margaret, his bride by proxy, when, touchingly pleased by the sight of her, he offers her a kiss, she inclines her head to take it on the lips, but he kisses her hand instead and retreats into contemplation of the divine. It is a good moment for Julia Foster as Margaret, too, as she demonstrates simultaneously her doubts about Henry as a man and her delighted anticipation of the power she will achieve by her marriage. Carrying through all four plays, this is a cruelly demanding role. Though Julia Foster does not bring to it the range of a Peggy Ashcroft, she can be both charming and vicious, a siren and a spitfire. A climactic scene is her taunting of Richard, Duke of York, played with splendid authority and fire by Bernard Hill.

Ron Cook plays York's son, Richard of Gloucester, as an amorally intelligent urchin. Short, physically and emotionally tough, he presents a Richard who can feign sympathy with complete conviction and remain stoically impassive in the face of his nephew's taunts and scorn. He is not vividly ironical; for example, he makes no comic point out of "Call them again" in the episode with the Lord Mayor and citizens. Nor does he attempt to dig deep into Richard's psychology. As a result *Richard III*, in which he is dominant, seems almost anticlimactically sombre; not being invited to share Richard's ironic perspective and to delight in his triumphs, we feel the more pity for his victims. It is not a virtuoso performance, but it is a legitimate interpretation, in line with the director's overall sympathy with the abhorrence of violence and the compassion with the suffering victims of aggressive ambition and of war that Shakespeare himself is at pains to stress.

It seems ungracious not to praise many other individual performances, among them Trevor Peacock's noble Talbot and egocentrically absurd but horrifying Jack Cade, Frank Middlemass's Beaufort, ghastly in death, Paul Chapman's glamorous Suffolk, and—among the smaller parts—Oengus MacNamara's fiery Young Clifford and Zoe Wanamaker's Lady Anne. But their success derives, in part at least, from the sustained power and imagination of Jane Howell's direction.

The method is uniformly honest, and sometimes it succeeds triumphantly, above all in the Cade episodes of Part II. Here, the death of the Clerk who perishes at the hands of the mob because he can write his name has the symbolic significance of the death of Cinna the poet in *Julius Caesar*, and the subsequent scenes, reaching a climax in the burning of "all the records of the realm," with Cade's exultant grimaces superimposed upon shots of slaughter, torture, and the pages of books torn up, cast into the air, and floating down onto a bonfire, have so timeless an impetus and vitality that they might belong to a modern play conceived entirely in televisual terms.

This is real translation of Shakespeare into the medium of television. Other stretches of the plays are more pedestrian, but the dedication with which, almost throughout the fourteen hours of playing time, Jane Howell has served Shakespeare is so admirable that she can be forgiven the indulgence of ending the tetralogy, following Richmond's prayer for peace after the stopping of "civil wounds," with a sequence in which we see a pile of bloodstained corpses, hear cackling laughter, and finally see Margaret, on top of the pyramid, exul-

tantly cradling in her arms the corpse of Richard III. It is a melodramatically simplistic conclusion to a richly varied experience.

John J. O'Connor, *NY Times* (10 Apr. 1983).

The set itself becomes a symbol of the plays' content, its bright colors gradually fading to a gloomy gray, its wooden slats covered with the scars of war and destruction. The blatantly theatrical device works splendidly for the purposes of television, a medium nearly always more interested in intense close-ups than in background visuals.

Miss Howell's repertory company was able to work together for about ten months. A duplicate set was constructed in a separate hall where extensive rehearsals were arranged. By the time the actors faced the cameras, they were as thoroughly prepared as any stage troupe. The intensive preparations are apparent in the finished product, in its assurance and energy. The performances are almost always substantial, never glaringly inadequate. Some, of course, are more impressive than others. Peter Benson's otherworldly Henry VI is a model of admirable yet infuriating piety. Brenda Blethyn's Joan la Pucelle turns the Maid of Orleans into a scheming fraud whose curse is nevertheless awesome. If one performance had to be chosen as outstanding, it would definitely be that of Julia Foster in the role of Margaret of Anjou, the woman who marries Henry VI. In Part I, she enters as a giggly but calculating 14-year-old princess. By *King Richard III*, she is an embittered 73-year-old widow, screaming for vengeance against her enemies. In between, she has some of the cycle's juiciest scenes, including one memorable sequence in which she taunts the about-to-be-executed Duke of York with news of the death of his young son. Miss Foster is truly formidable.

The cycle moves on, sweepingly and powerfully, to a shattering image devised for the end of *Richard III*: perched atop a huge mound of dead bodies, a keening Margaret caresses, "Pieta"-like, the bloody body of Richard. It is a stunning coda for this admirable production.

Michael Manheim, "The Shakespeare Plays on TV," *Shakespeare on Film Newsletter*, 8:2 Apr. 1984).

It has been observed before that the best television productions in the BBC Time/Life series seem to be those of the less popular Shakespearean plays. This observation certainly holds true for the production of the *Henry VI-Richard III* tetralogy, a sequence of plays which, despite its large number of events and personalities, is a fascinating, fast-paced, and surprisingly tight-knit study in political and national deterioration.

Covering nearly sixty years in England's tumultuous fifteenth century, the plays trace quite closely the progression of what later came to be called the "Wars of the Roses," that struggle for sovereignty which had its roots in the deposing of Richard II by his cousin Henry Bolingbroke (Henry IV) in 1399, and did not end until Henry of Richmond's triumph over Richard III at Bosworth Field in 1485.

The chief credit for the success of these productions must go, of course, to Jane Howell, who directed the entire tetralogy, and whose sense of their purposes strikes me as clear and accurate throughout. She sees the role of King Henry on the one hand and of the emerging Richard of Gloucester on the other as set apart from the many other important characters in the plays.

Her Henry is a non-political man in an era dominated by political men. He is here seen as an incipient pacifist living among power brokers who consider no means of resolving political differences other than violent ones.

Paralleling Henry, at the opposite end of the spectrum, is the figure of Richard, who also pulls away from the others—this time in the direction of still greater violence and relentless duplicity. Howell recognizes that the essential integrity of Shakespeare's first historical tetralogy rests firmly on the polar opposition of its "saintly" hero and its super villain.

Howell's staging of the many battle scenes supports the inherent pacifism she sees as central to these plays. In Part I, rapid reversals are conveyed by the simple device of swinging doors. At one instant, the English pursue the French through these doors with great cheers and flourishes; at another, they are themselves pursued back with the physical evidence of defeat suddenly plastered on their countenances.

While such devices enhance the sense of the pointlessness of battle in Part II, they also contribute to the somewhat comic quality of the early battles in these plays. But as the true Wars of the Roses begin late in Part II and Part III, there is little comedy. What we now see are montages of the false glory of battle (represented by trumpets and drums), followed by the very graphic examples of hand-to-hand combat which are quite free from any kind of glory.

Howell individualizes these battles, seemingly so similar to one another as one reads them on the printed page. Each has its own noteworthy feature. For example, there is Tewksbury, which, before it concludes with the brutal on-stage murder of the foolish Prince Edward, is preceded by marvelous, balletic montages of bloody winter battle which perhaps better than anything else in these productions suggest the cold absurdity of men killing each other for vaguely conceived ambition and senseless revenge. Since the three parts of H6 cover such a long sequence of years, one naturally needs actors who can show us something of the maturation, over the years, of the characters they play. The actor who does this most successfully is Bernard Hill

as the Duke of York, whom we see first as the debonair youth involved in what seems a trivial argument over a minor point of law in Part I (which is of course the beginning of the rivalry of the Roses).

Hill develops quite convincingly into the tough, middle-aged baron who almost achieves his kingly ambition, and he leaves us with a strong sense of the lingering medieval "honor" which underlies some of York's actions and the raw ambition which competes successfully with that honor.

Of course, the major woman's role in these plays is that of Queen Margaret, and Julia Foster is quite sufficient to the role. Her savagery is blood-curdling, and she gives Margaret's curses and prophecies in the last play a Hecate-like dimension. Howell makes her a kind of death-goddess at the conclusion of the tetralogy, as she sits atop the mound of corpses which have been steadily building up at the end of each play.

That Henry is defeated and finally slain by the most monstrous adventurer of all in no way takes away from his larger vision in these plays—a vision that invites the human race to survive.

G. M. Pearce, *Cahiers Elisabéthains* 24 (Oct. 1983).

The BBC, in their presentation of Shakespeare's complete works, have been going through the history plays in chronological order, except for *Henry VIII*, which was given as an hors d'oeuvre in their first season. It was particularly valuable to have an unbroken sequence between 3 *Henry VI* and *Richard III*, because it enabled one to follow the same personalities, played by the same actors and directed by the same person.

The events encompassed in these plays are on such an epic scale that the small screen could not hope to convey their scope. The huge cast was managed with a certain amount of doubling, sometimes rather disconcerting in its effect, as when Henry VI, played by Peter Benson, turned up as a priest early in *Richard III* after his sharp thin profile had been clearly recognized on his bier a few minutes before. The staging of the productions appeared to have been done in a theatre with a deliberate lack of realism. For instance the title of each play was shown at the beginning on the door through which the actors then burst or occasionally hacked their way; and the actors rode pantomime hobby horses (in 1 *Henry VI*). The audience were drawn even more closely into this game when Richard (Ron Cook) chalked his name, 'Richard III,' on a board before launching into his famous opening 'winter of discontent' speech. The same basic set was used for the four plays, but it was given a different angle in each case. It consisted of the currently fashionable and adaptable scaffolding with balconies and walkways as appropriate. It was never given undue prominence, although it was no doubt deliberate that the main doorway for exits and entrances was much in evidence.

The individual plays had their own specific flavour, with the smoothest transition being from 3 Henry VI to Richard III, both of which were produced by Shaun Sutton, whereas Jonathan Miller produced 1 and 2 Henry VI. Although forewarnings of Henry's future downfall were clear to see in Part I, it was still the most cheerful of the four plays. The costumes were colourful with plenty of contrast between the English and French nobles. Ian Saymor made an elegant Dauphin and Julia Foster, as Margaret, was still allowed to be attractive in a heavy embroidered cream dress to match her mass of blond hair. The small, determined mouth was just the same when she played Margaret, the old witch, in Richard III, but in other ways the transformation was complete. Henry VI himself, played by Peter Benson, changed disappointingly little during the three plays. Even if the inner character remains constant in Shakespeare's characterization, more attempt could have been made to indicate the passing of years. There was some effort to assume a youthful manner in Part I but for the most part one was guided by the words to reveal age and increasing disillusionment. His attachment to his childhood was seen in the fetal position he assumed as he rocked himself in grief at the death of Gloucester in Part II. Throughout, his voice was best suited to the part in its even, mellifluous softness.

The beginning of Part III was well adapted to television as a camera panned very slowly over an immense pile of bodies, dwelling now on a particularly horrific mutilation and now of the corpse of top of the pile in an attitude of crucifixion. Michael Wood has compared the cycle to the Greek tragic trilogies, where calamities crowd in thick and fast in the final part. Warwick was now grim-faced with dark hair plastered down as he bullied Richard and overreached himself. It was good to see Brian Protheroe's Edward IV still fresh and youthful and not the disease-ravaged wreck of Richard III. Rowena Cooper however was more convincing as his tragic queen, than the attractive widow he woos against all advice. Julia Foster's Margaret grew ever more Red Queen-like, dressed for war with her helmet awry.

There were more touching moments: Henry's soft melodious voice enhanced the beautiful soliloquy where he longs for the peaceful life, and his regret was infinite in the scene where he surveyed the son who had killed his father and the father who had killed his son. Such scenes highlighted the barbarity of the Wars of the Roses, and as their end-product, Richard, who is ever more prominent in 3 Henry VI, could hardly have been more corrupt and evil.

Evil was the hallmark of Ron Cook's Richard III

and he drew the audience into his devilish maneuverings by the force of his magnetic personality, directed at the camera. He needed this, because although his stature and physique were very well suited to the role, he was short on personal charm and brought out little of the element of black humour. It was hard indeed to believe that the spirited Lady Anne of Zoe Wanamaker would ever have succumbed to such a runt. One could better understand the pure loathing for him of the Duchess of York, his mother (a subdued but moving performance by Annette Crosbie). With his light northern intonation and flat voice, Ron Cook did not make the most of the poetry in the role, and the opening soliloquy was disappointingly pedestrian. However, in the ghost scene at the end where numerous candles burning low bore witness to the sleepless night caused by his guilty conscience, Richard's sense of remorse was strong and the horror he felt was tangible when he realized that the spirits who haunted him were encouraging Richmond. Richard III ended not with the final speech of Richmond as he surveyed the corpse-strewn battlefield, but with Margaret, hair wild in her frenzy, cackling like a hyena atop a pile of corpses even greater than the one at the beginning of 3 Henry VI. The links were strongest between these two plays, but the cohesion of all four together was of great advantage in viewing the turbulent period of the Wars of the Roses as a whole and in understanding Shakespeare's own interpretation of the historical facts. The cast appreciated the opportunity of a sustained development and were strong in their praise of Jane Howell as director. Despite certain weaknesses, only in part due to television, it was an interesting production, with a stronger sense of continuity than was possible even in the two parts of Henry IV and Henry V, also shown in sequence by the BBC.

Macbeth (BBC, 1983 [PBS, 17 October 1983])

Banquo: Ian Hogg. Duncan: Mark Dignam. Lady Macbeth: Jane Lapotaire. Macbeth: Nicol Williamson. Macduff: Tony Doyle. Malcolm: James Hazeldine. Porter: James Bolam.

Producer: Shaun Sutton. Director: Jack Gold. Designer: Gerry Scott.

Peter Ackroyd, London Times (7 Nov. 1983). "The closer the camera came to the Macbeths the more murky and formless they became."

G. M. Pearce, Cahiers Elisabéthains, 26 (Apr. 1984). "Ghosts and visions were only present in the heat-oppressed brain of Macbeth . . . and his anguished spouse. . . . Williamson assumed a strangled voice interspersed with rasping breathing which may have conveyed Macbeth's anguish effectively, but murdered most of the poetry. . . .

[The] lack of any relief gave a relentless concentration on the actual dramatic events and the breakdown of the individual[s] . . . but it sacrificed certain imaginative and poetical aspects of the play . . . essential [to] its . . . appeal."

Steven Reddicliffe, *Los Angeles Times* (17 Oct. 1983). Williamson is "competent, but [at times] seems a bit too frenzied. . . . The three witches are terrific."

David Richards, *Washington Post* (17 Oct. 1983). "One of the strongest offerings in the series to date. . . . Both lead performances have a lot of the panting beast in them. . . . Williamson['s] voice is as harsh as burlap and sharply nasal. . . . He . . . growls, hisses, rasps, and whines. . . . Lapotaire[s'] sleek grace as Lady Macbeth is that of the caged cat. . . . [Their] mating gives [this production] its true distinction."

Arthur Unger, *Christian Science Monitor* (17 Oct. 1983). "May be one of the . . . greatest versions of *Macbeth*. It would be hard to imagine a more savage and driven, a more naive and self-deceived, a more conscience-stricken and nearly understandable Macbeth than . . . Williamson's. . . . No matter that he alternately underplays and overplays, that he sometimes mumbles and sometimes speeds up his speech so much that he is almost incomprehensible. What matters is the overall character he creates indelibly in the viewer's mind and heart. . . . Lapotaire's Lady Macbeth is [too often] reciting Shakespeare rather than acting Shakespeare, and in several instances her exaggerated acting style borders on the ludicrous. I had the impression of watching a 'Saturday Night Live' takeoff of *Macbeth* rather than the real thing. . . . So, it is not a perfect *Macbeth*, but it is an unforgettable Macbeth."

Peter Kemp, "Schizoid Schemers," *Times Literary Supplement* (18 Nov. 1983).

The weirdest thing about Jack Gold's *Macbeth* isn't the three sisters but the gulf between the central performances and the rest of the production. In most ways, the play receives intelligently traditional treatment. Visually, Gold works tactfully and powerfully to highlight the pervading imagery. Blood spouts and cakes effectively. Mist and darkness thicken an atmosphere of uncertainty and evil. The sets have the slab-like simplicity of the play's structure: Dunsinane is a chunky assemblage of grim walls, forbidding corridors and few loopholes; the witches convene near a cromlech—and, when crouched motionless in their grey rags, look like eerie prehistoric boulders.

Massive and murky, the settings are solidly in keeping with the play, as are most of the performances. *Macbeth* doesn't allow much scope for a wide span of characterization, but here the subsidiary roles all show considerable strength—and not only in the rendering of lines. Besides delivering

their speeches with vigorous authenticity, thanes and hired assassins alike bring plenty of convincing toughness to the play's physical struggles. There is, too, a nicely inventive treatment of the bearing of Birnam Wood to Dunsinane: spring-like green light just flickers over the army supposedly carrying branches, giving an effect of freshly sprouting life.

This strategic handling of the Birnam branches is typical of the production's general chariness of the visually bizarre. Banquo's ghost never materializes; Macbeth does indeed, as the camera emphasizes, look but on a stool. The apparitions in Act IV don't appear either. Instead, the production has Macbeth inhaling narcotic fumes from the hags' cauldron and staring, mesmerized, into it, as the witches ventriloquize spirit voices. This generally cautious treatment of the occult makes the witches' preparation of their voodoo ragout seem particularly outlandish: as if demonstrating a recipe, they carefully display each ingredient—"Fillet of a fenny snake," "Liver of blaspheming Jew"—before popping it in the pot.

This eccentricity looms small, however, compared with that of the main performances. Apparently seeing Macbeth as schizophrenic, Nicol Williamson employs two different vocal registers for him—a ringing, resonant tone for public utterance, and a hoarse, introverted mutter for private disturbance. Increasingly exaggerated, this split-level approach eventually breaks up the character, as well as the sense of numerous lines. In particular, Macbeth's final scenes—all ogreish howls and rapid simian gibber—are drastically reduced to sound and fury, signifying nothing.

With the casting of Jane Lapotaire as Lady Macbeth, further damage is done. An actress who—in voice, looks and technique—is most suited to mannered comedy, she gives a fatally lightweight performance. The "fiendlike queen" becomes a girlish figure crooning "My husband!" in tones that would do credit to a Barbara Cartland heroine. Among many eccentricities, her response to the news of the witches' prophecy and Duncan's approach is especially memorable. Macbeth's prediction that his letter "will make joyful my wife's hearing" can seldom have received more striking vindication. Clutching the exciting scrap of parchment to her on a couch, panting, writhing, splay-legged and kneading her "woman's breasts," Lapotaire gasps out, "Unsex me here" in the throes of an orgasm. Only in the sleep-walking scene does she turn her ingenuity to bringing out what's in the play instead of superimposing things alien to it: in a neatly chilling touch, she uses the conventional outstretched-arms posture of the sleep-walker to portray Lady Macbeth pushing her rigid, tainted hands as far from her as possible.

Elsewhere, the play is treated with shrewd respect—apart from a few instances of tampering with the text: a couple of scenes with Lennox and Ross are shuffled; the third murderer kills his two accomplices without any warrant. There are some minor cuts and a regrettable major one: the omission of Malcolm's speech describing Edward the Confessor curing the King's evil—a passage that, in its calculated contrast of the benign English monarch with the malignant usurper across the border, is surely too significant to be dispensed with.

Michael Mullin, "The BBC *Macbeth,*" *Shakespeare on Film Newsletter,* 9:1 (Dec. 1984).

In this superbly acted production the BBC Shakespeare has fulfilled much of the promise so sadly lacking in its earlier work. Central to its interpretation are several basic production choices. The setting blends a quasi-realistic heath (large boulders and swirling mists and fogs) with a starkly expressionistic castle of angular stone slabs that create an acting space for all the interior scenes. A change of light, a different camera angle, some furniture, and the unit set is transformed from the battlements where Lady Macbeth reads the letter to the Macbeths' bedroom, the banqueting hall, the palace courtyard, even into sunny England.

The producer and director have obviously thought through the play to offer not just a fresh reading, but a clear cut reimagining. Discovered crouching beneath a massive stone lintel supported by three plinths, the ragged, disgusting Witches take on the power of druid hags without the insistence, a la Orson Welles, that they represent anything more cosmic than themselves. Eschewing the hocus-pocus special effects Polanski went for, director Jack Gold locates the ghostly apparitions in Macbeth's mind and concentrates our interest on his reaction to them. Therein lies their power, and the camera's ability to bring us close to Nicol Williamson's perfervid acting makes possible an intensity difficult to imagine in any but the smallest theater.

The tall and long-limbed Williamson looks like a Viking warrior. Having already played the role in the theater, he searches his way through lines, wringing from them new readings in every speech. To complain that his speech is sometimes slurred and often far from musical is to fault an actor who seems to be actually experiencing the struggles that the words convey.

Jane Lapotaire, who played Lady Macbeth opposite Bob Peck in the Royal Shakespeare Company's unhappy 1982 production, has found the right medium and the right approach to the role. Her snug gown and feline grace make her seductive power over Macbeth easily credible, a power underscored by her own arousal during the "unsexing" passage, where she lies stretched out and slowly writhing on a bed piled high with furs and animal skins, the same bed she draws Macbeth to when she asks him to "leave all the rest to me" (I.v.74). Her lack of foresight and feeling make a strong contrast to

Macbeth's overwrought personality, and, as he hardens himself to evil, her collapse suggests his greater strength.

In a play renowned for the title roles, the rest of the cast often fade into mediocrity. These actors do not. Banquo (Ian Hogg) is a shrewd soldier, quick to catch Macbeth's nuances and indeed a great danger to the new king. Macduff (Tony Doyle) seems just the sort of man whose strength has never suspected guile or threats; his grief at the news of his family's slaughter is terrifying in its power. Malcolm (James Hazeldine) grows from a callow son just through his first battle to an able leader, a development underlined by a beard that goes from scruffy whiskers to a nearly full growth in the course of the play.

[This production] offers fine performances by first-rate actors set in a convincing and consistent production. Yet the director takes risks, he alters the script, and he expands it with additional stage business. It will reward viewing again and again, and wherever possible it ought to be part of every student's *Macbeth* experience.

H. R. Coursen, "Murky *Macbeth,*" *Marlowe Society of America Newsletter,* 1 (Spring 1985).

The BBC-TV *Macbeth* was not the worst production within the vast wasteland of this series, but it wasn't very good.

A no-frills *Macbeth* with only the simplest of sets—not a bad concept for the rugged highland setting and the tightly woven tartans of the poetry. If the focus is to be on the acting, however, it had better be good.

Here it was only adequate. Nicol Williamson bombed in a *Macbeth* a few seasons back in The Apple. In the TV production, his voice varied from a timorous tadpole of a whisper to a bullfrog croak as if he had contacted croup in the murky air of the studio. Williamson blew a line: "Words to the heat of deeds too cold breath gives" should be there, but wasn't. His hand clenched and unclenched behind his back as Macduff called on the murder morning, a silly cueing of what the actor should show by other means. He added "tomorrow" number one to the end of the previous line, so that it came out "time for such a word tomorrow." He tossed his modified garbage-can-top aside on the line, "Before my body / I throw my warlike shield." That represented an absolute misreading of the script. Williamson's was not as fatuous a Macbeth as Albert Finney's, but the former came close. Too close for comfort.

A sexless Queen of the Nile in Dr. Miller's fiascopious *Antony and Cleopatra* a few seasons back, Jane Lapotaire was a bit better as Lady Macbeth. It may be that her efforts at sexuality here, although as inadequate as a maiden aunt's imitation of Theda Bara, are not as intrinsic to the role of Lady Macbeth as to Cleopatra. When Lapotaire suggested that Macbeth look like the innocent flower but be the serpent under it, she delivered an unsolicited grope that was, fortunately, below camera range. Williamson kept a stiff upper lip. Her mad scene, delivered in the hallway that had led to Duncan's chamber, went well until she mimed her previous effort to push Macbeth out from in front of the murder chamber. That earlier moment, as Macbeth turtled on about hangman's hands and raveled sweaters, made Lady Macbeth look as if she were trying to muscle a reluctant Maxwell towards the nearest Sinclair sign. Her "faint" worked well. It was a "feint"—an obvious effort to get her babbling husband off the left hook of his own bloody rhetoric.

The principals were not up to the standard set by the sensuous Janet Suzman and the disciplined Eric Porter almost a decade ago in the "Classic Theatre" version. Suzman proved that the TV camera is no barrier to the transmission of sexual energy. As Porter delivered the too-famous "Tomorrow" speech, the camera rose above him. Macbeth shouted his nihilism towards a sky emptied only for him. His words echoed back to surround the damned spot where he stood.

This latest production lacked effective directorial touches. While we discovered the Weird Sisters atop an outsized Ouija Board planchette—fair enough—they registered no reaction later to Macbeth's threat to curse them eternally. Thus was a potentially pregnant moment hollowed-out. Lady Macbeth did *not* "keep her state" at the banquet. She sat at the table and quaffed with the paltry band Macbeth had gathered. The script shows that *neither* Macbeth gets to the table, which represents a secular version of eucharist. This banquet scene was radically low-budget, with the excuse, one surmised, that Macbeth's reign has itself grown threadbare by this time.

This production was apparitionless. Fine. Better that we be the focal point of Macbeth's clutching of the dagger than that it be a meretricious glitter a la Polanski. But then we ask, "Say, who *were* those three old ladies anyway?" If the numina are primarily products of Macbeth's introverted sensation, we need a stronger actor than Williamson to convince us. Two actors I have seen in the role on stage—Michael Redgrave and Ian McKellen—*could* have convinced us that external visions were there without the sensible and true avouch of our own eyes.

Director Gold did establish Seyton early as Macbeth's henchperson—third murderer, impaler of Macduff junior, a neo-fascist punk-rocker. In drawing the character in our own image, however, Gold missed a chance at the Seyton-Satan equation. But then I cavil at a touch that did work in an otherwise leaden effort. The brutal scene at Macduff's castle was precisely directed in this version.

In the Polanski film, Donalbain suffered from a Richard-the-Thirdian truncated left leg. At the end

of the film, we saw him shuffling off to the Buffalo Sisters, ostensibly to develop foundation support for his own career. In the latest version, Donalbain (I think it was Donalbain!) slithered in to upstage King Malcolm's final speech. The concept was wrong in Polanski, but clear. Evil was a constantly recyclable can of newts. In the BBC production, however, the concept was merely confusing. Were we to take this pie-faced youth as a threat to the masterful Malcolm? If so, Macbeth had gained a kind of quirky victory, even as he cooled within his designer jeans. The BBC *Macbeth* introduced an ambiguity for which the production had not prepared us and, more importantly, that the medium is not prepared to accommodate. TV insists on a normalization of the script.

A murky *Macbeth*. Better perhaps than no *Macbeth* at all. But not by much.

King Lear (Granada, 1983 [Mobil Showcase Network, January 1984])

Albany: Robert Lang. *Cordelia*: Anna Calder-Marshall. *Cornwall*: Jeremy Kemp. *Edgar*: David Threlfall. *Edmund*: Robert Lindsay. *Fool*: John Hurt. *Gloucester*: Leo McKern. *Goneril*: Dorothy Tutin. *Kent*: Colin Blakely. *Lear*: Laurence Olivier. *Regan*: Diana Rigg.

Producer: David Plowright. *Director*: Michael Elliott. *Designer*: Roy Stonehouse.

Adam Mars-Jones, London *Times*, (10 Apr. 1983). "The production was . . . resolutely theatrical and studio-bound. . . . But you do at least actually see Olivier's risky and self-lacerating Lear, up close."

Christopher Andreae, *Christian Science Monitor* (2 May 1983). Olivier "casts over the entire proceedings a brittle, crackling magic. The whining of second childhood renders his Lear pitiable. . . . [He] also charts . . . Lear's madness and the delicate strength of his final gentle lucidity. Articulate precision is instilled into his entire performance. . . . [Olivier] undercut[s] the conscious exhibitionism of his acting [with] a scissors-like wit. . . . John Hurt is a troubled . . . Fool, prematurely old, who derives no more joy from his wisdom than he does from everyone else's foolishness. . . . The acting [is] helped . . . by a considerable and powerful use of the close-up. . . . Olivier's Lear is surely an instant classic."

Benny Green, *Punch* (13 Apr. 1983). Olivier "played right across the keyboard of his vocal range to convey the fluctuations of his fortune. But *King Lear* is one of those big plays that will not be squeezed into a small box. Reduced, as it must be by television, it cannot meet its emotional commitments, which end up looking nothing like the lineaments of tragedy and very much like Grand Guignol melodrama instead. The cast was spectacular, much of the acting beautiful, and most of

Shakespeare's lines came across. But the repertory theatre in our living room has no time to pander to works of genius."

Jack Kroll and Rita Dallas, "Return of the Prodigal King," *Newsweek* (8 Nov. 1982). A look at the relationship between Olivier the person and Olivier the actor. We learn that the rabbit he consumes in the production "was stuffed with cold salmon, a favorite dish of Olivier's."

G. M. Pearce, *Cahiers Elisabéthains*, 25 (Oct. 1983). "Olivier's Lear rose above . . . irritating distractions (advertisements for pet food, etc.) and a simple gesture of beckoning gently with a delicate frail hand to the words, 'Thou'lt come no more,' helped to make his performance into one of the very great Lears."

Caroline Seebohm, *Wall Street Journal* (23 Jan. 1984). "The supporting actors are . . . uniformly brilliant, [particularly] Colin Blakely . . . and John Hurt. . . . Olivier feels the king's weaknesses all right [but] is too mellow, too childlike to hurl forth [Lear's] imprecations [and] too cozy for the character's anguish." We do not see "great rage, largely, I suspect, because of the very thing Olivier claimed—his age. . . . That being said, this is of course still a rare and profound performance."

Tom Shales, *Washington Post* (26 Jan. 1984). A "forceful and fascinating performance [by Olivier]. . . . When he first enters in white beard and flowing white hair, he is the spitting image of God . . . a herculean Lear. . . . A determinedly full-throttle production."

Dan Sullivan, *Los Angeles Times* (26 Jan. 1984). Olivier "gives his best attention to sharing with the camera the serious things going on in the old man's head." Goneril and Regan are not the standard "twin viragoes. . . . Diana Rigg's Regan is a scheming, clever narcissist with very little grasp of anybody else's reality—since other people are basically figments, she has no compunctions about eliminating them. . . ." The "realistic settings . . . look . . . phony."

Stanley Wells, "The Sweetness of Age," *Times Literary Supplement* (8 Apr. 1983).

Michael Elliott's sensitive production of *King Lear* for Laurence Olivier does not aim at an intellectual exploration of the text such as is associated with the concept of director's theatre. It seeks rather to provide a framework in which the actors' energies may be fully released in the portrayal of individual characters. Roy Stonehouse's setting is in the pictorial tradition deriving from the nineteenth century. Though it is studio-based, it uses turf, sand, a stream, an oak tree, animals—horses, dogs, hens, a rabbit, a mouse, even butterflies—and lashings of studio rain. Tanya Moiseiwitsch's costumes are Ancient British; the action begins and ends in misty weather at Stonehenge. Irving and Wolfit would have been at home in this setting; the most recent theatre production that it recalls is

Glen Byam Shaw's for Charles Laughton at Stratford in 1959—the season in which Olivier gave his magnificent Coriolanus.

This is the right mode for a production clearly designed to enable Olivier, who has not been fit enough to appear on the stage for some years, and who has not acted in Shakespeare since 1974, to play Lear for the first time since 1946. Inevitably, the focus of interest is on his performance, though a very strong supporting cast has been assembled. Jeremy Kemp is a bleary, sinister Cornwall. Anna Calder-Marshall a touching Cordelia. Dorothy Tutin and Diana Rigg nicely differentiate the wicked sisters, the former authoritatively, sibilantly hard-boiled, the latter a sweetly smiling, eminently reasonable villainess. John Hurt is not permitted to develop much indivduality as the Fool, and Robert Lindsay is a bland Edmund, but David Threlfall copes intelligently with Edgar, Colin Blakely is an extremely sympathetic Kent, and Leo McKern passes from choleric geniality to powerful suffering as Gloucester.

The Lear who is at the centre of the composition is a white-haired, white-bearded, pink-cheeked old man who touches our hearts from the moment when, following upon all the other members of the court, he enters supported by Cordelia in a warm embrace. He relishes the love-contest that he imposes on his daughters; it's a bit of a game for him, though he insists that Goneril kiss the ground before she begins to speak. His affectionate commitment to Cordelia is evident. When she declares she can say nothing to compete with her sisters, he cups his hand playfully to his ear, indulgently asking her to "speak again" as if sure that she must be playing a game he doesn't quite understand. In "Mend your speech a little / Lest you may mar your fortunes," the second clause is given confidentially, as if he were still incredulous that she can mean what she says. When it becomes clear that she does, he reacts with pain rather than anger. The old man seems foolish rather than tyrannical; there is much reasonableness in his attitude; and he has immense charm: a quality not often associated with Lear, but which gains our sympathetic indulgence from the start.

Olivier's voice is occasionally hoarse, and there are a few fluffs. He may have given a more commanding performance in 1946, but can scarcely have given a more touching one. It is good that he has been given this late chance to demonstrate, to a new generation and in a new medium, his technical and interpretative genius in a great Shakespearean role.

Steven Urkowitz, "Lord Olivier's *King Lear*," *Shakespeare on Film Newsletter*, 8:1 (Dec. 1983).

From its opening moments to its closing credits, this video production gives us a superbly chosen company of British performers and scenic artists, at the height of their powers, working together with trust and daring on one of the world's great plays. Every aspect of televised drama works magnificently in this performance—acting, direction, scenic and costume design, camera-work, music, choreographed stage fighting, literary interpretation of Shakespearean poetry, subtle control of dramatic illusion and audience response.

When Lear enters, the members of the court prostrate themselves before him, and Olivier's eyes gleam as he leaves the nobles stretched out on the earth a moment before he says a word, we see him take delight in one of humankind's insatiable cravings, unconditional adulation. We will have no trouble recognizing a reprise of this egomania when it reappears viciously in Dorothy Tutin's Goneril and Diana Rigg's Regan. Later, noting Lear's equally profound sensitivity toward his Fool and his knight (John Cording), we can understand the deep humanity and loyalty he calls forth from Cordelia and Kent.

All of the performers find surprising life and variety in the characters they play. Unafraid to show us their ugliness or weakness, they are believable when they rise to ferocity, grace or grandeur. Bit parts like the Doctor (Paul Curran) and Edmund's Captain (Ian Ruskin) stand out as clearly as the tour de force portrayals of Gloucester, Edgar, and Edmund.

There are some problems. Shakespeare designed the great storm of Act III as a dialogue between the king and the thunder—the sky talks and Lear answers. But extravagant rain and swelling background music temporarily submerge Shakespeare's words under too much orchestrated sound. For technical verisimilitude to a real-life storm we pay the price of understanding what Lear says.

For viewers familiar with the text, too many intrusive changes appear in the screenplay. Just before the climactic battle, in the original scripts Edgar tells his father to "take the shadow of this tree for your good host" before leaving him alone onstage. Here instead Edgar says, "Take the protection of this holy stone" (perhaps to underscore the neolithic motifs of the set? perhaps to make Edgar seem more concerned for Gloucester's safety?). In the last scene, Goneril will "ne'er trust *poison*" rather than "medicine;" Edmund would send to "the prison" rather than "the castle." And too many speeches at the very end of the play have been cut, leaving Lear alone as the focus of attention, eliminating a broader view of a ruined society around him which fills the original.

Kenneth Rothwell, "Representing *King Lear* on Screen: From Metatheatre to Meta-Cinema," *Shakespeare Survey*, 39 (1987).

Since the 1953 Brook-Welles *King Lear*, television has undergone a technological growth that makes it unreasonable to discuss recent and past productions as though they were of the same genre. The three major televised *King Lears* of the past

two decades—those with James Earl Jones, Michael Hordern, and Laurence Olivier in the title roles—have been produced using studio equipment that was unimaginable in the 1950s with its 'live' performances fraught with potential disasters: an actor doing a swaggering Petruchio could stumble on the stairs or a Lady Macbeth could muff a cue in front of millions. And yet as television approaches the technical competence of film it gains an 'air-brushed' slickness at the expense of spontaneity, ironically the same complaint that theatre advocates have always made about filmed Shakespeare.

Even television reduces itself into further subsets when one considers that the 1977 broadcast in the United States of the James Earl Jones *King Lear* was actually a recording of an earlier Delacorte Theater production in New York City's Central Park. Camera becomes merely a tool or service to the stage, though even that assertion needs qualification because some recordings of stage productions have obviously been done with greater expertise than others. The Richard Burton/John Gielgud Electronovision *Hamlet*, for example, used no less than fifteen cameras,[1] which did not guarantee its success but does suggest the magnitude of the production's mechanical problems.

The chronicle of making a 'television movie' from *King Lear* will focus here on Jonathan Miller's 1982 BBC TV/Time-Life version starring Michael Hordern, and the 1983 Granada Studios *King Lear* starring Laurence Olivier. Both these television plays appeared at almost the same time, just as the two film versions of Brook and Kozintsev made their premieres within a few months of each other. Like the Brook and Kozintsev films, the Miller television version also gestated on stage before being subjected to the permanent record of the camera.

The television version apparently adhered very closely to the style of the stage production in its stress, as Miller put it, on an 'absence of regality' in the person of the old king. Indeed, anyone calling for 'regality' is in peril of being dismissed by Miller as a kind of lout with 'lower middle class' sensibilities.[2] There is not room here to do full justice to Hordern's thoroughly professional and competent performance in this startlingly original conception of the old king, nor to Frank Middlemass's Fool. The measure of how far it is removed from the cliché King Lear is to think of Albert Finney's Lear in *The Dresser*, which carries all the old stereotypes to the point of a *reductio ad absurdum*. Then again, however, one recollects the wild old hirsute king of Frederick Warde's nineteenth-century America and grave doubts settle in. Has the loss of regality been bought at the expense of innate dignity? Has the Jove figure been reduced to Job?

Whatever the answers to these questions, in putting the play into a monochromatic, late Renaissance ambiance and in attempting to turn the disadvantages of acting in a television studio into advantages, Miller used the medium to serve Shakespeare's words rather than Shakespeare's words to serve the medium. At the same time, there is no defensiveness about television's being neither a play script, nor a stage play, nor a film. Quite the contrary. One senses an aggressive, even robust, relish for working with the medium. With such an attitude, the technicians on the set replace the live audience in the theatre, as Hordern once commented. There is a willingness to work with what is on hand rather than a restless search to recover the lost glories of either stage or film. As with Kozintsev, most of Miller's thoughts about making a television movie out of Shakespearean tragedy apparently took place at the planning stage, not in production. This is not a *King Lear* that readily responds to a search for elements of either metatheatre or 'meta-television'; it both records and reaffirms the Shakespearean text. Its hidden agenda may be that the theatre origins partially subverted remaking of the play for television. Along the way, however, Michael Hordern, in becoming less the king-man and more the man-king, displays a special brand of competence, summed up in John J. O'Connor's homespun comment: 'While he is not overwhelming, he is mightily convincing.'[3]

To complete the figure, however, of metatheatre, the promise of my subtitle, the Olivier/ Elliott *King Lear* offers a splendid coda. What could possibly be more self-referential, more 'meta-television,' than the world's greatest actor playing himself as an aged monarch in the declining years of his career? More than that, the veteran supporting cast is virtually a real-life counterpart to the old king's hundred knights. From all accounts they also brought a Kent-like loyalty on the set to the aged monarch,[4] which in a way is reflected in the 'division of the kingdom' scene when they lie prostrate in awe of the king's majesty. A retinue of stars in their own right, they include Diana Rigg as a surprisingly reptilian Regan and Colin Blakely, a memorable Antony in the BBC *Antony and Cleopatra*, as Kent. Dorothy Tutin's Goneril is quietly degenerate, but no doubt Leo McKern as a throaty Gloucester offers the most memorable of the supporting performances.

The producers also constructed a studio replica of Stonehenge to endow the play with timelessness. Enormous hunks of cowhide make up the map of England in the first scene, and a Stonehenge setting at the beginning and ending of the play hint at dark druidic mysteries of sacrifice. Moreover Stonehenge, as Tucker Orbison recently observed,[5] is set off against an oak tree to punctuate the nihilistic and regenerative side of the Lear tale.

Olivier himself never loses his gift for canny stage business, particularly in the mad scenes when, to signify his pathetic vulnerability, he washes clothes, exposes the breasts of his withered body, slaughters a rabbit and consumes its raw flesh, makes a necklace of flowers, and plays with a mouse. Shorn of his beard at the end, not even grizzled like Hordern, Olivier is the very opposite of the Warde King Lear of the nineteenth century. This King Lear of the post-holocaust era, of the post-monarchical period, of the electronic age, cannot somehow achieve the sublimity of the past. He must be made, as with the Hordern King Lear, as much man as king. And yet neither the medium nor the director is actually decisive. It is the genius of the actor that makes audiences either sit up and take notice or switch to another channel. Olivier's remarkable voice, which can turn a vowel or a diphthong into discovery of a lost chord, does not desert him even in his advanced years and guarantees the enduring viability of this production.

Having said all that, however, one is still left uneasy about this representation of Shakespeare's greatest tragedy. In spite of the expenditure of huge sums of money by Granada Television, in spite of the star quality of the cast, and in spite of the brilliance of Olivier's performance, the result still illustrates the obstacles to literal representation of Shakespearean tragedy on screen. Something undergoes a sea change from stage to screen. What works perfectly at an RSC performance in the Barbican may turn leaden on screen. Only the star-quality performance of Olivier saves this production from sinking without a trace. As one reviewer said, the cast and Olivier were simply too large for the production.[6] It would seem that all attempts at literal representation only lead back to the conclusion that Shakespeare on film is most interesting when least representational.

As we have seen then, since the early twentieth century directors have undertaken to represent the unrepresentable by putting *King Lear* on the big screen of movies and then, subsequently, also on the small screen of television. Haunted by the stage traditions of the past, self-conscious about the film and television medium of the present, and anxiety-ridden by the burden of their responsibility to the world's greatest dramatist, they have inevitably allowed their perturbations to creep into their moving pictures. In turning our attention back to the inexhaustible problems of reading, acting, producing, interpreting, and filming the canon, 'meta-cinema' offers yet another way to approach and understand the art of William Shakespeare.

1. Brenda Davies, 'Hamlet,' *Monthly Film Bulletin*, 39 (1972), 163.

2. Henry Fenwick, 'The Production [of *King Lear*],' in *King Lear, The BBC TV Shakespeare*, ed. Peter Alexander *et al.* (London, 1983), p. 22.

3. 'TV: A No-Nonsense *King Lear*,' *New York Times*, 18 Oct. 1982, p. 16.

4. Peter Cowie, 'Olivier at 75 Returns to *Lear*,' *New York Times*, 1 May 1983, Entertainment sect., pp. 1–2.

5. 'The Stone and the Oak: Olivier's TV Film of *King Lear*,' *CEA Critic*, 47 (1984), 67–77. See also

Frank Occhiogrosso, ' "Give Me Thy Hand:" Manual Gesture in the Elliott-Olivier *King Lear*,' *Shakespeare Bulletin*, 2:9 (1984), 16–19.

6. Lloyd Rose, 'Television: A Winter's Tale,' *Atlantic*, Feb. 1983, p. 92. The production combines 'genius and schlock.'

The Comedy of Errors (BBC, 1984 [PBS, 1984])

Adriana: Suzanne Bertish. *Aegeon*: Cyril Cusack. *Aemilia*: Wendy Hiller. *Antipholi*: Michael Kitchen. *Dromios*: Roger Daltrey. *Luciana*: Joanne Pearce. *Solinus*: Charles Gray.

Producer: Shaun Sutton. *Director*: James Cellan Jones. *Designer*: Don Homfray.

Stanley Wells, *Times Literary Supplement* (6 Jan. 1984). The "comic techniques exploited and elaborated by Shakespeare in this brilliantly plotted comedy seemed strangely unrelated to . . . Jones's production. . . . The brilliantly sophisticated structure requires the direction of a master-chef's deftness of [balancing] one ingredient against another, so as to whip up the whole concoction with . . . verve and grace. Here it is not so much a soufflé as a pudding."

G. M. Pearce, *Cahiers Elisabéthains*, 26 (Apr. 1984). A "sparkling production. . . . Trick photography allowed the same [men] to play both [pairs of] twins, making the confusion over identity more realistic."

Jeanne Addison Roberts, "The Shakespeare Plays on TV," *Shakespeare on Film Newsletter*, 9:1 (Dec. 1984).

The Comedy of Errors ranks with the very best BBC productions of the Shakespeare plays to date. The producers have combined lush, delightfully varied sets with splendid acting and have used deliberate theatricality and calculated artifice in ways that sustain the delicate balance in the play between Greek romance and Plautine farce.

The production looked like a romance. It opened with a distant view of a fantastically garbed troupe of entertainers dancing on a map of the eastern Mediterranean. A narrowing focus on magicians, mimes, and tumblers established an image, periodically reinforced by the camera's return to these characters, of Ephesus as a town of "nimble jugglers," "Dark-working sorcerers," and "Soul-killing witches." The scenery throughout was beautiful: pastel "Mediterranean" stucco houses silhouetted against blue "Greek" sky; dusty roses and turquoises inside and out; Elizabethan costumes and interiors frequently verging on the fantastic, with elaborately ornate embroidery and intricate inlay work. The Duke rode a white horse and wore a silver helmet with grotesquely carved silver mask. A

sense of spaciousness, mystery, and hidden possibilities, rarely achieved on the stage and even more rarely on TV, pervaded the whole and made more superficially credible the deliciously incredible events of the play.

The aura of romance was greatly enhanced from the start by the superb performance of Cyril Cusack as Aegeon. He quickly persuaded us of the genuine pathos of his loss of family and the desolation of his futile search. He was aged, fragile, vulnerable, and yet stoically brave. His long recitation of his misfortunes was artfully and illuminatingly mimed, as he spoke, by the troupe of performers. Even though it flirted openly with self-parody by adding sentimental violin music to the sad story, the scene brought audiences both on and off the screen closer to tears than to laughter.

In dealing with *The Comedy of Errors* television has certain clear advantages over the stage. If one actor plays both twins, credibility is enhanced without the loss of potential for confrontation entailed in stage doubling. This production also steered an admirable course between the TV perils of monotonous talking heads such as those that marred the BBC *Julius Caesar* and the misguided "realism" that muffled the language of *Antony and Cleopatra* and *Pericles*. When Luciana spoke her pedagogic piece, the camera showed us her face clearly, but she sat considerably behind her sister, whose reactions we were able to follow close up. Most wonderfully, thanks to the skill of the actors and the intelligence of the filming, every word was crystal clear; the delight of eye and ear were superbly harmonized. We owe Director James Cellan Jones and his company an enduring debt of gratitude.

Roger Warren, "Shakespeare in England," *Shakespeare Quarterly*, 35 (Autumn 1984).

James Cellan Jones's production of *The Comedy of Errors* emphasized the varied origins of the play—the classical world, the Renaissance, and the commedia dell'arte—but it did so in a style well suited to television. It was set in the delightful colonnaded marketplace of a Renaissance seaport; the beautifully decorated, well-furnished interior of Adriana's house was clearly that of a wealthy merchant's wife. The Duke arrived in the marketplace on a white horse, as it were the emperor Charles V on horseback: he even changed the white plume in his resplendent silver helmet for a black one when he arrived for what he thought would be Egeon's execution at the end. But when the camera looked down into the market from above, the floor was decorated with a map of the Adriatic, on which a commedia dell'arte troupe, who also embodied the witches, sorcerers, and mountebanks that Antipholus of Syracuse is so afraid of, mimed Egeon's narrative as he delivered it. This was a legitimate adaptation of those gigantic speeches for television, but it failed to clarify the narrative because Cyril Cusack's irritating mannerism of running on phrases regardless of sense failed to sustain his narration, so that the ultimate effect of the mime was to distract rather than support.

Since there is of course no possibility of audience reaction in televised Shakespeare, the director staged the play in ways that did not depend upon such reactions. A key example was Adriana's first mistaking of Antipholus of Syracuse for her husband. This is usually played all out for riotous comic embarrassment, but here it was very cleverly directed to suggest that Adriana, who had fumed with jealousy when alone with her sister, played a different role with her husband, trying to humor him in the act of accusing him, luring him back home. And Antipholus responded with fascination as well as bewilderment, which is not against the text since he does after all take advantage of the situation: "I'll say as they say." Each pair of twins was played by one actor, again exploiting the possibilities of television. Michael Kitchen distinguished a quietly unnerved Antipholus of Syracuse from a boorish Antipholus of Ephesus, so the further realistic point could be made that Luciana's amazement in the wooing scene arose in part from the fact that she could not have expected such eloquence from her blunt brother-in-law.

The performances were rather muted, with the exception of Suzanne Bertish's precisely articulated Adriana, who took full advantage of the fact that the play was not sent up to present a serious picture of an unhappily married woman, not a harpy. Her scene with Wendy Hiller's formidable battleaxe of an Abbess made the brilliant point that strife between mother- and daughter-in-law began instinctively, before the two of them were even aware of the relationship! All in all, the quiet, small-scale realism of this Errors made a refreshing change from the extraneous gags and musical numbers which usually load down productions of the play.

Coriolanus (BBC, 1984 [PBS, 26 March 1984])

Aufidius: Mike Gwilym. Cominius: Patrick Godfrey. Coriolanus: Alan Howard. Menenius: Joss Ackland. Volumnia: Irene Worth.
    Producer: Shaun Sutton. Director: Elijah Moshinsky. Designer: Dick Coles.

John Engstrom, Boston Globe (26 Mar. 1984). Howard and Worth "give transcendent performances, even if they have about half Shakespeare's text to work with. . . . This version, alas, leaves out most of the politics—the result of cutting and reshuffling of . . . one of the most architecturally sound . . . of all Shakespeare's dramatic structures. . . . Worth [played] a woman of cultivation and appeal [so] her ruthlessness strikes us as even more horrific. . . ." Howard's "performance is peerless for its controlled passion, wit, venom, sexiness, irony, introspection—all expressed with and through a command of rhetoric that stamps him as [a] great declamatory actor."

G. M. Pearce, Cahiers Elisabéthains, 27 (Oct. 1984). Howard's "harsh and strident voice was perfectly attuned to the metallic resonance of the blank verse. . . . The intensity of the bond [between Volumnia and Coriolanus] made [his] capitulation to her . . . both inevitable and very moving. . . . Mike Gwilym [as] Aufidius . . . emphasized the . . . relatively uncivilized state [of the Volsces] when compared with the Romans. . . . [Gwilym's] was a sensitive and volatile performance."

Katherine Duncan-Jones, "Posturing to the Populace," Times Literary Supplement (4 May 1984).

Elijah Moshinsky's sombre production of Coriolanus has in heightened form the faults and virtues of his Cymbeline. Often visually static, its strength lies in peaceful, pictorially composed interiors, such as the charming sequence in which Virgilia works at her tapestry frame and Volumnia, in profile, stitches a white cloth. Several of the scenes in the Roman senate, with rugged-featured, black-suited figures marshalled along the length of a great wooden table, recall Van Dyck or even Holbein pictorially, while being redolent of C. P. Snow in atmosphere. The power game in its early stages comes alive through stillness and suspense, but fails ever to rise to real excitement. Frenetic theatricality is no substitute. In the scenes of military action atmosphere is wholly lacking. Smoke, elaborate helmets and murky slow motion shots of shields and battering rams fail to persuade us that we have seen Caius Marcius fluttering the Volscians in Corioli. And after this ample display of Roman weaponry, it seems perverse of Coriolanus to fight virtually naked with his chief enemy Aufidius—especially given the stubborn pudeur which will prevent him from exposing his scarred body to the Roman populace. Perhaps we are meant to remember the naked wrestling scene in Ken Russell's Women in Love: certainly some sort of Lawrentian blood-brotherhood between Coriolanus and Aufidius seems to be indicated. But the relationship never comes fully alive, and swinging cuts in the last two scenes make Aufidius' revulsion against his former chum unprepared and unexplained.

Alan Howard is seriously miscast as Coriolanus.

His extraordinarily affected diction could never be mistaken for military roughness, and his tedious, solipsistic posturings appear to test to their very limit the benign loyalty of Menenius (an admirable performance by Joss Ackland) and the steely maternal dedication of Volumnia (a magnetic rendering by Irene Worth, but one which never seems to achieve any rapport with Howard's). The only scene in which Howard's manner really comes off is, however, an important one. In II.iii, his sneering plea for citizens' "voices" has just the right lofty, annoying quality, and the confused reaction of the people (a lively mob, well led by Paul Fesson)—"'tis his kind of speech; he did not mock us"—matches the viewers' difficulty in knowing what to make of him. Coriolanus' rare moments of magnanimity—an important element, I would have thought, in any interpretation—are either unnoticeable or merely grotesque.

Roger Warren, "Shakespeare in England," *Shakespeare Quarterly*, 35 (Autumn 1984).

The very strong cast of the BBC television production of *Coriolanus* was fully capable of bringing off Elijah Moshinsky's interesting interpretation. Mr. Moshinsky set the play in the early seventeenth century. He fully exploited the possibilities of television by subdividing scenes into smaller units set in different locations. The opening scene, for instance, began in a corner of the marketplace for the encounter between the citizens, Menenius, and Coriolanus; but instead of an entry for the Senate after line 221, there was a cross-cut to the Senate in session, seated at a long table in a claustrophobic late-Renaissance room; for the final exchange between two tribunes, there was another cross-cut to a narrow back-street. The play was abbreviated quite drastically, and many of the omissions coincided with the cross-cutting. Coriolanus' soliloquy before Aufidius' house led straight into his conversations with Aufidius inside, the three serving-men being omitted entirely, and Menenius' resolve to plead with Coriolanus [led straight] into the plea itself, omitting the entire episode between Menenius and the watch.

The cross-cutting was most strikingly used to point the contrast between the worlds of the two people who most obsess Coriolanus, his mother and Aufidius. The women gossiped in a cool, light, domestic interior very obviously indebted to early seventeenth-century painting; but the armies at Corioli wore sinister classical-style helmets, while Coriolanus and Aufidius fought their duel virtually naked. After they had beaten the weapons out of each other's hands, they continued to grapple, their hands around one another's throats—but the stranglehold became almost an embrace: as they stared infatuated into each other's eyes, there was a cross-cut back to Rome. The effect was repeated when Coriolanus went to Antium. Aufidius took Coriolanus by the throat before embracing him and

massaging his chest slowly and intently as he said that to see Coriolanus there "more dances my rapt heart / Than when I first my wedded mistress saw / Bestride my threshold." He and Aufidius were locked together once again during their final exchange, one sword held by both of them: as Aufidius turned the point toward him, Coriolanus seemed to accept it almost willingly, aware that by yielding to his mother and sparing Rome he had destroyed himself, in personal terms by being false to his "absolute" nature, in practical terms by placing himself in Aufidius' power. The conspirators were omitted, and their line "Kill, kill" was obsessively repeated by both Coriolanus and Aufidius, united to the end.

This was an intimate personal, almost private approach to Coriolanus' tragedy, playing down the large-scale political issues and focusing attention upon Coriolanus' personal relationships with his family, friends, and enemies. The emphasis upon the love-hate obsession between Coriolanus and Aufidius clearly needed two actors of equal stature, and certainly found them in Alan Howard and Mike Gwilym.

Maurice Charney, "Alan Howard in Moshinsky's *Coriolanus*," *Shakespeare on Film Newsletter*, 9:1 (Dec. 1984).

Elijah Moshinsky's *Coriolanus* is strikingly painterly and static. In this version it is a play from Shakespeare's Blue Period, and the classical world is luminous and Mediterranean. There is a lot of talk and surprisingly little action. The aristocratic values of the patricians are assumed, so that plebeian aspirations, as expressed through the Tribunes, are seen to be intrusive and presumptuous. Although the Tribunes are represented as a couple of old-style Marxist scholars, the class war is heavily weighted against the revolutionary party.

There are some wonderful individual performances in this production, yet the overall conception doesn't make good critical sense of Shakespeare's play. We are, however, happily distracted from total meanings by vibrant and appealing details. Alan Howard is a very energetic and self-assured Coriolanus, who has no doubts about his own integrity and the baseness and vulgarity of the commoners. He appears so often on horseback in the early scenes that we think of him as an equestrian statue, grand and towering and commanding. He is obviously much too old for Shakespeare's Marcius, who can be stung by the accusation of "Boy" and whose attachment to his mother is still deeply oedipal. A Coriolanus of 35 disrupts the logic of the play. Despite this obstacle, Alan Howard is splendidly dismissive. All of his speeches to the plebeians are virtually asides because he doesn't believe them worth speaking to.

It was a brilliant stroke to match Alan Howard's Coriolanus with Mike Gwilym's Aufidius. The two actors are so radically different that they represent opposing lifestyles. This gives us a new insight into the play. Mike Gwilym is short, dark, wiry, and violent—no match for the heroic warrior invincibly portrayed by Alan Howard. Gwilym is threatening, melodramatic, and treacherous, whereas Howard has no need to dabble in the sinister. The scene in Act IV when Coriolanus, disguised and muffled, reappears in Antium at the house of his old enemy is full of surprises. Playing it with so many overtly homosexual caresses removes some of the ambiguity that hovers over the heroic ideal in Shakespeare's play. It literalizes and excessively motivates what is merely an undertone in the text.

If the whole BBC series, which now approaches its close, were now to do over again, everyone would have a much better sense of what the public wants. The more recent productions, like *Coriolanus*, are breaking free of a literal dependence on Shakespeare's written text—perhaps they are breaking so free as to leave the text far behind. It is, after all, other television programs that the Shakespeare plays must compete with. The sociology of a mass audience demands that these plays make it in the charts and the ratings. They must be, first and foremost, good television. If they are also good Shakespeare, that is an added benefit. We need creative television artists who can bring these two sets of values closer together.

Othello (Bard Productions, 1984)

Cassio: DeVeren Bookwalter. *Desdemona*: Jenny Agutter. *Emilia*: Leslie Paxton. *Iago*: Rod Moody. *Othello*: William Marshall. *Roderigo*: Joel Asher. *Director*: Frank Melton.

H. R. Coursen, "The Bard *Othello*."

Of the three Bard Productions I have seen this one is easily the best. In fact, it is at least the equal of the two other available versions. The Olivier, although a film produced at Shepperton, scales down to the shallow depth-field of TV and is a dull production, as exciting as it was on stage. The BBC version employs static camera angles that negate what a well-edited production can do for Shakespeare. The Bard version employs a stage setting, but is neither silly in its staginess as the *Macbeth* nor cramped by its set as the *Richard II*. Othello, a domestic tragedy, clenches in, as Bradley says, to "a close-shut murderous room." The one-on-one confrontations are suited to the dimensions of the tube, as one noticed by contrast in the somewhat awkward scenes from Cyprus Harbor and in the scene following the discovery of Desdemona's death—often difficult as everyone crowds into the chamber. Here, it was not only tedious but anticlimactic after the very moving scene in which Desdemona dies had pulled most of the emotion out of us. It was not that William Marshall threw Othello's finale away, as had James Earl Jones in the Winter Garden Production, but that we felt

that Othello deserved what he was going to give himself and wished he would be a bit more laconic in his leavetaking. On the whole, however, and with a few exceptions to be further noted, this production worked superbly within its various spaces, evoking the nocturnal scenes convincingly via the flicker of torch and candle, and creating vivid visual moments with its rich costumes—blues, reds and golds, pinks and purples. A lot can be said for an opulent foreground in a medium that can provide little or no background. The production was free of the self-conscious "old master" technique that can work well in a film (like *Romeo and Juliet*) but that can trap a TV production under old paint (as in Miller's *Antony and Cleopatra*).

Marshall gave us the basso Othello to which Robeson conditioned us in the Margaret Webster production of the 1940s. But Marshall was more in control of verse rhythms than Robeson and brought anguish to the role as Jones had not. Marshall's was an understated performance, appropriate for TV, but at times he seemed too "laid-back," as in his unemphatic "Naked in bed, Iago, and not mean harm?" He "peaked" in his "when we shall meet at compt" speech, which is about as late as an actor can choose to peak (Jones chose not to do so at all), but what we got was a restrained and quietly moving performance. Marshall's "her father lov'd me" was said, in some sorrow, right to Brabantio. On "a friend that lov'd her," Marshall put his arm around Cassio, a nice foreshadowing of what Othello will come to believe.

Jenny Agutter's Desdemona was a bit beyond the first bloom of youth, but not yet the sophisticated woman, a few years from spinsterhood, of Maggie Smith. Agutter really did seem to be the daughter of the gentle, merely saddened Brabantio of Peter MacLean. Human and humane, he had given Desdemona the qualities that allow her to endure convincingly the terrors Othello is to inflict upon her. Agutter was convincingly womanly *and* innocent. One could share Othello's sadness in having to kill her and understand why this script has such a record of audience intervention. The murder scene was powerful, so much so that it pretty well erased what was to follow. What was to come was almost superfluous, and the production should have ended with alacrity.

Moody's Iago was not a non-com up from the ranks but a fallen aristocrat to whom lack of promotion was motivation enough. Moody's social status made sense of his "relationship" with Joel Asher's Roderigo, who was Brabantio's best example of a "wealthy, curl'd darling" of Venice, and an embarrassing example who allowed Brabantio almost to understand Desdemona's choice of the Moor. Moody's bald head was a space to be drummed as he asked "How? How?" A superb moment came when Moody turned with a half-smile to the camera on "'til us'd." Since the "talking head" approach was used sparingly in this production, its brief employment was potent here. Iago with Roderigo was splendid, but he was even more convincing with Othello. The hinge on which Iago swung Othello here was the latter's sense that he was a winner over Brabantio, in a sense, a "rival" for Desdemona. Othello's arrogance, though mildly expressed, allowed Iago to give more weight to Desdemona's deceiving of Brabantio than, obviously, it should have, and helped Iago push Othello into the Brabantio "position," which included a declination into the vale of years. Thus this production showed Othello carrying out Brabantio's revenge upon Desdemona, unconsciously, of course, but brilliantly, as the initial gravamen is reiterated by Iago as Othello's mission.

A few sour grapes: one seldom realizes the importance of a small role until it is badly done, as was Leslie Paxton's Emilia, hardly an effective foil for her gentle mistress. When the Duke told Othello that he "must away tonight," Desdemona's dismay showed that she had had other plans. That instant nicely touched upon the matter of consummation of the marriage. But, later at Cyprus, Iago was robbed of his description of "bride and groom / Devesting them for bed"—that "innocent" simile which thrusts at Othello's possible sexual insecurity and describes what he and Desdemona have presumably just been doing. So—the earlier suggestion was, inexplicably, allowed to drop, as were Othello's lines about his "gentle love" being "raised up." Gone also was Iago's "Ha—I like not that!" Yet Othello alluded to the line a moment later.

While the editing left a lot to be desired, the brief scene in which Othello visits the fortifications of Cyprus (III.ii.) was left in. It gets Othello out of the way while Cassio visits Desdemona and shows us Shakespeare at work on thematics even while engaging in essential dramaturgy. External fortifications are rapidly becoming irrelevant as Iago's pestilence penetrates Othello's soul.

The Two Gentlemen of Verona (BBC, 1983 [PBS, 1984])

Julia: Tessa Peake-Jones. Launce: Tony Haygarth. Lucetta: Hetta Charnley. Proteus: Tyler Butterworth. Silvia: Joanne Pearce. Speed: Nicholas Kaby. Valentine: John Hudson.
Producer: Shaun Sutton. Director: Don Taylor. Designer: Barbara Gosnold.

Stanley Wells, *Times Literary Supplement* (6 Jan. 1984). "Joanne Pearce looks lovely in the unrewarding role of Silvia, but, as Julia, Tessa Peake-Jones plays against the verse and, like other actresses before her, falls into the trap of maudlin lachrymosity on finding herself betrayed."

G. M. Pearce, *Cahiers Elisabéthains*, 27 (Oct. 1984). Praises lighting, "rich colour," music which "perfectly echoed the lyrical mood of the lov-

ers. . . . Joanne Pearce . . . gave a dignity and distance to . . . Sylvia which justified both the famous song and the manifold interest in her."

Roger Warren, "Shakespeare in England," *Shakespeare Quarterly*, 35 (Autumn 1984).

Don Taylor set *The Two Gentlemen of Verona* in a beautiful, romantic world of vine-covered pillars and cypress-lined avenues, with Italian medieval and early Renaissance landscapes in the distance. Silvia, dressed like one of Botticelli's Graces, presided over a Court of Love, complete with masked—"blind"—cupids, in which it was natural for the men to act ostentatiously as "servants" to their "mistress" Silvia. It seemed at first as if this formal, fragile world in pastel colors was intended to "distance" the play and to provide a context for a debate between love and friendship; but the temple of Love was desecrated when Proteus arrived in it. His resolve to pursue Silvia and to betray Valentine and Julia was marked by a clap of thunder and a sudden wind dashing the blossom from the trees. It became darker still when the disguised Julia told Proteus bitterly, " 'Tis pity love should be so *contrary;*" Proteus was clearly attracted to the "page," thus preparing for their reunion at the end.

Harry Keyishian, "The Shakespeare Plays on TV," *Shakespeare on Film Newsletter*, 9:1 (Dec. 1984).

The major technical legacy of the BBC Shakespeare series may be its establishment of the two-shot (two heads in the "frame" conversing) as the basic mode of recording dialogue. When the television screen's borders enclose two heads—shot anywhere from waist-up to relatively tight close-ups—intimacy of expression is enhanced and formal declamation made absurd. The result is increased audience involvement.

Two Gentlemen of Verona, as an early work of Shakespeare's and relatively primitive in technique, relies heavily on "duologues" or "duets," as Bernard Beckerman has pointed out ("Shakespeare's Dramaturgy and Binary Form," *Theatre Journal*, 33 [1981], 5–17). It therefore lends itself especially well to the use of the close-up and the two-shot and, not surprisingly, very effective use is made of these shots in the BBC's television production. The conversations between Valentine and Proteus and the comic dialogues of Launce and Speed are given special vitality and charm on the small screen.

Director Don Taylor also employs a full range of other television techniques to give life to the production. Adroit camera placement, mobile framing, arresting composition, and other devices were used to good effect.

Pericles (BBC, 1983 [PBS, 11 June 1984])

Antiochus: John Woodvine. Boult: Trevor Peacock. Cleon: Norman Rodway. Dionyza: Annette Crosbie. Gower: Edward Petherbridge. Lysimachus: Pat-

rick Ryecart. *Marina*: Amanda Redman. *Pericles*:
Mike Gwilym. *Thaisa*: Juliet Stevenson.

   Producer: Shaun Sutton. *Director*: David Jones.
Designer: Don Taylor.

   John Engstrom, *Boston Globe* (16 June 1984).
Finds "formal beauty in the compositions, which
always light up the characters and their
plights. . . . This odd, remote play suddenly seems
as gripping and moving as a raw documentary. . . .
One of the strongest productions [of the Series]."
Praises Gwilym, Stevenson, and Redman.

   Roger Warren, *Shakespeare Quarterly*, 35
(1984). "Jones was content to take each episode as
it came, using a series of detailed, naturalistic sets
to suggest the constantly changing Mediterranean
locations. . . . Ryecart [gave] a very subtle performance as Lysimachus, shifty and uncertain . . .
beneath his breezy, confident exterior. . . . Mike
Gwilym . . . lacked the wide vocal range needed
for Pericles, and . . . missed the sublime tender-
ness of Pericles' reunion with Marina."

Peter Kemp, "Between Crest and Trough," *Times
Literary Supplement* (21 Dec. 1984).

   A medley of events that are as far-fetched as
they're far-flung, *Pericles* bristles with difficulties for
a director. Its text is grossly corrupt; its heroine,
ethereally pure. The central figure, Pericles, is passive, tossed around by high seas and life's ups and
downs. Around him the play strains in opposing directions. Miraculous survivals and supernatural intervention hoist it towards fantasy; low comedy tugs
it back to earth. To make something successfully
homogeneous of a work generally taken to be of
mixed authorship and which jumps not merely
around the Aegean but from Dumb Shows to lively
vernacular, from melodrama to poetic intensity,
constitutes a formidable challenge.

   In David Jones's fine version for the BBC Shakespeare series it's triumphantly met. Streamlined
and sumptuous, the production—by giving the
play's excitements their full due—shows why, in its
day, *Pericles* was so popular. It also brings out with
colour and clarity the underlying pattern of the
drama—demonstrating the play's coherence, paradoxically, by stressing the diversity of its settings.
Written close to *Antony and Cleopatra*, Pericles
shares that play's interest in contrasting cultures.
Helped by a variegated score from Mike Best and
atmospheric sets from Don Taylor, Jones's production highlights this. Each centre of action has its
very distinctive sights and sounds. Antioch, for instance, where incest and tyranny hold sway, is a
sinister compound of grilles, spikes, studded doors,
plants with razor-edged leaves, and whining, shud-
dering discords. Pentapolis, where courtesy reigns,
is emblazoned with white and gold, and rings with
vigorous harmonies.

   Marked changes of scene like this never let you
forget how much this play—awash with oceans and
sea imagery—relies upon undulation. Pericles's

career oscillates between crest and trough. The societies and characters he encounters represent contrasting extremes. What connects them is a concern with princeliness and parenthood, differing
attitudes towards subjects and offspring. There are
four royal fathers, each with a daughter, in *Pericles*.
The plot, as this production points up, carefully
juxtaposes them: so that to omit the play's early
scenes, as has sometimes been done, is to mutilate
its design. The opening moments of *Pericles*—
made tense and barbaric in this television version—plunge dramatically into a court where
butchery is resulting from the corrupt attachment
to his daughter of Antiochus (played with incisive
menace by John Woodvine): fatherhood and kingship are both perverted. Wheeling away from this,
Pericles finds his way to a régime that's its diamet-
ric opposite: Pentapolis under the benign rule of Si-
monides (a role rounded out with taking geniality
by Patrick Allen) and his daughter Thaisa (whose
demure, determined responsiveness to Pericles is
nicely caught by Juliet Stevenson). Instead of the
lethal, twisted riddle set in Antioch, testing of
mettle here takes the form of invigorating, chivalric
exercise—something the production does flamboyant justice to.

   Repeatedly, the production steers *Pericles* as
close as it can to high-coloured naturalism. Largely
because of this, it is a haunting experience.

Joan Hartwig, "*Pericles*: An Unclaimed World,"
Shakespeare on Film Newsletter, 9:2 (Apr. 1985).

   One of the more difficult concepts for modern
producers of Shakespeare to accept as intentional
on Shakespeare's part is the mixed mode of tragicomedy. Audiences have been trained to expect either realism or fantasy, and directors promote these
expectations. It seems clear that the BBC production of *Pericles* determined that a naturalistic
mode, in which every effect had a logical cause ex-
plainable by gesture if not by plot, was the purpose
of playing.

   The insistent realism of this 1983 production often is at odds with the remoteness and fairy-tale
world that Shakespeare created in the play. Shades
of ambiguity fall to morality's good versus evil
in the portrayal of this legendary hero and his
restored-from-ashes narrator, Gower.

   Gower, played by Edward Petherbridge, opens
the play, sitting by a fire on an island (which at the
end of the play is seen to be Ephesus, the isle of
restoration), suggesting visually the power of the
line, "from ashes ancient Gower is come." From
the brightly burning fire (whence we assume ashes
have come) Gower's image is superimposed upon
Antioch's green lushness—visually pointing up the
description of Antioch as the "fairest [city] in all
Syria."

   The first show of former suitors' skulls seems
small and insignificant, no more than dolls' heads
pinned to a wall, but when Pericles goes on to read

the riddle, these art objects become ominous. This is fairy tale taken seriously, as Shakespeare meant it to be taken. John Woodvine plays Antiochus as a strong character who finds a mysterious union in his daughter's love, not to be challenged lightly by youthful suitors.

When Pericles understands the riddle and begins to see—with an on-screen image of his insight into the truth—the hidden, lascivious embraces of Antiochus and his daughter, we understand what horror precludes revelation. And Pericles' hesitation to touch the daughter's face after he has deciphered the truth of the riddle is effective, especially since he had raptly soliloquized her charms before he understood her corruption. (The hesitation to touch her face becomes a motif carried throughout the performance, culminating in Pericles' touching of his own daughter's face in the recognition scene.)

The problem is that with such a strong Antiochus, Mike Gwilym's Pericles seems almost entirely a victim throughout the scene and the play that follows. Pericles should seem at least as strong as Antiochus except for age and experience, yet Gwilym's Pericles seems a coward in fleeing Antiochus' false promise of hospitality for forty days, even though we recognize with him that Antiochus is lying. Still, Pericles should have more dignity in flight. Gwilym's entrance into Tyre, as he flounces past nobles awaiting his return, to ruminate privately upon his bed only restates an immature and cowardly nature.

Trying to make things seem natural, to explain cause for effect, often defeats the rareness of Shakespeare's tragicomic vision. Consider the restoration scene between Marina and Pericles as an example of what happens when realism gets in the way of theater. Pericles repeatedly strikes out at Marina (once is called for in the text), his nose drips from his shedding of tears as he comes out of what seems more like a drug-withdrawal than a self-imposed mourning. Marina, sensitively and attractively played by Amanda Redman, valiantly withstands the repeated assaults from Pericles until he finally hears the music of the spheres after recognizing that his daughter is not dead. But Pericles stumbles about, embracing everyone, and generally destroys the delicacy of the merging of two different worlds—his ability to hear what no one else does comes across as a delusion of madness. Only the dream-shrouded descent of Diana offers evidence that Pericles is in tune with divine harmony.

The final effect of this production is that there is more tragedy and somberness here than comedy and a sense of hope; that joy is a "flat" state of mind rather than an elevating one; that "wonder" is a state we cannot know here and now, unless we strain mightily for it.

Perhaps it is rare to find the magic equivalent that Shakespeare discovered in this fairy tale play that touches so deeply upon the truth of our human experience. On occasion, when the director and the actors allow it to happen through the text that is extant, the magic works marvelously well.

Much Ado About Nothing (BBC, 1984 [PBS, 30 November 1984])

Beatrice: Cherie Lunghi. *Benedick*: Robert Lindsay. *Claudio*: Robert Reynolds. *Don John*: Vernon Dobtcheff. *Don Pedro*: Jon Finch. *Hero*: Katharine Levy. *Leonato*: Lee Montague.

Producer: Shaun Sutton. *Director*: Stuart Burge. *Designer*: Jan Spoczynski.

David Richards, *Washington Post* (30 Nov. 1984). A "handsome, thoughtful and . . . sober interpretation of a comedy that easily lends itself to flashy effects. . . ." Lindsay and Lunghi, Benedick and Beatrice, "make it deliciously obvious that the war of words is nothing compared to the conflict they are experiencing in their own hearts. . . . The self-doubts they allow themselves when others aren't looking . . . make them uncommonly attractive." Praises Vernon Dobtcheff and Michael Elphick [as Dogberry].

Peter Kemp, "Ambivalent Amiability," *Times Literary Supplement* (11 Jan. 1985).

Stuart Burge's rich production of *Much Ado About Nothing* brings the play's Sicilian setting very much to the fore. Messina is depicted as a handsome warren of honey-coloured courtyards, tapestried galleries, and formal gardens dotted with orange and lemon trees. Convincingly costumed characters stream down the gleaming reaches of elegant stairs or linger in gracefully vaulted cloisters. Giving added resonance to the shock of Claudio's vindictive shoving of Hero from the altar, the church where this occurs is all marbled tranquillity suffused with violet light. Later, the crypt housing her supposed tomb becomes the site for a penitential procession—torches, cowls, black robes and skulls—vibrating with the Sicilian fervour for mortuary exuberance.

This combination of grimness and gaiety is, as Burge keeps demonstrating, characteristic of the play. *Much Ado About Nothing* isn't merely a drama in which two obverse plots are held in counterpoise: malevolent deceit dividing a pair of lovers in one story, benevolent gulling drawing a couple together in the other. Nor is it simply a play where what's glimpsed or overheard turns out to be at variance with reality. It's a work—as serious as it is comic—in which people sway between ferocity and courtliness.

Psychologically acute performances from Cherie Lunghi and Robert Lindsay [as Beatrice and Benedick] stress that, for them, wit is an aspect of wariness. True to the claim that Beatrice "speaks poniards," her banter is kept pointed and polished. But the play's intimation that she has been hurt in some earlier involvement with Benedick emerges more noticeably here than usual. Resentful woundedness is entangled with fascination in her response to her verbal sparring-partner: the smartness, Lunghi makes it often seem, derives from smarting. Likewise, Lindsay's Benedick does justice both to the character's "quick wit and his queasy stomach." As with Beatrice, he appears simultaneously guarded and goading, clamping irony over emotional vulnerability. The couple's gradual *rapprochement*—tense and tentative—is invested with ambiguity to the end.

Around the lovers—taking his cue from the play's frequent reference to fashion, its imagery of traps and baits, its plethora of disguises—Burge assembles an aristocratic world of seigneurial whims, silky self-advantage, and stratagems ranging from the mildly to the viciously predatory. Vernon Dobtcheff's Don John, hooded eyes and droned tones only sharpening at the prospect of drawing blood, infuses what might seem an extinct piece of dramatic fauna—the saturnine Machiavellian—with creepy life.

Eschewing blatant theatrical effects for something more subtle and integrated, Burge takes pains to release even the most latent pleasures of the play.

Susan McCloskey, "The Shakespeare Plays on TV," *Shakespeare on Film Newsletter*, 9:2 (Apr. 1985).

The problem of harmonizing the play's comic and tragic elements is central to *Much Ado's* stage history. The solution, apparently, does not lie in splitting the difference between them, as Burge's production does.

The worst consequence is that the actors defy the sense of their lines. In the first act, for instance, this Beatrice (Cherie Lunghi) is seldom merry, though her companions repeatedly describe her so. Often praised for his wit and good fellowship, Benedick (Robert Lindsay) spends his early scenes in a prickly funk. Until they are tricked into the truth, their scenes foreshadow not the ultimate marriage of two lively minds, but the emotions that explode at Hero's and Claudio's abortive wedding—anger, jealousy, deep distrust.

Despite its uncertain first half, this production often challenges the claim that Shakespeare's plays cannot be adapted to the 19-inch screen. Burge clearly knows how to move in the space he commands.

At the party scene in the first act, for instance, we watch the unhappy Claudio watching Hero with Don Pedro, then Don John (Vernon Dobtcheff) watching Claudio. When the camera moves back to Claudio, the party has dissolved around him, leaving him the isolated prey to Don John's wiles. The arbor scenes, in which Benedick and Beatrice are duped into love, show how adroitly the camera can be used to manage action and reaction,

without merely panning from one face to the next. When pairs of characters begin to move down a colonnade towards a stationary camera, or when groups of characters pause and then descend a staircase, an image in two dimensions takes on a third.

Indeed, the spaces through which these characters move distinguish this production. Spoczynski's designs most frequently feature the motif of the arch. Arches frame Leonato's elegant courtyard, provide entrance to the arbor, lend majesty to the wedding chapel and Hero's coffin. They are not mere passageways through which characters enter and exit, but images of opposing forces maintained in perfect poise. They are the ideal emblem for *Much Ado's* beautifully orchestrated comedy and tragedy, an emblem Burge learns to read only late in this production.

King John (BBC, 1984 [PBS, 11 January 1985])

Constance: Claire Bloom. *Dauphin*: Jonathan Coy. *King John*: Leonard Rossiter. *Philip the Bastard*: George Costigan. *Queen Elinor*: Mary Morris.
Producer: Shaun Sutton. *Director*: David Giles. *Designer*: Chris Pemsel.

Peter Kemp, *Times Literary Supplement* (7 Dec. 1984). Discusses the problem of the script. Given the difficulties, this production is "very credible." Bloom "softens the notoriously intractable role of Constance . . . into something moving. . . . Mary Morris [plays Elinor] with poisonous aplomb . . . as a glittery-eyed, leathery-skinned old reptile. . . . Paradoxically [Rossiter] seems most in command [of the role of King John] in the scenes where John, teetering towards downfall, is at his wobbliest." George Costigan "brings a very engaging verve and trenchancy [to his] fresh, forceful performance [as the Bastard]."

Nicholas Shrimpton, *Times Educational Supplement* (30 Nov. 1984). Costigan "bounced through the production as a spring-heeled Jack the Lad . . . [while] Rossiter . . . sidled up to his victim with the air of a quizzical crab. . . . Disaster and disease allowed him to settle into a grander and more majestic style. . . . Claire Bloom played . . . Constance with fierce energy and flawless technique. . . . Even Shakespeare at his third best . . . gives scope for performances which leave the rest of our playwrights standing."

Dennis Hackett, London *Times* (26 Nov. 1984). "Rossiter made a good job of the shifty, untrusting, murderous king. . . . Claire Bloom . . . and George Costigan . . . were more than competitive [with] the insubstantial nature and limited mood of the sets."

John J. O'Connor, *NY Times* (11 Jan. 1985). Praises Rossiter, Costigan, and Bloom. Mary Morris "superb." "The sets . . . are singularly disappointing . . . more suitable to a children's production of 'Jack and the Beanstalk.' . . . The aim may have been clever stylization, but the effect is merely chintzy, and this *King John* ends up sounding a lot better than it looks."

John Engstrom, *Boston Globe* (11 Jan. 1985). *King John* is "one of [Shakespeare's] talkiest plays, hard to bring to life on stage, almost intractable on television." Praises visual contrast between French and English courts, and the acting of Rossiter, Bloom, and Costigan. "Finally, though . . . pretty tedious viewing."

Christopher Swan, "PBS's *King John* Is a Lesson in How Not to Do Shakespeare," *Christian Science Monitor* (7 Jan. 1985)

Much has been written about Shakespeare's chronicle plays, of which this is one: that they are labored and too loaded with historical detail—which accounts for the twilight fame this play enjoys. Hardly anyone undertakes it. And it would be altogether easy, sitting through director David Giles's presentation of it, to say, "No wonder." But the fact is inescapable that a play of particular moral force and uncommon imagery stands in these vestments.

It should prove helpful, therefore, to understand why its force seldom comes forth in this effort.

For one thing, most of the people here really seem not to believe in the play. It looks as if actors and director and scenic designers took it for a costume drama with some beautiful language, impossible scenes, and artless contrivances. Something, in short, to be gotten through, if one were mounting a complete series of Shakespeare plays.

Can it be enough, after all, to have yet another Shakespeare play set to war drums and trumpets, and not much real insight? The language here is as large and poetic as any Shakespeare ever wrote. It certainly calls for something more than the fleur-de-lis sky backdrops and stuffed robes we get here.

One longs to see the company strip away all this museum storehouse of materiel and get down to the play's rich marrow.

That happens now and again, mostly when Claire Bloom is about, giving us her obsessed, intelligent Constance. So, too, do we get lucid flashes from George Costigan as a Philip the Bastard who speaks as though fresh from Liverpool's pubs, yet makes the anachronism work. But the late Leonard Rossiter is not at his best in the title role. And the two child princes seem to be delivering high school valedictory addresses in their most important speeches.

Still, nitpicking about this or that performance misses the heart of the issue: that Giles should have set about to do this work as one does a brand new opera, full of wonderful dissonances and undiscovered beauties. Each line should have been read for clues to a world unimagined.

In this *King John*, Giles is too hasty to set up

scenes and breeze through them, as though they can be tossed off. Strangely, it is this very hurry that makes the play seem "as tedious as a twice told tale vexing the ear of drowsy man," to borrow a phrase from Philip.

Scott Colley, "The BBC-TV *King John*," *Shakespeare on Film Newsletter*, 9:1 (Dec. 1985)

David Giles's production of *King John* could strike some viewers as a brave effort in an ambiguous cause. Indeed, Giles might have recognized how Lewis of France felt in Act V when it became clear to him that victory was impossible. With supplies lost at sea and allies slipping away on all sides, Lewis settled for a truce. As it was, he lost heart too soon: the English forces were no match for him. We will never know if David Giles lost heart when victory was within his grasp. But through much of the production, Giles seems to have been trying simply to avoid a rout.

Shakespeare's play depicts the paradoxes and confusions of domestic and international politics, and alas, resembles too closely those parts of other history plays which have all of the long speeches and sennets. Giles's interpretation, at any rate, intensifies the declamatory nature of the play. Tight groups of actors strenuously recite their lines, and one looks for some movement or spark which will give life to this rarely-seen tragedy. True Shakespeareans surely appreciate the opportunity to see *King John* enacted, but less hardy souls will emulate Salisbury, Pembroke, and Bigot in deserting the campaign before it is done. In my living room, first one family member, then another, and eventually even the dog abandoned King John well before Salisbury and his crew did. This version will strike many of us as one which fills a gap in the series rather than one which alerts us to new dimensions of the canon.

It is too bad that the production is sometimes lifeless, for there are bright moments and some skillful acting. The late Leonard Rossiter, a quirky, mannered comic actor, surprisingly brings both menace and desperation to the role of King John. Scowling and smirking by turns, talking rapidly out of the side of his mouth, skulking about the set like a regal phantom of the opera, Rossiter makes John seem a king even true patriots would desert. This King John lives under a dark cloud—Rossiter certainly keeps him under one—and fails even at skullduggery and bravado. He is clearly a tyrant who is not certain what to do next.

George Costigan makes the part of the Bastard Faulconbridge dignified as well as satirical when he could have as easily remained a warring clown. Jonathan Coy's "Dolphin" is another of the surprises of the production. He grows up on camera, appearing first as an adolescent extra in someone else's crowd scene, and at the end as an exhausted and suddenly unidealistic warrior-prince. Coy brings a sense of self to his short scenes and, with

[Claire] Bloom, is one of the most assured voices heard in this costume drama of sententiousness.

The hard-core Shakespearean will benefit from watching this rarely-performed play. I will not show it to my classes, however, fearing the play and the interpretation will confirm some snap judgments my students may have reached about Shakespeare. David Giles's *King John* makes me recall fondly the splendid *Henry VIII* of the first television season— shot entirely on location. Some television productions can come to life in a studio. This one did not.

Love's Labour's Lost (BBC, 1985 [PBS, 31 May 1985])

Berowne: Mike Gwilym. *Boyet*: Clifford Rose. *Costard*: Paul Jesson. *Don Armado*: David Warner. *Dumain*: Geoffrey Burridge. *King*: Jonathan Kent. *Longaville*: Christopher Blake. *Princess of France*: Maureen Lipman. *Rosaline*: Jenny Agutter.

Producer: Shaun Sutton. *Director*: Elijah Moshinsky. *Designer*: Barbara Gosnold.

John J. O'Connor, *NY Times* (31 May 1985). "Mr. Moshinsky's conception and the performers' talents . . . are best realized in [the] sober closing moments [of the play.]" O'Connor quotes Moshinsky: "The play is not about love at all. It is a kind of situation comedy using love to explore the nature of the emotions."

Megan Rosenfeld, *Washington Post* (31 May 1985). "One of Shakespeare's sillier plays [and this] production swamp[s] whatever irony or poignance might be brought out [with] archness and artificiality. At times the band of wellborn would-be lovers . . . seem like nothing so much as a group of preppies, affected and superior and amusing themselves with witticisms coined at other people's expenses. . . . In the smaller parts . . . the acting shines, notably David Warner's foppish Don Armado [and] John Wells['] . . . gloriously funny [Holofernes]."

Dan Sullivan, *Los Angeles Times* (26 May 1985). "[T]ea-cup Shakespeare [not] particularly entertaining."

Peter Kemp, "Mellowness Is All," *Times Literary Supplement* (18 Jan. 1985).

Love's Labour's Lost is plugged into its period as into a life-support system. Pulled out of topical context, most of its jokes expire. And even in context, batteries of footnotes are needed to galvanize the play's petrified guyings of defunct absurdities back to life. Regrettably for the modern director, there's no easy means by which Shakespeare's burlesque of late-Elizabethan literary, dramatic and verbal extravagances can be made accessible nowadays. With its pastiche and its parody so rooted in a specific cultural phase, much of the comedy has an unavoidably antiquarian look. What makes its thickets of dead wood worth pushing through, of

course, is that the play also sees the sprouting of a fresher, more durable type of Shakespearean comedy. Characteristic themes emerge—such as the ousting of affectation by affection. Amid its stylistic contortions, the play looks both back and forward. Conflicting aims twist it into a highly artificial attack upon artificiality, a work that revels in the linguistic excesses it deplores.

Elijah Moshinsky's version, however, tries to give the play wider appeal by travestying it— starting with the wrenching of it from its Elizabethan context into the eighteenth century. At once wayward and unoriginal (Peter Brook offered a similar Watteau-esque treatment at Stratford-on-Avon in 1946), this approach proves unable to accommodate whole sections of the play: a problem Moshinsky resolves by discarding or reworking them.

His production divides the action between two main settings. Navarre's celibate Academe is located in a cold-lit library, across whose chilly spaces—littered with frigid statuary and leathern tomes—tread bewigged would-be *philosophes*. Opposed to this is the milieu of the French Princess (played with gentle delicacy by Maureen Lipman in the production's one notable performance). Here, a Watteau-like mellowness obtains. Ladies in panniered silks—old gold, greenish grey, dusty pink—arrange themselves, their fans and ruffed wrists into picturesque groupings against a background of amber haze or russet distances.

The play's final moment, when natural zest should well up simply and strongly in the ballad-like songs of Spring and Winter, gets titivated into a pseudo-Mozartian sequence of self-conscious operatic trills and cadenza fanciness. Ultimately, it's not so much love's labour that's lost in Moshinsky's production as the bulk of the play.

Frances Teague, "The Shakespeare Plays on TV," *Shakespeare on Film Newsletter*, 9:1 (Dec. 1985).

The last of the BBC Shakespeare plays, a handsome *Love's Labour's Lost*, pleased both eye and ear. How sad that this production should be so dull.

The director, Elijah Moshinsky, chose to set the play in the eighteenth century of Gainsborough, not of Blake or Hogarth. Save for Armado's dark house or the Muscovites' nighttime visit, the scenes were well lit; their composition was balanced and graceful. Exterior settings were clean, open spaces, while interiors showed a lovely twentieth-century re-creation of the period, and perhaps because of the care expended on setting, this production used little physical comedy.

The performances, which ought to sparkle, seemed heavy and drained of energy. One reason was characterization: Rosaline (Jenny Agutter) was sullen, Berowne surly, and Holofernes (John Wells) nastily arrogant. Most startling of all, Moth (John Kane) was full-grown, so that all the jokes about his size fell flat and he had to play the infant Hercules on his knees.

If Moshinsky felt that something was amiss, he did not try to change the tone of bittersweet melancholy, but instead changed the pace of the play, speeding it along with heavy cuts and rearranged speeches. Despite some imaginative cross-cutting, many changes were annoying. Immediately after the king's description of Armado in I.i, the scene moved to Armado's musings on love in I.ii. Then it was back to I.i for the rest of that scene, followed by the end of I.ii. Was there some fear that in 150 lines of blank verse the audience might forget who Armado was?

Again, Act III opened with Moshinsky's invention, a scene in which Berowne spoke to himself the opening of his letter to Rosaline. Only after his monologue did we see the actual III.i (minus about 60 lines) in which Costard receives the letters. Evidently the viewers were deemed too obtuse to realize that Berowne's letter was secret because it was a love letter.

Finally, why provide most of Holofernes's Latin-ate quibbling in IV.ii only to cut the delightful letter scene (IV.iii) to the bone? Such changes suggest that the director doubts Shakespeare's craftsmanship and the audience's intelligence.

Because the tone of the performance was at odds with the setting, the production was handicapped. Visually and aurally the production was so serene and careful that one lost sight of Shakespeare's quicksilver comedy. An air of melancholy, with an occasional flash of mean-spiritedness, obscured the play's charming, farcical wit. And without wit, Love's Labour's Lost is lifeless. In short, the production ignored what the eighteenth-century artist Blake knew: tastefulness is an enemy to art.

Had the setting been darker, more Hogarthian, and the performances even harsher, it might have been an interesting interpretation. Then when Holofernes protested, "This is not generous, not gentle, not humble," to an eighteenth-century French court, we might have recalled the Revolution and welcomed the play's somber ending. Had the performances been good-natured, flirtatious, teasing, we might have enjoyed the courtly *débats* and the mannered wit. As anyone knows who has seen the play performed well, it can be a delight, and here I betray my bias: the production done by John Houseman's Acting Company remains my ideal. The BBC production was pretty, but I found it pretty dull.

Titus Andronicus (BBC, 1985 [PBS, 19 April 1985])

Aaron the Moor: Hugh Quarshie. *Lavinia:* Anna Calder-Marshall. *Tamora:* Eileen Atkins. *Titus:* Trevor Peacock. *Young Lucius:* Paul Davies-Prowles.

Producer: Shaun Sutton. *Director:* Jane Howell. *Designer:* Tony Burrough.

Sean French, London *Times* (28 Apr. 1985). "Dull. . . . A blankly-lit studio set and some over-theatrical performances all apparently designed for export and schools."

Michael Billington, "Shaping a Gory Classic," *NY Times* (14 Apr. 1985). Interview with Jane Howell, Director of this production, *The Winter's Tale*, and the *Henry VI-Richard III* sequence. Howell says, "What you miss on television is the sense of overall design. You also miss the tension of actors performing to an audience. But I always bring a few people to a run-through to ginger the actors up."

John J. O'Connor, *NY Times* (19 Apr. 1985). "The action is seen through the eyes of a young, somber, bespectacled boy . . . grandson of Titus. The device allows Shakespeare to have his violence while openly questioning it, too. The production approaches the solemnity of a black mass. . . . Hugh Quarshie is, by turns, silkily smooth and abrasively horrifying as the complex Aaron."

David Richards, *Washington Post* (19 Apr. 1985). "When horror is this bald, it becomes inadvertently entertaining. . . ." Howell's devices "fail to ennoble the material and merely coat it with an unfortunate pretentiousness. . . . Sooner or later, they had to do this one."

Stanley Wells, "The Canon in the Can," *Times Literary Supplement* (10 May 1985).

Jane Howell's production of *Titus Andronicus* opens with the image of a grinning skull juxtaposed with the face of an earnest, anachronistically bespectacled boy. The same boy acts as an acolyte in the play's opening rituals. Gradually we realize that he is young Lucius, Titus's grandson. In the play as written, he first appears in the last scene of the third act. Jane Howell adds no lines to the role, but to make the boy a minor participant in many of the scenes in which he does not speak is a brilliant stroke. His wordless reactions to the often bloody deeds form a welcome contrast to the heavily verbalized responses of many of the other characters. His grave compassion reflects and directs our response: he is the viewer on the other side of the screen.

A few other changes help to adapt the play to its new medium. An alteration in the order of the opening episodes ensures that the initial focus is on Titus. A couple of Latin tags are translated, one or two phrases are modernized. After Lavinia, Tamora, Titus and Saturninus have been killed in rapid succession—a point at which the text is, in any case, suspect—Jane Howell cleverly breaks the action. The suggestion of a lapse in time adds dignity and plausibility to the closing passages.

Another interpretative point in the play's last minutes affects the boy. Marcus's words "Behold the child . . ." indicate that the infant son of Aaron the Moor and Tamora is on stage. In a manner that would not be possible in the theatre, Jane Howell has several times shown us close-ups of the half-caste baby, an endearing, touchingly helpless scrap. As Marcus speaks his words, an attendant produces not a baby, but a small black coffin. Young Lucius gazes at it in dismay. He is grieving over it when he is called to take his last farewell of Titus; then, as the play's final lines are spoken, he opens it, revealing the baby's body lying in a bed of straw. Marcus closes the lid, the boy looks towards us, and the image of the skull reappears.

Adaptive techniques such as these are common enough in the theatre; the text is altered here less than in most stage productions. Its notorious horrors are not flinched. We see the horribly bloody stump of Titus's arm after his hand is cut off; we see his sons' severed heads; his daughter, Lavinia, whose hands, too, have been lopped off, visibly carries his hand between her teeth, as he instructs; blood flows as Titus cuts her ravishers' throats.

Unconscious comedy is avoided, but the play's emotional impact is not fully realized. The production's most touching figures are its least articulate ones: the boy Lucius (Paul Davies-Prowles) and Lavinia (Anna Calder-Marshall), all pathos and horror after her tongue has been cut out. The play's tableaux of grief are comparatively unaffecting, partly because the camera dwells too much on the object of suffering, too little on the sufferer—as when Marcus describes his mutilated niece—partly because the performers do too little to move us. The play's rhetoric may need to be scaled down for television, but it must not be evaded. Edward Hardwicke, as Marcus, tries, and fails, to take command of the verse instead of letting it take command of him. Trevor Peacock begins splendidly as Titus, a grizzled, sombre warrior with the authority of experience, sternly stoical in the face of grief. But as his sufferings take the centre of the stage his gravelly voice does not realize the emotion latent in his anguished arias, there is no sense of consolation deriving from the power to verbalize sorrow; nor does he create any impression of madness, real or feigned.

The mixed merits and weaknesses of this production are characteristic of the ambitious series that it brings to an end. Most of the plays, like this one, are set and costumed more or less naturalistically, either in the historical period represented or in the period of their composition. An eighteenth-century Love's Labour's Lost is an unsuccessful exception. Sometimes the settings add reality to the text. Such a moment comes in Titus, when Lucius remarks that the slaughtered Alarbus's entrails "feed the sacrificing fire." Normally the fire is imagined off-stage; here, it is visible on an altar, and the entrails are sloshed into it. On a larger scale, Jonathan Miller's Timon of Athens includes an absorbing reconstruction of a Jacobean masque.

Often, especially in the plays which were filmed when Miller was in overall charge, settings and costumes give pleasure by their beauty, sometimes influenced by paintings: one remembers the Dutch interiors and deep perspectives of Miller's Taming of the Shrew, the baroque richness of Elijah Moshinsky's Midsummer Night's Dream. But at other times the impression is rather of an old-fashioned, ill-mounted stage production in the picturesque style. Jane Howell notably departs from the dominant mode in her remarkable mounting of the three parts of Henry VI along with Richard III, which for much of the time dare to admit that the action takes place in a studio, and which also achieve some stunning effects by using filmic techniques of slowed-down action and superimposed images.

Acting styles vary greatly. The plays' rhetoric is a recurrent problem. Some performances are too big for the small screen. Donald Sinden, as the king, bursts out of the frame of All's Well That Ends Well. Other actors, such as Jeremy Kemp playing Leontes, attempt to act at a drawing-room level; their success fluctuates according to their ability to convey inwardness of emotion without sacrificing the verse structure. Some productions record performances that have been admired on the stage—Derek Jacobi's Richard II and Hamlet, Elizabeth Spriggs's delightful Mistress Quickly (in The Merry Wives of Windsor), Anthony Quayle's ripe Falstaff (in Henry IV)—not always with a sense that the television director has reshaped them to fit into his production. Some admired performers are seen in roles they have not played on stage—Celia Johnson as the Nurse in a generally feeble Romeo and Juliet and as the Countess in Moshinsky's excellent All's Well That Ends Well, Claire Bloom as Queen Katherine in Henry VIII (one of the few productions to be filmed on location), Helen Mirren as an intense but humourless Imogen. And there are inspired pieces of unexpected casting: John Cleese as Petruchio, the Incredible Orlando (Jack Birkett) as Thersites.

The principal weakness of the series is in direction. Some directors, with the art that conceals art, succeed in creating the illusion that the plays are speaking for themselves, and a few—such as Moshinsky in Coriolanus—interpret them with real flair and originality. But some plays—such as King John—are seriously under-interpreted, and others display no more than routine competence. Comedy, particularly, suffers, perhaps through the absence of a participating audience: even "Pyramus and Thisbe" scarcely raises a laugh, and The Taming of the Shrew (stripped of the Sly framework) and The Comedy of Errors are reduced to a cosy domesticity.

One aim of the series (which has been widely distributed overseas) is to provide teaching aids in areas where productions of Shakespeare are few and far between. This aim has been fulfilled; some teachers may be grateful that the plays are given usually in fairly full texts and are not eccentrically interpreted. But few of these productions would grip a reluctant viewer by the throat, nor do they comprehensively tackle—let alone solve—the problems of adapting Shakespeare to the television medium.

Further Readings

Bentley, Eric, "The Tragedy of *King Lear*," *TV Guide*, 16 Oct. 1982, pp. 33–36. A discussion of modern versions of *King Lear* and of the BBC-TV production.

Champion, Larry S., "Hamlet and the Players: Jacobi and the Television Audience," *Hamlet Studies*, 5 (1983), 98–103.

Charney, Maurice, "Is Shakespeare Suitable for Television?" *Shakespeare on Film Newsletter*, 10:2 (Apr. 1986), 1–2. "The basic rationale for Shakespeare on television lies in Shakespeare's own connection with the popular theater."

Christiansen, Richard, "Shakespeare in Your Living Room," *Chicago Tribune*, 25 Feb. 1979. preview of Season One of The Shakespeare Series.

Cook, Ann Jennalie, "The Bard *Othello*," *Shakespeare on Film Newsletter*, 12:1 (Dec. 1987), 1, 4.

Clayton, Thomas, "'Should Brutus Never Taste of Portia's Death but Once?': Text and Performance in *Julius Caesar*," *Studies in English Literature*, 23 (Spring 1983), 237–55.

Dessen, Alan C., "The Supernatural on Television," *Shakespeare on Film Newsletter*, 11:1 (Dec. 1986), 1, 8. "Emphasis upon the psychological rather than the otherworldly. . . . Sidesteps effects that may strike television viewers as questionable, even laughable [as with the Ghost of Caesar and the disappearing Ariel in the BBC-TV productions]."

Gaertner, Johannes A., "Costumes and Design in BBC-TV," *Shakespeare on Film Newsletter*, 3:2 (Apr. 1979), 4:2 (Apr. 1980), and 5:2 (May 1981). Notes on the authenticity of costumes and props for the BBC-TV productions of *Julius Caesar, As You Like It, Romeo and Juliet, Richard II, Measure for Measure, Henry VIII, Twelfth Night,* and *Hamlet.*

Gelatt, Roland, "The Beeb's Bard," *Saturday Review*, 17 Feb. 1979, pp. 45–48. Examines the problems faced by the BBC in producing the canon for television.

Hapgood, Robert, "Shakespeare on Film and Television," *The Cambridge Companion to Shakespeare Studies*, ed. Stanley Wells (Cambridge: Cambridge University Press, 1986), pp. 273–286. J. Miller "has gone out of his way to make [the comedies] unfunny," p. 286.

Jones, Gordon P., "Long-Distance Shakespeare," *Shakespeare Quarterly*, 35 (1984), 590–596. "Drawing on the resources of modern technology for the study of Shakespeare's plays simply reconfirms their vitality and adaptability. . . . Television articulates and explains the text of Shakespeare's plays; but it also sends students back to the text as the primary reality and the final arbiter, with a fuller sense of its flexibility, its richness, and its multiplicity."

Kliman, Bernice, "An Unseen Interpreter," *Film Criticism*, 7 (Spring 1983), 29–37. An interview with George Schaefer, director of *Hamlet, Macbeth, Richard II, Shrew,* and *Twelfth Night* for Hallmark Hall of Fame in the early days of U.S. television.

Lusardi, James, and Schlueter, June, "Jonathan Miller on Dover Cliff," *Shakespeare on Film Newsletter*, 11:2 (1987), 5. Miller tricks the spectator as well as Gloucester. The latter may resent Edgar's deception.

Maher, Mary Z., "Moshinsky's *Love's Labour's Lost*," *Shakespeare on Film Newsletter*, 10:1 (Dec. 1985), 2. On Moshinsky's "film-like" approach to television—"'finding' the play through various camera angles . . . cutting and blending for visual effect."

———, "Video in Review," *Shakespeare on Film Newsletter*, 8:2 (Apr. 1984). A review of two of the tapes in the "Playing Shakespeare Series:" "Speaking Shakespearean Verse," and "Preparing to Perform Shakespeare," Royal Shakespeare Company Workshop.

Millard, Barbara, "Husbanded with Modesty," *Shakespeare Bulletin*, 4 (May/June 1986), 19–22. Deals with the stage play taped for TV and with a host of other generic issues.

Newlin, Louisa F., "Shakespeare Saved from Drowning," *Shakespeare Quarterly*, 35 (1984), 597–600. Examines the Royal Shakespeare Company series, "Playing Shakespeare," with John Barton and several outstanding members of the company.

Nightingale, Benedict, "TV or Not TV," *New York Times*, 24 Feb. 1980. Critics debate the BBC-TV Series.

Occhiogrosso, Frank, "Manual Gesture in the Elliott-Olivier *King Lear*," *Shakespeare Bulletin*, 2 (May/June 1984), 16–19.

O'Connor, John J., "The Bard's Genius Gets Through," *New York Times*, 29 Apr. 1979. Charts the "uneven record" of Season One of the BBC-TV Series.

Orbison, Tucker, "The Stone and the Oak: Olivier's *King Lear*," *CEA Critic*, 47:1–2 (Fall/Winter 1984), 61–77.

Oruch, Jack, "Shakespeare for the Millions: 'Kiss Me, Petruchio,' " *Shakespeare on Film Newsletter*, 11:2 (1987), 11. Review of "Moonlighting"'s version of *Shrew*.

Papp, Joseph, "Shakespeare Project—A British Preserve?" Letter to *New York Times*, 13 May 1979. Questions the "Anglophilic myth . . . that only the British can properly perform Shakespeare."

Pearce, G. M., "*As You Like It* [BBC-TV]," *Cahiers Elisabéthains*, 16 (1979), 82.

——, "*Macbeth* [Thames]," *Cahiers Elisabéthains*, 16 (1979), 82–83.

Perret, Marion D., " 'To Stage Me to Their Eyes': Visual Imagery in the BBC *Measure for Measure*," *Literature in Performance*, 2 (Apr. 1982), 12–22.

——, "The Making of *King Lear*," *Shakespeare on Film Newsletter*, 8:2 (Apr. 1984). On the Granada Production of *King Lear*.

Revzin, Philip, "Shakespeare Writes for Television," *Chicago Tribune*, 12 Feb. 1979. Preview of First Season. "The crowd scenes seem artificial, much as they must have seemed to Shakespeare's audience."

Robinson, Paul, "TV Can't Educate," *New Republic*, Aug. 1978, pp. 13–15. "Television is superbly fit to amuse . . . and it gives us a sense of union with humanity, if only in its foibles. Herbert Marcuse might even contend that it keeps alive the image of an unrepressed existence. . . . But it can't educate. . . . The only way to learn is by reading."

Rothwell, Kenneth, "The Bard *Richard II*," *Shakespeare on Film Newsletter*, 12:1 (Dec. 1987), 4.

Shakespeare à la Télévision, ed. Michèle Willems (Rouen: Publications de l'Université, 1987). Essays in French, with abstracts in English, by Jean-Louis Curtis, Jean-Pierre Maquerlot, François Laroque, Jean-Pierre Petit, Raymond Willems, and Michèle Willems, and interviews in English with Producer Shaun Sutton, Director David Jones, Director Jack Gold, Director David Giles, Director Jane Howell, and Actor Patrick Stewart. Reviewed by H. R. Coursen, *Shakespeare on Film Newsletter*, 12:1 (Dec. 1987), 8.

Shakespeare and the Arts, ed. Cecile Cary and Henry Limouze (Washington, D.C.: University Press of America, 1982). Reviewed by Harry Keyishian, *Shakespeare on Film Newsletter*, 8:1 (Dec. 1983), 6–7.

The Shakespeare Hour, ed. Edward Quinn (New York: Signet, 1986). Essays on A *Midsummer Night's Dream* (David Young), *Twelfth Night* (Jack Jorgens), *All's Well that Ends Well* (John Russell Brown), *Measure for Measure* (John Andrews), and *King Lear* (Frank Kermode), and a selected bibliography by Kenneth Rothwell.

Shakespeare Plays Television Course (Dubuque, Iowa: Kendall-Hunt, 1980). Reviewed by Martha Hopkins Keating, *Shakespeare on Film Newsletter*, 5:1 (1980), 6–8.

Siegel, Ed, "Laborious and Lost," *Boston Globe*, 31 May 1985. "Whatever theatrical values the series has had, it has been truly terrible television. . . . The BBC reduces Shakespeare to tacky sets, static direction and harsh declamation that seems totally foreign to television." Exceptions are *Twelfth Night* and *Two Gentlemen of Verona*. Siegel praises the Granada *King Lear* as proof that "Shakespeare can be adapted for television."

Simon, John, "TV or Not TV," *TV Guide*, 23 Feb. 1980, pp. 29–32. A debate about the pros and cons of Shakespeare on TV, using Season One as its context. The "complete televised Shakespeare may be only a partial and dubious blessing to sophisticated viewers."

Smith, Cecil, "Good Night, Sweet Series, Parting Is Such?" *Los Angeles Times*, 26 May 1985. Review of Series: *Caesar* "mediocre;" *Romeo and Juliet* "pallid;" *Tempest* "dreadfully leadfooted;" *Hamlet* "marvelous." Smith criticizes PBS's treatment of Series in scheduling plays for Sunday afternoons.

Styan, J. L., *All's Well That Ends Well*, *Shakespeare in Performance*, ed. James Bulman and J. R. Mulryne (Manchester: Manchester University Press, 1987). Styan incorporates the BBC-TV production into his purview. Reviewed by Bernice Kliman, *Shakespeare on Film Newsletter*, 10:2 (Apr. 1986), 2.

Symonds, Peggy Muñoz, "Jupiter, His Eagle and BBC-TV," *Shakespeare on Film Newsletter*, 10:1 (Dec. 1985), 3.

Unger, Arthur, "Shakespeare as They Hope They Like It," *Christian Science Monitor*, 5 May 1978. Preview of Season One.

Willis, Susan, "Making *All's Well*: The Arts of Televised Drama at the BBC" in *Shakespeare and the Arts*, ed. Cecile W. Cary and Henry S. Limouze (Washington, D.C.: University Press of America, 1982), pp. 155–63.

Willson, Robert, "The BBC-TV *Measure for Measure* and TV Aesthetics," *Shakespeare Bulletin*, 4 (Nov./Dec. 1986).

Abstracts of unpublished papers on Shakespeare and Television have appeared in *Shakespeare on Film Newsletter*. Some of these papers may have been published by the time this book goes to press.

Christiansen, Peter B., "The BBC-TV *Cymbeline* and the Idea of Presentation," SAA (1986), *Shakespeare on Film Newsletter*, 11:2 (Apr. 1987), 2.

Dash, Irene, "*All's Well That Ends Well* on TV," NEMLA (1983), *Shakespeare on Film Newsletter*, 7:1 (Dec. 1983), 7.

Eldridge, Elaine, "Sea Scenes in the BBC Shakespeare Productions," SAA (1986), *Shakespeare on Film Newsletter*, 11:2 (Apr. 1987), 8.

Hinman, Myra, "Words, Words, Words," SAA (1986), *Shakespeare on Film Newsletter*, 11:2 (Apr. 1987), 3.

Latimer, Kathleen, "Criticism and the Work of Dramatic Art," SAA (1986), *Shakespeare on Film Newsletter*, 11:2 (Apr. 1987), 7.

Lusardi, James, and Schlueter, June, "Reading Shakespeare in Performance: The Anonymous Captain in *King Lear*," SAA (1986), *Shakespeare on Film Newsletter*, 11:1 (Dec. 1986), 11.

Maher, Mary, and Labron, Elizabeth, "Derek Jacobi's *Hamlet*: A Video View," SAA (1983), *Shakespeare on Film Newsletter*, 8:1 (Dec. 1983), 3.

Manheim, Michael, "The History Play on Film and TV," MMLA (1986), *Shakespeare on Film Newsletter*, 11:1 (Dec. 1986), 6.

Perret, Marion, "'Thou torturest me': 3.1 and 4.1 of the BBC *Merchant of Venice*," NEMLA (1982), *Shakespeare on Film Newsletter*, 8:1 (Dec. 1983), 4.

Richmond, Hugh, "TV or Not TV: TV in Shakespeare Studies," SAA (1986), *Shakespeare on Film Newsletter*, 11:1 (Dec. 1986), 11.

Schlueter, June, "The Final Stage Image in Two *Lears*," SAA (1986), *Shakespeare on Film Newsletter*, 11:2 (Apr. 1987), 8.

Slights, William, "The Art of Limning," SAA (1986), *Shakespeare on Film Newsletter*, 11:2 (Apr. 1987), 2.

Walker, Lewis, "The BBC *Pericles*," SAA (1986), *Shakespeare on Film Newsletter*, 11:1 (Dec. 1986), 12.

Willis, Susan, "*Troilus and Cressida* and Jonathan Miller," NEMLA (1983), *Shakespeare on Film Newsletter*, 7:2 (Apr. 1983), 7–8.

Worthen, William, "The Shakespeare Plays and Spectator Play," MLA (1983), *Shakespeare on Film Newsletter*, 8:2 (Apr. 1984), 10–12.

Citations for interviews of actors, directors, and producers are scattered throughout the annotations of Part III. Below we list the persons interviewed.

Jon Finch, interviewed by Michael Kernan, *Washington Post*, 26 Mar. 1980.

Sir John Gielgud, interviewed by Henry Fenwick, *NY Times*, 25 Mar. 1979.

David Giles, interviewed by Michèle Willems *et al.*, in *Shakespeare à la télévision* (Rouen: Publications de l'Université, 1987).

Jack Gold, interviewed by Michèle Willems, *et. al. S à la TV*.

Michael Hardern, interviewed in The New Orleans *Times-Picayune* (4 May 1980)

Jane Howell, interviewed by Michael Billington, *NY Times*, 14 Apr. 1985.

Jane Howell, interviewed by Michèle Willems, in *S à la TV*.

David Jones, interviewed by Michèle Willems *et. al.*, in *S à la TV*.

Cedric Messina, interviewed by John Andrews, *Shakespeare Quarterly*, 30 (1979).

Jonathan Miller, interviewed by Tim Hallinan, *Shakespeare Quarterly*, 32 (1981).

Jonathan Miller, interviewed by Ann Pasternak-Slater, *Quarto*, Sept. 1980.

Jonathan Miller, interviewed by John N. Gundas, New Orleans *Times-Picayune*, 25 Jan. 1981.

Helen Mirren, interviewed by Sally O. Davis, *Chicago Tribune*, 20 Feb. 1979.

Richard Pasco, interviewed by Cecil Smith, *Los Angeles Times*, 28 Feb. 1979.

Alvin Rakoff, interviewed by Mike Silverman, New Orleans *Times-Picayune*, 14 Mar. 1979.

George Schaefer, interviewed by Bernice Kliman, *Film Criticism*, 7 (Spring 1983).

Patrick Stewart, interviewed by Michèle Willems, in *S à la TV*.

Shaun Sutton, interviewed by Michèle Willems, in *S à la TV*.

Orson Welles, interviewed by Val Adams, *NY Times*, 18 Oct. 1953.

Videography

In a field which is changing as rapidly as is "Shakespeare on Video Cassette," any videography is likely to require revision as soon as it appears. This one lists television productions only, is admittedly incomplete, and does not include items like "Kiss Me, Kate," "Kiss Me, Petruchio," "Kiss Me, Bottom," "Playing Shakespeare," etc. For more complete, definitive, and current information, see the Melzer-Rothwell Filmography. We include only a few prices, since they change, and urge potential buyers or renters to check price and available format directly with the distributor.

Productions in the BBC-TV Series (1979–1985) are available from Time-Life Video, Time & Life Bldg., New York, NY 10020 (1-800-526-4663). Prices as of April, 1987: $300/production, $8000/entire series.

Productions in the Globe Playhouse, Shakespeare Society Series (*Macbeth*, *Merry Wives*, *Othello*, and *Richard II*, for example) are available from R. Thad Taylor, The Globe Playhouse, 1107 N. Kings Road, Los Angeles, California 90069. In addition, "From Page to Stage," five half-hour kits based on productions at Stratford, Ontario (*As You Like It*, *Romeo and Juliet*, *Shrew*, *Tempest*, and *Twelfth Night*) with commentary by actors, is available at $149 per kit (VHS) from Beacon, 1251 Washington St., P.O. Box 575, Norwood, Massachusetts 02062.

Production	Distributor	Available by Special Arrangemnt
Julius Caesar (CBS, 1949)		Folger Shakespeare Library 201 E. Capital Street Washington, DC 20003
Julius Caesar (NBC, 1949)		Folger
Macbeth (NBC, 1949)		Folger
Othello (NBC, 1950)		ATAS/UCLA TV Archives UCLA Los Angeles, CA 90024 (Dan Einstein, Archivist)
Coriolanus (CBS, 1951)		New York Museum of Broadcasting 1 E. 53rd St. New York, NY 10022 (212-752-4690)

Production	Distributor	Available by Special Arrangement
Macbeth (CBS, 1951)		N.Y.M. of B.
Hamlet (NBC, 1953)		UCLA University Film Study Center M.I.T. Cambridge, Mass. 02139
King Lear (Welles, 1953)		Folger, N.Y.M. of B.
Richard II (NBC, 1954)		Folger, M.I.T., UCLA
Macbeth (NBC, 1954)	Facets Multimedia, Inc. 1517 West Fullerton Ave. Chicago, IL 60614 $19.95 (as of Apr. 1987) (1-800-331-6197)	M.I.T., UCLA
Shrew (NBC, 1956)		M.I.T., N.Y.M. of B., UCLA
Twelfth Night (NBC, 1957)		M.I.T., N.Y.M. of B., UCLA
Hamlet (Old Vic, 1959)		N.Y.M. of B., UCLA
Tempest (NBC, 1960)	Films for the Humanities Box 2053 Princeton, NJ 08540 The Writing Company 10,000 Culver Blvd. P.O. Box 802 Culver City, CA 90230	N.Y.M. of B., UCLA
Hamlet (Austria, 1960)	Syracuse Films 1455 East Colwin St. Syracuse, NY 13210 (16mm rental)	
Hamlet (NBC, 1970)		UCLA
Much Ado (Papp, 1973)	Serge Mogilat N.Y. Shakespeare Festival 425 Lafayette St. New York, NY 10003 (212-588-71099) (16mm rental) Films Incorporated 1144 Wilmette Avenue Wilmette, IL 60091 (16mm for sale: $795 [Apr. 1987]	
Merchant (Olivier, 1974)		Folger, N.Y.M. of B. Has been shown recently on A&E
King Lear (Papp, 1974)		Possible archival copy: New York Shakespeare Festi- val (above). Is shown occa- sionally on PBS. N.Y.M. of B.

Production	Distributor	Available by Special Arrangement
Antony & Cleopatra (Nunn, 1975)		Folger
Macbeth (Gorrie, 1975)	Time-Life Video	
Shrew (A.C.T., 1977)	WNET/Thirteen 3200 Eisenhower Parkway Ann Arbor, MI 48104	
Macbeth (Nunn, 1979)	Films for the Humanities	
Macbeth (Caldwell, 1982)	Films for the Humanities	
Dream (Papp, 1982)	Films for the Humanities	Folger
Shrew (CBC, 1982)	Embassy Home Entertainment 1901 Avenue of the Stars Los Angeles, CA 90067 (outside U.S. only)	
King Lear (Olivier, 1983)	Films for the Humanities	
	The Writing Company	

Index